Qualitative Reasoning about Physical Systems

Computational Models of Cognition and Perception

Editors

Jerome A. Feldman
Patrick J. Hayes
David E. Rumelhart

Qualitative Reasoning about Physical Systems, edited by
Daniel G. Bobrow, 1985

Qualitative Reasoning about Physical Systems

edited by

Daniel G. Bobrow

A Bradford Book
The MIT Press
Cambridge, Massachusetts

Third printing, 1988

First MIT Press edition, 1985

Reprinted from *Artificial Intelligence: An International Journal*,
volume 24 (ISSN: 0004-3702). The MIT Press has exclusive license
to sell this edition in North America.

Printed and bound by The Murray Printing Co. in the United States
of America.

Library of Congress Cataloging in Publication Data

Main entry under title:

Qualitative reasoning about physical systems.

"A Bradford book."
"Reprinted from Artificial intelligence: an international journal,
volume 24"—T.p. verso.
1. Artificial intelligence—Addresses, essays, lectures.
2. Reasoning—Addresses, essays, lectures. I. Bobrow,
Daniel Gureasko.
Q335.5.Q35   1985   001.53'5   84-28877
ISBN 0-262-02218-4

Contents

Qualitative Reasoning about Physical Systems:
An Introduction   1
Daniel G. Bobrow

A Qualitative Physics Based on Confluences   7
Johan de Kleer and John Seely Brown

Qualitative Process Theory   85
Kenneth D. Forbus

Commonsense Reasoning about Causality: Deriving
Behavior from Structure   169
Benjamin Kuipers

How Circuits Work   205
Johan de Kleer

Qualitative Analysis of MOS Circuits   281
Brian C. Williams

Diagnostic Reasoning Based on Structure and Behavior 347
Randall Davis

The Use of Design Descriptions in Automated
Diagnosis   411
Michael R. Genesereth

VERIFY: A Program for Proving Correctness of Digital
Hardware Designs   437
Harry G. Barrow

Index   493

Qualitative Reasoning about Physical Systems: An Introduction

Daniel G. Bobrow

XEROX Palo Alto Research Center, Palo Alto, CA 94304, U.S.A.

This volume brings together current work on qualitative reasoning. Previous publication has been primarily in scattered conference proceedings. The appearance of this volume reflects the maturity of qualitative reasoning as a research area, and the growing interest in problems of reasoning about physical systems. The papers present knowledge bases for a number of very different domains, from heat flow, to transistors, to digital computation. Anyone concerned with automated reasoning about the real (physical) world should read and understand this material.

Compositionality

A common theme of all these papers is explaining how physical systems work. An important shared criterion is that the behavioral description must be *compositional*, that is the description of a system's behavior must be derivable from the structure of the system. The term 'structure' refers to the components of the analysis, component behaviors, and the connections between components. The term 'behavior' refers to the time course of observable changes of state of the components and the system as a whole. Each component has some associated behavior, and the behavior of the system as a whole results from the interactions of the behaviors of the components through specified connections.

Locality

A shared criterion for explanation is that effects must propogate locally, through specified connections. Explanations which follow such local propagation rules are felt to be *causal*. This contrasts sharply with standard physics. In that paradigm, systems are described by differential equations which provide constraints on the dynamics of system state variables. Analytic techniques determine allowable time-varying behavior of these continuous state variables, but there is no sense from these solutions of how that time course comes to be. Descriptive terms for behavior such as 'oscillatory' and 'damped' are derived from examining the shapes of the resulting functions of time, rather than from an understanding of the causal processes which underly the system. (See the discussion in De Kleer and Brown on Physics.)

Function

Designed artifacts have a *function*: the relation between a goal of a human user and the behavior of a system. Functionality is a different level of description than behavior. For example, the behavior of the hour hand of a clock can be described in terms of rotation around a point, whereas its function is to indicate the hour to an observer. The function of a piece of a system relates the behavior of that piece to the function of the system as a whole.

Reasoning about function can facilitate understanding of system behavior. It may also allow interesting optimizations in system design. A completely different kind of structure may be substituted for a piece of a larger system if the two structures provide the same function; e.g., using a quartz crystal in a watch as a time standard instead of a balance wheel.

System Tasks

The authors describe how systems can perform a number of different qualitative reasoning tasks. We use this as a primary index into the papers in this volume, indicated by authors' names in parentheses.

Simulation: Starting with a structural description of some device or system, and some initial conditions, determine a likely course of future behavior. When there is ambiguity in the possible behavior which cannot be resolved, ask the user or decide arbitrarily (Forbus, Kuipers, Williams).

Envisionment: Starting with a structural description, determine all possible behavioral sequences (De Kleer, De Kleer and Brown). Two criteria must be met: all possible envisioned behaviors can be realized in some real system with some choice of parameters (realizability); and all possible real systems follow one of these behaviors (completeness).

Mental models: People reason about system behavior in ways inconsistent with physically realizable systems. Sometimes their models may be realizable, but not causal. Capturing such reasoning processes (Forbus, Kuipers) requires models which don't satisfy all the criteria for a good qualitative physics model (see the discussions of De Kleer and Brown, De Kleer, Williams). Nonetheless, the language of qualitative reasoning, particularly encapsulated histories, provide ways of modeling this process.

Diagnosis: A system is 'misbehaving' if its composed behavior (as computed from its assumed structure) is different than some specified desired behavior. For systems which previously behaved correctly, the problem is to find the change in the underlying structure which is causing the difference in behavior

(Davis, Genesereth). The problem is to limit the search for changes (since unlimited search can result in hypothesizing a completely new structure—an unlikely event).

Verification: Designed systems start with a behavior specification to achieve a system function. Any number of structures may be used to try to implement such a specification. The problem of verification (Barrow) is to ascertain that a particular implementation structure has a composite behavior which matches the desired behavior specification.

Deducing functionality: For people to understand explanations of complex devices, it is useful to identify the function of components in terms common to the field. Extracting functional descriptions from structural and behavioral descriptions can be done by examining the mechanism graph for an electric circuit (De Kleer).

Discrete versus Continuous Systems

Another distinction among qualitative reasoners is whether the devices and processes they reason about have state variables that are inherently discrete (a relatively small number of values), or continuous (real-valued functions). The diagnosis and verification programs (Genesereth, Davis, Barrow) all deal with digital computation, and are discrete systems. The rest all do qualitative reasoning about continuous systems.

Quantity Spaces

Qualitative reasoning about continuous domains requires quantization of the domain to a discrete symbol set. The values chosen reflect open regions of qualitatively uniform component behavior, and values at important boundaries where interesting transitions occur only at these boundary points. For example, with respect to a spring attached to a mass, the qualitative values of the force exerted by the spring can be mapped into three values for qualitative reasoning: positive (exerting force to the right, say), zero (at its rest length) or negative (exerting force to the left).

Following Hayes' discussion in his Naive Physics Manifesto, a discrete representation of a continuous space is called a 'quantity space'. Forbus has an extended discussion of quantity spaces. The simple quantity space $\{+, 0, -\}$ illustrated above suffices for many devices described in these papers (e.g., De Kleer, De Kleer and Brown, Williams). Williams also shows how more complex quantity spaces can be usefully mapped into this simpler space.

Ontological Primitives

There is another ontological choice to be made in a knowledge base for quantitative reasoning: what are the primitive elements of structural descriptions? Kuipers makes the jump from quantitative differential equations directly to qualitative constraints among state variables of a system. The components are only state variables, and the connections are the constraints. His simulation assumes that causality is identical to value propagation with constraints.

A device-centered ontology is used by De Kleer, Brown and Williams. The primitives are devices such as pipes, valves and springs, or resistors, capacitors and transistors. Network laws provide constraints at connection points (e.g. that the total current into a point is zero). Brown and De Kleer take much care to ensure that their device models do not embed unstated assumptions about the context in which these devices are placed. They have an important discussion of criteria for device-model selection for physics. The digital papers (Davis, Genesereth, Barrow) also use a device-centered ontology, but their choice of component models is much clearer since the devices are defined digitally.

Forbus uses an ontology based on the concept of process as the medium for transfer of causality. A single process is described as affecting a number of individuals; this combination of effects is expressed more easily than in device-centered ontology. However, in the process-centered ontology, it is harder to be sure that one has specified all ways a system can affect an individual than it is in the device-centered ontology where connections determine effects. Forbus has extended Pat Hayes' notion of 'history' to allow easier modeling of people's naive reasoning. Forbus also has a very interesting discussion of how processes and histories define the AI 'frame problem' out of existence, replacing it with the new and hopefully more tractable problems of local evolution and intersection/interaction.

Implementation

Most of the systems described here use propagation of constraints in their implementation. Of particular note is De Kleer's discussion of implementation problems, and his techniques for obtaining choices without backtracking. Davis uses successive suspension of constraints to control search for modifications to the structural descriptions to account for misbehavior. He uses both physical and electrical descriptions of a single system. Davis's system 'discovers' a failure caused by a bent connector pin which effectively added a wire to the system. Thus this short between two points changed the topology of the circuit. However, by using possible *close* 'pathways of interactions' this was discovered without having to examine very many possible circuit changes.

Barrow and Genesereth both use logic-based reasoners. Barrow uses PROLOG, and extends the proof procedures embedded in PROLOG to do case enumeration when appropriate, and unrolling of sequential behavior. Genesereth has extended the notion of resolution to use *resolution residue* to guide search in his diagnosis program.

Notation

The planning for this volume caused some convergence in the research, as can be seen in the occurrence of similar ideas in several papers. It also caused some convergence in the notation used by the authors, though not nearly enough for my taste. Williams, De Kleer and Brown use a common notation for qualitative values. Forbus uses a different one which separates magnitudes of quantities and their signs. Kuipers shows how new points in the quantity space can arise from analysis of the behavior of the system. Full convergence awaits the grand synthesis of all these ideas, and the appearance of a widely accepted teaching text.

ACKNOWLEDGMENT

I want to thank all of the authors, who in addition to writing and rewriting their own papers, contributed greatly to the quality and coherence of this volume by providing careful critiques of other papers. I am grateful to John Seely Brown who encouraged me to put together this special volume, to John and Johan De Kleer for seducing me into thinking about problems in qualitative reasoning, and to Mark Stefik for his aid and general support. Finally, I want to thank North-Holland for making a special effort to get this volume out in a timely manner, both in the AI Journal and as a book.

A Qualitative Physics Based on Confluences

Johan de Kleer and John Seely Brown
Xerox PARC, Intelligent Systems Laboratory, Palo Alto, CA 94304, U.S.A.

ABSTRACT

A qualitative physics predicts and explains the behavior of mechanisms in qualitative terms. The goals for the qualitative physics are (1) to be far simpler than the classical physics and yet retain all the important distinctions (e.g., state, oscillation, gain, momentum) without invoking the mathematics of continuously varying quantities and differential equations, (2) to produce causal accounts of physical mechanisms that are easy to understand, and (3) to provide the foundations for commonsense models for the next generation of expert systems.

This paper presents a fairly encompassing account of qualitative physics. First, we discuss the general subject of naive physics and some of its methodological considerations. Second, we present a framework for modeling the generic behavior of individual components of a device based on the notions of qualitative differential equations (confluences) and qualitative state. This requires developing a qualitative version of the calculus. The modeling primitives induce two kinds of behavior, intrastate and interstate, which are governed by different laws. Third, we present algorithms for determining the behavior of a composite device from the generic behavior of its components. Fourth, we examine a theory of explanation for these predictions based on logical proof. Fifth, we introduce causality as an ontological commitment for explaining how devices behave.

1. Introduction

Change is a ubiquitous characteristic of the physical world. But what is it? What causes it? How can it be described? Thousands of years of investigation have produced a rich and diverse physics that provides many answers. Important concepts and distinctions underlying change in physical systems are state, cause, law, equilibrium, oscillation, momentum, quasistatic approximation, contact force, feedback, etc. Notice that these terms are qualitative and can be intuitively understood. Admittedly they are commonly quantitatively defined. The behavior of a physical system can be described by the exact values of its variables (forces, velocities, positions, pressures, etc.) at each time instant. Such a description, although complete, fails to provide much insight into how the system functions. The insightful concepts and distinctions are usually qualitative, but they are embedded within the much more complex framework established by continuous real-valued variables and differential equations. Our long-term goal is to develop an alternate physics in which these same concepts are derived from a far simpler, but nevertheless formal, qualitative basis.

The motivations for developing a qualitative physics stem from outstanding problems in psychology, education, artificial intelligence, and physics. We want to identify the core knowledge that underlies physical intuition. Humans appear to use a qualitative causal calculus in reasoning about the behavior of their physical environment. Judging from the kinds of explanations humans give, this calculus is quite different from the classical physics taught in classrooms. This raises questions as to what this (naive) physics is like, and how it helps one to reason about the physical world.

In classical physics, the crucial distinctions for characterizing physical change are defined within a non-mechanistic framework and thus they are difficult to ground in the commonsense knowledge derived from interaction with the world. Qualitative physics provides an alternate and simpler way of arriving at the same conceptions and distinctions and thus provides a simpler pedagogical basis for educating students about physical mechanisms.

Artificial intelligence and (especially) its subfield of expert systems are producing very sophisticated computer programs capable of solving tasks that require extensive human expertise. A commonly recognized failing of such systems is their extremely narrow range of expertise and their inability to recognize when a problem posed to them is outside this range of expertise. In other words, they have no commonsense. In fact, expert systems usually cannot solve simpler versions of the problems they are designed to solve. The missing commonsense can be supplied, in part, by qualitative reasoning.

A qualitative causal physics provides an alternate way of describing physical phenomena. As compared to modern physics, this qualitative physics is only at its formative stages and does not have new explanatory value. However, the qualitative physics does suggest some promises of novelty, particularly in its explicit treatment of causality—something modern physics provides no formalism for treating.

Our proposal is to reduce the quantitative precision of the behavioral descriptions but retain the crucial distinctions. Instead of continuous real-valued variables, each variable is described qualitatively—taking on only a small number of values, usually $+$, $-$, or 0. Our central modeling tool is the qualitative differential equation, called a confluence. For example, the qualitative behavior of a valve is expressed by the confluence[1] $\partial P + \partial A - \partial Q = 0$ where Q is the flow through the valve, P is the pressure across the valve, A is

---

[1] We make no attempt to keep the units consistent.

the area available for flow, and ∂Q, ∂A, and ∂P represent changes in Q, A, and P. The confluence represents multiple competing tendencies: the change in area positively influences flow rate and negatively influences pressure, the change in pressure positively influences flow rate, etc. The same variable can appear in many confluences and thus can be influenced in many different ways. In an overall system each confluence must be satisfied individually. Thus if the area is increasing but the flow remains constant, the pressure must decrease no matter what the other influences on the pressure are. A single confluence often cannot characterize the behavior of a component over its entire operating range. In such cases, the range *must* be divided into subregions, each characterized by a different component state in which different confluences apply. For example, the behavior of the valve when it is completely open is quite different from that when it is completely closed. These two concepts, of confluence and of state, form the basis for a qualitative physics, a physics that maintains most of the important distinctions of the usual physics but is far simpler.

In presenting our qualitative physics, we rederive a large number of the concepts of classical physics. As the derivation is often novel, we simplify matters by drawing most of our examples from the same device: the pressure-regulator (see [16]). The pressure-regulator[2] illustrated in Fig. 1 is a device whose purpose is to maintain a constant output pressure (at C) even though the supply (connected to A) and loads (connected to C) vary. An explanation of how it achieves this function might be:

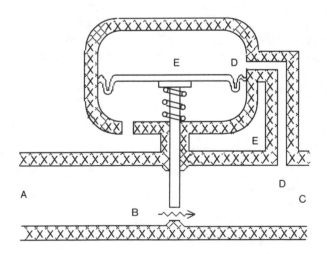

FIG. 1. Pressure-regulator.

[2] More sophisticated considerations than discussed in this paper dictate that most actual pressure-regulators be designed quite differently, but this figure accurately illustrates the central feedback action of regulators.

> An increase in source (A) pressure increases the pressure drop across the valve (B). Since the flow through the valve is proportional to the pressure across it, the flow through the valve also increases. This increased flow will increase the pressure at the load (C). However, this increased pressure is sensed (D) causing the diaphragm (E) to move downward against the spring pressure. The diaphragm is mechanically connected to the valve, so the downward movement of the diaphragm will tend to close the valve thereby pinching off the flow. Because the flow is now restricted the output pressure will rise much less than it otherwise would have.

This explanation characterizes the essential idea underlying the operation of the pressure-regulator that is designed to achieve a kind of homeostasis by sensing its own output and adjusting its operation. Systems that operate on this principle are subject to oscillation due to phase delay in the sensing and destructive feedback when used inappropriately. The foregoing explanation and analyses of feedback action are all derivable from our qualitative physics. No quantitative or analytical analysis is required, yet it is possible to identify the essential characteristics of the pressure-regulator's operation.

1.1. ENVISION

One of the central tenets of our methodology for exploring the ideas and techniques presented in this paper is to construct computer systems based on these ideas and compare their results with our expectations. Except when noted otherwise, everything has been implemented and tested in this way. The program ENVISION has been run successfully on hundreds of examples of various types of devices (electronic, translational, hydraulic, acoustic, etc.). Although we view constructing working programs as an important methodological strategy for doing research, the existence of a working implementation contributes little to the conceptual coherence of the theory. In this paper we focus on

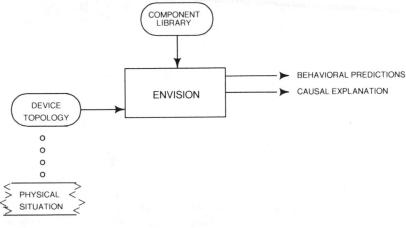

FIG. 2. ENVISION.

presenting the ideas of our conception of naive physics. We therefore leave out extensive examples, computer printouts or the algorithms that produce them.

Although the algorithms ENVISION uses are not the primary focus of this paper, a brief description of its inputs, outputs, and success criteria clarifies the stage for the following conceptual presentations. ENVISION's basic task is to derive function from structure for an arbitrary device. It relies on a single library of generic components and uses the same model library to analyze each device. The input to ENVISION is a description of a particular situation in terms of (a) a set of components and their allowable paths of interaction (i.e., the device's topology), (b) the input signals applied to the device (if any), and (c) a set of boundary conditions which constrain the device's behavior. ENVISION produces a description of the behavior of the system in terms of its allowable states, the values of the system's variables, and the direction these variables are changing. Most importantly, it produces complete causal accounts and logical proofs for that behavior. Both of these analyses provide explanations of how the system behaves with the causal analysis also identifying all possible feedback paths.

The success criteria for ENVISION are also important. Our physics is qualitative and hence sometimes underdetermines the behavior of a system. In these cases, ENVISION produces a set of behaviors (we call these interpretations). At a minimum, for a prediction to be correct, one of the interpretations must correspond to the actual behavior of the real device. A stronger criterion follows from observing that a structural description, abstracted qualitatively (i.e., the device topology), of a particular device implicitly characterizes a wide class of different physically realizable devices with the same device topology. The stronger criterion requires that (a) the behavior of each device in the class is described by one of the interpretations, and (b) every interpretation describes the behavior of some device of the class.

1.2. Organization

The remainder of this paper is divided into five major sections, each addressing a particular aspect of our qualitative physics. Each can be read as a separate unit. Section 2, 'Naive Physics', introduces the subject of naive physics and discusses some of its methodological considerations. We present the major paradigmatic assumptions that underlie the architectures and organizations of the remaining sections. Section 3, 'Modeling Structure', presents the techniques by which we can model the generic behavior of individual components of a device. We discuss the basic modeling primitives: the qualitative differential equation (confluence) and the notion of qualitative state. Section 4, 'Prediction of Behavior', discusses algorithms to determine the behavior of a composite device from the generic models of its individual components. In this section, we introduce the distinction of behavior within a state from behavior between states. The algorithms determine *what* the behavior is, not an explanation of it. In Section 5, 'Explanation of Behavior', we present a form of logical explanation of behavioral predictions—a kind of proof using a natural deduction scheme. The logical explanation turns out to be unsatisfactory as it makes no ontological commitments, just epistemological ones. In Section 6, 'Causality and Digital Physics', we present a completely different kind of explanation, one which explains device behavior in terms of *how* the device itself achieves its behavior. This information-processing view of causality may also serve as the basis for an alternate kind of physics.

We present a new unifying framework: the qualitative differential equation. This new research builds on the ideas of qualitative value, component models, and envisioning developed in earlier investigations [5–7]. These concepts and our methodology are discussed in more detail in our earlier papers. Some of the important concepts developed in this paper are:

– *Quasistatic approximation.* Most modeling, whether quantitative or qualitative, makes the approximation that behavior at some small time scale is unimportant. In modern thermodynamics, this concept is central to the definition of equilibrium. Until now, qualitative physics has treated this modeling issue in both an ad hoc and tacit manner. In our formulation, quasistatic assumptions play a theoretically motivated and explicit role.

– *Causality.* The behavior of a device is viewed as arising from the interactions of a set of processors, one for each component of the 'device'. The information-passing interactions of the individual components are the cause-effect interactions between the device's components. Within this framework, causal accounts are defined (as interactions that obey certain metaconstraints) and their limitations explored.

– *Mythical causality and mythical time.* Any set of component models makes some assumptions about device behavior (i.e., quasistatic assumptions) and hence cannot, in principle, yield *causal* accounts for the changes that must occur between equilibrium states of a system. In order to handle this problem we have defined new notions of causality and time (i.e., mythical causality and mythical time) cast in terms of information-passing 'negotiations' between processors of neighboring components.

– *Generalized machines.* Many physical situations can be viewed as some kind of generalized machine, whose behavior can be described in terms of variable values. These variables include force, velocity, pressure, flow, current, and voltage.

– *Proof as explanation.* Physical laws, viewed as constraints, are acausal. We discuss how a logical proof of the solution of a set of constraints is a kind of acausal explanation of behavior.

– *Qualitative calculus.* Qualitative physics is based on a qualitative calculus, the qualitative analog to the calculus of Newton and Leibniz. We define qualitative versions of value, continuity, differential, and integral.

– *Episodes*. Episodes are used to quantize time into periods within which the device's behavior is significantly different.

– *Digital physics*. Each component of a physical system can be viewed as a simple information processor. The overall behavior of the device is produced by causal interactions between physically adjacent components. Physical laws can then be viewed as emergent properties of the universal 'programs' executed by the processors. A new kind of physical law might thus be expressible as constraints on these programs, processors, or the information-flow among them.

2. Naive Physics

There is a growing amount of research in the area of naive physics, although often under different titles (e.g., qualitative process theory, qualitative physics, commonsense knowledge, or mechanistic mental models [5, 6, 7, 9, 10, 14, 15, 17, 21, 22]). All propose formalizing the commonsense knowledge about the everyday physical world, but each views this task rather differently. It is thus important to make clear what the current enterprise is all about. Naive physics is in itself an ambiguous term. Is it just bad physics? Is it psychology? Artificial intelligence? Physics? All these questions deserve to be asked and we take pains to answer them.

Naive physics concerns knowledge about the physical world. It would not be such an important area of investigation if it were not for two crucial facts: (a) people are very good at functioning in the physical world, and (b) no theory of this human capability exists that could serve as a basis for imparting it to computers. Modern science, which one might think should be of help here, does not provide much help. Although the modern mathematics in which most physical laws are expressed is relatively formal, the laws are all based on the presupposition of a shared unstated commonsense prephysics knowledge. Hence, it is not surprising that artificial intelligence has been rather unsuccessful at building systems that require physics problem-solving. The knowledge presented in textbooks is but the tip of the iceberg about what actually needs to be known to reason about the physical world [9]. Even the physicist will agree that he is not using his formal physics when avoiding an automobile collision or jumping back from his seat after someone has spilled hot coffee on the table. This is hardly an indictment of modern physics—why should it address itself to a subject area that every scientist takes as given? The formalisms of modern physics[3] do not provide much direct help; we need to look elsewhere.

Naive physics, as a theory, bears a resemblance to modern physics in two ways. First, it makes explicit claims about the knowledge necessary for deriving, from relatively meager evidence about the world, the kinds of com-

---

[3] Although some informal attempts are being made for pedagogical purposes such as "physics for poets" or texts such as *Conceptual Physics* [18].

monsense conclusions that modern physics takes as given. Second, naive physics makes claims about what constitutes information-rich idealizations about the world. For example, in Newtonian physics a crucial idealization is the notion of point mass; in our physics, direction of change is a crucial idealization.

Our naive physics is also an idealization in other senses. It is not intended to be a psychological theory per se—although we use observations of human behavior as hints. We are not concerned with human foibles. Nor do we focus on one domain in particular, nor on one particular set of laws for a domain. Rather, we are concerned with the general *form* of those laws and the calculi for deriving inferences from the laws.

As in the naive physics of Hayes [17], the actual mechanisms used to derive inferences of secondary importance, although we do want to characterize properties of the derivational apparatus. Unlike Hayes, we consider accounting for *how* the physical system achieves its behavior a proper task of naive physics; note that he does not view the world as a collection of devices, and thus distinguishing 'how' from 'what' carries little weight in his framework. Our physics is based on viewing the world as a machine (albeit a very complex one).

The main goal of our qualitative physics is to provide a theoretical framework for understanding the behavior of physical systems. We are particularly interested in prediction and explanation. It should be possible to predict (an important kind of inference) the future behavior of the physical system. It should also be possible to explain how the device achieves the predicted behavior. This kind of explanation is not based on *how* some algorithm constructs predictions, but rather *how* the device produces the behavior. To answer this latter kind of 'how' question requires an ontological commitment to nature as mechanism.

Our qualitative physics is based on a number of fundamental principles or paradigmatic assumptions. We briefly discuss each of these assumptions in turn, but first we need to make explicit the reasons why we chose dynamical systems (i.e., hydraulic, electrical, rotational, etc. systems) as a set of domains to focus our initial inquiry into qualitative physics.

2.1. Our basic strategic move

The essence of doing physics is modeling a physical situation, solving the resulting equations and then interpreting the results in physical terms. Modeling a physical situation requires a description of its physical structure. Although there does not exist a general methodology for describing the structure of all physical situations, system dynamics[4] [2, 20, 24] fortunately, provides a

---

[4] We mean the formalisms used in linear systems theory, not that of Forrester. System dynamics is used to model the behavior of dynamical systems of all types (e.g., mechanical, electrical, fluid and thermal) starting with a description of the system in terms of lumped ideal elements which interact through ideal interconnections.

methodology for describing a large and interesting collection of physical systems. Thus we initially focus our attention on this class of situations and on how behavior arises from structure and do not worry much about the extremely difficult issue of modeling more general physical situations. This move combined with our use of causality as an ontological principle results in a very mechanistic world view. Every physical situation is regarded as some type of physical device or machine made up of individual components, each component contributing to the behavior of the overall device.

2.2. Qualitativeness

The variables used to describe the behavior of the device can only take on a small predetermined number of values, and each value corresponds to some interval on the number line. Using a small number of values instead of a dense set of numbers means some information must be lost. However, our goal is to make a judicious choice for the qualitative intervals such that as little information as possible about the important features of device functioning is lost. Thus the divisions between intervals are best chosen to be at singularities such as at zeros and discontinuities. As such, the formalisms underlying our qualitative calculus relates to the branch of mathematics that characterizes the qualitative behavior of systems of differential equations, i.e., catastrophe theory [23].

By taking the qualitative approach, some loss of information cannot be avoided. Sometimes so much information is lost that it is not possible to determine unambiguously the qualitative behavior. Although the consequences of ambiguity are important, the definitions and concepts we define are not significantly affected by the presence of ambiguity. Therefore, in the main flow of this paper we usually assume no ambiguity. In the appendices we discuss the subtle consequences of ambiguity that are important, but tangential, to the main arguments in this paper.[5]

2.3. Structure to function

We want to be able to infer the behavior of a physical device from a description of its physical structure. The device consists of physically disjoint parts connected together. The structure of a device is described in terms of its components and interconnections. Each component has a type, whose generic model (i.e., laws governing its behavior) is available in the model library. The task is to determine the behavior of a device given its structure and access to the generic models in the model library.

---

[5] Our earlier work [7] focused almost exclusively on the problem of ambiguities and how representing ambiguities (i.e., multiple interpretations) can be useful in producing robust troubleshooting systems that handle faults that fundamentally alter the underlying mechanism of the device.

2.4. No-function-in-structure

The goal is to draw inferences about the behavior of the composite device solely from laws governing the behaviors of its parts. This view raises a difficult question: where do the laws and the descriptions of the device being studied come from? Unless we place some conditions on the laws and the descriptions, the inferences that can be made may be (implicitly) pre-encoded in the structural description or the model library.

The *no-function-in-structure* principle is central: the laws of the parts of the device may not presume the functioning of the whole. Take as a simple example a light switch. The model of a switch that states, "if the switch is off, no current flows; and if the switch is on, current flows", violates the no-function-in-structure principle. Although this model correctly describes the behavior of the switches in our offices, it is false as there are many closed switches through which current does not necessarily flow (such as, two switches in series). Current flows in the switch only if it is closed and there is a potential for current flow. One of the reasons why it is surprisingly difficult to create a 'context-free' description of a component is that whenever one thinks of how a component behaves, one must, almost by definition, think of it in some type of supporting context. Thus the properties of how the component functions in that particular supporting context are apt to influence subtly how one models it.

2.5. Class-wide assumptions

Those assumptions that are idiosyncratic to a particular device must be distinguished from those that are generic to the entire class of devices. For example, the explanation of the pressure-regulator's behavior ignored turbulence at the valve seat, Brownian motion of the fluid molecules, and the compressibility of the fluid; these are however all reasonable assumptions to make for a wide class of hydraulic devices. We call such assumptions *class-wide* assumptions, and they form a kind of universal resolution for the 'microscope' being used to study the physical device.

Given this definition for class-wide assumptions, the no-function-in-structure principle can be stated more clearly: the laws for the components of a device of a particular class may not make any other assumptions about the behavior of the particular device that are not made about the class in general. An example of an undesirable non-class-wide assumption would be if the law for the valve stated that the area available for flow decreases as pressure goes up. This law is valid for the valve in the pressure-regulator, not for valves in general.

Although as originally phrased, no-function-in-structure is unachievable, its essential idea is preserved through the use of class-wide assumptions. A presupposition behind no-function-in-structure is that it is possible to describe the laws and the parts of a particular device without making any assumptions about the behavior of interest. There is no neutral, objective, assumption-free way of determining the structure of the device and the laws of its components. The no-function-in-structure demands an infinite regress: a complete set of engineering drawings, a geometrical description, and the positions of each of its molecules all make some unwarranted assumptions for some behavior that is potentially of interest. Thus we admit that assumptions in general cannot be avoided in the identification of the parts and their laws, which is why class-wide assumptions are crucial.

Class-wide assumptions play two important roles in our qualitative physics. First, they play a definitional role. Formalizing the idealization (i.e., qualitative physics) demands that we be explicit about which assumptions we are making. Second, and as important but not discussed in this paper, they are important for building expert systems. In constructing an expert system to design, operate, or troubleshoot complex devices, it is critical to clearly state what assumptions are being used in modeling the given device. Thus, when the unexpected situation or casualty occurs, these assumptions can be examined to determine whether the 'knowledge base' can be relied on.

The most common kind of class-wide assumption is that behavior of short-enough duration can be ignored. Under this assumption the 'settling' behavior by which the device reaches equilibrium after a disturbance need not be modeled. As 'short-enough' is a relative term, this assumption can be made at many levels. This assumption plays a major role in studying the heating and cooling of gases. In classical physics, it is called the quasistatic approximation. For example, the lumped circuit formulation of electronics makes the quasistatic assumption that the dimensions of the physical circuit are small compared to the wavelength associated with the highest frequency of interest. Other examples of class-wide assumptions are that the mean free path of the fluid particles is small compared to the distances over which the pressure changes appreciably and that the rate of change of the fields is not too large.

A particular set of class-wide assumptions will suggest a procedure for determining the structural decomposition of a given situation into its constituent parts. The most common and well-known procedure is the derivation of a schematic for an electrical circuit. The procedure is well known, and usually tacit; all electrical engineers will agree whether a particular schematic is an accurate description of the circuit. In fact, the schematic is now considered a description of the structure of the electrical device. The situation is analogous in other domains such as acoustics, fluids, etc., but not as clean as it is for electronics.

Providing a coherent theory of class-wide assumptions would involve another paper in itself. For the purpose of this paper, it is sufficient to recognize they exist and to provide some examples. By and large we employ the same class-wide assumptions that are used in introductory system dynamics and classical mechanics tests. Some typical class-wide assumptions have already been mentioned. Some others are: all masses are rigid and do not deform or break; all flows are laminar; there are always enough particles in a pipe so that macroscopic laws hold; currents are low enough not to destroy components; and magnetic fields are small enough not to induce significant currents in physically adjacent wires. Under these kinds of class-wide assumptions, wires, pipes, cables, linkages can be modeled as ideal connections. Note that our formalisms do not presume those class-wide assumptions. It is possible to model a string as a part that breaks at a certain tension or a wire as melting away at a certain current. It is just that commonly one chooses not to model strings and wires this way.

Class-wide assumptions determine the kinds of interactions that can occur between parts. Under the usual class-wide assumptions of electronics, the only way two capacitors can interact is through wires. However, if the electric fields are strong enough each capacitor will affect the distribution of charges in the other. Thus neighboring, physically distinct parts can become coupled thereby changing the connectivity of the parts and the types of interactions that can occur between them.[6]

A sophisticated reasoning strategy, not discussed in this paper, concerns when and how to change the class-wide assumptions when reasoning about a particular device. Such concerns are critical for troubleshooting where faults can force devices into fundamentally new modes of operation [1, 3]. However, even a simple analysis can sometimes require departures from the usual set of class-wide assumptions. For example, it is sometimes important to remove a class-wide assumption for some localized part of the device, such as two wires running close together, which should be modeled as a transmission line. A fluids example of this phenomenon is discussed in the next section.

2.6. Locality

The principle of *locality* demands that the laws for a part cannot specifically refer to any other part. A part can only act on or be acted on by its immediate neighbors and its immediate neighbors must be identifiable a priori in the structure. To an extent, locality follows from no-function-in-structure. If a law for part of type A referred to a specific neighboring part of type B, it would be making a presupposition that every device which contained a part of type A also contained a part of type B. The locality principle also plays a crucial role in our definition of causality. Our theory does not apply to distributed parameter systems, where the locus of causal interactions cannot be determined a priori.

---

[6] A single device can be modeled using various sets of class-wide assumptions. Each such set leads to a different collection of device parts and different models for these parts (including their interconnections). Therefore, violation of no-function-in-structure can occur in the models for a part type or in the identification of the parts of a device. These two kinds of violations are arguably indistinguishable.

2.7. The importance of the principles

Violating the no-function-in-structure principle has no direct consequences on the representation and inference schemes presented later in the paper. Although the form of the structure and the laws are chosen to minimize blatant violations of the no-function-in-structure principle, it is possible to represent and draw inferences from arbitrary laws—in fact, it is too easy.

Without this principle, our proposed naive physics would be nothing but a proposal for an architecture for building handcrafted (and thus ad hoc) theories for specific devices and situations. It would provide no systematic way of ensuring that a particular class of laws did or did not already have built into them the answers to the questions that the laws were intended to answer. That is not to say that the handcrafted theories are uninteresting—quite the reverse, and the architecture proposed in this paper may well be appropriate for this task. This is especially true for constructing an account of the knowledge of any one individual about the given physical situation. We are doing something quite different; we want to develop a physics—not a psychological account— which is capable of supporting inferences about the world.

Another purpose for the principles is to draw a distinction between the 'work' our proposed naive physics does and the 'work' that must be done (outside of our naive physics) to identify the parts and laws. Only after making such a distinction is evaluation possible. Without making the distinction, a reader could always ask, in response to some complexity in an example, "Why didn't they model it differently?"; or in response to some clever inference in an example, "They built this into their models". As the principles define what can and what cannot be assumed within the models, the criticisms implied by these two questions are invalid. Of course, the principles themselves are open to challenge.

3. Modeling Structure

3.1. Device structure

Our approach is reductionist: the behavior of a physical structure can be completely accounted for by the behaviors of its physical constituents. We distinguish three kinds of constituents: materials, components and conduits. Physical behavior is accomplished by operating on and transporting materials such as water, air, electrons, etc. The components are constituents that can change the form and characteristics of material. Conduits are simple constituents which transport material from one component to another and cannot change any aspect of the material within them. Some examples of conduits are pipes, wires and cables.

The physical structure of a device can be represented by a topology in which nodes represent components and edges represent conduits. Fig. 3 illustrates the

V V (VALVE)

T1   IN   #1   #2   OUT   T2

FP   SNS (SENSOR)

T3

SMP (MAIN-SUMP)

FIG. 3. Device topology of the pressure-regulator.

TABLE 1. Icons

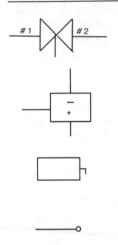

A valve, viewed in isolation, has no distinguished inputs or outputs so the two fluid terminals are labeled #1 and #2. The bottom terminal controls how much area is available for flow within the valve.

A pressure sensor takes as input the pressure from the conduit attached to terminal + to the conduit attached to terminal −, and produces an output signal proportional to it. In the pressure-regulator, increased pressure results in less area available for flow, so the −-terminal is attached to the regulator's output and +-terminal to the fluid reference.

By convention, most pressurelike variables have a common reference. For electrical systems it is ground, for mechanical system it is the fixed reference frame, and for fluid systems it is the main-sump. This is the icon for the main-sump. Note that strictly speaking a reference is a conduit, not a component.

Terminals indicate those terminals which are connected to the external world about which no information is provided in the device topology.

device topology of the pressure-regulator diagrammed in Fig. 1. In this device topology, the conduits IN and OUT transport material of type fluid and conduit FP transports material of type force.

In order to avoid ambiguity, the following is a description of the topology of Fig. 3 in a textural rather than graphical form. It is important to note that there is no information in the names of any of the components and conduits, these have been chosen (as well as the geometry of Fig. 3) solely for the reader's benefit. Each component is described by *name:type[conduits]*, where *name* is solely used to refer to the component, *type* is the generic type of the component, and *conduits* are the names of the conduits to which the terminals of the component are connected. Whenever there might be an ambiguity the conduits are prefixed by *terminal:* indicating the particular component terminal the conduit is attached to.

T1 : terminal[IN]
T2 : terminal[OUT]
T3 : terminal[SMP]
SNS : sensor[+ : SMP, − : OUT, FP]
VV : quantity-valve[#1 : IN, #2 : OUT, FP]

Behavior is described in terms of the attributes of the material. Most behavior can be described by dual attributes, one pressurelike and the other flowlike. For a fluid, the attributes are pressure and volumetric flow; for electricity, voltage and current; for translational conduits, velocity and force; for rotational conduits, angular velocity and torque.

By definition, conduits only transport, but do not process, material. Furthermore, we make the simplification that a conduit only transports one type of material. A conduit has a very simple structure: a collection of attachments to components with each attachment taking place at a terminal. For example, a flowlike attribute is associated with every such terminal, and a pressurelike attribute is associated with the entire conduit.

Conduits are poor for modeling distributed parameter systems (e.g., heat flow in a slab) or fields (e.g., gravitational field of the sun). In limited cases, where the paths of causal interaction can be determined *a priori*, a conduit can be used to model the effects of a field.

Unlike conduits, components process and transform material. The behavior of a component can either be modeled by a set of formal laws or by an interconnected set of lower-level components. In this latter case, the lawful behavior of the component emerges from the behavior of the lower-level device. Conduits can also be viewed as more detailed devices, but it is rarely profitable to do so.

3.2. Qualitative variables

An attribute represents a set of variable entities (e.g., a variable and its integrals and derivatives with respect to time), each of which can be referenced in a law. Unlike quantitative variables, qualitative variables can only take on one of a small number of values. This set of possible values is determined by the quantity space [15] it participates in. '$[\cdot]_Q$' is used to indicate the qualitative value of the expression within the brackets with respect to quantity space Q. Each qualitative value corresponds to some interval on the real-number line. These regions are completely determined by the laws and typically are disjoint.

The most important property of a quantity is whether it is increasing, decreasing or unchanging (or, equivalently, its derivative is positive, negative or zero). This simple, but most important, quantity space consists of only three values: +, − and 0. + represents the case when the quantity is positive, 0 represents the case when the quantity is zero, and − represents the case when the quantity is negative. This quantity space is notated: '$[\cdot]_0$.' More generally, the simple quantity space of $x < a$, $x = a$, and $x > a$ is notated by '$[\cdot]_a$.' Thus, $[x]_0 = +$ iff $x > 0$, $[x]_0 = 0$ iff $x = 0$, and $[x]_0 = -$ iff $x < 0$.

Addition and multiplication (Tables 2 and 3) are defined straight-forwardly (as $[\cdot]_0$ is so common it is abbreviated $[\cdot]$).

TABLE 2. $[X] + [Y]$

[Y] \ [X]	−	0	+
−	−	−	−
0	−	0	+
+	−	+	+

TABLE 3. $[X] \times [Y]$

[Y] \ [X]	−	0	+
−	+	0	−
0	0	0	0
+	−	0	+

Note that although $[xy] = [x][y]$, $[x + y] \neq [x] + [y]$.

This $+$, 0, $-$ value set is surprisingly versatile. For example, if we need to distinguish x with respect to landmark value a we define a new variable $y = x - a$. Then, $[y] = +$ corresponds to $x > a$, $[y] = 0$ corresponds to $x = a$, and $[y] = -$ corresponds to $x < a$.

"x is increasing" in the formalism is $[dx/dt] = +$. This notation tends to be cumbersome both for typography and computer input/output. Thus, ∂x is used as an abbreviation for $[dx/dt]$, and more generally $\partial^n x$ for $[d^n x/dt^n]$. Note that unlike in quantitative calculus, $\partial^{n+1} x$ cannot be obtained by differentiating $\partial^n x$. One always has to go back to the quantitative definition: $\partial^{n+1} x = [d^{n+1} x/dt^{n+1}]$. This fact has dramatic impact on the form of the component models.

It is important to note that ∂x and $[x]$ are only instantaneously independent. As time passes, $[x]$'s changes are governed by ∂x (i.e., integration). The laws must be time-invariant. Thus every law applies to a time-instant, and no law may depend on the value of the time variable. (Laws describing behavior over time require explicit integrals in their formulation.) The topic of time is described in more detail in its own section as it plays a central role in our qualitative physics.

The simplicity of this algebra is deceptive and the algebra of Tables 2 and 3 is often misunderstood. The change of a quantity is often confused with the change in the magnitude value of a quantity (i.e., whether it is moving towards or away from zero). For example, if x changes in value from -6 to -7 its value is decreasing, even though its magnitude is increasing from 6 to 7. Thus, the statements "x is increasing" and "$-x$ is decreasing" are equivalent: $[x] =$

$-[-x]$. $[d^2x/dt^2] = [x]\partial x = +$, if x is moving away from zero, and $[x]\partial x = -$, if x is moving towards zero.

3.3. Qualitative calculus

Some component laws must be described in terms of derivatives. In our physics, a simple theory of qualitative integration is constructed from the qualitative versions of continuity, Rolle's theorem, and the mean value theorem of the standard differential calculus.

Time, always the independent variable, is also quantized, but in a very different way than the qualitative values. In particular, the distinctions for values of time are not determined *a priori* but become determined as a consequence of analyzing the confluences. The actual value of the time variable is irrelevant, the only important property is the (partial) ordering of time values. Thus many of the theorems in the standard calculus, when applied to functions of time, are the axioms of time for ours.

– *Qualitative values.* Generally, the qualitative values a variable can have are $A_0, \ldots, A_z$, representing disjoint abutting intervals that cover the entire number line (the $A_0 = -$, $A_1 = 0$, $A_2 = +$ value set is an instance of this definition). The ends of the intervals can either be open or closed and the difference between being open and being closed is crucial. The left end of A_0 must be $-\infty$. If the right end of A_k is open, the left end of A_{k+1} must be closed. If the right end of A_k is closed, the left end of A_{k+1} must be open. The right end of A_z must be ∞.

– *Continuity.* As a function of time, every variable changes continuously: If $[X(T_1)]_Q = A_k$ and $[X(T_2)]_Q = A_m$, then for every A_n between A_k and A_m there exists some time $T_1 < T < T_2$ such that $[X(T)]_Q = A_n$. Put intuitively, no variable may jump over a qualitative value.

– *Mean value theorem.* Qualitative versions of Rolle's theorem and the mean value theorem also hold. If $[X(T_1)] = [X(T_2)]$ where $T_1 < T_2$, then $\partial X(T_i) = 0$ for some $T_1 \leq T_i \leq T_2$. If $T_1 < T_2$, then there exists a T_i such that $\partial X(T_i) = [X(T_2)] - [X(T_1)]$. However, as time is quantized, these well-known theorems can be stated far more strongly. In particular, as time is not dense, it makes sense to speak of two successive times. Call T' the time immediately after T. If $[X(T)] = [X(T')] = C$ where C is the qualitative value representing a point on the number line, then $\partial X(T) = 0$.

These theorems form the basis for reasoning about time in our qualitative physics. Consider some examples using the $+$, $-$, 0 value set. $[X(T)] = +$ followed by $[X(T')] = -$ violates continuity. In most contexts[7] the mean value

---

[7] If T is an instant and $\partial X(T) = 0$ this formulation of the mean value theorem is technically incorrect. More generally, $[X(T')] = [X(T)] + \partial^n X$ where n is the first non-zero derivative order. However, for many systems, and, in particular, the examples discussed in this paper, if $[X(T)] = 0$ and $\partial X(T) = 0$ then $\partial^n X(T) = 0$ for all n. So we will always use $[X(T')] = [X(T)] + \partial X(T)$. This issue is discussed in [4].

theorem can be restated as $[X(T')] = [X(T)] + \partial X(T)$. Thus if $[X(T)] = 0$ and $\partial X(T) = +$, then $[X(T')] = +$. If $[X(T)] = +$ and $\partial X(T) = +$ or $\partial X(T) = 0$, then $[X(T')] = +$. On the other hand, if $[X(T)] = +$ and $\partial X(T) = -$, $[X(T')]$ either remains $+$ or becomes 0. We discuss these issues in far greater detail in a later section.

3.4. Models

The component model characterizes all the potential behaviors that the component can manifest. The lawful behavior of a component is expressed as a set of confluence equations. Each model confluence consists of a set of terms which must sum to a constant: $\sum T_i = C$. A term can be a variable (i.e., an attribute), the negation of a variable, or the product of a 'constant' and a variable. Consider the form of the confluence $\partial P + \partial A - \partial Q = 0$. This confluence consists of three terms, ∂P, ∂A, and $-\partial Q$, which sum (we presume a $+$, 0, $-$ value set) to zero. For naturalness sake, we sometimes write the confluence $[x] - [y] = 0$ as $[x] = [y]$.

A set of values satisfies a confluence if either (a) the qualitative equality strictly holds using the arithmetic of Tables 2 and 3, or (b) if the left-hand side of the confluence cannot be evaluated as in the following case. When $\partial P = +$ and $\partial A = -$, the confluence $\partial P + \partial A - \partial Q = 0$ is satisfies because $\partial P + \partial A$ has no value. A set of values contradicts a confluence if (a) every variable has a value, (b) the left-hand side evaluates, and (c) the confluence is not satisfied. Thus $\partial P = +$, $\partial A = +$, and $\partial Q = -$ is contradictory. Note that by this definition a confluence need neither be satisfied nor contradicted if some of the variables do not have assigned values.

3.4.1. The notion of qualitative state

Confluence alone is an inadequate modeling primitive. The value model $\partial P + \partial A - \partial Q = 0$ violates fidelity: if the valve is closed, no flow (Q) is possible, the area (A) available for flow is unchanging, and the pressure (P) across the valve is unconstrained; but the confluence states that if $\partial A = 0$ and $\partial Q = 0$, then $\partial P = 0$. Thus $\partial P + \partial A - \partial Q = 0$ is too specific a model. It violates the no-function-in-structure principle by assuming the valve is never closed. Using confluences alone, no model for the valve exists which does not violate the no-function-in-structure principle.

The second qualitative modeling primitive is qualitative state. Qualitative states divide the behavior of a component into different regions, each of which is described by a different set of confluences. The notion of state is often not necessary in quantitative analysis since a single mathematical equation can adequately model the behavior of the component. Nevertheless it is often convenient to introduce state into quantitative analysis in order to delineate regions where certain effects are negligible or to form piecewise approximations. On the other hand, in the qualitative regime the notion of state is absolutely necessary, since it is often not possible to formulate a *single* qualitative equation set which adequately characterizes the behavior of the component over its entire operating range.

In order to satisfy the no-function-in-structure principle the region of operation is solely specified in terms of inequalities among variables (but not derivatives and integrals). These inequalities must always be of the form $x \, op \, y$, where op is one of $>$, $=$, $<$, $\leq$ or $\geq$ and x and y are non-derivative variables or symbolic constants. For example, the closed state of a valve is defined by the condition $[a = 0]$, stating that if the component is in state CLOSED there is no area available for flow and if there is no area available for flow the component is in state CLOSED. For each qualitative state, the component model provides the confluences which govern the behavior in that state. These specifications correspond to the quantity conditions of qualitative process theory [15]. However, we do not use his more general notion of a global quantity space for the entire device, instead we use a simpler, local quantity space for each component which suffices for our qualitative physics.

The full model for the valve is (the general form of the model is *state*:[*specifications*], *confluences*):

$$
\begin{array}{llll}
\text{OPEN:} & [A = A_{\text{MAX}}], & [P] = 0, & \partial P = 0, \\
\text{WORKING:} & [0 < A < A_{\text{MAX}}], & [P] = [Q], & \partial P + \partial A - \partial Q = 0, \\
\text{CLOSED:} & [A = 0], & [Q] = 0, & \partial Q = 0.
\end{array}
$$

In state OPEN, the valve functions as a simple conduit, there is no pressure drop across it, and the flow through it is unconstrained. Neither can the pressure across it change—that can only be caused by a change in position of the valve. The state CLOSED is the dual to state OPEN. In it the valve completely disconnects the input from the output. There is no flow through the valve and the pressure across it is unconstrained. The flow through it cannot change without changing the area available for flow.

3.4.2. *Pure and mixed models*

The model confluences are not always simple sums. The correct confluence for the WORKING state of the valve is actually $\partial P + [P]\partial A - \partial Q = 0$ not $\partial P + \partial A - \partial Q = 0$ as stated earlier. This can be illustrated by examining the case where P is negative. The basic behavioral characteristic of the valve is that an increase in the area available for flow always reduces the *absolute valve of the pressure drop across the valve*. If the pressure drop is a positive value, an increase in area decreases the drop to zero (as in the previous analysis). If the pressure drop is a negative value, an increase in area increases the drop to zero. Thus the second term of the valve confluence is $[P]\partial A$ not ∂A.

We call a confluence, which is a simple sum of variables, *pure* (e.g., $\partial P + \partial A - \partial Q = 0$) as opposed to a sum of products, which we call *mixed* (e.g.,

$\partial P + [P]\partial A - \partial Q = 0$). It is always possible to construct pure models from mixed ones by adding qualitative states. For example, the state for which $\partial P + [P]\partial A - \partial Q = 0$ holds can be split into three states thereby producing a pure model: one in which $P > 0$ so that $\partial P + \partial A - \partial Q = 0$, one in which $P = 0$ so that $\partial P - \partial Q = 0$, and one in which $P < 0$ so that $\partial P - \partial A - \partial Q = 0$. The resulting pure model is formally equivalent to the mixed one and the solution methods function as well for mixed models as well as for pure ones, but we generally presume the models to be pure. The pure five-state valve model is:

OPEN:	$[A = A_{MAX}]$,	$[P] = 0$,	$\partial P = 0$,
WORKING-+:	$[0 < A < A_{MAX}, P > 0]$,	$[P] = [Q]$,	$\partial P + \partial A - \partial Q = 0$,
WORKING-0:	$[0 < A < A_{MAX}, P = 0]$,	$[P] = [Q]$,	$\partial P - \partial Q = 0$,
WORKING--:	$[0 < A < A_{MAX}, P < 0]$,	$[P] = [Q]$,	$\partial P - \partial A - \partial Q = 0$,
CLOSED:	$[A = 0]$,	$[Q] = 0$,	$\partial Q = 0$.

This model illustrates, that for pure models, the set of all confluences can be divided into those involving solely derivatives and those involving solely the variables themselves.

3.4.3. Constructing the component models

Although the confluences can be derived from commonsense knowledge of component behavior, most are or can be viewed as adaptations of the conventional physical model. Often that adaptation is direct. For example, conservation of fluid for a pipe is exactly $q_{in} - q_{out} = 0$ and the corresponding confluence is $[q_{in}] - [q_{out}] = 0$. If the physical model is a linear function, $\sum c_i x_i = c_0$ where the c_i are constants, the confluence is $\sum [c_i][x_i] = [c_0]$. In general, a quantitative equation can be transformed to a qualitative one by rules of the following form: $[e_1 + e_2] \Rightarrow [e_1] + [e_2]$, $[e_1 e_2] \Rightarrow [e_1][e_2]$, $[0] + [e] \Rightarrow [e]$, $[0][e] \Rightarrow [0]$, $[+][e] \Rightarrow [e]$, and $[-][e] \Rightarrow - [e]$. Additionally, if e is a constant, or always of the same sign, substitute its qualitative value.

The original physical model need not be linear. The flow rate through an orifice is given by Cochin [2, p. 797]:

$$Q = CA\sqrt{2P/\rho}, \quad P > 0,$$

where Q is the flow rate through the orifice, C is the discharge coefficient of the orifice, P is the pressure across the valve, and ρ is the mass density of the fluid. Transforming:

$$[Q] = [C][A][\sqrt{2P/\rho}] = [+][+][\sqrt{2P/\rho}] = [P].$$

To obtain the confluence for the changes we must first differentiate the quantitative equation and then transform it. Differentiating,

$$\frac{dQ}{dt} = C\sqrt{\frac{2P}{\rho}}\frac{dA}{dt} + \frac{CA}{\rho}\sqrt{\frac{\rho}{2P}}\frac{dP}{dt}.$$

Transforming,

$$\partial Q = [C][\sqrt{2P/\rho}]\partial A + [C][A][\sqrt{\rho/2P}][P]\partial P.$$

Simplifying,

$$\partial Q = [P]\partial A + [A][P][P]\partial P.$$

As $P > 0$ and $A > 0$ we get

$$\partial Q = \partial A + \partial P.$$

The transformation process introduces component states in two ways. First, the original quantitative equation may be based on states. For example, the preceding valve model holds only for $P > 0$. Second, state specifications can be introduced to remove ambiguities. For example, the transformation $[e_1 + e_2] \Rightarrow [e_1] + [e_2]$ loses information. This information may be regained. For example, $[e_1 + e_2]$ may be + if $x > A$ in which case it is worth introducing a component state. In general, if the physical model is of the form $\sum [f_i]\partial x_i = [f_0]$, then it may be worth analyzing the regions of $[f_i]$ and introducing component states for each.

Another method is to linearize via the Taylor expansion producing an equation of the form $\sum g_i \, dx_i/dt = g_0$ where g_0 represents the contributions of higher-order derivatives. This equation is then transformed into a collection of states corresponding to the regions of g_i each with its individual confluences. Thus, provided that the original physical model is well-behaved, there is a simple procedure for determining the qualitative states and confluences for a component type.

3.4.4. *The laws for connections*

The laws for flowlike variables are based on the fact that conduits are always completely full of material and incompressible (by definition), and therefore any material added through one terminal must result in material leaving by some other terminal. In other words, material is instantaneously conserved. This rule is called the *continuity condition*.[8] For electrical circuits, it is called Kirchhoff's current law; for fluid systems, the law of conservation of matter, for thermal systems, the law of conservation of energy.[9] The continuity condition requires that the sum of the current, forces, heat-flows, etc., into a conduit (and most components) be zero. As these rules are simple sums they apply to the derivatives of attributes too. These can all be expressed as confluences.

As the value of the pressurelike variable in a conduit is the same everywhere in the conduit, there are no pressure laws for individual conduits or components. Furthermore, if there are no structural loops in the device (i.e., there

---

[8] From system dynamics.

[9] Assuming the common, and somewhat misleading, convention in which the two variables are taken to be temperature and heat-flow. Better would be temperature and entropy-flow.

is only one path of conduits and components between every two components), no pressure laws are needed. For these devices the continuity condition alone completely specifies the qualitatively significant behavior of the material in the conduits. Few devices have this property however. Most interesting devices contain many structural loops. For these loops, the behavior of the material has an additional relevant property. No matter which path the material takes from component A to B, the sum of the individual pressure drops along each path must be equal. This is called the *compatibility* condition.[10] For example, if the pressure between conduits A and B is x and the pressure between conduits B and C is y, then the pressure between conduits A and C is $x + y$ (and thus qualitatively $[x] + [y]$). Compatibility requires equal voltages, velocities, etc., at points where the components are connected.

It is a simple matter to construct all the continuity and compatibility equations from a device topology. However, this set of equations is usually highly redundant. In quantitative analysis every extra equation introduces added complexity, and therefore a great deal of effort is taken to ensure that a minimal number of equations are included. In the qualitative domain, the computational effort manipulating +, 0 and − is insignificant. However, the addition of redundant equations has numerous unfortunate side-effects for generating explanations and detecting feedback.[11] Therefore, as in the quantitative case, there is a motivation for having all the equations independent.

Only a few of the possible compatibility and continuity confluences are necessary to establish the compatibility and continuity conditions for the entire device. There are a number of theorems in system dynamics that indicate exactly how many equations are necessary and how to choose them. Most of those theorems are false in the qualitative domain, and we have not yet completed the theoretical analysis to determine how many confluences are actually necessary (n 'independent' confluences in n variables do not necessarily have a unique solution). We include a continuity confluence for every component and a compatibility confluence for every three conduits (between which paths exist and transport the same object type). This usually produces a few redundant confluences, but we have never found a case where adding more conduit confluences provided more information about behavior.

3.4.5. *A model of the pressure-regulator*

We have developed all the necessary modeling primitives. The specific confluences governing the behavior of the device can be constructed from the

---

[10] Again, from system dynamics.

[11] For example, in generating explanations redundant equations result in multiple explanations (derivations) for the same behavior. These explanations are superficially different, but essentially identical. Also, the behavior a redundant equation with three or more variables produces often looks superficially like feedback.

device topology, the library of component models and the composite device state. Assuming that the valve is in a state in which $P > 0$ and $0 < A < A_{MAX}$ (state WORKING-+), the derivative confluences for the pressure-regulator form seven confluences in eight variables. The pressure-regulator has only two components, each of which is modeled by one confluence. The remaining confluences describe the behavior of the material. We state all the confluences in terms of the variables of the pressure-regulator (Fig. 4). The subscripts on the variables indicate which terminals and conduits of the device topology the variable refers to. The confluence for the valve is

$$\partial P_{IN,OUT} - \partial Q_{\#1(VV)} + \partial X_{FP} = 0$$

where $P_{IN,OUT}$ is the pressure drop from input to output, $Q_{\#1(VV)}$ is the flow from terminal #1 into the valve, and ∂X_{FP} is the position of the valve control and is qualitatively equal to area available for flow. The confluence for the pressure-sensor is

$$\partial X_{FP} + \partial P_{OUT,SMP} = 0$$

where $P_{OUT,SMP}$ is the pressure at the output of the pressure-regulator. The position of the valve (equivalently the area available for flow) varies inversely

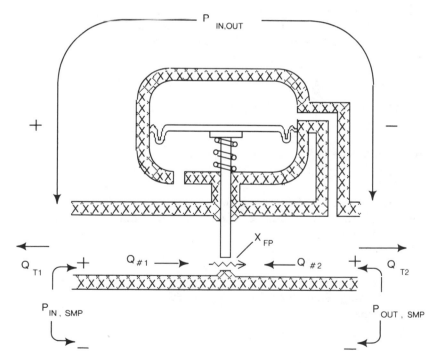

FIG. 4. Variables of the pressure-regulator.

with output pressure. As the pressure-regulator contains very few components, only one confluence is needed to establish the compatibility condition:

$$\partial P_{\text{IN,OUT}} + \partial P_{\text{OUT,SMP}} - \partial P_{\text{IN,SMP}} = 0 .$$

The pressure-regulator has three conduits (IN, OUT and SMP) and one component (VV) that processes fluid. We write continuity confluences for all except SMP (whose continuity confluence is redundant):

$$\partial Q_{\text{T2}} + \partial Q_{\#2(\text{VV})} = 0 ,$$

$$\partial Q_{\text{T1}} + \partial Q_{\#1(\text{VV})} = 0 ,$$

$$\partial Q_{\#1(\text{VV})} + \partial Q_{\#2(\text{VV})} = 0 .$$

A load is connected to the pressure-regulator

$$\partial Q_{\text{T2}} - \partial P_{\text{OUT,SMP}} = 0 .$$

Our interest in how change comes about results in a focus on the derivative variables. However, it is also possible to model the qualitative values of the device's variables. These values, although they do not direct indicate change, help determine the state of device and hence which derivative confluences apply. This confluence set is very similar to the derivative confluence set. The valve is modeled by three confluences. Unless the valve is completely open or closed, it is simply acting as a fluid resistor obeying the qualitative version of Ohm's law:

$$[P_{\text{IN,OUT}}] - [Q_{\#1(\text{VV})}] = 0 .$$

Since area is, by definition, always positive:

$$[X_{\text{FP}}] = + .$$

In state WORKING-+ $P > 0$:

$$[P_{\text{IN,OUT}}] = + .$$

Note that given the usual input condition $[P_{\text{IN,SMP}}] = +$, $[P_{\text{IN,OUT}}] = +$ necessarily follows given the remaining confluences. The confluence for the pressure sensor is more complex:

$$[X_{\text{FP}}] + [P_{\text{OUT,SMP}}] = + .$$

This confluence, coupled with the corresponding derivative confluence characterizes thresholding effect. The remaining confluences are identical. The compatibility confluence is:

$$[P_{\text{IN,OUT}}] + [P_{\text{OUT,SMP}}] - [P_{\text{IN,SMP}}] = 0 .$$

The three continuity confluences are:

$$[Q_{T2}] + [Q_{\#2(VV)}] = 0 \,,$$
$$[Q_{T1}] + [Q_{\#1(VV)}] = 0 \,,$$
$$[Q_{\#1(VV)}] + [Q_{\#2(VV)}] = 0 \,.$$

Lastly, the pressure-regulator is connected to a positive load:

$$[Q_{T2}] - [P_{OUT,SMP}] = 0 \,.$$

As a comparison, consider all of the confluences grouped by component and conduit:

$$\partial P_{IN,OUT} - \partial Q_{\#1(VV)} + \partial X_{FP} = 0 \,,$$
$$[P_{IN,OUT}] - [Q_{\#1(VV)}] = 0 \,, \qquad [X_{FP}] = + \,, \qquad [P_{IN,OUT}] = + \,,$$
$$\partial X_{FP} + \partial P_{OUT,SMP} = 0 \,, \qquad [X_{FP}] + [P_{OUT,SMP}] = + \,.$$
$$\partial P_{IN,OUT} + \partial P_{OUT,SMP} - \partial P_{IN,SMP} = 0 \,,$$
$$[P_{IN,OUT}] + [P_{OUT,SMP}] - [P_{IN,SMP}] = 0 \,,$$
$$\partial Q_{T2} + \partial Q_{\#2(VV)} = 0 \,, \qquad [Q_{T2}] + [Q_{\#2(VV)}] = 0 \,.$$
$$\partial Q_{T1} + \partial Q_{\#1(VV)} = 0 \,, \qquad [Q_{T1}] + [Q_{\#1(VV)}] = 0 \,,$$
$$\partial Q_{\#1(VV)} + \partial Q_{\#2(VV)} = 0 \,, \qquad [Q_{\#1(VV)}] + [Q_{\#2(VV)}] = 0 \,,$$
$$\partial Q_{T2} - \partial P_{OUT,SMP} = 0 \,, \qquad [Q_{T2}] - [P_{OUT,SMP}] = 0 \,.$$

The fact that these two sets of confluences are similar should not be surprising. If the underlying quantitative model is linear, i.e., all the equations of the form $\sum g_i x_i = g_0$, differentiation produces an almost identical expression except for the fact that g_0 is now zero. This is of course not true of the valve, the only nonlinear component of the pressure-regulator.

3.4.6. *The dependence of device topology on connection laws*

The way conduit and component were distinguished in the beginning of this section was purposefully vague; both components and conduits transport and process material. Conduits are simply an abstraction for those pieces of the device whose behavior is modeled extremely simply. Usually, constituents such as wires, pipes, linkages, shafts, etc., only serve the role of communicating information between the more complex components. The compatibility and continuity conditions define what can be modeled as a conduit. The components of a device are necessarily disjoint and thus must share information in order to operate. This sharing cannot be through other components. This is the role of the conduits—they are the informational glue that connects the device together.

The compatibility and continuity conditions follow primarily from the definition of what it means to be connected. Thus modeling the intuitively obvious physical connections will not have the expected result if that physical connection does not obey compatibility or continuity. A simple example illustrates this point. Consider the situation of Fig. 5. The pipe cannot be modeled as a conduit if the behavior of interest is the change of fluid level in the tanks. The compatibility condition is violated because the pressure at the left-hand side is different than the pressure at the right-hand side. It is not acting as a simple communicator of information. To analyze the device effectively, the pipe must be modeled as having a finite flow rate (i.e., modeled as a valve). The modified device topology is illustrated by Fig. 6. The two conduits now obey the compatibility condition without contradiction: the bottom of tank A is at the same pressure as the left-hand side of the valve and the bottom of tank B is at the same pressure as the right-hand side of the valve.

This example illustrates a violation of a class-wide quasistatic assumption: the material in the pipe takes as much time to reach equilibrium as the composite device. Thus this particular pipe cannot be modeled as a conduit. This example is a direct analog of the violation of a class-wide assumption of electronics that occurs when two capacitors charged to different potentials are placed in parallel. In these two cases, there is a violation of no-function-in-structure: wires are usually modeled as connections, but that model predicts behavior incorrectly. Knowledge of the behavior of the device is needed to determine what the structure is. No procedure for determining the device topology is foolproof, but every failure can be attributed to a violation of a class-wide assumption—as occurred in the previous two examples. However, at present we have not found an effective way to determine whether a topology that describes a particular device violates some class-wide assumption; this is a topic of ongoing research.

FIG. 5. Two tanks.

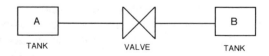

FIG. 6. A device topology for Fig. 5.

4. Prediction of Behavior

In order to better understand the technical issues concerning how the behavior of a device is derived from its structure, it may help first to sketch the intuitions underlying our formal theory. Our central concern is with change. That is, what causes a device to move from one equilibrium state to another, how does that change transpire and how can it be explained in terms of the laws defining the given equilibrium state? Our approach involves decomposing a device's behavior into two dimensions, one being its interstate behavior, the other being its intrastate behavior. From this perspective, a device changes state when one or more of its variables (i.e., a pressure, a current, etc.) exceeds some threshold that defines that state. Thus part of determining when a device changes state requires determining which thresholds are being exceeded and from that determining possible target transitions. *But what causes a variable to change in the first place?* Determining this requires figuring out what the first-order time derivatives are within the current state. The qualitative values of these derivatives act as 'tendencies' that sum over infinitesimal time intervals that cause a variable to change from its present value. These derivatives constitute intrastate behavior, 'forces', or said differently, the agents of change. Thus the time derivatives that are operative within an equilibrium state can eventually lead to a variable changing its value enough to cause the qualitative state to change. In Section 5, we discuss another kind of causality—mythical causality—that explains how a qualitative change in one derivative 'causes' another derivative to change all within the (potentially infinitesimal) time interval.

It is also possible to determine indirectly what the first-order derivatives must have been within a given state by comparing the values of the variables in the state and its successor state. In that approach, primacy is given to the state transition, itself, from which the values of the derivative can be deduced. However, in our scheme, primacy is given to the tendencies (i.e., values of the derivatives) operating within a state, from which the possible successor states can be determined. Thus our approach must accept the burden of deducing these tendencies directly from structural properties of the device and perturbations to its inputs.

The passage of time is modeled by episodes. Within an episode each component, viewed as a pure model, remains in the same state and all the device's variables keep on changing in the same way (i.e., the derivative variables do not change[12]). In the first set of examples, we tend to use pure models and derivative variables rarely change during a state; thus the states and episodes of a device are in one-to-one correspondence. Their fundamental

---

[12] As a consequence of ambiguity, the derivative values may change while no component changes state. In addition mythical time places an ordering upon the changes of values as a device changes state.

difference lies in the fact that a state is a mode of behavior of a device while an episode is a period of time during which the device is always in the same mode.

The approach outlined in this section does not result in a comprehensive causal account, for there is no causal explanation of the intrastate behavior. Constructing such explanations is discussed in Section 5.

4.1. Intrastate behavior

To determine the behavior within an episode, an assignment of $+$, 0, and $-$ to the variables must be found that satisfies the confluences of the device. Given the operating context where $[P_{IN,SMP}] = +$, it must be the case that the regulator is in state [WORKING-+] or [OPEN]. The $[x]$ column of Table 4 lists the only assignment of values of variables that satisfies the confluences. Given an input signal of $\partial P_{IN,SMP} = +$, there is only one assignment of values to variables that satisfies the derivative confluences for that state. (By coincidence, these two value sets are identical.)

Before discussing the types of algorithms that produce such a solution, consider the information contained in it. At first blush, it does not appear as if it contains very much information. However, it does capture the essential characteristic that the valve is closing ($\partial X_{FP} = -$). Admittedly, it does not state that the output pressure does not change ($\partial P_{OUT,SMP} = +$), but the fact that $\partial P_{IN,OUT} = +$ indicates the output pressure is not rising as fast as the input pressure, which indicates some attenuation. Of course, this solution does not explain why the valve is closing. We discuss this issue when we attempt to 'push a level' of detail in the analysis.

To determine the behavior (i.e., Table 4), the set of confluences must be solved. Each confluence is a constraint, and thus the problem of determining behavior is a constraint satisfaction problem. Unfortunately, simple propagation methods do not work. For example, consider propagation of constraints as a constraint satisfaction method: (a) start with a given, (b) find some as yet unsatisfied constraint and see if it can be used to determine a value for another variable, (c) repeat. In the foregoing example, the given is $\partial P_{IN,SMP} = +$, but there is no other constraint that provides additional information. The only

TABLE 4. Intrastate behavior of the pressure-regulator

x	$[x]$	∂x	x	$[x]$	∂x
$P_{IN,SMP}$	$+$	$+$	$Q_{\#1(VV)}$	$+$	$+$
Q_{T1}	$-$	$-$	X_{FP}	$-$	$-$
Q_{T2}	$+$	$+$	$P_{IN,OUT}$	$+$	$+$
$Q_{\#2(VV)}$	$-$	$-$	$P_{OUT,SMP}$	$+$	$+$

other constraint that even mentions $\partial P_{IN,SMP}$ is $\partial P_{IN,OUT} + \partial P_{OUT,SMP} - \partial P_{IN,SMP} = 0$, but nothing is known about the values of $\partial P_{OUT,IN}$ or $\partial P_{OUT,SMP}$. Nevertheless, unless $\partial P_{IN,OUT} = +$, the remaining confluences are contradictory. (This is a common problem for all local propagation schemes. We call such systems of simultaneous equations which cannot be solved by substitution alone inherently simultaneous [8].)

The seemingly obvious way around this problem is to solve the constraints using algebraic symbol manipulation. This is analogous to the situation where $x + y = 3$ and $2x + y = 4$ in which x must be 1 and y must be 3 although there is no sequence of simple propagations that can determine this. One resolves such inherent simultaneity by subtracting $x + y = 3$ from $2x + y = 4$, which yields $x = 1$. The analogous strategy fails in the qualitative domain because the operations outlined in Table 2 don't satisfy the field axioms which are required to do this kind of equation solving. ENVISION uses a combination of constraint propagation and generate and test to find all the solutions to the confluence equations.

Numerous schemes, for example, relaxation or generate and test can be used to solve sets of inherently simultaneous confluence equations. But because the qualitative calculus does not satisfy the field axioms multiple solutions result (note that just because our calculus is 'qualitative' does not, in itself, necessitate it producing ambiguous analyses). Multiple solutions often exist even when there are as many 'independent' confluences as qualitative unknowns. These multiple solutions are not just an artifact of our calculus, but are an important part of our theory. Each solution describes a behavior which can potentially occur in the actual operation of the modeled device.

We call each prediction resulting from the same set of confluences an *interpretation*. The issue of interpretations is a complex topic in its own right and is discussed in further detail in Appendix A.

4.2. Interstate behavior

The allowable states of a device are a subset of the cross-product of all the states of its constituent components. The interstate behavior is the possible transitions between these states. Thus the total solution to a set of qualitative models for the device, namely, a complete description of its behavior, is a set of assignments[13] of values to variables, one set for each composite device state. In addition, the total solution also specifies the state transitions and their causes. This latter information is illustrated graphically by a state-transition diagram. (Fig. 7 is an example of a state diagram, the details of which are discussed later.)

---

[13] Sets of assignments of values to variables if there is more than one interpretation for the confluences for a particular state.

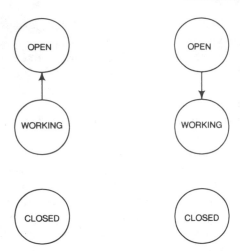

FIG. 7. State diagrams for the pressure-regulator with decreasing and increasing input. The spring and mass are not modeled and the load is presumed to be finite. Each circle represents a state and each edge represents a possible transition from the state to another. The contradictory state CLOSED is included purely for expository purposes—in all following examples contradictory states are deleted. This state is contradictory because there is no solution to the model confluences for that state.

Legal transitions between states are characterized by a set of conditions derived from the qualitative calculus. A sketch of the algorithm for constructing the total solution is as follows. Every composite device state is identified and the confluences solved for each in order to determine the qualitative values of each of the derivatives. The values of the derivatives indicate which direction the device's variables are changing and can thus be used to determine whether some state specification may cease to be valid and a transition occur. For example, suppose device state A has specification $[X < A]$ and solution $\partial X = +$ and device state B has specification $[X \geqslant A]$, then the state change from A to B is allowable.

Although the interstate behavior looks much like a result of a simulation, it is not. Instead, it simultaneously describes behaviors under all possible initial conditions of the generic device. The total solution is used to determine the behavior of a particular device using the initial conditions to determine the starting state and tracing through the possible state transitions. The state diagrams are always of finite size, but a particular device, given appropriate operating conditions, can undergo an infinite number of state transitions, never coming to rest in an any one state. This is the case with oscillators. The state diagram can also include ambiguities concerning possible state transitions. As a consequence, to determine the precise behavior of a particular device requires additional information. Nevertheless, the total solution describes all possible behaviors of all devices of the generic type *and no others*.

4.2.1. *The state diagram*

An example of interstate behavior can be illustrated in the operation of the pressure-regulator whose valve is modeled by the simplified model:

OPEN: $[A = A_{MAX}]$, $[P] = 0$, $\partial P = 0$,
WORKING: $[0 < A < A_{MAX}]$, $[P] = [Q]$, $\partial P + \partial A - \partial Q = 0$,
CLOSED: $[A = 0]$, $[Q] = 0$, $\partial Q = 0$.

This simple valve model has three states: OPEN, WORKING, and CLOSED. As the valve is the only component of the pressure-regulator that has state, the composite device, likewise, has only three states: [OPEN], [WORKING], and [CLOSED]. Suppose the input pressure is decreasing and the pressure-regulator is in state [WORKING], then $\partial X_{FP} = +$, which causes A, the cross-sectional area available for flow to increase. This raises the possibility that $A < A_{MAX}$ may no longer hold. If that happens, the state ends, and the device transitions into a new one with the valve pinned in state OPEN. In this state, the pressure-regulator provides no regulation at all because the input pressure is less than the regulator's target output pressure. The resulting state diagram is illustrated in Fig. 7(a). Fig. 7(b) illustrates the diagram in the case where the input pressure is increasing.

This example, although extremely simple, illustrates the task of drawing inferences concerning the termination of states and the determination of the next state. Note that no input disturbance can cause the valve to move to or from state CLOSED. In this device, every increase in input pressure results in a decrease in area available for flow. But even if the input pressure continues to grow unboundedly, the area will never become zero (if it were zero, the output pressure would be zero and hence the action of the sensor could be holding the valve closed). For any finite pressure, the area will be non-zero. Only as pressure tends to infinity does the area approach zero as the mathematical limit. This is a counter-example to the seductive fallacy that infinite sums of non-zero values always diverge. The point to be made here is that even though the qualitative algebra is extremely simple, it nevertheless concerns derivatives, integrals, and time, and one must be careful least one fall into the well-known pitfalls concerning infinitesimals.

Fig. 9 illustrates some of the more complex properties of a state diagram (the details are discussed later). States can have multiple outgoing edges because of qualitative ambiguity. Multiple ingoing edges correspond to cases where there is more than one route for reaching the state. Because derivative variables have one of three values, and the number of states in which any component can be is bounded, there are only a finite number of possible behaviors and possible episodes. Thus unbounded sequences of states can be represented by closed paths in the state diagram.

4.2.2. *Improved spring and valve models*

The previous models for the pressure-regulator are too simple to illustrate interstate behavior. With the more detailed models presented in this section *it is possible to make inferences about equilibrium, oscillation, ringing and dissipation in the pressure-regulator solely from the qualitative models and the qualitative differential calculus.* Although in pushing a level the class-wide assumptions have been changed, the device topology of Fig. 3 remains essentially the same. The same connection laws hold for force and velocity: as connections (points at which two or more physical objects attach) are massless, forces for every connection sum to zero (continuity), and velocities for attached parts must match (compatibility). Thus force and velocity fit into the connection scheme outlined earlier. (However, one usually doesn't think of any 'material' carrying this information. This material is momentum and it has all the usual properties of material. For example, momentum can be thought of as having flow (see [12]).

The model for the pressure-sensor is extremely simple. It relates pressure directly to force:

$$\partial P = \partial Q.$$

The effects of a force on an object with mass is based on Newton's law $f = ma$. As mass is always positive and unchanging, the confluence for this behavior is:

$$[F] = \partial V.$$

∂V is the qualitative derivative of velocity. This is a mixed confluence equation relating a derivative to a non-derivative so an object with mass can be modeled as three states:

$$\begin{aligned} F > 0: \quad & [F > 0], \quad \partial V = +, \\ F = 0: \quad & [F = 0], \quad \partial V = 0, \\ F < 0: \quad & [F < 0], \quad \partial V = -. \end{aligned}$$

The model for a spring is the dual (interchange V and F) of that for an object with mass and is derived from Hooke's law $f = kx$ or $dF/dt = kv$:

$$\partial F = [V].$$

This is also a mixed confluence equation which can be modeled as three states

$$\begin{aligned} V > 0: \quad & [V > 0], \quad \partial F = +, \\ V = 0: \quad & [V = 0], \quad \partial F = 0, \\ V < 0: \quad & [V < 0], \quad \partial F = -. \end{aligned}$$

The model for the valve is the same as the one used earlier, except for the fact that ∂A is the time derivative of distance (assuming area is proportional to the distance the valve is open) and hence it is a velocity (notated V). The confluence is thus still mixed (Q is flow rate):

$$\partial P - [V] - \partial Q = 0 .$$

To construct a pure model such confluences must be modeled by three states, resulting in a valve model with nine states. For simplicity, we only consider three of them.

$$V > 0: \quad [0 < A < A_{MAX}, \quad P < 0, \quad V > 0], \quad \partial P - \partial Q = + ,$$
$$V = 0: \quad [0 < A < A_{MAX}, \quad P < 0, \quad V = 0], \quad \partial P - \partial Q = 0 ,$$
$$V < 0: \quad [0 < A < A_{MAX}, \quad P < 0, \quad V < 0], \quad \partial P - \partial Q = - .$$

4.2.3. Total solution for expanded pressure-regulator

Fig. 9 is a state diagram for the behavior of the pressure-regulator based on these models. This diagram is produced by ENVISION using the rules discussed earlier. Table 5 describes the results of analyzing each of the nine global device states with an input signal of $\partial P_{IN,SMP} = +$. The new device topology (see Fig. 8) is like that of Fig. 3 but explicitly included the spring and the valve's mass (which we model by a separate object-with-mass component). Compared to the earlier analysis (Fig. 4) there are four new variables, $\partial F_{\#1(S)}$ and $\partial F_{\#2(S)}$ are the forces pulling at the spring from either side, $\partial F_{A(M)}$ is the force pushing the valve's mass, and ∂V_{FP} is the upward velocity of the point where the valve's mass, spring, and stem attach. The behavior in some of the states is ambiguous and hence all interpretations are stated. For example, state 3 has 5 interpretations.

TABLE 5. All pressure-regulator solutions

State	1	2	3	4	5	6	7	8	9
State specifications	$V=0$ $F=0$	$V=0$ $F<0$	$V<0$ $F<0$	$V<0$ $F=0$	$V<0$ $F>0$	$V=0$ $F>0$	$V>0$ $F>0$	$V>0$ $F=0$	$V>0$ $F<0$
Interpretation	1	1	1 2 3 4 5	1 2 3 4 5	1 2 3 4 5	1	1 2ı3	1 2 3	1 2 3
$\partial Q_{T1} =$	−	−	− − − 0 +	− − − 0 +	− − − 0 +	−	− − −	− − −	− − −
$\partial Q_{T2} =$	+	+	+ + + 0 −	+ + + 0 −	+ + + 0 −	+	+ + +	+ + +	+ + +
$\partial Q_{\#1(VV)} =$	+	+	+ + + 0 −	+ + + 0 −	+ + + 0 −	+	+ + +	+ + +	+ + +
$\partial Q_{\#2(VV)} =$	−	−	− − − 0 +	− − − 0 +	− − − 0 +	−	− − −	− − −	− − −
$\partial P_{IN,OUT} =$	+	+	+ + + + +	+ + + + +	+ + + + +	+	+ 0 −	+ 0 −	+ 0 −
$\partial P_{OUT,SMP} =$	+	+	+ + + 0 −	+ + + 0 −	+ + + 0 −	+	+ + +	+ + +	+ + +
$\partial F_{\#1(S)} =$	0	0	− − − − −	− − − − −	− − − − −	0	+ + +	+ + +	+ + +
$\partial F_{\#2(S)} =$	0	0	+ + + + +	+ + + + +	+ + + + +	0	− − −	− − −	− − −
$\partial F_{A(M)} =$	−	−	− 0 + + +	− 0 + + +	− 0 + + +	−	− − −	− − −	− − −
$\partial V_{FP} =$	0	−	− − − − −	0 0 0 0 0	+ + + + +	+	+ + +	0 0 0	− − −

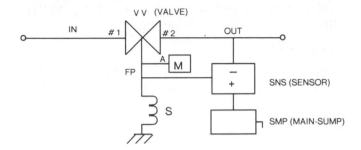

FIG. 8. Device topology of the pressure-regulator with mass and spring.

The device begins in state $V = 0$, $F = 0$. The confluences describing the behaviors of the valve's mass, valve, and spring are obtained from the models just presented. As $V = 0$ the confluence describing the pressure-regulator is

$$\partial P_{\text{IN,OUT}} - \partial Q_{\#1(VV)} = 0 .$$

Also, as $V = 0$, the spring obeys the confluence

$$\partial F_{\#1(S)} = 0 .$$

Since $F = 0$, the applicable valve mass confluence is

$$\partial V_{\text{FP}} = 0 .$$

The remaining confluences are the same for every state. The confluence for the pressure-sensor is

$$\partial P_{\text{OUT,SMP}} + \partial F_{\#1(S)} + \partial F_{A(M)} = 0 .$$

The remaining confluences are similar to those presented with Fig. 4.

$$\partial F_{\#1(S)} + \partial F_{\#2(S)} = 0 , \qquad \partial P_{\text{IN,OUT}} + \partial P_{\text{OUT,SMP}} - \partial P_{\text{IN,SMP}} - = 0 ,$$

$$\partial Q_{\text{T1}} + \partial Q_{\#1(VV)} = 0 , \qquad \partial Q_{\text{T1}} + \partial Q_{\#2(VV)} = 0 ,$$

$$\partial Q_{\#1(VV)} + \partial Q_{\#2(VV)} = 0 , \qquad \partial Q_{\text{T2}} - \partial P_{\text{OUT,SMP}} = 0 , \qquad \partial P_{\text{IN,SMP}} = + .$$

4.2.4. Constructing the state diagram

Constructing the state diagram is analogous to solving a set of simultaneous differential equations characterizing the behavior of a physical system. The process of constructing a particular state transition is equivalent to performing an integration involving the first-order derivatives operating in the original state. The process for constructing the state diagram outlined in this section, in essence, performs an integration of the set of differential equations describing the composite device.

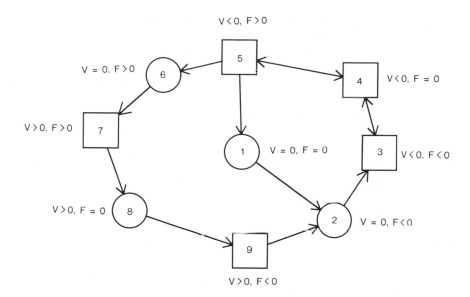

FIG. 9. State diagram for the pressure-regulator with continuing input signal, mass, spring, and no friction. Circles indicate momentary states, and squares indicate states that may exist for an interval of time.

As in quantitative analysis, there are diverse solution strategies, each applicable to a particular problem type. We present a number of different rules for constructing the state diagram, each based on some important property of the qualitative calculus.

Causality rule. The most basic rule for constructing the state diagram is that a component will not change state unless it is acted upon. (This is our analog to Newton's first law that a body will continue in its state of rest or uniform velocity until acted on by an external force.)

Limit rule. The qualitative mean value theorem is $[X(T')] = [X(T)] + \partial X(T)$ where T' immediately follows T; thus unless some ∂X is non-zero, the state cannot terminate. Only if $\partial X \neq 0$, may X move to its limit.[14] Thus every increasing variable ($\partial X = +$), which is bounded above ($X < A$), can produce a state termination. Similarly, every decreasing variable ($\partial X = -$) which is bounded below ($X > A$) can produce a state termination. There is no other way a state transition can occur.

---

[14] Note earlier footnote for the case $[x] = \partial x = 0$.

Ordering rule. Qualitative variables vary continuously, e.g., suppose $\partial X = +$ and the state could terminate by violating $x < m$ for component E or by violating $x < n$ for component B (the interesting case occurs when E and B are different components), and $n < m$. As x varies continuously, the only possible change for x is from $x < n$ to $n \leqslant x < m$. Thus component B changes state first.

Equality change rule. If $\partial X(T)$ is non-zero and $[X(T)] = A$, where A is a point interval $[k, k]$, then the state terminates immediately. For example, if $[X] = 0$ and $\partial X = +$, then the device must immediately move to a state where $[X] = +$. This rule applies in two situations: (a) where a model specification of the current state is of the form $[X = A]$ and (b) where $[X]$ is determined to be 0 by solving the confluences. (Forbus [15] calls this the equality change law.) Such momentary states play an important role and are specially marked.

With minor modification, these same rules apply to state specifications that refer to two variables, e.g., $x < y$ or $x = y$. The case of $x < y$ is transformed in $z = y - x$ and $z > 0$. If the introduced variable is unevaluable all cases must be considered. For example, in the case of $z = y - x$ and $z > 0$ the possibilities $\partial z = +$ and $\partial z = 0$, which cannot cause state change, and $\partial z = -$, which can cause state change must be considered. Similarly, $x = y$ is transformed to $z = x - y$ and $z = 0$.

The remaining rules restrict the results of the first four. Each applies to two states and the transition between them.

Epsilon ordering rule. Any change introduced by the equality change rule occurs first. For example, if $[X]$ is changing from 0 to $+$ and $[Y]$ is changing from $+$ to 0, then $[X]$ changes first. The rationale is that if $[Y]$ is $+$, then $Y > \varepsilon > 0$. As $Y(T)$ is a continuous function, it will take some finite time to change by ε but the change of X happens instantly.

Contradiction avoidance rule. Contradictions arise if the confluences are unsatisfiable, or two state specifications of different components have an empty interaction. If a state is contradictory in either way, a transition to it is impossible as well. This rule determines the valve cannot close, i.e., even though the area available for flow is decreasing it will never reach 0. Consider what would happen if the valve closed. If the valve closes then $[X_{FP}] = 0$, and by the valve and continuity equations $[Q_{T1}] = [Q_{T2}] = [Q_{\#1(VV)}] = [Q_{\#2(VV)}] = 0$. Using the confluence for the load, this implies $[P_{OUT,SMP}] = 0$. Substituting into the sensor equation $[X_{FP}] + [P_{OUT,SMP}] = +$ we get $0 + 0 = +$ which is impossible. Therefore, the valve cannot close and all transitions to this state cannot happen.

Continuity rule. Each variable varies continuously. For each variable, $[X(T)]$ must be adjacent to $[X(T')]$ otherwise the transition is impossible (similarly $\partial X(T)$ must be adjacent to $\partial X(T')$ and so on).

Mean value rule. The mean value theorem must hold for every variable if the transition is to be possible. For each variable, X, $[X(T')] = [X(T)] + \partial X(T)$. (This rule holds as a consequence of previously defined rules.)

Feedback rule. Knowledge about the feedback behavior of the device provides a crucial amount of information about the transition (the procedure for recognizing feedback is presented later). A negative feedback path that contains no 'momentum' components cannot overshoot. In cases of positive feedback, certain transitions cannot happen because the device will actively prevent the transition from happening. (The constraint satisfaction algorithm discussed earlier cannot detect feedback, but causal analysis, discussed later can.)

Appendix B discusses a procedure (which our program ENVISION uses) to construct the state diagram. It also handles cases where a global device state has multiple interpretations.

4.2.5. ENVISION's analysis

The following is ENVISION's brief analysis of each of the states and state transitions between them. For each state, the component(s) that may change state due to some threshold being reached are listed followed by the global device state changes which are possible. The state numbers correspond to those used in Fig. 8. The following analysis is simplified by avoiding reference to interpretations. The states are labeled by the specifications of the individual component states thereby equating the states of the valve and the valve's mass (both sets of state specifications reference velocity in exactly the same way). Constructing this simplified state diagram requires only three rules. The causality rule limits the transitions to those components undergoing some change, the limit rule specifies in which direction (if any) component changes occur, and the equality change rule indicates which states are momentary (indicated by the words 'immediately changes state' in the explanation). The ordering rule does not apply because the state specifications are too simple. If we had not made the simplification that the valve's mass and the spring change state in lock step, the contradiction avoidance rule would have applied. The reason the valve and spring change state in lock step is that both depend directly on the position of the valve, this position controls both the amount of material flowing and the stretch on the spring. If transitions within states had been considered (e.g., see Fig. 18), the continuity rule would have been needed. The mean value rule holds automatically and the feedback rule is inapplicable in this example.

At any given time, the state is determined by the values of velocity V_{FP} and force $F_{A(M)}$. State 1 is dependent on $V_{FP} = 0$ and $F_{A(M)} = 0$ thus; the values of ∂V_{FP} and $\partial F_{A(M)}$ determine the next state transition (if any). Table 5 indicates that $\partial V_{FP} = 0$ so the valve's mass cannot change state. However, the fact that $\partial F_{A(M)} = -$ means that $F_{A(M)}$ immediately becomes negative, thus causing the valve's mass to change state immediately. The new confluence for the valve's mass is $\partial V_{FP} = -$.

The analysis as printed out by ENVISION:

> In State 1, $V = 0$, $F = 0$:
>> Because $\partial F_{A(M)} = -$, M immediately changes state to $F < 0$.
>> The device immediately changes state to 2: $V = 0$, $F < 0$.
>
> In State 2, $V = 0$, $F < 0$:
>> Because $\partial V_{FP} = -$, S and VV immediately changes state to $V < 0$.
>> The device immediately changes state to 3: $V < 0$, $F < 0$.
>
> In State 3, $V < 0$, $F < 0$:
>> The value of $\partial F_{A(M)}$ is ambiguous.
>> If $\partial F_{A(M)} = +$, M may change state to $F = 0$.[15]
>> The device may change state to 4: $V < 0$, $F = 0$.
>
> In State 4, $V < 0$, $F = 0$:
>> The value of $\partial F_{A(M)}$ is ambiguous.
>> If $\partial F_{A(M)} = -$, M immediately changes state to $F < 0$.
>> If $\partial F_{A(M)} = +$, M immediately changes state to $F > 0$.
>> Therefore, the device may change state to one of:
>> 5: $V < 0$, $F > 0$; 3: $V < 0$, $F < 0$.
>
> In State 5, $V < 0$, $F > 0$:
>> The value of $\partial F_{A(M)}$ is ambiguous.
>> If $\partial F_{A(M)} = -$, M may change state to $F = 0$.
>> Because $\partial V_{FP} = +$, S and VV may change state to $V = 0$.
>> Therefore, the device may change state to one of:
>> 6: $V = 0$, $F > 0$; 1: $V = 0$, $F = 0$, 4: $V < 0$, $F = 0$.
>
> In State 6, $V = 0$, $F > 0$:
>> Because $\partial V_{FP} = +$, S and VV immediately changes state to $V > 0$.
>> Because $\partial F_{A(M)} = -$, M may change state to $F = 0$.
>> Therefore, the device must immediately change state to one of:
>> 8: $V > 0$, $F = 0$; 7: $V > 0$, $F > 0$.
>
> In State 7, $V > 0$, $F > 0$:
>> Because $\partial F_{A(M)} = -$, M may change state to $F = 0$.
>> The device may change state to 8: $V > 0$, $F = 0$.
>
> In State 8, $V > 0$, $F = 0$:
>> Because $\partial F_{A(M)} = -$, M immediately changes state to $F < 0$.
>> The device immediately changes state to 9: $V > 0$, $F < 0$.
>
> In State 9, $V > 0$, $F < 0$:
>> Because $\partial V_{FP} = -$, S and VV may change state to $V = 0$.
>> The device may change state to 2: $V = 0$, $F < 0$.

Said less baroquely: In the starting State 1, the valve is unmoving and the force from the sensor and from the spring are in balance. An increase in input pressure produces an increase in output pressure, which is sensed by the sensor and produces an increased downward force on the valve (State 2). The transition is mandatory, as even an infinitesimal change in value at zero must

---

[15] If ∂F is 0 or $-$ no state change can happen.

cause it to become non-zero. The increase of downward force on the valve (the coordinate system is chosen so that open valve positions correspond to positive distances and a closed valve is characterized by zero distance) causes the valve to acquire velocity and hence the valve begins to close (State 3). This transition is also mandatory because the velocity is being changed away from zero. In State 3, the value of the force on the valve is ambiguous. The closing of the valve could reduce the output pressure enough to equal the force of the spring, causing a transition to State 4. On the other hand, the rise in input pressure could continue to dominate behavior and thus the output pressure continues to rise. The same sort of situation arises in the two following states. Depending on the functional relationship between the input pressure, the input pressure function itself and the gain of the feedback loop, the system may move back and forth between these three states. If the pressure rise does not dominate, the moving valve will reduce the output pressure enough so that the restoring force of the spring is greater than the force exerted by the pressure. If the input pressure rise becomes negligible the pressure-regulator will continue to oscillate through States 2–9 (as suggested in Fig. 8 and verified by the analysis underlying Fig. 10).

4.2.6. *Physical rationale for the new component models*

With the models used in the pressure-regulator examples before Section 4.2.2, it is impossible to analyze the behavior of the pressure-regulator at small time durations. The particular quasistatic approximation demands that a change of output pressure 'instantly' results in a change of valve setting. The models we had been using are inherently incapable of describing the oscillatory and feedback behavior of the device. We needed to 'push a level' of detail and model behavior at smaller time gradations if oscillation is to be evidenced. (In Section 6 we present an alternative strategy for determining the presence of feedback and oscillation based on 'mythical causality', which does not require pushing a level.)

The time delay introduced by removing the quasistatic approximation is not the result of some explicit time delay in some component, but rather the direct consequence of the particular physical laws and the mathematical properties of integrals and derivatives. When small time durations are involved, the mass of the valve itself, although very small, must be taken into consideration. An increase in pressure increases the force on the mass of the valve. This force produces an acceleration on the valve that results in a velocity that in turn results in a change of position of the valve *after some time has elapsed*. Once the valve is given a non-zero velocity, it starts to close.

To operate successfully, the valve must also contain a spring, which provides a restoring force by tending to open the valve. At equilibrium the force provided by the pressure of the fluid on the diaphragm equals the restoring force of the compressed spring. As pressure increases, the force of the diaphragm increases, causing the forces on the valve to become unbalanced and forcing it to seek a new equilibrium position. The valve moves in the direction of closing the valve, thereby simultaneously increasing the restoring force of the spring and decreasing the force delivered by the pressure until these two forces balance. There is, however, one more effect that complicates matters: *momentum*. As the valve reaches equilibrium position it will have some non-zero velocity and as it has mass it will continue to move past this equilibrium position. Eventually the valve will reach its maximum overshoot position and will start moving back to equilibrium, but again it will overshoot. This ringing, or oscillation, around the new equilibrium position continues indefinitely unless there are some dissipative effects.

4.2.7. *Uses of the state diagram*

The state diagram is a complete description of all possible interstate behaviors of the generic device. It represents every possible interstate behavior the device can manifest, and enumerates how the device changes from one behavioral pattern to another. The state diagram can be used to directly answer 'what happens' type questions. The intrastate behavior is characterized by the assignment of values to variables, which satisfies the confluences of the state. The combined structure can be used to answer a variety of types of questions about device behavior in addition to basic prediction. The structure can be used to answer questions about whether something could happen. For example, to determine whether the output pressure could rise, each state is checked to see whether the pressure rises in that state, and then a further check is made to see whether any of those states can be reached given the initial conditions. State A can be reached from state B if there exists a sequence of transitions from A to B. Far more interesting inferences can be drawn about the state diagram concerning oscillation and energy dissipation, but we present those after describing how the state diagram can be constructed.

Fig. 9 indicates the system oscillates through States 2–9. A direct examination of Table 5 shows the second-order derivatives (i.e., the column differences between the first-order derivatives). The extrema of the variables occur within those states where the first-order derivatives can be zero (e.g., $\partial V_{FP} = 0$ in State 4) where $\partial X = 0$ and whether these are a maxima or minima can be determined by the second-order derivatives. For example, the velocity of the valve achieves a downward maximum in State 4 which is a momentary state at which forces of the spring and pressure-sensor perfectly balance ($[F_{A(M)}] = 0$). The position of the valve (whose value is the same as the force on the spring ($F = kx$)), has extrema in States 6 and 2 which are momentary states where the velocity of the valve is 0.

The state diagram for a device is a representation of the overall functioning of the generic device. Although it is constructed solely from the component models, many features of the global operation of a device only become evident in the structure of the state diagram. The state diagram is thus a representation of device behavior that itself can be examined to gain further insight into device functioning. In particular, issues such as oscillation, ringing, energy dissipation, and stability are identifiable as particular patterns in the state diagrams. Thus our qualitative physics is able to detect the presence of these important functional characteristics.

State diagrams reveal a great deal more about the potential behaviors of the device. Fig. 10 is the state diagram for the pressure-regulator when there is no applied input signal. It shows that if the pressure-regulator starts at quiescence ($V = 0$, $F = 0$) it will remain there (because in this state all the derivatives are also zero). If the device is in this quiescent state the only solution to the

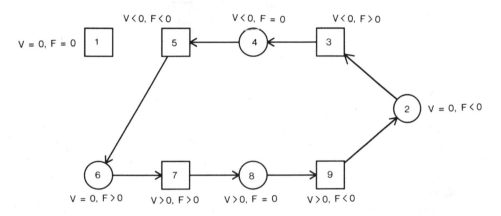

FIG. 10. No input signal, no friction.

TABLE 6. Solution given no input signal, no friction

State	1	2	3	4	5	6	7	8	9
State specifications	$V = 0$ $F = 0$	$V = 0$ $F < 0$	$V < 0$ $F < 0$	$V < 0$ $F = 0$	$V < 0$ $F > 0$	$V = 0$ $F > 0$	$V > 0$ $F > 0$	$V > 0$ $F = 0$	$V > 0$ $F < 0$
$\partial Q_{T1} =$	0	0	+	+	+	0	−	−	−
$\partial Q_{T2} =$	0	0	−	−	−	0	+	+	+
$\partial Q_{\#1(VV)} =$	0	0	−	−	−	0	+	+	+
$\partial Q_{\#2(VV)} =$	0	0	+	+	+	0	−	−	−
$\partial P_{IN,OUT} =$	0	0	+	+	+	0	−	−	−
$\partial P_{OUT,SMP} =$	0	0	−	−	−	0	+	+	+
$\partial F_{\#1(S)} =$	0	0	−	−	−	0	+	+	+
$\partial F_{\#2(S)} =$	0	0	+	+	+	0	−	−	−
$\partial F_{A(M)} =$	0	0	+	+	+	0	−	−	−
$\partial V_{FP} =$	0	−	−	0	+	+	+	0	−

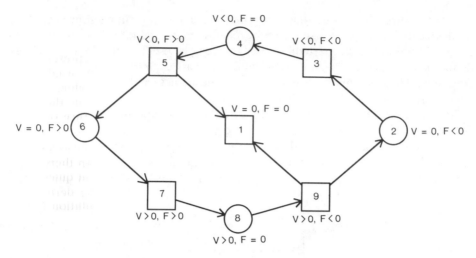

FIG. 11. State diagram with no input signal, friction.

confluence equations is that every derivative variable is zero. If the pressure-regulator starts in a non-quiescent state, it can never reach quiescence. Again this is directly deducible from the confluences. For each state, there is no solution to the confluence equations which results in a change of operating region to the quiescent state. Note that this deduction is possible solely from the component models themselves, models which do not reference or contain any idea of quiescence.

Any movement in the valve is resisted by imperfections in its components. A simple law that describes this effect is $df/dt = k\,dV/dt$, i.e., any change in velocity produces a corresponding increase in force acting against the change in velocity. (This is the mechanical analog to Ohm's law.) The resulting state diagram is illustrated in Fig. 11. It shows that it is now possible for the pressure-regulator to reach an equilibrium state and once it reaches it no further movement is possible.

The law of the form $F = kv$ is an instance of a general class of dissipative laws—laws which dictate that the device must lose energy. Hence oscillations involving[16] dissipative components must eventually damp out and ones that do not contain dissipative laws must not. However, it is possible to draw these kinds of inferences from constructing state diagrams and then analyzing their topological structure. The changed state diagram is solely the result of adding a component with the law $\partial F = \partial V$. This component model does not contain any explicit hint about damping or energy dissipation (i.e., no violation of no-function-in-structure). The major difference between Figs. 11 and 10 is that the

---

[16] And, of course, no sources of energy.

TABLE 7. Solution given no input signal, friction

State	1	2	3	4	5	6	7	8	9
State specifications	$V=0$ $F=0$	$V=0$ $F<0$	$V<0$ $F<0$	$V<0$ $F=0$	$V<0$ $F>0$	$V=0$ $F>0$	$V>0$ $F>0$	$V>0$ $F=0$	$V>0$ $F<0$
Interpretation	1	1	1	1	1 2 3	1	1	1	1 2 3
$\partial Q_{T1} =$	0	0	+	+	+ + +	0	−	−	− − −
$\partial Q_{T2} =$	0	0	−	−	− − −	0	+	+	+ + +
$\partial Q_{\#1(VV)} =$	0	0	−	−	− − −	0	+	+	+ + +
$\partial Q_{\#2(VV)} =$	0	0	+	+	+ + +	0	−	−	− − −
$\partial P_{IN,OUT} =$	0	0	+	+	+ + +	0	−	−	− − −
$\partial P_{OUT,SMP} =$	0	0	−	−	− − −	0	+	+	+ + +
$\partial F_{\#1(S)} =$	0	0	−	−	− − −	0	+	+	+ + +
$\partial F_{\#2(S)} =$	0	0	+	+	+ + +	0	−	−	− − −
$\partial F_{A(M)} =$	0	+	+	+	− 0 +	−	−	−	− 0 +
$\partial V_{FP} -$	0	−	−	0	+ + +	+	+	0	− − −
$\partial F_{\#2(D)} =$	0	+	+	0	− − −	−	−	0	+ + +
$\partial F_{\#1(D)} =$	0	−	−	0	+ + +	+	+	0	− − −

device may reach the quiescent state thus terminating the oscillation. From physics we know that the oscillation *must* eventually damp out, but our qualitative physics cannot capture this fine-grained detail.

4.2.8. *Qualitative vs. quantitative techniques*

Two interesting comparisons emerge between techniques used for qualitative analysis and those used for solving differential equations in physics. First, the usual quantitative analysis techniques produce solutions whose *form* we can interpret as being oscillatory, damped, etc. But this requires an interpretation of the solution. The qualitative techniques presented in this section provide a procedure for constructing such interpretations. However, instead of operating on a given quantitative solution, our techniques operate directly on the qualitative laws that describe the behavior of components.

Second, the construction of the state diagram provides an example of how the combinatorial symbol manipulation capabilities of a computer can be used to provide an analytic tool. The power of this tool comes to light when one can introduce an arbitrary number of 'nonlinear' distinctions for an individual component and then have these distinctions (i.e., states) collapsed through interactions between neighboring components as governed by the rules for constructing the state diagram. Thus this tool provides a new mechanism for analyzing nonlinear systems.

5. Explanation of Behavior

Qualitative physics is concerned with both prediction and explanation. Explanations should be testable, compelling and succinct. By testable, we mean that it is possible to syntactically identify valid explanations. Thus, in particular, an explanation may not contain hidden assumptions about the behavior of the device. An explanation must be compelling and leave no doubt as to the validity of its conclusions. We could define an explanation as the execution trace of whatever algorithm is used to make the prediction. Although this form of explanation certainly meets the foregoing two desiderata, explanations are intended to communicate information and thus they also should be succinct. One structure that meets the two criteria of compellingness and succinctness is logical proof.

An explanation consists of a sequence of statements $E_1, E_2, \ldots$, where each statement is justified by statements previous in the sequence. The confluences provided by the component models and the input signal(s) provide the givens. The justifications are in terms of simple logical inference steps on the statements. The explanation is expressed as a proof in a natural deduction system [25]. In this system the theorem is the prediction and the proof is the explanation; thus a theory of 'explanation' (or at least a taxonomy of different kinds of structures for explanation) can be discovered from examining the different kinds of proof structures.

Each line of the proof consists of a line number (so it can be referenced), a statement, a justification of the statement, and a set of premises upon which the statement depends. The following is part of an explanation of why the valve starts to close (i.e., $\partial X_{FP} = -$) when an input pressure rise is applied (i.e., $\partial P_{IN,SMP} = +$) when the pressure-regulator is in its 'normal' mode of operation (i.e., the valve is in state WORKING-+).

(1)	$\partial X_{FP} + \partial P_{OUT,SMP} = 0$	Given	$\{\ \}$
(2)	$\partial Q_{T2} - \partial P_{OUT,SMP} = 0$	Given	$\{\ \}$
(3)	$\partial Q_{\#2(VV)} + \partial Q_{T2} = 0$	Given	$\{\ \}$
(4)	$\partial Q_{\#1(VV)} + \partial Q_{\#2(VV)} = 0$	Given	$\{\ \}$
(5)	$\partial Q_{\#1(VV)} = +$	Premise	$\{5\}$
(6)	$\partial Q_{\#2(VV)} = -$	Substitution 5, 4	$\{5\}$
(7)	$\partial Q_{T2} = +$	Substitution 6, 3	$\{5\}$
(8)	$\partial P_{OUT,SMP} = +$	Substitution 7, 2	$\{5\}$
(9)	$\partial X_{FP} = -$	Substitution 8, 1	$\{5\}$

This explanation-proof can be rendered into English as follows (the givens have been put in a more natural order). Suppose the flow into the input side of the valve is increasing (5). As the valve conserves material (4), the flow into the output side of the valve must be decreasing (6). As no material is gained or lost in the connection from the output of the valve to the output of the pressure-regulator (3), the flow out of the output side of the pressure-regulator is increasing (7). As the flow through the load is proportional to the pressure across it (2), this results in an increased output pressure (8). This output pressure is sensed (1), and the area available for flow is reduced (9).

(All the explanation-proofs presented in this paper are constructed automatically by our program, i.e., lines (1)–(9) are a verbatim output. The English test is added by us for expository purposes. Our program, ENVISION, takes a description of the physical structure of the device and a library of component models, constructs a model for the overall device, solves the model thereby making predictions, and produces explanations as illustrated.)

This particular explanation used three kinds of justifications corresponding to the application of three inference rules. 'Given' indicates that the statement is a confluence obtained from the models or from the applied input signal. 'Substitution $n_1, \ldots, n_i, m$' indicates that value assignments $n_1, \ldots, n_i$ are substituted into confluence m. 'Premise' indicates an arbitrary unsubstantiated assignment introduced to make the explanation go through. Note that lines (1)–(9) do not explain the necessity of $\partial X_{FP} = -$ because the underlying premise (5) $\partial Q_{\#1(VV)} = +$ has not been substantiated. In a conventional natural deduction system one would derive the statement

(9') $\partial Q_{\#1(VV)} = + \supset \partial X_{FP} = -$ CP 9, 5   { }

by conditional proof. Namely, if it can be shown that $\partial Q_{\#1(VV)} = +$, then $\partial X_{FP} = -$. In English: suppose the flow into the input side of the valve is increasing, then the area available for flow is reduced. However, from the three inference rules, there is no way to show that $\partial Q_{\#1(VV)} = +$ necessarily follows.

5.1. The crucial role of indirect proof

It can, however, be shown that $\partial Q_{\#1(VV)} = +$ by arguing that $\partial Q_{\#1(VV)} \neq +$ is contradictory and thus by *reductio ad absurdum* (abbreviated RAA), $\partial Q_{\#1(VV)} = +$, namely by an indirect proof. As a qualitative variable can have only three values it is sufficient to show that $\partial Q_{\#1(VV)} = 0$ is contradictory and $\partial Q_{\#1(VV)} = -$ is contradictory. We need to introduce three new types of inference rules. 'Unique Value n, m' indicates that the assignments of lines n and m directly contradict each other. 'RAA n, m' indicates the contradictions of line n and m force an assignment by reductio ad absurdum. 'Discharge $n, m_1, \ldots, m_i$' indicates that the assignments of lines $m_1, \ldots, m_i$ can be used to remove unsubstantiated premises from line n. 'RAA' and 'Discharge' derive directly from natural deduction systems. 'Unique Value' is a short-hand for a lemma derived from a simple axiomatization of equality: every variable must have one and only one value. More formally:

$$x = + \lor x = 0 \lor x = -$$
$$x = + \supset x \neq - \land x \neq 0$$
$$x = 0 \supset x \neq + \land x \neq -$$
$$x = - \supset x \neq 0 \land x \neq +$$

With this additional inferential machinery, i.e., the machinery of indirect proof, we can proceed to prove or explain why the valve will start to close when the input pressure is increased. The remaining 21 steps of the proof for the pressure-regulator's behavior discharge the assumption that $\partial Q_{\#1(VV)} = +$. Note that some of the confluences only play a role in the discharging, hence they do not appear in the proof until these steps.

(10)	$\partial P_{IN,OUT} - \partial Q_{\#1(VV)} + \partial X_{FP} = 0$	Given	{ }
(11)	$\partial P_{IN,OUT} + \partial P_{OUT,SMP} - \partial P_{IN,SMP} = 0$	Given	{ }
(12)	$\partial P_{\#1(VV)} = 0$	Premise	{12}
(13)	$\partial Q_{\#2(VV)} = 0$	Substitution 12, 4	{12}
(14)	$\partial Q_{T2} = 0$	Substitution 13, 3	{12}
(15)	$\partial P_{OUT,SMP} = 0$	Substitution 14, 2	{12}
(16)	$\partial P_{IN,SMP} = +$	Given	{ }
(17)	$\partial P_{IN,OUT} = +$	Substitution 16, 15, 11	{12}
(18)	$\partial X_{FP} = -$	Substitution 12, 17, 10	{12}
(19)	$\partial X_{FP} = 0$	Substitution 15, 1	{12}
(20)	False	Unique Value 18, 19	{12}
(21)	$\partial Q_{\#1(VV)} = -$	Premise	{21}
(22)	$\partial Q_{\#2(VV)} =$	Substitution 21, 4	{21}
(23)	$\partial Q_{T2} = -$	Substitution 22, 3	{21}
(24)	$\partial P_{OUT,SMP} = -$	Substitution 23, 2	{21}
(25)	$\partial P_{IN,OUT} = +$	Substitution 16, 24, 11	{21}
(26)	$\partial X_{FP} = -$	Substitution 21, 25, 10	{21}
(27)	$\partial X_{FP} = +$	Substitution 24, 1	{21}
(28)	False	Unique Value 26, 27	{21}
(29)	$\partial Q_{\#1(VV)} = +$	RAA 28, 20	{ }
(30)	$\partial X_{FP} = -$	Discharge 9, 29	{ }

In English: Suppose the flow into the input side of the valve were not increasing, but unchanging (12). Then by conservation (4), the flow into the output side of the valve is also unchanging (13), and again by conservation (3), the output flow of the pressure-regulator is unchanging (15). As flow through the load is proportional to the pressure across it (2), there is no output pressure change (15). Now, we are given that the pressure-regulator input pressure is rising (16), and since the difference of pressure-regulator input and output pressures appears across the valve (11), the increased input pressure appears across the valve (17). In the situation where there is no change in flow and there is an increase in pressure, there must (10) be a decrease in area available for flow through the valve (18). On the other hand, if there is no change in output pressure there cannot be (1) a change in area (19). Thus assuming that the flow is unchanging leads to a contradiction (20); the flow cannot be unchanging. The only possibility that remains is that the flow into the valve is decreasing (21). By an identical line of argument, (21)–(28), that assumption also leads to a contradiction. Hence by indirect argument the flow into the input side of the valve is increasing (29). Thus the area available for flow is decreasing (30).

The intuitive notion of a compelling explanation can now be stated precisely, namely, one which does not depend on any undischarged premises. In the previous example, (30) $\partial X_{FP} = -$ must necessarily follow. Qualitative analysis can sometimes be ambiguous, thus it is not always possible to discharge all the premises. Consider the case where the input pressure is lower than the output pressure (i.e., in state WORKING--). In this situation all the confluences remain the same except the valve confluence:

$$\partial P_{IN,OUT} - \partial Q_{\#1(VV)} - \partial X_{FP} = 0 .$$

This is the same confluence as line (10) in the above explanation-proof, except that the sign of the area change is inverted. This is because of the behavioral characteristic of the valve that an increase in area available for flow always reduces the *absolute value of the pressure drop*. If the pressure drop is a positive value, an increase in area decreases it towards zero (as in the previous analysis). If the pressure drop is a negative value, an increase in area increases it towards zero. The resulting analysis is ambiguous, in principle, and no unique value can be found for ∂X_{FP}. Explanation-proofs for the two possible values for ∂X_{FP} are shown in Fig. 11A. (We could also show that $\partial X_{FP} \neq 0$.) The point is that no proof exists for discharging or contradicting the assumptions of either line (5). *When the analysis is ambiguous, compelling explanations cannot, in principle, exist.*

Allowing assumptions in explanation opens the floodgates to an extremely serious problem: arbitrarily many explanations are now syntactically valid and appear plausible. By allowing unsubstantiated premises we, in effect, allow a proof for $A \supset B$ to be an explanation of B. If A is false, the implication is still valid but the proof may provide no information about the validity or the plausibility of B. It is impossible to tell from an explanation alone whether or not its outstanding assumptions can be ruled out. It is hard to show that a particular premise will not be discharged or contradicted. For example, in the foregoing two proofs no further sequence of statements can contradict or discharge the remaining assumptions (without, of course, introducing other assumptions which themselves cannot be discharged, etc.). In general, to show that the theorem $A \supset B$ and its explanation-proof is the best result achievable requires showing that A is neither necessarily true nor false. (From a model theory point of view, the theory has at least two *logical interpretations*.) If A were true, we would have a compelling explanation of B alone. If A were false, $A \supset B$ is trivially true. However, one cannot tell from a proof for $A \supset B$ whether it is also possible to determine the validity of A. An even more difficult result to explain is that the given set of interpretations is complete, i.e., there exist no other theorems of the form $A \supset B$ for a behaviorally different B and for which A cannot be proved to be true or false.

For most devices, no explanation exists within the calculus which does not include premises. However, the local ambiguity can often be resolved because the device's behavior exhibits no global ambiguity (i.e., the premise can often be discharged). Thus there are two fundamentally different roles for assump-

(1)	$\partial X_{FP} + \partial P_{OUT,SMP} = 0$	Given	{ }
(2)	$\partial Q_{T2} - \partial P_{OUT,SMP} = 0$	Given	{ }
(3)	$\partial Q_{\#2(VV)} + \partial Q_{T2} = 0$	Given	{ }
(4)	$\partial Q_{\#1(VV)} + \partial Q_{\#2(VV)} = 0$	Given	{ }
(5)	$\partial Q_{\#1(VV)} = -$	Premise	{5}
(6)	$\partial Q_{\#2(VV)} = +$	Substitution 5, 4	{5}
(7)	$\partial Q_{T2} = -$	Substitution 6, 3	{5}
(8)	$\partial P_{OUT,SMP} = -$	Substitution 7, 2	{5}
(9)	$\partial X_{FP} = +$	Substitution 8, 1	{5}

(1)	$\partial X_{FP} + \partial P_{OUT,SMP} = 0$	Given	{ }
(2)	$\partial Q_{T2} - \partial P_{OUT,SMP} = 0$	Given	{ }
(3)	$\partial Q_{\#2(VV)} + \partial Q_{T2} = 0$	Given	{ }
(4)	$\partial Q_{\#1(VV)} + \partial Q_{\#2(VV)} = 0$	Given	{ }
(5)	$\partial Q_{\#1(VV)} = +$	Premise	{5}
(6)	$\partial Q_{\#2(VV)} = -$	Substitution 5, 4	{5}
(7)	$\partial Q_{T2} = +$	Substitution 6, 3	{5}
(8)	$\partial P_{OUT,SMP} = +$	Substitution 7, 2	{5}
(9)	$\partial X_{FP} = -$	Substitution 8, 1	{5}

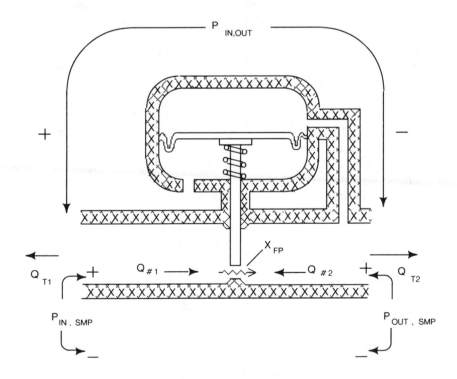

FIG. 11A.

tions which are locally indistinguishable. An assumption either can represent a global ambiguity or can be a temporary construction to enable an explanation-proof to go through. The latter type of local ambiguity arises because the system is inherently simultaneous.

5.2. Proof as explanation

There are four undesirable characteristics of explanation-proof that are symptomatic of its inadequacy as a theory of explanation: (a) the introduction of premises into an explanation is unmotivated and arbitrary; (b) indirect proofs are intuitively unsatisfying; (c) explanation-proofs are non-unique; and (d) explanation-proofs may be causally inverted. We explore each of these in detail.

Premises are introduced because of local ambiguity but can often be resolved because the device's behavior exhibits no global ambiguity. Even so, the premise must be introduced arbitrarily in the explanation-proof (and later discharged). Although this might seem plausible if the device's behavior were globally ambiguous, it seems questionable that explanations of unambiguous behavior should be so arbitrary. As the choice of assumption is not determined, usually many different assumptions will independently lead to valid explanations of the same behavior.

Indirect arguments are counterintuitive. One would like explanations to consist of steps, each describing correct behavior which follows by applying a component model rule to functionings described in earlier steps (something like the proof but without RAA). Neither is the case for indirect explanation-proofs. The steps may refer to hypothetical functionings which do not actually occur and a justification might be RAA. Indirect proofs explain a consequence by showing that all alternative consequences do not happen, and thus cannot establish a simple relationship between a cause and its effect.

The same conclusion can have many proofs, none of which can be identified as the 'correct' one. Hence, there may be multiple explanation-proofs of a device's functioning. Although it might make sense in a few cases to have two or three explanations of how a device behaves, it makes little sense to have multiple explanations of a device's behavior *at the same grain-size of analysis*. Remember that we are considering explanations of the same behavior in terms of the same component models. Multiple explanations can sometimes arise because the confluences are redundant, but more commonly arise due to the arbitrary choice of premise. In our framework there usually exist an extremely large number of syntactically acceptable valid proofs, but it is straightforward to eliminate most of them by employing a minimality condition. However, there still remain roughly fifteen different explanations of the pressure-regulator's unambiguous behavior, corresponding to the different minimal com-

(1) $\partial X_{FP} = -$ Premise   {1}
(2) $\partial Q_{\#2(VV)} + \partial Q_{T2} = 0$ Given   { }
(3) $\partial P_{IN,OUT} - \partial Q_{\#1(VV)} + \partial X_{FP} = 0$ Given   { }
(4) $\partial P_{IN,OUT} + \partial P_{OUT,SMP} - \partial P_{IN,SMP} = 0$ Given   { }
(5) $\partial X_{FP} + \partial P_{OUT,SMP} = 0$ Given   { }
(6) $\partial X_{FP} = 0$ Premise   {6}
(7) $\partial P_{OUT,SMP} = 0$ Substitution 6, 5   {6}
(8) $\partial P_{IN,SMP} = +$ Given   { }
(9) $\partial P_{IN,OUT} = +$ Substitution 8, 7, 4   {6}
(10) $\partial Q_{\#1(VV)} = +$ Substitution 6, 9, 3   {6}
(11) $\partial Q_{\#1(VV)} + \partial Q_{\#2(VV)} = 0$ Given   { }
(12) $\partial Q_{\#2(VV)} = -$ Substitution 10, 11   {6}
(13) $\partial Q_{T2} = +$ Substitution 12, 2   {6}
(14) $\partial Q_{T2} - \partial P_{OUT,SMP} = 0$ Given   { }
(15) $\partial Q_{T2} = 0$ Substitution 7, 14   {6}
(16) False   Unique Value 15, 13   {6}
(17) $\partial X_{FP} = +$ Premise   {17}
(18) $\partial P_{OUT,SMP} = -$ Substitution 17, 5   {17}
(19) $\partial P_{IN,OUT} = +$ Substitution 8, 18, 4   {17}
(20) $\partial Q_{\#1(VV)} = +$ Substitution 17, 19, 3   {17}
(21) $\partial Q_{\#2(VV)} = -$ Substitution 20, 11   {17}
(22) $\partial Q_{T2} = +$ Substitution 21, 2   {17}
(23) $\partial Q_{T2} = -$ Substitution 18, 14   {17}
(24) False   Unique Value 23, 22   {16}
(25) $\partial X_{FP} = -$ RAA 24, 16   { }

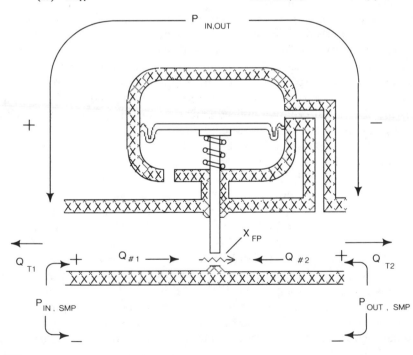

FIG. 11B.

binations of premises that can be introduced to analyze the device. A particularly undesirable one is obtained by introducing premises about ∂X_{FP}. The explanation is now totally indirect (see Fig. 11B).

In English: Suppose the area available for flow were not changing (6). Then the sensor does not (5) sense any output pressure change (7). As the input pressure is rising, this rise must (4) appear across the valve (9). If the area available for flow is unchanging and the pressure across the valve is increasing, the flow into the input side of the valve must (3) be increasing (10). As the valve conserves material (11) the flow into the output side of the valve is decreasing (12) and as the output connection also conserves material (2), the flow out of the output of the pressure-regulator must be increasing (13). However, it was shown earlier that the output pressure was unchanging (7), and hence there can be (14) no change in flow through the load (15). This contradiction shows that the area available for flow must be changing (16). On the other hand, suppose the area available for flow is increasing (17), then the sensor must sense (5) a decrease in output pressure (18). An increase in input pressure and a decrease in output pressure dictate (4) the valve pressure decrease (19). By the same argument used in (10)–(13), the flow out of the pressure-regulator increases. However, it was shown earlier that the output pressure was decreasing (18), and hence there can be (14) no increase in flow through the load (23). This contradiction shows that the area available for flow cannot be increasing (24). As the area must be changing, and cannot be decreasing, it must be increasing (25).

In this explanation we see another undesirable feature of indirect explanations: the steps in the explanation do not follow any notion of causal order. The explanation proceeds from output to input. The key problem is that the explanation-proof explains *why* the device must behave not *how* it behaves— the latter is the task of causal explanations.

6. Causality and Digital Physics

6.1. Causality

An explanation of device behavior may take many forms. For example, explanation-proofs explain behavior in terms of inference steps within a formal system. By causal account, we mean a particular kind of explanation that is consistent with our intuitions for how devices function, i.e., causality. Device behavior arises out of time-ordered, cause-effect interactions between neighboring components of the device. In these last two sections of the paper we attempt to derive a notion of causality within our qualitative framework. Our goal is to define a notion of causality that will make it possible to account for the behavior described in explanation-proofs in a causal manner like that of a state diagram.

The state diagram embodies the classical notion of causality. Every change of state is attributable to a change in a specific variable: effects have unique causes. Action is local as the variable causes state change in adjacent components: the cause is structurally near the effect. The states are time-ordered: a cause comes before the effect. The state diagram is unique not depending on external arbitrary choices of variables as explanation-proofs do.

While the state diagram provides causal explanations of state termination, it does not provide causal explanations of behavior within a state, i.e., why the behavior is what it is within a state. Few of the causal criteria hold for an explanation-proof which describes behavior within a state. In an explanation-proof, the reasons for a variable's value are non-unique. RAA, which is necessary, is non-local. There is no time-order among the settings for the variables. And there are multiple explanation-proofs of any particular variable value.

Why introduce the notion of causality when the predictive theory seems sufficient for accounting for behavior within a state? We want a theory that describes *how* devices function when there are no state changes and not just what their behavior is. The confluences and the solution algorithms say nothing about *how* the device functions. Instead the confluences are merely constraints on behavior and the algorithm a method of constraint satisfaction. The explanation-proof says little about how the device functions, and instead only proves that the particular instance of constraint satisfaction is correct. In short, it embodies the epistemological principle, "There is a reason for everything", at the expense of the ontological principle, "Everything has a cause".

Before delving into a detailed discussion of how causal explanations are produced, let us review the reasons why we care about creating them, both from an ontological and an epistemological perspective. Causality as a theory of how devices function provides many advantages. Because it is a theory of how the device achieves its behavior rather than just what its behavior is, it provides an ontologically justified connection between the structure of the device and its functioning. It is now possible to ask what functional changes result from hypothetical structural changes (a task important in troubleshooting). Without causality this question could only hope to be answered by a total reanalysis. (Thus, causality also provides an approach to solving the frame problem [17].) Because it describes how behavior is achieved by the device, more information about the behavior can be uncovered. For example, feedback, which alters the behavior of the device, can only be recognized definitively by understanding how the device achieves its behavior. This is because feedback is a property of functioning, not of behavior. Since causality is a universal mode of understanding functioning, it provides a medium by which the functioning of a device can be explained, by a designer to a user, by a teacher to a student, etc. Finally, since causal accounts are so universally adopted as the model of understanding, most common patterns of causal interactions around individual components have been identified and abstracted and often form the basic elements of the technical vocabularies of a given field. These abstractions are a kind of *canonical form* which can be used as indices into other knowledge about device behavior. For example, a transistor operating in the mode in which the base is the causal input and the collector the causal output has a technical name called the common-emitter configuration. Once a transistor's configuration has been identified as being an instance of the common-emitter (amplifier) then one knows important things about that circuit's gain and frequency response—things that would be impossible to derive from the prediction of the qualitative behavior alone.

6.2. Two impediments to causality

We want to devise a theory of causality which can explain behavior within a state, i.e., when there is no component state change involved. Two related problems concerning time and RAA make it difficult to define a coherent notion of intrastate causality that meets our intuitive criteria. Consider the analytical model for the valve discussed earlier

$$Q = CA\sqrt{2P/\rho} \, .$$

This equation is based on the assumption that any change in flow occurs simultaneously with any change in pressure. Of course, this is an approximation. Although it may be true that a change in pressure somehow causes a change in flow a moment later (through perhaps a pressure wave), this inference draws on knowledge about fluids not expressed in that equation. Mathematical laws of this type do not admit any such temporal or causal inferences.

Time-order remains a problem in the qualitative domain. Consider the confluence $\partial P - \partial Q = 0$. From this, one can infer that if $\partial P = +$, then $\partial Q = +$. But it is incorrect to say that $\partial Q = +$ was caused by $\partial P = +$, because ∂Q has to become + simultaneously with ∂P becoming +. If ∂Q cannot be +, ∂P cannot be +.

The basic intuition behind our notion of a causal account is that the behavior of the device is produced by interacting individual processors—one processor per component. Each processor (a) has limited ability to process and store information, (b) can only communicate with processors of neighboring components, (c) acts on its neighbors which in turn act on their neighbors, and (d) contributes only once to any particular behavior for each disturbing influence.

Each processor is programmed to satisfy the model confluences. Whenever all but one of the values around a component are known, they will (if possible) determine the last one. For example, if the model confluence were $\partial Q = \partial P_{in} - \partial P_{out}$ it would produce $\partial Q = +$ if it discovered from its immediate neighbors that $\partial P_{in} = +$ and $\partial P_{out} = 0$. Note that the logical power of these combined processors operating in this fashion is no greater than the natural deduction schemes described earlier without RAA. As the inclusion of RAA is critical to attaining completeness, programming the processors in this manner is inadequate for realizing the behavior of certain devices. Consider an example of two narrow pipes (i.e., constrictions not conduits) connected in series as illustrated in Fig. 12. The models are simplified to reference only flow variable ∂Q. Suppose $\partial P_3 = 0$ and $\partial P_1 = +$. The processor for constriction A cannot determine ∂Q or ∂P_2 because the value of only one of its confluence variables is known. The case for constriction B is similar. However, given $\partial P_3 = 0$ and $\partial P_1 = +$, then $+$ is the only possible value for ∂P_2. Suppose it were not. Then, either $\partial P_2 = 0$ or $\partial P_2 = -$. If $\partial P_2 = 0$, then the program for constriction B produces $\partial Q = 0$, and the processor for constriction A produces $\partial Q = +$. These two values are contradictory, hence ∂P_2 cannot be zero. If $\partial P_2 = -$, the processor for constriction A produces $\partial Q = +$, and the processor for constriction B produces $\partial Q = -$. Again a contradiction. Thus $\partial P_2 = +$ by a reductio ad absurdum argument. (This is exactly the type of problem that made it impossible to construct an explanation-proof of the behavior of the pressure-regulator; the first proof of Section 5 could not go through without introducing some assumption $(\partial Q_{\#1(VV)} = +)$.) There seems to be no way to change the confluences (nor their form) to satisfy locality and fidelity while avoiding the use of RAA.

The impediment to causality raised by RAA is not easily avoided. It is not solely a property of our qualitative physics. Consider the quantitative analysis of Fig. 12. The equations describing the behavior are (for brevity we use dx to refer to the time derivative of x)

$$dP_3 = 0 , \tag{1}$$

$$dP_1 = a > 0 , \tag{2}$$

$$dQ = k(dP_1 - dP_2) , \tag{3}$$

$$dQ = k(dP_2 - dP_3) . \tag{4}$$

These are four equations in four unknowns. There is no way to solve these

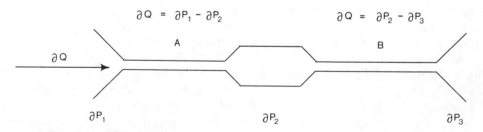

FIG. 12. Two narrow pipes (constrictions) in series.

equations one at a time. Both equations (3) and (4) reference unknowns dQ and dP_2. To solve this system, equations (3) and (4) have to be considered simultaneously. Equations (1) and (2) are easily eliminated through substitution:

$$dQ = k(a - dP_2), \tag{5}$$

$$dQ = k \, dP_2. \tag{6}$$

Equating (5) and (6) gives

$$k \, dP_2 = k(a - dP_2),$$

which can be solved

$$dP_2 = a/2.$$

Thus the quantitative analysis also cannot be done in single steps and requires something like RAA to determine a solution.

Even if we 'push a level' the RAA problem is not avoided. Suppose the constrictions are modeled as a sequence of smaller constrictions. If the same contriction model is used, the RAA problem only becomes more complex as one is required for each constriction fragment. Of course, if the fragment is modeled as a simple pressure transporter (i.e., $\partial P_{in} = \partial P_{out}$), each smaller constriction can directly communicate a pressure rise without using RAA. Although this model successfully shows that the P_2 rises and seems intuitively compelling, it is only a post-hoc rationalization. This simple constriction fragment model does not, in general, predict correctly. For instance, in this same example, as P_2 rises, so must P_3, but this cannot be since P_3 is fixed as a given. The simple model (i.e., $\partial P_{in} = \partial P_{out}$) only applies in limited situations, e.g., all cases where $\partial Q = 0$, but the confluence gives no aid in identifying these situations. The correct model for the constriction fragment at this level is $\partial Q = \partial P_{in} - \partial P_{out}$, but nothing is gained by pushing a level and keeping the component models the same.

A more appropriate way to 'push a level' is to model the material in the constrictions as having momentum and the constrictions themselves as having storage capacity. A quantitative analysis of this behavior results in a fourth-order differential equation. The essential characteristic of the solution is that it is oscillatory (but damped). The pressures and amounts in the two constrictions rise and fall repeatedly, but each time the rise is a little less than the previous time and the fall is not as far. Each constriction can contain more or less material and once the material starts to move left or right it gathers momentum and overshoots its quiescent position. Thus not much has been gained. In order for this lower-level system to 'find' the higher-level equilibrium solution requires repetitive oscillation back and forth of material between the two constrictions. This kind of 'negotiation' does not satisfy the one interaction per disturbance criterion for a causal account.

This lower-level or finer-grain analysis can also be done qualitatively. Each constriction is described by two mixed confluences one characterizing momentum and the other storage capacity. As a result there are four mixed confluences resulting in a state diagram with 81 states. Thus two immediate problems come to the fore. First, the resulting state diagram has additional states and state transitions which can only be resolved with unavailable lower-level information. Second, even if the ambiguities could be resolved, it would show behavior of no interest at the original level. For example, if the 'correct' state trajectory could be determined through the ambiguous state diagram, it would be a lengthy sequence representing a damped oscillation to the final values, not a simple direct state transition to the final values. In summary, pushing a level brings up distinctions about which we have no information at the original grain-size and results in an extremely complex state diagram most of whose details are of no concern. Pushing a level may introduce more harm than good.

All these complications and impediments concerning causality come as a result of asking the question "How does change come about?" Modern physics tends to sidestep this question by adopting a modeling perspective which cannot, in principle, account for change. The central thermodynamical principle that underlies the construction of almost every model is that of quasistatic approximation: the device is presumed always to be infinitesimally near equilibrium. Of course, if the actual device behavior is examined in sufficient detail, one must observe some non-equilibrium intermediate states, otherwise the device could not change state! It is extremely important to note that this problem does not come from the particular laws we have been working with but rather the form of these laws. As was practically illustrated in the previous paragraphs pushing a level without changing the form of the laws does not help. It does not help, because it cannot help. Therefore, in our physics we do not futilely change the level of analysis to obtain causality, but rather change the interpretation of the laws.

6.3. The correspondence principle of mythical causality

"Time and space are not things but orders of things."—Gottfried Leibniz.

Our solution is to leave the original models unchanged, but define a new kind of causality (which we call *mythical* causality) that describes the trajectory of non-equilibrium 'states' the device goes through before it reachieves a situation where the quasistatic models are valid. We introduce the idea of mythical time, which has most of the properties of conventional time, except that it imposes a partial not total order. No conventional time passes between mythical time instants. During mythical time instants, the component laws may be violated, but eventually (in mythical time) all the component laws must hold again.

The component laws and the definition of mythical time are insufficient to unambiguously specify what occurs during the mythical time instants, and a set of criteria must be laid down to restrict some of the options. These additional criteria help to *reconstruct* what the behavior below the quasistatic level *must have been* if the world were causal. The first criterion is to *presume* that the causal action below the grain-size of analysis (of the class-wide assumptions) is of a similar form as the causal action that is explicitly represented in the state diagrams. Thus, interactions are local, a cause is always before an effect, every effect has a cause, etc.

The second criterion is deceptively simple: whatever behavior occurs below the quasistatic level, the values of the variables must start with one set of equilibrium values and eventually reach another. We assume that this intervening behavior is as simple as possible.

A difference between the causal action above the grain-size level and below it is that the first takes time and the second does not. If A causes B we will always say B occurs after A, but no time need pass between A and B. We call causal action below the grain-size level mythical causality and time flow below the grain-size level mythical time.

Mythical causality is, of course, summarizing physical action taking place at a lower level. As discussed in the previous section, no model of the form we have been discussing is adequate. Here is one approach adapted from Feynman, Leighton, and Sands [13]. Assume that the constriction is made of a sequence of *identical* constriction fragments, each having 'momentum' and 'storage capacity'. The idea is that every constriction fragment gets a small piece of the total 'momentum' and 'storage capacity'. So far we have made one simplifying assumption (all fragments are identical) and one complicating assumption (many fragments), and the analysis is still subject to the just stated problems. Now take the limit, that is, break the constriction into an 'infinite' number of fragments where each piece has an infinitesimal amount of 'momentum' and 'storage capacity'. If the mathematics is done correctly the resulting equation describing the behavior of the constriction is

$$u_{tt} = c^2 u_{xx},$$

where $u(x, t)$ is either the pressure or flow at position x at time t. u_{tt} is the second partial derivative of $u(x, t)$ with respect to t and u_{xx} is the second partial derivative of $u(x, t)$ with respect to position. This expression is known as the wave equation because its only solutions are of the form

$$u(x, t) = f(x - ct).$$

This is a wave because as time passes the overall pattern of values of u just shifts with velocity c, e.g., as t changes from 0 to 1 the values of $u(0, 0)$, $u(1, 0)$, and $u(2, 0)$ become the values for $u(0, c)$, $u(1, c)$, and $u(2, c)$. Applying this equation to the constriction (under appropriate boundary conditions) results in

a solution of a wave traveling back and forth between the component producing the effect and the component which is recipient of the effect. The wave
itself traverses the constriction undiminished, but every time the receiving component reflects it back the amplitude is slightly reduced and the wave eventually damps out. We can interpret this solution as a kind of negotiation
underlying RAA that sends information back and forth between the causing
and caused component in order to decide what the equilibrium effect will be.
Of course this view is an interpretation of the observed wave transmissions and
reflections and is not explicit in the mathematics.

6.4. The causal process

Having dealt with some conceptual objections we now return to the main
theme: how can the processors be programmed such that the informational
interactions between neighboring processors satisfy our desiderata for causality? Before proceeding, let us summarize the stage of development we have
reached. The device is initially presumed to be at equilibrium, i.e., the
confluences of all the component processors are satisfied. Then a disturbance
arrives which causes a disequilibrium. The device then equilibrates in mythical
time until an equilibrium is again established. At mythical time instants, the
confluences are not necessarily satisfied. Quite the opposite; *it is the violation of
the confluences that result in causal action*. In the previous subsections, we
presented various schemes for programming the processors, none of which met
our desiderata for causality. In these subsections, we introduce additional processor architecture and a set of heuristics that enable the processors to meet our
desiderata for causality.

We extend the architecture to allow the processors to distinguish between a
new equilibrium value and an old equilibrium value. Furthermore, for a single
disturbance each variable can change value exactly once, from its old equilibrium value to its new equilibrium value. (Note that the new equilibrium values
are not necessarily different than the old equilibrium values.) Each processor is
programmed to produce new equilibrium values that satisfy its component's
confluences. Whenever all but one of the new equilibrium values of a component confluence are known, the final variable is set to its new equilibrium
value (as dictated by our qualitative arithmetic).

One result of this processor architecture is that the set of variables with new
equilibrium values grows monotonically in mythical time, while the set of old
equilibrium values decreases monotonically. In addition the set of new equilibrium values is topologically connected (with respect to the device's structure),
and slowly grows outwards from the initial disturbance. Therefore, there is
always a well-defined *fringe* of processors between the new and old equilibrium
values.

This approach does not prevent the processors from becoming 'stuck' in the sense of needing RAA (as demonstrated by Fig. 12). Indeed, the need for RAA is inescapable—a fundamental challenge to the classical notions of causality. Suppose we introduce RAA, but in a limited form. A processor can introduce an assumption[17] by assigning +, −, or 0 value to a variable, but only if: (a) it is just beyond the fringe, i.e., it still has an old equilibrium value and a component confluence exists linking this variable to a variable having a new equilibrium value; and (b) every other processor on the fringe is also stuck. This severely restricts RAA, avoiding spuriously introducing assumptions for already known variables, variables remote from the fringe and variables directly determinable without introducing additional assumptions. Although this solution severely limits the introduction of RAA, it is still needed: Every time all the fringe processors are stuck, one of the stuck processors must be arbitrarily selected and be allowed to arbitrarily assign +, −, or 0 to one of its variables such that it becomes unstuck. Because of this arbitrariness, the same device behavior may have many causal accounts. Thus RAA is still there with a vengeance.

At this stage in our research we do not have any principled way of distinguishing between these multiple accounts or identifying which ones are causal. Our desiderata of causality underconstrains the possibilities. To get around this obstacle, in the next section we introduce three heuristic rules for good guessing. Crucially, these rules are just part of the programming of the processors; they do not require access to global information and hence do not violate our desiderata for causality. We employ these three rules to push the fringe causally forward whenever it's stuck. In the next sections we present and make plausibility arguments for these rules, but we have no independent justification for them, except that they work for most of the cases we have tried (the cases on which they fail can be characterized). The causal account produced using them is a representative element of the equivalence class of possible causal accounts using the RAA scheme of the previous paragraph. We thus call these rules the canonicality heuristics.

The canonicality heuristics, or 'rules for good guessing', turn out to be better than one might think to be reasonable given that they were chosen empirically. They largely eliminate ambiguity and the necessity for backtracking yet produce causal accounts for all the possible behaviors. The rules eliminate ambiguity in that for most fringes of stuck processors, the rules introduce a single assumption, no less, and no more. This is somewhat remarkable because these processors are topologically disjoint and thus cannot make their 'guesses' by consulting each other. Using these heuristics, we have never seen a case where an entire fringe got stuck (although we can easily invent pathological cases). In the few cases where assumptions are introduced (by multiple proces-

---

[17] This is an oversimplification. More accurately, it is the variables which are 'stuck', not the processors.

sors), the order rarely turns out to matter because the ensuing propagations do not interact (i.e., 'race'). If the propagations do 'race', then unwanted ambiguity in causal attributions results. In addition, the rules eliminate backtracking because the guesses are rarely wrong (i.e., in the sense that there does not exist an assignment of values to the remaining old equilibrium values which satisfies the confluences).

This state of affairs is not perfect. Although we propose no solutions to the outstanding problems, it is important to summarize how the theory of mythical causality we have arrived at is unsatisfactory. First, we have proposed no mechanism by which the processors on the fringe decide they are all stuck, except by postulating some kind of global polling that violates locality. Second, the canonicality heuristics seem to work, but not for any reason we yet understand. Do these rules reflect a property of the physical world, or perhaps just a cultural property of how humans understand? Third, the canonicality heuristics sometimes produce ambiguity (which is not too bad), but sometimes produces a wrong value (if backtracking which is antithetical to our desiderata for causality is not introduced).[18]

These objections make it impossible to 'causally simulate' the behavior of a device. In our study of this theory, we have therefore taken a different approach. Our program ENVISION constructs *all* possible behaviors and *all* causal accounts for those behaviors which satisfy our theory of mythical causality. In this way, we sidestep the final objections. Ambiguity is not a problem: ENVISION produces all accounts. The problem of wrong values is sidestepped by eliminating all accounts that eventually contain contradictions. The price we wind up paying for this is that the resulting causal accounts do not have the compelling force of an explanation-proof: A particular causal account does not indicate why alternate behaviors and causal accounts are not possible. The causal accounts produced by ENVISION are often just extremely good rationalizations.

The inability to 'causally produce' a causal account of a device's behavior is not a fatal flaw from either an AI or psychological viewpoint. From a psychological perspective there is no reason to expect that the kind of problem-solving that underlies constructing a causal account of how a device behaves would in its own right be causal—that is, never need to have access to global information, to backtrack from a decision, etc. Said differently, the problem solving underlying the construction of a causal account need have no relation-

---

[18]The fourth objection is the most serious, but also the least obvious: we propose no mechanism for dealing with intrinsic ambiguity resulting from multiple interpretations. Presumably a particular physical device has a single behavior and, in addition, the behavior of this particular device has a single causal account. (Note that a different physical device may have the same behavior, yet have a different causal account for this behavior.) However, both the behavior and its causal account are ambiguous in our formulation. How can a particular physical device select amongst the possibilities proposed by our theory?

ship to the nearly trivial problem solving involving in executing a causal simulation. Envisioning is not just simulation. However, from a physics perspective the inability to causally produce a behavior is fatal. After all, nature seems to be able to determine what to do next in ways that satisfy our causal criteria. The need for RAA, as discussed previously, dashed that hope. Here, we have been exploring how to minimize the RAA damage in order to bring the machinery to produce a causal account into maximal alignment with the causal account itself. We can argue for this on the basis of simplicity alone, or from the point of view of probing the limits of causality in a digital physics.

6.5. Canonicality heuristics

There may be many sets of canonicality heuristics that work. Ours, however, have one very important additional property: they have been abstracted from the kinds of arguments people tend to use, i.e., from verbal and written explanations of device behavior. Therefore, a causal account generated by these three heuristics, in addition to having the desirable characteristics of causality, is the one human experts use. Thus the explanations generated are ones human's prefer. Of course, this set of particular heuristics is not only good for explanation, but as it is the conventional terms our culture uses to explain behavior, it is at the base of the hierarchical abstract language our engineering culture uses to describe device behavior. Thus, for example, an expert AI system using our terminology can have access to the functional vocabularies and libraries engineers use. It is an intriguing question whether the particular set of rules and heuristics presented here are necessary as well as sufficient for accounting for device behavior.

On the one hand we want enough heuristics to be able to predict the behavior of all devices, while on the other hand we want them to be as few and as simple as possible. Furthermore, the heuristics should not predict behaviors which are not physically realizable.

Metaphorically speaking, the device can be viewed as the surface of a lake. The water surface is completely flat—the device is at equilibrium. The input disturbance corresponds to dropping a pebble in a lake which causes a wavefront to propagate from the spot where the pebble is dropped disturbing the surface of the entire lake. Complicating matters are the obstacles in the lake which cause the waves to reflect and interact with each other. The values of the device's variables correspond to the heights of the water at different places.

The wave on the lake surface metaphor best conveys the difficulty and the intuition behind the three heuristics that solve the problem. Take the simple case where a single disturbance propagates outwards without reflecting from intervening objects. The wave propagating outwards divides the surface into three regions: the region through which the wavefront has already passed, the region that no wave has yet reached and the region at the boundary between these two. The region that the wave has already passed has re-established a new equilibrium, and the region it yet has to reach remains at its original equilibrium. As the wave propagates, the old equilibrium region decreases and the new equilibrium region increases. Eventually the new equilibrium completely dominates. The only disequilibrium exists exactly at the wavefront itself. A component 'balanced' on the wavefront is partly within the region of the 'old equilibrium' and partly in the region of the 'new equilibrium'. How does the component behave in this third region?

The confluence models apply directly to the equilibrium regions, and as a consequence of our correspondence principle, the equilibrium confluence models also apply to the third region. The confluences underdetermine what happens in the disequilibrium region. As a disturbance first reaches a component, some of its variables may be known, but not enough to apply a confluence. In exactly those situations where RAA is required in the logical analysis, the processors get 'stuck', but the metaphorical wave continues on. The three heuristics are based on the intuition of an expanding wavefront, and prevent the processors from ever becoming stuck.

The confluence cannot capture the characteristic that a wavefront causes the new equilibrium to dominate the old. For components on the wavefront, behavior at connections within the new equilibrium region cause behavior at connections within the old equilibrium and dominate it. This is how the wave moves. At the moment the wave passes a component the new equilibrium values are assumed to be dominant (i.e., causal) and the old equilibrium values are assumed to be causally insignificant (i.e., as if they were zero). If some of the old equilibrium inputs are assumed to be zero, the confluences immediately apply and the processors are no longer 'stuck'. Now as the wave passes, the region of new equilibrium values grows slightly covering the old equilibrium values still attached to the component. Although the old equilibrium values are taken as zero, they need not be zero or become zero; more than likely they are not. The point is that just before the wave passed their values were insignificant with respect to the new equilibrium values and after the wave passed their values are consistent with the confluences. The heuristics capture the behavior of components in the short 'blip' in which variables switch from their old equilibrium values to their new equilibrium values.

In summary, each heuristic applies only as a wavefront passes a component and introduces a particular assumption that allows the processors to continue propagating the disturbance *as if it were a wave*. The processor architecture and its associated criteria, define the form of mythical causal accounts, the heuristics dictate their content. Different sets of heuristics would result in different causal accounts although their form would be identical. These differing causal accounts are all of the same behavior but each may assign a different sequence of cause-effect interactions that produces it. Said differently, a theory of causality must assign causal directions to every possible interaction between components, but different sets of heuristics will assign different directions. Without any canonicality heuristics, the notion of causality would be very weak for it would admit many causal accounts for exactly the same behavior.

Significantly, the three canonicality heuristics apply for all disciplines (fluid, electrical, acoustic, rotational, etc.). They are presented here in terms of the pressure-regulator and thus are stated in terms of pressure and flow. In electrical systems, the same heuristics apply, but for voltage and current, etc.

The heuristics presented here will not always work for devices which contain negative resistances (e.g., in the mechanical domain an object with negative mass—easily stated in confluences but rare in the world). As negative resistances do occur, the heuristics can be modified to work for these as well although that is beyond the scope of the paper. We believe (but cannot prove) that the heuristics presented in the next section will work for all devices which do not contain negative impedance, have one disturbance, and have a single common reference.[19]

The component heuristic. If one 'pushes' or 'pulls' on one side of a component and nothing else is known yet to be acting on the component, the component responds as if the unknown actions are negligible.

Suppose the input disturbance has propagated to a change in a pressurelike variable at some component, say conduit 1 of component D (see Fig. 13). (The pressure is changing significantly with respect to some common reference such as the main-sump, ground, etc.) Further, suppose that the disturbance has not yet reached conduits 2 and 3. In this case, it seems reasonable to assume that whatever behavior results in conduits 2 and 3 is caused by the disturbance in conduit 1 propagated through component D. Although the behavior of D may

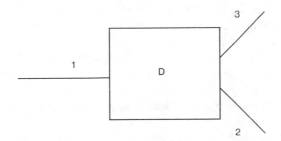

FIG. 13. Component D.

[19]An example of a device for which the heuristics, even embellished to handle negative resistance, fail are mechanical widgets which do analog multiplication (without logarithmic inputs, of course).

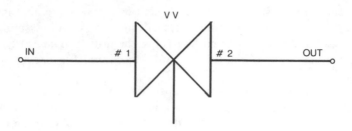

F<small>IG</small>. 14. Component heuristic.

depend on the pressure between conduits 1 and 2 (e.g., a pressure drop) and thus be inapplicable, it is plausible to assume that conduit 2 changes in response to conduit 1. The pressure change between conduits 1 and 2 is thus assumed to be the same as that between conduit 1 and the common reference. Thus component D will exhibit some behavior.

This heuristic is illustrated in the causal argument for the pressure-regulator. E<small>NVISION</small> states an application of the component heuristic as (see Fig. 14):

> The PRESSURE between conduits IN and OUT is increasing.
> Assume that the change in P#1(PRESSURE from terminal #1 to reference SMP) of QUANTITY-VALVE VV causes a corresponding change in P(PRESSURE between terminals #1 and #2).

The confluence for the valve is $\partial P + \partial A - \partial Q = 0$, where ∂P refers to the pressure across the valve—the pressure from conduit IN to conduit OUT. The input pressure rise is with respect to the reference conduit SMP, not conduit OUT. Therefore this confluence cannot be directly used. However, the disturbance has not yet reached conduit OUT, so its pressure cannot be changing with respect to the main-sump as the system is still at equilibrium there. Therefore the total input pressure rise must appear across the valve.

As the rest of the causal argument for the behavior of the pressure-regulator shows, the pressure at conduit OUT rises as a consequence (which is consistent with the overall causal argument). It is interesting to note that if the pressure rise in conduit OUT has been reached first, the pressure in conduit IN would also be predicted to rise but *the change of flow through the valve would be of opposite sign.* The causal order has a direct effect on the predictions of the heuristics. The latter behavior can arise only if the input disturbance has been applied to the conduit OUT, not to the conduit IN.

An application of an heuristic can be incorrect. For instance, it might be mistaken that the input disturbance reaches terminal #1 of the valve first. There might be an alternate path from the initial input disturbance to terminal #2 of the valve. This might cause the change in pressure drop across the valve of result in the terminal #2 dominating terminal #1.

The conduit heuristic. If some component 'sucks' stuff out of a conduit or 'forces' stuff into a conduit the conduit's pressure drops or rises respectively.

The conduit heuristic is the only one that relates pressurelike and flowlike variables in a conduit. Like the other heuristic, this relationship describes the behavior of the components attached to the conduit, and not the behavior of the conduit in particular. It does not refer to 'compressibility' of the material in the conduit. Suppose the input disturbance has propagated to a change in a flowlike variable of some conduit, say terminal #1 of conduit C (see Fig. 15). Further, suppose that the disturbance has not yet reached terminals #2 and #3, nor the pressure of conduit C. In this case it seems reasonable to assume that whatever behavior results in conduit C is caused by the disturbance in terminal #1. The change of pressure in conduit C (with respect to the reference) is assumed to be the same as the change of flow out of terminal #1.

This heuristic is illustrated in the causal argument for the pressure-regulator. ENVISION states the application of a conduit heuristic as:

> The PRESSURE between conduits OUT and SMP is increasing.
> Assume that VOLUMETRIC-FLOW(s) produced by QUANTITY-VALVE VV cause a change in PRESSURE of conduit OUT.

The conduit OUT has three terminals, one connected to the valve, another to the pressure sensor and yet another to the load. The input disturbance propagates through the valve producing an increase of flow into the conduit OUT. By the conduit heuristic, the flow pushes up the pressure.

This heuristic is similar to the component heuristic in many ways. We may eventually discover that the flow into the load also increases. If that had been reached first, it would be regarded as pulling the pressure at the conduit OUT

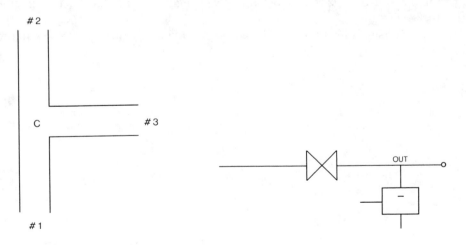

FIG. 15. Conduit heuristic.   FIG. 16. Conduit assumption for pressure-regulator.

down. Thus the causal order has a direct effect on the prediction of the conduit heuristic. The latter behavior can only arise if the input disturbance originates in the load instead of the source of the pressure-regulator.

An application of the conduit heuristic can be incorrect. There might be an alternate path from the initial input disturbance to one of the other two terminals of the conduit OUT. This might determine the change in pressure at the conduit directly from the components attached to this conduit or result in the assumption that the changes in flows in these other terminals dominate the effects of the valve terminal.

The confluence heuristic. If some, but not enough, of the variables of a component confluence are known, propagate as if all but one of the unknown variables is zero. (This heuristic does not apply to compatibility and continuity constraints and only makes sense for model confluences having three or more variables—which are relatively rare.)

The confluence heuristic is a generalization of the previous two. It applies when some of the quantities mentioned by a component confluence are known, but not enough to make a prediction. Suppose the input disturbance has propagated to a change in a variable at terminal #1 of component D (see Fig. 17). Further, suppose that the disturbance has not yet reached terminals #2 or #3. In this case, it seems reasonable to assume that whatever behavior results around component D is caused by the disturbance at terminal #1. Thus the effects of the disturbance at terminal #1 can be predicted by assuming there is no disturbance at terminals #2 or #3.

Suppose the confluence for component D is $\partial x + \partial y + \partial z = 0$, where ∂x is associated with terminal #1, ∂y is associated with terminal #2, and ∂z is associated with terminal #3. From $\partial x = +$, we might assume that ∂y is negligible and that $\partial z = -$. Conversely we might assume that ∂z is negligible and that $\partial y = -$.

This heuristic is illustrated in the causal argument for the pressure-regulator.

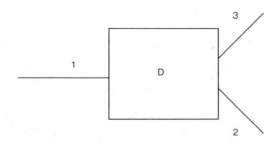

FIG. 17. Confluence heuristic.

The VOLUMETRIC-FLOW into terminal #1 of QUANTITY-VALVE VV is increasing.

Assume, given the confluence rule $\partial P + \partial A - \partial Q = 0$ for QUANTITY-VALVE VV, that the change(s) in P(PRESSURE between terminals #1 and #2) cause corresponding change in Q(VOLUMETRIC-FLOW into terminal #2).

The valve confluence $\partial P + \partial A - \partial Q = 0$ mentions three variables: ∂Q, the flow through the valve; ∂P, the pressure across the valve; and ∂A, the change in area available for flow. The input pressure increase has propagated to an increase in pressure across the valve. By the confluence heuristic, the area available for flow can be assumed to be negligible and thus the increase in pressure causes an increase in flow through the valve. In the specific case of the valve, the converse (where the area is changed) is impossible as the area is an input-only variable of the valve.

A particular application of the confluence heuristic can be incorrect. However, the prediction of at least one of the possible applications for a particular confluence must hold. For example, from $\partial x = +$ and $\partial x + \partial y + \partial z = 0$, it must be the case that either $\partial y = -$, or $\partial z = -$, or both.

The three heuristics are all very similar. Each embodies the same intuition: places where the disturbance has not yet reached are not changing. This assumption is only plausible because the device is at equilibrium before the disturbance is applied. Eventually more or different heuristics may be needed, but all heuristics should be of this general form. These three types work for a wide class of devices, but they do not work for all possible devices. In order for the heuristics to apply successfully: the device must be at equilibrium, the disturbance must originate at a single point, the disturbance must either be in a flowlike variable or a pressurelike variable with respect to a common reference conduit, the device must not contain any incremental negative resistances, and the device must have a distinguished conduit which can serve as a reference. By reference, we mean a common return, or sink, for all the material flowing in the conduits. For fluid systems the reference is main-sump, for electrical systems it is ground, for translational systems it is the fixed reference frame.

6.6. Feedback

One of the additional advantages of mythical causal analysis over simple relaxation or explanation-proof is that it is possible to determine the presence and effect of feedback. Relaxation predicts what the behavior would be (i.e., assignments of values to variables) but does not describe how the device achieves that behavior—a causal account does. Thus feedback, which is a characteristic of *how* the device functions, is only detectable using causal analysis.

In the words of Norbert Wiener [26] "feedback is a method of controlling a system by reinserting into it the results of its past performance". More technically, feedback is defined as the transmission of a signal from a later to an earlier stage. We define feedback as occurring when a sequence of cause-effect interactions produces an effect on antecedents in the sequence. There is no new information to be gained by propagating this fedback signal around the loop again (ad infinitum), it is only important that this event occurs. Thus, once a processor has made a propagation, it becomes quiescent until the next state change no matter what variable values are discovered around it. Feedback is detected by noting when an attempt is made to reactivate it.

Most attempts to reactivate a processor are unimportant. Consider some of the possibilities if reactivation were permitted. When a processor produces a new value, the presence of this new value technically should reactivate the processor, but reactivating the processor could never produce anything different. Sometimes the same value can be produced two different ways, this would again reactivate neighboring processors but to no avail. An intuition behind the causal account is that neighbors act on neighbors until the input disturbance reaches the output. However, a neighbor will usually produce a backwards response as well as passing along the disturbance. For example, if the regulator output pressure across the load is increased, the load responds by drawing more flow from the regulator. This kind of degenerate feedback (which we call reflection) is, in fact, so common that its absence rather than its presence is a sign of something unusual. We define feedback as occurring when the processors of the cause-effect loop also form a loop in the structure (thus ruling out reflections which form a cause-effect loop, but not a structural loop).

Feedback is potentially present when a signal reaches a variable which was assumed to be insignificant according to an heuristic used in one of the signal's antecedents. The analysis of the pressure-regulator required the application of three heuristics, each of which could lead to feedback. The component heuristic (Fig. 17) produces increased pressure drop across the valve, which results in increased flow through the valve which produces an increased flow out of the pressure-regulator and hence an increased output pressure. As there is no structural loop, there is no feedback (reflection, perhaps from an attached output load). The conduit heuristic (Fig. 15) produces an increased output pressure for which there is no reflection. ENVISION would remark about this, except for the fact that this is a port to the external world about which it knows nothing. The component heuristic (Fig. 14) is the only one that results in bona-fide feedback. The confluence for the valve is $\partial P + \partial A - \partial Q = 0$ but only ∂P is known thus far. This heuristic makes the assumption that ∂A is approximately zero, and thus ∂Q must be $+$. This results in increased output pressure which is detected by the sensor producing a decrease in A (i.e., $\partial A = -$). This cause-effect loop corresponds to a loop in the structure and hence represents feedback.

In addition to being able to detect the presence of feedback it is also possible to determine whether it is acting with or against the initial disturbance. In the example, a component heuristic for the valve applied an input disturbance ($\partial P = +$), to the confluence $\partial P + \partial A - \partial Q = 0$, assuming ∂A was insignificant to produce $\partial Q = +$. The subsequent chain of cause-effect interactions produces $\partial A = -$. Consider the effect of $\partial A = -$ would have if ∂P were insignificant. If ∂P were approximately 0, then the confluence would be $\partial A - \partial Q = 0$ and hence $\partial A = -$ would imply $\partial Q = -$. Thus the effect on Q is of opposite sign, and the feedback is negative. Note that $\partial A = -$ cannot completely dominate, because $\partial A = -$ only holds if $\partial Q = +$!

During the causal analysis no additional processing is done for the sake of feedback except that the above facts are noted. Having detected this property of the pressure-regulator's functioning, we can finally say something significant about its regulating action. The presence of negative feedback always reduces the gain of a stage, which is exactly what the pressure-regulator tries to do: lower the amplitude of any disturbance. The lower the gain of the pressure-regulator, the better it regulates pressure.

A causal account can also be represented graphically (see [7, 11] for examples). In the causal diagram, a node represents the assignment of a value to a variable and a directed edge represents the causal action of some component processor. Loops in the causal diagram correspond to feedback in the functioning of the device.

7. Summary

Intrastate behavior describes action within a state (i.e., the confluences governing behavior do not change), while interstate behavior describes action between states (i.e., as the confluences governing behavior change). We have discussed three techniques for analyzing behavior within a state. The first two, relaxation and natural deduction, produce acausal accounts. The third, which embodies the canonicality heuristics, produces causal accounts. We presented one technique for constructing the state (or episode) diagram. In addition, we have presented two sets of models for the pressure-regulator's components. The first set of models, call them the level-1 models, (first presented in Section 3) did not take account of the spring or the mass of the value. The second set of models, call these the level-2 models, including models for the mass of the valve and the spring. Table 8 reviews the results of applying the analysis

TABLE 8. Summary of modeling results

	Acausal	Causal
Level 1:	Table 4	Section 7
Level 2:	Table 5 and Figure 9	

techniques to the different sets of models (we combine relaxation and natural deduction under the heading 'acausal'). The result of applying acausal analysis to level-1 models was a simple assignment of values to derivatives (Table 4, Section 3). This analysis was inadequate in that it neither explained how that behavior was produced, nor revealed important characteristics about its operation such as oscillation. We then discussed two approaches to overcoming these shortcomings. The first of these (discussed in Section 4) took the approach of 'pushing a level' in order to capture important properties about its operation in a greatly expanded state diagram. The second (discussed in Section 6) introduced mythical causality as an alternative analysis technique and did not 'push a level'.

It is crucial to observe that the account (causal diagram) produced using causal analysis with level-1 models is very similar to the account (state diagram) produced using acausal analysis with level-2 models. Both reveal important characteristics concerning the operation of the pressure-regulator. In particular, each reveals a loop indicating that the cause-effect interactions eventually fold back on themselves. However, in the causal analysis this is evidenced as feedback, while in the acausal analysis this is evidenced as oscillation. This is because oscillation and feedback are strongly related. Physically speaking, it always takes some time for the output to affect the functioning. Thus, if the output is changing, the device is always correcting its internal functioning based on an output value monitored earlier. As a consequence, all feedback devices tend to over- or undercorrect, thereby producing oscillation. The point is that any device that exhibits feedback necessarily exhibits oscillation when viewed at a lower-level. However, this oscillation often damps out so quickly (i.e., a quasistatic assumption) that it can be ignored.

As both analyses say similar things about the pressure-regulator's behavior, the question rearises whether introducing mythical causality was worth the bother. There are two independent answers to this question. First, note that Fig. 9 combined with Table 4 does not explain how the state transitions themselves happen, so there cannot be an unbroken path of cause-effect interactions (covering many states) from the initial input behavior to eventual output. In causal analysis this path is unbroken. Second, the tremendous advantage of mythical causal analysis is that it did not have to 'push a level' to detect feedback. Furthermore, in order to 'push a level' more complex component models are needed and these might not be available.

7.1. Digital physics

In a previous section, we discussed how to construct causal accounts for device behavior. These accounts were however constructed by viewing the device from outside. Can we construct a theory for how the device *itself* achieves its behavior? Can the device 'decide' what to do next given the constraints that each component processor (a) has access to only local information, (b) has finite memory, and (c) is allowed one cause-effect interaction per disturbance.

RAA demands these three cannot be achieved simultaneously. One of these criteria must be relaxed.

If we relax the criteria that the processors only have access to local information, i.e., that they can access as much information about all the components and all the variables as needed, a digital physics is possible although rather uninteresting. Each component processor could contain part of the algorithm discussed in the previous section and thus always make the 'correct' assumption about what happens next.

If each processor or interprocessor message is allowed potentially unbounded memory a variety of strategies are available that trade off time against memory requirements. It is possible to include with each value a description of the processing steps that produced it. Then when a contradiction is discovered, this audit trail is consulted to determine which assumption to change. This is equivalent to chronological backtracking and tends to be inefficient in time but relatively efficient in memory usage. In this procedure values will be discovered in their mythical time-order. Another method is to propagate multiple values (only one of which is correct) whenever a choice is encountered. No backtracking is ever required: whenever a contradiction is discovered, values which depend on it are ignored. This strategy trades off memory for a gain in speed.

If more than one cause-effect interaction is allowed per disturbance, the processors can negotiate amongst neighbors in mythical time to determine what happens next. This negotiation process, if it is to succeed at all, needs to be carefully designed as the processors have limited memory. This approach makes an extreme trade-off, utilizing only local information and little memory at a potentially enormous time cost. A simple negotiation scheme suggested by Hopfield [19] is based on an idea of local stress or energy. Local energy is defined as how far a variable is away from satisfying all neighboring constraints. If each variable is changed (repetitively) to minimize local energy, the device will eventually find an assignment of values to variables which minimizes the local energy for each component. Such a state corresponds to a global energy minimum and thus the device has reachieved equilibrium.

These three approaches are somewhat speculative, but point out some of the ways that a computational approach might be used to account for physical phenomena. Each approach has different predictions. If one of these approaches could be partially validated we would have the basis for a new branch of physics, one in which the flow of information plays as fundamental a role as the flow of energy and momentum.

Appendix A. Interpretations

Although the pressure-regulator is intended always to be operated under the conditions where the input pressure is higher than the output pressure (i.e., its valve always in state WORKING-+), the component models should correctly predict the behavior of the pressure-regulator under other boundary conditions

TABLE 9

Interpretation	1	2	3	4
$\partial Q_{\#1(VV)} =$	−	+	+	+
$\partial Q_{\#2(VV)} =$	+	−	−	−
$\partial Q_{T2} =$	−	+	+	+
$\partial Q_{T1} =$	+	−	−	−
$\partial P_{IN,SMP} =$	+	+	+	+
$\partial P_{IN,OUT} =$	+	−	0	+
$\partial P_{OUT,SMP} =$	−	+	+	+
$\partial X_{FP} =$	+	−	−	−

as well. Otherwise the models for the components are presumed to be part of a working pressure-regulator—a violation of no-function-in-structure. The situation where the output pressure is higher than the input pressure is an unusual operating context for the pressure-regulator, and its behavior illustrates some interesting features. In this situation, all of the same confluences remain in force except that the valve is in state WORKING-− and thus the valve confluence is

$$\partial P_{IN,OUT} - \partial Q_{\#1(VV)} - \partial X_{FP} = 0 .$$

Including the input disturbance, there are eight confluences in eight unknowns. Unlike the case when the pressure drop is positive, the pressure-regulator confluences have four solutions. That is there are four different assignments of values to variables that satisfies all the confluences (Table 9).

The device can only manifest one of these behaviors at a time, but the confluences provide no information about which one is correct. We call these different behaviors for the same episode interpretations. Although these interpretations describe potentially unstable behavior (and hence only occur momentarily if they occur at all), it is possible to design pressure-regulators and to select operating conditions such that each interpretation arises. These potential problems with operating the valve in the reverse of its usual orientation is the reason systems are often designed to prevent such situations from arising.

The set of interpretations is the solution space of the confluences. This solution space describes physical reality in the sense that it specifies the behavior of the generic device. The behavior of each device of the generic type is accounted for within the solution space and every interpretation of the solution space is manifested by some device of the generic type within some operating context. This result is not a desideratum on our modeling but rather a direct consequence of obeying fidelity (and the no-function-in-structure principle) in modeling the individual components of the device correctly. It also provides an interesting example of qualitative prediction. Namely, as we originally modeled the pressure-regulator we had not considered the possibility of operating the pressure-regulator in the 'reverse' mode (although a possibility we might have considered as part of some more global context) nor had we ever imagined that there would be multiple possible behaviors.

Interpretations 2, 3, and 4 are nearly identical except for $\partial P_{IN,OUT}$, which is left unconstrained. These three interpretations have the same explanation. As the input pressure rises towards the output pressure ($\partial P_{IN,SMP} = +$) the flow from the high-pressure side decreases ($\partial Q_{\#2(VV)} = -$), and thus the pressure at the output rises ($\partial P_{OUT,SMP} = +$). This increased pressure is sensed and fed back to the valve ($\partial X_{FP} = -$) which closes. This causality is the same as in the normal situation where the input is at higher pressure. In this situation, however, closing the valve reduces the flow from the high-pressure side even further, causing the output pressure to rise even more and thus resulting in positive feedback.

The reason why $\partial P_{IN,OUT}$ cannot be determined for these three interpretations is that there are two tendencies acting on it whose combination cannot be resolved. The valve confluence can be restated as

$$\partial P_{IN,OUT} = \partial X_{FP} + \partial Q_{\#1(VV)} .$$

On the one hand, the increase in flow from the high-pressure side ($\partial Q_{\#1(VV)} = +$) causes $\partial Q_{\#1(VV)} = -$ tends to cause the pressure at the input to rise with respect to the pressure at the output ($\partial P_{IN,OUT} = +$). On the other hand, the increase in pressure at the output ($\partial P_{OUT,SMP} = +$) causes the valve to close ($\partial X_{FP} = -$), which tends to cause the pressure at the input to drop with respect to the pressure at the output ($\partial P_{IN,OUT} = -$). The result is that the change in pressure difference between input and output is not determinable:

$$\partial P_{IN,OUT} = \partial X_{FP} + \partial Q_{\#1(VV)} ,$$

$$\partial P_{IN,OUT} = (-) + (+) ,$$

$$\partial P_{IN,OUT} = ?$$

In this situation no other value depends on $\partial P_{IN,OUT}$ and the ambiguity is completely localized to one variable.

The first interpretation is radically different from the remaining three. As just illustrated, the pressure-regulator contains (potentially unstable) positive feedback. The positive feedback can make a device behave as if it contains a *negative resistance*. (We use the term negative resistance to describe the general situation where a pressurelike variable between two conduits varies inversely with the flow between these two conduits.) It is extremely unusual for an individual component to exhibit negative resistance. A device can exhibit a negative resistance without containing a negative resistor. In Interpretation 1 an increased input pressure results in an increased flow *out of* the input, and thus from the point of view of the source, the pressure-regulator is acting like a negative resistance.

A.1. Origin of ambiguity and its importance

Depending on one's perspective, ambiguity is either a problem or advantage. Ambiguity is purely a result of inadequate information about the device. However, if we devised a modeling system which was less subject to ambiguity (e.g., the usual quantitative one), more detailed information might always be needed—detailed information that might not be available. Therefore a middle ground must be chosen that can utilize additional information, but does not require it. In this sense, ambiguity is an advantage. Given only the qualitative models, *the solution space of interpretations* is the best, in principle, that can be achieved. The results of the process outlined in Section 4 is thus not so much a prediction of future behavior, but rather a set of options which delimit the behaviors that are possible. This set of options describes the behavior of the generic device, any particular device will manifest one of the options (at a time).

To see what kind of additional information would be useful, we must examine why qualitative analysis is ambiguous and why quantitative analysis is not. Ambiguity is a consequence of the particular kind of qualitative value set we have chosen to use. In conventional quantitative analysis it is easy to construct n independent equations for n variables of the physical system, and n independent equations are always solvable for n unknowns. There are eight confluences in eight unknowns describing the pressure-regulator's behavior, yet there are four solutions to those confluences. The conventional theorems rely on the field axioms; however, the addition operation of Table 2 does not even form an algebraic group. Hence there is no reason to expect unique solutions.

While it is important to consider what sources of information are available for disambiguation, it is important to define the results of an ambiguous analysis first. An ambiguous analysis produces a set of interpretations, but that set characterizes *every* possibility. Any piece of additional information will serve to reduce the size of this set. To make effective use of new information the starting interpretation set must be complete; otherwise in the cases where the desired interpretation is missing, no additional information can result in a valid analysis.

The contents of Table 2 suggest an additional source of information to deal with ambiguity. The cases where addition is underdetermined could be resolved using information about the ordering of the variables. For example, $[X] + [Y] = +$, if $[X] = +$, $[Y] = -$ and $X > -Y$. Forbus suggests maintaining a partial order data structure among all the variables, and using this ordering information to resolve such ambiguous cases. He calls this partial order the quantity-space representation. To be effective, the models must also include additional information about inequalities. Nevertheless, only a few of the inequalities will probably be known and therefore the behavior may still be ambiguous or may require drawing very sophisticated inferences about inequalities. For example, suppose we wanted to determine the qualitative value of the sum $X + Y + Z + Q$ where $X = +$, $Y = +$, $Z = -$ and $Q = -$. In the qualitative algebra, this value $([X] + [Y] + [Z] + [Q])$ is underdetermined, but if the quantity space contained $X > -Z$ and $Y > -Q$ the qualitative value of the sum must be $+$.

Appendix B. A Procedure for Constructing the Expanded Episode Diagram

The existence of multiple interpretations introduces another measure of complexity. Within a given composite device state the device can change its behavior by exhibiting first one interpretation and then another. Thus the same composite state may give rise to multiple episodes.

If the requirement is added that all non-derivative variables be constant during an episode then the procedures outlined in this section work as well for pure as mixed component models. By allowing mixed confluences, more interpretations but less composite states result. For example, suppose we used the mixed valve model $\partial P + [P]\partial A - \partial Q = 0$. If $[P]$ is unknown, constraint satisfaction results in six interpretations corresponding to $[P] = +$, $[P] = 0$ and four in which $[P] = -$, but there is only one composite state. Using pure confluences results in three states ([WORKING-+], [WORKING-0] and [WORKING--]) where the third has four interpretations. Both definitions of episode ultimately result in the same number of episodes and the same variable values within them. In both cases time is defined in terms of qualitative state and interpretation. The methods we present work with either representation, although we will generally presume the models are pure.

Here is a procedure, based on the rules of Section 4 that constructs the expanded episode diagram. (This algorithm does not take advantage of the initial device boundary conditions.) First the set of possible composite device states is determined by considering every possible component state. Constraint satisfaction is applied to the confluence set for each such composite state. If there are no solutions, the state is ruled out as contradictory. If there are multiple solutions, each interpretation corresponds to a new episode. Each episode is examined individually to determine under what circumstances it terminates and what the subsequent episode is. Each case $\partial X = +$ where X is bounded above or $\partial X = -$ where X is bounded below indicates a possible transition (always consider only the smallest such bound). In addition, if $X = [c, c]$, the transition is immediate and mandatory. There are sometimes many possible and mandatory transitions for an episode. Except for mandatory transitions, all, some, or none of the transitions may occur. Thus

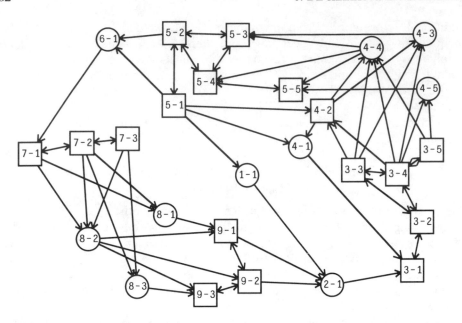

Fɪɢ. 18. Expanded (of Fig. 9) episode diagram for the pressure-regulator with continuing input signal, no friction.

each subset is examined, and the next state is computed on the basis of which thresholds are exceeded. The destination state may have many episodes (corresponding to its interpretations) and a transition is possible to each one as long as no variable need vary discontinuously. In addition, if there are no mandatory transitions out of the state, each episode may transition to an episode of the same state, again as long as no variable change discontinuously. Fig. 18 is the expansion of Fig. 9.

ACKNOWLEDGMENT

This paper has existed in draft forms for so long (about two and one-half years) that innumerable people have read it and provided useful comments and arguments. We collectively thank them. In particular, the content of this paper benefited from extensive discussions with Ken Forbus, Daniel Bobrow and Brian Williams. (This does not imply they agree with the contents however.) They read this paper many times and we have incorporated many of their suggestions and good ideas. We also thank Jim Greeno, Russ Greiner, Tom Kehler, Kurt van Lehn, Robert Lindsay, Steve Locke, and Charles Smith for their useful comments. We thank Jackie Guibert and Janice Hayashi for drawing figures, and assembling, editing and copying countless drafts.

REFERENCES

1. Brown, J.S., Burton, R.R. and De Kleer, J., Pedagogical, natural language and knowledge engineering techniques in SOPHIE I, II and III, in: D. Sleeman and J.S. Brown (Eds.), *Intelligent Tutoring Systems* (Academic Press, New York, 1982) 227–282.

2. Cochin, I., *Analysis and Design of Dynamic Systems* (Harper and Row, New York, 1980).
3. Davis, R., Shrobe, H., Hamscher, W., Wieckert, K., Shirley, M. and Polit, S., Diagnosis based on description of structure and function, in: *Proceedings National Conference on Artificial Intelligence*, Pittsburgh, PA (August, 1982) 137–142.
4. De Kleer, J. and Bobrow, D.G., Qualitative reasoning with higher-order derivatives, in: *Proceedings National Conference on Artificial Intelligence*, Austin, TX, August, 1984.
5. De Kleer, J. and Brown, J.S., Mental models of physical mechanisms and their acquisition, in: J.R. Anderson (Ed.), *Cognitive Skills and their Acquistion* (Erlbaum, Hillsdale, NJ, 1981) 285–309.
6. De Kleer, J. and Brown, J.S., Mental models of physical mechanisms, CIS-3 Cognitive and Instructional Sciences, Xerox PARC, Palo Alto, CA, 1981.
7. De Kleer, J. and Brown, J.S., Assumptions and ambiguities in mechanistic mental models, in: D. Gentner and A.S. Stevens (Eds.), *Mental Models* (Erlbaum, Hillsdale, NJ, 1983) 155–190.
8. De Kleer, J. and Sussman, G.J., Propagation of constraints applied to circuit synthesis, *Circuit Theory and Applications* 8 (1980) 127–144.
9. De Kleer, J., Qualitative and quantitative knowledge in classical mechanics, Artificial Intelligence Laboratory, TR-352, MIT, Cambridge, MA, 1975.
10. De Kleer, J., Causal and teleological reasoning in circuit recognition, Artificial Intelligence Laboratory, TR-529, MIT, Cambridge, MA, 1979.
11. De Kleer, J., The origin and resolution of ambiguities in causal arguments, in: *Proceedings Sixth International Joint Conference on Artificial Intelligence*, Tokyo, Japan (August, 1979) 197–203.
12. DiSessa, A.A., Momentum flow as a world view in elementary mechanics, Division for Study and Research in Education, MIT, Cambridge, MA, 1979.
13. Feynman, R.P., Leighton, R.B. and Sands, M., *The Feynman Lectures on Physics*, Vol. 1 (Addison-Wesley, Reading, MA, 1963).
14. Forbus, K.D., Qualitative reasoning about physical processes, in: *Proceedings Seventh International Joint Conference on Artificial Intelligence*, Vancouver, BC (August, 1981) 326–330.
15. Forbus, K.D., Qualitative process theory, *Artificial Intelligence* 24 (1984) this volume.
16. Forbus, K.D. and Stevens, A., Using qualitative simulation to generate explanations, Rept. No. 4490, Bolt Beranek and Newman, Cambridge, MA, 1981.
17. Hayes, P.J., The naive physics manifesto, in: D. Michie (Ed.), *Expert Systems in the Microelectronic Age* (Edinburgh University Press, Edinburgh, 1979).
18. Hewitt, P.G., *Conceptual Physics* (Little and Brown, Boston, MA, 1974).
19. Hopfield, J.J., Neural networks and physical systems with emergent collective computational abilities, in: *Proceedings National Academy of Sciences, U.S.A.* (1982) 2554–2558.
20. Karnopp, D. and Rosenberg, R., *System Dynamics: A Unified Approach* (Wiley, New York, 1975).
21. Kuipers, B., Commonsense reasoning about causality: Deriving behavior from structure, *Artificial Intelligence* 24 (1984) this volume.
22. Kuipers, B., Getting the envisionment right, in: *Proceedings National Conference on Artificial Intelligence*, Pittsburgh, PA (August, 1982) 209–212.
23. Poston, T. and Stewart, I., *Catastrophe Theory and its Applications* (Pitman, London, 1978).
24. Shearer, J.L., Murphy, A.T. and Richardson, H.H., *Introduction to System Dynamics* (Addison-Wesley, Reading, MA, 1971).
25. Suppes, P.S., *Introduction to Logic* (Van Nostrand, New York, 1957).
26. Wiener, N., *The Human Use of Human Beings: Cybernetics and Society* (Houghton Mifflin, Boston, 1950).

Qualitative Process Theory

Kenneth D. Forbus*

The Artificial Intelligence Laboratory,
Massachusetts Institute of Technology,
Cambridge, MA 02139, U.S.A.

ABSTRACT

Objects move, collide, flow, bend, heat up, cool down, stretch, compress, and boil. These and other things that cause changes in objects over time are intuitively characterized as processes. *To understand commonsense physical reasoning and make programs that interact with the physical world as well as people do we must understand qualitative reasoning about processes, when they will occur, their effects, and when they will stop. Qualitative process theory defines a simple notion of physical process that appears useful as a language in which to write dynamical theories. Reasoning about processes also motivates a new qualitative representation for quantity in terms of inequalities, called the* quantity space. *This paper describes the basic concepts of qualitative process theory, several different kinds of reasoning that can be performed with them, and discusses its implications for causal reasoning. Several extended examples illustrate the utility of the theory, including figuring out that a boiler can blow up, that an oscillator with friction will eventually stop, and how to say that you can pull with a string, but not push with it.*

1. Introduction

Many kinds of changes occur in physical situations. Objects move, collide, flow, bend, heat up, cool down, stretch, compress, and boil. These and the other things that cause changes in objects over time are intuitively characterized by *processes*. Much of formal physics consists of characterizations of processes by differential equations that describe how the parameters of objects change over time. But the notion of process is richer and more structured than this. We often reach conclusions about physical processes based on very little information. For example, we know that if we heat water in a sealed container the water can eventually boil, and if we continue to do so the container can explode. To understand commonsense physical reasoning we must understand how to reason qualitatively about processes, when they will occur, their effects, and when they will stop. This paper describes *qualitative process theory*, which I have been developing for this purpose.

In addition to providing a major part of the representational framework for

* Present address: Department of Computer Science, 1304 West Springfield Avenue, Urbana, IL 61801, U.S.A.

commonsense physical reasoning, I expect qualitative process theory to be useful in reasoning about complex physical systems. Programs that explain, repair and operate complex engineered systems such as nuclear power plants and steam machinery will need to draw the kinds of conclusions discussed here. Fig. 1 illustrates some of the commonsense conclusions about physical situations that are discussed in this paper.

Many schemes have been tried for qualitative reasoning about quantities, including simple symbolic vocabularies (TALL, VERY-TALL, etc.), real numbers, intervals, and fuzzy logic. None are very satisfying. The reason is that none of the above schemes makes distinctions that are relevant to physical reasoning. Reasoning about processes provides a strong constraint on the choice of

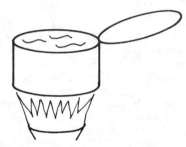

Q: What might happen when the heat source is turned on?
A: The water inside might boil, and if the container is sealed it might blow up.

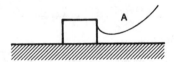

Q: Can we push the block with A if it is a string?
A: No, but you can pull the block if it is taut.
Q: Assuming A is an elastic band and the block is fixed in position, what might happen if we pull on it?
A: It would stretch and if pulled hard enough would break.

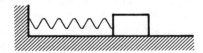

Q: What happens if we release the block?
A: Assuming the spring doesn't collapse, the block will oscillate back and forth. If there is friction it will eventually stop.
Q: What if it gets pumped?
A: If there is no friction the spring will eventually break. If there is friction and the pumping energy is constant then there will be a stable oscillation.

FIG. 1. Some conclusions QP theory can be used to draw.

representation for quantities. Processes usually start and stop when orderings between quantities change (such as unequal temperatures causing a heat flow). In qualitative process theory the value of a number is represented by a *quantity space*, a partial ordering of quantities determined by the domain physics and the analysis being performed. The quantity-space representation appears both useful and natural in modeling a wide range of physical phenomena.

1.1. Motivation

The goal of *naive physics* [21] is to represent the commonsense knowledge people have about the physical world. Here we examine why a theory of processes is needed, what representational burden it carries in naive physics, and the properties such a theory must have.

1.1.1. *Change, histories, and processes*

Reasoning about the physical world requires reasoning about the kinds of changes that occur and their effects. The classic problem which arises is the frame problem [29], namely when something happens, how do we tell what facts change and what facts don't? Using the situational calculus to represent the changing states of the world requires writing explicit axioms that describe what things change and what things remain the same. The number of axioms needed rises as the product of the number of predicates and the number of actions, and so adding a new action potentially requires adding a large number of new axioms. There have been several attempts to fix this problem (e.g., [11, 34], but none of them have seemed adequate. Hayes [21] argues that the situational calculus is fundamentally impoverished, and has developed the notion of *histories* as an alternative.

In situational calculus, situations are used to model the world at different instants in time. Temporally each situation is an instant, but is spatially unbounded. Situations are connected by actions, and actions are specified in terms of what facts can be deduced about the situation which results from performing the action. By contrast, histories are descriptions of objects that are extended through time but are always spatially bounded. Histories are divided into pieces called *episodes*, corresponding to a particular kind of thing happening to the object (episodes will be defined more precisely later on).

Histories help solve the frame problem because objects can interact only when their histories intersect. For example, suppose we are building a clock in our basement. In testing parts of this gadget we look to see what parts touch each other, what parts will touch each other if they move in certain ways, and so on. By doing so we build descriptions of what can happen to the pieces of the clock. We do not usually consider interactions with the furnace sitting in the corner of the basement, because whatever is happening in there is spatially isolated from us (if it is summer it can also be 'temporally isolated').

The assumption that things interact only when they touch in some way also permeates 'non-naive' physics—action at a distance is banished, with fields and particle exchanges introduced to prevent its return. It means that spatial and temporal representations bear most of the burden for detecting interactions. While not easy, developing such representations seems far more productive than trying to develop clever frame axioms. In particular, the qualitative representations of space and time developed in artificial intelligence have precisely the desired properties for reasoning with histories—they often allow ruling out interactions even with very little information.[1]

Histories are to qualitative physical reasoning what descriptions of state parameters over time are to classical numerical simulations. Processes are the analog of the differential equations used to describe the dynamics of the system.

While the classical version of the frame problem is solved, two new problems arise to take its place.

(1) The *local evolution* problem: How are histories generated? Under what circumstances can they be generated for pieces of a situation independently, and then pieced together to describe the whole situation?

In the basement example above, for instance, we could safely ignore the furnace in the corner and concentrate on figuring out how pieces of the clock we are building will move. The divisions are only semi-independent, because certain kinds of changes can violate the conditions for isolation. For example, if the internal thermostat of the furnace gets stuck and it explodes, we can no longer safely ignore it.[2]

(2) The *intersection/interaction* problem: Which intersections of histories actually correspond to interactions between the objects?

Dropping a large steel ball through a flame, for example, won't affect its motion even if the flame is hot enough to melt it unless the gases are moving fast enough to impart significant momentum. Solving these problems in general requires knowing what kinds of things can happen and how they can affect each other—in other words, a theory of processes.

---

[1]For an example of histories in use, see [12] which describes a program called FROB that reasons about motion through space. FROB used a diagram to compute qualitative spatial representations which served as the spatial framework for its most abstract histories, while the diagram itself was used for the spatial framework in the most exact histories. The description of possible motions it computed was used to assimilate assumptions about the character of the motion (such as assuming a ball would never reach a particular place) and to rule out potential collisions between objects.

[2]Unless the physical situation is simulated by some incremental time scheme, the reasoning involved in extending histories is inherently 'non-monotonic' in the sense of [31]. The reason is that conclusions reached by considering one part of a system may have to be reconsidered in the light of unexpected interactions. In standard incremental time simulations the changes in the entire system are computed over a very short timespan, and then the system is tested to see if any new interactions occur, such as objects colliding. The timespan is usually chosen to be small enough that interactions during a step can be ignored. The cost is that the work required to simulate a system is a function of the time scale rather than the actual complexity of the system's behavior.

In classical mechanics *dynamics* describes how forces bring about changes in physical systems. For any particular domain, such as particles or fluids, a dynamics consists of identifying the kinds of forces that act between the classes of objects in the domain and the events that reslt from these forces. In general, we can view a *qualitative dynamics* as a qualitative theory about the kinds of things that 'can happen' in a physical situation. Qualitative process theory claims that such theories have a common character, in that they are organized around the notion of *physical processes*.

1.1.2. *Reasoning tasks involving qualitative dynamics*

Aside from the role of dynamics in representing change, there are a number of reasoning tasks involving naive physics in which dynamics is central. Each of them is a different 'style' of reasoning, appropriate for solving different classes of problems. The catalog below, while surely incomplete, covers a large proportion of the cases. Examples of inferences from several of these categories are being presented later.

Determining activity: Deducing what is happening in a situation at a particular time. Besides providing direct answers to a class of questions ("what is happening here"?), it is also a basic operation in the other reasoning tasks.

Prediction: Deducing what will happen in the future of some situation. We usually must work with incomplete information, so we can only generate descriptions of possible futures, rather than a single future. De Kleer's notion of *envisioning* is a powerful theory about this type of deduction.[3]

Postdiction: Deducing how a particular state of affairs might have come about. Hayes [22] contains a good example of this kind of deduction. Postdiction is harder than prediction because of the potential necessity of postulating individuals. If we have complete knowledge of a situation and have a complete dynamics, we know what individuals will vanish and appear. But usually there are many ways for any particular situation to have come about. Consider walking back to our basement and finding a small pile of broken glass on the floor. Looking at it we may deduce that a coke bottle was dropped, but we do not know much about its history before that, or about anything else that might have been in the room before we looked. There could have been a troupe of jugglers filling the basement, each manipulating six bottles, and a minor mishap occurred. The simplest explanation is that a single bottle was dropped, but our criteria for simplicity is not due solely to our theories of physics. Postdiction will not be considered further here.

Skeptical analysis: Determining if the description of a physical situation is consistent. An example of this task is evaluating a proposed perpetual motion

---

[3]Useful as it is, envisioning has certain limitations, especially as a sufficient model of human behavior on this task. See [17] for details.

machine. This kind of reasoning is essential if a reasoner is to recover from inconsistent data and discover inadequacies in its theories about the world.

Measurement interpretation: Given a partial description of the individuals in the situation and some observations of their behavior, inferring what other individuals exist and what else is happening.[4] The first part of a QP-based theory of measurement interpretation is described in [18].

Experiment planning: Given knowledge of what can be observed and what can be manipulated, planning actions that will yield more information about the situation.

Causal reasoning: Computing a description of behavior that attributes changes to particular parts of the situation and particular other changes. Not all physical reasoning is causal, especially as more expert kinds of deductions are considered.[5] Causality seems mainly a tool for assigning credit to hypotheses for observed or postulated behavior. Thus it is quite useful for generating explanations, measurement interpretation, planning experiments, and learning (see [19]).

1.1.3. *Desiderata for qualitative dynamics theories*

There are three properties a theory of dynamics must have if it is to be useful for commonsense physical reasoning. First, a dynamics theory must explicitly *specify direct effects* and *specify the means by which effects are propagated*. Without specifying what can happen and how the things that happen can interact, there is no hope of solving either the local evolution or inter-section/interaction problems. Second, the descriptions the theory provides must be *composable*. It should be possible to describe a very complicated situation by describing its parts and how they relate.[6] This property is especially important as we move towards a more complete naive physics that encompasses several 'domains'. In dealing with a single style of reasoning in a particular class of situations an ad hoc domain representation may suffice, but sadly the world does not consist of completely separate domains. Transferring results between several ad hoc representations may be far more complex than developing a useful common form for dynamics theories.[7] Finally, the theory should allow *graceful extension*. First, it should be possible to draw at least the same conclusions with more precise data as can be drawn with weak data. Second, it

---

[4]Simmons [42] explores the related problem of reconstructing a sequence of events from a static final state, an interesting combination of measurement interpretation and postdiction.

[5]Experts often use arguments based on constraints, such as conservation laws. It seems unlikely that such constraint arguments are central in naive physics, since usually some kind of animistic explanation is proposed to justify them to non-experts (e.g., "the particle senses which path has the least action").

[6]Producing models with this property is a primary motivation for the 'no function in structure' principle [8].

[7]An initial exploration of linking results from reasoning within multiple domains is described in [44].

should be possible to resolve the ambiguities that arise from weak data with more precise information.

These properties are not independent—for example, specifying direct and indirect effects cleanly is necessary to insure composability. Nevertheless, they are not easy to achieve. Graceful extension is bound up with the notion of good qualitative representations. Qualitative representations allow the construction of descriptions that include the possibilities inherent in incomplete information. If designed properly, more precise information can be used to decide between these alternatives as well as perform more sophisticated analyses. Representing quantities by symbols like TALL and VERY-TALL or free space by a uniform grid, for instance, does not allow more precise information to be easily integrated.

It is important to notice that, while qualitative descriptions are approximations, not all approximations are good qualitative descriptions. Changing a value in a qualitative represention should lead to qualitatively distinct behavior. Consider, for example, heating a pan of water on a stove. Suppose we represent the value of the temperature of the water at any time by an interval, and the initial temperature is represented by the interval [70.0, 80.0], indicating that its actual temperature is somewhere between 70 and 80 degrees Fahrenheit. Changing the 'value' of its temperature to [70.0, 85.0] doesn't change our description of what's happening to it (namely, a heat flow), whereas changing it to [70.0, 220.0] changes what we think can be happening to it—it could be boiling as well. While an interval representation makes certain distinctions, they usually are *not* distinctions relevant to physical reasoning.

A purely qualitative theory cannot hope to capture the full scope of human reasoning about physical domains. However, by defining a basic theory using qualitative representations, we can later add theories involving more precise information—perhaps such as intervals—to allow more precise conclusions. In other words, we would like extensions to our basic theory to have the logical character of extension theories—more information should result in a wider class of deductions, not changing details of conclusions previously drawn. In this way we can add theories onto a common base that capture more sophisticated reasoning, such as an engineer uses when estimating circuit parameters or stresses on a bridge.

1.2. Perspective

The present theory has evolved from several strands of work in artificial intelligence. The first strand is the work on *envisioning*, started by De Kleer [6] (see also [7, 12]). Envisioning is a particular style of qualitative reasoning. Situations are modeled by collections of objects with *qualitative states*, and what happens in a situation is determined by running simulation rules on the initial qualitative states and analyzing the results. The weak nature of the information means the result is a directed graph of qualitative states that corresponds to the set of all possible sequences of events that can occur from the initial qualitative state. This description itself is enough to answer certain simple questions, and more precise information can be used to determine what will actually happen if so desired.

The second strand of work concerns the representation of quantity. Most AI schemes for qualitative reasoning about quantities violate what I call the *relevance principle* of qualitative reasoning—qualitative reasoning about something continuous requires some kind of quantization to form a discrete set of symbols; the distinctions made by the quantization must be relevant to the kind of reasoning being performed. Almost all previous qualitative representations for quantity violate this principle. One exception is the notion of quantity introduced by De Kleer as part of incremental qualitative (IQ) analysis [7], which represented quantities according to how they changed when a system imput was perturbed—increasing, decreasing, constant, or indeterminate. For more general physical reasoning a richer theory of quantity is necessary. IQ analysis alone does not allow the limits of processes to be deduced. For instance, IQ analysis can deduce that the water in a kettle on a lit stove would heat up, but not that it would boil. IQ analysis does not represent rates, so we could not deduce that if the fire on the stove were turned down the water would take longer to boil (Section 5.4 describes how this conclusion might be drawn). The richer notion of quantity provided by QP theory is useful for a wider range of inferences about physical situations than the IQ notion.

The final strand relevant to the theory is, of course, the naive physics enterprise initiated by Pat Hayes [21]. The goal of naive physics is to develop a formalization of our commonsense physical knowledge. From the perspective of naive physics, qualitative process theory is a *cluster*—a collection of knowledge and inference procedures that is sensible to consider as a module. The introduction of explicit processes into the ontology of naive physics should prove quite useful. For instance, in Hayes' axioms for liquids [22] information about processes is encoded in a form very much like the qualitative state idea (see for example axioms 52 through 62). This makes it difficult to reason about what happens in situations where more than one process is occurring at once—Hayes' example is pouring water into a leaky tin can. In fact, difficulties encountered in trying to implement a program based on his axioms for liquids were a primary motivation for developing qualitative process theory.

1.3. Overview of the paper

This paper is an expanded treatment of the central ideas of qualitative process theory [15, 16]. While at this writing certain portions of the theory are still under active development, the ideas described here are fairly stable and other workers have already found these concepts useful. It is hoped that this exposition will stimulate further work in the area.

The next two sections provide the basic definitions for the qualitative representation of objects, quantities and physical processes. Objects and quantities are discussed first in Section 2 because they are required for defining processes in Section 3. The basic deductions sanctioned by the theory are discussed as well, including analyzing the net effects of processes and the limits of their activity. Section 4 illustrates these deductions by several extended examples, including modeling a boiler, motion, materials, and an oscillator. Further implications of the theory, including causal reasoning, are discussed in Section 5. Section 6 provides a summary, discusses potential applications, and places the theory into the perspective of other recent work in artificial intelligence.

A word on notation. Axioms are used only when they help the reader interested in the fine details. Although a full axiomatic description might be desirable, there are a host of complex technical details involved, few of which essentially contribute to understanding the ideas. When used, axioms are written in a more or less standard sorted predicate calculus notation. The following notational conventions are used for axioms: Predicates and relations are capitalized (e.g., Fluid-Connection), and functions are in lower case (e.g., amount-of, made-of). Sorts are italicized (e.g., *time*). Individuals (often physical objects) are in upper case (e.g., WA) and variables are in lower case (e.g., p). Small finite sets are enclosed by braces ('{',`}'). When non-standard notation is introduced an effort is made to show an interpretation of it in terms of logic. This should not necessarily be taken as an endorsement of logic as 'the meaning of' the statements.

At this writing, major parts of the theory have been tested via implementation. The basic deductions sanctioned by the theory (see Section 3.6) are coded, as well as an envisioner for predicting possible behaviors of systems and an algorithm for interpreting measurements taken at an instant. However, the domain models used by the program are still primitive and some of the more sophisticated analyses used in the examples presented here are not yet implemented. In particular, the examples presented should not be taken as representative of the results of a currently running program. This paper does not discuss the implementation at all.

2. Objects and Quantities

To talk about change we first establish some conventions for describing objects and their properties at various times. In this section we describe the temporal notation used and develop the representation of quantity and the *quantity-space* representation for numerical values. *Individual views* are then introduced to describe both the contingent existence of objects and object properties that change drastically with time. The idea of a *qualitative proportionality* ($\propto_Q$) is then introduced to describe functional dependencies between quantities. Finally *histories* are introduced to represent what happens to objects over time.

2.1. Time

We use the representation of time introduced by Allen [1]. To summarize, time is composed of intervals that may be related in several ways, such as one interval being before, after, or equal to another. A novel feature of this representation is that two intervals can *meet*; that is, the start of one interval can be directly after the end of another interval such that no interval lies between them (i.e., time is not dense). Instants are represented as 'very short' intervals which have zero duration but still have distinct beginnings and ends.

Some additional notation is required. We will assume the functions start and end which map from an interval to the instants that serve as its start or end points. The function during maps from an interval to the set of intervals and instants contained within it. We will assume a function time which maps from instants to some (implicit) global ordering, and a function duration which maps from an interval to a number equal to the difference between the times for the start and the end of the interval. We further assume that the time of the end of a piece of time is never less than the time of its start, so that the duration of an instant is zero while the duration of an interval is greater than zero. Finally, we use the modal operator T to say that a particular statement is true at some time, such as

     (T Aligned(PIPE3) I1)

to say that PIPE3 is aligned at (or during) I1. Often the temporal scope of a statement is clear in context, in which case we will not bother with using T.

2.2. Quantities

Processes affect objects in various ways. Many of these effects can be modeled by changing *parameters* of the object, properties whose values are drawn from a continuous range. The representation of a parameter for an object is called a *quantity*. Examples of parameters that can be represented by quantities include

Quantity-Type(amount-of)
Quantity-Type(level)
Quantity-Type(pressure)
Quantity-Type(volume)

Has-Quantity(WC, amount-of)
Has-Quantity(WC, level)
Has-Quantity(WC, pressure)
Has-Quantity(WC, volume)

FIG. 2. Types of quantities. Quantities represent continuous parameters of objects. Here are some quantities that are used in representing the liquid in the cup.

the pressure of a gas inside a container, one-dimensional position, the temperature of some fluid, and the magnitude of the net force on an object.

The predicate Quantity-Type indicates that a symbol is used as a function that maps objects to quantities. To say that an object has a quantity of a particular type we use the relationship Has-Quantity. Fig. 2 illustrates some quantities that pertain to the liquid in a cup.

2.3. Parts of quantities

A quantity consists of two parts, an *amount* and a *derivative*. The derivative of a quantity can in turn be the amount of another quantity (for example, the derivative of (one-dimensional) position is the amount of (one-dimensional) velocity). Amounts and derivatives are *numbers*, and the functions A and D map from quantities to amounts and derivatives respectively. Every number has distinguished parts *sign* and *magnitude*. The functions s and m map from numbers to signs and magnitudes respectively. For conciseness, the combinations of these functions that select parts of quantities are noted as:

> A_m – magnitude of the amount,
> A_s – sign of the amount,
> D_m – magnitude of the derivative, or rate,
> D_s – sign of the derivative.

Numbers, magnitudes, and signs take on *values* at particular times. When we wish to refer to the value of a number or part of a number, we write

> (M Q t) .

This statement is read as "the value of Q measured at t". (Notice that M is not the same as m.) Often it is convenient to speak of the value of a quantity, meaning the value of its amount. Fig. 3 illustrates the use of M.

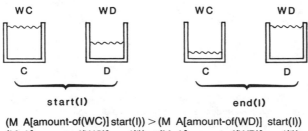

(M A[amount-of(WC)] start(I)) > (M A[amount-of(WD)] start(I))
(M A[amount-of(WC)] end(I)) < (M A[amount-of(WD)] end(I))
(M D_s[amount-of(WC)] I) = −1
(M D_s[amount-of(WD)] I) = 1

FIG. 3. M describes values at different times. Some facts about the two containers expressed as relationships between their quantities.

Signs can take on the values −1, 0, and 1. We take the real numbers as our model for the values of numbers and elements of the non-negative reals as our model for the values of magnitudes so that operations of comparison and combination are well defined.[8] Note however that in basic qualitative process theory we never know numerical values. What we do know about values is described next.

2.4. The quantity space

The value of a number or magnitude is described in terms of its *quantity space*. A quantity space is a collection of numbers which form a partial order. Fig. 4 illustrates a quantity space for the levels of fluid in two tanks C and D connected by a pipe. The orderings and even the elements of a quantity space are not fixed over time. The elements in a particular quantity space are determined by the comparisons needed to establish certain kinds of facts, such as whether or not processes are acting. This means there are only a finite number of elements in any reasonable quantity space, hence there are only a finite number of distinguishable values. Thus the quantity space is a good symbolic description, because it supports case analyses and reasoning by exclusion.

Two elements that are ordered and with no elements in the ordering known to be between them are called *neighbors*. For the quantity space in Fig. 4, level(WD) has height(bottom(D)), height(top(D)), and level(WC) as neighbors, but not height(top(C)). Determining neighbors will be important in determining when processes start and stop acting.

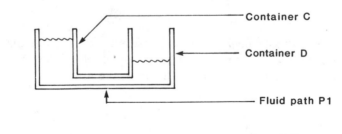

Fig. 4. Graphical notation for a quantity space. WC and WD are the pieces of liquid in containers C and D respectively. The arrow indicates that the quantity at the head is greater than the quantity at the tail. As drawn, level(WC) and height(top(D)) are unordered. For simplicity, we ignore temporal references here.

---

[8]In this model, m becomes absolute value and s becomes signum, hence the choice of values for signs.

We shall now be a bit more formal about defining quantity spaces and the relationships between parts of quantities. Readers who are uninterested in the details may wish to skip to the next section.

The quantity space of a number consists of a set of elements (numbers or magnitudes, often the amounts of quantities) B and a set of orderings. In basic QP theory the value of a number n is described by the ordering relations between n and the other elements in the quantity space. The value is completely specified only if the orderings among the elements in B is known (i.e., the orderings form a total order), and is incomplete otherwise. Every quantity space can in principle be completely specified. A collection of inequality statements whose union with the orderings of an incompletely specified quantity space results in the quantity space being completely specified is called a *completion* of that quantity space.

All quantity spaces have the distinguished element ZERO. ZERO serves to connect the sign of a number with inequality statements, as follows:

$$\forall n \in number \ \forall t \in time$$
$$(M \ n \ t) > ZERO \leftrightarrow (M \ s[n] \ t) = 1$$
$$\wedge \ (M \ n \ t) = ZERO \leftrightarrow (M \ s[n] \ t) = 0$$
$$\wedge \ (M \ n \ t) < ZERO \leftrightarrow (M \ s[n] \ t) = -1$$

Note also that the values of magnitudes are related to the values of signs and the value of the number, in that:

$$\forall n \in number \ \forall t \in time$$
$$Taxonomy((M \ m[n] \ t) > ZERO, (M \ m[n] \ t) = ZERO)$$
$$\wedge \ ((M \ m[n] \ t) = ZERO \leftrightarrow (M \ s[n] \ t) = 0)$$

(Taxonomy is drawn from [22] and means that exactly one of its arguments is true.) Thus if the value of D_s for some quantity is 0, then the derivative itself is zero and the quantity is unchanging. We sometimes need to combine sign values across addition. Fig. 5 illustrates the algebra used.

For s[A + B]:

B A	−1	0	1
−1	−1	−1	N1
0	−1	0	1
1	N1	1	1

N1: if m[A] > m[B] then s[A]
    if m[A] < m[B] then s[B]
    if m[A] = m[B] then 0

FIG. 5. Combining sign values. This table specifies how sign values combine across addition. The cases marked by notes require additional information to determine the result.

2.5. Individual views

Objects can be created and destroyed, and their properties can change dramatically. Water can be poured into a cup and then drunk, for example, and a spring can be stretched so far that it breaks. Some of these changes depend on values of quantities—when the amount of a piece of fluid becomes zero we can consider it gone, and when a spring breaks, it does so at a particular length (which may depend on other continuous parameters such as temperature). To model these kinds of changes we use *individual views*.

An individual view consists of four parts. It must contain a list of *individuals*, the objects that must exist before it is applicable. It has *quantity conditions*, statements about inequalities between quantities of the individuals and statements about whether or not certain other individual views (or processes) hold, and *preconditions* that are still further conditions that must be true for the view to hold. Finally, it must have a collection of *relations*, statements that are true whenever the view is true. Fig. 6 illustrates a simple description of the fluid in a cup.

For every collection of objects that satisfies the description of the individuals for a particular type of individual view, there is a *view instance*, or VI, that relates them. Whenever the preconditions and quantity conditions for a VI hold we say that its status is Active, and Inactive otherwise. Whenever a VI is active the specified relations hold between its individuals. An individual view can be thought of as defining a predicate on (or relation between) the individual(s) in the individuals field, and we will often write them that way. The contained liquid description of the previous figure is translated into logical notation in Fig. 7 to illustrate.

```
; we take "amount-of-in" to map from substances and
; containers to quantities

Individual View Contained-Liquid(p)
    Individuals:
        con a container
        sub a liquid
    Preconditions:
        Can-Contain-Substance(con, sub)
    QuantityConditions:
        A[amount-of-in(sub, con)] > ZERO
    Relations:
        There is p ∈ piece-of-stuff
        amount-of(p) = amount-of-in(sub, con)
        made-of(p) = sub
        container(p) = con
```

FIG. 6. Individual views describe objects and states of objects. Here is a simple description of the fluid contained in a cup. This description says that whenever there is a container that contains some liquid substance then there is a piece of that kind of stuff in that container. More elaborate descriptions are developed later on.

$\forall$ c $\in$ *container* $\forall$ s $\in$ *liquid*
  Container(c) $\wedge$ Liquid(s) $\Rightarrow$
    ($\exists$ IV $\in$ *view-instance*
    ; names of individuals are used as selector functions
    con(IV) = c $\wedge$ sub(IV) = s
    ; logical existence of individual is timeless
    $\wedge$ ($\exists$ p $\in$ *piece-of-stuff*
      container(p) = c $\wedge$ made-of(p) = s)
    $\wedge$ ($\forall$ t $\in$ *time*
      ; it is active whenever Preconditions and Quantity Conditions hold
      (T Status(IV, Active) t)
      $\leftrightarrow$ [(T Can-Contain-Substance(con(IV), sub(IV)) t)
        $\wedge$ (T A[amount-of-in(sub(IV), con(IV))] > ZERO t)]
      ; when active, p exists physically and its amount is the
      ; amount of that kind of substance in the container
      $\wedge$ (T Status(IV, Active) t) $\Rightarrow$
        ((T Contained-Liquid(p) t)
        $\wedge$ Exists-In(p, t)
        $\wedge$ (M amount-of(p) t) = (M amount-of-in(s, c) t))))
; In general,
$\forall$ IV $\in$ *view-instance* $\forall$ t $\in$ *time*
  (T Taxonomy(Status(IV, Active), Status(IV, Inactive)) t)

FIG. 7. The contained liquid description of Fig. 6 translated into logical notation.

The distinction between preconditions and quantity conditions is important. The intuition is to separate changes that can be predicted solely within dynamics (quantity conditions) from those which cannot (preconditions). If we know how a quantity is changing (its D_s-value) and its value (specified as a quantity space), then we can predict how that value will change (Section 3.6). It cannot be predicted within a purely physical theory that someone will walk by a collection of pipes through which fluid is flowing and turn off a valve. Despite their unpredictability, we still want to be able to reason about the effects of such changes when they do occur, hence any dependence on these facts must be explicitly represented. That is the role of preconditions.

2.6. Functional relationships

A key notion of qualitative process theory is that the physical processes and individual views in a situation induce functional dependencies between the parameters of a situation. In other words, by knowing the physics you can tell what, if anything, will happen to one parameter when you vary another. In keeping with the exploration of weak information, we define

$$Q_1 \propto_{Q+} Q_2$$

(read "Q_1 is *qualitatively proportional* to Q_2", or "Q_1 q-prop Q_2") to mean "there exists a function that determines Q_1, and is increasing monotonic (i.e., strictly increasing) in its dependence on Q_2". In algebraic notation, we would write

$$Q_1 = f(\ldots , Q_2 , \ldots) .$$

If the function is decreasing monotonic (i.e., strictly decreasing) in its dependence on Q_2, we write

$$Q_1 \propto_{Q-} Q_2$$

and if we don't wish to specify if it is increasing or decreasing,

$$Q_1 \propto_Q Q_2$$

For example, we would express the fact that the level of water in a cup increases as the amount of water in the cup increases by adding into the relations of the Contained-Liquid description:

$$level(p) \propto_{Q+} amount\text{-}of(p).$$

It is important to notice how little information $\propto_Q$ carries. Consider the relationship between level and amount-of stated above. Effectively, all we know is that, barring other changes, when amount-of rises or falls level will also. From this statement alone we do not know what other parameters might affect level, nor do we know the exact way level varies with amount-of. In fact, that $\propto_{Q+}$ statement is satisfied by all of the following equations (assuming appropriate range restrictions):

$$level(p) = amount\text{-}of(p) ,$$
$$level(p) = [amount\text{-}of(p)]^2 ,$$
$$level(p) = sin(amount\text{-}of(p)) ,$$
$$level(p) = amount\text{-}of(p) * temperature(p) ,$$

and many more.

Often we leave the function implied by $\propto_Q$ implicit. When it is necessary to name the function, we write

$$\text{Function-Spec}(\langle id \rangle, \langle specs \rangle)$$

where $\langle id \rangle$ is the name of the function being described and $\langle spec \rangle$ is a set of $\propto_Q$ statements and correspondences (see below) that further specify that function. Suppose for example that level is expressed in a global coordinate system, so

that whenever two open containers whose bottoms are at the same height have
fluid at the same level the pressure the fluid exerts (on the bottom, say) is the
same. We might introduce a function p-l-fun that relates pressures to levels:

Function-Spec(p-l-fun, {pressure(p) $\propto_{Q+}$ level(p)}) .

Then if c1 and c2 are containers such that

(M level(c1) t0) = (M level(c2) t0)

then since

pressure(c1) = p-l-fun(level(c1)) ,
pressure(c2) = p-l-fun(level(c2)) ,

by the equalities above we have

(M pressure(c1) t0) = (M pressure(c2) t0) .

Sometimes we want to express the fact that a function depends on something
that is not a quantity. In that case we say

F-dependency(⟨id⟩, ⟨thing⟩) .

In the contained-liquid description, for instance, the level depends on the size
and shape of the cup as well as the amount of water. Assuming shape and size are
functions whose range is something other than quantities, we would write

Function-Spec(level-function, {Level(p) $\propto_{Q+}$ Amount-of(p)})
F-dependency(level-function, Shape(container(p)))
F-dependency(level-function, Size(container(p)))

to express this fact. Thus if two containers have the same size and shape, a
particular amount of water will result in the same level, but if the size or shape
is different we cannot deduce anything about the level of water.

The definition of $\propto_Q$ is motivated in part by issues involved in learning and
causal reasoning, and we postpone further discussion of its variants until
Section 5. There is one other kind of information that can be specified about
the function implied by $\propto_Q$, and that is a finite set of *correspondences* it induces
between points in the quantity spaces it connects. An example of a correspondence is that the force exerted by an elastic band B is zero when it is at
rest. This would be written:

Correspondence((internal-force(B), ZERO) ,

(length(B), rest-length(B)))

Correspondences are the means of mapping value information (inequalities) from one quantity space to another via $\propto_Q$. For example, if the length of the band described above is greater than its rest length the internal force is greater than zero. Fig. 8 illustrates.

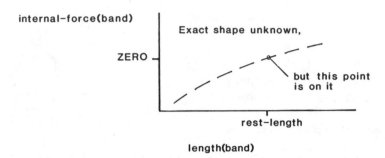

internal-force(band) $\propto_{Q+}$ length(band)
Correspondence ((internal-force(band), ZERO) ,
(length(band), rest-length(band)))

FIG. 8. Correspondences link quantity spaces across $\propto_Q$. A correspondence statement allows information about inequalities to be transferred across qualitative proportionalities ($\propto_Q$). The rough shape of the graph is determined by the $\propto_Q$, the equality between the two points is determined by the correspondence.

2.7. Histories

To represent how things change through time we use Hayes' notion of a *history*. We assume the concepts introduced in [22] as our starting point. To summarize, the history of an object is made up of *episodes* and *events*. Episodes and events differ in their temporal aspects. Events always last for an instant, while episodes usually occur over an interval of time. Each episode has a start and an end which are events that serve as its boundaries. Following [1], we assume that episodes and events meet, that is, the start of some piece of history is directly after the end of the previous piece with no time in between. This allows us to say, for example, that the episode of heating water on a stove is ended by event of the water reaching its boiling temperature, yet during the episode the temperature was below the boiling point.

The particular class of histories Hayes introduced are called *parameter* histories, since they are concerned with how a particular parameter of a specific individual changes.[9] Objects can have more than one parameter, and these

[9]In fact, Hayes' examples are parameter histories for 'amount of stuff', representing an object solely as a piece of space-time. The representation introduced here can be thought of as pieces of space-time that are 'bristling with properties'.

parameters often can change independently. For example, if we drop a steel ball past a flame, the ball will heat up a bit but the motion won't be affected (unless the combustion gases impart significant momentum to it). Thus the history of an object includes the union of its parameter histories. Fig. 9 illustrates the parameter histories for the situation just described. The criteria for individuation, for breaking up time into episodes and events (the spatial component of parameter histories is inherited from the object they are a parameter of) are changes in the values of quantities and their parts. In Fig. 9, for example, the events consist of the ball's position reaching h2 and h1, because different values hold before and after that time. The final component of an object's history are the histories for the processes it participates in, which are described in Section 3.7.

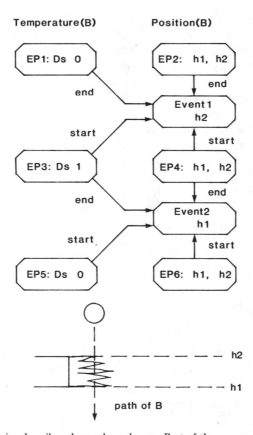

FIG. 9. Parameter histories describe when values change. Part of the parameter histories for a ball being dropped through a flame are depicted below. Time runs from top to bottom, and the portion of the history that depicts what is happening (motion and heat flow) is not shown.

Again following Hayes, a *slice* of a history denotes a piece of an object's history at a particular time. We denote the slice of an individual i at time t by

    at(i, t) .

If we let all functions, predicates, and relations that apply to objects apply to slices as well, with functions that map from objects to quantities map from slices to values, then we could be rid of T and M and just talk in terms of slices. For instance, instead of writing

    (T Aligned(P1) t0)
    (M A[amount-of(WC)] t0) > (M A[amount-of(WB)] t0)

we could write

    Aligned(at(P1, t0))
    A[amount-of(at(WC, t0))] > A[amount-of(at(WB, t0))]

For clarity of exposition, however, we continue to use T and M.

The notion of history so far is 'object-centered'. Since processes will often act between several objects, we need a way of talking about several objects at a particular time. We recycle the term *situation* to mean a collection of slices for a set of objects under consideration at some particular time. Unlike situational calculus, the temporal aspect of a situation can be either an instant or an interval. Also, a situation is now spatially bounded—its spatial extent is that of the slices that comprise it. In formulae where times are required, we assume a coercion from a situation or event to its time so that we can freely use the names of situations in expressions involving T and M.

The question of what constitutes a useful situation brings us back to the local evolution problem described in the introduction. We may now state it more precisely: Given some collection of objects that we know about at a particular time, can we figure out some way to divide them up into situations that can be considered semi-independently?[10] For the moment we leave the criteria of what constitutes useful situations unspecified, returning to this problem in Section 3.7 after discussing processes.

3. Processes

A physical situation is usually described in terms of a collection of objects, their properties, and the relationships between them. So far our description of the world has been static—we can say that things are different from one time to another, but have not provided the means by which changes actually occur. The ways in which things change are intuitively characterized as processes. A *physical process* is something that acts through time to change the parameters

---

[10]In current AI systems this problem usually does not arise because the situations under consideration are composed solely of relevant objects. However, as we attempt to make programs that can deal with more realistic problems this issue will become very important.

of objects in a situation. Examples of processes include fluid and heat flow, boiling, motion, stretching and compressing.

This section describes what processes are, including how to specify them, and elaborates the notion of *influences*. A catalog of basic deductions involving processes illustrates the kinds of conclusions that can be drawn within QP theory. Histories are extended to include occurrences of processes, and the role of processes in specifying a language of behavior is discussed.

3.1. Specifying processes

A process is specified by five parts:

(1) the *individuals* it applies to;

(2) a set of *preconditions*, statements about the individuals and their relationships other than quantity conditions;

(3) a set of *quantity conditions*, that are either statements of inequalities between quantities belonging to the individuals (including domain-dependent constants and functions of them) or statements about the status of processes and individual views;

(4) a set of *relations* the process imposes between the parameters of the individuals, along with any new entities that are created;

(5) a set of *influences* imposed by the process on the parameters of the individuals.

Fig. 10 illustrates process specifications for heat flow and boiling. (For fans of logic, Fig. 11 illustrates how the boiling process would look translated into predicate calculus.)

Basically, a process is just like an individual view—it is a time-dependent thing—except it has something called *influences*. To recapitulate, for every collection of objects that satisfy the individuals specification for a particular type of process, there is a *process instance* (PI) that relates them. The process instance is active, representing the process acting between these individuals, exactly whenever both the preconditions and the quantity conditions are true. Preconditions are those factors that are outside QP theory, such as someone opening or closing a valve to establish a fluid path, but still relevant to whether or not a process occurs. The quantity conditions are those statements that can be expressed solely within QP theory, such as requiring the temperature of two bodies to be different for heat flow to occur, or a heat flow to occur as a prerequisite to boiling. The set of relations associated with a process are the relationships it imposes between the objects it is acting on. The relations component usually describes, but is not limited to, indirect effects via functional relationships between quantities, such as the flow rate in fluid flow being qualitatively proportional to the difference in the pressures of the contained fluids involved. The relations also include descriptions of any new individuals created by the process, as for example the steam generated by boiling, and facts needed by external representations, such as describing appearances. We discuss influences next.

process heat-flow

Individuals:
   src an object,Has-Quantity(src, heat)
   dst an object,Has-Quantity(dst, heat)
   path a Heat-Path, Heat-Connection(path, src, dst)

Preconditions:
   Heat-Aligned(path)

QuantityConditions:
   $A[temperature(src)] > A[temperature(dst)]$

Relations:
   Let flow-rate be a quantity
   $A[flow\text{-}rate] > ZERO$
   flow-rate $\propto_{Q+}$ (temperature(src) − temperature(dst))

Influences:
   I−(heat(src), A[flow-rate])
   I+(heat(dst), A[flow-rate])

process boiling

Individuals:
   w a contained-liquid
   hf a process-instance, process(hf) = heat-flow
                        ∧ dst(hf) = w

QuantityConditions:
   Status(hf, Active)
   ¬ $A[temperature(w)] < A[t\text{-}boil(w)]$

Relations:
   There is g ∈ *piece-of-stuff*
   gas(g)
   substance(g) = substance(w)
   temperature(w) = temperature(g)
   Let generation-rate be a quantity
   $A[generation\text{-}rate] > ZERO$
   generation-rate $\propto_{Q+}$ flow-rate(hf)

Influences:
   I-(heat(w), A[flow-rate(hf)])
   ; The above counteracts the heat flow's influence
   I−(amount-of(w), A[generation-rate])
   I+(amount-of(g), A[generation-rate])
   I−(heat(w), A[generation-rate])
   I+(heat(g), A[generation-rate])

FIG. 10. Two examples of process specifications. Heat flow happens between two objects that have heats and are connected via some path through which heat can flow. The predicate Heat-Aligned is true exactly when heat can flow through the path. Boiling happens to a contained liquid being heated, and creates a gas made of the same stuff as the liquid. t-boil represents the boiling point for the piece of stuff involved.

∀ w ∈ *contained-liquid* ∀ hf ∈ *process-instance*
(process(hf) = heat-flow ∧ dst(hf) = w ⇒
  [∃ pi ∈ *process-instance*
  process(pi) = boiling ∧ w(pi) = w ∧ hf(pi) = hf
  ∧ [(Status(hf, active) ∧ A[temperature(w)] = A[t-boil(w)])
     ↔ Status(pi, Active)]
  ∧ [Status(pi, Active) ⇒
     [∃ g ∈ *piece-of-stuff* ∃ generation-rate ∈ *quantity*
     Boiling(w, hf)
       ∧ gas(g)
       ∧ substance(g) = substance(w)
       ∧ temperature(w) = temparature(g)
       ∧ A[generation-rate] > ZERO
       ∧ generation-rate ∝ Q+ flow-rate(hf)
       ∧ A[flow-rate(hf)] ∈ minus-imputs(influence-adder(heat(w)))
       ∧ A[generation-rate]
          ∈ minus-inputs(influence-adder(amount-of(w)))
       ∧ A[generation-rate]
          ∈ plus-inputs(influence-adder(amount-of(g)))
       ∧ A[generation-rate]
          ∈ minus-inputs(influence-adder(heat(w)))
       ∧ A[generation-rate]
          ∈ plus-inputs(influence-adder(heat(g)))]]]

; a directly influenced quantity has an "influence adder",
; which determines its derivative
∀ q ∈ *quantity*
  ([¬minus-inputs(influence-adder(q)) = { }
  ∨¬plus-inputs(influence-adder(q)) = { }] ⇒
     D[q] = Sum(influence-adder(q)))

FIG. 11. Boiling expressed as an axiom. How the boiling description could be written as an axiom. For clarity, temporal references have been omitted.

3.2. Influences and integration

Influences specify what can cause a quantity to change. There are two kinds of influences, *direct* and *indirect*. The influences component of a process specifies the direct influences imposed by that process. For example, in a flow process (see Fig. 10) the flow rate will make the amount of 'stuff' at the source tend to decrease and the amount of 'stuff' at the destination tend to increase. If the number n is a direct influence on the quantity Q, we write

$$I+(Q, n) \qquad I-(Q, n) \qquad I\pm(Q, n)$$

according to whether its influence is positive, negative, or unspecified. Importantly, processes are the only source of direct influences. If at least one process is directly influencing a quantity Q at some particular time, then we say that Q is *directly influenced*. If a quantity is directly influenced, its derivative equals the sum of all of the direct influences on it.

An indirect influence occurs when a quantity is a function of some other quantity that is changing. Qualitative proportionalities ($\propto_Q$), introduced earlier, are the means of specifying these effects. Sometimes we will refer to a process or quantity *indirectly influencing* some quantity. One quantity indirectly influences another if the second quantity is qualitatively proportional to the first. A process indirectly influences a quantity Q_1 if it directly influences some quantity Q_2 which in turn indirectly influences Q_1.

Notice that direct influences tell us much more about the relationship between quantities than indirect influences as specified by $\propto_Q$. Given two direct influences on a quantity we know they combine by addition, but we do not know how multiple indirect influences combine because $\propto_Q$ provides little information on the exact form of the underlying function. We will discuss this in more detail in Section 3.6.3.

At any particular time a quantity must be either directly influenced, indirectly influenced, or not influenced at all. Importantly, we assume that no quantity is both directly and indirectly influenced at once. A domain physics that allows a quantity to be both directly and indirectly influenced at the same time is considered to be inconsistent. This may seem odd, given that relationships between quantities in 'real' physics are often specified as constraint equations. For example, we could express the equation $F = m * a$ in three different ways using qualitative proportionalities, each corresponding to one parameter being described as a function of the other two. How, and why, do we select a particular function to represent the constraint relationship?

The choice is made to reflect the way causality works in the domain. In thinking about motion, for instance, we cannot directly apply an acceleration— we can only cause acceleration by imposing a force. Similarly, we cannot by accelerating something or pushing on it cause the mass of a solid object to change, yet its mass will affect how much acceleration we get for a given push. These considerations suggest the proper rendering of $F = m * a$ is:

$$a \propto_{Q+} F \qquad a \propto_{Q-} m.$$

There is a subtle issue lurking here. In a sense, quantities that can be directly influenced are 'independent', in that we can cause changes in them directly via active processes. All other quantities must be changed indirectly as a consequence of the changes processes make on the directly influenced parameters. The choice of directionality when transforming a constraint equation into a function must respect this fact. The full importance of this distinction is discussed later on when examining causal reasoning (Section 5.2).

The influences on a quantity are combined to determine its derivative (we describe just how later). A notion of integrability—the relationship between the derivative of a quantity and its amount—is needed. Essentially, if the derivative is negative then the amount will decrease over an interval, if positive then the amount will increase, and if zero then the amount will be the same:

$\forall$ q $\in$ *quantity* $\forall$ I $\in$ *time*
(constant-sign(D[q], I) $\Rightarrow$
  (M D$_s$[q] during(I)) = -1
  $\leftrightarrow$ (M A[q] end(I)) $<$ (M A[q] start(I))
  $\wedge$ (M D$_s$[q] during(I)) = 1
    $\leftrightarrow$ (M A[q] end(I)) $>$ (M A[q] start(I))
    $\wedge$ (M D$_s$[q] during(I)) = 0
    $\leftrightarrow$ (M A[q] end(I)) = (M A[q] start(I))

where

$\forall$ n $\in$ *numbers* $\forall$ I $\in$ *time*
constant-sign(n I) $\equiv$ ($\forall$ i$_1$, i$_2$ $\in$ during(I) (M s[n] i$_1$) = (M s[n] i$_2$)) .

This statement is very weak compared to our usual notion of integrability.[11] In particular, it does not rest on knowing an explicit function describing the derivative and thus does not require an explicit notion of integral.

3.3. Limit points

Recall that a quantity space consists of a collection of elements and ordering relations between them. The major source of elements for the quantity space of some quantity Q are the numbers and constants that are compared to Q via quantity conditions. Because they correspond to discontinuous changes in the processes that are occurring (or individual views that hold), they are called *limit points*. Limit points serve as boundary conditions. For example, the temperature quantity space for an object W might include the limit points t-melt(W) and t-boil(W), where the object undergoes phase changes that result in qualitatively distinct behavior. These different modes of behavior are modeled by individual views.

3.4. The sole mechanism assumption and process vocabularies

The central assumption of qualitative process theory is the *sole mechanism* assumption, namely:

Sole mechanism assumption. *All changes in physical systems are caused directly or indirectly by processes.*

---

[11]If the time involved is an instant (i.e., an interval of duration ZERO), then we also assume that the quantity "doesn't change very much" during this time. To be more exact, we assume in that case the quantity is only different by an infinitesimal amount, or equivalently, that influences are finite. This assumption underlies case (2) of the equality change law, which is discussed shortly.

As a consequence, the physics for a domain must include a vocabulary of processes that occur in that domain. This *process vocabulary* can be viewed as specifying the dynamics theory for the domain. A physical situation, then, is described by a collection of objects, their properties, the relations between them (including individual views), *and* the processes that are occurring. The sole mechanism assumption allows us to reason by exclusion. If we make the additional assumption that our process vocabulary for a domain is complete, then we know what types of quantities can be directly influenced. If we understand the objects and relationships between them well enough, we know all the ways quantities can be indirectly influenced. Thus we know all the potential ways any physical situation will change. Without these closed-world assumptions (see [5, 35, 38]), it is hard to see how a reasoning entity could use, much less debug or extend, its physical knowledge.

3.5. Reprise

Processes should be first-class entities in the ontology of naive physics. It may be tempting to think that processes are mere abbreviations for 'deeper' representations, such as constraint laws. However, they are not. The temptation arises both because constraint laws are often judged to be the most elegant physical descriptions in 'non-naive' physics, and because constraint-based computer models have been fairly successful for analyzing engineered systems [9, 43]. However, the aims of naive physics are not the same as the aims of physics or engineering analysis. In physics we are trying to construct the simplest models that can make detailed predictions about physical phenomena. When performing an engineering analysis, even a qualitative one, we have chosen a particular point of view on the system and abstracted away certain objects. Unlike either of these enterprises, naive physics attempts to uncover the ideas of physical reality that people actually use in daily life. Thus the notions that physics throws away (objects, processes, causality) for conciseness in its formal theory—the equations—are precisely what we must keep.

Qualitative process theory concerns the form of dynamical theories, not their specific content. For example, the heat flow process illustrated previously adheres to energy conservation, and does not specify that 'stuff' is transferred between the source and destination. The language provided by the theory also allows one to write a heat flow process that violates energy conservation and transfers 'caloric fluid' between the source and destination. The assumptions made about the content of dynamical theories are quite weak. Aside from the ability to write a wide variety of physical models, the weakness of its assumptions allow other theories to be written that impose further constraints on the legal vocabularies of processes. For example, conservation of energy can be expressed as a theory about certain types of quantities and the allowable patterns of influences in processes that affect those types of quantities (see

Section 4.5). We do not, however, wish to saddle QP theory with these assumptions.

3.6. Basic deductions

To be useful, a representation must support deductions. Several basic deductions involving the constructs of QP theory are catalogued below. It may be helpful to skip momentarily to the example in Section 4.1, which illustrates these deductions step by step.

3.6.1. Finding possible processes

A process vocabulary specifies the types of processes that can occur. Given a collection of individuals and a process vocabulary, the individual specifications from the elements in the process vocabulary must be used to find collections of individuals that can participate in each kind of process. These process instances (PIs) represent the potential processes that can occur between a set of individuals. A similar deduction is used for finding view instances.

3.6.2. Determining activity

A process instance has a status of Active or Inactive according to whether or not the particular process it represents is acting between its individuals. By determining whether or not the preconditions and quantity conditions are true, a status can be assigned to each process instance for a situation.[12] The collection of active PIs is called the *process structure* of the situation. The process structure represents "what's happening" to the individuals in a particular situation. Similarly, the *view structure* is the collection of active VIs in the situation. Whenever we discuss the process structure, we usually include the view structure as well.

3.6.3. Determining changes

Most of the changes in an individual are represented by the D_s-values for its quantities. A D_s-value of -1 indicates the quantity is decreasing, a value of 1 indicates that it is increasing, and a value of 0 indicates that it remains constant. As stated previously, there are two ways for a quantity to change. A quantity can be directly influenced by a process, or it can be indirectly influenced via $\propto_Q$. (By the sole mechanism assumption, if a quantity is uninfluenced its D_s-value is 0.) Determining the D_s-value for a quantity is called *resolving* its influences, by analogy to resolving forces in classical mechanics.

Resolving a quantity which is directly influenced requires adding up the

---

[12]This can require searching the completions of the relevant quantity spaces if the required orderings cannot be deduced from what is already known about the value.

influences. If all the signs of the influences are the same then the D_s-value is simply that sign. Since we do not have numerical information, ambiguities can arise. Sometimes an answer can be found by sorting the influences into positive and negative sets and using inequality information to prove that one set of influences must, taken together, be larger than the other set. However, there is not always enough information to do this, so direct influences are not always resolvable.

Resolving an indirectly influenced quantity involves gathering the $\propto_Q$ statements that specify it as a function of other quantities. Because we lack detailed information about the form of the function, in many cases indirect influences cannot be resolved within basic QP theory. An example will make this point clearer. Suppose we have a quantity Q_0 such that in a particular process structure:

$$Q_0 \propto_{Q+} Q_1 \wedge Q_0 \propto_{Q-} Q_2 .$$

If we also know that

$$D_s[Q_1] = 1 \wedge D_s[Q_2] = 1$$

then we cannot determine $D_s[Q_0]$, because we do not have enough information to determine which indirect influence dominates. However, if we had

$$D_s[Q_1] = 1 \wedge D_s[Q_2] = 0$$

then we can conclude that

$$D_s[Q_0] = 1$$

because Q_1 is now the only active indirect influence.

Importantly, we assume the collection of qualitative proportionalities which hold at any particular time is loop-free, that is, if A is qualitatively proportional to B then it cannot also be the case that B is qualitatively proportional to A. At first glance it might seem that this assumption makes it impossible to model systems where two parameters are interdependent, such as feedback systems. This is not the case; the key observation is that, in physical systems, such loops always contain a derivative relationship—which is modeled by a direct influence, not a qualitative proportionality. In thinking about fluid flow, for example, we might observe that a change in amount of liquid causes a change in flow rate, which in turn acts to change the amount of liquid. But while flow rate is qualitatively proportional to the amount of liquid (via its dependence on pressure, which depends on the level, which in turn depends on the amount of liquid), the flow rate is a direct influence on the amount of liquid. The integral connection between them serves to 'break' the loop, thus ensuring that the system of qualitative proportionalities is loop-free.

Domain-specific and problem-specific knowledge often plays a role in resolving influences. We may know that a certain influence can be ignored, such as when we ignore heat loss from a kettle on a stove to the air surrounding it if the stove is on. Our knowledge about particular functions may tell us which way things combine. Suppose for instance that our model of fluid flow included influences to model the changes in heat and temperature that result from mass transfer. In the source and destination temperature would be indirectly influenced (via Amount-of and heat), and if we knew only the D_s-values we could say nothing about how they will change. From Black's Law, however, we know that the temperature of the source is unchanged and the temperature of the destination will rise or fall according to whether the temperature of the source is greater or less than the temperature of the destination.

3.6.4. *Limit analysis*

Changes in quantities can result in the process and view structures themselves changing. Determining these changes and changes in D_s-values is called *limit analysis*. Limit analysis is carried out by using the current D_s-values and quantity spaces to determine how the quantity spaces (and hence the truth of quantity conditions) can change.

The first step is to find the neighboring points within the quantity spaces of each changing quantity. If there is no neighbor in some direction, then a change in that direction cannot affect the status of any process. The ordering between each neighbor and the current amount of the quantity can be combined with the D_s-values of each to determine if the relationship will change (see Fig. 12). If the neighbor is a limit point, some processes may end there and others begin. Thus the set of possible changes in orderings involving limit points determines the ways the current set of active processes might change.[13] The set of changes between single inequalities plus consistent conjunctions of changes (corresponding to the occurrence of simultaneous changes) forms the set of *quantity hypotheses* for the current situation. A quantity hypothesis that imposes a change in either the view or process structure (as opposed to merely indicating a change in a D_s-value) will be called a *limit hypothesis*.

Determining which changes and conjunctions of changes are consistent involves several types of knowledge. First, one change might render another

---

[13]This assumes that rates are not infinitesimals, so that if a quantity is 'moving' towards some point in its quantity space it will actually reach that value in some finite time. This assumption rules out a simple form of Zeno's paradox. Note, however, that relaxing this assumption would result in only one additional state in the possibilities returned by the limit analysis—that the current set of active processes never changes.

For A > B:

A \ B	−1	0	1
−1	N1	=	=
0	>	>	=
1	>	>	N2

N1: If $D_m[A] > D_m[B]$ then $=$; $>$ otherwise
N2: If $D_m[A] < D_m[B]$ then $=$; $>$ otherwise

For A = B:

A \ B	−1	0	1
−1	N3	<	<
0	>	=	<
1	>	>	N4

N3: If $D_m[A] > D_m[B]$ then $<$;
    If $D_m[A] < D_m[B]$ then $>$;
    If $D_m[A] = D_m[B]$ then $=$;

N4: If $D_m[A] > D_m[B]$ then $>$;
    If $D_m[A] < D_m[B]$ then $<$;
    If $D_m[A] = D_m[B]$ then $=$;

FIG. 12. Linking derivatives with inequalities. This table summarizes how the ordering relationship between two quantities may change according to the sign of their derivatives over some interval.

change moot. For example, if a particular change causes an individual to vanish, then any other changes involving that individual are irrelevant. Second, we assume that changes must be continuous both in quantity spaces and in D_s-values. Continuous in quantity spaces means that all order relations must go through equality, i.e., that the relationship between N_1 and N_2 cannot change directly from $>$ to $<$ or from $<$ to $>$. Continuous in D_s-values means a D_s-value cannot jump directly from 1 to −1 or from −1 to 1. Finally, domain-dependent information can be used to determine that the situation resulting from the change is inconsistent. For example, if the bottoms of two open containers are at the same height and the only thing happening is a fluid flow from one to the other, then it is impossible for the source of the flow to run out of liquid.

Typically more than one change is possible, as the examples in the next section illustrate. There are three reasons for this. First, if the ordering within a quantity space is not a total order more than one neighbor can exist. Second, a process can influence more than one quantity. Finally more than one process can be occurring simultaneously. The basic theory does not in general allow the determination of which alternative actually occurs. Using calculus as the model for quantities, the alternative which occurs next is the one for which time to integrate the quantities involved to their limit points is minimal. Since the basic theory does not include explicit integrals, this question typically cannot be decided.

There are some special situations, due to the nature of quantities, where sometimes we can rule out classes of hypotheses without detailed domain-specific information. Consider two quantities A and B that are equal, and C and D that are unequal. If all of the quantities are changing (D_s-value of -1 or 1) in ways that insure the relationships between them will change, then the finite difference between C and D implies that the change in the equality between A and B occurs first. In fact, we assume that the change *from* equality occurs in an instant, while the change *to* equality usually will take some interval. We further assume that the only time a change *to* equality will take an instant is when the change in value was due to a process that acted only for an instant. We will summarize this as the *equality change law*:

Equality change law. *With two exceptions, a process structure lasts over an interval of time. It lasts for an instant only when either*
  (1) *a change from equality occurs, or*
  (2) *a change to equality occurs between quantities that were influenced away from equality for only an instant.*

The first case assumes that the values of numbers are not 'fuzzy', and the second case assumes that the changes wrought by processes are finite (i.e., no impulses).

Remember that the set of quantity hypotheses consists of single changes and conjunctions of single changes. Consider the set of conjunctive hypotheses which contain only changes that occur in an instant, and in particular, the maximal element (in terms of inclusion) of the set. The quantity hypotheses that contain this maximal element are the ones which can occur next, because the duration of an instant is shorter than the duration of an interval. By using the equality change law to identify those quantity hypotheses that represent changes that occur in an instant, we can sometimes get a unique result from limit analysis within the basic theory.

For some kinds of tasks just knowing the possible changes is enough (e.g., envisioning). If required, knowledge outside the scope of QP theory can be used to disambiguate the possibilities. Depending on the domain and the style of reasoning to be performed there are several choices; among them simulation [2], algebraic manipulation [6], teleology [7], or possibly default assumptions or observations [17].

3.7. Processes and histories

Adding processes to the ontology of naive physics requires extending the history representation of change. In addition to parameter histories, we will also use *process histories* to describe what processes are occurring when. The temporal extent of a process episode is the maximal time during which the status of the instance is constant, and the spatial extent is the spatial extent of the individuals involved in it. The events that bound episodes in the process history occur at the instants at which quantity conditions, preconditions, or the existence of objects involved in the instance change. *View histories*, describing the status of view instances, are defined similarly. Process and view episodes are included in the histories of the objects that participate in the process, and the union of the object's parameter histories and the histories of the processes and views it participates in comprise its total history. Fig. 13 illustrates the full

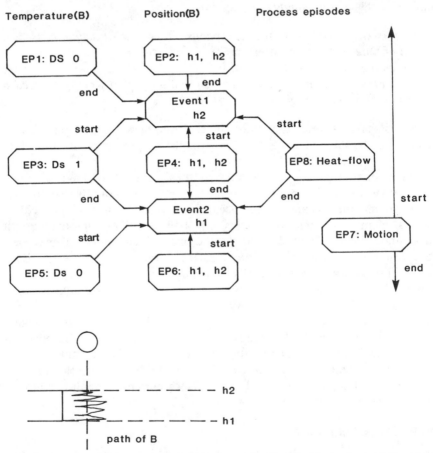

FIG. 13. History for a ball dropping through a flame. A piece of the history for the ball again, but with process episodes added. As before, EP⟨n⟩ are episodes, and time runs from top to bottom.

history over a small interval for the ball being dropped through a flame discussed previously.

As mentioned previously, the two key problems in reasoning with histories are the *local evolution* problem (extending the known portion of an object's history, preferably by carving up the situation into pieces that can be reasoned about semi-independently) and the *intersection/interaction* problem. The key to solving them lies in having explicit descriptions of the ways changes are caused.

Recall that the processes active in a situation form its process structure (as usual, we also implicitly include the view structure to simplify discussion). Processes interact by shared influences; two processes which affect the same parameter or a process that affects a parameter mentioned in the quantity conditions of another must be considered together when figuring out if, and how, they will change. If there is no way for two processes to 'communicate' by common effects, then they can be considered independently. This suggests carving up what is happening at a particular time into 'non-overlapping' pieces, subsets of the process structure that do not interact.

We define *p-components* as equivalence classes on the process structure as follows. A process instance P1 is in the same p-component as another process instance P2 (or view instance) if either: (a) P1 influences a quantity mentioned in P2's quantity conditions, (b) P1 influences a quantity influenced by P2, (c) P1's quantity conditions mention a quantity mentioned in the quantity conditions of P2, or (d) P2 contains a $\propto_Q$ that propagates an influence of P1.

As long as a particular process structure lasts, the p-components can be reasoned about independently. For example, we usually don't worry about getting our feet wet in a basement despite the proximity of flowing water and steam in our plumbing. Changes in the process structure can bring about changes in p-components, so the conclusions made in each p-component may have to be modified depending on how the process structure changes. If our plumbing leaks, for instance, there are now ways for our feet to get wet.

The individuals affected by the processes in each p-component define a

If shared wall is not a heat path,
    PS: Fluid-Flow(WB, channel), no interaction
Otherwise, if A[Temperature(WA)] = A[Temperature(WB)]
    PS: Fluid-Flow(WB, channel), no interaction
    Otherwise, PS: Fluid-Flow(WB, channel) and a heat flow, hence they interact.

FIG. 14. Determining interactions. Suppose WA and WB are liquids, with WB the fluid flowing through the channel below WA's container. The process structures that result from different assumptions about the situation are shown, with potential interactions indicated.

collection of objects that can be reasoned about in isolation, barring certain changes in process structure. Thus we can generate object histories by evolving situations that correspond to p-components, combining the results when the process structure changes to get new p-components, and so forth. The inter-action part of the intersection/interaction problem becomes trivial—two episodes interact if and only if the processes that give rise to them are part of the same p-conponent of a process structure on a situation made up of slices from those particular episodes. Fig. 14 provides a graphical illustration.

3.8. A language for behavior

QP theory concerns the structure of qualitative dynamics. We can view it as specifying a language in which certain commonsense physical models can be written. Can this language be extended to form a full language of behavior for physical systems? Although I have not yet done so, I will argue that the answer is yes, and that several advantages would result from the extension.

A language should have primitives, a means of combining these primitives, and some means of abstraction to allow new entities to be defined. Processes and individual views are obviously the primitives in this language.[14] There are two sensible kinds of compound processes. The first kind consists of processes that form a p-component, a shared-parameter combination. An example of a shared-parameter combination is the intake stroke of a four-cycle engine, which consists of a flow of air and gas into a cylinder and motion of the piston. The second kind consists of sequences of processes occurring over the same individuals. An example of a sequential combination is the sequence of intake, compression, combustion and exhaust strokes of a four-cycle engine. Treating these combinations as new 'things' then allows properties of the system they describe to be reasoned about.

It should be clear that the shared-parameter combination can be treated exactly as a simple process, specified by the union of the properties of the component processes. In other words, a shared-parameter combination will have individuals, preconditions, quantity conditions, relations, and influences that work just like any other process. However, the sequential combination is *not* a process, because the same influences and relations do not hold over every distinct time within the occurrences of the sequential combination. A sequential combination is really a piece of a history! In particular, it is an abstraction of the history of the individuals affected by the processes, viewed as a system.

---

[14]The choice of what is primitive in any particular domain's vocabulary will of course vary—for example, the description of a gas we use later is macroscopic. Presumably a richer process vocabulary would contain the 'mechanisms' that induce these relations (i.e., the kinetic theory of gases), but there is no reason to always include such detail. Consider for example a resistor in a circuit that never exceeds its electrical capacity. The detailed mechanics of conduction hinder rather than help when calculating the current that will result from a voltage across it.

In honor of this mixed ontological status such descriptions will be called *encapsulated histories*. Encapsulated histories (EH) are important for two reasons. First, some phenomena which can be described in that form seem irreducible in terms of processes—collisions, for example. Second, they serve as abstract descriptions for more complex behavior, e.g. in describing the pattern of activity in an oscillator.

When writing encapsulated histories, we will use most of the syntactic structure of processes and individual views, in that the combination will have individuals, preconditions, quantity conditions, and relations. However, the relations component is restricted to holding a description of a piece of the history for the individuals, and the preconditions and quantity conditions are written relative to episodes in that piece of history. If the preconditions and quantity conditions are ever true for a partial history of a collection of objects matching the individual specifications, then the schematic history described in its relations is instantiated as part of the history of those objects.[15] We will see colliding described as an encapsulated history in Section 4.3.

For those phenomena which are irreducible, the encapsulated history may be the only way to evolve the history of the object past that point. For systems where the encapsulated history serves as a summary, an interesting kind of perturbation analysis becomes possible (as we will see in Section 4.5.1). In performing an energy analysis, for example, the quantity conditions are re-written in terms of energy. Changes to the system, such as adding friction, are modeled by processes that influence energy, and the effects of these changes are determined by examining the episodes that comprise the encapsulated history.

3.9. Classification and abstraction

A classification hierarchy is needed to account for the various kinds of conditions under which processes occur. For example, Hayes [22] elucidates several distinct conditions under which fluid flow occurs. Another example is the process of motion—flying, sliding, swinging, and rolling are distinct types of motion, despite sharing certain common features. Sliding and rolling are examples of motion along a surface, and along with swinging comprise the motions involving constant contact with another object. Each of these conditions has slightly different properties, but they are sufficiently similar in the individuals they involve and the pattern of influences they engender to be considered the same kind of process. Having explicit abstract descriptions of processes should also be useful because they are often easier to rule out than more detailed descriptions. If, for instance, there is no path between two places

---

[15]Many of diSessa's "phenomenological primitives" [10] appear to be representable as encapsulated histories. Encapsulated histories are also good candidates for the first models people make of a new domain [19].

through which an object can be moved, it cannot get there by sliding, flying, rolling, or any other kind of motion that might exist.

Theoretically, disjunctions could be used within a single-process description to cover the various cases. Doing so would lead to complicated descriptions that could not easily be reasoned about. Instead, every case will be represented by a different process. We will indicate that P1 is a case of P2, such as:

Case-of(Swinging, Motion) .

The following restrictions hold on cases:

Specificity: There is a subset of the individuals specified for P1 such that they or individuals whose existence is implied by them match the individual specifications of P2. The preconditions and quantity conditions for P1 imply the preconditions and quantity conditions for P2 respectively.

Inheritance: All statements in the relations and influences fields of P2 hold for P1 unless explicitly excluded.

Fig. 15 illustrates some specializations of the abstract motion process that will be discussed in Section 4.3.

Process Motion(B, dir)

Individuals:
  B an Object, Mobile(B)
  dir a direction

Preconditions:
  Free-direction(B, dir)
  Direction-Of(dir, velocity(B))

QuantityConditions:
  A_m[velocity(B)] > ZERO

Influences:
  I+ (position(B), A[velocity (B)])

Process Slide	Process Roll
Case-of: Motion	Case-of: Motion

Individuals:
  S a surface
	Individuals:
	  S a Surface

Preconditions:
  Sliding-Contact(B, S)
  AlongSurface(dir, B, S)
	Preconditions:
	  Contact(B, S)
	  Round(B)
	  AlongSurface(dir, B, S)

FIG. 15. Some specialized descriptions of motion. Cases of motion are organized around constraints on kinematics. The abstract motion process already includes the individuals B, a movable object, and dir, a direction. The abstract motion process will be explained in more detail later. In sliding and rolling there is contact with a surface, but different constraints on the kind of contact. Otherwise the same facts pertain to them as to the abstract version of motion.

4. Examples

At this point a great deal of representational machinery has been introduced. It is time to illustrate how QP theory can be used in physical reasoning. The examples are fairly informal for two reasons. First, the formalization of the domains is still underway.[16] Second, while QP theory provides the means to represent an important part of a domain's theory, a complete model usually has to address several considerations besides dynamics, such as spatial reasoning (qualitative kinematics, as it were). Still, these examples are complex enough to provide an indication of the theory's utility. The assumptions about other kinds of required knowledge are noted as they occur.

4.1. Modeling fluids and fluid flow

This example illustrates some of the basic deductions sanctioned by qualitative process theory and introduces the representations of fluids that are used in other examples. These representations are slightly more complex than the contained-liquid description we have been using. Consider the two containers illustrated in Fig. 16. What will happen here?

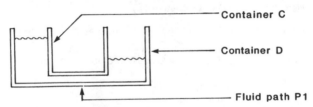

; structural description

Open-Container(C)
Open-Container(D)
Fluid-Path(P1)
Fluid-Connected(C, D, P1)

; some substances are in the containers
Contains-Substance(C, water)
Contains-Substance(D, water)

; the levels are related
(M Level-in(C, water) Initial) > (M Level-in(D, water) Initial)

FIG. 16. Two partially filled containers. Containers C and D are connected by a pipe. Initially C contains more water than D. In general, an "-in" suffix indicates a function that maps from a container and a substance to a quantity.

---

[16]At present work is focusing on two domains: the *mechanism world*, and the *fluids world*. The mechanism world includes the blocks world but also more complex shapes and some non-rigid materials. The aim of work in the mechanism world is to understand devices such as mechanical watches and automobile transmissions. The fluids world is an attempt to extend Hayes' theory of liquids to include gases and more complex fluid systems such as found in steam plants.

We first introduce descriptions of the fluids. Following Hayes [22], we individuate liquids according to what contains them. Fig. 17 describes 'pieces of stuff', independently of the particular criteria used for individuating them. Fig. 18 describes a particular class of pieces of stuff that are individuated by being the stuff inside a container. Any piece of stuff must be in some state, either solid, liquid, or gas. Fig. 19 describes the states of substances. The interaction of state and containment is described in Fig. 20. Since the containers initially contain some water, we will create individuals corresponding to the water in

```
; A piece of stuff consists of several quantities, a substance, and
; a location
(∀ p ∈ piece-of-stuff
   Has-Quantity(p, amount-of)
   ∧ Has-Quantity(p, volume) ∧ Has-Quantity(p, pressure)
   ∧ Has-Quantity(p, temperature) ∧ Has-Quantity(p, heat)
   ∧ Substance(made-of(p)) ∧ Place(location(p))
   ∧ temperature(p) ∝_{Q+} heat(p))

; where
(∀ p ∈ things ∀ q ∈ quantity-type
   Has-Quantity(p, q) ↔ Quantity(q(p)))
```

FIG. 17. Pieces of stuff. A piece of stuff is mainly described by several quantities and its location.

```
Individual-View Contained-Stuff

Individuals:
   c a container
   s a substance

Preconditions:
   Contains-Substance(c, s)

QuantityConditions:
   A[amount-of-in(c, s)] > ZERO

Relations:
   There is p ∈ piece-of-stuff
   amount-of-in(c, s) = amount-of(p)
   s = made-of(p)
   inside(c) = location(p)
```

FIG. 18. Contained stuff. Contained-Stuff describes the conditions under which pieces of stuff exist inside a container.

each container. Call the pieces of stuff in containers C and D WC and WD respectively. We will assume their temperatures are such that they are both liquids. For simplicity we will ignore the liquid in the pipe P1. We will also ignore the precise definition of fluid paths, except to note that P1 is one, connecting the two contained fluids.

Individual-View Solid(p)

Individuals:
  p a piece-of-stuff

QuantityConditions:
  $\neg$ A[temperature(p)] > A[t-melt(p)]
  $\neg$ Liquid(p)

Individual-View Liquid(p)

Individuals:
  p a piece-of-stuff

QuantityConditions:
  $\neg$ A[temperature(p)] < A[t-melt(p)]
  $\neg$ A[temperature(p)] > A[t-boil(p)]
  $\neg$ Solid(p)
  $\neg$ Gas(p)

Relations:
  volume(p) $\propto_{Q+}$ amount-of(p)
  t-boil(p) $\propto_{Q+}$ pressure(p)

Individual-View Gas(p)

Individuals:
  p a piece-of-stuff

QuantityConditions:
  $\neg$ A[temperature(p)] < A[t-boil(p)]
  $\neg$ Liquid(p)

Relations:
  temperature(p) $\propto_{Q+}$ pressure(p)
  pressure(p) $\propto_{Q+}$ amount-of(p)
  pressure(p) $\propto_{Q-}$ volume(p)
  pressure(p) $\propto_{Q+}$ heat(p)

FIG. 19. States of matter. The temperatures at which state changes occur are modeled by two functions t-melt and t-boil. t-melt and t-boil map pieces of stuff onto quantities, and we assume A[t-boil] is never less than A[t-melt]. The quantity conditions express the fact that a substance can be in either state at a phase boundary, but that a particular piece cannot be in both states at once. To determine the state of a piece of stuff at the phase boundary requires either knowing its history or making an assumption.

  ; Contained stuff has states as well –

($\forall$ p $\in$ *piece-of-stuff*
  (Contained-Gas(p) $\leftrightarrow$ (Contained-Stuff(p) $\wedge$ Gas(p)))
  $\wedge$ (Contained-Liquid(p) $\leftrightarrow$ (Contained-Stuff(p) $\wedge$ Liquid(p)))
  $\wedge$ (Contained-Solid(p) $\leftrightarrow$ (Contained-Stuff(p) $\wedge$ Solid(p))))

  ; Contained liquids have levels, which are tied to amounts
  ; and in turn (assuming an open container) determines pressure

($\forall$ c $\in$ *contained-liquid*
  Has-Quantity(c, level)
  $\wedge$ level(c) $\propto_{Q+}$ amount-of(c)
  $\wedge$ (Open-Container(space-of(location(c))) $\Rightarrow$
    Function-Spec(p-l-fun, {pressure(c) $\propto_{Q+}$ level(c)})))

FIG. 20. Effects of state on containment.

Suppose our process vocabulary consists of fluid flow, whose description is illustrated in Fig. 21. This model is very simple, because it ignores the possibility of different kinds of fluids and the details of how fluids move through the fluid paths ([22] illustrates some of the distinctions that should be drawn in a more detailed model).

With the situation we have so far, there are two process instances, one corresponding to flow from WC to WD and the other corresponding to flow from WD to WC. To determine if either is active (thus determining the process structure) we have to know the relative pressures of WC and WD. Assume we deduce from the relative levels that the pressure of WC is greater than the pressure of WD. Then the process instance representing fluid flow from WC to WD will be active, and the process instance representing fluid flow from WD to WC will be inactive. Thus the process structure is the set consisting of Fluid-Flow(WC, WD, P1).

To find out what changes are occurring we must resolve the influences. In this situation resolving influences is simple. The fluid flow from C to D is the only cause of direct influences, changing amount-of for WC and WD. Each of

process fluid-flow

Individuals:
   src a contained-liquid
   dst a contained-liquid
   path a fluid path, Fluid-Connected(src, dst, path)

Preconditions:
   Aligned(path)

QuantityConditions:
   A[pressure(scr)] > A[pressure(dst)]

Relation:
   Let flow-rate be a quantity
   flow-rate $\propto_{Q+}$ (A[pressure(src)] − A[pressure(dst)])

Influences:
   I + (amount-of(dst), A[flow-rate])
   I − (amount-of(src), A[flow-rate])

; A fluid path is aligned if only if either it has no valves or every valve is open
($\forall$ p $\in$ fluid-path
   ((number-of-valves(p) = 0) $\Rightarrow$ Aligned(p))
   $\wedge$ ((number-of-valves(p) > 0) $\Rightarrow$ ($\forall$ v $\in$ valves(p) Open(v)) $\leftrightarrow$ Aligned(p))
   $\wedge$ $\neg$ (number-of-valves(p) < 0))

; A heat path is defined in terms of objects in contact, and aligned
; indicates that the contact is unbroken. We ignore heating
; by radiation and by convection, as well as temperature changes
; caused by mixing.

FIG. 21. A process description of fluid flow. This simple model does not describe the existence and behavior of the fluid within the fluid path.

them has only one influence, hence

$$D_s[\text{amount-of(WC)}] = -1 \quad \text{and} \quad D_s[\text{amount-of(WD)}] = 1 \,.$$

These in turn influence volume, level and pressure, each of which has only one $\propto_Q$ applicable (see Fig. 20). Thus we can deduce that the volume, level and pressure of WC are all decreasing, and the volume, level and pressure of WD are all increasing. All other quantities are uninfluenced, hence unchanging. Limit analysis is similarly simple. The pressures will eventually be equal, which means the fluid flow will stop. It is also possible that the container C will run out of water, thus ending WC's existence (although it is not possible in the particular drawing shown). These results are summarized in Fig. 22. This graph of process structures can be used to generate a history by first creating the appropriate episodes for objects and processes from their initial slices, and then selecting one or the other limit hypothesis as the end-event for that episode. Usually we will just represent the interconnections between possible process structures as we have done here. With only a single process and simple relationships between quantities, resolving influences and limit analysis are simple. In more complex situations resolving influences and disambiguating the possibilities raised by limit analysis will require more information, as we will see below.

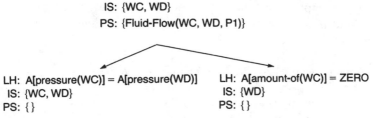

$D_s[\text{amount-of(WC)}] = -1 \qquad D_s[\text{amount-of(WD)}] = 1$
$D_s[\text{volume(WC)}] = -1 \qquad D_s[\text{volume(WD)}] = 1$
$D_s[\text{level(WC)}] = -1 \qquad D_s[\text{level(WD)}] = 1$
$D_s[\text{pressure(WC)}] = -1 \qquad D_s[\text{pressure(WD)}] = 1$
$D_s[\text{heat(WC)}] = 0 \qquad D_s[\text{heat(WD)}] = 0$
$D_s[\text{temperature(WC)}] = 0 \qquad D_s[\text{temperature(WD)}] = 0$

Limit Analysis:

IS: {WC, WD}
PS: {Fluid-Flow(WC, WD, P1)}

LH: A[pressure(WC)] = A[pressure(WD)]   LH: A[amount-of(WC)] = ZERO
IS: {WC, WD}   IS: {WD}
PS: {}   PS: {}

FIG. 22. Resolved influences and limit analysis. The results of resolving influences and limit analysis for the situation involving two containers are summarized. The individuals in the situation are labeled IS, the process structure by PS, and limit hypotheses by LH.

4.2. Modeling a boiler

Let us consider the possible consequences of the situation shown in Fig. 23. The situation consists of a container partially filled with water. Initially the lid of the container is open; we stipulate that if boiling ever occurs, the lid will be closed and sealed. A flame, modeled as a temperature source, is placed so that heat can be conducted to the container and water (i.e., there is an aligned heat path between them). What sorts of things can happen?

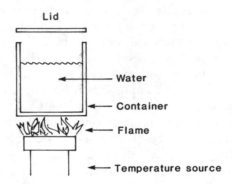

FIG. 23. A simple boiler.

To begin with, we need the contained substances defined in the previous example and a model of containers. We assume that if the pressure inside the container exceeds a particular pressure p-burst(CAN), the container will explode. Fig. 24 describes the container model. We will assume that, in addition to fluid flow, the process vocabulary includes heat flow and boiling, as presented in Section 3.1. We will ignore the rest of the details, such as the nature of heat and fluid paths and the detailed geometry of containers.

We start by assuming that no processes are active before the heat source is turned on; in other words that all temperatures, pressures, etc. are equal so there are no flows, and that the temperatures are in the appropriate regions of their quantity spaces so that no state changes are occurring. (Note that, as usual, we are making a closed-world assumption both in assuming our process vocabulary is complete and that we know all of the relevant individuals.) Since there is a heat path between the source and the container, if we turn the heat source on and if

$$A[\text{temperature(SOURCE)}] > A[\text{temperature(WATER)}]$$

there is a heat flow from the source to the water. We ignore the influence of the heat flow on the source by assuming

$$D_s[\text{temperature(SOURCE)}] = 0 .$$

∀ c ∈ *container*
  [Has-Quantity(c, volume) ∧ Has-Quantity(c, pressure)
    ∧ Has-Quantity(c, temperature) ∧ Has-Quantity(c, heat)
    ∧ (Rigid(c) ⇒ D_s[volume(c)] = 0)
    ∧¬Open-Container(c) ⇒
      (∀ p ∈ contents(c)
        pressure(c) = pressure(p)
        ∧ temperature(c) = temperature(p))]

; note we are assuming instantaneous equilibration
; within the container

Encapsulated History Explode

Individuals:
  c a container, rigid(c)
  e an episode

Preconditions:
  (T ¬ Open-Container(c) e)

QuantityConditions:
  (M A[pressure(c)] end(e)) = (M A[p-burst(c)] end(e))
  (M A[pressure(c)] during(e)) < (M A[p-burst(c)] during(e))

Relations:
  Let EV1 be an event
  end(e) = EV1
  (T Explodes(c) EV1)
  Terminates(c, EV1)

; The relation Terminates indicates that the object does not exist past
; that particular event

FIG. 24. A simple container model. For simplicity we will model a container only as a collection of quantities, a set of pieces of stuff which are its contents, and an encapsulated history to describe the possibility of it exploding. The geometric information necessary to determine flow paths and the spatial arrangement of the contents will be ignored.

The only influence on temperature(CAN) is that of the heat flow, so

$$D_s[\text{temperature(CAN)}] = 1 .$$

This in turn causes a heat flow to the air surrounding the container and to the air and the water inside the container. Since we are only thinking about the container and its contents the loss of heat to the air will be ignored, and from now on when we refer to heat flow it will be the flow from the flame to the contained stuff, using the container as the heat path. The temperature quantity space that results is illustrated in Fig. 25. If A[temperature(SOURCE)] > A[t-boil(WATER)] and the process is unimpeded (i.e., the preconditions for the heat flow remain true), the next process structure to occur will include a boiling.

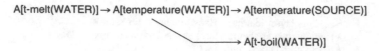

FIG. 25. Quantity space for water temperature. The heat flow is increasing the heat, and thus (via $\propto_{Q+}$) the temperature of the water. The lack of ordering information between the temperature of the source and the boiling temperature leads to uncertainty about what will occur next.

Suppose the preconditions for the heat flow continue to be met and boiling occurs. Then by our initial assumptions the lid will be sealed, closing all fluid flow paths and thus preventing any flows. The amount-of quantity spaces that result are illustrated in Fig. 26. The influence of the boiling on amount-of(WATER) moves it towards ZERO. So one of the ways the process structure might change is that all of the water is converted to steam.

If all the water is converted to steam, the only active process is a heat flow from the heat source to the steam. Thus the sole influence on the heat of the steam is positive, and (because of $\propto_Q$) the temperature also rises. Heat indirectly influences pressure, so the pressure of the steam will also rise. By examining the quantity spaces for temperatures and pressures we find there are two limit points which may be reached, namely that the temperature of the steam can reach the temperature of the heat source and that the pressure of the container (which is equal to the pressure of the steam) can reach the explosion point. In the first case there are no active processes, and in the second an explosion occurs. We have found one possible disaster, are there more? To find out, we must go back to the boiling episode and check the indirect consequences of the changes in amount-of(STEAM).

$$ZERO \rightarrow A[amount\text{-}of(WATER)]$$

$$ZERO \rightarrow A[amount\text{-}of(STEAM)]$$

FIG. 26. amount-of quantity spaces.

Consider some arbitrary instant I within the boiling episode. Because the steam is still in contact with the water their temperatures will be the same. Since we assumed the container would be sealed when boiling began, there are no fluid paths hence no fluid flows. Therefore during I the only influence on amount-of(STEAM) and on amount-of(WATER) is from boiling. So

$$D_s[amount\text{-}of(STEAM)] = 1 \quad \text{and} \quad D_s[amount\text{-}of(WATER)] = -1 .$$

Because steam is a gas, there are several indirect influences on temperature(STEAM) and pressure(STEAM) (see Fig. 19). In particular,

temperature(STEAM) $\propto_{Q+}$ pressure(STEAM)
temperature(STEAM) $\propto_{Q+}$ heat(STEAM)
pressure(STEAM) $\propto_{Q+}$ amount-of(STEAM)
pressure(STEAM) $\propto_{Q-}$ volume(STEAM)
pressure(STEAM) $\propto_{Q+}$ heat(STEAM)

Assuming the container is rigid, D_s[volume(CAN)] = 0, and since the spaces of the steam and and water are separate and fill the container,

volume(CAN) = volume(WATER) + volume(STEAM) .

Since

D_s[volume(WATER)] = -1 , D_s[volume(STEAM)] = 1

and

D_m[volume(STEAM)] = D_m[volume(WATER)] .

Assume the function that determines pressure(STEAM) is continuous in amount-of(STEAM), heat(STEAM), and volume(STEAM). Then for any particular D[amount-of(STEAM)] and D[heat(STEAM)], we can find a corresponding D[volume(STEAM)] such that

(M D_s[pressure(STEAM)] I) = 0

i.e., the pressure at the end of I will be the same as it was at the start of I. Let β stand for that value of D[volume(STEAM)]. Then

(M A[volume(STEAM)] end(I)) = (M A[volume(STEAM)] start(I)) + β

is necessary for D_s[pressure(STEAM)] to be zero. A fact about steam is that, at any particular pressure and temperature, the volume of steam is very much greater than the volume of water it was produced from.[17] In other words,

D_s[pressure(STEAM)] = 0 $\Rightarrow$ D_m[volume(WATER)] $\ll$ D_m[volume(STEAM)] .

But in fact,

D_m[volume(STEAM)] = D_m[volume(WATER)] ,

---

[17]At standard temperature and pressure, about 220 times greater in fact.

so

$$D[volume(STEAM)] < \beta.$$

This means that (M A[volume(STEAM)] end(I)) will be less than

$$(M\ A[volume(STEAM)]\ start(I)) + \beta\ ,$$

and because

$$pressure(STEAM) \propto_{Q-} volume(STEAM)\ .$$

the pressure of the steam will be greater than it was, i.e.,

$$D_s[pressure(STEAM)] = 1\ .$$

Since

$$D_s[heat(STEAM)] = 1\ ,$$

both of the influences on temperature(STEAM) are positive, so

$$D_s[temperature(STEAM)] = 1\ .$$

So far we have discovered that

$$D_s[pressure(STEAM)] = D_s[temperature(STEAM)] = 1\ .$$

Since the water and steam are in contact their pressures will be equal, and since pressure indirectly affects the boiling temperature, the boiling temperature will also rise. The possible relative rates introduce three cases. If the boiling temperature is rising faster, i.e.,

$$(D_m[t\text{-}boil(WATER)] > D_m[temperature(STEAM)])$$

then the boiling will stop, the heat flow will increase heat(WATER) again, the temperature will rise, and the boiling will begin again.[18] In the other two cases

$$(D_m[t\text{-}boil(WATER)] = D_m[temperature(STEAM)]$$

---

[18]The astute reader will notice that this situation gives rise to a cycle of states that corresponds to a rising equilibrium rather than an oscillation. We will discuss how to use the equality change law to distinguish between these cases in Section 5.1.

and

$$D_m[\text{t-boil(WATER)}] < D_m[\text{temperature(STEAM)}])$$

the boiling will continue, albeit at a higher temperature and pressure. In all three cases, the increasing pressure makes

$$A[\text{pressure(CAN)}] = A[\text{p-burst(CAN)}]$$

possible, in which case the container explodes. The alternatives are summarized in Fig. 27. To actually determine which of these occurs requires more information, but at least we have a warning of potential disaster.

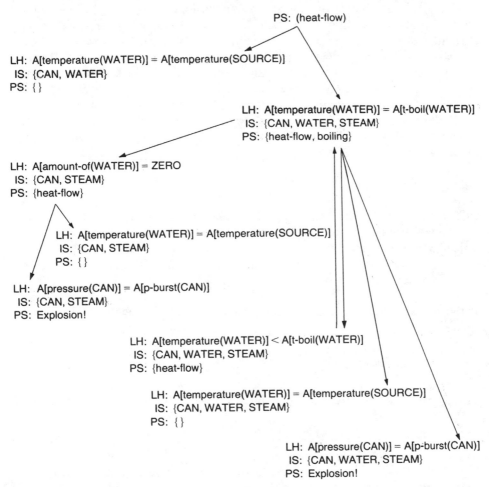

FIG. 27. Alternative behaviors for the boiler. The process structures are envisioned for water being heated in a sealed container, generated by repeated limit analysis.

4.3. Modeling motion

One process we reason about every day is motion. Motion is complex because it is intimately connected with our concepts of space and shape. Since QP theory describes the form of qualitative dynamics theories, it can only carry part of the representational burden imposed by motion. After developing a simple motion vocabulary, we compare the QP descriptions with the earlier qualitative-state representation in order to illustrate the strengths and weaknesses of the QP model.

4.3.1. A simple motion vocabulary

Consider a single object moving in one dimension. By ignoring the particular kind of motion it exhibits (FLY, SLIDE, SWING, ROLL) which depends on the particular shape and type of contact with other surfaces, we can develop an abstract vocabulary for describing motion. While very weak, such abstract descriptions have certain uses—we can deduce that if we kick something but it is blocked, for instance, then it will not move, and by ruling out most abstract motion possible, we rule out all the more specific kinds.

First we will need some simple descriptions of spatial relationships. The symbols 1 and −1 will denote distinct directions along some axis, and for some quantity Q and direction dir

Direction-Of(dir, Q)

will be true exactly when $A_s[Q]$ equals dir. The location of an object is modeled by a quantity position, and if there is no immobile object directly against an object B in direction dir we say

Free-Direction(B, dir) .

If there is an object in that direction which is directly in contact with it, say C, then we say

Contact(B, C, dir) ,

Finally, when some object C lies along direction dir from object B, we will say

Direction-Towards(B, C, dir) .

Fig. 28 contains the process specifications for motion and acceleration. The motion process occurs when a mobile object has a non-zero velocity and is free to move in the direction of its velocity (i.e., no other objects in the way). Motion has a positive influence on position of an object, in that if the velocity

Process Motion(B, dir)

Individuals:
  B an object, Mobile(B)
  dir a direction

Preconditions:
  Free-direction(B, dir)
  Direction-Of(dir, velocity(B))

QuantityConditions:
  A_m[velocity(B)] > ZERO

Influences:
  I + (postiion(B), A[velocity(B)])

Process Acceleration(B, dir)

Individuals:
  B an object, Mobile(B)
  dir a direction

Preconditions:
  Free-Direction(B, dir)
  Direction-Of(dir, net-force(B))

QuantityConditions:
  A_m[net-force(B)] > ZERO

Relations:
  Let Acc be a quantity
  Acc $\propto_{Q+}$ net-force(B)
  Acc $\propto_{Q-}$ mass(B)
  ; The basic QP version of F = m * a
  Correspondence((Acc ZERO)
               (net-force(B) ZERO))

Influences:
  I + (velocity(B) A[Acc])

FIG. 28. Process descriptions of Newtonian motion and acceleration. In this motion vocabulary we have abstracted away the kind of motion occurring (flying, sliding, swinging, etc.) and the complexities of motion in more than one dimension. We assume sign values are assigned to directions along some axis, with magnitudes indicating distance from some arbitrarily chosen origin.

is positive the position will 'increase' and if the velocity is negative the position will 'decrease'. (The problem of mapping a quantity space onto more complex geometric frames of reference will be considered in more detail below). Acceleration occurs when a mobile object has some non-zero net force in a free direction. Acceleration provides a positive influence on velocity, and in fact the influence is qualitatively proportional to the net force and qualitatively inversely proportional to the mass of the object (the QP version of Newton's Second Law).

While this description is Newtonian, Aristotelian and impetus theories can also be described.[19] One form of Aristotelian motion, for example, can be written as in Fig. 29. Here motion only occurs when an object is being pushed. An impetus theory is described in Fig. 30. Aristotelian theory has the problem of explaining what keeps a moving object going once it doesn't touch anything; impetus theory explains this by the push giving an object a kind of internal force or 'impetus'. While superficially like momentum, impetus kinematics is very different.[20] Impetus also differs from momentum in that it can spontaneously dissipate. Compare the dissipation of impetus with the Newtonian model of sliding friction in Fig. 31. Here friction occurs when there is surface contact, and produces a force on the object that is qualitatively proportional to the normal force and acts in a direction opposite that of the motion. The effect of friction occurs indirectly, through providing a force that changes acceleration, rather than directly as in the impetus theory.

Process Motion

Individuals:
  B an object, Mobile(B)
  dir a direction

Preconditions:
  Free-Direction(B, dir)
  Direction-Of(dir, net-force(B))

QuantityConditions:
  A_m[net-force(B)] > ZERO

Relations:
  Let velocity be a quantity
  velocity $\propto_{Q+}$ net-force(B)
  velocity $\propto_{Q-}$ mass(B)

Influences:
  I+(position(B), A[velocity])

FIG. 29. Aristotelian motion. Aristotle theorized that objects required a constant push to keep them going. Note that velocity does not have an existence independent of the motion process.

Collisions are complicated in any theory of motion. The reason collisions are complicated is that they are usually described in terms of a piece of history. We will use an encapsulated history, as described in Section 3.8. The simplest description of a collision just involves a reversal of velocity, as illustrated in

[19]McCloskey [28] and Clement [50] argue that naive theories of motion in our culture correspond to impetus theories, rather than Aristotelian theories as previously suggested.

[20]In particular, impetus is not a vector quantity. Subjects vary in their beliefs as to the means of combination for impetus; they include rules like "the motion is in the direction of the biggest impetus." There are other oddities as well—for example, impetus 'remembers' not just the direction of the push but some of the previous history of directions, so that leaving a spiral tube will result in spiral motion for a little while. See [28] for details.

Process Motion   Process Impart

Individuals: Individuals:
  B an object, Mobile(B)   B an object, Mobile(B)
  dir a direction   dir a direction

Preconditions: Preconditions:
  Free-Direction(B, dir)   Free-Direction(B, dir)
  Direction-Of(dir, impetus(B))   Direction-Of(dir, net-force(B))

QuantityConditions: QuantityConditions:
  A_m[impetus(B)] > ZERO A_m[net-force(B)] > ZERO

Relations: Relations:
  Let vel be a quantity   Let acc be a quantity
  vel $\propto_{Q+}$ impetus(B)   acc $\propto_{Q+}$ net-force(B)
                                   acc $\propto_{Q-}$ mass(B)

Influences: Influences:
  I +(position(B), A[vel])   I +(impetus(B), A[acc])

Process Dissipate

Individuals:
  B an object, Mobile(B)

QuantityConditions:
  A_m[impetus(B)] > ZERO

Relations:
  Let acc by a quantity
  A_s[acc] = A_s[impetus(B)]

Influences:
  I −(impetus(B), A[acc])

FIG. 30. An impetus dynamics for motion. In impetus theories of motion, a push imparts 'impetus' to an object. An object's impetus is an internalized force that keeps on pushing the object, thus causing motion. Motion eventually stops because impetus spontaneously dissipates with time.

Fig. 32. As a simplification we have assumed C is immobile so that we won't have to worry about momentum transfer between moving objects and changes of direction in more than one dimension. Even our more complicated models of collisions appear to use such encapsulated histories, such as a compound history consisting of contacting the surface, compression, expansion, and finally breaking contact. The type of collision—elastic or inelastic—that occurs could be specified by referring to a theory of materials for the objects involved.

4.3.2. Relationship to qualitative states

Previous work on representing motion used a *qualitative-state* representation for motion [6, 12], an abstraction of the notion of state in classical mechanics.

Individual View Moving-Friction

Individuals:
  B an object, Mobile(B)
  S a surface
  dir a direction

Preconditions:
  Sliding-Contact(B, S)

QuantityConditions:
  Motion(B, dir)

Relations:
  Let fr be a quantity
  $fr \propto_{Q+}$ normal-force(B)
  $A_s[fr] = -A_s[velocity(B)]$
  $fr \in$ forces-on(B)

FIG. 31. Moving friction in Newtonian sliding. Objects have a set forces-on, whose sum is the net force on the object. Friction is modeled by an individual view rather than a process because it contributes directly to the force on an object, rather than the derivative of the force.

Encapsulated-History Collide(B, C, dir)

Individuals:
  B an object, Mobile(B)
  C an object, Immobile(C)
  dir a direction
  E an event

Preconditions:
  (T contact(B, C, dir) start(E))
  (T direction-of(dir, velocity(B)) start(E))

QuantityCondition:
  (T Motion(B, dir) start(E))

Relations:
  (M A[velocity(B)] start(E)) = −(M A[velocity(B)] end(E))
  (M A[velocity(B)] during(E)) = ZERO
  duration(E) = ZERO
  (T contact(B, C, dir) end(E))

FIG. 32. Colliding modeled as an encapsulated history. Sometimes all that is known about a situation is the particular kind of behavior that will occur. While violating composability, encapsulated histories are the only way to evolve a history in such cases. This particular encapsulated history describes a perfectly-elastic collision with a fixed object in one dimension.

Some of the parameters that would appear in a classical description of state are represented abstractly—typically position is represented by a piece of space, and velocity by a symbolic heading. While in classical physics the type of activity is left implicit in the choice of descriptive equations, the qualitative-state representation explicitly names the type of activity (FLY, SLIDE, etc.). Qualitative states are linked by simulation rules that map a qualitative state into the set of qualitative states that can occur next. Envisioning using such simulation rules is simple; given an initial state, use the rules to generate a set of new states. Apply the simulation rules to these states in turn, and continue in this fashion until no distinct new states are generated. Fig. 33 illustrates a physical situation and the envisionment that results. The envisionment can be used to answer simple questions directly, assimilate certain global assumptions about motion (such as assuming that a ball must or must not ever be in a particular place), and plan solutions to more complex questions. By examining the relationship between the qualitative state representation and the QP representation we will understand both more clearly.

Consider a process vocabulary comprised solely of motion and acceleration. The limit analysis for a moving object will include only the possibilities raised by dynamics, such as the acceleration due to gravity reversing the velocity of a ball or friction bringing a sliding block to a halt. The possible changes in process structure caused by kinematics—such as the ball hitting a wall or the block flying off a table—are not predicted within this vocabulary. To include them would require encoding the relevant geometry in such a way that it can be moved out of the preconditions and into the quantity conditions. To do this, we must first describe space by a *place vocabulary*[21], because we must break space up into distinct pieces that can be reasoned about symbolically. We might then try to use the entities in the place vocabulary as elements in the quantity space for position. Then the kinematic changes would be discovered by limit analysis just as the dynamical ones are.

Unfortunately, things are not so simple. First of all, we need to introduce an ordering between elements of the place vocabulary. (This ordering need not be total; we can use ambiguity in the ordering to represent our lack of knowledge about the precise heading of the moving object.) For motion in two or three dimensions this requires specifying a direction to obtain a partial order. And because we have specified a direction, we now must also specify the place we are starting from, since that will determine what the neighbors in the position quantity space are. (Consider walking out your front-door while throwing a ball up in the air. What the ball might hit changes dramatically.) However, this means the place and direction must be included in the specification of the motion process. If we could successfully add such information, an instance of the motion process in this vocabulary would begin to look like a qualitative state for the same collection of places and type of motion. The qualitative simulation rules would thus roughly correspond to a compilation of the limit analysis on this new motion vocabulary.

[21]Forbus [12] describes the principles involved and defines a place vocabulary for motion through space in a simple domain.

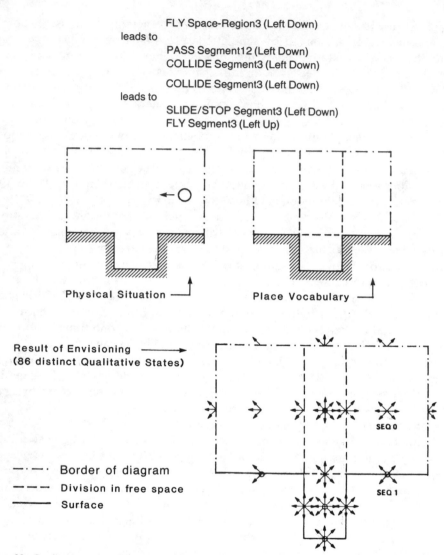

FIG. 33. Qualitative-state description of motion. Consider the ball moving leftwards. A qualitative description of space (*place vocabulary*) can be computed from the diagram and the possible ways the ball can move given that initial state are depicted schematically over the places they occur. A detailed description of two states and their relationships with other states is also shown.

From this perspective we can see the relative strengths of the two representations. For evolving descriptions of motion the qualitative-state representation seems superior, because kinematic constraints are essential to motion. However, simulation rules are an opaque form of dynamics theory— they do not contain the assumptions under which they operate. Their 'compiled' nature makes the qualitative-state representation inappropriate for very simple deductions (where only part of a qualitative state is known), or for more subtle analyses that involve perturbing a system. In particular, the qualitative-state representations for motion are not easily composable to form descriptions of more complex systems. The example of Section 4.5 illustrates a more subtle analysis of motion made possible by the ontology of QP theory.

4.4. Modeling materials

Let us consider what happens when we pull on something. If it doesn't move, then its internal structure is 'taking up' the force (this can happen even if it does move—try hitting an egg with a baseball bat—but we will ignore this case). Three things can happen: (1) it might do nothing (rigid behavior); (2) it might stretch (elastic behavior); or (3) it might break. For a push, (2) becomes compressed and (3) becomes crushed. We can use the notions of quantity and process provided by QP theory to state these facts. In particular, we can express the changes between these kinds of behavior by creating individual views describing these properties, introducing new elements into a quantity space for forces on an object.

The concepts involved with elasticity can be thought of in terms of applied force versus internal force. If the magnitude of the applied force is greater than that of the internal force the length of the object will change. The change in length results in an internal force that will counterbalance the applied force. Three individual views describe the states of an elastic object, either stretched, relaxed, or compressed. Fig. 34 illustrates the individual view for elastic objects and their states. To avoid the complications of shape and connectivity, we only model one-dimensional objects that have a fixed end. By convention, forces into an object (pushes) will be negative and applied forces directed outwards (pulls) will be positive.

Imagine that we apply a constant force to an elastic object (with, say, a robot hand under force, rather than position, control). An imbalance between internal and applied forces will result in the length changing. Exactly what occurs depends on the state of the elastic object (stretched, relaxed, compressed), the sign of the applied force, and the relative magnitudes of the forces (the dependence on the sign of the internal force is encoded in the state of the object via the $\propto_Q$ and correspondence). The four possibilities are stretching, compressing, and two kinds of relaxing. These processes are described in Fig. 35.

Of course, objects are not perfectly elastic. If the applied force is very small, objects will often behave rigidly. If too much force is applied an object can break or crush. The rigidity under small forces can be modeled by adding another quantity condition to stretching and compressing. For a partially-elastic object the thresholds for compressing and stretching will be called $f_{compress}$ and

Individual-View Elastic-Object

Individuals:
  B an object

Preconditions:
  Elastic-Substance(made-of(B))

Relations:
  Has-Quantity(B, length)
  Has-Quantity(B, Internal-force)
  Has-Quantity(B, rest-length)
  $D_s[\text{rest-length}(B)] = 0$
  internal-force(B) $\propto_{Q+}$ length(B)
  Correspondence((internal-force(B) ZERO)
                  (length(B) rest-length(B)))

Individual-View Relaxed   Individual-View Stretched

Individuals: Individuals:
  B an elastic-object   B an elastic-object

QuantityConditions: QuantityConditions:
  A[length(B)] = A[rest-length(B)]   A[length(B)] > A[rest-length(B)]

Individual-View Compressed

Individuals:
  B an elastic-object

QuantityConditions:
  A[length(B)] < A[rest-length(B)]

FIG. 34. Descriptions of elastic objects. An elastic object stores energy in reversible deformations of shape. The basic view of an elastic object relates the internal force and length, and the other three views describe the states it can be in.

f_{stretch} respectively. The conditions under which crushing and breaking can be captured similarly by thresholds f_{crush} and f_{break}, which are functions of both the material and the object (to allow for dependence on the shape). The process descriptions for crushing and breaking, however, are more complex than compressing and stretching because they involve irreversible changes. This requires statements in the relations field that explicitly mention time, turning the description into an encapsulated history rather than a true process. Much of the information that must be included concerns deformations of shape and transformation of one object into several. As with kinematics, these issues are beyond the scope of QP theory.

Fig. 36 illustrates the force quantity spaces that describe different kinds of materials. In theory a taxonomy such as this one could be used for classifying a process Stretching

Individuals:
  B an elastic object

Preconditions:
  $\neg$ Position-Constrained(B)

QuantityConditions:
  $\neg$ Compressed(B)
  A_s[applied-force(B)] = 1
  A_m[Applied-force(B)]
    $> A_m$[internal-force(B)]

Relations:
  Let SR be a quantity
  SR $\propto_{Q+}$ (A_m[applied-force(B)]
    $- A_m$[internal-force(B)])

Influences:
  I+(length(B), SR)

process Compressing

Individuals:
  B an elastic object

Preconditions:
  $\neg$ Position-Constrained(B)

QuantityConditions:
  $\neg$ Stretched(B)
  A_s[applied-force(B)] = -1
  A_m[applied-force(B)]
    $> A_m$[internal-force(B)]

Relations:
  Let SR be a quantity
  SR $\propto_{Q+}$ (A_m[applied-force(B)]
    $- A_m$[internal-force(B)])

Influences:
  I−(length(B), SR)

process Relaxing-Minus

Individuals:
  B an elastic object

Preconditions:
  $\neg$ Position-Constrained(B)

QuantityConditions:
  Stretched(B)
  A_m[applied-force(B)]
    $< A_m$[internal-force(B)]

Relations:
  Let SR be a quantity
  SR $\propto_{Q+}$ (A_m[applied-force(B)]
    $- A_m$[internal-force(B)])

Influences:
  I−(length(B), SR)

process Relaxing-Plus

Individuals:
  B an elastic object

Preconditions:
  $\neg$ Position-Constrained(B)

QuantityConditions:
  Compressed(B)
  A_m[applied-force(B)]
    $< A_m$[internal-force(B)]

Relations:
  Let SR be a quantity
  SR $\propto_{Q+}$ (A_m[applied-force(B)]
    A_m[internal-force(B)])

Influences:
  I+(length(B), SR)

FIG. 35. Stretching, compressing, and relaxing. The continuous changes that can occur to elastic objects when constrained by an applied force are described. The individual views of stretched, compressed, and relaxed are described in Fig. 34.

material by applying forces to it and seeing what sorts of behavior result. In a richer model of materials forces along different directions could result in different behavior (such as attempting to bend balsa wood against its grain instead of along the grain) and the effects of plastic deformation would be included.

Rigid:
    ⟨no processes affecting length⟩
Elastic:
    ⟨stretching and compressing apply⟩
Breakable:
    $ZERO < f_{break}$
Crushable:
    $f_{crush} < ZERO$
Partially stretchable:
    $ZERO < f_{stretch}$
Partially compressible:
    $f_{compress} < ZERO$
Brittle:
    $f_{crush} < ZERO < f_{break}$
Partially elastic:
    $f_{compress} < ZERO < f_{stretch}$
Normal:
    $f_{crush} < f_{compress} < ZERO < f_{stretch} < f_{break}$

FIG. 36. Materials classified by quantity spaces. Distinct kinds of materials give rise to different quantity spaces because different combinations of processes can occur. This taxonomy should allow a material to be classified by applying forces and observing what kinds of things actually occur.

A classic AI conundrum is to be able to express in some usable form that "you can pull with a string, but not push with it" [33]. This fact can be succinctly stated, at least to a first approximation, using QP theory. First, consider what pushes and pulls are. Both concepts imply one object making contact with another to apply force. Recall that if the direction of the force is towards the object it is a push, and if the direction is away from the object then it is a pull. Obviously a push can occur with any kind of contact, but pulls cannot occur with an abutting.

Understanding how pushes and pulls are transmitted is fundamental to understanding mechanisms. For a first-pass model, consider the notion of *push-transmitters* and *pull-transmitters*. We say an object is a push-transmitter if when it is pushed, it will in turn push an object that is in contact with it, in the direction between the two contact points. Pull-transmitters can be similarly defined. This particular set of definitions is obviously inadequate for mechanisms,[22] and is only for illustration. Note also that push-transmitters and pull-transmitters need not be reflexive relations. Rigid objects are an exceptional case:

[22]Consider for example a rocker arm connected to a pivot or two blocks resting on the floor that are tied together by a length of string. In the first case a push will be transmitted in a different direction, and in the second case it can be transformed into a pull. Better theories of push- and pull-transmitters will require representing kinematics in two and three dimensions.

∀ B ∈ *object*
  rigid(B) ⇒ (∀ c_1, c_2 ∈ contact-points(B)
      Push-Transmitter(c_1, c_2)
    ∧ Push-Transmitter(c_2, c_1)
    ∧ Pull-Transmitter(c_1, c_2)
    ∧ Pull-Transmitter(c_2, c_1))

Strings, however, are more complicated. A string can never be a push-transmitter:

∀ s ∈ *string*
  (∀ t ∈ *time* (T(¬ Push-Transmitter(end1(s), end2(s))
          ∧ ¬ Push-Transmitter(end2(s), end1(s))) t))

But if it is taut it can be a pull-transmitter:

∀ s ∈ *string*
  (∀ t ∈ *time*
    (T Taut(s) t) ⇒ (T Pull-Transmitter(end1(s), end2(s)) t)
          ∧ (T Pull-Transmitter(end2(s) end1(s)) t))

Now the problem becomes how to define Taut. As a first pass, let ends-distance be a type of quantity representing the distance between the ends of the string. Then we can define Taut as an individual view:

Individual-View Taut

Individuals:
  s a string

QuantityConditions:
  ¬ A_m[ends-distance(s)] < A_m[length(s)]

This model assumes that only the ends of the string contact other objects—it would fail for a rope hanging over a pulley, for instance. A better model is to divide up the string into segments according to whether or not that part of the string is in contact with a surface. A string is then taut if each segment that is not in contact with a surface is taut:

∀ S ∈ *string*
  (∀ seg ∈ segments(geometry(S)) Free-Segment(seg, S) ⇒ Taut(seg)) ⇒
    Taut(S)

This of course ignores the fact that the non-free segments may not be tight, as say for string lying on the floor. A full definition would also require tension along the entire string, but we have strayed far enough from dynamics already.

4.5. An oscillator

Dynamical reasoning involves more than just simulation. By analyzing the possible behaviors of a situation we can produce a summary of its behavior and eventual disposition (e.g., [12]). In classical physics these analyses are often concerned with stability. Here we will examine a simple situation involving motion and materials, ascertain that it oscillates, and perturb it to figure out under what conditions it will remain stable.

Consider the block B connected to the spring S in Fig. 37. We will model the spring S as device satisfying Hooke's Law (see Fig. 34). Initially we will assume the spring cannot break. To model the position constraint imposed on the spring's length by being rigidly connected to the block, and to set the origin of position to the location at which the spring is relaxed, we assume:

$$\text{length(S)} \propto_{Q+} \text{position(B)}$$
$$\text{Correspondence(length(S) rest-length(S)) (position(B) ZERO))}$$

Suppose the block is pulled back so that the spring is extended. Initially, we also assume that the contact between the block and the floor is frictionless. What will happen?

Since initially the spring is stretched (i.e., A[length(S)] > A[rest-length(S)]), the spring will exert a force. This will in turn exert a force on the block which, since the block is free to move leftwards (S is not immobile), will cause an

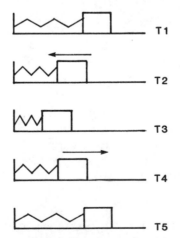

FIG. 37. A sliding block. Here is a system we will analyze to determine what it does and how different factors, such as whether or not there is friction, affect its behavior.

acceleration. So the initial view and process structures are:

> VS: {Stretched(S)}
> PS: {Acceleration(B, −1)} .

However, A[velocity(B)] will change from ZERO in an instant (by case (1) of the equality change law), so the process structure will become

> PS: {Acceleration(B, −1), Motion(B, −1)} .

Since D_s[position(B)] = −1, by the $\propto_{Q+}$ above we have D_s[length(S)] = −1 as well, and by the correspondence in the definition of elastic objects, D_s[internal-force(S)] = −1 as well. The next limit point is reached when A[length(S)] = A[rest-length(S)], making S relaxed instead of stretched. When this occurs A[net-force(B)] = ZERO, thus ending the acceleration. The motion, however, continues. The process and view structures become:

> VS: {Relaxed(S)}
> PS: {Motion(B, −1)} .

This state of affairs will last but an instant, since position is still decreasing. As the position moves past ZERO we will have

> VS: {Compressed(S)}
> PS: {Motion(B, −1), Acceleration(B, 1)} .

The only limit point that can be reached occurs in the quantity space for B's velocity, i.e., A[velocity(B)] = ZERO. When that occurs the motion will stop, leaving:

> VS: {Compressed(S)}
> PS: {Acceleration(B, 1)}

Since Acceleration directly influences velocity, this state of affairs will instantly change to:

> VS: {Compressed(S)}
> PS: {Motion{B, 1), Acceleration(B, 1)} .

The conclusion that the next change results in

> VS: {Relaxed(S)}
> PS: {Motion(B, 1)}

with an instantaneous change to

> VS: {Stretched(S)}
> PS: {Motion(B, 1), Acceleration(B, −1)}

which lasts for an interval and then yields

> VS: {Stretched(S)}
> PS: {Acceleration(B, −1)}

follows in the same way. However, this situation matches the initial situation—the quantity spaces, view and process structures, and D_s-values are the same. Thus we can conclude that an oscillation is occurring. Note that the view and process structures must be the same, because in principle the preconditions might have changed.

Some of the assumptions made in producing the process history can now be perturbed to examine the effects of different physical models. For instance, suppose the spring is crushable and breakable, as defined previously. Then there are limit points around rest-length(S) that correspond to the occurrence of crushing or breaking. It seems crushing must be ruled out by assumption, since the machinery we have developed so far does not allow us to rule it out via contradiction. We can however deduce that the spring won't break under the conditions above.

If we can prove that the block will go out no further than when it started then we can claim that it won't break because it didn't break in the first place. This requires an energy argument. The energy theory we will use is very simple. There are certain types of quantities that are *energy-quantities*, which are qualitatively proportional to certain other quantities and exist whenever they do. Two kinds of energy are kinetic energy and 'spring' energy. For every object there is a total energy, which is the sum of its energy quantities (Fig. 38 describes systems and energy quantities more formally, and Fig. 39 describes sources, sinks, and conservation laws).

Here the system is the mass and spring combination. At time t1, the block is still but the spring is streched, i.e.,

> (M A[Velocity(B)] t1) = ZERO
> (M A[length(S)] t1) > A[rest-length(S)]

which means that

> (M total-energy(SYSTEM) t1) > ZERO .

If energy is conserved and there is no influx of energy, then we know

> ∀ t ∈ *time*
>   After(t, t1) ⇒
>   ¬ (M total-energy(SYSTEM) t) > (M total-energy(SYSTEM) t1)

Energy-Quantity(kinetic-energy)

; velocity gives rise to kinetic energy

$\forall$ B $\in$ *object*
  Has-Quantity(B, velocity) $\Rightarrow$
    (Has-Quantity(B, kinetic-energy)
      $\wedge$ kinetic-energy(B) $\propto_{Q+}$ m[velocity(B)]
      $\wedge$ (A[kinetic-energy(B)] = ZERO
        $\leftrightarrow$ A[velocity(B)] = ZERO))

Energy-Quantity(spring-energy)

; an internal force gives rise to "spring" energy

$\forall$ B $\in$ *object*
  Has-Quantity(B, internal-force) $\Rightarrow$
    (Has-Quantity(B, spring-energy)
      $\wedge$ spring-energy(B) $\propto_{Q+}$ m[internal-force(B)]
      $\wedge$ (A[spring-energy(B)] = ZERO
        $\leftrightarrow$ A[internal-force(B)] = ZERO))

; the total energy of an object is the sum of its energy quantities

$\forall$ B $\in$ *object*
  Has-Quantity(B, total-energy) $\wedge$ Set(energy-quantities(B))
    $\wedge$ $\forall$ q $\in$ quantities(B) Energy-Quantity(q) $\Rightarrow$ q(B) $\in$ energy-quantities(B)
    $\wedge$ total-energy(B) = sum-over(energy-quantities(B))

; the energy of a system is the sum of the energy in its objects

$\forall$ sys $\in$ *system* Set(objects(sys)) $\wedge$ ($\forall$ b $\in$ objects(sys) Physob(B) $\vee$ System(B))
    $\wedge$ Has-Quantity(sys, total-energy) $\wedge$ Set(energy-quantities(sys))
    $\wedge$ ($\forall$ B $\in$ objects(sys)
      Subset(energy-quantities(B), energy-quantities(sys)))
    ; ignore converse case (assume all members must be from some part)
    $\wedge$ total-energy(sys) = sum-over(energy-quantities(sys))

FIG. 38. A simple energy theory—energy and systems. The predicate Energy-Quantity asserts that its argument is a quantity representing a kind of energy. Energy quantities occur as a consequence of objects having particular types of quantities. The energy of a system is the sum of the energy quantities for its parts.

This means that the block can only go out as far as it was at t1, since if it ever went out farther we would contradict the previous statement.

4.5.1. *Stability analysis*

To further analyze this system, we must treat the processes that occur as a compound process. We can start by writing an encapsulated history, including properties of the objects taken over the piece of history (a cycle of the oscillator) so defined. We want to perform an energy analysis, so we will include the total energy of the system (total-energy(SYSTEM)) and the maximum length of the spring over a cycle (max-length(S)), since length(S) gives us an

; processes can be sources and sinks w.r.t. a system

$\forall$ pi $\in$ *process-instance* $\forall$ sys $\in$ *system* $\forall$ q $\in$ *quantity-type*
  Source(pi, sys, q) $\equiv$
  ($\exists$ B $\in$ objects(sys) Influences(pi, q(B), +1))
  $\wedge$ $\neg$ ($\exists$ B $\in$ objects(sys) Influences(pi, Q(B), $-$1))
; define sinks similarly, ignore cross-flows

$\forall$ pi $\in$ *process-instance* $\forall$ sys $\in$ *system*
  Energy-Source(pi, sys) $\equiv$
  ($\forall$ q $\in$ *quantity* Energy-Quantity(q) $\wedge$ Source(pi, sys, q))
  $\wedge$ ($\forall$ q $\in$ *quantity* Energy-Quantity(q) $\Rightarrow$ $\neg$ Sink(pi, sys, q))
; energy sinks are defined analogously

; simple form of conservation:

; if you don't kick it it won't get any higher. .

$\forall$ sys $\in$ *system* $\forall$ i $\in$ *time*
  ($\forall$ pi $\in$ *process-instance*
    Energy-source(pi, sys) $\Rightarrow$
      ($\forall$ l_1 $\in$ during(i) (T Status(pi, INACTIVE) l_1))) $\Rightarrow$
      $\neg$ (M total-energy(sys) end(i)) > (M total-energy(sys) start(i))

; more complex version:

$\forall$ sys $\in$ *system* $\forall$ i $\in$ *interval*
  ($\forall$ pi $\in$ *process-instance*
    Energy-Source(pi, sys) $\Rightarrow$
      ($\forall$ l_1 $\in$ during(i) (T Status(pi, INACTIVE) l_1)))
  $\wedge$ ($\forall$ pi $\in$ *process-instance*
    Energy-Sink(pi, sys) $\Rightarrow$
      ($\forall$ l_1 $\in$ during(i) (T Status(pi, INACTIVE) l_1))) $\Rightarrow$
      (M A[total-energy(sys)] start(i)) = (M A[total-energy(sys)] end(i))

FIG. 39. A simple energy theory—sources, sinks, and conservation. There are several forms of energy conservation, some stronger than others. The weakest says that if there is no inflow then the energy never increases. The strongest says that in a closed system the energy is always the same.

indication of 'spring energy'. We assume the relations for the compound process include:

max-length(S) $\propto_{Q+}$ total-energy(SYSTEM)
correspondence((max-length(S), ZERO), (total-energy(SYSTEM) ZERO))

since during each cycle there will be some time during which all of the energy is in the spring. To perform an energy analysis we must re-write any inequalities in the quantity conditions in terms of energy, to wit:

QuantityConditions:
A[total-energy(SYSTEM)] > ZERO .

Thus if the total energy of the system ever reaches ZERO during an occurrence of the compound process it will no longer be active, because the total energy of the system is zero only when the spring is relaxed and the block is unmoving. Note that the quantity condition is no longer tied to a particular episode of the encapsulated history. This means that, unlike the encapsulated histories previously encountered, we cannot use this one for simulation. Instead, we use it to analyze global properties of the system's behavior.

We can use the basic QP deductions on this new description to determine the consequences of perturbing the model of the situation in various ways. Each perturbation is represented by a process that influences one of the parameters that determines the energy of the system. For example, suppose friction were introduced into the system. Its effect will be modeled by introducing a new quantity, e-loss(SYSTEM), the energy lost during a cycle. Then

$$D_s[\text{total-energy(SYSTEM)}] = -1 \, ,$$

and we can deduce, via limit analysis, that the quantity condition above will eventually be false, and so the oscillation will eventually stop. Suppose the system is pumped so that its energy is increasing (i.e., $D_s[\text{total-energy(SYSTEM)}] = 1$). Then while the quantity condition above will remain true, the energy will be continually increasing, which means the force on the spring will increase over time (since during part of the cycle the energy is all in the spring, and the spring energy is qualitatively proportional to the internal force of the spring). If the spring is breakable, then there will be a limit point in the quantity space for the spring's force that will eventually be reached. So the spring could break if the system is frictionless and pumped.

Let us examine in detail what happens if the oscillator is subject to friction, but we pump it with some fixed amount of energy per cycle, as would happen in a mechanism such as a clock. Is such a system stable? We will call the energy lost to friction over a cycle e-loss(SYSTEM) and the energy added to the system over a cycle e-pump(SYSTEM). The only things we will assume about the friction process in the system is that

> Relations:
> e-loss(SYSTEM) $\propto_{Q+}$ total-energy(SYSTEM)
> correspondence((e-loss(SYSTEM), ZERO), (total-energy(SYSTEM), ZERO))

> Influences:
> I−(total-energy(SYSTEM), A[e-loss(SYSTEM)])

The loss being qualitatively proportional to the energy is based on the fact that the energy lost by friction is proportional to the distance traveled, which in turn is proportional to the maximum length of the spring, which itself is qualitatively proportional to the energy of the system, as stated above.

The lower bound for the energy of the system is ZERO, and an upper bound for energy is implicit in the possibility of the parts breaking. The result, via the $\propto_Q$-statement above, is a set of limit points on the quantity space for e-pump(SYSTEM). If we assume e-pump(SYSTEM) is within these limit points then there will be a value for total-energy(SYSTEM), call it e-stable(SYSTEM), such that:

$$\forall\ t \in cycle$$
$$(M\ A[\text{total-energy(SYSTEM)}]\ t) = (M\ A[\text{e-stable(SYSTEM)}]\ t)) \Rightarrow$$
$$(M\ A[\text{e-loss(SYSTEM)}]\ t) = (M\ A[\text{e-pump(SYSTEM)}]\ t)$$

Note that e-stable(SYSTEM) is unique because $\propto_Q$ is monotonic. If the energy of the system is at this point, the influences of friction and pumping will cancel and the system will stay at this energy. Suppose

$$(M\ A[\text{total-energy(SYSTEM)}]\ t) > (M\ A[\text{e-stable(SYSTEM)}]\ t)$$

over some cycle. Then because the loss is qualitatively proportional to the energy, the energy loss will be greater than the energy gained by pumping, i.e., $D_s[\text{total-energy(SYSTEM)}] = -1$, and the energy will drop until it reaches e-stable(SYSTEM). Similarly, if total-energy(SYSTEM) is less than e-stable(SYSTEM) the influence of friction on the energy will be less than that of the pumping, thus $D_s[\text{total-energy(SYSTEM)}] = 1$. This will continue until the energy of the system is again equal to e-stable(SYSTEM). Therefore for any particular pumping energy there will be a stable oscillation point. This result is actually a qualitative version of the proof of the existence and stability of limit cycles in the solution of a differential equation. It is surprising just how little information about the system we needed to draw these conclusions, and it will be interesting to see what other results from the classical theory of differential equations can be derived from qualitative information alone.

5. Further Consequences

Qualitative process theory provides a representational framework for a certain class of deductions about the physical world. In this section we examine the consequences of this framework for several 'higher-level' issues in common-sense physical reasoning. Several of these issues arise in reasoning about designed systems, while others arise more generally.

5.1. Distinguishing oscillation from stutter

We have seen that envisioning—generating all the possible behaviors of a system—can be performed by repeated limit analysis. The result is a graph of situations which can be traversed to form any of the possible histories for the objects involved. In walking this graph we may find a terminal state (either because the situation is quiescent, because we do not know how to evolve a history past a certain kind of event or because we simply haven't bothered) or we might find a loop. A loop must be summarized if we are to get a finite description of the system's behavior. There are several ways to produce such summaries. In some domains the major regularity is spatial, in which case we would produce descriptions like "the ball is bouncing around inside the well" [12]. Another type of concise summary is possible when a system is oscillating, since there is a pattern of activity that occurs over and over again.

While oscillation in the physical system results in loops in the envisionment, there are other circumstances that give rise to loops as well. In part this is due to the qualitative nature of the descriptions used. Consider the situation illustrated in Fig. 40. Initially there are two flows, one from A to B and the other from B to C. What can happen? Limit analysis reveals three alternatives, corresponding to each of the flows stopping individually and to both ending simultaneously (see Fig. 41). In the cases where one flow stops before the other, the flow that continues will decrease the amount, and hence pressure, of the water in container B so the other flow will start again. These cycles of activity do not correspond to physical oscillations; they are an artifact of our qualitative physics. A better description of this behavior is that the change in level 'follows' the other change. In other words, we have a decaying equilibrium. We will call the behavior represented by these degenerate cycles *stutter*. How can we distinguish stutter from true oscillation?

Physically an oscillation requires that the system have some form of inertia or hysteresis. This means that, at least for some part of the system, when the cause of the change stops acting, the change will continue for a while afterwards. A real oscillation will therefore include process episodes that last over an interval, whereas stutter—a kind of 'mythical oscillation—will only include process episodes that last but an instant.

Fortunately the equality change law (Section 3.6.4) provides a way of distinguishing these cases. In Fig. 41, for example, the transitions marked with an 'i' take place in an instant. Therefore we have two instances of stutter, corresponding to the two fluids participating in a decaying equilibrium.

A similar phenomena occurred in the boiler model presented earlier (Section 5.2). Fig. 42 depicts the envisionment. Notice that if t-boil(WATER) rises faster than temperature(WATER) (due to the increasing pressure), the boiling will

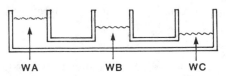

WA   WB   WC

FIG. 40. Three container example. Suppose we have three containers partially filled with water and connected by pipes, as shown. If we assume the water moves slowly, what can happen?

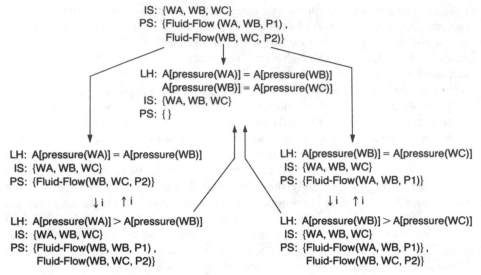

IS: {WA, WB, WC}
PS: {Fluid-Flow (WA, WB, P1) ,
          Fluid-Flow(WB, WC, P2)}

LH: A[pressure(WA)] = A[pressure(WB)]
      A[pressure(WB)] = A[pressure(WC)]
IS: {WA, WB, WC}
PS: { }

LH: A[pressure(WA)] = A[pressure(WB)]
IS: {WA, WB, WC}
PS: {Fluid-Flow(WB, WC, P2)}

↓i   ↑i

LH: A[pressure(WA)] > A[pressure(WB)]
IS: {WA, WB, WC}
PS: {Fluid-Flow(WB, WB, P1) ,
          Fluid-Flow(WB, WC, P2)}

LH: A[pressure(WB)] = A[pressure(WC)]
IS: {WA, WB, WC}
PS: {Fluid-Flow(WA, WB, P1)}

↓i   ↑i

LH: A[pressure(WB)] > A[pressure(WC)]
IS: {WA, WB, WC}
PS: {Fluid-Flow(WA, WB, P1)} ,
          Fluid-Flow(WB, WC, P2)}

FIG. 41. Stutter in fluid flow. This graph of transitions between process structures formed by repeated limit analysis contains two cycles, neither of which correspond to physical oscillations. For simplicity, we ignore the possibility of the contained liquids vanishing as a result of the flows.

stop. Since this change in the inequality relationship between the quantities is a change from equality, by case (1) of the equality change law it will occur in an instant. This in turn means that t-boil(WATER) was only influenced for an instant. When the boiling stops only the heat flow is acting, so temperature(WATER) will rise, and thus by case (2) of the equality change law the return to equality will occur in an instant. Therefore this cycle is an instance of stutter as well, corresponding to a rising equilibrium.

Being able to distinguish stutter from oscillation means we can write rules that summarize the process history. For example, when stutter occurs we can note the D_s-values for the quantities involved and assert that one kind of change is 'following' another, a decaying or rising equilibrium. Informal observations suggest that novices in a domain often confuse stutter and oscillation, and even experts who describe the situation as decaying or rising equilibrium are able to reconstruct the view of stutter as an oscillation. These informal observations need to be examined in the light of empirical data, but if true it may be useful in testing QP theory as a psychological model.

5.2. Causal reasoning

We use causality to impose order upon the world. When we think that "A causes B", we believe that if we want B to happen we should bring about A, and that if we see B happening then A might be the reason for it. Causal

FIG. 42. Stutter in the boiler model. The temperature and pressure will be continuously increasing in the boiler, but unless the changes in the links marked 'i' are recognized as occurring in an instant, the system will appear to be oscillating.

reasoning is especially important for understanding physical systems, as noted in [7, 39]. Exactly what underlies our notion of causation in physical systems is still something of a mystery.

Consider the representations used in physics. Typically equations are used to express constraints that hold between physical parameters. A salient feature of equations is that they can be used in several different ways. For example, if we know "X = A + B", then if we have A and B we can compute X, but also if we have X and A we can compute B. It has been noted that in causal reasoning people do *not* use equations in all possible ways [10, 40]. Only certain directions of information flow intuitively correspond to causal changes. I propose the following *causal directedness* hypothesis:

Causal directedness hypothesis. *Changes in physical situations which are perceived as causal are due to our interpretation of them as corresponding either to direct changes caused by processes or propagation of those direct effects through functional dependencies.*

This section will attempt to justify that hypothesis.

First, I propose that causality requires some notion of mechanism.[23] Imagine an abstract rectangle of a particular length and width. If we imagine a rectangle that is longer, it will have greater area. There is no sense of causality in the change from one to the other. If however we imagine the rectangle to be made of some elastic material and we bring about the increased length by stretching it, then we are comfortable with saying "the increased length causes the area to increase". Qualitative process theory asserts that processes are the mechanisms that directly cause changes. The quantities that can be directly influenced by processes are in some sense independent parameters, because they are what can be directly affected. All other quantities are dependent, in that to affect them some independent parameter or set of independent parameters must be changed. This suggests representing the relationships between parameters for causal reasoning in terms of functions rather than constraint relations.

Some examples will make this clearer, as well as emphasizing that the point is not academic. In generating explanations of physical systems, it is often useful to characterize how the system responds to some kind of change (this variety of qualitative perturbation analysis was invented by De Kleer, who calls it *incremental qualitative analysis* (IQ)). One way to perform IQ analysis is to model the system by a constraint network, in which the relationships are modeled by 'devices' that contain local rules that enforce the desired semantics.[24] The values of quantities are modeled by the sign of their change—

---

[23]In its most general form, this proposal is not new (Bunge [4] surveys various proposals concerning the nature of causality). For example, Heise [23] proposes *operators* as a mechanism that underlies all causal relations. The proposal presented here is more specific.

[24]These examples are drawn from systems implemented in CONLAN [14], a constraint language. The graphical notation for constraint networks is similar to logic diagrams, except that 'terminals' are given explicit names and the 'devices' are multi-functional. The technique described here is actually a simplification of De Kleer's algorithm. However, the models in [7] sometimes used directional rules rather than constraint laws, although no criteria was provided for selecting which direction in a constraint law is appropriate for causal reasoning.

increasing, decreasing, or constant. To perform an analysis, a value corresponding to a hypothesized change is placed in a cell of the constraint network representing the system. The rules associated with the constraint network are then used to deduce new values for other cells in the network. The propagation of information models the propagation of changes in the system, with dependency relationships between the cell values corresponding to causal connections. For example, if the value of cell A was used to deduce the value of cell B, we would interpret this as "The change in A caused the change in B". Fig. 43 illustrates fragments from two different models.[25] The top fragment states that heat is the product of the temperature of the 'stuff' and the amount of 'stuff', and the bottom fragment is the definition of sodium concentration in a solution.

In building a causal argument it is possible to reach an impasse—a quantity receives a value, but no further values can be computed unless an assumption is made. The safest assumption is that, unless you know otherwise, a quantity doesn't change. The problem lies in determining which quantity to make the assumption about. Suppose we assume that the amount of stuff is constant. Then we would conclude that an increase in heat causes an increase in temperature, which makes sense. However, suppose we assume instead that the temperature remains constant. We are left with the conclusion that an increase in heat *causes* the amount of stuff to decrease! Barring state changes, this does not

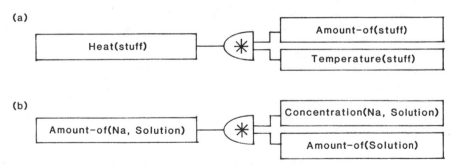

FIG. 43. Constraint representation of relationships. In the constraint networks, the boxes (cells) denote quantities. The relationship between the parameters is expressed by a multiplier constraint connecting them. Box (a) is drawn from the model for a piece of 'stuff' used in an effort to represent a student's understanding of heat exchangers. Box (b) is drawn from a model of a kidney to be used in explaining the syndrome of inappropriate secretion of anti-diuretic hormone (SIADH).

[25]These model fragments are drawn from an attempt to implement the model of a student's understanding of a heat exchanger described in [49], and an early version of the kidney model described in [2].

correspond to our notion of causality. In the second fragment the problem is more serious—increasing sodium will cause the amount of water to increase, *if* the rest of the kidney is working as it should! To do this requires a complicated feedback mechanism that is triggered by detecting an increased sodium concentration, not by the definition of concentration itself.

The problem lies in the ontological impoverishment of the constraint representation. Temperature and concentration are not directly influenced by processes (at least in most people's naive physics). Physically, they are *dependent* variables, and thus are not proper subjects of assumptions when constructing causal arguments. Amount of stuff, on the other hand, can be directly affected, so assuming it does not change will avoid generating ill-formed causal arguments. Fig. 44 illustrates.

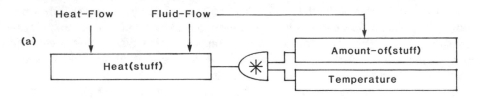

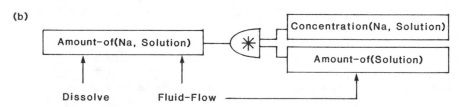

FIG. 44. Model fragments with possible processes. Models from Fig. 43 with the quantities annotated with the (likely) processes that might affect them. Note that certain quantities (temperature, concentration) cannot be directly changed. These are *dependent* quantities, and should not be the subject of assumptions in building causal arguments.

Of course, the proper assumptions to make really concern which processes are active and how influences are resolved. If we do not represent processes, we can only assume facts about quantities. If we assume a quantity is constant and later discover that assumption is wrong, we are left in the dark about *why* that assumption was wrong. For example, if the amount of stuff turns out not to be constant, we can look for fluid flows or state changes to explain why it isn't. Since processes tend to have more than one effect, there is some chance that the contradiction can lead to discovering more about the system rather than just being a bad guess.

5.3. Qualitative proportionalities revisited

The previous section argued that functional dependence is central to the kind of 'incremental' causality that people find useful in reasoning about the physical world. As discussed earlier, one goal of naive physics should be to develop a theory of observation. One use of observation is to interpret measurements in terms of theories [18], but another role for observation is in developing the physical theories themselves. While this problem has been studied before (c.f. [27]), the target representations have been equations. As a result the learning procedure has relied on numerical data and cannot build theories around weaker information. Learning constraint laws also differs from learning causal connections. As noted previously, an equation carries only part of what we know about a domain. Construction a learning theory for physical domains will require ways to learn process descriptions and causal connections.

One way to learn about a system is to 'poke' it and see what it does. The observed behavior can be used to make conjectures about causal connections between the parts of the system, and further experiments can be made to test the conjectures. This requires some notation to express the local causal connections conjectured on the basis of these simple observations. This requirement helped motivate the definition of $\propto_Q$ (see Section 2), which asserts that a functional dependence exists between two quantities. If whenever we increase parameter A in a system we observe that parameter B increases, the result can be expressed as:

$$B \propto_{Q+} A ,$$

A physical explanation for the dependence comes from writing the $\propto_Q$ within the scope of an individual view or process.

More powerful statements about a system or domain will require extensions of $\propto_Q$. To see what is involved, consider the analogous problem of learning how an old-fashioned typewriter works.[26] If the space bar is pushed, the carriage will move to the left. This is analogous to the kind of statement that can be made with $\propto_Q$. But lots of other things can happen to move the carriage, namely all of the letter keys and a few more. Thus it would be useful to be able to state that we know *all* of the influences (at least, within the current grasp of the situation) on some particular parameter. Suppose also that we just wanted to move the paper up without changing anything else. The return bar would move the paper up, but before doing so would return the carriage to the right. Being able to say there are no (known) intervening parameters is then also a useful ability.

To see how these notions can be expressed, consider the collection of $\propto_Q$ relations that hold at some instant in time. For any quantity, the $\propto_Q$-statements

---

[26]This is not proposed as a serious example because the quantity definitions and $\propto_Q$ would apply only in some very abstract sense.

relevant to it can be thought of as a tree with the dependent quantity at the root and the 'independent' quantities at the leaves. A plus or minus denotes the sense of the connection (whether or not it will reverse the sign of the change in the input). Thus

$$Q_0 \propto_Q Q_1$$

only specifies that Q_0 is on some branch 'above' Q_1.

Fig. 45 illustrates such a dependency tree. Suppose we are trying to cause Q_0 to change. If we don't want to change Q_2, then Q_3 or Q_1 are our only choices. We need a way to express that (at least within our knowledge of the situation) there are no intervening parameters. To say this, we use

$$\propto_Q\text{-immediate}(Q_0, Q_1)$$

which can be modified by $+$ or $-$ as before. $\propto_Q$-immediate adds a single link to the tree of dependencies. Another problem is to find all the ways to bring a change about, or to prove that changing one thing won't cause a change in some other quantity of interest. We do this by stating that a particular collection of quantities together 'closes off' the tree—there will be exactly one quantity for each branch. Out notation will be

$$\propto_Q\text{-all}(\langle\text{quantity}\rangle, \langle\text{plus-set}\rangle, \langle\text{minus-set}\rangle)$$

which means that there is a function which determines the quantity, relies on the quantities in the two sets solely, and is strictly increasing in its dependence on the quantities in the plus-set and strictly decreasing in its dependence on the quantities in the minus-set. If a quantity is not mentioned in a $\propto_Q$-all statement, then either it is irrelevant to the quantity of interest, it depends on some quantity in the $\propto_Q$-all statement (above the slice of the tree it represents), or some quantity in the $\propto_Q$-all statement depends on it. By ruling out the other two possibilities, independence can be established.

As a rule $\propto_Q$-statements will not hold for all time. In the typewriter analogy, imagine the carriage at the end of its travel—hitting the space bar will no longer result in movement. More to the point, consider Q_0 given by:

$$Q_0 = (a - b * Q_2) * Q_1 .$$

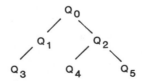

FIG. 45. A tree of functional dependencies.

Note that:

$$\text{if } a > b * Q_2, \quad Q_0 \propto_{Q+} Q_1$$
$$a = b * Q_2, \quad \neg \; Q_0 \propto_{Q-} Q_1$$
$$a < b * Q_2, \quad Q_0 \propto_{Q-} Q_1$$

In the case of equality, Q_0 and Q_1 are not related at all, and in the other two cases the sign of the function connecting them is different. Thus the collection of $\propto_Q$-statements that are true for a system can vary as a function of the values of the quantities, which is why they usually appear within some individual view or process. The idea of a *mode* of a system in 'real' physics roughly corresponds to particular process and view structures which hold during the system's operation.

5.4. Differential qualitative analysis

The idea of a comparison in IQ analysis suggests a complementary qualitative reasoning technique. IQ analysis concerns the relationship between two situations, one of which is the direct result of things happening in the other. Another case of interest concerns situations that are just slightly different from one another—an 'alternate-world' interpretation. For instance, we often have an idea of the different consequences that would result if something were changing a bit faster—if we put the heat up on the stove the water in the kettle would boil sooner, and if our arm were quicker the serve would have been returned. Such inferences are essential in debugging and monitoring execution of plans that involve physical action, and performing sensitivity analyses to evaluate a proposed design. The language needed to express such conclusions is in part the same as that used in IQ analysis—amounts are either the same, increased, decreased, or indeterminate as compared with the old situation. Answering these kinds of questions will be called *differential qualitative* analysis.

Let us consider a situation S_1. If we can get a new situation S_1 by changing a single ordering in S_1 or by changing the status of a single process or view instance in S_1, we will call S_2 an *alternate* of S_1. There are two kinds of changes that may occur as a result of perturbing S_1. First, other quantities can change. Second, the process history for the situation itself may change, apart from any changes made to define S_2 in the first place. For example, punching a hole in the bottom of a kettle could let all the water drain out before it boils. Even changes in orderings can lead to further changes in the histories of the individuals involved—e.g., if we reduce the intensity of a flame but still turn it off in five minutes, boiling may be prevented.

Let $DQ(q, S_1, S_2)$ for some quantity q be the sign of the difference between it in two alternate situations S_1 and S_2. Then the inequality order between them defines DQ-values, as follows:

$$(M \, q \, S_1) > (M \, q \, S_2) \leftrightarrow DQ(q, S_1, S_2) = -1$$
$$(M \, q \, S_1) < (M \, q \, S_2) \leftrightarrow DQ(q, S_1, S_2) = 1$$
$$(M \, q \, S_1) = (M \, q \, S_2) \leftrightarrow DQ(q, S_1, S_2) = 0$$

Since situations can occur over intervals, the inequality orderings for instants must be extended. For equality this is simple:

$$\forall \, q_1, q_2 \in quantity \; \forall \, i \in time$$
$$(M \, q_1 \, i) = (M \, q_2 \, i) \equiv \forall \, i_1 \in during(i) \, (M \, q_1 \, i_1) = (M \, q_2 \, i_1)$$

For the other cases the choice is less clear. The strongest version of greater-than is having it hold over every instant in the interval:

$$\forall q_1, q_2 \in quantity, i \in interval$$
$$(M \, q_1 \, i) > (M \, q_2 \, i) \equiv$$
$$(\forall \, i_1 \in during(i) \, (M \, q_1 \, i_1) > (M \, q_2 \, i_1))$$

however, the following will also suffice:

$$\forall q_1, q_2 \in quantity, i \in interval$$
$$(M \, q_1 \, i) > (M \, q_2 \, i) \equiv$$
$$[(\exists \, i_1 \in during(i) \, (M \, q_1 \, i_1) > (M \, q_2 \, i_1))$$
$$\wedge \, (\forall \, i_1 \in during(i) \, \neg \, (M \, q_1 \, i_1) < (M \, q_2 \, i_1))]$$

A version of $<$ for intervals may be similarly defined.

An episode in a parameter history has several numbers associated with it. The relationships between these numbers allows new DQ-values to be determined. The first number is *rate*, e.g., the D_m of the quantity the parameter history is about. The second number is the duration of the interval associated with the episode. The third number is the difference in the value measured at the beginning and end of the interval, which we will call the *distance*.

How are these numbers related? Intuitively we know that if the rate changes, the duration of time will vary inversely, or the distance the value moves will vary accordingly for the same duration. Implicit in this simple intuition is the assumption that the rate is constant during the interval, i.e., that the function defining the change of the quantity is linear and time invariant. This often is not the case, so we must require that either the beginning or the end of the two episodes being compared are the same. If we apply DQ analysis only to alternate situations as defined above this restriction will be satisfied.

With these assumptions, the DQ-value of the distance is just the product of the DQ-values of the rate and duration. Thus we can draw conclusions such as "if the rate is higher then over the same time the distance traveled will be greater" and "if the duration is shorter and the rate is the same then the distance traveled will be less." These inferences are illustrated in Fig. 46.

The direct historical consequences of these changes can be characterized by their effects on limit analysis. Consider a collection of limit hypotheses for a p-component. Recall that each hypothesis concerns a possible change in the process structure, brought about by changes in quantities that cause changes in quantity conditions. Suppose a particular limit hypothesis is chosen as representing what actually occurs. This means the change it stands for happens before the changes represented by the other hypotheses. If in an alternate situation this hypothesis has an increased duration (a DQ-value of 1) or one of the other limit hypotheses has a decreased duration (a DQ-value of −1), then in fact a different change could occur. Once again, the weak nature of our information prevents us from actually deciding if a different change would occur—but we at least know that it is possible in these circumstances.

```
; definition of distance
∀ S ∈ episode distance(Q) = (M A[Q] end(S)) − (M A[Q] start(S))

Suppose we have alternate situations S₁ and S₂, with a
quantity Q in both of them.

DQ[distance(Q, S), S₁, S₂] = DQ[rate(Q), S₁, S₂] * DQ[duration(Q), S₁, S₂]

Then assuming time(start(S₁)) = time(start(S₂)).

   DQ[rate(Q), S₁, S₂] = 1 ∧ DQ[duration(Q), S₁, S₂] = 0
     ⇒ DQ[distance(Q), S₁, S₂] = 1

   DQ[rate(Q), S₁, S₂] = −1 ∧ DQ[distance(Q), S₁, S₂] = 0
     ⇒ DQ[duration(Q), S₁, S₂] = 1

i.e., "If Q is going faster then it will get farther in the same time" and
"If Q is going slower it will take longer to go the same distance."
```

FIG. 46. Differential qualitative analysis. Differential qualitative analysis answers questions about how a situation would change if parts of it are perturbed.

6. Discussion

This paper has described qualitative process theory, which attempts to model aspects of commonsense reasoning about physical domains. To summarize:

(1) Our theories about how things change in the physical world have a common character. Physical processes are the mechanisms by which change occurs. Reasoning about processes—their effects and limits—form an important part of our commonsense physical reasoning.

(2) Numerical values can be usefully represented by the quantity space, which describes the value of a number in terms of inequalities. The quantity space is an appropriate representation because processes usually start and stop when order relationships between particular quantities change.

(3) QP theory provides the means to draw several types of basic, qualitative, deductions, including describing what is happening in a physical situation (finding view and process structures), reasoning about the combined effects of several processes (resolving influences), and predicting when processes will start and stop (limit analysis). These basic deductions can be woven together to perform more complex inferential tasks, such as envisioning.

(4) QP theory can be used to model several interesting physical phenomena for commonsense reasoning, including flows, state changes, motion, materials, energy, changing equilibria, and oscillation.

(5) QP theory provides a highly constrained account of physical causality (all changes are due to a finite vocabulary of processes) and a useful notation for expressing causal connections between quantities ($\propto_Q$).

(6) QP theory provides a structured role for the use of experiential and default knowledge in physical reasoning—for example, in resolving influences and choosing or ruling out alternatives in limit analysis.

(7) QP theory partially specifies a language for writing qualitative dynamics theories. In particular, the primitives are simple processes and individual views, the means of combination are sequentiality and shared parameters, and the means of abstraction are naming these combinations, including encapsulating a piece of a history.

6.1. Application areas

While designed to be a theory about naive physics, qualitative process theory has other potential applications. Two are discussed below.

6.1.1. ICAI and engineering problem solving

Since many engineered devices are implemented as physical systems, QP theory should be useful in reasoning about them. Perhaps the most immediately feasible application is providing part of a representation language for intelligent computer-aided instruction (ICAI). An important part of expert's knowledge of a system is a qualitative understanding of how it works. To the extent that QP theory models our qualitative understanding of dynamical systems, a program using it can generate explanations that a student will find easy to understand. Indeed, QP theory was developed in part to be used in the STEAMER project, whose goal is to provide instruction about steam propulsion plants for Navy trainees.[27]

---

[27]The STEAMER project is a joint enterprise of the Navy Personnel Research and Development Center and Bolt, Beranek, and Newman, Inc. See [46] for an overview.

One interesting implementation strategy is to construct a *tutor compiler*. Current qualitative-reasoning programs work from first principles in constructing explanations. This is analogous to setting a human domain expert down in front of a system he has never seen before and expecting him to understand it well enough to generate coherent explanations in real time. Using human instructors to teach this way is obviously a bad idea, so why should we expect our programs to do better? One alternative is to construct a program which takes as its input a system to be understood and a specification of the class of questions which are to be asked about it. The output of this program would be a specialized tutoring program that could, in real time, answer that class of questions about the system in question. This technique would have several advantages, for example, the qualitative-reasoning system in the compiler itself need not be especially fast, and more sophisticated techniques for generating explanations could be exployed than would otherwise be possible (such as McDonald's MUMBLE [32].

As extension theories are developed, QP theory should become useful in other kinds of engineering and control tasks as well. Individual views could be used to express desirable and undesirable operational characteristics. For example, in operating a boiler the fuel-air ratio must not become too rich or too lean; in either case smoke pours out the boiler stack, which is bad if you want not to be seen and combustion efficiency, hence fuel economy, will drop. A good boiler design will provide operating regions in which the individual views representing these undesired conditions are inactive. Similarly, these descriptions could be used in synthesizing control strategies, by determining what measurements indicate a state from which a view instance representing an undersirable condition will become active and what corrective action must be taken to ensure that the particular change will not occur.

Another interesting possibility is building a *hypothesizer*. A hypothesizer is an interpretation module which either takes measurements from operators of a system or gathers data itself from instruments, and will evaluate an operator's theories about what is happening in the system. Such a program could serve as a devil's advocate, pointing out inconsistencies in an operator's theory or suggesting alternate interpretations for the data. This would be useful because it seems that a common source of human error in operating complex systems (such as nuclear power plants) is premature commitment to a particular theory about the state of the system (see [37]). For example, the incident at the Three Mile Island reactor might not have happened if the operators had thought of the alternate explanation for the overpressure in the reactor vessel—that instead of being too high, the level of cooling water was too low, thus causing a boiling that raised the pressure.

6.1.2. *Economic modeling and decision support systems*

Historically, the success of differential equations in physics led to attempts to apply them to problems from other fields, such as economics. To the extent that differential equations prove useful in reasoning about a domain, QP theory should be similarly useful. In economics, for example, physical limitations often prove important. Storage capacities, transportation capacities, and rates of manufacture are important examples (see [20, 45]).[28] The features which make qualitative models useful for physical reasoning, such as the ability to characterize the classes of things that can happen even with very little data, should be useful in other domains, especially in domains where numerical data is unreliable or hard to come by.

However, caution seems advisable in attempting such applications. There seems to be no real agreement on what mathematical descriptions are appropriate in economics, hence it will be hard to judge whether a qualitative model is correct. In addition, the very structure of the domain can change with time; for instance, the tax code can change. These factors make modeling economics much harder than modeling physics.

6.2. Other work

The first attempts to formalize processes modeled them as collections of interacting automata [3] or extended STRIPS-like operators [24]. Let us examine each in turn.

Brown's automata-based system was designed to generate explanations for intelligent computer-aided instruction. Quantities and processes were represented by individual automata whose states represented classes of values or activities (such as a quantity decreasing or a particular activity in a sequence occurring). Time was modeled by specifying that automata representing quantities changed instantly while automata representing processes took an interval of time to change. Although arbitrary LISP code was permitted in specifying state transitions, in practice state changes were predicted on state changes in other automata. While adequate for generating explanations of fixed phenomena, the automata representation is too brittle for most reasoning tasks. For example, there is no influence-like mechanism for dynamically combining effects, thus all interactions must be foreseen in advance by the model builder. The process models are similar to encapsulated histories, in that they presuppose the outcome of the activity of the processes they describe. Hence such models will be insensitive to changing conditions.

Hendrix's system was designed to provide a world model for robot planning. While a significant advance over the models of action available at the time, the importance of qualitative descriptions had not yet been understood. For example, all quantities were real numbers, and relationships between

---

[28]Interestingly, Samuelson was one of the first to describe the possibility of using qualitative models and to point out that their inherent ambiguity would make prediction difficult. Subsequent developments in qualitative modeling, however, suggest his views were overly pessimistic, at least for physical domains.

parameters were expressed as numerical constraint equations. The process descriptions were used in simulation, solving simultaneous equations in the process descriptions to determine when the collection of active processes would change. Since the goal was to model general processes (non-physical as well as physical), add lists and delete lists were also used to specify effects. Qualitative process theory, by using qualitative descriptions and focusing on physical processes only, can be used in several other kinds of deductions in addition to simulation, often requiring less information to draw interesting conclusions.

Recently several attempts have been made to model temporal reasoning by Allen [1] and McDermott [30]. Allen's model is the one assumed here, both because meet seems to be the appropriate relationship between pieces of a history and because modeling instants as 'very short' intervals makes formalizing certain facts involving derivatives easier. McDermott's axioms for time contain several interesting ideas, including the chronicle representation of possible futures and its implications for planning. Unfortunately, McDermott expects too much of the temporal logic. For example, the logic includes the notion of a 'lifetime', how long you can assume a fact to be true once you have observed it to be true. McDermott claims lifetimes must be provided outside the logic, by fiat ("The senses actually tell you about persistences"), because having axioms that provide persistences can lead to contradictions. This ad hoc notion is needed precisely because the logic is developed independently from a theory of dynamics. Given a dynamics (and the ability to make closed-world assumptions about individuals and relationships), we can *deduce* what will and will not change. If we need an estimate of how long something will remain true, we can figure out how long it is likely to be before something that can change it occurs. To use McDermott's example, if you look at a boulder you might be able to estimate that if you came back in 50 years it would still be there (a weaker conclusion than implied by the notion of lifetimes, but it will do). However, if you are told that there is dynamite underneath, your estimate will be considerably different. In either case, if you came back the next day and discovered the boulder was some distance from its original location, you would have some theory about why, not just the feeling that your senses had lied to you. In addition, McDermott's model of quantities uses average rate instead of derivatives, which means many of the dynamical conclusions described here (such as distinguishing oscillation from stutter) cannot be drawn.

6.3. Current directions

Since the original publication of qualitative process theory, several projects have adopted or extended some of its ideas. In particular:

(1) Ben Kuipers has adopted a subset of QP theory for analyzing protocols of causal reasoning in medicine, including an implementation of rules to reason about changes within a process structure [25, 26].

(2) Reid Simmons has developed process representations for geologic inter-

pretation by qualitative simulation, including the use of a diagram. His system extends the quantity-space representation by using quantitative information, including representing values by intervals and using specific equations to describe functional dependencies [42].

(3) Johan De Kleer and John Seely Brown have extended their device-centered qualitative physics for machines to include inequality information so that state transitions can be more precisely modeled (see this volume). Also, Brian Williams has developed a similar device-centered physics for reasoning about VLSI circuits, focusing on the interrelationships between intuitive and formal mathematical models and the importance of continuity (also in this volume).

(4) Al Stevens, Dan Weld, and Albert Boulanger are using qualitative process theory in constructing a theory of explanations for machines [47].

(5) Alan Collins and Dedre Gentner are using qualitative process theory to express theories of evaporation in order to understand how to shift from one level of description to another. Also, we are using QP theory in developing a psychological theory of learning for physical domains [19].

ACKNOWLEDGMENT

Mike Brady, John Seely Brown, Alan Collins, Johan De Kleer, Dedre Gentner, Pat Hayes, David McAllester, Drew McDermott, Bruce Roberts, Reid Simmons, Al Stevens, Gerald Sussman, Dan Weld, Brian Williams, and Patrick Winston have all influenced the development of this theory in various ways. The bulk of this research was carried out at the MIT Artificial Intelligence Laboratory, under support from the Defense Advanced Research Projects Agency. Portions of this work were supported by the Navy Personnel Research and Development Center as part of the STEAMER project at Bolt, Beranek, and Newman, Inc.

REFERENCES

1. Allen, J., Maintaining knowledge about temporal intervals, TR-86, Computer Science Department, University of Rochester, Rochester, NY, 1981.
2. Asbell, I., A constraint representation and explanation facility for renal physiology, MIT SM Thesis, Cambridge, MA, 1982.
3. Brown, J.S., Burton, R.R. and Zdybel, F., A model-driven question-answering system for mixed-initiative computer-assisted instruction, *IEEE Trans. Systems Man Cybernet.* **3** (3) (1973).
4. Bunge, M., *Causality and Modern Science* (Dover, New York, 1979).
5. Collins, A., Warnock, E., Aiello, N. and Miller, M., Reasoning from incomplete knowledge, in: D. Bobrow and A. Collins (Eds.), *Representation and Understanding* (Academic Press, New York, 1975).
6. De Kleer, J., Qualitative and quantitative knowledge in classical mechanics, TR-352, MIT AI Lab, Cambridge, MA, 1975.
7. De Kleer, J., Causal and teleological reasoning in circuit recognition, TR-529, MIT AI Lab, Cambridge, MA, 1979.
8. De Kleer, J. and Brown, J., Assumptions and ambiguities in mechanistic mental models in: D. Gentner and A. Stevens (Eds.), *Mental Models* (Erlbaum, Hillsdale, NJ, 1983).

9. De Kleer, J. and Sussman, G., Propagation of constraints applied to circuit synthesis, MIT AI Lab Memo No. 485, Cambridge, MA, 1978.
10. diSessa, A., Phenomenology and the evolution of intuition, in: D. Gentner and A. Stevens (Eds.), *Mental Models* (Erlbaum, Hillsdale, NJ, 1983).
11. Fikes, R. and Nillson, N., STRIPS: A new approach to the application of theorem proving to problem solving, *Artificial Intelligence* 2 (1971) 189–208.
12. Forbus, K., A study of qualitative and geometric knowledge in reasoning about motion, TR-615, MIT AI Lab, Cambridge, MA, 1981.
13. Forbus, K. and Stevens, A., Using qualitative simulation to generate explanations, BBN Tech. Rept. No. 4490, prepared for Navy Personnel Research and Development Center, 1981; also in: *Proceedings Third Annual Conference of the Cognitive Science Society*, August, 1981.
14. Forbus, K., A CONLAN primer, BBN Tech. Rept. No. 4491, prepared for Navy Personnel Research and Development Center, 1981.
15. Forbus, K., Qualitative reasoning about physical processes, in: *Proceedings Seventh International Joint Conference on Artificial Intelligence*, Vancouver, BC, August, 1981.
16. Forbus, K., Qualitative process theory, MIT AI Lab Memo No. 664, Cambridge, MA, 1982; revised 1983.
17. Forbus, K., Qualitative reasoning about space and motion in: D. Gentner and A. Stevens (Eds.), *Mental Models* (Erlbaum, Hillsdale, NJ, 1983).
18. Forbus, K., Measurement interpretation in qualitative process theory, in: *Proceedings Eighth International Joint Conference on Artificial Intelligence*, Karlsruhe, Germany, August, 1983.
19. Forbus, K. and Gentner, D., Learning physical domains: Towards a theoretical framework, in: *Proceedings Second International Machine Learning Workshop*, June, 1983.
20. Forrester, J.W., *Principles of Systems* (MIT Press, Cambridge, MA, 1968).
21. Hayes, P.J., The naive physics manifesto, in: D. Michie (Ed.), *Expert Systems in the Micro-Electronic Age* (Edinburgh University Press, Edinburgh, 1979).
22. Hayes, P.J., Naive physics 1 – Ontology for Liquids, Memo, Centre pour les Études Semantiques et Cognitives, Geneva, Switzerland, 1979.
23. Heise, D.R., *Causal Analysis* (Wiley, New York, 1975).
24. Hendrix, G., Modeling simultaneous actions and continuous processes, *Artificial Intelligence* 4 (1973) 145–180.
25. Kuipers, B., Getting the envisionment right, in: *Proceedings National Conference on Artificial Intelligence*, Pittsburgh, PA, 1982.
26. Kuipers, B. and Kassirer, J., How to discover a knowledge representation for causal reasoning by studying an expert physician in: *Proceedings Eighth International Joint Conference on Artificial Intelligence*, Karlsruhe, Germany, August, 1983.
27. Langley, P., Rediscovering physics with BACON.3, in: *Proceedings Sixth International Joint Conference on Artificial Intelligence*, Tokyo, Japan, August, 1979.
28. McClosky, M., Naive theories of motion, in: D. Gentner and A. Stevens (Eds.), *Mental Models* (Erlbaum, Hillsdale, NJ, 1983).
29. McCarthy, J. and Hayes, P.J., Some philosophical problems from the standpoint of artificial intelligence, in: B. Mettzer and D. Michie (Eds.), *Machine Intelligence* 4 (Edinburgh University Press, Edinburgh, 1969).
30. McDermott, D., A temporal logic for reasoning about processes and plans, *Cognitive Sci.* 6 (2) (1982).
31. McDermott, D. and Doyle, J., Non-monotonic logic I, *Artificial Intelligence* 13 (1980) 41–72.
32. McDonald, D., Natural language generation as a computational problem: an introduction, in: J.M. Brady and R.C. Berwick (Eds.), *Computational Models of Discourse* (MIT Press, Cambridge, MA, 1983).
33. Minsky, M., Personal communication.

34. Minsky, M., A framework for representing knowledge, MIT AI Lab Memo No. 306, Cambridge, MA, 1974.
35. Moore, R., Reasoning from incomplete knowledge in a procedural deduction system, MIT AI Lab, TR-347, Cambridge, MA, 1975.
36. Moore, R., Reasoning about knowledge and action, MIT Ph.D. Thesis, Cambridge, MA, 1979.
37. Pew, R., Miller, D. and Feeher, C., Evaluation of proposed control room improvements through analysis of critical operator decisions, Electric Power Research Institute Rept. NP-1982, 1982.
38. Reiter, R., A logic for default reasoning, *Artificial Intelligence* **13** (1980) 81–132.
39. Rieger, C. and Grinberg, M., The declarative representation and procedural simulation of causality in physical mechanisms, in: *Proceedings Fifth International Joint Conference on Artificial Intelligence*, Cambridge, MA, 1977.
40. Riley, M., Bee, N. and Mokwa, J., Representations in early learning: The acquisition of problem solving strategies in basic electricity/electronics, University of Pittsburgh Learning Research and Development Center, Pittsburgh, PA, 1981.
41. Shearer, J., Murphy, A. and Richardson, H., *Introduction to System Dynamics* (Addison-Wesley, Reading, MA, 1967).
42. Simmons, R., Representing and reasoning about change in geologic interpretation, TR-749, MIT AI Lab, Cambridge, MA, 1983.
43. Stallman, R. and Sussman, G., Forward reasoning and dependency-directed backtracking in a system for computer-aided circuit analysis, *Artificial Intelligence* **9** (1977) 135–196.
44. Stanfill, C., The decomposition of a large domain: Reasoning about machines, in: *Proceedings National Conference on Artificial Intelligence*, Washington, DC, August, 1983.
45. Stansfield, J., Conclusions from the commodity expert project, MIT AI Lab Memo 601, Cambridge, MA, 1980.
46. Stevens, A. et al., STEAMER: Advanced computer aided instruction in propulsion engineering, BBN Tech. Rept. No. 4702, Cambridge, MA, 1981.
47. Weld, D., Explaining complex engineered devices, BBN Tech. Rept. No. 5489, Cambridge, MA, 1984.
48. Williams, B., Qualitative analysis of MOS circuits, *Artificial Intelligence* **24** (1984) this volume.
49. Williams, M., Hollan, J. and Stevens, A., Human reasoning about a simple physical system, in: D. Gentner and A. Stevens (Eds.), *Mental Models* (Erlbaum, Hillsdale, NJ, 1983).   (Eds.),
50. Clement, J., A conceptual model discussed by Gallileo and used intuitively by physics students, in: D. Gentner and A. Stevens (Eds.), *Mental Models* (Erlbaum, Hillsdale, NJ, 1983).

Received March 1982; revised version received July 1983

Commonsense Reasoning about Causality: Deriving Behavior from Structure*

Benjamin Kuipers

Laboratory for Computer Science, Massachusetts Institute of Technology, Cambridge, MA 02139, U.S.A.

ABSTRACT

This paper presents a qualitative-reasoning method for predicting the behavior of mechanisms characterized by continuous, time-varying parameters. The structure of a mechanism is described in terms of a set of parameters and the constraints that hold among them: essentially a 'qualitative differential equation'. The qualitative-behavior description consists of a discrete set of time-points, at which the values of the parameters are described in terms of ordinal relations and directions of change. The behavioral description, or envisionment, is derived by two sets of rules: propagation rules which elaborate the description of the current time-point, and prediction rules which determine what is known about the next qualitatively distinct state of the mechanism. A detailed example shows how the envisionment method can detect a previously unsuspected landmark point at which the system is in stable equilibrium.

1. Introduction

People have a fundamental desire to understand how things work, and an equally fundamental desire to explain their understanding to others. In this paper, I describe a class of knowledge structures to support prediction, explanation and question answering using causal descriptions of physical systems. Within the following framework for causal reasoning (inspired by De Kleer [6, 7]), I address the problem of how a qualitative description of the behavior of a system is derived from a qualitative description of its structure.

$$\text{Structural} \atop \text{description} \quad \rightarrow \quad {\text{Behavioral} \atop \text{description}} \quad \rightarrow \quad {\text{Functional} \atop \text{description}}$$

*This research was supported in part by NIH Grant LM 03603 from the National Library of Medicine.

The *structural description* consists of the individual variables that characterize the system and their interactions; it is derived from the components of the physical device and their physical connections. The *behavioral description* (or *envisionment*) describes the potential behaviors of the system as a network of the possible qualitatively distinct states of the system. I reserve the term *functional description* for a description that reveals the purpose of a structural component or connection in producing the behavior of a system. Thus, the *function* of a steam-release valve in a boiler is to prevent an explosion; the *behavior* of the system is simply that the pressure remains below a certain limit. The existing literature frequently obscures this distinction by using the term 'function' to refer to behavior.

The goal of this research is to develop a knowledge representation capable of describing human commonsense reasoning and explanation about physical causality. *Commonsense* causal reasoning is qualitative reasoning about the behavior of a mechanism which can be done without external memory or calculation aids, although it may draw on concepts learned from the advanced study of a particular domain, e.g. automobile mechanics, computer architecture, or medical physiology. In order to be useful for modeling human commonsense knowledge, the computational primitives of our representation must not require excessive memory or processing resources.

Simulation of the behavior of a mechanism is useful, for example in medical diagnosis, for determining the consequences of a hypothesized primary change, for predicting the expected course of the patient's disease, and for investigating the effects of hypothetical therapies. *Qualitative* simulation is important because the physician typically lacks precise numerical values for many parameters characterizing the patient's state, and some parameters may be difficult or impossible to measure. In spite of this, the physician is clearly capable of making useful predictions. The knowledge representation described here was inspired by the attempt to capture the knowledge revealed by a physician explaining a case of kidney disease with an unusual presentation. A detailed analysis of the physician's behavior is presented elsewhere [20].

In this paper, I propose a simple but very general descriptive language for structural descriptions, and a qualitative-simulation process for producing the behavioral description. The representation described here begins with a description of the structure of a mechanism that is similar to, but weaker than, a differential equation. The qualitative simulation produces a description of its behavior that corresponds to, but is weaker than, the continuous function that is a solution to the differential equation. Thus, the representation is intended to produce a useful qualitative description of behavior, starting with a qualitative description of structure that would be too weak to support more traditional reasoning methods (see Fig. 1).

Within the structural description, a mechanism is described as a collection of *constraints* holding among time-varying, real-valued *parameters*. The behavioral

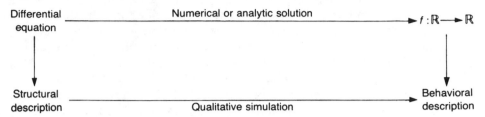

FIG. 1. The qualitative structural description is capable of capturing a less complete state of knowledge than a differential equation, and the qualitative simulation produces a partial description of the mechanism's behavior. Because the qualitative simulation uses heuristics, the two paths through the above diagram do not always yield the same result.

description consists of a finite set of *time-points* representing the qualitatively distinct states of the system, and *values* for each parameter at each time-point. A *value* is a description of the real number corresponding to a parameter at a particular time-point. This description consists of the *ordinal relations* holding among the different values in the behavioral description, and the *IQ value* (the sign of the time derivative) of the parameter at that time. The envisionment proceeds first by *propagating* the implications of initial facts through the constraints to complete a description of the system's state at the current time-point, and second by *predicting* the characteristics of the next distinct qualitative-state description.

After reviewing related work, a simple example demonstrates the basic properties of the representation and the envisionment process. Then a more elaborate example shows how, without external information, the simulation process deduces the existence of a previously unsuspected landmark value, and shows that the mechanism moves to a stable equilibrium about that value. The envisionment process has been implemented in MACLISP, as a program called ENV [10], which has run all the examples included here. The figures presenting the results of the envisionment have been laid out by hand for publication and are not in the actual output format. Appendices provide more formal specifications of the representation and the envisionment process, as well as an additional example addressing related issues.

2. Related Research

Answering a question about the behavior of a physical system involves two quite different operations. Problem *formulation* includes selecting which of several ways the physical situation should be described to allow a deeper examination. Problem *solving*, in the narrow sense, starts with a formal description of a well-structured problem and derives an acceptable solution. The different approaches to problem formulation taken by experts and novices have been examined by psychologists such as Chi, Feltovich, and Glaser [3] and

Larkin, McDermott, Simon, and Simon [22]. In particular, when solving problems in physics Chi et al. show that experts describe the given situation in terms appropriate to the underlying physical principle (e.g. conservation of momentum) required for a solution, while novices describe the same situation in terms of the physical objects in the surface statement of the problem. Naturally, the expert is then able to proceed directly to the solution, while the novice must search a larger space of alternate solutions. The work described here is a method of solving problems previously formulated, applicable at either level of expertise.

Artificial intelligence methods for qualitative reasoning about mechanisms were first developed by Rieger and Grinberg [25], whose knowledge representation consists of *events*, *tendencies*, *states*, and *state changes*, related by several different types of *causal links*. Their system produces realistic qualitative simulations of the behavior of mechanisms. However, their representation lacks a strong distinction between the structure and behavior of a mechanism, which we feel is critical to causal reasoning. More generally, their representation is ambiguous about whether its elements refer to the structure, potential behavior, or actual behavior of the mechanism being described. The CASNET program of Weiss, Kulikowski, Amarel and Safir [27] uses causal links to propagate confirmation scores among pathophysiological states describing the progression of glaucoma. However, the program has no knowledge of the relationship between physiological mechanisms and pathophysiological states, and so expresses causal relationships known to its authors, rather than doing causal reasoning itself. McDermott [24] has proposed an ambitious temporal logic for reasoning about events, actions, and plans as well as processes involving continuously varying parameters. In a sense, he has taken Rieger and Grinberg's representation based on states and events, and created a much extended representation on a better logical foundation, that is capable of addressing a larger set of issues. His logic, however, is oriented toward expressing the behavioral description as actions and events of various kinds, so the structural description is stated as conditionalized events, not as a separate type of description. Since McDermott's goal is to establish a logical framework for temporal reasoning, he demonstrates his logic by expressing many small example sentences rather than larger inference scenarios. Thus, he does not present a detailed set of rules and axioms for inferring behavior from structure. The aim of the present paper is to specify such a set of rules for causal inference, and to use only those features of a logic needed to express the rules.

The *envisionment* approach to reasoning about mechanisms based on the relationship between structure and behavior, rather than between actions and events, has been developed by researchers such as De Kleer [6, 7] and Forbus [11, 12]. When the qualitative description of a system's state is not strong enough to specify which of several futures it will actually follow, the envisionment becomes non-deterministic and the behavioral description contains a branch. Much of the research on envisionment processes has studied the use of external sources of information (e.g. quantitative [6] or teleological [7]) to resolve non-determinism in the envisionment.

There is little agreement on the exact role or expressive power of the *functional description*, which shows how the structure and components of the system contribute to its ability to perform its overall function [8, 19]. The functional description of a system should make explicit not only what behaviors are possible for a system, but why. Thus, a functional description must include terms that refer implicitly to changes past the final state of the system (e.g. *stable equilibrium*), or even to states that do not occur in the envisionment (e.g. *the steam-release valve prevents explosions*). The *function* of the steam-release valve, for example, must include a teleological relationship with the design process, in which the valve was added to the structure in order to prevent a certain behavior.

There is significant disagreement, as well, about the exact nature of the envisionment process. The main issue is the means for describing continuously variable parameters. De Kleer [6, 7] describes changing parameters according to the sign of the derivative (the *IQ value*, standing for *incremental qualitative value*), and an algebra for propagating IQ values across addition constraints. Forbus [11] observes that IQ values alone are inadequate for more than incremental-perturbation analysis, and expands the description to include the signs and magnitudes of both the amount and the derivative of a parameter. In practice, his system uses only the ordinal relations among quantities belonging to partially ordered *quantity spaces*, rather than performing arithmetic operations on numerical magnitudes. Hayes [16, 17] initially proposed the concept of a quantity space, but his efforts were directed toward developing an adequate ontology for causality involving liquids, and he did not use the quantity space in a significant way in his examples, remaining agnostic about its properties. Thus, there is a recognized need for a qualitative method for reasoning about quantities without losing the fine distinctions needed in particular applications.

Another important issue, not fully addressed by previous proposals, is the ability of the envisionment to detect previously unsuspected points at which qualitatively significant changes take place. Forbus [11] and Hayes [16] both assume that landmark values indicating qualitatively significant changes are provided as part of the initial description of the situation. De Kleer's "roller coaster" envisionment [6] usually makes the same assumption, although it is able to posit a change taking place within an interval if the roller coaster's behavior is different at the two ends. However, the point at which the change takes place is not then introduced into the envisionment for further qualitative reasoning. Determining where that point is, and what its properties are, is passed off to the quantitative-reasoning component. As we shall see in Section 5, the envisionment process proposed here is able to detect a previously unsuspected point at which qualitatively significant changes occur and determine many of its properties, without going beyond qualitative reasoning.

A number of researchers are developing methods for deriving behavior from structure in digital electronics, for the purpose of circuit verification (Barrow [1]) or fault diagnosis (Davis [4, 5], Genesereth [14]). Because of the discrete nature of the parameter values, digital electronics is a significantly different domain from physical systems characterized by continuous, analog parameters. In particular, although the simulation of the device may be symbolic [1], the precise values of the parameters can be described and used, so the simulation is not, strictly speaking, qualitative. Furthermore, current work has studied the propagation of information to establish a coherent state for the circuit at a single instant in time. These reasoning techniques do not address (yet) the *evolution* of the state of a circuit over time. Finally, as we shall see below, there is a relatively small set of possible constraints that may hold among parameters in an analog system, and relatively few ways that a set of changing parameters can change over time. In digital electronics, on the other hand, the constraints that can hold among parameters, and the way future states can depend on the past, are limited only by the set of available or constructible component types. Thus, many of the important issues in deriving behavior from structure will be different in the two domains.

3. Two Other Ways to Reason about Physical Systems

We can develop certain aspects of our qualitative-reasoning method by comparison with other formal reasoning methods using differential equations. Physical scientists reason about physical systems by describing the structure of a system with a differential equation, then determining its behavior by solving the equation, either analytically or by numerical simulation. The solution can then be analyzed to detect previously unsuspected landmark values of the system's parameters where its behavior changes qualitatively: zero-crossings, maximum or minimum values, and inflection points. Perturbation analysis of the system in the neighborhood of such a point can reveal the existence of (e.g.) a stable equilibrium. There are two costs to using such a reasoning method: the computational resources to perform its primitive operations, and an interpretation process to construct a meaningful description from its output.

Consider an example of a simple physical system (Fig. 2) consisting of a closed container of gas (at temperature T) receiving heat from a source (at T_s).

A commonsense description of the behavior of this system is *"The temperature of the gas increases until it is equal to the temperature of the source"* Our goal is a causal reasoner which can produce a description of this form from a description of the causally-relevant structure of the system.

A numerical simulation [13] of this system requires a complete description, in that the value of each parameter at each point in time must be given as a

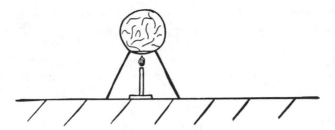

FIG. 2. A container of gas (at temperature T) receiving heat from a source (at a constant temperature T_s). There is no heat loss. The rate of flow of heat into the gas (inflow) is a function of the difference ($\Delta T = T_s - T$) between the two temperatures, with $\Delta T = 0$ corresponding to inflow = 0.

real number. The relationship between ΔT and inflow must also be specified precisely, so we assume strict proportionality with a numerically specified constant. The simulation algorithm is conceptually simple, computing the values of all parameters at a time-point from their values in the previous time-point. It does, however, require arithmetic operations on real numbers, which are more than we might be willing to assume as primitive operations in the human. Fig. 3 gives the structural and behavioral description of the simple heat-flow system, as appropriate for numerical simulation.

The output of the numerical simulation requires substantial further interpretation to recognize and classify important events in the behavior of the system. There is no information about the nature of the dependencies between the different parameters, or how the outcome might vary for different values of the numerical parameters. The fundamental problem is that the numerical description required for this type of simulation has very few states of partial

The structural description:

$$\Delta T = T_s - T$$

$$\text{inflow} = \frac{\Delta T}{10}$$

$$\frac{\mathrm{d}}{\mathrm{d}t} T = \text{inflow}$$

The behavioral description produced by numerical simulation:

t	1	2	3	4	
T	300	370	433	490	
T_s	1000	1000	1000	1000	etc.
ΔT	700	630	567	510	
inflow	70	63	57	51	

FIG. 3. The structural and behavioral description of the simple heat-flow system for numerical simulation. The behavior of the system is described in terms of a discrete set of time-points, each of which specifies the numerical values for the system's parameters.

knowledge: either the value of a parameter is known or it is not. The simulation process cannot run without complete knowledge, and its output can only be matched to a numerically identical system.

The analytic solution of a differential equation provides a substantially different description of the system. In order to describe the causal structure of the simple heat-flow system (Fig. 2) as a differential equation we must specify the relationship between inflow and ΔT explicitly, in this case as a strict proportionality, but with a symbolic constant k. It can then be solved analytically as is shown in Fig. 4.

The language of differential equations provides very useful states of partial knowledge about the system, in that quantities may be represented symbolically instead of as real values. There is also a very rich symbolic vocabulary of relationships that may be asserted between quantities in formulating the problem or describing the solution: the arithmetic operators, the trigonometric functions, logarithm, exponentiation, and many others. While these properties make differential equations the fundamental descriptive tool of the physical sciences, they cannot be solved analytically by humans without external memory resources. In spite of this descriptive power, the analytic solution of differential equations requires global and knowledge-intensive operations such as indefinite integration.

We have seen two quite distinct treatments of continuously varying parameters in these two representations. One treats quantities as real numbers, revealing their changes in the course of incremental simulation, but requires a sophisticated interpretation to derive an understanding of the behavior of the mechanism given the simulation. The other representation treats parameters as real-valued continuous functions, and yields an easily interpretable solution, but requires a sophisticated mathematical inference method which often fails to produce a closed-form solution. Qualitative reasoning about physical systems must be able to handle states of incomplete knowledge such as weakly specified functional relationships, and non-numerical initial parameter values. As a form of human commonsense reasoning, it must also require only modest computational facilities [18], but must still be able to handle systems without

$$\frac{d}{dt} T = \text{inflow} = k \Delta T = k(T_s - T)$$

$$\int \frac{dT}{T_s - T} = \int k \, dt$$

$$\ln(T_s - T) = -kt + C$$

$$T_s - T = C' e^{-kt}$$

$$T = T_s - C' e^{-kt}$$

FIG. 4. The first equation is the structural description of the simple heat-flow system (Fig. 2), and the final equation is its behavioral description, created by solving the differential equation analytically.

closed-form solutions, and must be able to recognize unexpected points of qualitative change.

4. Qualitative Simulation with Ordinal Quantities

The qualitative simulation, like the other formal models, begins with a structural description which consists of a set of constraints holding among time-varying, real-valued parameters. The three principal types of constraints are:

(1) *Arithmetic*: $(X = Y + Z)$. The values of the parameters must have the indicated relationship at each point in time.

(2) *Functional*: $(Y = M^+(X))$. Y is a strictly increasing function of X (decreasing if M^-). M_z^+ and M_z^- pass through the origin as well.

(3) *Derivative*: $(Y = dX/dt)$. At each time-point, Y is the rate of change of X.

The functional relationship, in particular, provides a weaker level of description than is possible with numerical or analytic solutions of differential equations. The relationship inflow $= M_z^+(\Delta T)$ in Fig. 5 states only that the relationship is strictly monotonically increasing, and that inflow $= 0$ corresponds to $\Delta T = 0$. Fig. 5 gives the qualitative structure description for the simple heat-flow system in Fig. 2.

The problem we observed in the last section with numerical simulation and analytic solutions of differential equations lies in the restricted states of partial knowledge and in the excessively powerful computational machinery required. In order for qualitative reasoning about physical causality to have more states of partial knowledge with a weaker set of primitive relations, it must operate,

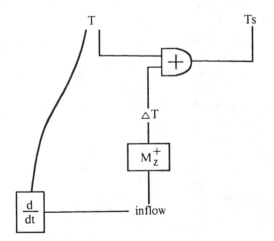

```
(defnet heat-flow
  (unit (temp t-in t-s delta-t)
    (heat inflow)
    (constant (t-s (*range* 0 nil)))
  (constraint
    (adder add A t-in
              B delta-t
              C t-s)
    (m0 + foo X delta-t
              Y inflow)
    (d//dt deriv RATE inflow
              X t-in))
  (initialize (lt t-in t-s)))
```

FIG. 5. The qualitative causal structure description for the simple heat-flow system (Fig. 2). Note that the M_z^+ constraint is a strictly weaker description of the functional relationship than was required for numerical simulation or analytic solution. The defnet form on the right is the actual internal form of the structure description.

not on real numbers, but on symbolic *descriptions* of real numbers and the relations among them. The behavioral description consists of a finite set of *time-points* representing the qualitatively distinct states of the system, and *values* for each parameter at each time-point. A *value* is a description of the real number corresponding to a parameter at a particular time-point. This description consists of the *ordinal relations* (i.e. $>$, $<$, and $=$) holding among the different values in the behavioral description, and the *IQ value* (stated as *increasing*, *steady*, or *decreasing*) of the parameter at that time. Certain values are distinguished or *landmark* values which play a special role in the qualitative simulation. Table 1 summarizes the terminology of this model of qualitative causal reasoning.

Beginning with a set of assertions about the initial state of the system, the envisionment process takes place through the *propagation/prediction cycle*.

Propagation. The consequences of information known about the state of the mechanism at the current time-point are propagated through the constraints to create a more complete qualitative description. The current time-point is complete when the direction of change for each value is known. Appendix B provides the detailed specification of the propagation rules.

Prediction. The configuration of changing values is examined to determine what can be inferred about the next qualitatively distinct state of the mechanism. A new time-point is defined (or three in case of a branch) and those conclusions asserted within its context. Appendix C provides the detailed specification of the prediction rules.

The prediction rules for determining the next qualitatively distinct state are elaborations on the following three types of qualitative changes, which depend on the ordinal relationship between the current value of a parameter and nearby landmark values.

(1) *Move from landmark value*: If the current value of a changing parameter is equal to a landmark value, then let the next value be perturbed in the direction of change, closer to the starting point than any other landmark value.

(2) *Move to limit*: If the current value of a changing parameter is not equal to a landmark value, and there is a landmark value in the direction of change, let the value of that parameter in the next time-point be equal to the next landmark value.

(3) *Collision*: If there are two changing values moving toward each other, not equal to landmark values nor separated by a landmark value, let their next values be equal, and make that new value a landmark.

Fig. 6 demonstrates these rules graphically.

When the description of the system's current state is not sufficiently complete to determine the next state uniquely, the envisionment branches on the possible states of a particular IQ value or ordinal relation. An additional set of recognition rules (Appendix C) detect properties of the behavioral description, such as cycles, case joins, and quiescence.

Fig. 7 demonstrates that the result of the qualitative simulation is a two-state

TABLE 1. The objects and relations in the qualitative causal reasoning representation. Appendix A provides a more formal definition. Appendix B contains the rules by which individual constraints propagate ordinal and IQ value assertions. The representation for causal knowledge consists of the following objects. They are described here in terms of the real values and real-valued functions for which they provide a partial description.

Object	Description
Parameter	A term corresponding to a continuous real-valued function of time.
Switch	A term corresponding to a Boolean-valued function of time.
Value	A term corresponding to a real number, the value of a parameter at a particular point in time.
Landmark value	A specially designated value.
Boolean	A term corresponding to the Boolean value of a switch at a particular point in time.
Time-point	A value of the special parameter, *time*.
IQ value	A term corresponding to the sign of the derivative of a parameter at a particular point in time. It may have one of three values: increasing (inc), steady (std), or decreasing (dec).
Assertion	One of the predicates describing the relation between two values, or between a value and the IQ value at the same time. The reasoning system acquires knowledge about the magnitudes of quantities by inferring new assertions.
Ordinal	$(\langle rel \rangle \langle value \rangle \langle value \rangle)$; $\langle rel \rangle :: = gt \mid eql \mid lt$.
IQ	$(IQ \langle value \rangle \langle iq\text{-}value \rangle)$; $\langle iq\text{-}value \rangle :: = inc \mid std \mid dec$
Constant	$(constant \langle value \rangle)$.
Value space	The set of values, partially ordered by the transitive closure of the ordinal assertions. Its primary use is to retrieve the next landmark value in a given direction from a given value.
Correspondence	An alist of (parameter landmark-value) pairs consisting of all the parameters at a particular time-point whose values are equal to landmark values.
Constraint	One of five types of predicate describing the relationship between several parameters and switches. A set of parameters, switches, and constraints constitutes the structural description of a mechanism, whose behavioral description is determined by examining the assertions generated through qualitative simulation.
Arithmetic	$(\langle parameter \rangle \langle parameter \rangle \langle parameter \rangle) [+^*]$
Functional	$(\langle parameter \rangle \langle parameter \rangle) [M^+ \ M^- \ M_z^+ \ M_z^-]$.
Derivative	$(\langle parameter \rangle \langle parameter \rangle \langle switch \rangle) [d/dt]$.
Inequality	$(\langle parameter \rangle \langle parameter \rangle \langle switch \rangle) [= \ne < > \leqslant \geqslant]$.
Conditional	$(\langle switch \rangle \langle parameter \rangle \langle parameter \rangle \langle parameter \rangle)$.

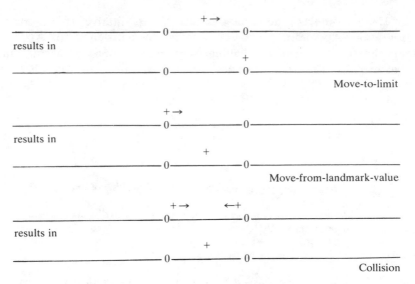

FIG. 6. A graphical illustration of three of the simple prediction rules. The actual set of rules is considerably more complex because there are frequently more than one or two changing values.

envisionment that corresponds closely with the commonsense description of the simple heat-flow system: "*The temperature of the gas increases until it is equal to the temperature of the source*". The qualitative structural and behavioral descriptions offer simplicity of mechanism, in that the qualitative-simulation process depends on the ability to create and match simple assertions, rather than on arithmetic operations or symbolic integration. They also offer the ability to represent partial knowledge, in that both values and functional relationships are only constrained to lie in qualitatively defined classes. Both simplicity of mechanism and states of partial knowledge are valuable properties of a commonsense knowledge representation.

The next example shows that the qualitative simulation can also provide an essential property of a description of physical causality: the ability to detect previously unsuspected values at which qualitatively significant changes take place.

5. Detecting and Establishing a Stable Equilibrium

We have seen that the qualitative-simulation process can handle a simple heat-flow problem like the one above, where the system reaches an equilibrium at a previously known landmark value. However, one important product of causal reasoning about a physical system is the existence of previously unsuspected values at which qualitatively significant changes take place. We can explore this issue in the context of a more realistic heat-flow problem, where there are flows of heat both into the gas from the source, and away from the gas into the surrounding cooler air. The causal structure description of the constant(T_s)

---

(1) $T < T_s$
     $\Delta T > 0$
     inflow > 0
     increasing(T)
     decreasing(ΔT)
     decreasing(inflow)

(2)
     $T = T_s$
     $\Delta T = 0$
     inflow $= 0$
     steady(T)
     steady(ΔT)
     steady(inflow)

- Initial conditions are constant (T_s) and $T < T_s$.
- In time-point (1), the addition constraint propagates $T < T_s \Rightarrow \Delta T > 0$.
- The functional constraint propagates $\Delta T > 0 \Rightarrow$ inflow > 0.
- The derivative constraint yields inflow $> 0 \Rightarrow$ increasing(T).
- The IQ values propagate similarly to complete the description of time-point (1).
- A version of the move-to-limit rule determines that T, ΔT, and inflow are all changing toward landmark values, and that they must reach their limits simultaneously.
- Time-point (2) is created with the initial assertions $T = T_s$, $\Delta T = 0$, and inflow $= 0$.
- The constraints propagate ordinal assertions and IQ values until the description of time-point (2) is complete.
- Since all IQ values are steady, the system is quiescent.
- *"The temperature of the gas increases until it is equal to the temperature of the source"*.

FIG. 7. The envisionment of Fig. 5 produced by qualitative simulation.

double heat-flow system (Fig. 8) is constructed by merging two descriptions of simple heat flows. The problem is to deduce the existence of an equilibrium temperature (T_e) between the temperatures of the heat source (T_s) and the air (T_a), and to show that the system moves to a stable equilibrium about that temperature.

This description is a qualitative version of the differential equation

$$\frac{d}{dt} T = k(T_s - T) - k'(T - T_a)$$

whose solution is

$$T = \frac{kT_s + k'T_a}{k + k'} - C' \, e^{-(k+k')t} .$$

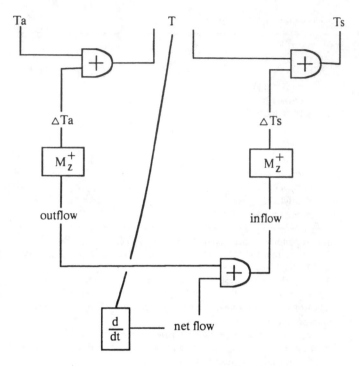

FIG. 8. The causal structure description of the container of gas with two heat flows.

A commonsense description of the behavior of this system is "*The temperature of the gas moves to a temperature between the temperature of the air and that of the source, and remains steady*".

The envisionment process attempts to produce a complete description of the system's behavior through time. As we shall see, it first propagates newly discovered information through the constraints to complete the description of the system at a given time-point. Once that description is sufficiently complete, the envisionment process examines the set of currently changing values to determine the next qualitatively distinct state. If the description of the current state is not sufficiently well specified to determine the next state uniquely, the behavioral description branches according to the three possible states of an unspecified IQ value or ordinal relation. If the alternating cycle of sprouting a new time-point and propagating information among its values should become bogged down in intractible branching, the causal-structure description may be summarized and simplified (cf. Fig. 10 and Appendix D). The new description is less constrained, hence weaker than the old one, but by being simpler it may avoid branching and allow the envisionment process to continue. The envisionment process continues to simulate the system until some terminating condition is detected: quiescence, a cycle, a contradiction, or intractible branching.

The set of values in the behavioral description, partially ordered by the ordinal assertions that are currently known, is called the *value space*. The prediction rules that determine the next state of the system give special status to landmark values. The prediction rules consider only the subset of the value

constant(T_a)
constant(T_s)

(1) $T_a < T < T_s$
  $\Delta T_a > 0$ $\Delta T_s > 0$
  outflow > 0 inflow > 0
  net flow = unknown

Case split: relation(net flow, 0)

(1G)	(1L)	(1E)
net flow > 0	net flow < 0	net flow $= 0$
inflow $>$ outflow > 0	$0 <$ inflow $<$ outflow	inflow $=$ outflow > 0
$T_a < T < T_s$	$T_a < T < T_s$	$T_a < T < T_s$
$\Delta T_a, \Delta T_s > 0$	$\Delta T_a, \Delta T_s > 0$	$\Delta T_a, \Delta T_s > 0$
increasing(T)	decreasing(T)	steady(T)
increasing(ΔT_a)	decreasing(ΔT_a)	steady(ΔT_a)
increasing(outflow)	increasing(outflow)	steady(outflow)
decreasing(ΔT_s)	increasing(ΔT_s)	steady(ΔT_s)
decreasing(inflow)	increasing(inflow)	steady(inflow)
decreasing(net flow)	increasing(net flow)	steady(net flow)

– In time-point (1), starting with the condition that $T_a < T < T_s$, ordinal assertions propagate through the network, producing the succeeding facts, but failing to provide information about net flow.
– In order to allow the derivative constraint to derive IQ values, the envisionment is split into cases according to the sign of net flow. In the branches, with net flow specified, IQ values propagate through the network to complete the description.
– Time-point (1E) is quiescent, with all IQ values steady, so new landmark values are created, and the correspondence between parameters taking on landmark values is recorded.
  (net flow: 0) ⇔ (inflow: flow*) ⇔ (outflow: flow*)
   ⇔ (ΔT_a: ΔT_a^*) ⇔ (ΔT_s: ΔT_s^*) ⇔ (T: T_θ)
– Time-points (1G) and (1L) each contain *six* changing values. However, not enough is known to show that they arrive at their limits simultaneously, making the required case split intractibly large, so the envisionment halts.

FIG. 9. Envisionment of the double heat-flow system. The envisionment diagrams (Figs. 9 and 11) are read from top to bottom, each line following from those above. Each cell contains assertions relevant to a single time-point. Time progresses from top to bottom, and alternate branches are side by side.

space consisting of the current values plus the landmark values. Initially, zero is the only landmark value; the current value of a parameter becomes a landmark when that value has an IQ value of steady.

Figs. 9, 10 and 11 show the stages of the qualitative simulation as it creates the envisionment. Fig. 9 shows how the envisionment of the double-flow system branches in order to derive missing IQ values, how a new landmark point is discovered on one of the branches, and how a set of corresponding values is recorded when several parameters take on landmark values simultaneously. Fig. 10 shows how the structural description is summarized when the first envisionment bogs down at an intractible branch, creating a much more manageable structural description which, though containing much less information, is still a valid description of the system. Fig. 11 shows how the summarized structural description, and the newly discovered correspondence, allow the successor time-points on the remaining two branches to be determined uniquely so the envisionment can be completed. Diagnosis of a stable equilibrium takes place using the final envisionment structure, by showing that a perturbation from the final quiescent state places the system into one of the previously described states from which there is a restoring change.

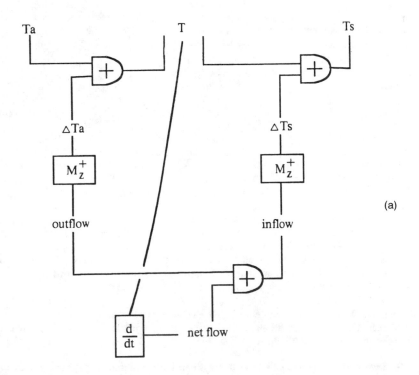

FIG. 10(a).

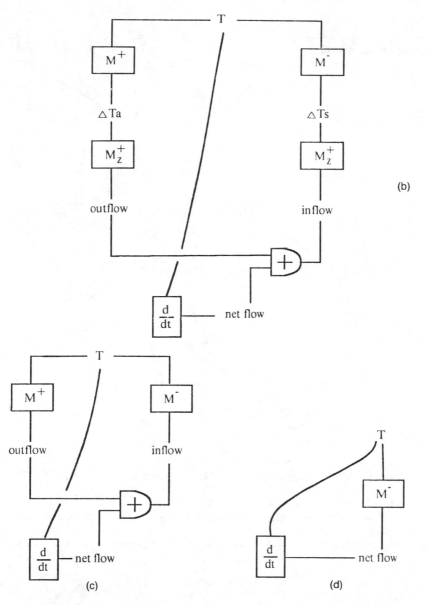

FIG. 10 (b), (c), (d). The arithmetic and functional parts of the causal-structure description are simplified in three steps, applying the following simplification rules. (See Appendix D.) The rules are applied repeatedly until the structural description can not be simplified further.

$$x + y = z \ \& \ \text{constant}(y) \Rightarrow z = M^+(x) \qquad (a) \rightarrow (b)$$
$$x + y = z \ \& \ \text{constant}(z) \Rightarrow y = M^-(x) \qquad (a) \rightarrow (b)$$
$$y = M^+(M^+(x)) \Rightarrow y = M^+(x) \qquad (b) \rightarrow (c)$$
$$y = M^-(M^+(x)) \Rightarrow y = M^-(x) \qquad (b) \rightarrow (c)$$
$$y = M^-(x) - M^+(x) \Rightarrow y = M^-(x) \qquad (c) \rightarrow (d)$$

185

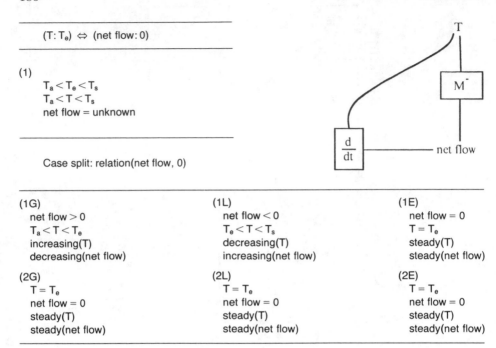

$$(T : T_e) \Leftrightarrow (\text{net flow} : 0)$$

(1)

    $T_a < T_e < T_s$
    $T_a < T < T_s$
    net flow = unknown

Case split: relation(net flow, 0)

(1G)	(1L)	(1E)
net flow > 0	net flow < 0	net flow $= 0$
$T_a < T < T_e$	$T_e < T < T_s$	$T = T_e$
increasing(T)	decreasing(T)	steady(T)
decreasing(net flow)	increasing(net flow)	steady(net flow)
(2G)	(2L)	(2E)
$T = T_e$	$T = T_e$	$T = T_e$
net flow $= 0$	net flow $= 0$	net flow $= 0$
steady(T)	steady(T)	steady(T)
steady(net flow)	steady(net flow)	steady(net flow)

Case join: identical outcomes on all branches

(2)

    net flow $= 0$
    $T = T_e$
    steady(T)
    steady(net flow)

– In time-point (1), ordinal assertions propagate as before, and the need for IQ values prompts a case split.
– Time-point (1E) is quiescent as before.
– The previously determined correspondence makes it possible to infer the relation between T and T_e in time-points (1G) and (1L).
– Since time-points (1G) and (1L) each contain only two changing parameters and their limits are known to correspond, their subsequent states, (2G) and (2L), are easily and unambiguously determined by the move-to-limit rule.
– Since the three branches of the split have identical end-states, they are joined to create state (2). The quiescent state (1E) is copied to an identical but temporally later state (2E) so that the temporal relation between states (1) and (2) is well defined.

FIG. 11. Envisionment of the summarized double heat-flow description.

The envisionment structure, or behavioral description, is now complete, since each state with changing values has a well-defined successor. The overall structure of the envisionment is shown in Fig. 12. Since the envisionment structure has only eight states, it is feasible to examine it for global properties such as the nature of its equilibrium.

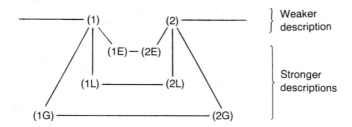

FIG. 12. The qualitative description of behavior is sufficiently compact that it can be examined for global properties such as stable equilibrium.

Since the system ends in a quiescent state, a set of recognition rules is applied to determine whether the quiescence can be diagnosed as some type of equilibrium. Perturbations from state (2) put the system into states (1G) or (1L), from which they return to (2), so the system is in stable equilibrium.

It is worth noting that almost the same conclusion would have been reached if the double heat-flow structure (Fig. 8) had been simplified immediately, without the initial envisionment. The reader may find it instructive to work through the envisionment in Fig. 11 without the correspondence given ahead of time. The more complete description is required, however, to show that $T_a < T_e < T_s$, if it is not initially assumed. Furthermore, there is no reason, before doing the initial simulation, for the envisionment process to transform a stronger description into a weaker (though simpler) one.

6. On the Qualitative Description of Time

A mechanism changes continuously with time. Thus, there is no 'next' instant after the current one. The qualitative simulation we use here, however, consists of a discrete set of time-points, and we frequently speak of the prediction phase as predicting the "next qualitatively distinct state" of the system.

Consider the example of a ball thrown into the air with velocity $v_0 > 0$ at time $t = 0$. The ball passes through a continuum of states during its journey up, the down again. However, these states are mapped into five distinct qualitative-state descriptions (see Fig. 13).

Each time-point in the sequence produced by the qualitative simulation corresponds to either a point or an open interval in physical time. In the open-interval case, the physical system clearly continues to change, but within the scope of the same qualitative-state description.

7. Individual Variation

Individual variation is an important characteristic of commonsense knowledge (cf. [23]). An individual might have the structural description shown in Fig. 14 for the single heat-flow system. The qualitative simulation is similar to that in Fig. 7, in that it matches the commonsense description: "*The temperature of the*

The quantitative-structure description:

$$\frac{d}{dt}y = v, \qquad \frac{d}{dt}v = a = -32 \text{ ft/sec}^2.$$

The quantitative-behavior description:

$$v(0) = 32 \text{ ft/sec} \Rightarrow y(t) = -16t^2 + 32t \text{ ft}.$$
$$y(0) = 0 \text{ ft}.$$

The qualitative-structure description:

$$\frac{d}{dt}y = v, \qquad \frac{d}{dt}v = a < 0.$$

The qualitative-behavior description:

	(0)	(1)	(2)	(3)	(4)
Y	$Y_0 = 0$	$0 < Y_1 < \text{YMAX}$	$Y_2 = \text{YMAX}$	$0 < Y_3 < \text{YMAX}$	$Y_4 = 0$
V	$V_{0'} > 0$	$0 < V_1 < V_0$	$V_2 = 0$	$V_3 < 0$	$V_4 < V_3 < 0$
A	$A_0 < 0$	$A_1 < 0$	$A_2 < 0$	$A_3 < 0$	$A_4 < 0$

FIG. 13. The structural and behavioral descriptions of the ball system, described both quantitatively and qualitatively. For all t in the open interval $0 < t < 1$, the quantitative descriptions are mapped into the same qualitative description (State (1)). Thus state (1) is the next qualitatively distinct state description after state (0), even though there is clearly no 'next' value of t after $t = 0$.

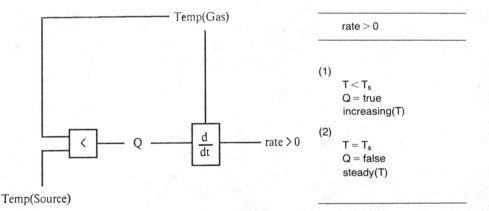

FIG. 14. An alternate causal-structure description of the single heat-flow system, and the corresponding behavioral description. Although the behavioral description is effectively the same as that in Fig. 7 for the simple heat-flow system, the structure description does not generalize to handle the double heat-flow situation.

gas increases until it is equal to the temperature of the source". The structural description is correct, but is at the wrong level of detail to support productive causal reasoning because it does not include the fact that the difference between the temperatures of the gas and the source controls the rate of heat increase. This structural description could not be generalized to produce a reasonable envisionment of the double heat-flow example.

We may speculate that some physics students learn models of physical phenomena such as shown in Fig. 14 which are accurately predictive for a certain class of simple mechanisms, but lead to intractible or incoherent structural descriptions when generalized. The Repair Theory approach of Brown and Van Lehn [2], applied to the composition of simple mechanism descriptions to produce more complex ones, may illuminate the misconceptions of naive physics students [15].

8. Conclusion

This paper is concerned with the qualitative simulation of physical systems whose descriptions are stated in terms of continuously varying parameters. These continuous systems are interesting because they pose unsolved problems in the representation of knowledge, and because they appear fundamental to commonsense knowledge of causality in the physical world. There appears to be a 'cluster' of knowledge of manageable size about the possible interactions among continuously changing parameters which we can hope to capture and represent [16].

The examples presented above demonstrate a representation for qualitative reasoning about causality in physical mechanisms. The system as described in this paper has been completely implemented in MACLISP. The structural description is essentially a qualitative form of a differential equation, specifying a set of parameters which characterize the state of the mechanism and a set of constraints holding among the parameters. Qualitative simulation produces a behavioral description which specifies the ordinal relationships and directions of change of the parameter values at each point in time.

Just as differential equations do not provide a theory of physics, but rather a language for stating theories of physics, the work presented here is a 'qualitative mathematics' intended as a language for stating theories of qualitative reasoning about particular mechanisms [9]. The preceding discussion of individual variation illustrates this point. Qualitative simulation of behavior from structure is a key element in a complete theory of 'naive physics'. Other critical elements include specifying *which* knowledge to represent to capture the properties of particular domains [17, 21], and specifying how the right structural descriptions can be evoked to handle particular physical situations [11, 12].

Future directions for research on these 'qualitative differential equations' include a mathematical exploration of their properties and the correctness of the qualitative-simulation algorithm (cf. Fig. 1), a reformulation of the prediction rules (Appendix C), and an extension to the formalism to allow time to be treated as a structural, as well as a behavioral, parameter.

Appendix A. A Formal Definition of the Causal Representation

Def. A *parameter* is symbol denoting a continuously differentiable real-valued function of time ($p_i : \mathbb{R} \to \mathbb{R}$).

Def. A *constraint* is a pair $\langle P, A \rangle$ consisting of:
  (1) a set P of parameters,
  (2) a set A of axioms stating relationships between the values and IQ values of the parameters in P. (See Appendix B.)

Def. A *structural description* is a 4-tuple $\langle P, U, C, A \rangle$ consisting of:
  (1) a set P of parameters,
  (2) a set U of subsets of P, called *units*, partitioning P into mutually exclusive subsets,
  (3) a set C of constraints, holding among the parameters in P,
  (4) a set A of axioms stating additional, situation-specific relationships between the values and IQ values of the parameters in P.
  (E.g. constant(p) $\Rightarrow$ (for-all (t) (IQ-value(p, t) = steady)).)

Def. A *time-point* is a symbol denoting a real number in the domain of some parameter.

Def. A *value* is a symbol denoting a real number in the range of some parameter.

Def. An *IQ value* is one of the three symbols {increasing, steady, decreasing}, denoting the sign of the derivative of a parameter at a particular time-point.

Def. Two landmark values d_i and d_j are *corresponding values* if there is some time-point t and two parameters p_i and p_j related by a monotonic function constraint, such that val(p_i, t) = d_i and val(p_j, t) = d_j.

Def. An *envisionment* is a 7-tuple $\langle SD, T, V, D, R, IQ\text{-value}, Corr \rangle$ consisting of:
  (1) a structural description SD,
  (2) a set T of time-points, with a subset T* designated as *active* time-points,
  (3) a set V of values, with a mapping val : $P \times T \to V$ which is a 1-1 correspondence,
  (4) a subset D of V called the *landmark values*,
  (5) an order relation R on the elements of V which is a total order when restricted to

the landmark values D in a given unit U_i plus any other value corresponding to a parameter in U_i.

(6) a partial mapping $IQ : P \times T \rightarrow$ {increasing, steady, decreasing}, which assigns to each parameter at each time the sign of the derivative of its parameter at that time,

(7) a set Corr of subsets of D denoting corresponding values.

Def. An *envisionment process* is a sequence $E_0 \ldots E_n$ of envisionments, where

(1) E_0 consists of a structural description SD, and the sets T, V, D, R, IQ, and Corr contain a description of a single, active, initial time-point t_0,

(2) E_{k+1} is derived from E_k by selecting an active time-point from E_k, and applying the rules in Appendix C below to that time-point to determine 1 (or 3 in the case of a branch) successor time-points which are added to T, along with a corresponding set of values to V, and possibly additional information to D, R, IQ-value, and Corr,

(3) none of the rules below apply to the final state E_n.

Appendix B. Definition of the Constraints

Constraints are relationships among parameters, but assert ordinal relations and IQ values among the values associated with those parameters at a given time, and also among the values associated with a single parameter at different times. The rules by which these assertions are created are given below. The constraint propagation mechanism is inspired by the scheme developed by Steele [26], modified to propagate ordinal and IQ value assertions rather than integers.

The *addition constraint*:

Ordinal relations can propagate among the values of the adder pins at any given time:

$$A = 0 \Leftrightarrow B = C$$
$$B = 0 \Leftrightarrow A = C$$
$$A > 0 \Leftrightarrow B < C$$
$$A < 0 \Leftrightarrow B > C$$
$$B > 0 \Leftrightarrow A < C$$
$$B < 0 \Leftrightarrow A > C$$

The sign of the derivative of A, B, and C at a given time can propagate through the adder.

$$C = A + B$$

+ IQ(A) IQ(B)	inc	std	dec
inc	inc	inc	?
std	inc	std	dec
dec	?	dec	dec

$$B = C - A$$

− IQ(C) IQ(A)	inc	std	dec
inc	?	inc	inc
std	dec	std	inc
dec	dec	dec	?

When inequalities are derived between values taken on by adder pins at different times, they can be propagated through the adder as well.

$$A1 = A2 \ \& \ B1 = B2 \Rightarrow C1 = C2$$
$$A1 = A2 \ \& \ B1 > B2 \Rightarrow C1 > C2$$
$$A1 = A2 \ \& \ B1 < B2 \Rightarrow C1 < C2$$
$$A1 > A2 \ \& \ B1 = B2 \Rightarrow C1 > C2$$
$$A1 > A2 \ \& \ B1 > B2 \Rightarrow C1 > C2$$
$$A1 < A2 \ \& \ B1 = B2 \Rightarrow C1 < C2$$
$$A1 < A2 \ \& \ B1 < B2 \Rightarrow C1 < C2$$

$$A1 = A2 \ \& \ C1 = C2 \Rightarrow B1 = B2$$
$$A1 = A2 \ \& \ C1 > C2 \Rightarrow B1 > B2$$
$$A1 = A2 \ \& \ C1 < C2 \Rightarrow B1 < B2$$
$$A1 > A2 \ \& \ C1 = C2 \Rightarrow B1 < B2$$
$$A1 > A2 \ \& \ C1 < C2 \Rightarrow B1 < B2$$
$$A1 < A2 \ \& \ C1 = C2 \Rightarrow B1 > B2$$
$$A1 < A2 \ \& \ C1 > C2 \Rightarrow B1 > B2$$

The *multiplication constraint*:

Ordinal relations can propagate among the values of the multiplier pins at any given time:

$$A = 0 \Rightarrow C = 0$$
$$B = 0 \Rightarrow C = 0$$

$$A > 0 \ \& \ B > 0 \Rightarrow C > 0$$
$$A < 0 \ \& \ B < 0 \Rightarrow C > 0$$
$$A > 0 \ \& \ B < 0 \Rightarrow C < 0$$
$$A < 0 \ \& \ B > 0 \Rightarrow C < 0$$

$$A > 0 \ \& \ C > 0 \Rightarrow B > 0$$
$$A < 0 \ \& \ C < 0 \Rightarrow B > 0$$
$$A > 0 \ \& \ C < 0 \Rightarrow B < 0$$
$$A < 0 \ \& \ C > 0 \Rightarrow B < 0$$

[The following rules are only valid assuming A, B, C $>$ 0. However, the only examples of multiplication so far are the calculations of concentration and pressure, which all involve physically positive values.]

The sign of the derivative of A, B, and C at a given time can propagate through the multiplier.

$C = A * B$					$B = C/A$			
$* IQ(A)$	inc	std	dec		$/ IQ(C)$	inc	std	dec
$IQ(B)$					$IQ(A)$			
inc	inc	inc	?		inc	?	inc	inc
std	inc	std	dec		std	dec	std	inc
dec	?	dec	dec		dec	dec	dec	?

When inequalities are derived between values taken on by multiplier pins at different times, they can be propagated through the multiplier as well.

$$A1 = A2 \ \& \ B1 = B2 \Rightarrow C1 = C2$$
$$A1 = A2 \ \& \ B1 > B2 \Rightarrow C1 > C2$$
$$A1 = A2 \ \& \ B1 < B2 \Rightarrow C1 < C2$$
$$A1 > A2 \ \& \ B1 = B2 \Rightarrow C1 > C2$$
$$A1 > A2 \ \& \ B1 > B2 \Rightarrow C1 > C2$$
$$A1 < A2 \ \& \ B1 = B2 \Rightarrow C1 < C2$$
$$A1 < A2 \ \& \ B1 < B2 \Rightarrow C1 < C2$$

$$A1 = A2 \ \& \ C1 = C2 \Rightarrow B1 = B2$$
$$A1 = A2 \ \& \ C1 > C2 \Rightarrow B1 > B2$$
$$A1 = A2 \ \& \ C1 < C2 \Rightarrow B1 < B2$$
$$A1 > A2 \ \& \ C1 = C2 \Rightarrow B1 < B2$$
$$A1 > A2 \ \& \ C1 < C2 \Rightarrow B1 < B2$$
$$A1 < A2 \ \& \ C1 = C2 \Rightarrow B1 > B2$$
$$A1 < A2 \ \& \ C1 > C2 \Rightarrow B1 > B2$$

The *functional relationship constraints* state that the two parameters so linked have a functional relationship which is either monotonically increasing (M^+) or monotonically decreasing (M^-), and possibly in which zero corresponds to zero (subscript z).

Y is a *strictly monotonically increasing function* of X:

$$X \longrightarrow \boxed{M_z^+} \longrightarrow Y$$

Information about values of X and Y at a given time can only be propagated if the function passes through the origin (subscript z)

$$X > 0 \Leftrightarrow Y > 0$$
$$X = 0 \Leftrightarrow Y = 0$$
$$X < 0 \Leftrightarrow Y < 0$$

The sign of the derivative at a given time can be propagated.

$$IQ(X) = inc \Leftrightarrow IQ(Y) = inc$$
$$IQ(X) = std \Leftrightarrow IQ(Y) = std$$
$$IQ(X) = dec \Leftrightarrow IQ(Y) = dec$$

An inequality between values of one of the pins at two different times can be propagated to the other pin.

$$X1 > X2 \Leftrightarrow Y1 > Y2$$
$$X1 = X2 \Leftrightarrow Y1 = Y2$$
$$X1 < X2 \Leftrightarrow Y1 < Y2$$

Y is a *strictly monotonically decreasing function* of X:

The sign of the derivative at a given time can also be propagated.

$$IQ(X) = inc \Leftrightarrow IQ(Y) = dec$$
$$IQ(X) = std \Leftrightarrow IQ(Y) = std$$
$$IQ(X) = dec \Leftrightarrow IQ(Y) = inc$$

An inequality between values of one of the pins at two different times can be propagated to the other pin.

$$X1 > X2 \Leftrightarrow Y1 < Y2$$
$$X1 = X2 \Leftrightarrow Y1 = Y2$$
$$X1 < X2 \Leftrightarrow Y1 > Y2$$

The *derivative constraint* holds between a parameter and a rate.

X

| $\frac{d}{dt}$ | ← R

At any given time, the sign of the rate can be propagated to the sign of the derivative of X.

$$R > 0 \Leftrightarrow IQ(X) = inc$$
$$R = 0 \Leftrightarrow IQ(X) = std$$
$$R < 0 \Leftrightarrow IQ(X) = dec$$

There are two versions of these rules, named after the classical theories of motion they resemble [23]. The Aristotelian rule has the benefit of simplicity, while the Newtonian rules are mathematically correct. Appendix E presents an example that illustrates the differences in the behavioral description produced.

Aristotelian:
$IQ(X1) = std \Rightarrow X2 = X1$

Newtonian
$IQ(X1) = std \ \& \ IQ(X2) = std \Rightarrow X2 = X1$
$IQ(X1) = std \ \& \ IQ(X2) = inc \Rightarrow X2 > X1$
$IQ(X1) = std \ \& \ IQ(X2) = dec \Rightarrow X2 < X1$

The *inequality constraint* holds between two parameters and a switch, so that the switch holds the boolean value corresponding to the truth of the given relationship between the values of the parameters at that time.

$A > B \Rightarrow cond = true$
$A = B \Rightarrow cond = false$
$A < B \Rightarrow cond = false$

$cond = true \Rightarrow A > B$

The *conditional constraint* (gate) holds among three parameters, A, B, and C, and a boolean switch, implementing the relationship

if cond = true then C = A else C = B .

$cond = true \Rightarrow C = A$
$cond = false \Rightarrow C = B$

$C = A \Rightarrow cond = true$
$C = B \ \& \ C \neq A \Rightarrow cond = false$

Appendix C. The Envisionment Rules

The *envisionment*, or qualitative simulation of the behavior of a device, proceeds using three types of rules.

(1) *Propagation rules* propagate information across constraints about the values of parameters at a given time-point.

(2) *Prediction rules* determine the nature of the next distinct qualitative-state description from what is known about the current state.

(3) *Recognition rules* detect global properties of the envisionment such as cycles, case-joins, and quiescence.

C.1. Propagation rules

Propagation rules propagate information about the values of parameters at the current time-point according to the relationships among the parameters and constraints describing the structure of the mechanism.

Rule P1. Propagate information (i.e. create a new assertion) for a constraint if enough of its arguments holds new information. (Rules given in Appendix B.)

Rule P2 (Make landmark value). If a value's IQ-value = steady, make that value a landmark value.

Rule P3 (Correspondences). If more than one of the values at the current time-point are landmark values, create a *correspondence*: an alist of (parameter landmark-value) pairs consisting of all the parameters whose current values are landmarks, and which are linked directly or indirectly by monotonic function constraints.

Rule P4 (Contradiction). If propagation derives a contradiction refute the branch containing the value which received the assertion causing the contradiction. If this is the main branch, the entire structural description is at fault.

Rule P5 (Branch on undetermined rate). If the IQ value of a parameter is unknown at the current time-point, and if it is the 'X' argument of a derivative relation, then branch the envisionment according to the assumptions:

$$IQ(X) = inc; \ IQ(X) = std; \ IQ(X) = dec \ .$$

Landmark values are only acquired by being built into the structural description (e.g. the speed limit is 55 mph), or being detected as critical points of functions (Rule P2).

C.2. Prediction rules

The configuration of changing values (the parameters whose current IQ value is not steady) can be analyzed to select the state or states that immediately succeed the current state. The decision tree below can be seen by inspection to exhaust all cases.

The notation specifies only the values of those parameters which are changing; all others are assumed steady. The current value of a parameter is given by a capital letter, followed by its IQ value (direction of change) in parentheses: A(inc) or B(dec). The value of the same parameter in the time-point created by the envisionment rule is A' or B' respectively. Landmark values are starred; sharing the same letter (A and A*) simply signifies that A* is a landmark value which does or will have some important relationship with A. If the result of an envisionment rule is a branch, the rule is written with multiple arrows ('⇒') and consequents.

0. No changing values ⇒ no next state.
1. One changing value (A)
   1.1 equal to a landmark value: (move from landmark value)
      [A(inc) = A*] ⇒ [A* < A']
   1.2 moving toward a landmark value: (move to limit)
      [A(inc) < A*] ⇒ [A* = A']
   1.3 not moving toward a landmark value:
      [A(inc)] ⇒ [A < A'] (next state will have same description as current state)
2. Two changing values (A and B)
   2.1 both equal to landmark values:
      [A(inc) = A*; B(inc) = B*] ⇒ [A* < A'; B* < B']
   2.2 one equal to landmark value:
      [A(inc) = A*; B(inc)] ⇒ [A* < A; B < B']
   2.3 neither equal to landmark values:
      2.3.1 A and B in different units: not comparable.
         2.3.1.1 neither approaching a limit:
            [A(inc); B(inc)] ⇒ [A < A'; B < B']
         2.3.1.2 one approaching a limit:
            [A(inc) < A*; B(inc) ⇒ [A* = A'; B < B']
         2.3.1.3 both approaching limits: (non-deterministic move-to-limit)
            [A(inc) < A*; B(inc) < B*] ⇒ [A* = A'; B* = B']
                                ⇒ [A* = A'; B < B' < B*]
                                  ⇒ [A < A' < A*; B* = B']
      2.3.2 A < B
         2.3.2.1 both moving the same way: A(inc) < B(inc)
           (a) no limits:
              [A(inc) < B(inc)] ⇒ [A' = B']
                             ⇒ [A' < B']
           (b) one limit for both values:
              [A(inc) < B(inc) < L*] ⇒ [A' = B' = L*]
                                  ⇒ [A' < B' = L*]
                                  ⇒ [B < A' = B' < L*]

(c) one limit point between A and B: (= case 2.3.1.2)

$[A(inc) < A^* < B(inc)] \Rightarrow [A' = A^* < B < B']$

(d) two separate limit points: (= case 2.3.1.3)

$[A(inc) < A^* < B(inc) < B^*] \Rightarrow [A^* = A' < B^* = B']$

$\Rightarrow [A^* = A' < B < B' < B^*]$

$\Rightarrow [A < A' < A^* < B^* = B']$

2.3.2.2 moving toward each other: A(inc) < B(dec)

(a) no limits between them:

$[A(inc) < B(dec)] \Rightarrow [A' = B']$

(b) one limit point between them: (= case 2.3.1.3)

$[A(inc) < L < B(dec)] \Rightarrow [A' = L^* = B']$

$\Rightarrow [A' = L^* < B']$

$\Rightarrow [A' < L^* = B']$

(c) two limit points between them: (= case 2.3.1.3)

$[A(inc) < A^* < B^* < B(dec)] \Rightarrow [A' = A^* < B^* = B']$

$\Rightarrow [A' = A^* < B^* < B']$

$\Rightarrow [A' < A^* < B^* = B']$

2.3.2.3 moving away from each other: A(dec) < B(inc)

(a) no limits on either side:

$[A(dec) < B(inc)] \Rightarrow [A' < A < B < B']$

(b) one limit point: (= case 2.3.1.2)

$[A^* < A(dec) < B(inc)] \Rightarrow [A^* = A' < B']$

(c) a limit point on each side: (= case 2.3.1.3)

$[A^* < A(dec) < B(inc) < B^*] \Rightarrow [A^* = A' < B' = B^*]$

$\Rightarrow [A^* = A' < B' < B^*]$

$\Rightarrow [A^* < A' < B' = B^*]$

2.3.3 A = B

2.3.3.1 moving same way:

$[A(inc) = B(inc)] \Rightarrow [A' = B']$

$\Rightarrow [A' < B']$

$\Rightarrow [A' > B']$

2.3.3.2 moving opposite ways:

$[A(dec) = B(inc)] \Rightarrow [A' < B']$

2.3.4 comparable but unknown relationship:

(branch on relation; then use cases 2.3.2 and 2.3.3)

3. More than two changing values

3.1 If any changing value is equal to a landmark value
or moving in a direction with no limit point,
then perturb each value in the direction of motion
(see cases 1.1 and 1.3).

3.2 If no changing values are equal to landmark values
and some changing values are moving toward limit points
and a correspondence exists among all those limit points,

then the next values of those changing parameters are equal to their limit points
and any changing parameters without limits are perturbed in their direction of
change.

3.3 If no changing values are equal to landmark values
and some changing values are moving toward limit points
and the limit points divide into exactly two sets of corresponding values,
then branch according to the non-deterministic move-to-limit rule (case 2.3.1.3)
and any changing parameters without limits are perturbed in their direction of
change.

3.4 Otherwise the current state is declared "Intractible".

We are currently experimenting with alternate formulations of the prediction
rules which may enable us to handle certain cases difficult to express in the
decision-tree format. Thus the definition of 'intractible' for the envisionment
system is likely to change.

C.3. Recognition rules

Recognition rules recognize global configurations in the envisionment that
allow the set of time-points to be simplified.

Rule R1. If all IQ values are steady, then *recognize a quiescent system*. Remove the
current time-point from the set of active time-points. If there are no more active
time-points, stop.

Rule R2. If all values at the current time-point are equal to landmark values, and all
values were equal to the same landmark values at a previous time-point, and all IQ
values match in the two time-points, then *recognize a cycle*. Replace the current
time-point with a pointer to the previous, identical, time-point, and remove the current
time-point from the set of active time-points, since its successors are now known.

Rule R3. If all values at the current time-point are equal to landmark values, and there
is a time-point on an alternate branch all of whose values are equal to the same
landmark values, and all of the IQ values match, then *recognize a case-join*. Replace
both time-points with pointers to a special case-join descriptor. In case the case-join
captures all the surviving branches of a case-split, map the join into a new time-point
related to the one at which the case-split occurred. (See Fig. 12 in the text.)

Appendix D. Summarizing the Structural Description

The syntactic transformation rules for summarizing the causal-structure description are the following (in mathematical notation, rather than graph
diagrams). They are applied repeatedly until the structural description cannot
be simplified further.

The transformation is implemented by installing the new constraint, linked with the existing parameters. The existing constraints are left in place but 'turned off' so their rules are no longer activated in response to newly asserted values.

1. Arithmetic constraint with one constant.

$$x + y = z \ \& \ \text{constant}(y) \Rightarrow z = M^+(x)$$
$$x + y = z \ \& \ \text{constant}(z) \Rightarrow y = M^-(x)$$

$$x * y = z \ \& \ y > 0 \ \& \ \text{constant}(y) \Rightarrow z = M_z^+(x)$$
$$x * y = z \ \& \ z > 0 \ \& \ \text{constant}(z) \Rightarrow y = M^-(x)$$

2. Composition of functional constraints.

$$y = M^+(M^+(x)) \Rightarrow y = M^+(x)$$
$$y = M^+(M^-(x)) \Rightarrow y = M^-(x)$$
$$y = M^-(M^+(x)) \Rightarrow y = M^-(x)$$
$$y = M^-(M^-(x)) \Rightarrow y = M^+(x)$$

$$y = M_z^+(M_z^+(x)) \Rightarrow y = M_z^+(x)$$
$$y = M_z^+(M_{\bar{z}}^-(x)) \Rightarrow y = M_{\bar{z}}^-(x)$$
$$y = M_{\bar{z}}^-(M_z^+(x)) \Rightarrow y = M_{\bar{z}}^-(x)$$
$$y = M_{\bar{z}}^-(M_{\bar{z}}^-(x)) \Rightarrow y = M_z^+(x)$$

3. Sum of functional constraints with same net effect.

$$y = M^+(x) + M^+(x) \Rightarrow y = M^+(x)$$
$$y = M^-(x) + M^-(x) \Rightarrow y = M^-(x)$$

$$y = M^+(x) - M^-(x) \Rightarrow y = M^+(x)$$
$$y = M^-(x) - M^+(x) \Rightarrow y = M^-(x)$$

$$y = M_z^+(x) + M_z^+(x) \Rightarrow y = M_z^+(x)$$
$$y = M_{\bar{z}}^-(x) + M_{\bar{z}}^-(x) \Rightarrow y = M_{\bar{z}}^-(x)$$

$$y = M_z^+(x) - M_{\bar{z}}^-(x) \Rightarrow y = M_z^+(x)$$
$$y = M_{\bar{z}}^-(x) - M_z^+(x) \Rightarrow y = M_{\bar{z}}^-(x)$$

Appendix E. Momentum and Cyclic Behavior

In examining the envisionment of the double heat-flow system, people occasionally ask about momentum: *"What if the value keeps on going rather than stopping at its limit?"* Naturally, this can only occur if the system is sufficiently complex to support that behavior, and if that complexity is reflected in the causal structure description. The example of the oscillating spring demonstrates both momentum and the creation of important new landmark values. This system is governed by the differential equation:

$$\frac{d^2}{dt^2} X = M_z^-(X),$$

or, more precisely, by the system of equations:

$$\frac{d}{dt} X = V, \qquad \frac{d}{dt} V = A, \qquad A = M_z^-(X).$$

In addition to demonstrating cyclic behavior, the oscillating spring (Fig. 15) demonstrates the use of the Aristotelian and Newtonian motion rules associated with the derivative constraint (see Appendix B). In particular, the chart below uses the Aristotelian rule applied to the variable V, in the transition from (3) to (4). This has the curious effect that the IQ value of V changes from steady to increasing while V remains equal to VMIN. Only in the transition from (4) to (5) does the change to the IQ value propagate to cause V > VMIN. Thus, when comparing the behavioral description with the physical world, state (4) is not actually distinct from states (3) and (5), but is a computationally required transitional pseudo-state.

The more complex Newtonian motion rule makes the correct transition from (3) directly to (5). It produces the same behavioral description as shown below, omitting states (4), (7), (10), and (14). One may speculate that the obvious differences in rule complexity is one reason for the observed differences in theories of motion, both across history and in naive subjects [23].

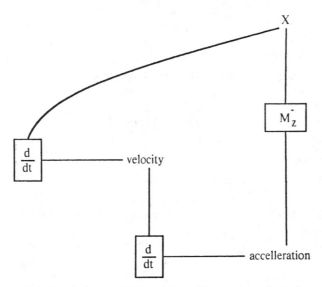

FIG. 15. Causal-structure description: oscillating spring without energy dissipation.

The following chart gives the ordinal assertions and the IQ value assertion for the value of x, v, and a, respectively, at each time-point. The last column gives the rules, other than simple propagation, used to generate each value (Appendix C). The terms that are underlined in each row are the initial information with which that time-point was created from its predecessor.

(1)	$x \geq 0$	std	$v = 0$	dec	$a < 0$	std	given
(2)	$x > 0$	dec	$v \leq 0$	dec	$a < 0$	inc	Rule 1.1
(3)	$x = 0$	dec	$v < 0$	std	$a = 0$	inc	Rule 3.2
			$vmin = v3$				Rule P2 (v)
(4)	$x \leq 0$	dec	$v = vmin < 0$	inc	$a \geq 0$	inc	Rule 2.1
(5)	$x < 0$	dec	$vmin < v < 0$	inc	$a > 0$	inc	Rule 3.1
(6)	$x < 0$	std	$v = 0$	inc	$a > 0$	std	Rule 3.2
	$xmin = x6$				$amax = a6$		Rule P2 (x, a)
(7)	$x = xmin < 0$	inc	$v \geq 0$	inc	$a = amax > 0$	dec	Rule 1.1
(8)	$xmin \leq x \leq 0$	inc	$v > 0$	inc	$0 < a \leq amax$	dec	Rule 3.1
(9)	$x = 0$	inc	$v > 0$	std	$a = 0$	dec	Rule 3.2
			$vmax = v9$				Rule P2 (v)
(10)	$x \geq 0$	inc	$v = vmax > 0$	dec	$a < 0$	dec	Rule 2.1
(11)	$x > 0$	inc	$0 < v < vmax$	dec	$a < 0$	dec	Rule 3.1
(12)	$x > 0$	std	$v = 0$	dec	$a < 0$	std	Rule 3.2
	$xmax = x12$				$amin = a12$		Rule P2 (x, a)
(13)	$x = xmax$	dec	$vmin < v < 0$	dec	$a = amin$	inc	Rule 1.1
(14)	$0 \leq x \leq xmax$	dec	$vmin < v < 0$	dec	$amin \leq a < 0$	inc	Rule 3.1
(15)	$x = 0$	dec	$v = vmin$	std	$a = 0$	inc	Rule 3.2

MATCH detected with state (3).   Rule R2

Summarized cycle (landmark values only):

(3)	$x = 0$	dec	$v = vmin$	std	$a = 0$	inc
(6)	$x = xmin$	std	$v = 0$	inc	$a = amax$	std
(9)	$x = 0$	inc	$v = vmax$	std	$a = 0$	dec
(12)	$x = xmax$	std	$v = 0$	dec	$a = amin$	std
(3)	$x = 0$	dec	$v = vmin$	std	$a = 0$	inc

ACKNOWLEDGMENT

Christopher Eliot is responsible for the implementation of this system, and has made substantial contributions to its design. Ken Church, Ken Forbus, Ramesh Patil, and Peter Szolovits have also provided helpful comments.

REFERENCES

1. Barrow, H., Proving the correctness of digital hardware designs, in: *Proceedings National Conference on Artificial Intelligence*, Washington, DC, August, 1983.
2. Brown, J.S. and Van Lehn, K., Repair theory: a generative theory of bugs in procedural skills, *Cognitive Sci.* **4**(4) (1980).

3. Chi, M.T.H., Feltovich, P.J. and Glaser, R., Categorization and representation of physics problems by experts and novices, *Cognitive Sci.* **5** (1981) 121–152.
4. Davis, R., Shrobe, H., Hamscher, W., Wieckert, K., Shirley, M. and Polit, S., Diagnosis based on description of structure and function, in: *Proceedings National Conference on Artificial Intelligence*, Pittsburgh, PA (August, 1982) 137–142.
5. Davis, R., Diagnosis via causal reasoning: Paths of interaction and the locality principle, in: *Proceedings National Conference on Artificial Intelligence*, Washington, DC, August, 1983.
6. De Kleer, J., Multiple representations of knowledge in a mechanics problem-solver, in: *Proceedings Fifth International Joint Conference on Artificial Intelligence*, Cambridge, MA, August, 1977.
7. De Kleer, J., The origin and resolution of ambiguities in causal arguments, in: *Proceedings Sixth International Joint Conference on Artificial Intelligence*, Tokyo, Japan (August, 1979) 197–203.
8. De Kleer, J. and Brown, J.S., Mental models of physical mechanisms and their acquisition, in: J.R. Anderson (Ed.), *Cognitive Skills and Their Acquisition* (Erlbaum, Hillsdale, NJ, 1981).
9. De Kleer, J. and Brown, J.S., The origin, form and logic of qualitative physical laws, in: *Proceedings Eighth International Joint Conference on Artificial Intelligence*, Karlsruhe, West-Germany, August, 1983.
10. Eliot, C. and Kuipers, B., *ENV manual*, Tufts University TMX Memo No. 15, Medford, MA, 1983.
11. Forbus, K.D., Qualitative reasoning about physical processes, in: *Proceedings Seventh International Joint Conference on Artificial Intelligence*, Vancouver, BC, August 1981.
12. Forbus, K.D., Qualitative process theory, *Artificial Intelligence* **24** (1984) this volume.
13. Forrester, J., *Urban Dynamics* (MIT, Cambridge, MA, 1969).
14. Genesereth, M.R., Diagnosis using hierarchical design models, in: *Proceedings National Conference on Artificial Intelligence*, Pittsburgh, PA, August, 1982.
15. Gentner, D. and Stevens, A. (Eds.), *Mental Models* (Erlbaum, Hillsdale, NJ, 1983).
16. Hayes, P.J., The naive physics manifesto, in: D. Michie (Ed.), *Expert Systems in the Micro Electronic Age* (Edinburgh University Press, Edinburgh, 1979).
17. Hayes, P.J., Naive physics I: Ontology for liquids, Department of Computer Science, University of Essex, 1978.
18. Kuipers, B.J., On representing commonsense knowledge, in: N.V. Findler (Ed.), *Associative Networks: The Representation and Use of Knowledge by Computers* (Academic Press, New York, 1979).
19. Kuipers, B.J., De Kleer and Brown's "Mental Models"; A critique, Tufts University Working Papers in Cognitive Science, No. 17, Medford, MA, 1981.
20. Kuipers, B.J. and Kassirer, J.P., Causal reasoning in medicine: Analysis of a protocol, *Cognitive Sci.* **8** (1984) 363–385.
21. Kuipers, B.J., Programs that understand how the body works, in: *Proceedings Second IEEE Computer Society International Conference and 1983 Stocker Symposium on Medical Computer Science and Computational Medicine (MEDCOMP '83)*, Athens County, OH, September, 1983.
22. Larkin, J., McDermott, J., Simon, D.P. and Simon, H.A., Expert and novice performance in solving physics problems, *Science* **208** (1980) 1335–1342.
23. McCloskey, M., Caramazza, A. and Green, B., Curvilinear motion in the absence of external forces: Naive beliefs about the motion of objects, *Science* **210** (1980) 1139–1141.
24. McDermott, D., A temporal logic for reasoning about processes and plans, *Cognitive Sci.* **6** (1982) 101–155.
25. Rieger, C. and Grinberg, M., The declarative representation and procedural simulation of causality in physical mechanisms, in: *Proceedings Fifth International Joint Conference on Artificial Intelligence*, Cambridge, MA, August, 1977.
26. Steele, G.L., Jr., The definition and implementation of a computer programming language based on constraints, MIT Artificial Intelligence Laboratory TR-595, Cambridge, MA, 1980.
27. Weiss, S.M., Kulikowski, C.A., Amarel, S. and Safir, A., A model-based method for computer-aided medical decision-making, *Artificial Intelligence* **11** (1970) 145–172.

Received October 1983

How Circuits Work

Johan de Kleer

Xerox PARC, Intelligent Systems Laboratory, Palo Alto, CA 94304, U.S.A.

ABSTRACT

This paper presents a theory of commonsense understanding of the behavior of electronic circuits. It is based on the intuitive qualitative reasoning electrical engineers use when they analyze circuits. This intuitive reasoning provides a great deal of important information about the operation of the circuit, which although qualitative in nature, describes important quantitative aspects of circuit functioning (feedback paths, stability, impedance and gain estimates, etc.).

One aspect of the theory, causal analysis, describes how the behavior of the individual components can be combined to explain the behavior of composite systems. Another aspect of the theory, teleological analysis, describes how the notion that the system has a purpose can be used to structure and aid this causal analysis. The theory is implemented in a computer program, EQUAL, which, given a circuit topology, can construct by qualitative causal analysis a description of the mechanism by which the circuit operates. This mechanism is then parsed by a grammar for circuit functions.

1. Introduction

This theory explains how the function of a circuit (i.e., its purpose) is related to its structure (i.e., its schematic). This issue is explored by showing how the function of a circuit is derived from its structure. The intermediate point between structure and function is behavior. Structure is what the device is, and function is what the device is for, but behavior is what the device does. Causal reasoning analyzes how disturbances from an operating point propagate through a circuit. It thereby determines the qualitative behavior of a circuit from its structure. In addition, unlike quantitative predictions it produces intuitive, causal explanations for the behavioral predictions. These behavioral predictions, combined with their explanations, form the basis for reasoning which explains how the purposes of the circuit are achieved by that behavior.

The research reported here contributes to the field of qualitative reasoning in six ways:

(1) *Qualitative physics.* The causal reasoning used for analyzing circuits is based on earlier work on qualitative physics [6–8]. This paper restates only the

barest essentials of qualitative physics. Those papers are concerned with the broad fundamental issues and (purposely) neither present any detailed examples nor explore any domain in particular. This paper contains a detailed qualitative physics for a particular domain: electronics. It shows how the concepts and distinctions of qualitative physics are used to analyze a wide variety of electronic circuits. The power of these techniques, which seem artificial when applied to the simple examples of the earlier papers, can thus be illustrated. In addition, it is possible to be explicit about AI applications for a qualitative theory of circuit behavior.

(2) *Teleological reasoning*. Although qualitative physics describes the behavior of physical artifacts, it says little about their function. Devices are designed by man to achieve some purpose. These purposes provide an alternative method for understanding the behaviors of physical systems. This paper presents a theory of teleology for physical systems and develops the details of one for electronic circuits.

(3) *Structure and function*. Qualitative physics integrates with other kinds of knowledge. This paper presents a theory for how the function of a device is related to its structure. The basic idea is that the qualitative physics relates structure to behavior and teleology relates behavior to function. Thus it is able to construct a complete account for how a particular device achieves its intended function.

(4) *Qualitative vs. quantitative*. One of the central driving intuitions behind qualitative physics is the idea that in reasoning about an artifact one first obtains a deep intuitive understanding of how the artifact works and then uses this deep understanding to guide further, perhaps quantitative analysis. Most of the potential applications of qualitative reasoning to electronics discussed in the conclusions are based on this idea.

(5) *Architecture*. The computation which uses the qualitative physics to produce accounts for behavior is surprisingly complex. This paper includes discussion of some of the critical architectural decisions involved in implementing the system. The necessity for the complications only becomes clear by considering more complex examples than those discussed in the earlier qualitative physics papers.

(6) *Electronics*. All the major contributions of this paper require working through the details of a particular qualitative physics. I have chosen electronics, primarily because of my familiarity with that subject matter. As a consequence, some of the sections may be difficult to follow. Section 2 on the qualitative physics of circuits is sufficiently elementary that if the reader did not know how a transistor worked before he or she can learn that from reading the paper. However, Section 6 on teleological reasoning may be harder to follow. This should not be surprising: teleology relates behavior to function and the function is expressed within the technical jargon of electrical engineering. If it were otherwise, my project would be a failure. The research contribution here

is not for electrical engineers—they already know their own jargon. The contribution is to AI: a technique for constructing accounts in the language of the experts (i.e., electrical engineers).

Although this paper concentrates on electronics, the underlying qualitative physics, the framework of teleological analysis, and the algorithms are all domain-independent. Only the component models, component configurations, and some of the teleological parsing rules are idiosyncratically electrical. For example, the ideas and techniques apply to hydraulic, acoustic, thermal as well as electrical systems.

1.1. Methodology

One of the ultimate goals of qualitative physics research is to develop a sufficiently complete account of reasoning about designed artifacts (such as electrical circuits) so that it can be automated. This research programme presumes that there is a coherent and parsimonious collection of theories which underlie expert human performance which needs to be uncovered before any reasonable fragment of an engineer's skill can be automated. These different theories are hard to identify, and must be studied in isolation in order to uncover their power and limitations.

This paper presents two related theories of the many engineers must use to understand circuit behavior. This is not intended to be a psychological theory of how human engineers actually work. Engineers use a variety of techniques for reasoning about circuits, most of which are not discussed in this paper. Perhaps, the most relevant of these involves geometry and teleology. Presented with a circuit, an engineer will recognize familiar circuit fragments and recall their function. In fact, engineers have explicit geometric conventions for drawing well-known circuit fragments. Furthermore, an engineer usually has a pretty good idea of what the new circuit is for, and he uses this teleological information to help guide his analysis of the circuit.

Studying causal reasoning in isolation is not taking an easy road. Causal reasoning encounters severe complexities which can usually be resolved by incorporating teleological or geometrical knowledge. If I were interested in building a performance program, the temptation for including this extra knowledge would be overwhelming. However, that would be shortsighted. To understand what causal reasoning, or teleological reasoning is, one must study it in isolation uncorrupted by other forms of reasoning. Otherwise one has merged two types of reasoning without ever identifying either one individually. In addition little scientific progress is made and we are not much closer to the ultimate goal as the limitations of the resulting system are completely unclear and extending the system may prove impossible. To achieve robust performance, the underlying theories must be identified.

This methodology stands in sharp contradistinction with the popular expert-systems methodology. Expert systems are aimed at producing what performance is possible in the short term without consideration of the longer term. Typically this is achieved by recording as many of the heuristics and rules of thumb that experts actually use in practice, as possible. This is misguided. The reasoning of experts is based on underlying theories that must be teased out. The expert systems approach can be caricatured as a stimulus–response model—good for some purposes, but ineffective in the long run.

The primary reason for initially starting with causal and teleological reasoning is that these two are basic to most of the other forms of reasoning about artifacts. For example, although recognition plays various roles in reasoning about circuits, its major task is to reduce the new device to something previously analyzed. Thus recognition is parasitic on other forms of reasoning. An additional pragmatic reason for isolating teleological reasoning from causal reasoning is that teleology is an external point of view established by the designer on the circuit. The circuit may or may not behave as intended, therefore it is important for causal reasoning to be able to identify all the possibilities independent of teleology.

1.2. EQUAL

Both the causal reasoning and teleological reasoning components have been completely implemented and run on hundreds of circuits. The program, EQUAL, takes as input the schematic for the circuit. As output it produces a qualitative prediction of the circuit's behavior, an explanation for that behavior, and a teleological parse which relates every component to the purposes of the overall circuit.

EQUAL need not be told the purpose of the circuit, as it can infer this itself. This is not as difficult a task as it might seem as the circuit is presumed to be a power-supply, logic-gate, amplifier or multivibrator where AC affects are unimportant.

In performing its causal analysis, EQUAL utilizes a component model library which describes the behavior of every type of electrical component. The teleological reasoning, on the other hand, utilizes a grammar of basic mechanisms (*not schematic fragments*), to parse the circuit's behavior.

2. The Basics of a Qualitative Physics for Circuits

Most circuits are designed to deal with changing inputs or loads. For example, an amplifier must amplify changes in its input, digital circuits must switch their internal states as applied signals change, and power-supplies must provide constant current or voltage in the face of changing loads and power sources. The purposes of these kinds of circuits is best understood by examining how they respond to change. Thus, causal analysis is primarily concerned with how circuits, in some equilibrium state, respond to input perturbations.

2.1. Causal analysis

When an electrical engineer is asked to explain the operation of an electrical system he will often describe it in terms of a sequence of events each of which is 'caused' by previous events. Each event is an assertion about some behavioral parameter of some constituent of the system (e.g., current through a resistor). Sequential descriptions are ubiquitous in engineers' verbal and text-book explanations. Consider the Schmitt trigger (Fig. 1). The explanation reads as if a time flow has been imposed on it.

> "... An increase in v_I augments the forward bias on the emitter junction of the first transistor, thereby causing an incremental increase in the collector current, i_{C1} of that transistor. Consequently both the collector-to-ground voltage v_1 of the first transistor, and the base-to-ground voltage of the second transistor v_3, decrease. The second transistor operates as an emitter follower which has an additional load resistor on the collector. Therefore, there is a decrease in the emitter-to-ground voltage v_2. This decrease in v_2 causes the forward bias at the emitter of the first transistor to increase even more than would occur as a consequence of the initial increase in v_I alone ..." [19, p. 68]

The theories of qualitative, causal, and teleological reasoning provide the inference mechanisms to support this kind of explanation. The basic characteristics of the theory are evident in the preceding quote.

The usual notion of variable. The variables mentioned, e.g., v_I, v_1, etc., are the same ones used in quantitative analysis.

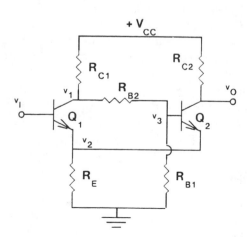

FIG. 1. The Schmitt trigger.

The explanation focuses on change. The most significant arena of behavior is how the circuit responds to input perturbations such as an increase in input.

Change is described qualitatively. All circuit quantities are described qualitatively: increasing, decreasing or unchanging.

The explanation contains unstated assumptions. Why does the v_1 increment appear across Q_1 instead of R_E? Why does the voltage v_1 drop, as Q_2's turning-off should raise it? Why is the current contributed by Q_2's turning-off more than the current taken by Q_1's turning-on? All of these undesired possibilities occur if the component parameters are chosen inappropriately. Thus, they truly are assumptions. Although the actual values of the parameters can be used to validate assumptions, engineers rarely do so. Rather teleological reasoning is used to differentiate among the possibilities.

Flow of causality. The explanation is in terms of a sequence of events each caused by preceding events. The increase in v_1 causes the increase in forward bias, which in turn causes an increase in i_{C1}, etc.

Prediction and explanation. The description of the Schmitt trigger both predicts qualitative values for circuit quantities and explains these values. Causal analysis is just one of many ways for explaining qualitative behavior. A causal explanation is a qualitative description of the equilibrating process that ensues when a signal is applied to the circuit. Before examining causal explanation, we must consider qualitative values and qualitative component models.

2.2. Forms of causality

Circuit theory is based on the notion of equilibrium conditions (see Section 3.3 for more details), and not on any notion of causality. Causality is a framework externally imposed by electrical engineers. One view of this causality is that it is a crude rendition of what actually happens when the circuit is examined closely (i.e., propagation of electrical fields) and that causality arises out of the solution of partial differential equations. Another view (and not necessarily inconsistent with the first), upon which this paper is based, is that causality arises out of viewing the system has a collection of information processors. Causation arises out of the passing of information between the parts of the system. Therefore we begin by examining the language for describing the behavior of system components.

2.3. Qualitative variables

The qualitative value of the expression x is denoted $[x]$. For brevity sake, $[d^n x/dt^n]$ is abbreviated $\partial^n x$ and $\partial^0 x$ sometimes used for $[x]$. A qualitative variable can only take on one of a small number of values. These values correspond to intervals separated by points at which transitions of interest occur. One quantity space [16] of particular interest is the sign of a quantity: $[x] = +$ iff $x > 0$, $[x] = 0$ iff $x = 0$ and $[x] = -$ iff $x < 0$.

The behavior of components is described by qualitative equations (called confluences). Qualitative multiplication is easily defined for this quantity space as $[x][y] = [xy]$. Unfortunately, addition is more complicated. $[x] + [y] = [x + y]$ unless $[x] = -[y] \neq 0$ in which case addition is undefined.

2.4. Qualitative quiescent and incremental analysis

Qualitative analysis utilizes a generalization of the electrical engineering distinction between quiescent and incremental analysis. The quiescent value of the quantity refers to the operating-point value (or steady-state value after the transients have died out). The incremental value is the deviation from the quiescent value. Using this distinction, circuit analysis is subdivided into two relatively independent subtasks: quiescent analysis with quiescent models and incremental analysis with incremental models.

Qualitative analysis generalizes this approach in two ways. First, the quiescent value of a quantity is defined to be its qualitative value and the incremental value of a quantity is defined to be the qualitative value of its rate of change.[1] Second, instead of having only quiescent and incremental models, qualitative analysis has models for every derivative order. The zero-order models are the quiescent models and the first-order models are the incremental models. As change is of primary interest, this paper concentrates on incremental qualitative analyis.

2.5. Qualitative models for simple components

As in conventional electrical engineering we must take care in constructing the component models. The no-function-in-structure principle of qualitative physics states that each component of the same type must be modeled in the same way: we may not choose an idiosyncratic component model to handle a behavior of a particular circuit. Said differently, the component model must characterize the essential generic behavior of the component type. Otherwise, the structure-to-function analysis would be of little value because the structural choices already contained functional information.

Admittedly, a human engineer will use different quantitative models for different tasks, but he will only do so because he already understands how the circuit works and which approximations are valid. Presumably an analogous

---

[1]This does some violence to the usual electrical engineering notions. Usually, the total variable is defined to be the sum of the quiescent and incremental values for some small deviations from the operating point. In qualitative analysis, the quiescent value is defined to be the qualitative value of the total variable. The only reason this makes sense with regard to the usual engineering conventions is that the coarseness of the qualitative-value space makes deviations in a unit time interval and derivatives indistinguishable.

process occurs in selecting the qualitative models. However, the validity of the qualitative predictions directly depend on the quality of the component models he chooses. Unsubstantiated violations of the no-function-in-structure principle will lead to a faulty understanding of circuit behavior and function.

Constructing component models is a surprisingly difficult task. The standard engineering models that describe the behavior of electrical components are widely agreed upon. However, the causal qualitative models that people use to reason about circuits are not. These models are rarely articulated, even though the tacit models that underlie people's arguments appear to be very similar. One of the contributions of this research is a specification of these qualitative models. The approach for constructing the models is to start with the classical constraint models [13, 18] and reformulate them in qualitative terms. For simple components this process is relatively direct. Kirchhoff's laws are particularly easy to model qualitatively.

2.5.1. *Kirchhoff's current law*

The most basic network constraint is Kirchhoff's current law (KCL). It states that the sum of the currents i_j flowing into a component or node (or set of components and nodes) must be zero:

$$\sum i_j = 0 , \tag{1}$$

where i_j are the currents in the terminals of the node, component or the boundary terminals of a set of nodes and components. In qualitative terms KCL is:

$$\sum [i_j] = 0 . \tag{2}$$

However, for causal analysis the change in the quantities is more important than the quantities themselves. Differentiating equation (1) gives:

$$\sum di_j/dt = 0 . \tag{3}$$

Thus, qualitatively:

$$\sum \partial i_i = 0 . \tag{4}$$

Note that while equation (1) implies (3), equation (2) does not imply (4). An unfortunate fact of the qualitative algebra is that $d[x]/dt$ cannot be defined in terms of $[x]$, but rather as $d[x]/dt = [dx/dt]$. Just because $[x] = [y]$ does not imply that $[dx/dt] = [dy/dt]$. For example, $[1] = [1 + x^2]$, but $[0] \neq [2x]$. Thus, although the qualitative calculus has the notion of derivative, it has no general definition of differentiation. As a consequence, in general, a separate qualitative equation must be written each time a higher-order derivative is introduced. Fortunately, if a component is linear, all of its higher-order models have the same form. KCL is linear, thus the complete KCL model is:

i_0 = current in terminal 0 ,

.

.

.

i_n = current in terminal n ,

$\sum \partial^k i_j = 0$ for $k = 0, 1, \ldots$.

A law like Kirchhoff's current law is needed for many physical domains. The analogous law for fluid systems is conservation of matter, for thermal systems, conservation of energy, for mechanical systems, Newton's law for equilibrium of forces at a point.[2]

2.5.2. *Kirchhoff's voltage law*

Kirchhoff's voltage law states the sum of all voltages around any loop is zero. Qualitatively, for every loop of k nodes $n_1, \ldots, n_k, n_{k+1} = n_1$:

$$\sum_{i=1}^{k} \partial^m v_{n_i, n_{i+1}} = 0 \quad \text{for } m = 0, 1, \ldots .$$

A law like Kirchhoff's voltage law is needed for many physical domains. The analogous law for fluid systems is that pressures must add (e.g., the sum of the pressure from point A to point B and the pressure from point B to point C must equal the pressure from point A to point C). For thermal and mechanical systems, temperatures and velocities must sum similarly.[3]

2.5.3. *Ohm's law*

Ohm's law has a particularly simple formulation. Assuming that resistors have fixed positive resistance, Ohm's law $v = iR$ is expressed qualitatively as $[v] = [i]$. Currents are defined to flow into components away from nodes. The complete resistor model is:

i = the current in terminal 1 ,
v = the voltage from terminal 1 to terminal 2 ,
$\partial^k v = \partial^k i$.

---

[2]These are all instances of the continuity condition of system dynamics [27] which is incorporated into qualitative physics [6].

[3]These are all instances of the compatibility condition of system dynamics [27]. which is incorporated into qualitative physics [6].

2.5.4. *Batteries*

Batteries are also modeled simply. An ideal battery supplies constant voltage:

v = voltage from terminal 1 to terminal 2 ,

$[v] = +$, $\qquad \partial^n v = 0$, $\quad n > 0$.

2.5.5. *Bipolar transistors*

Transistors[4] have the incremental model

$\partial v_{b,e}$ = voltage from the base to emitter ,

∂i_c = current flowing into the collector ,

∂i_e = current flowing into the emitter ,

∂i_b = current flowing into the base ,

$\partial v_{b,e} \Rightarrow \partial i_c$, $\quad \partial v_{b,e} - \Rightarrow \partial i_e$, $\quad \partial v_{b,e} \Rightarrow \partial i_b$.

$\partial v_{b,e} \Rightarrow \partial i_c$ indicates that $\partial v_{b,e} = \partial i_c$, but $\partial v_{b,e}$ causes ∂i_c, not vice versa. Likewise, $\partial v_{b,e} - \Rightarrow \partial i_e$ indicates that $\partial v_{b,e} = -\partial i_e$, but that the change in $v_{b,e}$ causes the change in ∂i_c. (The model for the transistor's other operating regions is presented in Section 9.)

2.6. Sign conventions

To readers familiar with the problems of sign conventions, this section is hopelessly pedantic and can be ignored.

There is an immense amount of confusion surrounding sign conventions. This is not helped by the fact that engineers are often rather cavalier about choosing them and often the precise meanings of variables are never made explicit. However, to formulate the component models and present the arguments constructed by EQUAL the sign conventions must be consistent. Admittedly, there is no significant information content in the sign conventions of variables, but without a precise definition of the quantities involved, the models and explanations are meaningless. The voltage from node 1 to 2 is notated $v_{1,2}$. The current flowing into R1 through terminal #1 is notated $i_{\rightarrow \#1(R1)}$ (which is sometimes abbreviated $i_{\#1(R1)}$) and the current out of R1, $i_{\leftarrow \#1(R1)}$.

As a consequence every circuit quantity can be expressed in two ways: $v_{1,2} = -v_{2,1}$ and $i_{\rightarrow \#1(R1)} = -i_{\leftarrow \#1(R1)}$. In causal analysis, these choices are irrelevant. However, for engineers they are very significant. For example, ground (G) is often taken as a common node to which all voltages are references. Thus $v_{1,G}$ is much preferred over $v_{G,1}$. When the voltage is referenced to ground, ground is dropped:

---

[4] NPN or PNP.

$v_{1,G} = v_1$. If $v_{1,2}$ is negative it is much more intuitive to use $v_{2,1}$ because it refers to a change in a positive quantity. An NPN transistor has positive base and collector currents but negative emitter currents. As a consequence, engineers will often define i_C and i_B to be the currents flowing into the transistor, and i_E to be the current flowing out of the transistor. I notate these $i_{\rightarrow C(Q)}$, $i_{\rightarrow B(Q)}$ and $i_{\leftarrow E(Q)}$.

3. Incremental Causal Analysis

The central aspect of how a circuit works is its response to change. Thus, in this section, I ignore quiescent models, higher-order models, and how they are used. Likewise, the determination of the state of a component or its state transitions is discussed later. Changing variables over time (i.e., integration) is also left until later. All components are assumed to behave linearly within a state. Finally, qualitative analysis is assumed to be unambiguous. All these assumptions are important and are dealt with later, but are unnecessary to understand the basic structure-to-function framework.

3.1. Causal propagation

The essential intuition behind causal analysis is that each component acts as an individual information processor which only performs an action when a signal reaches it from one of its neighbors. Then it passes along the signal to its neighbors according to its component model.

This notion of causality is based on two fundamental tenets: locality and directionality. Each component acts only when it is acted upon by neighboring components, and then it only acts on its neighbors. Thus, each interaction only has access to local information (i.e., from its neighboring components), and produces only local information. Finally, each component propagates information in one and only one direction. Thus, negotiation between component processors is impossible.

Causal analysis produces a causal argument which is a qualitative description of how the circuit equilibrates—how it responds to perturbations from its equilibrium. This description is, in effect, a simulation of the circuit's equilibration. This kind of explanation is often what people mean by a description of how something 'works'. Not surprisingly, the causal analysis process itself uses simulation in producing its analyses (complications which are introduced later require a great deal of additional problem-solving effort).

Consider as an example the circuit of Fig. 2. This circuit contains a transistor (Q1), a resistor (R1), and a battery (B1). These are connected by four groups of wires (i.e., nodes) IN, OUT, VCC, and G.

Components interact with each other by placing currents and voltages on their adjacent terminals. Thus, two components can only interact if there is a wire connecting them. The topology of potential causal interactions can be laid out as a topology of alternating component models and variables as is illus-

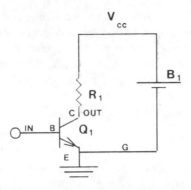

$$V_{cc}$$

FIG. 2. Simple amplifier.

trated in Fig. 3. Each circle indicates a component model which can only communicate information through shared variables. Causal analysis proceeds by propagating an input disturbance through this information topology. In this example, the propagation is very simple. Fig. 4 illustrates the causal topology for the simple amplifier when an increase is applied. Notice that the edges in the causal topology are directed corresponding to the direction of propagation and that only a subset of the potential causal interactions are utilized. The fundamental task of causal analysis is to determine that subset of potential interactions that 'best' describes the functioning of the circuit. We will see in a moment that for simple circuits such as that of Fig. 2 this task is relatively simple, but fundamental complexities arise for more complex circuits.

The causal argument for an output consists of a sequence of steps, starting with the input disturbance, each depending on previous steps in the sequence

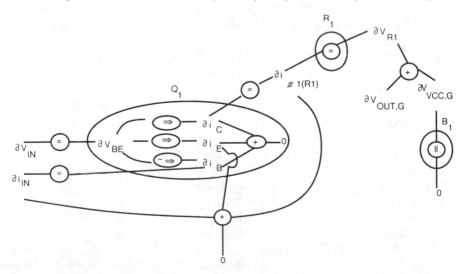

FIG. 3. Potential causal topology of Fig. 2.

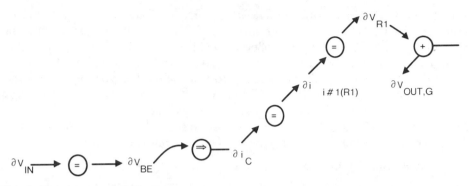

FIG. 4. Causal topology of Fig. 2.

and terminating in the output. The following is EQUAL's formulation of the
causal argument of the simple amplifier. Each step in the argument is placed on
a single line. The steps are organized into four columns. The first column
indicates the antecedents to the step. If the second column is blank, that step is
a premise (e.g., an input disturbance). $\Rightarrow$ indicates that the step follows directly
from its antecedents. If none are listed in the first column and the second
column is $\Rightarrow$ the step's antecedent is the previous line. The third column
indicates the variable assigned a value in that step. The final column provides
the reason which always refers to some component model. Note that Ohm's
law is defined with respect to the #1 terminal of a resistor. As #1 is the top
terminal in this circuit, this current must be propagated by KCL from #2
which is connected to the collector to #1 which is connected to the battery. As
quiescent current is flowing down through the resistor to the collector, EQUAL
has chosen sign conventions such that current flows out of the bottom of R1
and into the tops of R1 and Q1.[5]

Antecedents	Event	Reason
	$\partial v_{IN} = +$	Given
	$\Rightarrow \partial i_{\to C(Q1)} = +$	$\partial v_{B,E} \Rightarrow \partial i_C$ for NPN-transistor Q1
	$\Rightarrow \partial i_{\leftarrow \#2(R1)} = +$	KCL for node OUT
	$\Rightarrow \partial i_{\to \#1(R1)} = +$	KCL for resistor R1
	$\Rightarrow \partial v_{VCC,OUT} = +$	$\partial i_{\#1} \Rightarrow \partial v_{\#1,\#2}$ for resistor R1
	$\partial v_{VCC} = 0$	$\partial v_{+,-} = 0$ for battery B1
$\partial v_{VCC} = 0, \partial v_{VCC,OUT} = +$	$\Rightarrow \partial v_{OUT} = -$	KVL applied to nodes OUT, VCC, GROUND .

[5]EQUAL tries to determine the signs of the quantities and all the causal arguments presented in
this paper adopt sign conventions such that the underlying quantity is positive. In a few cases,
EQUAL cannot determine the sign of the underlying quantity, in which case the voltage choice is
arbitrary and currents are chosen to flow into components. These sign conventions do not affect the
chain of causal interactions produced by the disturbance, and are thus irrelevant to teleological
analysis. The necessary quiescent analysis is discussed later. However, without adopting these sign
conventions the causal explanations would be nearly incomprehensible.

In English: The increasing voltage at node IN is applied to the base-emitter junction of Q1. By the transistor law $\partial v_{B,E} \Rightarrow \partial i_C$ this causes an increase in current from node OUT into the collector of Q1. By Kirchhoff's current law, this same current is flowing out of the bottom of R1 into node OUT. By Ohm's law, this causes an increased voltage across it. Thus, the voltage from node VCC to OUT increases. Batteries supply constant voltage so the voltage between VCC and GROUND is constant. Thus, the increase in the voltage from VCC to OUT also produces an increase in the voltage from GROUND to OUT. Hence, the voltage at OUT drops with respect to GROUND.

3.1.1. *Nonlocality of KCL and KVL*

The formulations of KCL (Section 2.5.1) and KVL (Section 2.5.2) violate the locality tenet of causality. Fortunately, no important information is lost if KCL is restricted to be local (i.e., only applies to single components and nodes). However, KVL is inherently nonlocal: $v_{i,j} + v_{j,k} = v_{i,k}$ where nodes i, j and k may range over all the nodes in the circuit. If KVL were restricted to be purely local, i.e., only apply if nodes i, j and k are all connected to the same component, the causal propagation of the previous section could not go through.

The nonlocality of KVL is inescapable as it arises from the definition of voltage. The identical problem arises with temperatures, velocities, pressures, etc. The KVL-like law arises out of the very definition of voltage, pressure, temperature or velocity. This is illustrated by the more commonsense quantity of temperature. If the temperature difference between points A and B is t_1 and the temperature difference between points B and C is t_2 then the temperature difference between points A and C is $t_1 + t_2$. This non-local inference arises out of the basic defintion of temperature.[6]

3.2. Implementation

Causal analysis uses propagation of constraints [10,28,29,30] to determine circuit values. The propagator is designed to find the simplest explanation first. KCL and KVL deductions are considered simpler than component models, thus all KCL and KVL deductions are done first. On rare occasions the same cell value can be found in two different ways. EQUAL adopts the simple heuristic of picking the value utilizing fewest components in its argument. The breadth-first phase of the propagations is implemented using a queue to hold newly assigned values which have not yet been propagated.

---

[6]Under the approximations of conventional circuit theory, Maxwell's equations can be solved by a scalar potential, this potential is the definition of voltage. A scalar potential has the property its change from point A to point B is independent of the path taken to reach B from A. This is exactly KVL.

The data structure that propagation operates on is a set of cells representing the voltages and currents of the circuit and a set of constraints linking those cells. A new cell is allocated for each derivative of every variable. This data structure is constructed from the schematic by creating a voltage cell for every pair of nodes and a current cell for every component terminal. Then the component models, KCL and KVL are instantiated for each component and node by linking each confluence to their corresponding cells. The result is a data structure of cells and constraints linking those cells.

Each cell may have a value. This value may come from outside the circuit or may be deduced from values in other cells via the constraint confluences. When a cell is assigned a value each constraint it participates in is examined to determine if enough information is available to enable it to use that constraint to deduce a value for another cell. Discovering a new value may thus determine yet other values, thus 'propagating the constraints'. Associated with each value is a justification indicating how it derives from values in other cells. A complete audit trail of a value's propagation is constructed by tracing this justification path back to the initial inputs. The audit trail is the causal argument.

Sometimes two values are found for the same cell. This does not mean there are two competing tendencies on the cell: causality demands that once a cell receives a value it remains at that value. If the two values of such a coincidence conflict, the component models are faulty (e.g., a transistor model with a voltage source on the collector instead of a current source), the circuit cannot exist (e.g., two current sources in series) or the inputs are impossible (e.g., specifying that the current into the #1 terminal of a resistor is + and that the current into the #2 terminal is also +). If the two values of a coincidence corroborate, propagation of the second value is halted as no additional information can be gained by propagating it. The trivial cases of corroborations are avoided by a refraction rule disallowing the result of a constraint to trigger itself.

It is important to discover conflicts as early as possible. It makes no sense to create a long propagation chain only to discover that some simple antecedent is contradictory. This is why the propagation proceeds breadth-first.

Unilateral constraints such as $\partial v_{b,e} \Rightarrow \partial i_c$ for transistors require special handling. However, for well-designed circuits and correct models this unilateral restriction is never necessary and no analysis in this paper requires it.

KVL presents two sorts of problems. The first, discussed in more depth later, concerns how many KVL confluences to use. Including a confluence for *every* loop is extremely redundant. Redundancy is undesirable not because it introduces inefficiency, but rather that it gives rise to multiple syntactically different explanations for the same behavior. Using the conventional quantitative methods for formulating KVL confluences produces insufficient confluences. EQUAL includes a KVL confluence for every set of three nodes:

For every set of three nodes: i, j, and k

$v_{i,j}$ = voltage from node i to node j,

$v_{j,k}$ = voltage from node j to node k,

$v_{i,k}$ = voltage from node i to node k,

$\partial^n v_{i,j} + \partial^n v_{j,k} = \partial^n v_{i,k}$ for $n = 0, 1, \ldots$.

However, this formulation is still a source of redundancy. EQUAL implements KVL as a procedure which is invoked whenever a new voltage is discovered. It only 'creates' three-node KVL constraints when necessary, thus increasing efficiency by avoiding explicitly encoding all the KVL confluences and reducing redundant corroborations by not introducing KVL confluences when they are not needed. Unfortunately, it is not possible to avoid all redundancy.

3.3. What is causality?

The notion of causality is not that well understood or agreed upon. As the arguments of this paper depend crucially on a particular notion of causality, this section briefly outlines the basic intuitions behind my notion of causality. Consider these steps of the causal argument for the circuit of Fig. 2:

Antecedents	Event	Reason
$\Rightarrow \partial i_{\leftarrow \#2(R1)} = +$		KCL for node OUT
$\Rightarrow \partial i_{\rightarrow \#1(R1)} = +$		KCL for resistor R1
$\Rightarrow \partial v_{VCC,OUT} = +$		$\partial i_{\#1} \Rightarrow \partial v_{\#1,\#2}$ for resistor R1

This argument is written as if the change in current in R1 somehow causes the change in voltage across R1. This is absurd, as according to Ohm's law $v = iR$ any change in v must co-occur with any change in i. So what is causality?

There is no notion of delay in equilibrium models—all signals propagate in zero time and all circuit quantities change simultaneously when an input is applied. The network laws, KCL, KVL, etc., are all equilibrium conditions. They are quasistatic approximations which only apply if the wavelengths of the signals are long enough, energy levels of the signals are low enough and observation times of the signals long enough. Mathematically the behavior of the lumped-parameter system is described by *ordinary* differential equations.

On the other hand our intuitive notion of causality is quite different. The change in input causes a disequilibrium in the components near the input. This disequilibrium propagates through the circuit at finite speed until the circuit reaches a new overall equilibrium state. This equilibrating process is described by causal analysis. Note that during the equilibrating process, circuit laws do not apply.

In a way, this intuition corresponds to what actually happens if we examine the circuit closely. A far more accurate quantitative model is based on

Maxwell's field equations. The lumped-parameter circuit model is an idealization and simplification of the behavior of the electromagnetic fields in and around the circuit components. As changes in these fields propagate at finite speeds, this process takes a certain amount of time. The differential equations of the lumped-parameter circuit model cannot account for what happens during this period of disequilibrium. Within this period the changing fields of the input signals propagate until global equilibrium is reached. This propagation can be viewed as a kind of causal flow: the input field changes and propagates to other materials causing further fields to change. These changes can be partially ordered in a time sequence in which each change is caused by changes earlier in the sequence and earlier in time.

The quantitative calculation of the causal flow that happens during the period of disequilibrium is intractable. Although the electromagnetic laws that govern the physics are known, there is no practical way to quantitatively describe this causal process. This means that the electrical engineer can never completely analyze a circuit.

When an electrical engineer reasons about a circuit, he reintroduces a kind of causality that the lumped-circuit model throws away. He does this by using local causal models and imposing a time flow on the changes in circuit quantities. Only by creating local causal models that throw away much of the detail that of the quantitative view is he able to make the causal analysis tractable. The models are not based on Maxwell's equations, rather each circuit component is viewed as an active agent which attempts to re-establish a local equilibrium within its own vicinity. The engineer's qualitative theory of circuit causality explains the period of equilibration by introducing finite time flow and permitting the circuit to be in disequilibrium.

The formal linkage between the causal models derived earlier and Maxwell's equations is unexplored. However, the sense of causality presented in this paper seems to be an accurate description of engineer's reasoning and hence connects with the conventional language of electrical engineering. The models are sufficient to produce accurate predictions and explanations for circuits.

3.4. Causal heuristics

The component models alone are insufficient to construct causal analyses of some circuits. Consider the simple circuit fragment illustrated in Fig. 5. This circuit is like that of Fig. 2 except that an extra resistor is placed in the emitter and unspecified circuitry is attached to the emitter and collector. In the present framework there is no causal analysis for this circuit fragment.

The propagator can get no further than the voltage at the input. The only component that even references the input variable and hence has any hope of propagating the value is Q1. But Q1 responds to voltage across its base and emitter, not the voltage between its base and ground. Hence the propagation gets stuck. (In quantitative analysis this would be a point at which to introduce a new unknown variable to propagate around the loop.)

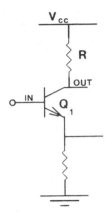

Fig. 5. Amplifier input.

3.4.1. *The three causal heuristics*

Propagation impasses can only occur at sums of three or more quantities. The propagation cannot halt at $x = y$ since if x is known y can be computed and vice versa. Sums of three or more quantities arise from KVL, KCL and (rarely) the component models themselves. EQUAL incorporates three heuristics to circumvent impasses at each of the types of sums: the KVL-heuristic, KCL-heuristic, and the confluence heuristic.

These heuristics are domain-independent. No matter what the domain, propagation will encounter impasses. The general solution is the introduction of three domain-independent heuristics: the component heuristic, the conduit heuristic and the confluence heuristic which are identical to the electrical KVL-, KCL- and confluence heuristics.

Unlike KVL, KCL and component-confluence deductions, the conclusions of heuristics are necessarily tentative being based on assumptions about circuit functioning that may later be found to be incorrect.

3.4.2. *The KVL-heuristic*

The KVL-heuristic handles the case where the propagation reaches an impasse at the KVL confluence $\partial v_{n,G} = \partial v_{n,m} + \partial v_{m,G}$ where n and m are nodes connected to different terminals of the same component and $\partial v_{n,G}$ is $+$ or $-$. The propagator always employs the rule $\partial v_{n,G} \Rightarrow \partial v_{n,m}$. In addition, if $\partial v_{n,G} = \partial v_{m,G}$ the propagator also employs $\partial v_{m,n} = 0$.

It is now possible to propagate past the initial impasse of Fig. 2:

$$\partial v_{IN} = + \qquad \text{Given}$$

$$\Rightarrow \partial v_{IN,E1} = + \qquad \partial v_B \Rightarrow \partial v_{B,E} \text{ KVL-heuristic for NPN-transistor Q1}$$

$$\Rightarrow \partial i_{\to C(Q1)} = + \qquad \partial v_{B,E} \Rightarrow \partial i_C \text{ for NPN-transistor Q1} .$$

The intuitive rationale for this heuristic is as follows. Consider the simple case where $\partial v_{n,m}$ and $\partial v_{m,G}$ are unknown. No causal path has yet been found which affects $\partial v_{m,G}$. Thus, $\partial v_{n,G}$ can be viewed as causing the changes in $v_{n,m}$ and $v_{m,G}$. The KVL-heuristic assumes that the change of voltage at node n produces an equal-valued change in the voltage across the component and that the voltage at m is insignificant (i.e., $v_{m,G} \approx 0$). It is very likely that, as a consequence, $v_{m,G}$ is affected as well: $\partial v_{n,G} \Rightarrow \partial v_{n,m} \Rightarrow \cdots \Rightarrow \partial v_{m,G}$. Thus the KVL-heuristic is based on the presupposition that the change in $v_{m,G}$ produced by the change in $v_{n,G}$ cannot swamp the change in $v_{m,G}$.

In the case where $\partial v_{n,G} = \partial v_{m,G} \neq 0$, the KVL-heuristic will already have produced two conflicting propagations: $\partial v_{n,G} \Rightarrow \partial v_{n,m}$ and $\partial v_{m,G} \Rightarrow \partial v_{m,n}$. However, the two changes might exactly cancel requiring the consideration of the third possibility: $\partial v_{n,m} = 0$. (No one would ever design a circuit that depended on this, but nevertheless it is a mathematical possibility.)

From a network theory point of view the KVL-heuristic is based on the presupposition that all incremental impedances are positive. If the situation can be modeled as illustrated in Fig. 6 a positive component impedance in series with an unknown composite positive impedance, then KVL-heuristic is correct.

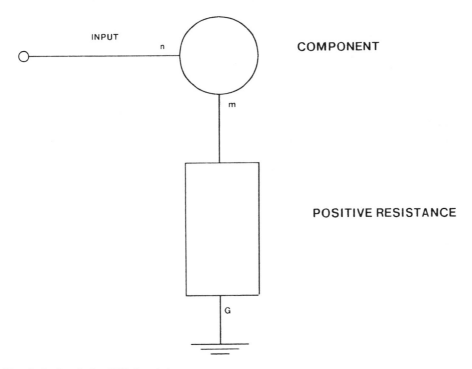

FIG. 6. Rationale for KVL-heuristic.

3.4.3. *The KCL-heuristic*

The KCL-heuristic handles the case where the propagation reaches an impasse at a KCL confluence for some node (which can only happen if the node has three or more component terminals connected to it). The rule is that if components directly cause terminal currents of a node, the voltage at the node is determined by the equation $\sum \partial i_{j_k} - \Rightarrow \partial v$. In addition, if some $\partial i_j = -\partial i_n$ the propagator employs $\partial v = 0$.

It is now possible to complete the causal argument for the output of Fig. 2:

$$\partial v_{\text{IN}} = + \qquad \text{Given}$$

$$\Rightarrow \partial v_{\text{IN,E1}} = + \qquad \partial v_{\text{B}} \Rightarrow \partial v_{\text{B,E}} \text{ KVL-heuristic for NPN-transistor Q1}$$

$$\Rightarrow \partial i_{\rightarrow \text{C(Q1)}} = + \qquad \partial v_{\text{B,E}} \Rightarrow \partial i_{\text{C}} \text{ for NPN-transistor Q1}$$

$$\Rightarrow \partial v_{\text{OUT}} = - \qquad \partial i_{\rightarrow \text{C(Q1)}} - \Rightarrow \partial v_{\text{OUT}} \text{ KCL-heuristic for node OUT.}$$

The KCL-heuristic is extremely common in an engineer's analyses: "Increasing current *out of* the node pulls it down, increasing current *into* the node forces it to rise."

The KCL-heuristic makes the presupposition that terminals which are causing current flow into nodes can be modeled as the output terminal of a current source. This current source sees an incremental positive impedance to ground. Fig. 7 illustrates this situation. If this is an accurate depiction of the situation, the voltage at the node can be determined directly from Ohm's law.

3.4.4. *The confluence heuristic*

The final source of three or more variable confluences is the component models themselves. However, such confluences are relatively rare. One such case occurs when the transistor is saturated. When the transistor is saturated, the change in base current is controlled by the combined action of the two junctions: $\partial v_{\text{b,e}} - \partial v_{\text{c,b}} \Rightarrow \partial i_{\text{b}}$. The '$\Rightarrow$' in this context indicates the $\partial v_{\text{b,e}} - \partial v_{\text{c,b}} = \partial i_{\text{b}}$, but the change in voltages cause the change in the current. If the propagation reaches an impasse on this confluence, the confluence heuristic, is invoked. Two other cases are a valve where the area available for flow controls both flow and pressure [6] and a mosfet [34].

All the cases I have encountered where this heuristic is used are of the form

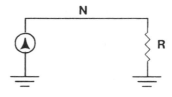

FIG. 7. Rationale for KCL-heuristic.

$\partial x + \partial y \Rightarrow \partial z$ where ∂x or ∂y are known. In such circumstances the propagation proceeds with $\partial z \Rightarrow \partial x$ or $\partial z \Rightarrow \partial y$ leaving the unknown ∂y or ∂x alone.[7]

3.4.5. *Interestingness*

These three heuristics are designed to find values for the important (i.e., interesting) circuit variables. The heuristics will not attempt to find a value for a voltage unless it is a component input, or it is a voltage which is (a) with respect to ground, and (b) has current flowing into the non-ground node. The heuristics will never directly attempt to find a value for a current unless it is part of a component confluence of more than two variables. The remaining variables are presumed to be of no causal importance, or automatically follow from important variables so that their values can be safely ignored. EQUAL adopts the convention that uncaused uninteresting variables are zero.

3.5. Causal analysis of the Schmitt trigger

We are now in a position to completely analyze the behavior of the Schmitt trigger. When an increase is applied to the input of the Schmitt trigger (Fig. 8), the voltage at the emitter drops. EQUAL produces the following causal argument for the drop in emitter voltage:

$\partial v_{B1} = +$	Given
$\Rightarrow \partial v_{B1,E1} = +$	$\partial v_B \Rightarrow \partial v_{B,E}$ KVL-heuristic for NPN-transistor Q1
$\Rightarrow \partial i_{\rightarrow C(Q1)} = +$	$\partial v_{B,E} \Rightarrow \partial i_C$ for NPN-transistor Q1
$\Rightarrow \partial v_{C1} = -$	$\partial i_{\rightarrow C(Q1)} - \Rightarrow \partial v_{C1}$ KCL-heuristic for node C1
$\Rightarrow \partial v_{C1,B2} = -$	$\partial v_{\#1} \Rightarrow \partial v_{\#1,\#2}$ KVL-heuristic for resistor RB2
$\Rightarrow \partial i_{\rightarrow \#1(RB2)} = -$	$\partial v_{\#1,\#2} \Rightarrow \partial i_{\#1}$ for resistor RB2
$\Rightarrow \partial i_{\rightarrow \#2(RB2)} = +$	KCL for resistor RB2
$\Rightarrow \partial v_{B2} = -$	$\partial i_{\rightarrow \#2(RB2)} - \Rightarrow \partial v_{B2}$ KCL-heuristic for node B2
$\Rightarrow \partial v_{B2,E1} = -$	$\partial v_B \Rightarrow \partial v_{B,E}$ KVL-heuristic for NPN-transistor Q2
$\Rightarrow \partial i_{\leftarrow 2E(Q2)} = -$	$\partial v_{B,E} \Rightarrow \partial i_E$ for NPN-transistor Q2
$\Rightarrow \partial i_{\leftarrow 2E(Q2)} = -$	$\partial i_{\leftarrow E(Q2)} \Rightarrow \partial v_{E1}$ KCL-heuristic for node E1

Of course, this argument only holds if the transistors are in their correct operating regions, the resistances and gains are just right, and that the input level is high enough—these issues are all discussed in later sections. If the conditions are right for the Schmitt trigger to operate as intended, it behaves as described by the preceding argument.

[7]The generalization is straightforward. The confluence is of the form $\Sigma \partial x \Rightarrow \Sigma \partial y$. The heuristic computes a value for the left-hand side assuming all unknown ∂x are zero. Then it hypothesizes all possible assignments to the unknown ∂y which are consistent with the computed value for the right-hand side.

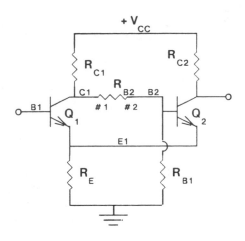

FIG. 8. Schmitt trigger.

3.6. Implementation

As all of the rules and heuristics are order-insensitive, a heuristic may be applied at any time in the propagation process. As an application of a heuristic may later be shown to be invalid or superfluous, an explicit assumption is recorded for each use of a heuristic. This assumption may need to be retracted if subsequent contradictions are encountered. For example, when the KVL-heuristic notices a voltage at the base of a transistor, it triggers the transistor model on the base-emitter voltage. In doing so, the heuristic makes the assumption that the emitter voltage's effect is negligible compared to that of the base voltage. If it is discovered later that the emitter voltage is significant, the assumption and all its ensuing propagations need to be retracted.

As the signal propagates through the circuit it may accumulate a number of such assumptions. Although the assumptions of a value can be computed from its justification, it is more convenient to propagate the assumptions of a value along as well. Thus, the assumptions of a newly deduced value is computed by constructing the set union of the assumptions of its antecedents. More precisely, EQUAL propagates value triples of the form $\langle qvalue, \{assumptions\}, justification(s)\rangle$ (where $qvalue$ is one of $+$, $-$ or 0). For example, if $\partial x = \partial y + \partial z$, and $\partial y = \alpha$: $\langle +, A_\alpha, \rangle$ and $\partial z = \beta$: $\langle +, B_\beta, \rangle$, then the propagator would deduce $\partial x = \gamma$: $\langle +, A_\alpha \cup B_\beta, + (\alpha, \beta)\rangle$.

Although the ordering of the propagation steps is irrelevant to completeness, it has significant effect on efficiency. There is no point propagating a value for a cell which is subsequently replaced by a simpler value or contradicted. EQUAL orders its propagations such that it finds contradictions as early as possible and finds the simplest causal argument for each value. EQUAL has three priorities for propagation, first KCL and KVL deductions, second component model deductions, and third KVL- and KCL-heuristics. The highest priority value is always propagated first. For example, if there are two possible independent KCL-heuristics pending and one is run, the next propagation will be KVL deductions from the new voltage, not the other KCL-heuristic. All three priorities are propagated breadth-first.

In order to distinguish values under different assumptions the notation $[C\, x]$ is used to indicate the assumption that x is the dominant input to C. The assumption that v_B is the dominant input to Q is written $[Q\, v_B]$. Assumptions $[Q\, v_E]$ and $[Q\, v_B]$ can both be active, potentially producing contradictory values for i_C. Assumptions introduced by the KCL-heuristic are notated analogously. For example, the KCL-heuristic used in analyzing Fig. 5 is notated $[OUT\, Q1]$ as Q1 is the dominant input to node OUT.

4. Feedback

Feedback, the idea of a device sensing its own output to control its own behavior, is one of the most powerful strategies for designing and analyzing circuits, mechanical systems, economic systems, biological systems, etc. Feedback is as important and prevalent to machine design as loop constructs are to programming. The benefits of negative feedback to circuit design are varied and extremely important. Feedback is primarily used to compensate for non-ideal components or operating conditions. In using feedback, the designer embeds the circuit fragment whose behavior is to be modified within a feedback loop, thereby mitigating undesirable behavior and enhancing the desirable behavior. Feedback can be used to stabilize circuit gain against variations in circuit parameters due to manufacturing or temperature. It allows the designer to modify the input and output impedances of the circuit, reduce distortion by improving linearity, and increase the bandwidth characteristic of amplifiers. For these reasons the use of feedback is ubiquitous in circuit design.

Feedback is also critical for understanding circuit behavior. It is the basic building block for designing analog circuits. It is also extremely important as a design strategy. Troubleshooting circuits with feedback requires understanding the feedback action. In addition to detecting it, the feedback must be characterized in the standard conventions of electrical engineers. This section presents how causal analysis is used to locally detect and analyze feedback.

4.1. Definition of feedback

Feedback cannot be directly observed in the voltage and current values. The quantitative behavior of a circuit is determined by solving the simultaneous set of equations obtained from characteristics of each component, KCL and KVL using either the node or mesh method [13]. Whether the circuit contains feedback or not has no effect on this process. It is impossible to tell from the solution whether the circuit utilizes feedback. But an engineer examining a circuit can determine whether it uses feedback. He does not do this using conventional network theory, but relies on something quite different—the topology or causality of the circuit.

A feedback amplifier can be viewed as a basic amplifier surrounded by extra circuitry to modify its behavior. Fig. 9 illustrates the basic parts of a feedback system. The input signal passes through the summing network, is amplified and subsequently output. However, as well as being connected to the overall circuit output, the main amplifier is connected to another network. The signal passes through this network and is subtracted from the input signal. Thus a fraction of the output is sampled and subtracted from the input. The advantage of this arrangement can be seen by considering what happens if the gain of the basic amplifier is suddenly disturbed. As the gain is reduced, the output signal drops. Thus less signal is fedback and less is subtracted from the input signal. As there is now more input to the main amplifier, the output increases again, thereby correcting for the disturbance.

When an engineer recognizes feedback in a circuit, he is noticing that the circuit somehow abstractly matches Fig. 9. He could try to recognize the basic amplifier, network and summing and sampling points. Recognizing these modules requires considerably more expertise than just knowledge of network theory. For example, most topological loops in the circuit schematic do not correspond to instances of feedback loops, let alone important ones.

Feedback is ultimately a property of the circuit's function (i.e., how it works), not its behavior (i.e., what it does). Although quantitative analysis (i.e., using network theory) cannot be used to identify feedback, causal analysis can. That is because causal analysis explains the *how* as well as the *what* of circuit behavior.

Feedback is an elusive concept. Devices based on feedback have been with mankind since antiquity [35] but feedback was not appreciated as an explicit design tool until James Watt's invention of the centrifugal governor in the late

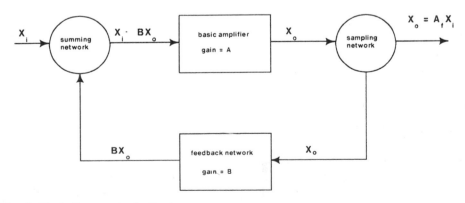

FIG. 9. Block diagram of a feedback system.

18th century. The abstraction of Fig. 9 is an invention of the twentieth century. Mayr's book "The Origins of Feedback Control" takes some pains to define the criteria for feedback in order to identify which machines in antiquity used feedback. Analogous care must be taken in causal analysis, for otherwise, feedback is seen everywhere. Intuitively, feedback occurs when a chain of causal interactions falls back on itself (as is the case with the Schmitt trigger) producing an endless chain of causal interactions. However, by that definition two resistors in series manifest feedback! Mayr introduces a very important criteria "The system includes a sensing element and a comparator, at least one of which can be distinguished as a physically separate element."

4.2. Feedback detection

The heuristics provide a clean way to detect feedback. All occurrences of the heuristics are at sums of three or more variables. Each occurrence where two or more of the variables are unknown are potentially points at which feedback occurs. The variables at each such point can be divided into three classes: inputs, outputs and insignificants. For example, given $\partial x + \partial y + \partial z = 0$, the heuristic might have, given ∂x, propagated $\partial x \Rightarrow \partial y$ assuming ∂z to be insignificant. *Feedback is present if, as a consequence of propagating the output variable(s), a value is propagated (perhaps after many steps) for the variables assumed to be insignificant.* For example, if $\partial x \Rightarrow \partial y \Rightarrow \cdots \Rightarrow \partial z$, the circuit contains a feedback loop from ∂x through ∂y to ∂z. In particular, the propagator has discovered that $\partial z = f(\partial y)$ and thus that $\partial y = -f(\partial y) - \partial x$, a clear indication of feedback.

Consider the Schmitt trigger. Section 3.6 presented the causal argument for why the emitter voltage dropped in response to an increase in input:

$$\partial v_{B1} = + \qquad \text{Given}$$
$$\Rightarrow \partial v_{B1,E1} = + \qquad \partial v_B \Rightarrow \partial v_{B,E} \text{ KVL-heuristic for NPN-transistor Q1}$$
$$\vdots$$
$$\Rightarrow \partial v_{E1} = - \qquad \partial i_{\leftarrow E(Q2)} \Rightarrow \partial v_{E1} \text{ KCL-heuristic for node E1}$$
$$\Rightarrow \partial v_{E1} = -\partial v_{B1} \qquad \text{Positive feedback at NPN-transistor Q1.}$$

As ∂v_{E1} was assumed insignificant in the KVL-heuristic propagation for $\partial v_{B1,E1}$, the propagation indicates a feedback loop starting with ∂v_{B1}, through $\partial v_{B1,E1}$ back to ∂v_{E1}. Thus, $\partial v_{B1,E1} = f(\partial v_{B1,E1}) + \partial v_{E1}$.[8]

---

[8]The delay between the initial input and the emitter drop is mythical. As there are no delay elements in the loop, formally, the input rises and emitter drops at exactly the same time. In the causal analysis, the first causes the second, but no time elapses. As there are no delay elements, there cannot be any overshoot or ringing. If this time delay is important, it should be included by adding capacitors or inductors in the loop. These additional components cause explicit time delays, resulting in overshoot and ringing (as discussed later).

4.3. Feedback configurations

Electrical engineering has developed a tremendous amount of theory concerning feedback [32]. There are a variety of different nomenclatures for describing feedback configurations. The terminology used here is from [18]. Table 1 outlines the 8 possible configurations, each important to electrical engineering. The type of feedback exhibited by a circuit is classified according its sign, comparison type, and sampling type. The sign of the feedback indicates whether the fedback signal acts with or against the input signal. For example, the Schmitt trigger exhibits positive feedback. The point at which the feedback is detected is the *comparison point* because it compares an input signal with a fedback signal to produce a composite of the two. The other distinguished point of a feedback loop is the last value which causally affects a circuit output. At this point a split occurs and one signal continues to the output of the circuit while the other is fed back. This value is called the *sampling point* as most of the signal goes on to circuit output, while rest (i.e., a sample) is fed back to the circuit input.

The presence of feedback, its sign, the comparison point and its type, and the sampling point and its type can all be determined from the causal analysis. The sign is computed directly from comparison the feedback signal to the input. Each application of a heuristic introduces a comparison point. For feedback detected via the KCL-heuristic this point is a node in the circuit. For feedback detected via the KVL-heuristic this point is a component. The sampling point is the last shared point on the causal argument for the output and fedback signals. The details (and definitions) for determining the type of the comparison point and sampling point can be found in [11].

Not every occurrence of feedback is on a path to the output. For example, feedback loops may be nested so that a feedback path itself contains feedback. For these loops the notion of sampling point must be redefined to be that last vertex of the loop that either directly affects the output or is a member of another feedback loop whose comparison point affects the output (recursively).

TABLE 1. Taxonomy of feedback types

Sign	Comparison type	Sampling type	Figure
−	Node	Node	
−	Node	Loop	10
−	Loop	Node	11
−	Loop	Loop	
+	Node	Node	
+	Node	Loop	
+	Loop	Node	
+	Loop	Loop	8

4.4. Two examples

Fig. 10 illustrates a circuit which contains negative feedback recognized using the KCL-heuristic. The input signal is an increase in current into the input. By the KCL-heuristic, the voltage at the input rises as well. This assumes the currents in the base of Q1 and RF are not relevant. However, the signal loops back through Q1, Q2, RB1 and RF producing an additional current into the input node at which the KCL-heuristic applied. Hence, feedback is present. As this current is of opposite sign to the input, the feedback is negative. (Note that the negative feedback signal cannot completely cancel or dominate the input, for it is the input itself which causes the fedback signal.)

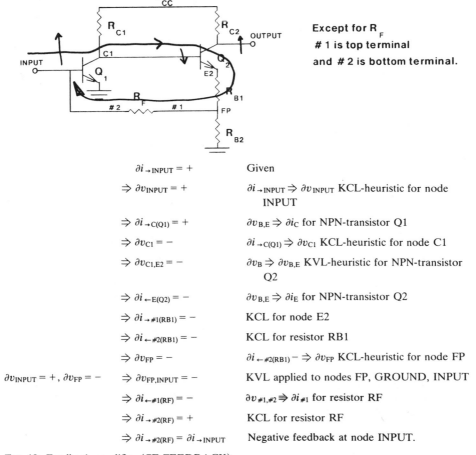

$$\partial i_{\to \text{INPUT}} = +$$ Given

$$\Rightarrow \partial v_{\text{INPUT}} = +$$ $\partial i_{\to \text{INPUT}} \Rightarrow \partial v_{\text{INPUT}}$ KCL-heuristic for node INPUT

$$\Rightarrow \partial i_{\to \text{C(Q1)}} = +$$ $\partial v_{\text{B,E}} \Rightarrow \partial i_C$ for NPN-transistor Q1

$$\Rightarrow \partial v_{\text{C1}} = -$$ $\partial i_{\to \text{C(Q1)}} \Rightarrow \partial v_{\text{C1}}$ KCL-heuristic for node C1

$$\Rightarrow \partial v_{\text{C1,E2}} = -$$ $\partial v_B \Rightarrow \partial v_{\text{B,E}}$ KVL-heuristic for NPN-transistor Q2

$$\Rightarrow \partial i_{\leftarrow \text{E(Q2)}} = -$$ $\partial v_{\text{B,E}} \Rightarrow \partial i_E$ for NPN-transistor Q2

$$\Rightarrow \partial i_{\to \#1(\text{RB1})} = -$$ KCL for node E2

$$\Rightarrow \partial i_{\leftarrow \#2(\text{RB1})} = -$$ KCL for resistor RB1

$$\Rightarrow \partial v_{\text{FP}} = -$$ $\partial i_{\leftarrow \#2(\text{RB1})} - \Rightarrow \partial v_{\text{FP}}$ KCL-heuristic for node FP

$\partial v_{\text{INPUT}} = +, \partial v_{\text{FP}} = -$ $\Rightarrow \partial v_{\text{FP,INPUT}} = -$ KVL applied to nodes FP, GROUND, INPUT

$$\Rightarrow \partial i_{\leftarrow \#1(\text{RF})} = -$$ $\partial v_{\#1,\#2} \Rightarrow \partial i_{\#1}$ for resistor RF

$$\Rightarrow \partial i_{\to \#2(\text{RF})} = +$$ KCL for resistor RF

$$\Rightarrow \partial i_{\to \#2(\text{RF})} = \partial i_{\to \text{INPUT}}$$ Negative feedback at node INPUT.

FIG. 10. Feedback amplifier (CE-FEEDBACK).

Fig. 11 illustrates a negative feedback amplifier with node sampling. The sampling point is $v_{\text{OUTPUT}} = +$ and it causes both $v_{\text{OUTPUT,E1}}$ and the overall circuit output.

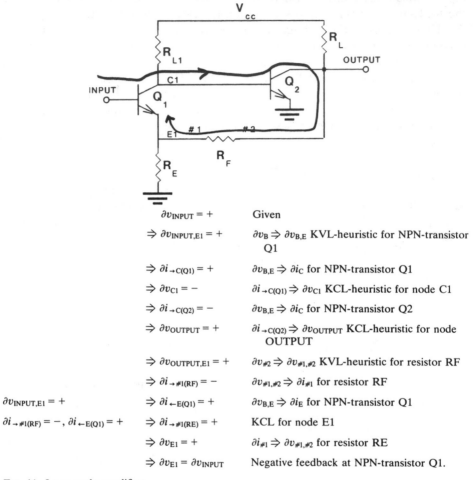

$$\partial v_{\text{INPUT}} = +$$ Given

$$\Rightarrow \partial v_{\text{INPUT,E1}} = +$$ $\partial v_B \Rightarrow \partial v_{\text{B,E}}$ KVL-heuristic for NPN-transistor Q1

$$\Rightarrow \partial i_{\to C(Q1)} = +$$ $\partial v_{\text{B,E}} \Rightarrow \partial i_C$ for NPN-transistor Q1

$$\Rightarrow \partial v_{\text{C1}} = -$$ $\partial i_{\to C(Q1)} \Rightarrow \partial v_{\text{C1}}$ KCL-heuristic for node C1

$$\Rightarrow \partial i_{\to C(Q2)} = -$$ $\partial v_{\text{B,E}} \Rightarrow \partial i_C$ for NPN-transistor Q2

$$\Rightarrow \partial v_{\text{OUTPUT}} = +$$ $\partial i_{\to C(Q2)} \Rightarrow \partial v_{\text{OUTPUT}}$ KCL-heuristic for node OUTPUT

$$\Rightarrow \partial v_{\text{OUTPUT,E1}} = +$$ $\partial v_{\#2} \Rightarrow \partial v_{\#1,\#2}$ KVL-heuristic for resistor RF

$$\Rightarrow \partial i_{\to \#1(RF)} = -$$ $\partial v_{\#1,\#2} \Rightarrow \partial i_{\#1}$ for resistor RF

$\partial v_{\text{INPUT,E1}} = +$ $\Rightarrow \partial i_{\leftarrow E(Q1)} = +$ $\partial v_{\text{B,E}} \Rightarrow \partial i_E$ for NPN-transistor Q1

$\partial i_{\to \#1(RF)} = -, \ \partial i_{\leftarrow E(Q1)} = +$ $\Rightarrow \partial i_{\to \#1(RE)} = +$ KCL for node E1

$$\Rightarrow \partial v_{\text{E1}} = +$$ $\partial i_{\#1} \Rightarrow \partial v_{\#1,\#2}$ for resistor RE

$$\Rightarrow \partial v_{\text{E1}} = \partial v_{\text{INPUT}}$$ Negative feedback at NPN-transistor Q1.

FIG. 11. Loop-node amplifier.

4.5. Local feedback

Electrical engineers distinguish a subclass of feedback called local feedback, in which the sampled signal is immediately fed back. Consider the first few steps of the analysis of the circuit of Fig. 11:

$$\partial v_{\text{INPUT}} = +$$ Given

$$\Rightarrow \partial v_{\text{INPUT,E1}} = +$$ $\partial v_B \Rightarrow \partial v_{\text{B,E}}$ KVL-heuristic for NPN-transistor Q1

$$\Rightarrow \partial i_{\to C(Q1)} = +$$ $\partial v_{\text{B,E}} \Rightarrow \partial i_C$ for NPN-transistor Q1

$$\Rightarrow \partial v_{\text{C1}} = -$$ $\partial i_{\to C(Q1)} \Rightarrow \partial v_{\text{C1}}$ KCL-heuristic for node C1.

The causal argument for RL1's current continues:

$$\Rightarrow \partial v_{C1} = - \qquad\qquad \partial i_{\rightarrow C(Q1)} \Rightarrow \partial v_{C1} \quad \text{KCL-heuristic for node C1}$$

$$\partial v_{VCC} = 0 \qquad\qquad \partial v_{+,-} = 0 \text{ for battery B}$$

$$\partial v_{VCC} = 0, \partial v_{C1} = - \quad \Rightarrow \partial v_{C1,VCC} = - \qquad \text{KVL applied to nodes C1,GROUND,VCC}$$

$$\Rightarrow \partial i_{\rightarrow \#1(RL1)} = + \qquad \partial v_{\#1,\#2} \Rightarrow \partial i_{\#1} \text{ for resistor RL1}$$

$$\Rightarrow \partial i_{\leftarrow \#2(RL1)} = + \qquad \text{KCL for resistor RL1.}$$

Thus, as a consequence of utilizing a KCL-heuristic at the collector of Q1, an additional current is propagated into the node. By the criteria of Section 4.1 this is evidence for feedback.

An analogous situation arises with the KVL-heuristic. Consider the simple amplifier of Fig. 12. An increase in input voltage causes (via the KVL-heuristic) an increased base-emitter voltage across Q1. As a consequence, the transistor conducts more current, increasing the flow out of its emitter and into the emitter resistor. The increased current causes increased emitter voltage, negatively influencing the base-emitter voltage.

Both of these examples meet the strict dictionary definition of feedback, and are detected by the mechanism of the previous section. However, the feedback is local because the fedback signal path does not form a loop in the circuit schematic (but, of course, a loop in the potential causal topology). Local feedback, although it exhibits all of the characteristics of feedback, can usually be ignored in analyzing the global behavior of the circuit. Local feedback does, however, perform an important validation function. A local feedback loop represents the loading effect of a load on a source. Thus, every KCL- or KVL-heuristic should have a local feedback (i.e., a reflection) as the heuristics presume the presence of a load. If there is no load, the heuristic is invalid.

4.6. Negative impedances

The KCL- and KVL-heuristics assume the circuitry connected to the component or node acts as a positive impedance. Thus, if the circuit fragment contains a negative impedance, any heuristic propagating a signal into it will get a reflected or fedback signal opposite to what it expected. Negative

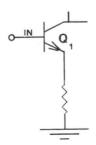

FIG. 12. Common-emitter amplifier.

impedance appears as a positive reflection. (It is important to note that even though none of the components individually may manifest negative resistance, the overall circuit might e.g., the Schmitt trigger can provide a negative impedance load to its input signal.) As a consequence it is always possible to tell whether the circuit contains negative impedances as well as which particular nodes see the negative impedances. The KCL- and KVL-heuristics are therefore implemented to only propagate a negative impedance signal after they have received a positive reflection assuming positive impedances. Thus causal analysis applies to negative impedances as well.[9]

5. The Mechanism Graph

With the inclusion of feedback detection, causal analysis is complete. Sections 5 and 6 discuss how the information constructed by the causal analysis process is analyzed to construct more abstract descriptions of the behavior and to relate this description to the ultimate purpose of the circuit. The *mechanism graph* provides a primitive representation for describing the mechanism by which a circuit achieves its input/output behavior. In Section 6 I describe how the mechanism graph is parsed into higher-level descriptions.

Fig. 13 illustrates the mechanism graph for the circuit of Fig. 10. A vertex in this graph represents information contained in a cell. An edge represents the fact that the information in the vertex adjacent from the edge contributes to the information in the vertex adjacent to the edge. Thus, the mechanism graph describes how information in one cell affects the information in other cells (i.e., causality).

As change is of interest, the mechanism graph only contains vertices which represent changing quantities. The only uncaused vertices are inputs and thus are the vertices with in-degree zero. The mechanism graph only includes quantities which causally affect circuit outputs (the black vertices). An edge is dashed if it depends on a heuristic, solid if it is deduced via a component rule. Circle vertices represent currents and square vertices represent voltages. In order to avoid cluttering the mechanism graphs, only a minimal amount of annotation is included on the graphs. If the quantity is a current, it is labeled by

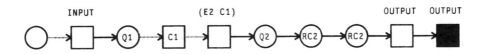

FIG. 13. Mechanism graph for the circuit of Fig. 10's output.

[9]With one exception, I haven't figured out what to do if the circuit contains both positive feedback involving positive impedances and negative feedback using negative impedances—I doubt that any circuit in existence depends on it.

FIG. 14. Splits and joins.

the component it is a current of. If the quantity is a voltage with respect to ground, it is labeled by the name of the non-ground node. Otherwise the voltage vertex is labeled by its pair of circuit nodes. If there is room, the label is printed inside the vertex, otherwise it is printed above it.

Not all causal graphs are straight lines. A causal graph may contain *splits* and *joins* (Fig. 14). A split occurs at a vertex with out-degree greater than one. Such a vertex represents a quantity that directly causes two other quantities to change, both of which eventually contribute to the output. A join occurs at a vertex with in-degree greater than one. In this case the change in the quantity is caused by the simultaneous change in all the antecedent quantities. A graph represents a single argument. Most splits and joins are the direct result of particular circuit mechanisms, but some splits and joins are necessary to account for the difference in number of inputs and outputs. *Feedforward* is used to describe the situation where two paths originating at a split recombine at a join.

5.1. Feedback in the mechanism graph

In order to represent feedback, the mechanism graph is augmented to include the graphs for the error signals, where extra dashed edges are included to indicate where signals feed back into comparison points. As a consequence of this modification, the mechanism graph is a digraph containing cycles.

Fig. 16 is the complete mechanism graph for Fig. 15. The feedback signal is

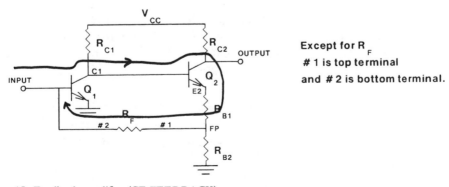

FIG. 15. Feedback amplifier (CE-FEEDBACK).

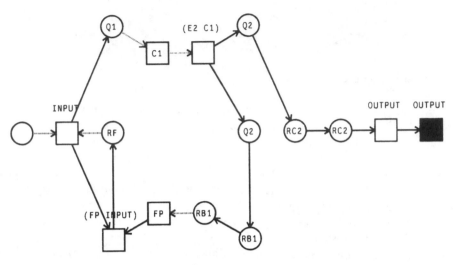

FIG. 16. Complete mechanism graph for Fig. 15.

the current flowing from resistor RF into node INPUT. This current is deduced by applying Ohm's law to the voltage determined by applying KVL to nodes INPUT, FP and GROUND. So both the voltage at INPUT and the voltage at FP contribute to the fedback signal.

6. Teleological Analysis

Circuits are designed and manufactured to achieve specific functions. As these artifacts have to be conveniently designed, efficiently manufactured and easily maintained, the designer attempts to make his circuits as simple as possible. These desiderata dictate that every component must contribute in some way to the ultimate purpose of the circuit. For designed artifacts, every component can be related to the ultimate function of the device. This is the *teleological* perspective.

Teleology plays such a fundamental role in understanding circuits, that electrical engineering has agreed upon a language for discussing it. Causal analysis provides a method for automatically determining the teleology of a circuit in the nomenclature of electrical engineers.

6.1. Configurations

The question, "What is the purpose of R1?" can be answered at many levels. A very simple kind of teleology can be defined using the mechanism graph of a circuit. The mechanism graph is a global description of how the circuit achieves its input/output behavior, and the purpose of an individual component is defined by how it contributes to this mechanism. In particular, a taxonomy of roles a component can play defines all the possible local causal patterns (called configurations) in which it can appear in the mechanism graph. By local, I mean propagations made using the component models and their immediate antecedents and consequents. The taxonomy proposed here is an expanded and formalized version of the language electrical engineers use. A great amount of lore, rules of thumb and advice is associated with each component configuration. The configuration provides a kind of index key into the data base of knowledge available about the component.

Consider the resistor as an example. The resistor is a relatively simple passive component and electrical engineers do not have a formal vocabulary for describing its functions. Nevertheless, its simplicity makes it easy to see how causal analysis distinguishes roles for components. A similar analysis can be done for each component type. The basic resistor law is $\partial v = \partial i$. This formulation suggests two basic causal patterns for the resistor: one in which the voltage causes the current (i.e., $\partial v \Rightarrow \partial i$) and one in which the current causes the voltage (i.e., $\partial i \Rightarrow \partial v$). By definition, within any particular mechanism graph the resistor is used in one of these two ways. The resistor may contribute to the mechanism graph as a voltage-to-current converter or as a current-to-voltage converter. In this view a resistor has two possible functions. However, closer examination shows that the resistor has far more possible roles.

The simplicity of the equation $\partial v = \partial i$ hides most of the options. In actual fact, the resistor has 18 possible configurations. As KCL applies to resistors, we must also take into account the equation $\partial i_{\#1} = \partial i_{\#2}$. Thus, a resistor might convert an input voltage to a current in terminal #1 which is then propagated out, or to a current in terminal #2. Analogously, the input to the resistor might be one of those two currents. These considerations result in two types of current-to-voltage conversion, two types of voltage-to-current conversion, and two types of current propagation (i.e., KCL alone).

Although a component voltage intrinsically refers to two terminals of a component, it is often possible to identify a distinguished voltage terminal. If a KVL deduction is used to determine the input voltage, i.e., $\partial v_{\#1,\#2} = \partial v_{\#1,x} + \partial v_{x,\#2}$, where $\partial v_{\#1,x} = 0$ or $\partial v_{x,\#2} = 0$, then the input terminal is #2 or #1 respectively. If a KVL-heuristic is applied to a component, the terminal connected to the node at which the KVL-heuristic is applied is considered the input terminal. If the output current of the resistor is an immediate antecedent to a KCL-heuristic, the output is really a voltage-to-ground at the terminal.

Tables 2 and 3 illustrate the 18 primitive causal patterns for a resistor (as the resistor is symmetric, #2 inputs are left out).

Examine the mechanism graph of Fig. 17. It mentions resistors RF, RC2 and RB1. As can be seen from the diagram, the two inputs to RF are the voltages at its two ends and the output is a current. Hence, it is functioning in a V-SENSOR configuration. The input to RC2 is a current and the output is a voltage at the same node, thus it is functioning in an I-LOAD configuration. On

TABLE 2. Resistor causal patterns

	Output	
Input	$i_{\#1}$	$i_{\#2}$
$i_{\#1}$	*	BIAS
$v_{\#1}$	V-LOAD	V-TO-I-COUPLE
$v_{\#1,\#2}$	V-SENSOR	V-SENSOR

TABLE 3. Resistor causal patterns

	Output		
Input	$v_{\#1}$	$v_{\#2}$	$v_{\#1,\#2}$
$i_{\#1}$	I-LOAD	I-TO-V-COUPLE	I-SENSOR
$v_{\#1}$	*	DIVIDER	DIVIDER

the other hand, the input to RB1 is a current and the output is a voltage so RB1 is functioning in the I-TO-V-COUPLE configuration.

Components that only participate in local feedback loops do not explicitly appear in the mechanism graph. The causal configurations of these components are determined by applying the standard configuration patterns as if the reflected

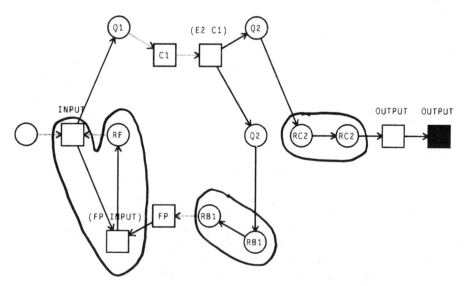

FIG. 17. Mechanism graph with resistor configurations.

signal were the input, and the heuristically deduced value the output. For example, RC1 does not appear in the mechanism graph but it contributes to a reflected current substantiating a KCL-heuristic, and thus causally it functions as an I-LOAD. So does RB2.

It is important to note that the same component may contribute in more than one way to the circuit mechanism. A resistor may be exhibiting more than one of the configurations listed in Tables 2 and 3. For example, a resistor may be converting a voltage to two different currents which propagate through different regions of the circuit. However, none of the resistors of the circuit of Fig. 10 exhibits a dual purpose.

6.2. No-function-in-structure

One of the central tenets of qualitative physics is the no-function-in-structure principle (NFIS): the laws of the parts of a component may not presume the functioning of the whole [6]. I have not stressed this issue earlier as it is implicit in electrical engineering. The definition of causal configuration just presented provides a simple means to motivate the concept by illustrating how easy it is to violate this principle.

Electrical engineering incorporates NFIS implicitly in its choice of conventions and notations. Likewise, the notation of qualitative physics is chosen to make it difficult to violate NFIS. However, if we were more liberal in writing components models, it would be quite easy to violate NFIS.

Tables 2 and 3 present 18 different causal configurations for resistor functioning. Given a more general notation, each of these 18 different causal configurations could be encoded as separate component models. For example, a V-LOAD model is $\partial v_t \Rightarrow \partial i_t$, and a V-TO-I-COUPLE is $\partial v_{\#1} \Rightarrow \partial i_{\#2}$. If causal analysis used these 18 models (using similarly developed models for the other component types), there would be no need for the heuristics or the causally ambiguous Ohm's law. The task of causal analysis would be to identify which of the possible models for a component were applicable in the given circuit being analyzed. The attraction of this approach is that the causal heuristics become superfluous, as a choice of component model implicitly involves making an assumption.

This approach unfortunately leads to incomplete models. In qualitative analysis generally there is a seductive tendency to confuse function with structure. For example, one might analyze a few circuits, notice that resistors were either BIAS's, V-TO-I-COUPLE's or I-LOAD's and build a model which incorporated only those possibilities. This model would be a gross violation of the no-function-in-structure principle as it would presume that the resistor does not ever function as, say, a V-SENSOR. The circuit of Fig. 10 could not be analyzed correctly. However, those circuits which only used resistors as BIAS's, V-TO-I-COUPLE's or I-LOAD's would be analyzed correctly.

Qualitative physics attempts to achieve no-function-in-structure by insisting that the models are as general and context-free as possible. Thus, for example, although the KCL- and KVL-heuristics could be incorporated into the component models, they are not. Instead, each model and law is general, local and parsimonious. A side benefit of this approach is that it is now possible to identify systematically all the possible functional roles of a resistor by looking at all the possible mechanism graph contexts in which the resistor can appear.

6.3. Transistor configurations

Electrical engineering distinguishes three configurations in which the transistor is capable of providing useful amplification. Each configuration has a unique combination of input impedance, output impedance, voltage gain, and current gain. The most familiar transistor configuration is the common-emitter (CE) in which the input is applied to the base and the output is taken off of the collector. The emitter provides the common terminal between input and output. In the common-base (CB) configuration the input is applied to the emitter and the output is taken off of the collector. The base provides the common terminal. In the common-collector configuration the input is applied to the base and the output is taken off of the emitter. This configuration is also called the emitter-follower configuration.

The correct transistor configuration is determined by the input and output variables of the transistor and these are determined in the same way as for resistor configurations. However, in laying out the possibilities many more transistor configurations come to the fore. A transistor can be used to compare two independent signals (the SUM configuration). As it also can be viewed as two back-to-back diodes it has many of the analogous configurations as a resistor (i.e., loading, sensing, and coupling). Table 4 summarizes the possible transistor configurations.

TABLE 4. Transistor configurations for forward active region

Input	Output			
	i_E	i_B	i_C	$v_{B,E}$
v_E	LOAD-Q	COUPLE-Q	CB	
v_B	CC	LOAD-Q	CE	SENSE-Q
$v_{B,E}$	SENSE-Q	SENSE-Q	SUM	*

Table 5 summarizes all the configurations for the circuit of Fig. 10. '(C)' indicates a causal (i.e., part of mechanism graph) configuration; '(F)' indicates a (non-local) feedback (i.e., part of mechanism graph but on a feedback path); and '(R)'

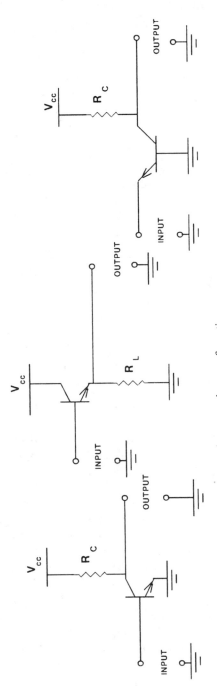

Fig. 18. Common-emitter, common-collector, and common-base configurations.

TABLE 5. Configurations for CE-FEEDBACK

Component	Configuration
Q1	CE(C)
	LOAD-Q(R)
Q2	CE(C)
	CC(F)
	LOAD-Q(R)
RC1	I-LOAD(R)
RC2	I-LOAD(C)
RB2	I-LOAD(R)
RB1	I-TO-V-COUPLE(F)
RF	V-SENSOR(F)
	I-LOAD(R)

indicates a reflection (i.e., supporting a heuristic propagation in the mechanism graph) configuration. Q1 functions in the common-emitter configuration on the signal path and LOAD-Q configuration in a reflection to the input signal. Q2 functions as a common-emitter stage to the output and as a common-collector stage feeding the signal back to the input. RC1 is functioning as an I-LOAD in a reflection configuration, RC2 is functioning as an I-LOAD on the causal path to the circuit output. RF is functioning as a V-SENSOR for the feedback path and as a reflection for the input signal. RB1 (with RB2) converts the transistor's output current to a voltage to be compared and fed back.

6.4. Fragment graph

The taxonomy of component configurations developed in Sections 6.1 and 6.4 can be used to parse the mechanism graph. Each component functioning in a particular configuration characterizes a subgraph of connected edges and vertices in the mechanism graph. These are the *primitive teleological fragments* of the circuit. As the output of every component is connected to the input of some other component, the fragments can be connected together in a topology homomorphic to that of the original mechanism graph. The result of this process is an abstract description of the functioning of the circuit in terms of the basic roles of the components. Fig. 19 is the fragment graph corresponding to the mechanism graph of Fig. 16.

Vertices corresponding to the component roles are labeled by their type. The different configurations are grouped into eight different classes which delineate the generic actions of fragments (e.g., input/output, coupling and amplification stage). Most classes are broken down further into types (e.g., the common-emitter, common-collector and common-base transistor configurations). The complete ontology used by EQUAL is given in Table 6.

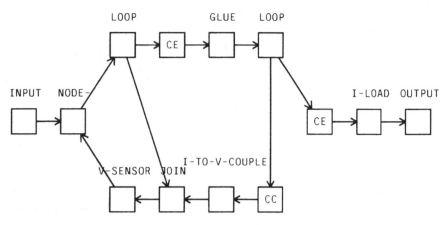

FIG. 19. Primitive fragments of mechanism graph for CE-FEEDBACK.

Not all these fragments types occur in the circuit CE-FEEDBACK or the component configuration tables. Fragment types SPLIT and JOIN are used to describe feedforward mechanisms where two signals split and later rejoin. CASCADE and FEEDBACK configurations are abstract fragments introduced in the Section 6.5.

As in the mechanism graph, the same component may fulfill multiple roles. Hence, for example, Q2 appears twice in the fragment graph: once in the common-emitter configuration in the main signal path and once in the common-collector configuration on the feedback path.

6.5. An amplifier parser

In the first two steps of the recognition process causal analysis applied to the

TABLE 6

Class	Type	Description
IO	INPUT,OUTPUT	signals on boundary
SAMPLING	NODE,LOOP	feedback sampling point
COMPARISON	NODE,LOOP	feedback comparison point
SPLIT	unused	signal splits n ways
JOIN	VOLTAGES,CURRENTS	n signals combine
STAGE	CE,CC,CB,CASCADE,FEEDBACK	amplifying stage
DIFF-2-1	SUM	differential amplifier
COUPLING	GLUE,V-LOAD,WIRE,I-LOAD,	
	V-SENSOR,V-TO-I-COUPLING,	
	I-TO-V-COUPLING,SENSE-Q,LOAD-Q,	
	COUPLE-Q,BIAS,LEVEL	signal couplers

circuit's topology constructs a representation of the circuit's abstract mechanism (Fig. 16) and the role each component plays in this mechanism (Fig. 19). The final step performs topological manipulations on this representation of circuit mechanism in order to construct a hierarchical decomposition of the mechanism with the ultimate purpose at the most abstract level using the fragment graph as its base.

COUPLING fragments only couple signals from one part of the circuit to another. As they perform no useful amplification, fan-in or fan-out roles the first parsing step is to incorporate all of them into their adjacent fragments. The result is Fig. 20.

Although pure reflections are never included in the mechanism graph, feedback which is both local and global must be included. A parsing rule is required to remove the local feedback loop, leaving the global one in place. The substitution rule is given in Fig. 21. The resultant fragment graph is Fig. 22.

The circuit can now be (correctly) parsed as a feedback amplifier followed by a common-emitter stage. However, there is an alternate parsing of the circuit which gives a better account of the gains (a topic discussed in more detail in [11]). EQUAL is also concerned with determining the input/output characteristics of each circuit fragment in terms of input impedance, output impedance, transresistance, current gain, voltage gain, and transconductance. In particular, it determines approximate ranges for their values and how stable they are. The fragment graph of Fig. 22 implies that the feedback action does not stabilize the gain of Q2's CE configuration. However, Q2's collector and emitter currents are identical, thus the feedback action also stabilizes the gain of Q2's configuration. For this reason EQUAL employs an additional parsing rule to rewrite the fragment graph (and the gains of the fragments—although that is

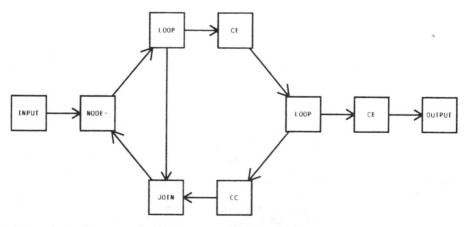

FIG. 20. Parse of CE-FEEDBACK after removing COUPLING.

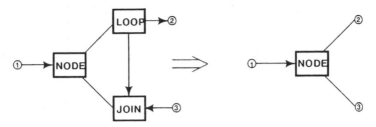

FIG. 21. Local feedback substitution rule.

not discussed here). Fig. 23 illustrates this rule. The resultant fragment graph is Fig. 24.

Two active component configurations (stages) can be combined into a single fragment called a CASCADE. After applying this cascade rule the fragment graph is Fig. 25. All feedback loops are of the form of Fig. 26 and may be summarized. The result of applying this rule is Fig. 27. The parse terminates at the point as the pattern of input-amplifier-output is a valid amplifier.

The purpose of a fragment is given by the role it plays in the more abstract fragments in which it participates. The role name is provided by the rewrite rule. For example, the two antecedent stages for the cascade rule are called STAGE1 and STAGE2. The rewrite rules in order of application are (the antecedent roles, if any, are listed in parentheses):

1 FLUSH-GLUE( )
   Remove all COUPLING and FEEDBACK COUPLING
2 CASCADE(STAGE1,STAGE2)
   Combine successive stages

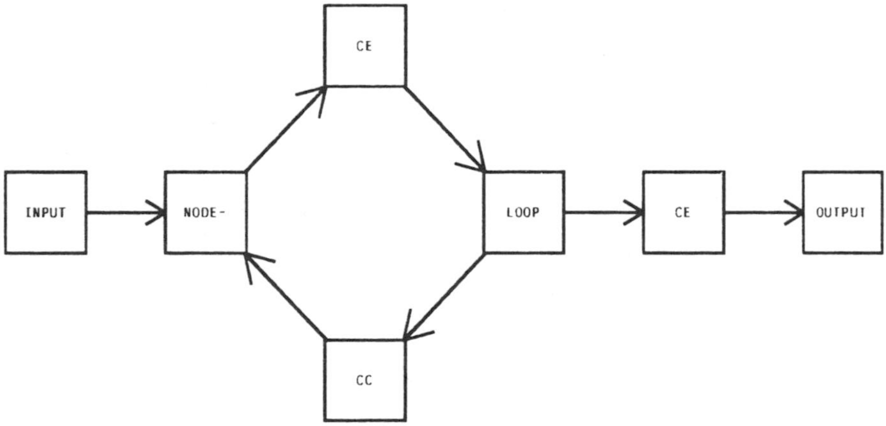

FIG. 22. Parse of CE-FEEDBACK after removing local feedback.

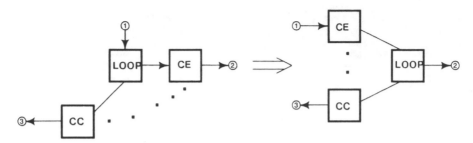

FIG. 23. Sampling rewrite rule.

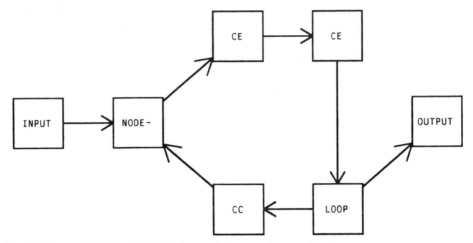

FIG. 24. Parse of CE-FEEDBACK after applying sampling rewrite rule.

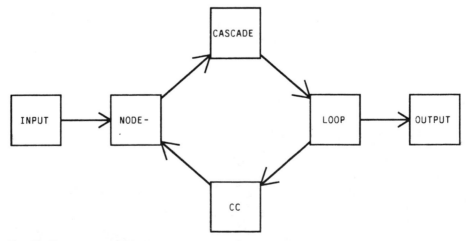

FIG. 25. Parse of CE-FEEDBACK after cascading stages.

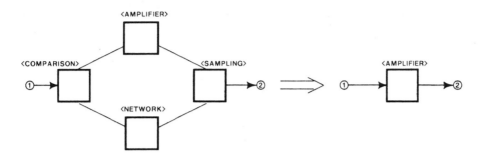

FIG. 26. Feedback rewrite rule.

3 LOCAL-FEEDBACK( )
  Remove local feedback
4 UNLOOPS( )
  Move sampling point backward
5 FEEDBACK(COMPARISON,BASIC-AMPLIFIER,SAMPLING,FEEDBACK-
    NETWORK)
  Feedback amplifier
6 TOP-LEVEL(INPUT-NETWORK,STAGE,OUTPUT-NETWORK)
  Termination

The ordering of these rules is important. For example, interchanging the rules UNLOOPS and FEEDBACK causes faulty analyses.

The hierarchical description generated by the fragment rewrite rules provides a detailed description of the role of each component of the circuit. The following is EQUAL's explanation for the purpose of each of the components in CE-FEEDBACK. Reflection configurations are left out unless and component is functioning only in a reflection configuration (i.e., LOAD-Q for Q2 is left out, while I-LOAD for RC1 is included). Each rewrite rule assigns role names to each fragment on its right-hand sides. A separate explanation is included for each configuration of each component. The first line of each component's description is its configuration. This is typically followed by a sequence of lines of the form "Which is ⟨role⟩ or ⟨rule⟩" which indicates how the fragments the component is part of are parsed. Passive components in load configurations

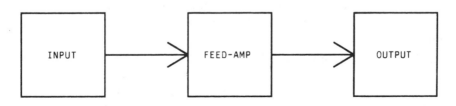

FIG. 27. Parse of CE-FEEDBACK after eliminating feedback.

(which are otherwise removed by the FLUSH-GLUE rule) are related to the
active components they load.

Q1 is functioning in CE configuration.
Which is STAGE1 of CASCADE
Which is BASIC-AMPLIFIER of FEEDBACK
Which is STAGE of TOP-LEVEL

Q2 is functioning in LOOP configuration.
Which is SAMPLING of FEEDBACK
Which is STAGE of TOP-LEVEL
And,

Q2 is functioning in CE configuration.
Which is STAGE2 of CASCADE
Which is BASIC-AMPLIFIER of FEEDBACK
Which is STAGE of TOP-LEVEL
And,

Q2 is functioning in CC configuration.
Which is FEEDBACK-COUPLING of FEEDBACK-NETWORK
Which is FEEDBACK-NETWORK of FEEDBACK
Which is STAGE of TOP-LEVEL

RC1 is functioning in I-LOAD configuration.
For Q1 functioning in CE configuration.
Which is STAGE1 of CASCADE
Which is BASIC-AMPLIFIER of FEEDBACK
Which is STAGE of TOP-LEVEL

RC2 is functioning in I-LOAD configuration.
Which is COUPLING of OUTPUT-NETWORK
Which is OUTPUT-NETWORK of TOP-LEVEL

RB1 is functioning in I-TO-V-COUPLE configuration.
Which is FEEDBACK-COUPLING of FEEDBACK-NETWORK
Which is FEEDBACK-NETWORK of FEEDBACK
Which is STAGE of TOP-LEVEL

RB2 is functioning in I-LOAD configuration.
For Q2 functioning in CC configuration.
Which is FEEDBACK-COUPLING of FEEDBACK-NETWORK
Which is FEEDBACK-NETWORK of FEEDBACK
Which is STAGE of TOP-LEVEL

RF is functioning in V-SENSOR configuration.
Which is FEEDBACK-COUPLING of FEEDBACK-NETWORK
Which is FEEDBACK-NETWORK of FEEDBACK
Which is STAGE of TOP-LEVEL

Much more work can be gotten out of teleology than is presented here. First,
it is possible to define the set of rewrite rules to cover a wide class of amplifiers
and power-supplies. Second, it is possible to include estimates of the gain and
impedances of stages and adjust these in the parsing process. For example,
feedback has a dramatic effect on gains and impedances. Third, voltage and

current sources need to be analyzed with different types of rules. Another report [11] extends the outline presented in this paper into these three areas.

6.6. The power of the teleological parse

The teleological analysis constructs a canonical form for circuit functioning. This has two immediate advantages. First, it identifies the role each component plays in the composite device. Electrical engineers associate with each configuration a large body of knowledge of how it is used, what its peculiar characteristics are, what its failure modes are, etc. Thus, the parse provides an index into this body of knowledge. For example, once it is recognized that the transistor is acting as a common-emitter amplifier, knowledge about its problems, frequency response, etc. can be accessed. Second, canonicalization helps identify similar circuits. For example, two circuits may have radically different schematics, but at a given level of abstraction they may both be series-regulated power-supplies. The techniques outlined here apply to fluid, hydraulic, mechanical, etc. systems as well, so the language of mechanism is sufficiently powerful to notice a mechanical analog of some electrical system, because at some level they have the same fragment graph.

7. Ambiguity

Sections 3–6 developed the structure-to-function analysis very quickly, glossing over many details. In these concluding sections, we step back and examine some of these glossed-over issues in more detail. The advantage of showing the role of teleology first, is that it now provides a motivation and organization for dealing with some of these harder problems.

Qualitative analysis is fundamentally ambiguous. It is often possible to find more than one qualitative value or more than one causal argument for a circuit quantity. When this occurs EQUAL considers both possibilities simultaneously and produces multiple causal arguments for the circuit's behavior(s). Other, non-causal, reasoning must be used to select amongst the possibilities. However, before dealing with the mechanics of selection it is important to consider the origin of ambiguity and the generation of the possibilities.

7.1. The origin of ambiguity

Due to the coarse distinctions of the qualitative value set, qualitative analysis is ambiguous compared to quantitative analysis. However, one would have hoped that qualitative analysis were unambiguous with respect to itself, i.e., that given a qualitative description of a situation it produces a distinct qualitative description of the behavior. Unfortunately, this is not possible and, even qualitatively, behavior is ambiguous. The root cause of this ambiguity is that the qualitative operators do not define a field and hence most of the usual theorems of linear algebra and network theory upon which our intuitions are based fail to hold. For a more detailed discussion see [6].

It is important to note that the ambiguity does not result from the implementation choices discussed in Section 3.2. Adding KCL or KVL confluences does not remove any ambiguity.

7.2. Global ambiguity

The task of causal analysis is to identify all possible globally consistent behaviors. The only way more than one behavior can arise is if there are some ambiguities in the propagation. It is important to note that a single heuristic, by itself, does not introduce any ambiguity. Rather, an ambiguity is only introduced if at some point in the propagation two or more heuristics apply. The ambiguity is whether either one or both of the heuristics are valid. However, it is not possible to tell, locally, which is the case. Only additional propagation can distinguish among the possibilities.

The only mechanism for disambiguation is contradiction detection. Suppose heuristics A and B apply at some impasse. There is now a potential ambiguity between {A}, {B} and {A, B}. A contradiction involving only A, rules out {A} and {A, B} leaving B as the only option. Likewise a contradiction involving only B, leaves A as the only option. Both these contradictions completely remove the local ambiguity (and hence the global ambiguity). However, there is a third case which we haven't yet considered, neither A nor B may individually contradict, however their combination {A, B} might. In this situation either A or B holds, but not at once. Then, and only then, is there a global ambiguity.

7.3. Implementation

The algorithm explores all possibilities at once, never backtracking (which is unnecessary if the underlying algorithm will find all the possibilities). The propagator is essentially the same as the one used earlier propagating KCL and KVL first, then component rules, and finally heuristics.

The implementation makes no commitments about global ambiguity until propagation finishes. As each value triple (i.e., $\langle qvalue,\{assumptions\},$ $justifications(s)\rangle$) carries with it the set of assumptions under which it holds, each value carries with it the ambiguities that matter to it. This design decision has other important benefits. It is not necessary to have a completely separate causal argument structure for each global ambiguity. For example, a multi-stage amplifier may have no ambiguity until the last stage. All of the cells for the earlier stages will have only one value which applies to all global ambiguities. The causal argument for any value in the last stage only differs within that final part of the argument within the last stage. Aside from the obvious efficiency advantages of this approach, with this representation it is trivial to see where two global ambiguities differ.

In the simple propagator each cell representing a circuit quantity could have at most one value. When a second value was discovered, one of the two would be chosen and propagated further. Now each cell may have any number of value triples and each propagated. It is important to note that when a cell receives a second value, the other values in the cell are not changed. In particular, the justification tree of a propagation does not change even if other values are discovered for the cells of its antecedent values. As a consequence, the set of assumptions underlying a propagated value never change.

Care must be taken to identify all contradictions and ensure that only the simplest argument is propagated. Both of these goals are achieved by the algorithm which adds a new value to a cell. If the qualitative expression of a new value triple differs from the qualitative expression of an existing value triple, the union of the set of assumptions of the old and new value triples is marked as contradictory. (And all superset assumption sets are also marked contradictory and all other value triples depending on these assumptions sets are removed from the cells and EQUAL's propagation queues.) If the new value triple is equal to an old value triple (i.e., same qualitative expression, same justification, and same assumption set) it is ignored. Simpler value triples have fewer assumptions. If the assumption set of the new value triple is a superset of an old value triple's, the new value triple is likewise discarded. If the assumption set of the new value triple is a subset of an old value triple's, the old value triple is discarded instead and all its consequents are removed from the cells and the queues. Only if the new value triple passes these tests is it added to the cell and allowed to propagate further. Thus, the simplest causal argument is found for each cell, and no contradictory value triples are propagated.

The implementation for the constraints themselves must also be modified to accept multiple-valued antecedents and to run multiple times. Naively, if a rule has two antecedents the first having n values, the second m values, the rule is applied nm times producing nm results. Unfortunately, the situation is far more subtle: this simple scheme is extremely inefficient and produces faulty propagations. It is unnecessary to apply the rule to cell values present the last time the rule was run. The new values can be easily distinguished from old values: the new values are on the queue of pending propagations. In addition, it is not worth the effort of generating the result if it is known to be contradictory. This is done by precomputing the union of the antecedent assumption sets to determine whether they are contradictory (i.e., contain a contradiction as a subset).

Suppose a particular heuristic is used twice during a causal analysis with the same antecedent cells, but different values of those cells. And furthermore, suppose the ensuing propagations from the two assumptions interact. This case, which occurs rarely, is clearly wrong by the preceding argument. This is avoided by treating each instance of a heuristic, even those having the same antecedent cells as mutually contradictory.

Applications of heuristics require special care. A heuristic usefully applies only if there is an impasse in the causal propagation, but if cells contain multiple value triples it is harder to see whether an impasse has been reached within some assumption set. The algorithm used is complex, but it is equivalent to an efficient implementation of the following simple and inefficient scheme. As usual run heuristic rules last, and just assume that every value is at an impasse. The pruning algorithm which applies when multiple values are added to a cell eliminates at the unnecessary heuristic applications. The actual implementation of the algorithm looks ahead to see whether the pruning algorithm would immediately eliminate the heuristic.

As manipulation of sets of assumptions is the most fundamental and common type of operation of causal analysis, some care must be taken to implement these potentially complex algorithms. EQUAL uses a subset of a full TMS algorithm (see [5] for a description) which is highly optimized for the operations needed for qualitative reasoning. Each assumption and set of assumptions is made unique and hashed into a lattice structure. This lattice structure directly represents superset and subset relationships among sets. Contradictions are automatically inherited along superset links and the data base of values is updated. The data structure is optimized for the two most common operations: adding an assumption to a set and computing the union of two sets. Aside from being optimized for causal analysis, this simple TMS has another significant advantage over Doyle's and McAllester's [14, 25]. Those TMS's force the data base to hold one consistent set of facts in at a time. Every contradiction brings different facts in and changes justifications for deductions. In EQUAL's scheme, multiple inconsistent views can be represented and compared at the same time, and additionally the justifications for deductions are never changed. The latter property is critical for causal analysis, and the former property is critical for comparing alternative causal arguments for a circuit quantity (discussed in Section 8.2).

8. Interpretations

An *interpretation* is a global point of view for circuit behavior which selects a single value for every cell, a coherent overall framework for circuit behavior, and a single mechanism graph. If the analysis is ambiguous, the circuit will have multiple interpretations. A fundamental success criteria of qualitative analysis is that the set of interpretations must be *complete* and *realizable*. Every possible behavior of every possible ideal circuit must be described by some interpretation (*completeness*) and every interpretation generated by causal reasoning must correspond to an ideal physically realizable circuit (*realizabil-*

ity). Put concretely, each of the six interpretations for CE-FEEDBACK (see Table 7) corresponds to the behavior of a version of CE-FEEDBACK with parameter values picked appropriately, and the behavior produced by any assignment of parameter values for CE-FEEDBACK is described by one of the interpretations.

Table 7 includes every circuit variable except the second current for two-terminal components. '#' indicates that no causal value is found for these quantities. Causal propagation only finds values for the interesting circuit variables.

As realizability and completeness are fundamental to qualitative reasoning, I want to be very precise by what I mean by 'ideal': an ideal circuit behaves in accordance with the component models of electrical engineers. Although these quantitative models are extremely accurate and almost always adequate, they may not completely describe the precise behavior of real physical components. Realizability and completeness can only be applied to the idealizations of electrical engineering. (Admittedly, I would like these criteria to also hold with respect to the real physical world but that would force this research into an empirical methodology.) Of course, electrical engineers sometimes use different quantitative models and therefore realizability and completeness should be stated differently: given *any* set of quantitative models, causal analysis working with the corresponding qualitative models should produce realizable and complete interpretations with respect to those quantitative models.

TABLE 7. Causal interpretations.

	1	2	3	4	5	6		1	2	3	4	5	6
$\partial i_{\rightarrow \text{INPUT}} =$	+	+	+	+	+	+	$\partial v_{\text{C1,VCC}} =$	+	0	−	−	−	−
$\partial i_{\rightarrow +(B1)} =$	+	+	#	#	#	#	$\partial v_{\text{C1}} =$	+	0	−	−	−	−
$\partial i_{\rightarrow \#1(RC2)} =$	−	−	−	−	−	−	$\partial v_{\text{E2,OUTPUT}} =$	#	#	−	#	−	−
$\partial i_{\rightarrow \#1(RF)} =$	+	+	+	+	+	+	$\partial v_{\text{E2,VCC}} =$	+	+	−	+	−	−
$\partial i_{\rightarrow \#1(RB2)} =$	−	−	−	−	0	+	$\partial v_{\text{E2}} =$	+	+	−	+	−	−
$\partial i_{\rightarrow \#1(RB1)} =$	−	−	−	−	−	−	$\partial v_{\text{E2,C1}} =$	+	+	+	+	+	+
$\partial i_{\rightarrow \#1(RC1)} =$	−	0	+	+	+	+	$\partial v_{\text{INPUT,OUTPUT}} =$	#	#	#	#	#	#
$\partial i_{\rightarrow C(Q2)} =$	−	−	−	−	−	−	$\partial v_{\text{INPUT,VCC}} =$	+	+	+	+	+	+
$\partial i_{\rightarrow B(Q2)} =$	−	−	−	−	−	−	$\partial v_{\text{INPUT}} =$	+	+	+	+	+	+
$\partial i_{\rightarrow E(Q2)} =$	+	+	+	+	+	+	$\partial v_{\text{INPUT,C1}} =$	+	+	+	+	+	+
$\partial i_{\rightarrow C(Q1)} =$	+	+	+	+	+	+	$\partial v_{\text{INPUT,E2}} =$	+	+	+	+	+	+
$\partial i_{\rightarrow B(Q1)} =$	+	+	+	+	+	+	$\partial v_{\text{FP,OUTPUT}} =$	#	#	#	#	−	−
$\partial i_{\rightarrow E(Q1)} =$	−	−	−	−	−	−	$\partial v_{\text{FP,VCC}} =$	+	+	+	+	0	−
$\partial v_{\text{VCC,OUTPUT}} =$	−	−	−	−	−	−	$\partial v_{\text{FP}} =$	+	+	+	+	0	−
$\partial v_{\text{OUTPUT}} =$	+	+	+	+	+	+	$\partial v_{\text{FP,C1}} =$	+	+	+	+	+	+
$\partial v_{\text{VCC}} =$	0	0	0	0	0	0	$\partial v_{\text{FP,E2}} =$	+	+	+	+	+	+
$\partial v_{\text{C1,OUTPUT}} =$	#	−	−	−	−	−	$\partial v_{\text{FP,INPUT}} =$	−	−	−	−	−	−

8.1. Constraint satisfaction vs. causal analysis

Although realizability and completeness define the goal of causal analysis, they are very hard to attain in practice. However, it is possible to apply them partially and this partial technique was used to debug EQUAL, the component models and the heuristics. The ultimate test of qualitative analysis can be broken down into three steps: (1) quantitative models describe physical components, (2) qualitative models describe 'ideal' quantitative models, and (3) causal arguments describe each qualitative behavior. We avoid the first step by simply leaving quantitative modeling to the electrical engineers and physicists. The correctness of the second step is achieved by being systematic in constructing the component models (see [6]). The correctness of the last step can be evaluated explicitly. In particular, every qualitatively possible behavior should have a causal argument. This can be tested by explicitly stating every qualitative equation that causal propagation uses and solving the system of equations thus produced with a conventional constraint satisfaction technique which is unencumbered with producing causal arguments. The constraint satisfaction algorithm is equivalent to generate and test so it is guaranteed to find every possible solution. Every possible qualitative behavior should have a corresponding causal analysis and every possible causal analysis should correspond to a possible qualitative behavior.

For example, CE-FEEDBACK is described by 64 qualitative equations in 41 variables (adding more equations neither improves, or eliminates interpretations).

Each transistor is modeled by three qualitative equations:

$$\partial v_{\text{E2,C1}} + \partial i_{\rightarrow \text{C(Q2)}} = 0 , \qquad \partial i_{\rightarrow \text{E(Q2)}} - \partial v_{\text{E2,C1}} = 0 ,$$

$$\partial v_{\text{E2,C1}} + \partial i_{\rightarrow \text{B(Q2)}} = 0 , \qquad \partial v_{\text{INPUT}} - \partial i_{\rightarrow \text{C(Q1)}} = 0 ,$$

$$\partial v_{\text{INPUT}} + \partial i_{\rightarrow \text{E(Q1)}} = 0 , \qquad \partial v_{\text{INPUT}} - \partial i_{\rightarrow \text{B(Q1)}} = 0 .$$

Ohm's law for each resistor is:

$$\partial v_{\text{C1,VCC}} + \partial i_{\rightarrow \#1(\text{RC1})} = 0 , \qquad \partial v_{\text{FP,E2}} + \partial i_{\rightarrow \#1(\text{RB1})} = 0 ,$$

$$\partial v_{\text{FP}} + \partial i_{\rightarrow \#1(\text{RB2})} = 0 , \qquad \partial v_{\text{FP,INPUT}} + \partial i_{\rightarrow \#1(\text{RF})} = 0 ,$$

$$\partial i_{\rightarrow \#1(\text{RC2})} - \partial v_{\text{VCC,OUTPUT}} = 0 .$$

The battery model is:

$$\partial v_{\text{VCC}} = 0 .$$

The input signal is:

$$\partial i_{\rightarrow \text{INPUT}} = + .$$

A KCL confluence is required for each component and node:

$$\partial i_{\to \text{INPUT}} - \partial i_{\to \#1(\text{RF})} - \partial i_{\to B(Q1)} = 0 ,$$

$$\partial i_{\to +(\text{B1})} + \partial i_{\to -(\text{B1})} = 0 ,$$

$$\partial i_{\to +(\text{B1})} + \partial i_{\to \#1(\text{RC2})} + \partial i_{\to \#1(\text{RC1})} = 0 , \quad \text{etc.}$$

A KVL equation is required for every three circuit nodes (35 equations).

$$\partial v_{\text{FP,E2}} - \partial v_{\text{FP,INPUT}} - \partial v_{\text{INPUT,E2}} = 0 ,$$

$$\partial v_{\text{FP,C1}} - \partial v_{\text{FP,INPUT}} - \partial v_{\text{INPUT,C1}} = 0 ,$$

$$\partial v_{\text{FP}} - \partial v_{\text{FP,INPUT}} - \partial v_{\text{INPUT}} = 0 , \quad \text{etc.}$$

In quantitative analysis such a set of equations has a unique solution. However, constraint satisfaction reveals that the above set of confluences has 85 solutions! Many of these interpretations result because some variable is completely underconstrained. If totally unconstrained quantities are eliminated there are 41 interpretations (See Table 8; '?' is used to indicate the totally unconstrained variables; for brevity, quantities with constant value are left out and only one terminal current is included for two-terminal components). Constraint satisfaction discovers far more interpretations than causal analysis because values for causally unimportant variables are included (as defined in Section 3.4.5). Table 7 can be collapsed by merging causally unimportant variables. In particular, if two interpretations differ only in a causally unimportant variable, the interpretations are merged and a '*' substituted for the uninteresting variable. Note that the values for uninteresting variables which need not be merged are left unchanged. The result after merging is five interpretations (Table 9).

Table 9 matches Table 7 as follows: 1 to 4, 2 to 5, 3 to 3, 4 to 3, 5 to 2, and 6 to 1. A comparison of the results of causal analysis and constraint satisfaction reveals two curiosities. As expected, constraint satisfaction discovers many more values, but always for causally uninteresting variables. Second, there are fewer interpretations generated by constraint satisfaction than with causal analysis. Constraint satisfaction interpretation 3 (Table 9) corresponds to causal interpretations 3 and 4 (Table 7). Causal interpretations 3 and 4 differ only in uninteresting variables $\partial v_{\text{E2,OUTPUT}}$, $\partial v_{\text{E2,VCC}}$ and ∂v_{E2}. Causal analysis produced differing values for these uninteresting quantities because these two interpretations have differing mechanism graphs. Note that causal analysis does not reliably produce all values for uninteresting quantities. For example, the full 41 interpretation constraint satisfaction (Table 8) shows that $\partial v_{\text{E2,VCC}}$ and ∂v_{E2} can both be zero, while no causal interpretation shows this.

It is more difficult to collapse causal interpretations than constraint satisfaction interpretations because the causal arguments and mechanism graphs need to be merged as well. However, on the basis of qualitative values alone,

TABLE 8

Interpretation	1	2	3	4	5	6	7	8	9	10	11	12	13	14	15	16	17	18	19	20	21	22	23	24	25	26	27	28	29	30	31	32	33	34	35	36	37	38	39	40	41
$\partial i_{-\to+(B1)} =$	+	+	+	+	+	+	+	+	+	+	+	+	+	+	+	+	+	+	0	0	0	0	0	0	0	0	0	0	0	0	−	−	−	−	−	−	−	−	−	−	−
$\partial i_{-\neq I(RF)} =$	+	+	+	+	+	+	+	+	+	+	+	+	+	+	+	+	+	+	+	+	+	+	+	+	+	+	+	+	+	+	+	+	+	+	+	+	+	+	+	+	+
$\partial i_{-\neq I(RB2)} =$	−	−	+	−	−	−	−	−	−	−	−	−	−	−	−	−	+	+	−	−	−	−	−	−	−	−	−	−	−	−	+	+	+	+	+	+	+	+	+	+	+
$\partial i_{-\neq I(RC1)} =$	−	−	−	0	−	0	0	−	0	−	−	+	+	0	−	+	+	0	+	+	+	−	+	+	+	+	+	+	+	+	+	−	−	−	−	−	−	−	−	0	+
$\partial v_{C1,OUTPUT} =$	+	0	−	−	−	+	+	+	+	+	+	−	0	+	+	−	−	−	−	−	−	−	−	−	−	−	−	−	−	−	−	−	−	−	−	−	−	−	−	−	−
$\partial v_{C1,VCC} =$	+	+	−	0	+	−	−	−	0	+	−	−	0	0	0	−	−	−	−	−	−	−	−	−	−	−	−	−	−	−	−	−	−	−	−	−	−	−	−	−	−
$\partial v_{C1} =$	+	+	−	0	+	−	−	−	0	+	−	−	0	0	+	−	−	−	−	−	−	−	−	−	−	−	−	−	−	−	−	−	−	−	−	−	−	−	−	−	−
$\partial v_{E2,OUTPUT} =$	+	+	?	?	?	0	−	−	−	−	−	−	−	−	−	0	−	−	?	?	−	−	−	−	−	−	−	−	−	−	?	−	−	−	−	−	−	−	−	−	−
$\partial v_{E2,VCC} =$	+	+	+	+	+	−	0	−	−	−	−	−	+	+	+	0	−	−	+	0	0	−	0	0	−	0	0	−	0	−	0	0	−	+	0	0	−	0	−	−	−
$\partial v_{E2} =$	+	+	+	+	+	+	−	+	+	+	+	+	+	+	+	?	−	−	+	0	0	−	−	0	−	−	−	−	−	−	+	+	+	+	−	−	+	−	−	−	−
$\partial v_{INPUT,OUTPUT} =$	+	+	+	+	+	+	+	0	0	0	+	0	?	?	?	−	+	?	+	0	0	+	+	0	+	+	0	−	?	?	+	+	+	+	+	+	+	0	+	0	?
$\partial v_{FP,OUTPUT} =$	+	+	+	+	+	+	+	+	+	0	0	+	?	?	?	?	−	?	+	0	0	+	0	0	0	0	0	0	?	?	+	+	+	0	0	+	+	+	?	?	?
$\partial v_{FP,VCC} =$	+	+	+	+	+	+	+	+	+	+	+	+	+	+	+	−	+	0	+	+	+	+	+	+	+	+	+	+	−	−	+	+	+	+	+	0	−	+	+	0	−
$\partial v_{FP} =$	+	+	+	+	+	+	+	+	+	+	+	+	+	+	+	+	+	0	+	+	+	+	+	+	+	+	+	+	0	−	+	+	+	+	+	+	+	+	+	0	−

TABLE 9. Satisfaction interpretations

	1	2	3	4	5		1	2	3	4	5
$\partial i_{\rightarrow \text{INPUT}} =$	+	+	+	+	+	$\partial v_{\text{C1,VCC}} =$	−	−	−	+	0
$\partial i_{\rightarrow +(\text{B1})} =$	*	*	*	+	+	$\partial v_{\text{C1}} =$	−	−	−	+	0
$\partial i_{\rightarrow \#1(\text{RC2})} =$	−	−	−	−	−	$\partial v_{\text{E2,OUTPUT}} =$	−	−	*	*	*
$\partial i_{\rightarrow \#1(\text{RF})} =$	+	+	+	+	+	$\partial v_{\text{E2,VCC}} =$	−	−	*	+	+
$\partial i_{\rightarrow \#1(\text{RB2})} =$	+	0	−	−	−	$\partial v_{\text{E2}} =$	−	−	*	+	+
$\partial i_{\rightarrow \#1((\text{RB1})} =$	−	−	−	−	−	$\partial v_{\text{E2,C1}} =$	+	+	+	+	+
$\partial i_{\rightarrow \#1(\text{RC1})} =$	+	+	+	−	0	$\partial v_{\text{INPUT,OUTPUT}} =$	?	?	*	*	*
$\partial i_{\rightarrow \text{C(Q2)}} =$	−	−	−	−	−	$\partial v_{\text{INPUT,VCC}} =$	+	+	+	+	+
$\partial i_{\rightarrow \text{B(Q2)}} =$	−	−	−	−	−	$\partial v_{\text{INPUT}} =$	+	+	+	+	+
$\partial i_{\rightarrow \text{E(Q2)}} =$	+	+	+	+	+	$\partial v_{\text{INPUT,C1}} =$	+	+	+	+	+
$\partial i_{\rightarrow \text{C(Q1)}} =$	+	+	+	+	+	$\partial v_{\text{INPUT,E2}} =$	+	+	+	+	+
$\partial i_{\rightarrow \text{B(Q1)}} =$	+	+	+	+	+	$\partial v_{\text{FP,OUTPUT}} =$	−	−	*	*	*
$\partial i_{\rightarrow \text{E(Q1)}} =$	−	−	−	−	−	$\partial v_{\text{FP,VCC}} =$	−	0	+	+	+
$\partial v_{\text{VCC,OUTPUT}} =$	−	−	−	−	−	$\partial v_{\text{FP}} =$	−	0	+	+	+
$\partial v_{\text{OUTPUT}} =$	+	+	+	+	+	$\partial v_{\text{FP,C1}} =$	+	+	+	+	+
$\partial v_{\text{VCC}} =$	0	0	0	0	0	$\partial v_{\text{FP,E2}} =$	+	+	+	+	+
$\partial v_{\text{C1,OUTPUT}} =$	−	−	−	*	−	$\partial v_{\text{FP,INPUT}} =$	−	−	−	−	−

causal analysis and constraint satisfaction predict the same set of behaviors. Thus, for CE-FEEDBACK every possible behavior has a causal argument and every possible causal argument corresponds to a possible behavior. The desideratum is that this be true for every possible circuit. Note, however, that the number of interpretations need not always match. Sometimes, as is the case with CE-FEEDBACK the same constraint satisfaction analysis may have multiple causal analyses. This also occurs in the few rare instances where the identical behavior (interesting and uninteresting quantities) has multiple causal explanations. There will never be more constraint satisfaction interpretations than causal interpretations due to the merging of uninteresting variables.

The technique of constraint satisfaction is used extensively in debugging EQUAL and its models as well as experimenting with differing heuristics. EQUAL has been run on hundreds of examples. For each, the causal and constraint satisfaction interpretations have been compared (via another program) to confirm that every possible behavior has a causal argument. The evidence on the adequacy of the KVL and KCL equation formulation was obtained using these means.

8.2. Causal interpretations

Although causal analysis finds values for each circuit quantity, it does not separate out which values belong to which causal argument or global behavior. This is the role of causal interpretations. Unlike the notion of constraint-satisfaction interpretations which arise out of differences in qualitative values, causal interpretations arise out of differences in causal assumptions. A causal interpretation is defined by a set of assumptions and selects those value triples whose assumption set is a subset of the interpretation assumption set. Each interpretation is intended to correspond to a single global behavior and the values for a single well-formed mechanism graph.

The remainder of this section presents criteria for selecting among these interpretations to identify which one best describes the 'normal' behavior of the circuit. The set of tentative interpretations is generated by finding all sets of assumptions which (1) could be a valid assumption set for a value; imagine a final circuit value whose antecedents were every circuit quantity: the assumption set must be contradiction-free, (2) is maximal, i.e., the inclusion of any additional assumption either introduces a contradiction or adds no information, and (3) is minimal, i.e., the removal of any assumption removes all values from some circuit quantity. CE-FEEDBACK has 6 causal interpretations:

1: $\{[\text{INPUT IN}][\text{FP RB1}][\text{Q2 } v_B][\text{C1 Q1}]\}$
2: $\{[\text{INPUT IN}][\text{FP RF RB1}][\text{Q2 } v_B][\text{C1 Q1}][\text{RF } v_{\#1}]\}$
3: $\{[\text{INPUT IN}][\text{C1 Q1}][\text{E2 RB1}][\text{RB1 } v_{\#2}][\text{FP RF}][\text{RF } v_{\#1}]\}$
4: $\{[\text{INPUT IN}][\text{E2 Q2}][\text{Q2 } v_B][\text{C1 Q1}][\text{FP RF}][\text{RF } v_{\#1}]\}$
5: $\{[\text{INPUT IN}][\text{C1 Q2 Q1}][\text{Q2 } v_E][\text{E2 RB1}][\text{RB1 } v_{\#2}][\text{FP RF}][\text{RF } v_{\#1}]\}$
6: $\{[\text{INPUT IN}][\text{C1 Q2}][\text{Q2 } v_E][\text{E2 RB1}][\text{RB1 } v_{\#2}][\text{FP RF}][\text{RF } v_{\#1}]\}$

This numbering corresponds to that of Table 7.

Coincidentally, Interpretation 1 is the one the designer probably intended. Its mechanism graph corresponds to the one we have been using earlier (Fig. 16). Interpretations 2 and 4 arise when there is no feedback in the circuit, but the signal is being amplified normally. Interpretations 2 and 4 differ in the behaviors of circuit quantities (around node FP) not on the main signal path so they have the same mechanism graph. Fig. 13 illustrates the mechanism graph. Interpretation 3 arises when the signal travels forward instead of backward on the feedback path and combines with the main signal at the base-emitter of Q2. Its mechanism graph is Fig. 28 and the flow is illustrated by Fig. 29.

Interpretations 5 and 6 occur when the signal reversing the feedback path dominates and the gain along the normal signal path is non-existent. The differences between Interpretations 5 and 6 (around node C1) do not affect the output value so their mechanism graphs are the same. Fig. 30 is the mechanism graph and Fig. 31 illustrates the causal flow.

All but one of these interpretations are nonsensical. The second and fourth interpretations have a useless RF. The third interpretation feeds forward a signal that is orders of magnitude smaller than the signal it is added to at Q2. The smaller signal through RF serves no purpose. The fifth and sixth interpretations

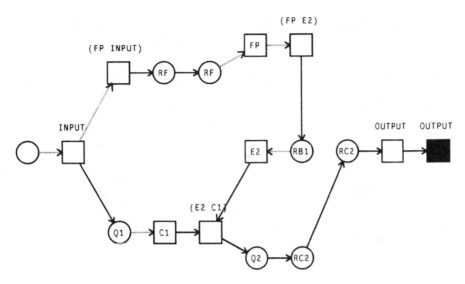

FIG. 28. Interpretation 3 (Feedforward) of CE-FEEDBACK.

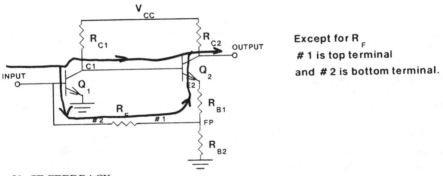

FIG. 29. CE-FEEDBACK.

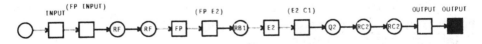

FIG. 30. Interpretations 5 and 6 (Unity Gain) of CE-FEEDBACK.

have no gain and Q1 and RC1 need not even be part of the circuit. These kinds of judgments for choosing the 'correct' interpretation are made by EQUAL's teleological reasoning. The task of causal analysis is to produce all the theoretical possibilities. With appropriate choices of resistor values and transistor gains each of these interpretations could arise.

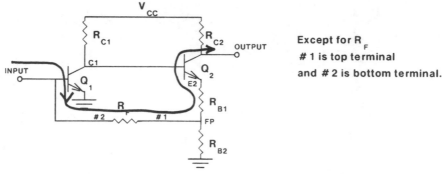

FIG. 31. CE-FEEDBACK.

8.3. Quantitative criteria

If the circuit is linear, given the numerical values of circuit parameters and inputs, quantitative analysis produces a single solution for the circuit. The signs of the variables describe the correct interpretation. As a consequence a particular linear circuit can exhibit only one of its interpretations and this interpretation can be determined using numerical analysis or symbolic algebra. Both of these quantitative techniques can be avoided, as a small set of easily applied rules usually selects the correct interpretation.

8.4. Teleological criteria

The causal interpretations define all the physically realizable behaviors of the circuit. For most the circuits, one of these interpretations can often be identified as the one the designer originally intended. Knowing the ultimate purpose of the circuit makes it easy to identify the correct interpretation. Surprisingly, the correct interpretation can be identified without knowing the circuit's ultimate purpose. The conventions for circuit design are so stylized and the designer is under such tight economic constraints that one interpretation usually stands out as the one the designer intended. This section presents a number of selection criteria for identifying the correct interpretation.

These selection criteria all depend on the fact that the circuit is well-designed in the first place using functional criteria alone. If an engineer adds a resistor because it makes the schematic look like a picture of his house, or adds a useless transistor so he can advertise it as a six instead of five transistor radio, the criteria may fail. The same is true for badly designed circuits or circuits which cannot possibly work.

The first criterion is that the circuit has a non-zero (i.e., changing) output signal. The designer cannot have intended the circuit to have no output signal. CE-FEEDBACK has no such interpretations.

The second criterion is that the circuit does not propagate a zero-value assuming two currents or voltages exactly cancel. Such situations can exist only if the signals perfectly balance, which is impossible in practice given that they come from different circuit paths and, in any case, can only exist momentarily in the face of a changing input signal. This criterion rules out Interpretations 2 and 6 of CE-FEEDBACK. Interpretation 2 had the current from RF perfectly balancing the current from RB1. In Interpretation 6 the collector current of Q1 exactly equaled the base current of Q2. Note that both of these are mathematical possibilities, but no circuit could utilize such a perfect balance.

Third, each component should have a known causal configuration. Fourth, causal or feedback configurations are preferred over reflection configurations which are preferred over no configurations at all. Finally, there are some configurations which are known, a priori, to be unlikely. These three criteria implement the intuition that the correct interpretation is the one which has the 'best' teleological explanation for each component of the circuit. This is based on two presuppositions. First, causal analysis finds every possible behavior. Second, that the taxonomy of component configurations is complete or *or at least corresponds to the ones design engineers are actually using.*

The preference criteria are best illustrated by an example. Table 10 lists all the component configurations. CE-FEEDBACK has four interpretations: correct (Fig. 16, Interpretation 1), feedbackless (Fig. 13, Interpretation 4), feedforward (Fig. 28, Interpretation 3) and unity gain (Fig. 30, Interpretation 5). '(C)', '(F)' and '(R)' indicate causal, feedback and reflection configurations.

The interpretation which assigns the best purpose to each component is preferred. As a causal or feedback configuration contributes directly to a circuit

TABLE 10. Interpretation configurations for CE-FEEDBACK

Component	Configuration			
	Correct (1)	Feedbackless (4)	Feedforward (3)	Unity gain (5)
Q1	CE(C)	CE(C)	CE(C)	LOAD-Q(R)
	LOAD-Q(R)	LOAD-Q(R)	LOAD-Q(R)	
Q2	CE(C)	CE(C)	SUM(C)	CB(C)
	CC(F)	LOAD-Q(R)	SENSE-Q(R)	
	LOAD-Q(R)			
RC1	I-LOAD(R)	I-LOAD(R)	I-LOAD(R)	I-LOAD(R)
RC2	I-LOAD(C)	I-LOAD(C)	I-LOAD(C)	I-LOAD(C)
RB2	I-LOAD(R)	I-LOAD(R)	I-LOAD(R)	I-LOAD(R)
RB1	I-TO-V-COUPLE(F)	I-LOAD(R)	DIVIDER(C)	DIVIDER(C)
			I-LOAD(R)	I-LOAD(R)
RF	V-SENSOR(F)	I-LOAD(R)	DIVIDER(C)	DIVIDER(C)
	I-LOAD(R)		I-LOAD(R)	I-LOAD(R)

output it is preferred over a reflection configuration. A reflection configuration is preferred over no configuration at all. This preference ordering on individual component configurations places a partial order on interpretations which can be represented as a lattice. The maximal elements of the resulting lattice are the feedforward and the correct interpretations. The feedforward interpretation is preferred over the unity gain interpretation because it assigns a causal purpose to Q1 (they both assign the same purpose types to the remaining components, e.g., Q2 functions in a causal configuration in both interpretations). The correct interpretation is preferred over the feedbackless interpretation because it uses RF in a causal configuration.

Certain component configurations are unlikely *a priori*. For example, it is very unlikely that a transistor is functioning in a SUM configuration (adding the voltages at its emitter and base) because the gains and input impedances of the base and emitter signal paths are so different. Also, it is unlikely that a transistor is only functioning in LOAD-Q, COUPLING-Q, or SENSE-Q configurations. All these roles can be achieved far more cheaply with a diode. This preference establishes another partial order which almost always has a single maximum. In the case of CE-FEEDBACK, the correct interpretation is preferred over the feedforward configuration as it is unlikely Q2 is functioning in a SUM configuration.

8.4.1. *More selection criteria*

If the circuit has more than one input or output (perhaps both), then that interpretation which has each input affecting as many outputs as possible is preferred.

Only the feedback path from a single sampling point with the most active components along it is included in the mechanism graph used to generate configurations and select interpretations. This final criterion applies when the circuit has multiple intertwined feedback loops (in particular multiple comparison points from a single sampling point). With the rules so far, the wrong interpretation would be selected.

The only cases where these criteria have been observed to fail are circuits which have some kind of symmetry (e.g., a push-pull output stage). For such circuits, either the two interpretations are identical and selecting either one would produce a correct analysis, or the circuit switches interpretations in its normal functioning (a situation which cannot be represented in EQUAL).

It is not hard to design a circuit for which they fail, but it is surprisingly difficult to design a circuit for which it both fails and would sensibly be designed by an experienced analog circuit designer. To construct a counter-example, one must come up with a circuit whose desired behavior was not expected by an electrical engineer *and* whose design cannot be simplified (i.e., badly designed circuits in which only a subset of the components were performing any useful function).

9. Operating Regions

Electrical engineers describe the behavior of nonlinear components with piece-wise linear approximations. The entire region of operation is broken down into a collection of subregions, or states, within which the behavior is approximately linear. For example, the diode model is

$$i = I_s(e^{qv/kT} - 1),$$

and its behavior is modeled by two regions. If v is small, $e^{qv/kT}$ is nearly one and the current is nearly zero. If v is large, the exponential is nearly a straight line and can be modeled by a simple resistor. These are called the *on* and *off* regions.

The qualitative model uses the same regions:

i_A = current into anode ,
$v_{A,C}$ = voltage from anode to cathode,
OFF: $(v_{A,C} \leqslant v_T)$, $\partial i_A = 0$,
ON: $(v_{A,C} > v_T)$, $\partial v_{A,C} \Rightarrow \partial i_A$.

The parenthesized conditions define the regions. Thus, if the voltage across the diode is less than some threshold, the diode is off and its current constant. For silicon diodes $v_T = 0.55$ volts, for germanium diodes the threshold is much less.

In qualitative analysis, nonlinearity is not as much of a problem as for quantitative analysis. For example, the equation $\partial v_{A,C} = \partial i_A$ equally well de-scribes the behavior of a linear resistance or an exponential diode effect. Component states are still important in qualitative analysis when behavior is qualitatively different in different regions, however, it is not necessary to assume linearity. Thus, qualitative modeling has not precluded the analysis of nonlinear systems.

The transistor is typically modeled by three regions: on, off and saturated. However, there is a fourth, often ignored, region important to digital circuitry called the reverse-active (R-ON in the model) region. The following is a model for the NPN transistor (the PNP model is identical except that the state specifications are all reversed):

ON:

$(v_{b,c} < v_T, v_{b,e} \geqslant v_T)$,

$\partial v_{b,e} \Rightarrow \partial i_c$, $\partial v_{b,e} - \Rightarrow \partial i_e$, $\partial v_{b,e} \Rightarrow \partial i_b$;

R-ON:

$$(v_{b,c} \geq v_T, v_{b,e} < v_T),$$

$$\partial v_{c,b} \Rightarrow \partial i_c, \quad \partial v_{c,b} - \Rightarrow \partial i_e = 0, \quad \partial v_{c,b} \Rightarrow \partial i_b = 0 ;$$

OFF:

$$(v_{b,c} < v_T, v_{b,e} < v_T),$$

$$\partial i_c = 0 ;$$

SATURATED:

$$(v_{b,e} \geq v_T, v_{b,c} \geq v_T),$$

$$\partial v_{b,e} - \partial v_{c,b} \Rightarrow \partial i_b .$$

9.1. Composite circuit state

The composite state of the overall circuit is defined in terms of the states of its individual components. All of the analyses of CE-FEEDBACK presumed that both its transistors were in their forward-active regions. This composite circuit state is represented as {(Q1 ON) (Q2 ON)}. Using the above transistor model it can be seen that the CE-FEEDBACK has 16 possible circuit states. For many circuits, it is quite reasonable to assume that unless shown to the contrary, all transistors are in their forward-active region. However, it is not necessary to depend on this presupposition as the 'normal' composite state can usually be determined directly. First, some composite states are contradictory in that they have no causal interpretations at all. Second, many composite states have contradictory quiescent models or violate the boundary conditions. Third, of the remaining possible states, the same teleological techniques used to select the correct interpretation are used to select the correct state.

9.2. Implementation

The introduction of component states requires little additional machinery. Component states are treated exactly as assumptions. The different regions of operation for a component are incompatible assumptions. This has the computational advantage that composite states share values and that any set of contradictory component states immediately rules out any superset component state set. Typically, in larger circuits, the state of one transistor determines the states of its neighbors. As a consequence, the set of circuit states needed to be explored only grows linearly in the number of active components.

9.3. Quiescent analysis

Quiescent analysis, unlike causal analysis, determines the values of the quantities, not how they change. Neither causal analysis, teleological analysis nor interpretation selection utilizes quiescent analysis. This should not be too surprising, as most circuits achieve their function by responding to changing inputs or producing changing outputs. Quiescent analysis is important for determining the possible composite states of a circuit and for establishing sign conventions for the printout of causal arguments.

For linear components, the quiescent and incremental models are identical. Thus most of the quiescent models were presented in the beginning the paper. The transistor, a nonlinear component, has a quite different quiescent model. The values of the voltages can often be determined from the state specifications. This is the NPN transistor model.

ON:

$$(v_{b,c} < v_T, v_{b,e} \geq v_T),$$

$$[i_b] = +, \quad [i_c] = +, \quad [i_e] = -, \quad [v_{b,e}] - +, \quad [v_{c,e}] = + ;$$

R-ON:

$$(v_{b,c} \geq v_T, v_{b,e} < v_T),$$

$$[i_b] = +, \quad [i_c] = -, \quad [i_e] = +, \quad [v_{c,e}] = -, \quad [v_{c,b}] = - ;$$

OFF:

$$(v_{b,c} < v_T, v_{b,e} < v_T),$$

$$[i_b] = 0, \quad [i_c] = 0, \quad [i_e] = 0 ;$$

SATURATED:

$$(v_{b,e} \geq v_T, v_{b,c} \geq v_T),$$

$$[i_b] = +, \quad [v_{b,e}] = +, \quad [v_{c,b}] = - .$$

The propagation algorithm of causal analysis can be used to determine the quiescent values, but the heuristics make little sense and the propagation may reach an impasse. As causal explanations are unimportant for quiescent analysis, brute-force constraint satisfaction suffices to obtain the values (however, the logical framework presented in [6] will provide explanations for the conclusions, but they are just not causal explanations).

Constraint satisfaction on CE-FEEDBACK uses 66 confluences in 39 unknowns. The transistor confluences are:

$$[i_{\rightarrow B(Q2)}] = + \qquad [i_{\rightarrow C(Q2)}] = + \qquad [i_{\rightarrow E(Q2)}] = -$$

$$[v_{E2,C1}] = - \qquad [v_{E2,OUTPUT}] = - \qquad [i_{\rightarrow B(Q1)}] = +$$

$$[i_{\rightarrow C(Q1)}] = + \qquad [i_{\rightarrow E(Q1)}] = - \qquad [v_{INPUT}] = + \qquad [v_{C1}] = +$$

The quiescent model for the battery is:

$$[v_{VCC}] = + .$$

The remaining quiescent confluences are analogous to the incremental confluences presented earlier. Ohm's law, KCL and KVL are all linear constraints and thus the quiescent confluences are the same as the incremental confluences. There is one less KCL confluence as the input port is presumed to supply zero bias.

These confluences have three solutions (only because the uninteresting quantity $v_{C1,OUTPUT}$ can be $+$, 0 or $-$.

$$[i_{\to -(B1)}] = +$$ $$[i_{\to B(Q2)}] = +$$ $$[v_{E2}] = +$$

$$[i_{\to +(B1)}] = -$$ $$[i_{\to E(Q2)}] = -$$ $$[v_{E2,C1}] = -$$

$$[i_{\to \#2(R2)}] = -$$ $$[i_{\to C(Q1)}] = +$$ $$[v_{INPUT,OUTPUT}] = -$$

$$[i_{\to \#1(RC2)}] = +$$ $$[i_{\to B(Q1)}] = +$$ $$[v_{INPUT,VCC}] = -$$

$$[i_{\to \#2(RF)}] = +$$ $$[i_{\to E(Q1)}] = -$$ $$[v_{INPUT}] = +$$

$$[i_{\to \#1(RF)}] = -$$ $$[v_{VCC,OUTPUT}] = +$$ $$[v_{INPUT,C1}] = -$$

$$[i_{\to \#2(RB2)}] = +$$ $$[v_{OUTPUT}] = +$$ $$[v_{INPUT,E2}] = -$$

$$[i_{\to \#1(RB2)}] = -$$ $$[v_{VCC}] = +$$ $$[v_{FP,OUTPUT}] = -$$

$$[i_{\to \#2(RB1)}] = -$$ $$[v_{C1,OUTPUT}] = ?$$ $$[v_{FP,VCC}] = -$$

$$[i_{\to \#1(RB1)}] = +$$ $$[v_{C1,VCC}] = -$$ $$[v_{FP}] = +$$

$$[i_{\to \#2(RC1)}] = -$$ $$[v_{C1}] = +$$ $$[v_{FP,C1}] = -$$

$$[i_{\to \#1(RC1)}] = +$$ $$[v_{E2,OUTPUT}] = -$$ $$[v_{FP,E2}] = -$$

$$[i_{\to C(Q2)}] = +$$ $$[v_{E2,VCC}] = -$$ $$[v_{FP,INPUT}] = +$$

Quiescent analysis shows that 31 of the possible 36 composite states of CE-FEEDBACK are contradictory. For example, Q1 cannot be ON if Q2 is OFF. For Q1 to be ON, it must be supplied a bias, this bias can only come through RF, node FP can only be pulled up from RB1, but if Q2 is OFF no current can be flowing through RB1 pulling up FP and thus Q1 cannot be receiving any bias. Similar, proof-by-contradiction arguments eliminate the remaining 30 circuit states. The 5 possible consistent circuit states are:

{(Q1 OFF)(Q2 SAT)}   {(Q1 ON)(Q2 SAT)}   {(Q1 OFF)(Q2 OFF)}

{(Q1 OFF)(Q2 ON)}   {(Q1 ON)(Q2 ON)}

Only the last two states allow the input to propagate all the way to the output, producing an interesting behavior. Using the interpretation selection rules, state {(Q1 OFF)(Q2 ON)} is an unlikely choice because it doesn't use Q1 in any useful configuration at all. Hence, the normal operating state of CE-FEEDBACK is {(Q1 ON)(Q2 ON)}.

9.4. Energy storage elements

With the models presented thus far quiescent ambiguity within a state has no effect on the causal analysis. It only matters whether a state is contradictory or not. This is because no incremental confluence references a quiescent variable (or vice versa). This is not the case for models described by differential equations (e.g., inductors and capacitors). The behavior of a capacitor is described quantitatively by the differential equation

i = current flowing into the capacitor,

v = voltage across the capacitor,

C = capacitance which is a fixed positive quantity,

$i = C \, dv/dt$.

In qualitative terms this is

$$[i] = \left[C \frac{dv}{dt} \right] = [C]\left[\frac{dv}{dt}\right] = \left[\frac{dv}{dt}\right] = \partial v .$$

Or more generally, as it is a linear element:

$$\partial^{n-1} i = \partial^{n} v .$$

Analogously, the inductor modeled quantitatively as

$$v = L \, di/dt$$

has the model:

i = current flowing into the inductor,

v = voltage across the inductor,

$[v] = \partial i$.

Or more generally:

$$\partial^{n-1} v = \partial^{n} i .$$

Consider the simple RC circuit of Fig. 32. This circuit is modeled with 5 quiescent confluences, one Ohm's law confluence, four KCL confluences and no KVL confluences. Note that the capacitor introduces no quiescent confluence[10] other than a KCL. A capacitor places no constraints on the quiescent behavior, that is left to the rest of the circuit. However, the quiescent possibilities that result, directly affect the causal analysis.

[10]Assuming its charge is not known.

FIG. 32. Simple RC circuit.

$$[i_{\to \#1(R)}] - [v_N] = 0 ,$$

$$[i_{\to \#2(C)}] + [i_{\to \#1(C)}] = 0 ,$$

$$[i_{\to \#2(R)}] + [i_{\to \#2(C)}] = 0 ,$$

$$[i_{\to \#1(R)}] + [i_{\to \#1(C)}] = 0 ,$$

$$[i_{\to \#2(R)}] + [i_{\to \#1(R)}] = 0 .$$

Not surprisingly there are 3 possible quiescent interpretations, each corresponding to one of the possible qualitative capacitor currents, see Table 11. Each one of the quiescent interpretations yields a different causal analysis, see Table 12.

Notice that unlike circuits considered thus far, a single RC network can exhibit all these interpretations without changing circuit conditions. Not one interpretation can be said to be the correct one. This is a consequence of the presence of energy storage elements. As $[x]\partial x$ is $-$ for all non-zero circuit quantities, they are moving towards zero.

Thus quiescent interpretations select incremental models in very much the same way as composite circuit state selects the incremental models. For the purpose of analysis, EQUAL considers the quiescent interpretations as introducing additional circuit states. However, it is only necessary to distinguish quiescent interpretations differing in the variables of energy storage elements. Thus, the three quiescent interpretations of CE-FEEDBACK differing in $[v_{C1,OUTPUT}]$ collapse as no incremental confluence depends on its value. Said differently, capacitor currents and inductor voltages are the only interesting

TABLE 11			
Interpretation	1	2	3
$[i_{\to \#1(C)}] =$	+	0	−
$[i_{\to \#2(C)}] =$	−	0	+
$[i_{\to \#1(R)}] =$	−	0	+
$[i_{\to \#2(R)}] =$	+	0	−
$[v_N] =$	−	0	+

TABLE 12			
Solution	1	2	3
$\partial i_{\to \#1(C)} =$	−	0	+
$\partial i_{\to \#2(C)} =$	+	0	−
$\partial i_{\to \#1(R)} =$	+	0	−
$\partial i_{\to \#2(R)} =$	−	0	+
$\partial v_N =$	+	0	−

variables of quiescent interpretations contributing to the composite circuit state.

10. Time

As time passes the behavior and the causality of the circuit may change, either as a consequence of a new input behavior or of the internal workings of the circuit. For circuits such as CE-FEEDBACK, not much will change. The qualitative values continue to hold as long as the input signal is present. In other words the causal analysis (the qualitative values and the mechanism graph) holds for an extensive interval of time. This is not surprising, as CE-FEEDBACK has only one useful interpretation and state of behavior. The input signal may vary, first increasing then decreasing, but that just flips all the qualitative values, the interpretation and mechanism graph remain unchanged. Change induced by new inputs is uninteresting.

In general, two significant things can happen as time passes. First, qualitative integration takes place. Any non-zero incremental variable will cause changes in the quiescent variables. $\partial x = +$ means x increases. If a significant amount of time passes this increase in x may become significant and qualitatively noticeable. For example, suppose a transistor is in the OFF state. $\partial v_{b,e} = +$ causes $v_{b,e}$ to increase which in turn causes $v_{b,e}$ to become greater than the threshold v_T. As a consequence the transistor changes to state ON and the incremental behavior changes.

Second, the behavioral interpretations can change. If there is more than one quiescent interpretation, the non-zero incremental quantities may cause the quiescent interpretation to change. This can only happen if the circuit is either nonlinear or contains energy storage elements (otherwise the interpretation is uniquely determined by circuit conditions (component parameters and input signals).) In the simple RC circuit considered earlier the capacitor's current $[i]$ is ambiguous producing three quiescent interpretations each having one incremental interpretation. In this example when $[i] = + \partial i = -$, so the quiescent interpretation may change to one in which $[i] = 0$. The RC and transistor examples illustrate a fundamental problem of qualitative analysis. Although it is possible to identify which transitions might happen, it is difficult to determine whether they indeed do happen. Just because $\partial v_{b,e} = +$ does not mean $v_{b,e}$ will ever pass threshold v_T. In fact, for the RC circuit we know (from solving the differential equations) that even though $\partial i = -$, i never reaches zero: it dies out exponentially. In fact, no matter what interpretation it starts in, it will approach Interpretation 2 asymptotically. More generally, a linear circuit will approach the same interpretation no matter what the initial conditions are.

A circuit may also change its incremental interpretation. The Schmitt trigger is an example of such a circuit. There is very little that can be said concerning changes between incremental interpretations without doing a second-order analysis [4]. After all, it is $\partial^2 i$ which is causing the change in ∂i. To determine the movement between causal interpretations one needs to solve for the second-order derivatives. For linear circuits, this is easy as the models do not change and thus it is not necessary to redo the analysis, but for nonlinear circuits the higher-order models can be completely different and require an entire reanalysis.

10.1. Interstate behavior

Fortunately, state changes and quiescent interpretation shifts obey numerous constraints which can be used to generate the state-transition diagram for the circuit. The state-transition diagram describes the interstate behavior of the circuit, while causal analysis and the mechanism graph describes the intrastate behavior of the circuit. Fig. 33 illustrates the state-transition diagram for CE-FEEDBACK in response to a rising input. Unless the circuit contains negative resistances uncovered by the heuristics, the state diagram for a falling input is identical except for change in direction of arrowhead.

The state-transition diagram is constructed using a very basic algorithm to generate all the possibilities and then apply constraints to prune down the space of possibilities. The basic envisioning algorithm proceeds as follows. The

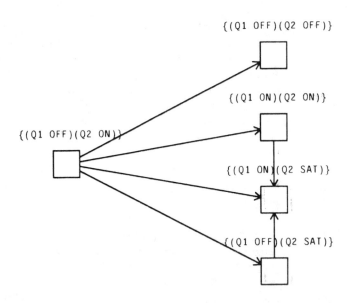

FIG. 33. State-transition diagram for CE-FEEDBACK.

circuit is presumed to be in some given initial condition. In this state, causal analysis identifies the values of all the circuit quantities. Identify all the quiescent quantities which are approaching some threshold: these are the causes for possible state transitions. The state transitions define a set of possible next states (usually there is only one). If this state has not been considered before, analyze it. If there is more than one next state, explore state space breadth-first.

The above algorithm includes three kinds of ambiguities. First, the incremental variable may be ambiguous, so we do not know whether the variable is approaching its threshold. Second, even though the variable may be approaching its threshold, we do not know whether it will reach it. Finally, more than one variable may be approaching thresholds (the case of the same variable approaching two different thresholds is handled by presuming that all inequality relationships between constants are known), and it is hard to tell whether one crosses its threshold before the other or whether they both cross simultaneously. Without additional constraints, all possible combinations of threshold crossings are possible. For example, in state {(Q1 OFF)(Q2 ON)}, the changing quantities tend to turn Q1 ON and Q2 OFF. But Q1 can turn ON before Q2 turns OFF or Q1 turns OFF before Q2 turns ON, or they both change state simultaneously.

The following is the list of legal states of CE-FEEDBACK and an indication of which threshold is being approached. This list and state diagram of Fig. 33 presumes all incremental interpretations are possible, thus some circuit values are ambiguous.

> In State 1, {(Q1 OFF)(Q2 ON)}
>> The value of $\partial v_{C1,OUTPUT}$ is ambiguous.
>> If $\partial v_{C1,OUTPUT} = +$, Q2 may change state to SAT because $v_{C,B}$ may drop past threshold $-v_T$.
>> Because $\partial v_{E2,C1} = +$, Q2 may change state to OFF because $v_{B,E}$ may drop past threshold v_T.
>> Because $\partial v_{INPUT,C1} = +$, Q1 may change state to R-ON because $v_{C,B}$ may drop past threshold $-v_T$.
>> Because $\partial v_{INPUT} = +$, Q1 may change state to ON because $v_{B,E}$ may rise past threshold v_T.
> In State 3, {(Q1 OFF)(Q2 OFF)}
>> Because $\partial v_{INPUT,C1} = +$, Q1 may change state to R-ON because $v_{C,B}$ may drop past threshold $-v_T$.
>> Because $\partial v_{INPUT} = +$, Q1 may change state to ON because $v_{B,E}$ may rise past threshold v_T.
> In State 2, {(Q1 ON)(Q2 ON)}
>> The value of $\partial v_{C1,OUTPUT}$ is ambiguous.
>> If $\partial v_{C1,OUTPUT} = +$, Q2 may change state to SAT because $v_{C,B}$ may drop past threshold $-v_T$.
>> Because $\partial v_{E2,C1} = +$, Q2 may change state to OFF because $v_{B,E}$ may drop past threshold v_T.
>> Because $\partial v_{INPUT,C1} = +$, Q1 may change state to SAT because $v_{C,B}$ may drop past threshold $-v_T$.

In State 5, {(Q1 ON)(Q2 SAT)}

Because $\partial v_{E2,C1} = +$, Q2 may change state to R-ON because $v_{B,E}$ may drop past threshold v_T.

Because $\partial v_{INPUT,C1} = +$, Q1 may change state to SAT because $v_{C,B}$ may drop past threshold $-v_T$.

The value of $\partial v_{C1,OUTPUT}$ is ambiguous.

If $\partial v_{C1,OUTPUT} = -$, Q2 may change state to ON because $v_{C,B}$ may rise past threshold $-v_T$.

In State 4, {(Q1 OFF)(Q2 SAT)}

Because $\partial v_{E2,C1} = +$, Q2 may change state to R-ON because $v_{B,E}$ may drop past threshold v_T.

Because $\partial v_{INPUT,C1} = +$, Q1 may change state to R-ON because $v_{C,B}$ may drop past threshold $-v_T$.

Because $\partial v_{INPUT} = +$, Q1 may change state to ON because $v_{B,E}$ may rise past threshold v_T.

Most of these transitions cannot happen individually because the resulting state is not consistent with the confluences. For example, in state {(Q1 OFF) (Q2 ON)} Q1 tends to turn ON while Q2 turns OFF, but this target state is inconsistent and therefore it cannot become the next circuit state.

The second constraint on state diagrams is that variables must change value continuously. This restriction applies to both quiescent and incremental variables. For example, x may not change from $+$ to $-$ without an intervening state within which it is 0. This rule is used only twice in the CE-FEEDBACK's state diagram. If a state has more than one incremental interpretation, that individual interpretation which is causing the state change must be continuous with some interpretation of the target state. For example, in state {(Q1 ON) (Q2 SAT)}, Q2 may turn ON, causing a circuit state change to {(Q1 ON) (Q2 ON)}. However, this does not make much sense as the circuit would immediately tend to make Q2 saturate again. More formally, this transition does not happen because the derivatives would have to vary discontinuously [34]. In state {(Q1 ON)(Q2 SAT)} $\partial i_{\rightarrow \#2(RC2)} = -$, in {(Q1 ON)(Q2 ON)} $\partial i_{\rightarrow \#2(RC2)} = +$, which requires a discontinuous transition. The reason it is possible for the state change to happen in the reverse direction is that there is an interpretation of {(Q1 ON)(Q2 SAT)} in which $\partial i_{\rightarrow \#2(RC2)} = +$ or 0 (this interpretation is continuous with one of {(Q1 ON)(Q2 ON)}, but no circuit quantity is heading towards a threshold which would cause a transition to {(Q1 ON)(Q2 ON)}.

These are all the rules required to construct the state diagram for CE-FEEDBACK. Here is EQUAL's analysis of the preceding possibilities.

In State 1, {(Q1 OFF)(Q2 ON)}

But some combinations lead to contradictory states: {(Q1 R-ON)(Q2 SAT)}*, {(Q1 ON)(Q2 OFF)}*, {(Q1 R-ON)(Q2 OFF)}* or {(Q1 R-ON)(Q2 ON)}*.

Therefore the device may change state to one of:

4: {(Q1 OFF)(Q2 SAT)},   5: {(Q1 ON)(Q2 SAT)}

3: {(Q1 OFF)(Q2 OFF)},   2: {(Q1 ON)(Q2 ON)}.

In State 3, {(Q1 OFF)(Q2 OFF)}
   But all combinations lead to contradictory states: {(Q1 R-ON)(Q2 OFF)}* or {(Q1 ON)(Q2 OFF)}*.
   Therefore there are no transitions out of this state.
In State 2, {(Q1 ON)(Q2 ON)}
   But some combinations lead to contradictory states: {(Q1 SAT)(Q2 SAT)}*, {(Q1 ON)(Q2 OFF)}*, {(Q1 SAT)(Q2 OFF)}* or {(Q1 SAT)(Q2 ON)}*.
   The device may change state to 5: {(Q1 ON)(Q2 SAT)}
In State 5, {(Q1 ON)(Q2 SAT)}
   But some combinations lead to contradictory states: {(Q1 SAT)(Q2 ON)}*, {(Q1 ON)(Q2 R-ON)}*, {(Q1 SAT)(Q2 R-ON)}* or {(Q1 SAT)(Q2 SAT)}*.
   $\partial i_{\rightarrow - (B1)}$ changes discontinuously from + to − to State 2: {(Q1 ON)(Q2 ON)}
   $\partial i_{\rightarrow \#2(RC2)}$ changes discontinuously from − to + to State 2: {(Q1 ON)(Q2 ON)}
   Therefore there are no transitions out of this state.
In State 4, {(Q1 OFF)(Q2 SAT)}
   But some combinations lead to contradictory states: {(Q1 OFF)(Q2 R-ON)}*, {(Q1 ON)(Q2 R-ON)}*, {(Q1 R-ON)(Q2 R-ON)}* or {(Q1 R-ON)(Q2 SAT)}*.
   The device may change state to 5: {(Q1 ON)(Q2 SAT)}

10.2. Ontology for time

This section is a direct application of the rules of [4, 6] to electrical circuits. So far we have assumed that every operating region or interpretation exists for

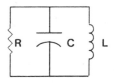

| Episode | 1 | 2 | 3 | 4 | | | 5 | 6 | 7 | 8 | | | 9 |
Interpretation	1	1	1	1	2	3	1	1	1	1	2	3	1
$\partial i_{\rightarrow \#1(C)} =$	0	−	−	−	0	+	+	+	+	−	0	+	−
$\partial i_{\rightarrow \#1(R)} =$	0	+	0	−	−	−	−	−	0	+	+	+	+
$\partial i_{\rightarrow \#1(L)} =$	0	+	+	+	+	+	0	−	−	−	−	−	0
$\partial v_N =$	0	+	0	−	−	−	−	−	0	+	+	+	+
Episode	1	2	3	4			5	6	7	8			9
Interpretation	1	1	1	1	2	3	1	1	1	1	2	3	1
$[i_{\rightarrow \#1(C)}] =$	0	+	0	−	−	−	−	−	0	+	+	+	+
$[i_{\rightarrow \#1(R)}] =$	0	+	+	+	+	+	0	−	−	−	−	−	0
$[i_{\rightarrow \#1(L)}] =$	0	−	−	−	0	+	+	+	+	−	0	+	−
$[v_N] =$	0	+	+	+	+	+	0	−	−	−	−	−	0

FIG. 34. RLC circuit.

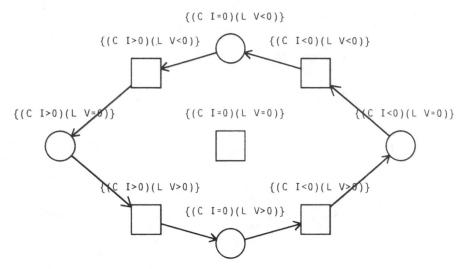

FIG. 35. State diagram for RLC circuit.

some interval time. However, some operating regions and interpretations may only exist momentarily. An operating region for which $x = a$ and $\partial x = -$ will only exist momentarily because x will immediately drop below a. Similarly a quiescent interpretation with $x = 0$ and $\partial x = +$ exists only for an instant. It is important to distinguish instants from intervals, because instants do not take any time and are always guaranteed to end, unlike intervals. This new ontology is illustrated by a simple RLC circuit (Fig. 34).

The set of confluences have 13 solutions, but these can be collapsed into 9 as v_N and $i_{\to \#1(C)}$ are the only interesting variables. The corresponding state diagram is Fig. 35. Circles represent states that exist momentarily, squares represent states that may exist over a time interval. The state diagram embodies two additional constraints. First, every quantity changes from zero before any quantity changes to zero. Second, computing higher-order derivatives shows that any transition to state $\{(C\,I = 0)(L\,V = 0)\}$ is impossible (see [4] for an explanation of this rule).

11. Applications

The goal of qualitative physics is to predict and explain the important behavior of physical systems without recourse to quantitative methods. This paper has presented a qualitative physics for circuits which achieves this goal. In addition, it is possible to identify the mechanism by which the circuit functions in the standard language used by electrical engineers. This concluding section briefly outlines a few of the potential applications of this theory to analysis, design, troubleshooting and training.

11.1. Quantitative analysis

The electrical engineer's most fundamental task is circuit analysis. He can perform this analysis either symbolically [10] or numerically [26]. A good engineer will first understand how the circuit functions qualitatively. Then based on this understanding, he will select component models, important variables, approximations and integration step sizes, then perform the necessary symbolic or numerical computation, and finally interpret the results in terms of his commonsensical understanding of how the circuit works. In other words, an engineer does not perform a quantitative analysis unless he first understands the circuit at a qualitative level. In [10] we constructed a program SYN which analyzed circuits symbolically in order to determine circuit parameters. Many of the problems of SYN were due to the fact that it has no understanding of the behavior of the circuit it was analyzing.

SYN can only work on very simple circuits because the algebraic expressions generated quickly fill up program memory. On the other hand, an engineer can analyze the circuit quickly just using pencil and paper. Comparing the engineer to SYN reveals four interesting facts. First, the engineer chooses approximations which simplify the algebra enormously without significantly changing the answer. Second, the engineer chooses models which are algebraically more tractable. Third, the engineer chooses variable substitutions and equation formulations which keep equation size relatively small. Finally, he uses standard rules of thumb to analyze well-known circuit configurations. Qualitative analysis addresses all four of these.

11.1.1. *Approximations*

As SYN does not know how a particular component is being used, it must always use the most complex model available. In most situations simpler models are sufficient which lead to far simpler algebra. EQUAL can give advice to SYN as to how a component is being used so that it can choose an

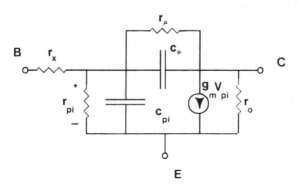

FIG. 36. Complete hybrid-π model.

appropriate simplification of the complex model. For example, the complete hybrid-π model for a transistor is shown in Fig. 36. (The circle containing a downward arrow represents a source which produces a downwards current of $g_m V_\pi$.) At reasonable currents, $r_x \ll r_\pi$ so r_x can be ignored unless the circuit is driven by an extremely low source impedance. Analogously r_μ and r_0 can be ignored unless the load is of extremely high impedance. As only the common-emitter configuration is ever used with extremely high loads, r_μ and r_0 can be ignored in the common-base and common-collector configurations. c_μ can be ignored unless the circuit is of high impedance. When the circuit is being driven by a very low impedance, c_π can be ignored. In the common-base configuration c_μ is usually not important.

11.1.2. Choosing tractable models

The hybrid-π model is particularly useful for analyzing the common-emitter and common-collector configurations. In the common-base configuration a different model—the T model—makes the analysis easier. Although the T model is quantitatively equivalent to the hybrid-π model, the resulting symbolic equations are more tractable because the source does not appear across the input. In many cases, the output signal can be computed directly from the input without having to solve simultaneous equations.

11.1.3. Choosing tractable formulations

Causal analysis helps choose the important variables in which to formulate circuit quantities. The causal analysis identifies the important circuit feedback paths and the instances of local feedback. These feedback paths appear as simultaneities in the symbolic analysis. The causal heuristics of the correct interpretation indicate places where simultaneity must be broken. Choosing these variables as the places to break feedback loops simplifies the form of the equations and formulates intermediate results in terms familiar to the electrical engineer.

11.1.4. Rules of thumb

Common combinations such as cascode, differential pair, and Darlington have well-known rules of thumb for making their quantitative analysis easier. EQUAL can recognize these situations for SYN. Certain combinations of transistors occur so frequently that it is useful to consider them as single fragments. A common-collector stage followed by a common-emitter stage forms an amplifier with high input impedance and moderate output impedance. This combination is known as a Darlington pair. The common-emitter/common-base combination is called a cascode and has very good frequency response. The common-collector/common-base connection forms a circuit widely used in

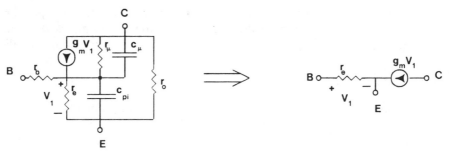

FIG. 37. T models.

operational amplifiers. The emitter-coupled pair provides differential outputs and can be direct coupled. The recognition of these combinations is not critical to EQUAL since it can calculate the impedance-gain specifications of these combinations with its composition rules, but it is of use to SYN.

The type of the feedback configuration provides direct advice about how to analytically determine the behavior of the circuit. For example, the following advice can be found in most textbooks on feedback amplifiers. In order to analyze a loop-loop configuration you should:

(1) Use z parameters to model the two-ports.

(2) Calculate the gain of the feedback network by driving the feedback network with a current and determining the voltage produced into an open circuit.

(3) Calculate feedback loading at the amplifier input by open circuiting the output node.

(4) Calculate feedback loading at the amplifier output by open circuiting the input node.

This simplifying technique can only be applied if feedback is known to be present, and only causal analysis not quantitative analysis can do that.

11.2. Design

Analysis is a key component of design and thus the techniques of the previous section apply to the design task as well. This observation lies at the heart of SYN's synthesis-by-analysis approach. Thus SYN can both construct a symbolic transfer function of a circuit, and determine values of circuit parameters given desiderata for circuit behavior.

Interpretation construction is also an important design tool. Causal analysis identifies all possible interpretations, including behaviors the designer does not intend. By identifying all the possible interpretations, causal analysis identifies possible pathological modes of circuit behavior that the designer must avoid.

In many ways the design task is the inverse of the recognition task around which this paper is organized. Recognition starts with a schematic of a particular circuit and constructs an abstract account for its behavior. Design, on the other hand, starts with an abstract description of the desired behavior and constructs a schematic which achieves this abstract description. The algorithms for recognition, are thus entirely different from those of design, nevertheless the languages for describing the levels of abstraction are probably quite similar.

11.3. Troubleshooting

Troubleshooting involves determining why a particular correctly designed circuit is not functioning as intended, the explanation for the faulty behavior being that the particular instance of that circuit under consideration is at variance in some way with its design. Starting with the external symptom, the troubleshooter makes a series of measurements in order to localize the fault. Quantitative analysis is ruled out as a troubleshooting strategy both because it is impractical and the circuit parameters are not precisely known. Thus, qualitative reasoning plays a key role in troubleshooting.

Causal analysis can quickly evaluate the plausibility of hypothetical faults. One simply substitutes a faulty component model for the correct one and performs the qualitative analysis again to see whether the predicted results are consistent with measurements made thus far in the troubleshooting session.

Fortunately, causal analysis can be used for much more than evaluating hypotheses. The causal interpretation for the intended behavior also provides a causal explanation for how the outputs are caused by the inputs. The components mentioned in this explanation are prime candidates for possible faults and the fault modes can be determined by examining the argument. The resulting hypotheses can be evaluated to determine which faults in which of these components are consistent with the symptoms. This technique works well if some component has shifted in value, but fails if circuit behavior has radically changed. The interpretation may have changed in the presence of the fault. If a causal assumption is violated, the entire argument may be invalidated. Since the designer never intended that the circuit behave in that way, no appeal can be made to the original intention. When this happens, the troubleshooter must first make measurements to determine the unintended interpretation within which the circuit is operating.

Causal analysis can also be run backwards if the models and the heuristics are changed. This technique can be used to identify circuit faults. The input is the difference between measured and intended outputs and the propagation engine works identically. Now, the propagation identifies "what could have caused x" instead of "What does x cause"—the only difference between these two questions is that time flow is reversed.

As part of the SOPHIE project [1] we built a general-purpose troubleshooting expert. Although the troubleshooting expert was very general, it was not powerful enough to troubleshoot using the schematic alone. It had to be provided a small collection of rules which characterized circuit behavior and with those it could troubleshoot every possible fault of the power-supply. Each of these rules was based on an abstract, qualitative analysis of how the circuit functioned. Causal analysis is powerful enough to construct some, if not all, of these rules. Thus, there is now a possibility of constructing a troubleshooter which can troubleshoot circuits which it has never seen before given only their schematic. This troubleshooter would operate by first doing a causal and teleological analysis of the circuit and then use this analysis to construct the needed abstract rules. The SOPHIE's troubleshooter could use these rules in combination with its other inference mechanisms to troubleshoot the circuit.

One of the original motivations for the no-function-in-structure principle and for studying causal reasoning in isolation was to achieve robustness in a computer-based troubleshooter. When a circuit is faulted, the circuit is no longer working as originally intended by the designer. A reasoner which presumes the use of teleological assumptions in choosing the component models or disambiguating interpretations will be of no value because the circuit functioning is radically changed. Thus, for troubleshooting, it is extremely important to identify all the possible interpretations.

11.4. ICAI

Computer-based instructional systems for electronics and electronic trouble-shooting need to explain their conclusions in terms that the student under-stands in order to enable him to build his own qualitative models of circuit functioning. Causal analysis provides a theory of explanation for humans and thus provides the basis for an explanation facility in an ICAI system. SOPHIE was first and foremost an ICAI system; the expert troubleshooter was constructed, not because it was itself important, but rather to provide explanations for troubleshooting interferences that SOPHIE itself could not give. For example, SOPHIE evaluated students hypotheses by running a numerical simulation with the modified model to see if it was consistent with observed measurements. This strategy evaluates hypotheses, but produces no explanation for why a particular hypothesis is valid or invalid. Causal reasoning provides a way to both evaluate hypotheses and produce explanations for their plausibility.

ACKNOWLEDGMENT

I thank John Seely Brown and Gerald Jay Sussman for continuing guidance in this research. Harry Barrow, Dan Bobrow, Randy Davis, Jeff Shrager, and Brian Williams provided many useful comments on the paper.

REFERENCES

1. Brown, J. S., Burton, R.R. and De Kleer, J., Pedagogical, natural language and knowledge engineering techniques in SOPHIE I, II and III, in: D. Sleeman and J.S. Brown (Eds.), *Intelligent Tutoring Systems* (Academic Press, New York, 1982) 227–282.
2. Cochin, I., *Analysis and Design of Dynamic Systems* (Harper and Row, New York, 1980).
3. Davis, R., Shrobe, H., Hamscher, W., Wieckert, K., Shirley, M. and Polit, S., Diagnosis based on description of structure and function, in: *Proceedings National Conference on Artificial Intelligence*, Pittsburgh, PA (August, 1982) 137–142.
4. De Kleer, J. and Bobrow, D.G., Qualitative reasoning with higher-order qualitative derivatives, in: *Proceedings National Conference on Artificial Intelligence*, Austin, TX, August, 1984.

5. De Kleer, J., Choices without backtracking, in: *Proceedings National Conference on Artificial Intelligence*, Austin, TX, August, 1984.
6. De Kleer, J. and Brown, J.S., A qualitative physics based on confluences, *Artificial Intelligence* **24** (1984) this volume.
7. De Kleer, J. and Brown, J.S., Assumptions and ambiguities in mechanistic mental models, in: D. Gentner and A.S. Stevens (Eds.), *Mental Models* (Erlbaum, Hillsdale, NJ, 1983) 155–190.
8. De Kleer, J. and Brown, J.S., Mental models of physical mechanisms and their acquisition, in: J.R. Anderson (Ed.), *Cognitive Skills and their Acquisition* (Erlbaum, Hillsdale, NJ, 1981) 285–309.
9. De Kleer, J. and Brown, J.S., Mental models of physical mechanisms, CIS-3 Cognitive and Instructional Sciences, Xerox PARC, Palo Alto, CA, 1981.
10. De Kleer, J. and Sussman, G.J., Propagation of constraints applied to circuit synthesis, *Circuit Theory and Applications* **8** (1980) 127–144.
11. De Kleer, J., Causal and teleological reasoning in circuit recognition, Artificial Intelligence Laboratory, TR-529, MIT, Cambridge, MA, 1979.
12. De Kleer, J., Qualitative and quantitative knowledge in classical mechanics, Artificial Intelligence Laboratory, TR-352, MIT, Cambridge, MA, 1975.
13. Desoer, C.A. and Kuh, E.S., *Basic Circuit Theory* (McGraw-Hill, New York, 1969).
14. Doyle, J., A truth maintenance system, *Artificial Intelligence* **12** (1979) 231–272.
15. Forbus, K.D. and Stevens, A., Using qualitative simulation to generate explanations, Rept. No. 4490, Bolt Beranek and Newman, Cambridge, MA, 1981.
16. Forbus, K.D., Qualitative process theory, *Artificial Intelligence* **24** (1984) this volume.
17. Forbus, K.D., Qualitative reasoning about physical processes, in: *Proceedings Seventh International Joint Conference on Artificial Intelligence*, Vancouver, BC (August, 1981) 326–330.
18. Gray, P.E. and Searle, C.L., *Electronic Principles: Physics, Models, and Circuits* (Wiley, New York, 1969).
19. Harris, J.N., Gray, P.E. and Searle, C.L., *Digital Transistor Circuits* (Wiley, New York, 1966).
20. Hayes, P.J., The naive physics manifesto, in: D. Michie (Ed.), *Expert Systems in the Microelectronic Age* (Edinburgh University Press, Edinburgh, 1979).
21. Hewitt, P.G., *Conceptual Physics* (Little and Brown, Boston, MA, 1974).
22. Karnopp, D. and Rosenberg, R., *System Dynamics: A Unified Approach* (Wiley, New York, 1975).
23. Kuipers, B., Getting the envisionment right, in: *Proceedings National Conference on Artificial Intelligence*, Pittsburgh, PA (August, 1982) 209–212.
24. Kuipers, B., Commonsense reasoning about causality: Deriving behavior from structure, *Artificial Intelligence* **24** (1984) this volume.
25. McAllester, D., An outlook on truth maintenance, Artificial Intelligence Laboratory, AIM-551, MIT, Cambridge, MA, 1980.
26. Nagel, L.W. and Pederson, D.O., Simulation program with integrated circuit emphasis, in: *Proceedings Sixteenth Midwest Symposium on Circuit Theory*, Waterloo, Canada, 1973.
27. Shearer, J.L., Murphy, A.T. and Richardson, H.H., *Introduction to System Dynamics* (Addison-Wesley, Reading, MA, 1971).
28. Stallman, R.M. and Sussman, G.J., Forward reasoning and dependency-directed backtracking in a system for computer-aided circuit analysis, *Artificial Intelligence* **9** (1977) 135–196.
29. Steele, G.L., The definition and implementation of a computer programming language based on constraints, Artificial Intelligence Laboratory, TR-595, MIT, Cambridge, MA, 1980.
30. Steele, G.L. and Sussman, G.J. CONSTRAINTS – A language for expressing almost-hierarchical descriptions, *Artificial Intelligence* **14** (1980) 1–39.
31. Suppes, P.S., *Introduction to Logic* (Van Nostrand, New York, 1957).
32. Waldhauer, F.D., *Feedback* (Wiley, New York, 1982).
33. Wiener, N., *The Human Use of Human Beings: Cybernetics and Society* (Houghton Mifflin, Boston, 1950).
34. Williams, B.C., Qualitative analysis of MOS circuits, *Artificial Intelligence* **24** (1984) this volume.
35. Mayr, O., *The Origins of Feedback Control* (MIT Press, Cambridge, MA, 1970).

Qualitative Analysis of MOS Circuits*

Brian C. Williams

*The Artificial Intelligence Laboratory, Massachusetts Institute of
Technology, Cambridge, MA 02139, U.S.A.*

ABSTRACT

*With the push towards submicron technology, transistor models have become increasingly complex.
The number of components in integrated circuits has forced designers' efforts and skills towards higher
levels of design. This has created a gap between design expertise and the performance demands
increasingly imposed by the technology. To alleviate this problem, software tools must be developed
that provide the designer with expert advice on circuit performance and design. This requires a theory
that links the intuitions of an expert circuit analyst with the corresponding principles of formal theory
(i.e., algebra, calculus, feedback analysis, network theory, and electrodynamics), and that makes
each underlying assumption explicit.*

*Temporal qualitative analysis is a technique for analyzing the qualitative large signal behavior of
MOS circuits that straddle the line between the digital and analog domains. Temporal qualitative
analysis is based on the following four components: First, a qualitative representation is composed of
a set of open regions separated by boundaries. These boundaries are chosen at the appropriate level of
detail for the analysis. This concept is used in modeling time, space, circuit state variables, and device
operating regions. Second, constraints between circuit state variables are established by circuit theory.
At a finer time scale, the designer's intuition of electrodynamics is used to impose a causal
relationship among these constraints. Third, large signal behavior is modeled by transition analysis,
using continuity and theorems of calculus to determine how quantities pass between regions over time.
Finally, feedback analysis uses knowledge about the structure of equations and the properties of
structure classes to resolve ambiguities.*

1. Introduction

Advances in integrated circuit technology in the last decade have presented
circuit designers with new problems and challenges not dealt with previously.
Interest in the potential of VLSI (Very Large Scale Integration) has grown
tremendously in recent years, both in the academic and industrial settings. The
ability to place large systems on a single piece of silicon has made more

*This report describes research done at the Artificial Intelligence Laboratory of the Mas-
sachusetts Institute of Technology. Support for the laboratory's artificial intelligence research is
provided in part by the Advanced Research Projects Agency of the Department of Defense under
Office of Naval Research Contract numbers N0014-80-C-0505 and N00014-80-C-0622.

advanced systems realizable. However, this increase in capability brings with it new problems for the designer.

One major problem is how to manage the design and analysis of systems with a large number of components. Potential solutions to this problem include developing methodologies which exploit regularity and hierarchy during the design phase, and computer-aided design tools which take over some of the lower-level tasks of design and analysis. Much of the design takes place at an abstract level where, for example, the mosfet is modeled as a charge controlled switch. This allows the designer to ignore unnecessary detail.

An equally important problem arises when designing digitial circuits, such as superbuffers, bootstrap clockdrivers, and memory sense amplifiers, which must meet tight performance criteria. These circuits sit on the boundary between the analog and the digital domains; although they are used in digital systems, they must be viewed by the designer as analog circuits in order to meet speed, power and voltage-level requirements. These circuits usually consist of a small set of components; however, *the models necessary to analyze the circuit's performance are complex*. The switch-level mosfet model used to analyze the digital behavior of circuits is not adequate to describe such characteristics as switching speed, power dissipation, gain, capacitive coupling, or noise immunity, and so the designer must use analog device models to analyze the circuit's behavior.

Few tools are currently available to designers for analyzing the electrical characteristics of high-performance digital circuits. Existing tools are primarily electrical simulators which use numerical techniques to produce a set of waveforms showing the circuit's quantitative behavior during successive increments of time in response to a set inputs [20]. These systems can only provide quantitative answers about what the circuit is doing. The circuit analyst is responsible for using this and other information to provide answers to questions like:
– How does this circuit work?
– Why didn't the circuit behave as I expected?
– Which device parameters should I change to make it work?
– Which parameters should I change to increase the circuit's performance (speed, power, voltage thresholds, etc.)?
The knowledge necessary to answer these and similar questions is usually classified under *designer's intuition*. To produce systems which will assist the designer in answering these questions, we must develop a theory which captures some of these intuitions.

1.1. An explanation for a complex bootstrap driver

We can examine the type of reasoning involved in describing a circuit's behavior by looking at explanations of circuits which appear in journal articles. The following is a description of a 5-volt bootstrap driver modeled after one used in the INTEL 218 16K dynamic RAM [4] (Fig. 1.1). The reader is not

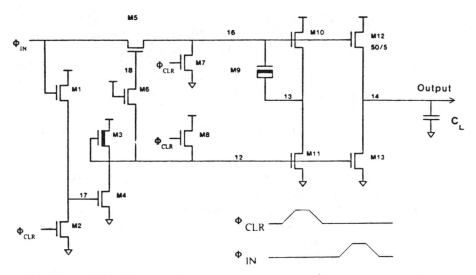

FIG. 1.1. Bootstrap driver.

expected to understand the details of this explanation but should just get a feel
for the style of reasoning involved. Most of the remaining examples in this
paper are very simple and require only a rudimentary knowledge of electronics.

> Initially Φ_{CLR} produces a step which precharges the gates of M11 and M13 high,
> turning them on and holding the output at ground. When Φ_{IN} starts to rise, it charges
> capacitor M9 through M5 and starts to turn M10 and M12 on. M6 isolates node 18,
> which allows that node to bootstrap with M5's gate capacitance, keeping M5 turned
> on hard. M1 and M4 form a comparator that notices when Φ_{IN} has gone above 2
> threshold drops. When this happens, M4 turns on and pulls nodes 12 and 18 down to
> ground. When node 18 discharges, M5 turns off, isolating node 16. Also, when node
> 12 discharges, M11 and M13, which had been holding down nodes 13 and 14, now
> turn off, letting those nodes rise. Capacitor M9 then bootstraps node 16 (which was
> isolated by M5 when M5's gate fell), turning M10 and M12 on hard. M12 pulls the
> output node voltage up. Φ_{IN} can now fall without affecting the rest of the circuit because
> M5 is off. When Φ_{CLR} rises again, M11 and M13 turn on and M10 and M12 turn off,
> forcing the output low and resetting the circuit. The bootstrapping capacitor M9 is
> driven from node 13 and not from node 14 to get more gate drive on M12 which
> significantly improves the output rise time.

Much can be learned by examining this and similar explanations. The terms
used in the explanation are primarily qualitative; when a quantity is used, it is
usually a symbolic quantity such as '2 threshold drops' ($2V_{Th}$), 'high' (V_{DD}), or
'ground'. The behavior of circuit state variables is described primarily in terms
of their rate of change; phrases like 'rises', 'fall', 'starts to rise', and 'discharges'
are commonly used. In addition, terms like 'high' and 'low' are used to describe
a region in which the circuit state variable lies. High usually identifies the

region above V_{DD} minus a noise margin ($x > V_{DD} - NM_H$), while low identifies a region between the threshold voltage minus a noise margin and ground ($V_{Th} - NM_L > x > 0$). The behavior of each device is described in terms of its current region of operation and its movement between these regions (e.g., 'on', 'off', 'turns off', 'starts to turn on', and 'resetting'). From these phrases we see that the notion of *qualitative analysis* plays a very important role in analyzing circuit behavior.

Many of the qualitative phrases above are connected with words like 'affecting', 'turning', 'causing', 'pulls', and 'holding'. The use of these words gives the explanation a strong sense of cause and effect. Except for the initial inputs, all changes of circuit state variables are described in terms of other circuit state variables which caused the change. We even notice phrases such as "... can now fall without affecting ... ", where a lack of effect is made explicit. Thus the notion of *causality* also plays an important role in circuit analysis.

In addition, most of the explanation is given in terms of *local interactions* between devices which are physically connected together. Furthermore, the description of the circuit's overall behavior is inferred from the behavior of each individual component and the way in which they are interconnected. This is a common notion of circuit analysis, which is captured formally by the network laws and device models of circuit theory.

The explanation also uses a number of *cliches*, each of which has a special meaning commonly understood by the designer and the readers. These cliches serve two purposes: to concisely refer to a complex behavior and to assign an intended purpose (teleology) to a set of one or more devices. A cliche like 'precharges' conjures up in the mind of the reader a complex set of events whereby turning on a device will charge a particular node up to V_{DD} or some other understood value. A cliche like 'bootstrapping capacitor' implies that the function of the capacitor will be to appear as a fixed voltage source during certain periods of circuit operation. This is achieved by isolating one of the capacitor's terminals from the rest of the circuit, causing the voltage at a node connected to that terminal of the capacitor to follow any changes in the voltage of the node connected to the other terminal of the capacitor.

Finally, certain statements reflect particular design decisions and assign purpose to certain devices; for example, "the bootstrapping capacitor M9 is driven from node 13 and not from node 14 to get more gate drive on M12, which significantly improves the output rise time". Notice that node 13 doesn't have nearly as much capacitance as node 14, which is connected to C_L. Thus, node 13 will rise much faster than node 14. By connecting the bootstrap capacitor to node 13, rather than node 14, node 16 rises faster providing M12 with a strong drive quickly.

The explanation also makes a number of implicit assumptions and leaves out parts of the explanation which, hopefully, are obvious to the audience to whom the explanation is addressed. A system which analyzes circuits must be able to make these assumptions explicit. This is important in understanding the limitations of the analysis technique and understanding where exactly these limitations arise. Furthermore, the generality of the components of an analysis technique depends on the specific assumptions made for that component.

A number of properties have been identified above which are important in reasoning about circuits. *Qualitative analysis* is an approach to capturing these properties.

1.2. Temporal qualitative analysis: an overview

The remainder of this paper describes *temporal qualitative* (*TQ*) *analysis*, a technique for analyzing MOS circuits whose important behavior straddles the boundary between the analog and the digital domains. TQ analysis describes the causal qualitative behavior of a circuit in response to an input over 'elapsed' time, where time is viewed as a set of intervals in which devices move through different operating regions. A major objective of this work is to show a close link between the intuitions of expert circuit analysts and the formal theories of calculus, circuit theory and feedback analysis.

The analysis of electrical systems involves two steps:

(1) developing models for electrical devices which accurately model their physical behavior,

(2) predicting the behavior of systems which obey these models.

Circuit theory is only concerned with the second step and assumes that the models provided are sound. In this paper a similar assumption is made, although particular properties of the analysis (e.g., continuity) will constrain the models used.

Many of the ideas in TQ analysis have evolved from work by De Kleer on the causal qualitative analysis of bipolar analog circuits [7]. De Kleer's Ph.D. work concentrated mostly on the incremental qualitative (IQ) analysis of devices within a single operating region. TQ analysis differs from De Kleer's work in two important ways:

(1) Because our interest is in analyzing the *electrical performance* of *digital* circuits we must be able to describe the circuit's large-signal behavior. This involves providing a mechanism for determining how devices move between operating regions (*transitions*), as well as describing their incremental behavior. Although De Kleer provided a mechanism for recognizing transitions, this was not central to his thesis and is inadequate for the types of circuits which we would like to analyze.

(2) Unlike the analog bipolar domain, an understanding of *charge flow* and *capacitive storage* is essential in the analysis of digital MOS circuits. A mechanism is provided for representing 'capacitive memory', which is based on the continuity of electrical quantities (e.g., charge) over time.

Each of the remaining sections of this paper will describe a major conceptual component of TQ analysis.

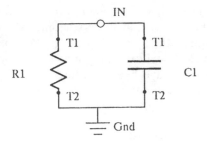

FIG. 1.2. RC example.

Section 2 provides the basic definitions for qualitative representations of electrical networks, time, state variables, and device-operating regions. Each of these representations is based on the notion that a qualitative representation consists of a network of open regions, separated by boundaries. These boundaries are chosen at the appropriate level of detail for the analysis.

Sections 3 and 4 discuss the two basic types of reasoning involved in TQ analysis: *causal propagation* and *transition analysis* [27]. These two sections will be illustrated by a parallel RC circuit (Fig. 1.2) which exhibits the following behavior:

> We will assume that at instant $t = 0$ the voltage across the capacitor is positive ($[V_{IN,GND}] = +$).[1] This causes the voltage across the resistor to be positive, producing a positive current through the resistor, which begins to discharge the capacitor, decreasing $V_{IN,GND}$. $V_{IN,GND}$ decreases for an interval of time and eventually reaches zero.[2] At this point the current stops flowing and the circuit has reached a steady state[3] at zero volts.

This description is marked by a series of events such as $V_{IN,GND}$ being initially positive or $V_{IN,GND}$ moving to zero, which break the description into a series of time intervals. Two types of reasoning are required to analyze the circuit during each interval.

One type of reasoning involves determining the instantaneous response of the circuit to a set of primary causes which mark the event; for example, "a positive voltage across the resistor, produces a positive current through the resistor ..." and so on. The mechanism corresponding to this type of reasoning in TQ analysis is causal propagation and is described in Section 3. Causal propagation occurs at the start of a time interval when a set of qualitative inputs are propagated forward, using a set of causal relations to determine their instantaneous effect on other circuit quantities. This may be viewed as a

---

[1]The notation $[V_{IN,GND}]$ indicates the sign of the voltage from the node IN to GND.
[2]Since $V_{IN,GND}$ is a decaying exponential it is positive for $t < \infty$ and reaches zero at ∞.
[3]By steady state we mean that all the voltages and currents in the circuit are constant.

qualitative small-signal analysis. The mechanism in this section is similar to De Kleer's incremental qualitative analysis.

The second type of reasoning determines the long-term effects of these qualitative inputs; for example, "$V_{IN,GND}$ decreases for an interval of time and eventually reaches zero." This type of reasoning is modeled by transition analysis and is described in Section 4. Transition analysis determines whether or not a quantity will move between two regions of interest (e.g., moving from positive to zero or saturation to cutoff) at the end of a time interval. This analysis is based on the assumption that real systems are modeled by *continuous functions* and builds on a few simple theorems of calculus. Transition analysis may be viewed as a qualitative large-signal analysis.

An understanding of both positive and negative feedback is essential to understanding digital circuits and restoring logic. Section 5 examines the qualitative properties of feedback and discusses a mechanism for recognizing and dealing with feedback in general.[4]

The examples used in the first five sections consist only of simple RC networks. In Section 6 the above mechanism is extended to describe the behavior of devices with multiple operating regions. A qualitative model is created for an enhancement-mode n-channel mosfet and is used to generate an explanation for a simple mosfet circuit.

Section 7 concludes the paper with a discussion of the material presented, comparing it to other qualitative systems, pointing out its limitations, and suggesting directions for future work.

2. Qualitative Values

People use a variety of terms which are considered qualitative. Some examples are positive, negative, increasing, decreasing, forward, saturation, yesterday, tomorrow, office and mosfet. What all of these have in common is that they are regions over time, space, or some other set of quantities which the explainer considers 'interesting'. In addition, these regions, which we call *qualitative regions*, are separated by boundaries. For example, zero is a boundary between plus and minus, midnight is a boundary between today and tomorrow, and the office walls define the space which is called the office.

In temporal qualitative analysis, the space of values which the quantity of interest can take on is broken into a set of open intervals or regions separated by a set of boundaries. These boundaries are chosen at the appropriate level of detail for the analysis. For a particular domain, the construction of a set of qualitative representations may be viewed as a mapping between continuous functions to functions of discrete intervals. In circuit analysis we are mapping from the continuous equations of device physics to a set of qualitative relations

---

[4]Our feedback mechanism was inspired by a set of feedback heuristics presented in De Kleer's Ph.D. Thesis and is a generalization of these concepts.

in circuit theory. The following sections describe the qualitative representation used in TQ analysis for space, time, state variables (e.g., voltage and current), and device behavior. For each section, we make the case that the qualitative representation consists of a set of open regions separated by boundaries. Many of these representations exist in formal circuit theory, while others are implied through common usage.

2.1. The network model

An integrated circuit is implemented as a semiconductor wafer with different ions diffused or implanted into its surface. The equations necessary to describe a complex circuit at the device physics level are not easily solvable and, more importantly, would not provide the designer with much insight into the overall circuit behavior.

In circuit theory, the complexity of these equations is reduced by modeling a region of space with a uniform electrical behavior as a single lumped element (e.g., a resistor, capacitor or mosfet). Each element has a set of terminals which allows it to interact with other elements. The electrical behavior of an element is described by a set of *constitutive* relations between state variables associated with the element's terminals.

An electrical circuit is described as a set of elements connected together in a network. Each member of a set of locally interacting elements has a terminal connected to a common node. The interactions between elements are described by a set of network laws known as Kirchoff's Voltage and Current Laws. These network laws only hold as long as the circuit is small enough that electromagnetic waves propagate across it instantaneously, that is:

$$d \ll c * dt$$
where:
    d is the largest distance across the circuit
    dt is the smallest time interval of interest
    c is the speed of light

This is known as the lumped-circuit approximation, and is important later in our discussion of causality.

A network is described by a set of devices, nodes, and connections between the two. The field Devices specifies the name of each component in the circuit, along with its corresponding type (e.g., resistor(R1) means that the component R1 is a resistor). Nodes is a list of node names used in the circuit. Finally, Connections consist of a set of assertions, each of which specifies the device terminals connected to a specific node. For example, if terminal one of C1 (denoted T1(C1)) and T2(R1) are connected to node IN, then this is specified as: connect(IN T1(C1) T2(R1)).

The following is a specification for the parallel RC network in Fig. 1.2:

```
Network: Parallel RC
    Devices: resistor(R1), capacitor(C1)
        Nodes: IN, GND
    Connections:
        connect(IN T1(R1), T1(C1))
        connect(GND T2(R1) T2(C1))
```

2.2. Time

We represent time as a linear, non-overlapping sequence of alternating in-stants[5] and open intervals. The duration of each interval is determined by transition analysis. During a single time interval, all quantities of interest have a single qualitative value. In other words, each quantity lies within a single qualitative region throughout the duration of an interval. Using this represen-tation, quantities can only interact if they are spatially local and they occur during the same time interval. A linear representation of time has been chosen for simplicity; however, none of the concepts presented in this paper depend strongly on this representation being a linear sequence.

2.3. State variables

The representation we choose for describing electrical quantities depends on which type of circuit and which properties we are interested in. For example, if we are interested in verifying a circuit's behavior at the digital abstraction level, we might want to segment the range of input and output voltages into the following set of regions:

Valid "0" Out	Noise Margin Low	Forbidden Zone	Noise Margin High	Valid "1" Out

Qualitative representation of a digital signal

To look at the analog performance of digital circuits, the components must be viewed as analog devices. At this level, a state variable is described in terms of its sign and the sign of its derivatives;[6] for example, the voltage is positive or the current is decreasing. Sign separates the real-number line into two open intervals, positive and negative, with a boundary at zero. The sign of a quantity, A, will be denoted by $[A]$ and the sign of the quantities nth

---

[5]An instant is a closed interval with zero duration.
[6]Unless otherwise stated, all derivatives discussed in this paper are partials with respect to time.

derivative by $[d^n A/dt^n]$.

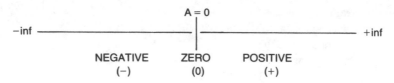

Qualitative representation of a real number A

2.4. Qualitative expressions

To describe the network laws and the element relations of circuit theory, a qualitative algebra in terms of the signs of quantities is necessary. The arithmetic operations necessary for modeling the MOS domain are negation, addition, and multiplication.[7] Tables describing these operations are shown below:

Addition: [A] + [B]

[A]\\[B]	+	0	−
+	+	+	?
0	+	0	−
−	?	−	−

Multiplication: [A] × [B]

[A]\\[B]	+	0	−
+	+	0	−
0	0	0	0
−	−	0	+

also ? × 0 = 0

Negation:

[A]	−[A]
+	−
0	0
−	+

where:
+ = positive
0 = zero
− = negative
? = ambiguous

In the table for addition the symbol (?) means that the result of the sum is *ambiguous*. The sign of the sum cannot be determined without additional information. Techniques for resolving this ambiguity are discussed in later sections. Also notice in the multiplication table that the product of two quantities can be deduced even when one quantity is ambiguous, as long as the other quantity is zero. More complex arithmetic operations, such as subtraction, summation, and exponentiation by a positive integer, can be constructed from these basic arithmetic operations. Finally, it is important to note that the variables participating in a qualitative expression are not limited to quantities and their first derivatives, but may include a mixture of second- and higher-order derivatives as well.

2.5. Operating regions

Often nonlinear devices, such as diodes, bipolar transistors and mosfets cannot

---

[7]The qualitative arithmetic used here is similar to the one used in De Kleer and Brown's Qual and Envision Systems and Forbus' Qualitative Process Theory [7, 14].

be described by a single set of relations without making these relations overly complex. Instead we consider the behavior of the device in each of several distinct operating regions, each described by a different set of equations. The mechanism for representing operating regions and describing how quantities move between operating regions is presented in Section 6.

2.6. Summary

In TQ analysis, a qualitative representation consists of a network of open regions, separated by boundaries which are chosen at the appropriate level of detail for the analysis. The following table summarizes the qualitative representations used in this paper for circuit analysis:

Representation	Open region	Boundary
space	lumped elements	nodes
time	open intervals	instants
state variables	positive, negative	zero
relations	operating regions	edge of op. regions

3. Causal Propagation

Causal propagation is a technique which uses knowledge of circuit theory and qualitative arithmetic to describe the behavior of a circuit during an instant or interval of time; it may be viewed as a qualitative small-signal analysis. In circuit analysis, the values of the state variables of a network can be determined at some instant of time from the network laws, each device's behavior, and the initial conditions. Using the qualitative quantities and expressions described in the previous section, we can perform a similar analysis at a qualitative level. Returning to the RC example (Fig. 1.2), a set of qualitative relations for the network is:

$$[V(IN,GND)] = [I(T1(R1))] \quad \text{Ohm's Law}$$
$$-[I(T1(R1))] = [I(T1(C1))] \quad \text{Kirchoff's Current Law}$$
$$[I(T1(C1))] = [dV(IN,GND)/dt] \quad \text{Capacitor Law}$$

and the initial condition is:

$$[V(IN,GND)] = +$$

From these relations and the initial condition we can deduce, for example, that $[I_{T1(R1)}] = +$, $[I_{T1(C1)}] = -$ and $[dV_{IN,GND}/dt] = -$. The qualitative equations act as a set of constraints on the electrical quantities; as long as $[V_{IN,GND}]$ remains positive the other electrical quantities are constrained to be the values shown above. Furthermore, during any time interval, all qualitative quantities must be single-valued, i.e., a quantity cannot move between qualitative regions or boundaries during the interval.

The qualitative model described thus far tells us what each qualitative value is, but does not explain how they came about. The qualitative description given by an engineer for the RC circuit (Fig. 1.2) gives a *causal* account of the circuit behavior. For example, when $V_{IN,GND}$ becomes positive, this causes a positive current through the resistor, discharging the capacitor and causing $V_{IN,GND}$ to decrease. This causality is not provided in a circuit-theory model. Where then does this causality come from? The answer lies in the assumptions made in modeling a circuit as a network of lumped elements.

3.1. Causality and the lumped-circuit approximation

The lumped-circuit approximation (Section 2.1) states that the network laws hold only as long as the smallest time interval of interest is sufficiently large that electromagnetic waves appear to propagate across the circuit instantaneously. When generating a causal description, the analyst breaks this assumption by viewing the circuit behavior at a time-scale close to the speed of light. On this time-scale, for example, there is a finite delay between the time an electromagnetic wave enters one end of a wire and the time the wave exits the other end. One can imagine the wire as a pipe connected to a faucet. When the faucet is turned on, there is a short delay before the water comes out of the pipe. Only after the water has begun to come out of the pipe and the flow has *stabilized*, can we say that the flow rate out of the pipe equals the flow rate out of the faucet. Similarly, once the current into the wire has had time to stabilize, we can say that the current out of the wire equals the current into it.

In general, the analyst uses multiple viewpoints in describing the behavior of a circuit. A microscopic, electrodynamic-level model is used initially to describe the effects of a set of changes on the system.[8] Once these effects have stabilized the analyst moves to a macroscopic viewpoint (i.e., the network model), where these effects propagate instantaneously. Using the macroscopic viewpoint, the set of initial changes provides a set of constraints on the rest of the system.

One way of modeling these two different viewpoints is to provide two sets of models, one which describes the electrodynamic behavior of devices in terms of Maxwell's equations and a second set which describes the circuit-level behavior in terms of the constraints established by network theory. The former model, however, is both intractable and undesirable. The primary reason for using a circuit model, in the first place, is to avoid the detail and number of interactions which occur in the electrodynamic model. To then reintroduce such a model would be counter-productive. Furthermore, supposing we could produce an electrodynamic model, we are still faced with the problem of assigning a

---

[8]De Kleer and Brown refer to this microscopic time-scale as "mythical time" since, from the macroscopic view of network theory, this time-scale doesn't exist.

causal ordering to the events which occur at the electrodynamics level. Of course, we could produce another model at an even lower level (e.g., quantum physics); however, this simply pushes the problem away one level and doesn't solve it.

The solution which causal propagation takes is to build in the intuition, which a designer has about causality from the electrodynamic level into the network level. This is done by initially imposing a sense of causality on the device relations and network laws in response to a set of changes; these will be referred to as *causal relations*. For example, if we know that $[V] = [I]$ by Ohm's Law, and the voltage across the resistor has begun to increase (i.e., $[dV/dt] = +$), then we say that an increase in V *causes* an increase in I by Ohm's Law.[9] If instead the current through the resistor was changing, then we would say that the change in current causes a change in voltage by Ohm's Law. In the above example, Ohm's Law is a *bi-directional* relation, since the causality can run in either direction. In general, if all but one qualitative value is known in a bi-directional relation, the known values are used to determine their effect on the unknown quantity.

In a few instances the engineer views this causality as occurring in only one direction. (E.g., as we will see in Section 6, an engineer will say that a voltage across the gate of a mosfet produces a current through the device's channel but not the converse.) In this case we refer to the relation as *uni-directional* and indicate the direction of the causality by replacing = with an arrow ($\rightarrow$) pointing from the cause(s) to the effect.[10] Once the circuit has had time to stabilize, the causal relations revert to a set of *constraints* between state variables without imposing a causal ordering. For example. Ohm's Law becomes a constraint between the current and voltage of the resistor and we say that V and I are constrained to be positive by the input.

In TQ analysis, the beginning of a time interval is marked by the *transition* of one or more quantities from one qualitative value to another. The transitioning quantities are referred to as the *primary causes* for that interval.[11] The microscopic viewpoint is used to determine the effects of these primary causes, i.e., to determine the qualitative value for each state variable in the circuit at the beginning of the interval. Moving to the macroscopic viewpoint, these quantities are then constrained by the qualitative network relations for that

[9]Where "*A* causes *B*" means that *B* is functionally dependent on *A*, i.e., the value that *B* has is caused by the value that *A* has.

[10]A bi-directional relation (R) is implemented as a set of uni-directional relations, where each uni-directional relation contains one of R's quantities as an effect and the rest of R's quantities as the cause. For example: $[I1] + [I2] + [I3] = 0$ is equivalent to: $[I1] + [I2] \rightarrow -[I3]$, $[I1] + [I3] \rightarrow -[I2]$, and $[I2] + [I3] \rightarrow -[I1]$. During the causal propagation phase of analysis for a particular interval, at most one of a set of uni-directional relations will be used.

[11]Each primary cause is either an externally driven input or the independent variable of a memory element (e.g., the voltage across a capacitor).

time interval. The end of the interval is marked when one or more quantities transition, creating a new set of primary causes for the next interval of time.[12]

3.2. Implementing causal propagation

Causal propagation is implemented as a set of assertions and rules in AMORD [6], a rule-based inference engine with a truth maintenance system. An assertion consists of a fact statement, which is an arbitrary LISP expression, and a supporting justification. The justification is a reason for the fact to be true, along with a set of facts which support this reason. A rule is composed of a pattern and a rule body which consists of arbitrary LISP code. The rule body is run whenever a set of assertions is found which matches the rule pattern.

Each uni-directional causal relation is implemented as an AMORD rule. The rule pattern consists of the quantities (i.e., 'causes') in the relation's qualitative expression; the expression is evaluated as LISP code in the rule body, and the effect is an assertion made by the rule body. Each assertion is recorded with a justification describing its cause.

Causal propagation begins at the start of a time interval by asserting a set of primary causes with their corresponding qualitative values. Rules function in a demon-like manner. When all of a rule's patterns are matched with a set of assertions, the rule body is run, possibly creating more assertions. Causal propagation terminates when all of the relevant rules have fired.[13]

3.3. Domain knowledge

In this section the domain-specific knowledge for analyzing electrical networks is discussed. This knowledge is broken into two parts: network laws and device models. The network laws describe how current and voltage quantities of connected devices interact, while the device models describe the behavior of a device via the voltages and currents associated with its terminals. Current is measured going *into* a device's terminals and voltage is measured between network nodes.

3.3.1. *Network laws*

Kirchoff's Voltage and Current Laws describe the network behavior of electrical circuits. Kirchoff's Current Law (KCL) states: the sum of the currents out of a Gaussian surface is zero. If the Gaussian surface is put around a single node, then the sum of the currents out of the node is zero. The *qualitative* KCL rule says that the *signs* of the currents out of a node must sum to zero.

---

[12]The duration of the interval is irrelevant to causal propagation. The interval may last to infinity or for only an instant. The duration of an interval and the set of transitioning quantities which mark the end of the interval is determined through transition analysis.

[13]This is not a complete constraint-satisfaction system since some relations can only fire in one direction.

Intuitively, this means that a node cannot source or sink current; that is, each node must contain at least one current flowing into the node and one current flowing out (except when all the currents for that node are zero). In addition, the KCL rule says that the signs of the ith derivative of the currents out of a node also sum to zero.

The qualitative KCL rule is shown below. This rule[14] consists of a set of *preconditions* and a set of *relations*. The preconditions are a mix of patterns for assertions which must exist and conditions which must be true in order for the rule to be applicable. KCL has one precondition: an assertion must exist which specifies all of the terminals connected to a particular node. The relations section consists of causal relations as described above.

> Law: n-Terminal KCL
>   Preconditions:
>   connect(Node-1 T1 T2 ... Tn)
>   Relations:
> $0 = [I(T1)] + [I(T2)] + \cdots + [I(Tn)]$
> $0 = [d^n I(T1)/dt^n)] + [(d^n I(T2)/dt^n] + \cdots + [d^n I(Tn)/dt^n]$

Kirchoff's Voltage Law (KVL) states that the sum of the branch voltages around any loop in the network graph is zero. The qualitative KVL rule states that the sum of the *signs* of the branch voltages around a loop is zero. For loops containing two nodes, the KVL rule (Voltage Negation) is equivalent to saying that voltage is path independent. For loops containing three nodes, the KVL rule states that the voltage between two nodes is the sum of the voltages between each of the two nodes and an intermediate node.

> Law: Voltage Negation
>   Relations:
> $[V(N1, N2)] = -[V(N2, N1)]$
> $[d^n V(N1, N2)/dt^n] = -[d^n V(N2, N1)/dt^n]$

> Law: Three Node KVL
>   Preconditions:
>   When $N1 \neq N2 \neq N3$
>   Relations:
> $[V(N1, N2)] + [V(N2, N3)] = [V(N1, N3)]$
> $[d^n V(N1, N2)/dt^n] + [d^n V(N2, N3)/dt^n] = [d^n V(N1, N3)/dt^n]$

3.3.2. *Device models*

In this section we will first discuss a general property of network elements and then present the specific device models for some simple network elements.

---

[14]TQ analysis considers the words **Law** and **Model** to be synonymous with **Rule** and these words are used purely for documentation purposes.

3.3.2.1. *KCL applied to devices*
Above KCL was stated as: "The sum of the currents out of a Gaussian surface is zero." By placing a Gaussian surface around a device this becomes: "The sum of the currents into a device is zero." Qualitatively this means that no device can source or sink current. All of the devices we are interested in have either two or three terminals. KCL for a three-terminal device is shown below:

>
> Law: Three Terminal Device KCL
>   Preconditions:
>   three-terminal-device(D)
>   Relations:
> $0 = [I(T1(D))] + [I(T2(D))] + [I(T3(D))]$
> $0 = [d^n I(T1(D))/dt^n] + [d^n I(T2(D))/dt^n] + [d^n I(T3(D))/dt^n]$

3.3.2.2. *Network elements*
The basic two-terminal elements are resistors, capacitors and inductors. The constitutive relation for each of these elements is $V = IR$, $I = C \, dV/dt$ and $V = L \, dI/dt$, respectively. A circuit designer views these relations as being bi-directional; that is, a change in voltage will produce a change in current and vice-versa. The models for the resistor and capacitor are shown below. The fields Terminals and Corresponding Nodes list the device's terminals and the nodes connected to these terminals, respectively. These models have an additional field called Assertions consisting of facts which are asserted as a result of running the rule.

>
> Model: Resistor(R)
>   Terminals: T1 T2
>   Corresponding Nodes: N1 N2
>   Relations:
> $[V(N1, N2)] = [I(T1(R))]$
> $[d^n V(N1, N2)/dt^n] = [d^n I(T1(R))/dt^n]$
>   Assertions:
>   two-terminal-device(R)

>
> Model: Capacitor(C)
>   Terminals: T1 T2
>   Corresponding Nodes: N1 N2
>   Relations:
> $[dV(N1, N2)/dt] = [I(T1(C))]$
> $[d^{n+1} V(N1, N2)/dt^{n+1}] = d^n I(T1(C))/dt^n$
>   Assertions:
>   two-terminal-device(C)

3.4. Example

Using the mechanism described thus far, we can determine the behavior of the parallel RC circuit (Fig. 1.2) for a particular instant of time. The analysis begins by inputting the network description shown in Section 2.1. At Instant-0 the initial condition (and the primary cause) is $[V_{IN,GND}$ @ Instant-0$] = +$.[15] This value is asserted and the causal propagator is invoked. We can then ask the system for the qualitative value of any quantity in the network, along with a causal explanation for that quantity:[16]

Explanation for FACT-24: dV(IN,GND)/dt @ Instant-0 is negative:

It was given that V(IN,GND) during Instant-0 is +.
  This causes I(T1(R1)) during Instant-0 to be +,
  since from rule RESISTOR: [V12] → [I1].
    This causes I(T1(C1)) during Instant-0 to be −,
    since from rule 2-T-KCL: [I2] → − [I1].
      This causes dV(IN,GND)/dt during Instant-0 to be −
      since from rule CAPACITOR: [I1] → [dV12/dt].

3.5. Ambiguities

The analysis technique described thus far is not powerful enough to deduce a set of qualitative values under every condition. We have already seen one example of this ambiguity in the addition table in Section 2.4. If $A + B = C$ and A and B have opposite signs, then C is ambiguous; that is, C could be positive, negative or zero.

Each ambiguity which arises in qualitative analysis can be categorized as one of three types:
– ambiguous effect;
– simultaneity;
– unknown primary cause.

First, an ambiguous effect occurs when all of the causes in a qualitative relation are known and the effect cannot be deduced. In the present system such an ambiguity only results from addition. Second, if a quantity (A) is a function of one of its effects (B) then B cannot be deduced without knowing A and A cannot be deduced without B. This cyclic behavior is commonly referred to as a simultaneity. Finally, we need a means of determining how each primary cause changes between time intervals, as they are the inputs to causal propagation.

Analysts use a variety of information, both qualitative and quantitative, in

---

[15]The symbol @ means 'at time' for example, $[A$ @ $t_1] = +$ translates to "the sign of A at time t_1 is positive".

[16]This explanation was generated by the current implementation of TQ analysis.

resolving these ambiguities. The next two sections discuss two techniques which use qualitative information to resolve these ambiguities. The first technique, *transition analysis*, uses information about continuity to resolve some of these ambiguities. The second technique, *feedback analysis*, reasons about the structure of the causal relations to resolve ambiguities which arise from simultaneities along a feedback loop. These two techniques do not resolve all types of ambiguities and other, more quantitative techniques, are needed.

3.6. Summary

Key concepts:
   (1) Causal propagation models the incremental behavior of a circuit and may be viewed as a qualitative small-signal analysis.
   (2) Interactions between circuit state variables are described at two levels:
      – Circuit theory views time at a macroscopic level and describes the interactions between circuit state variables using a set of qualitative network laws and device constitutive relations.
      – Electrodynamics views time at a microscopic level and allows the designer to impose a causality on the network laws and device relations.
   (3) Causal propagation cannot always deduce the sign of every state variable in the circuit unambiguously. These ambiguities are dealt with by transition analysis and feedback analysis.

4. Transition Analysis

In Section 3 we discussed the causal qualitative relationship between different state variables over an interval of time. During a time interval it is assumed that each quantity of interest remains within a single qualitative region (e.g., "the voltage is positive" or "the mosfet is in saturation during the interval"). Causal propagation, however, makes no predictions about if and when a quantity will move to another qualitative region. The goal of *transition analysis* is to make these predictions.

   Causal propagation may be viewed as a qualitative small-signal analysis; similarly, transition analysis may be viewed as a qualitative large-signal analysis. In transition analysis we are concerned with the way quantities move from one qualitative region to another, such as a mosfet becoming saturated or a current becoming positive and increasing. For each state variable in the circuit, transition analysis tries to determine whether or not it will remain in the same qualitative region or transition into another region at the end of a time interval.

   As we discussed at the end of Section 3, causal propagation sometimes cannot determine the qualitative value for one or more quantities during a particular time interval. When this occurs, the results of transition analysis can often be used to resolve the ambiguous quantity by determining how the quantity has changed (i.e., whether or not it has transitioned) between the previous and current time intervals. In the event that transition analysis cannot determine if a quantity has transitioned, other techniques must be used to resolve the ambiguity, such as feedback analysis (Section 5).

Transition analysis is broken into two steps: *transition recognition* and *transition ordering*. Transition recognition attempts to determine whether or not a quantity is moving towards another qualitative region or boundary (e.g., the positive charge on the capacitor is decreasing towards zero, or a mosfet is moving from the boundary between ON and OFF to the region ON). Transition recognition often determines that more than one quantity is moving towards another region or boundary. Transition ordering determines which subset of these quantities will *transition* into a new region or boundary first, marking the end of that interval. This section only discusses transitions across zero. In Section 6 the mechanism described here is extended to recognize transitions across boundaries other than zero.

4.1. Transition recognition

The basic assumption underlying transition analysis is:

The behavior of real physical systems is continuous.[17]

More precisely, it is the functions which describe a physical system that are continuous. This is not to say that the models that an engineer uses are always continuous. For example, only the currents, voltages and their first derivatives are continuous in the Shichman–Hodges model [22] of the mosfet. However, an engineer knows that this model is only an approximation and the behavior of a mosfet in the real world is continuous and infinitely differentiable.

There are a number of simple theorems of calculus which describe the behavior of continuous functions over time intervals. In this section we discuss the intuition which these theorems provide in determining how quantities move between and within qualitative regions. These theorems are then used to derive two rules about qualitative quantities: the *Continuity Rule* and the *Integration Rule*. The first rule requires that a quantity is continuous over the interval of interest, while the second assumes that a quantity is both continuous and differentiable.

4.1.1. *The Intermediate Value Theorem*

When describing the behavior of some quantity over time, we need a set of rules for determining how a quantity changes from one interval or instant to

---

[17]Continuity: "The function f is continuous if a small change in x produces only a small change in $f(x)$, and if we can keep the change in $f(x)$ as small as we wish by holding the change in x sufficiently small" [19].

the next. If, for example, a quantity is positive during some interval of time, will it be positive, zero or negative during the next interval of time?

Zero-crossing Principle. If f is continuous on the closed interval $[a, b]$ and if $f(a) < 0 < f(b)$ then $f(X) = 0$ for some number X in $[a, b]$ [19].

Intuitively, this means that a continuous quantity must cross zero when moving between the positive and negative regions. In the above example, the positive quantity will be positive or zero during the next interval of time, however, it cannot be negative.

The Zero-crossing Principle is a specialization of the following *Intermediate Value Theorem*.

Intermediate Value Theorem. *If f is continuous on the closed interval $[a, b]$ and if l is any number between $f(a)$ and $f(b)$, then there is at least one point X in $[a, b]$ for which $f(X) = l$* [19].

From this we can infer, in general, that a quantity will *always* cross a boundary when moving from one qualitative open region to another.

4.1.2. *State variables and time*

By assuming that quantities are continuous and by using the results of the Intermediate Value Theorem, a relationship can now be drawn between the representations for state variables and time. Recall that the representation for time consists of a series of *instants* separated by *open intervals*. An instant marks a quantity moving from an open region to a boundary or from a boundary to an open region. Also, recall that the range of a state variable is represented by the open regions *positive* $(0, +\infty)$ and *negative* $(-\infty, 0)$ separated by the boundary *zero*, which we denote $+$, $-$ and 0, respectively. If some quantity (Q) is positive at some time instant t_1 $(Q @ t_1 = \varepsilon$ where $\varepsilon > 0)$, then there exists some finite open interval $(\varepsilon, 0)$ separating Q from zero.[18]

If we assume that Q is described by a continuous function of time, then it will take some finite interval of time $\{(t_1, t_2)$ where $t_1 \neq t_2\}$ to move from ε to 0, traversing the interval $(\varepsilon, 0)$. Similarly, it will take a finite interval of time to move from 0 to some positive value ε (Fig. 4.1). Furthermore, we can say that a quantity moving from 0 to ε will leave zero at the *beginning* of an open interval of time, arriving at ε at the end of the interval. Conversely, a quantity moving from ε to 0 will leave ε at the beginning of an open interval and arrive at 0 at the *end* of the open interval. Another way of viewing this is that a quantity will move through an open region during an open interval of time, and a quantity

---

[18]Any two distinct points are separated by an open interval.

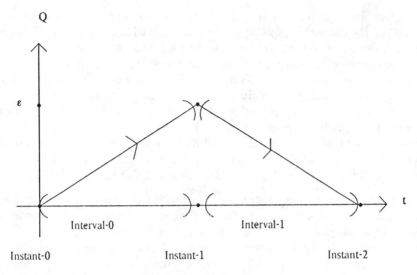

FIG. 4.1. Relationship between state variables and time.

will remain on a boundary for some closed interval of time (possibly for only an instant).

The notion of continuity is captured with the following rule (Fig. 4.2).

Continuity Rule. (1) If some quantity Q is positive (negative) at an instant, it will remain positive (negative) for an open interval of time immediately following that instant.

(2) If some quantity Q is zero during some open interval of time, it will remain zero at the instant following the open interval.

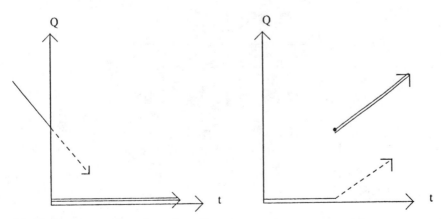

FIG. 4.2. Continuity. --- allowed; = discontinuous.

For example, suppose that $A - B = C$, $[A] = +$ and $[B] = 0$ for some instant of time (t_1). By causal propagation we deduce that $[C @ t_1] = +$. If B becomes positive for the next open interval (I_1), then we cannot deduce C during I_1 by the above causal relation, since the sum is ambiguous (i.e., $[C @ I_1] = (+) - (+) = ?$). Using the first part of the Continuity Rule, however, we predict that C remains positive during I_1. This agrees with our intuition since C is the difference between A and B and we know that it will take some interval of time before B 'catches' up to A (Fig. 4.3).

Using the fact that a state variable will only move off zero at the beginning of an open interval and will only arrive at zero at the end of an open interval, we can now sketch an outline of the steps involved in TQ analysis:[19]

Step 1. Given a set of primary causes for an instant, run causal propagation.

Step 2. Determine which quantities may transition from zero to a positive or negative region at the beginning of the next open interval.

Step 3. Use the results of transition analysis to determine the values of the primary causes for the next open interval of time. Run causal propagation for that interval.

Step 4. Use transition recognition to determine which quantities are moving from positive or negative towards zero.

Step 5. Use transition ordering to determine which quantities will transition

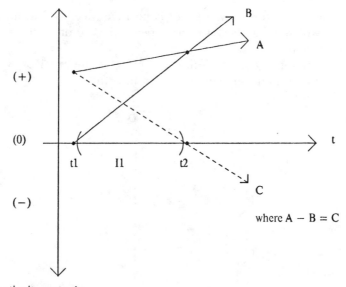

FIG. 4.3. Continuity example.

[19]In the actual implementation the first four steps are performed concurrently.

to zero first. These transitions define the end of that interval and the beginning of the next instant.

Step 6. Repeat this process for the next time instant.

4.1.3. *Mean Value Theorem*

In addition to looking at the continuity of quantities, information can also be derived by looking at the relationship between quantities and their derivatives. The following two corollaries of the Mean Value Theorem [26] are of particular interest to TQ analysis:

Corollary 1. *If a function f has a derivative which is equal to zero for all values of x in an interval (a, b), then the function is constant throughout the interval.*

Corollary 2. *Let f be continuous on [a, b] and differentiable on (a, b). If f'(x) is positive throughout (a, b), then f is an increasing function on [a, b], and if f'(x) is negative throughout (a, b), then f is decreasing on [a, b].*

By combining these two corollaries with the Intermediate Value Theorem, the behavior of a state variable is described over an interval (instant) in terms of its value during the previous instant (interval) and its derivative. At the qualitative level, this is similar to integration and is captured by the following rule (Fig. 4.4):

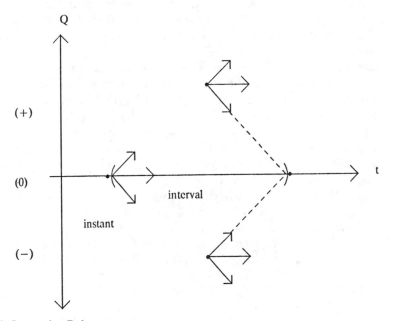

FIG. 4.4. Integration Rule.

Qualitative Integration Rule.

(1) *Transitions to zero*:

(i) If a quantity is positive and decreasing[20] (negative and increasing) over an open time interval, then it will move towards zero during that interval and possibly transition to zero at the end of the interval.

(ii) If a quantity is positive but not decreasing[21] (negative and not increasing) over an open time interval, then it cannot transition to zero and will remain positive (negative) during the following instant.

(2) *Transitions off zero*:

(i) If a quantity is increasing (decreasing) during some open time interval and was zero at the previous instant, then it will be positive (negative) during the interval.

(ii) If a quantity is constant during some open time interval and was zero at the previous instant, then it will be zero during that interval.

Note that in Part (1) of the rule the derivative of the quantity affects how it behaves at the following instant, while in Part (2) the derivative of a quantity affects that quantity during the same interval. For example, suppose that a quantity (Q) is resting at zero at some instant (t_1) (i.e., $[q]$ @ $t_1 = 0$ and $[dQ/dt]$ @ $t_1 = 0$). If dQ/dt becomes positive for the next open interval (I_2), then it will cause Q to increase during that interval and become positive. Furthermore, Q moves off zero instantaneously, thus Q is also positive during I_2. In the above case, the causal relationship between a quantity and its derivative is similar to that between two different quantities related by a qualitative expression (e.g., in a resistor a change in current instantaneously causes a change in voltage).

If we are interested in analyzing a system which includes a number of higher-order derivatives, then the Integration Rule may also be applied between each derivative and the next higher-order derivative. For example, suppose the system being analyzed involves the position (x), velocity (v) and acceleration (a) of a mass (where $dv/dt = a$) and that all three quantities are constant at some instant (t_1). If a becomes positive for the next open interval (I_2), then it will cause an increase in v, making it positive for I_2. Similarly, positive v causes an increase in x, making it positive for I_2. Thus the Integration Rule uses the relation between each quantity and its derivative to locally propagate the effects of changes along a chain from higher-order derivatives down towards the lower-order derivatives.

De Kleer and Bobrow [12] suggest an alternate formulation of Part (2) of the Integration Rule which, for example, says that: When a quantity (Q) is zero at some instant (t_1), if all of its derivatives are zero at t_1, then Q will remain zero during the following interval (I_1), otherwise $[Q] = [dQ^n/dt^n]$ during I_1 (where

[20]where "Q is decreasing" means that $[dQ/dt] = -$.
[21]where "Q is not decreasing" means that $[dQ/dt] = +$ or 0.

$[dQ^n/dt^n]$ is the first non-zero derivative). This formulation has a number of problems. First, it is overly restrictive since it requires each quantity and all of its higher-order derivatives to be continuous. This restriction rarely holds when modeling nonlinear systems, such as MOS circuits, where a device model usually contains a discontinuity in at least one level of derivative. Thus the formulation is inadequate for many complex systems. The Integration Rule only requires that a quantity is continuous and differentiable, making the rule applicable for a wider class of systems. Second, their formulation is non-local in the sense that it looks at the relationship between a quantity and *all* of its higher-order derivatives to determine the behavior of that quantity. The Integration Rule only looks at the relationship between a quantity and its *first derivative*, allowing changes in higher-order derivatives to propagate up locally towards the lower-order derivatives. Finally, De Kleer and Bobrow's formulation can produce a description consisting of a sequence of instants which are not separated by open intervals, thus their model of time is not dense.

As we have seen above, the Integration Rule describes the direction a quantity is moving with respect to zero (e.g., towards or away from zero). Recall that if a quantity is zero and increasing or decreasing during the next interval, then the quantity must transition from zero. If, however, a quantity (A) is moving towards zero for some interval of time, it may or may not reach zero by the end of the interval. Suppose some other quantity (B) reaches zero first and B causes dA/dt to become zero, then A will not reach zero. Thus we need a mechanism for determining which quantity or set of quantities will reach zero first during an open interval of time. One mechanism for doing this is called *transition ordering* and is described in the following section.

4.2. Transition ordering

As a result of transition recognition we have divided the set of all quantities into (1) those which may transition (they are moving monotonically towards zero); (2) those which can't transition (they are constant or moving monotonically away from zero); and (3) those whose status is unknown (their direction is unknown or is not monotonic).

Next we want to determine which subsets of these quantities can transition by eliminating those transitions which lead to (1) quantities which are inconsistent with the set of qualitative relations (e.g., $[A] = +$ and $[B] = 0$ when $[A] = [B]$), and (2) quantities which violate the Intermediate Value Theorem and thus are discontinuous (e.g., Q is caused to jump from $+$ to $-$ without crossing 0).

The simplest solution to this is to enumerate all sets of possible transitions and test each for the above two criteria. However, the number of sets of possible transitions grows exponentially with the number of quantities which can transition; thus this solution becomes intractable for large systems (De

Kleer and Bobrow [12] use a similar approach, but only need to consider the transitions of the independent state variables).

Instead, transition ordering uses (1) the direction each quantity is moving with respect to zero, and (2) the qualitative relations between these quantities to formulate a set of constraints. These constraints determine which quantities can transition first while still satisfying the criteria of consistency and continuity. If in the worst case, every qualitative relation is used during transition ordering, then this solution grows linearly with the number of relations in the system.

If the derivative of a non-zero quantity (Q) is known then its direction will be monotonic over the interval (Q's derivative has a single qualitative value during that interval) and can always be determined by transition recognition. However, even if the derivative of Q is unknown, it is still sometimes possible to determine Q's direction using one of the qualitative relations associated with Q, along with the directions of the other quantities involved in that relation. This is similar to determining the derivative of Q in that, given the value of Q and its direction we can compute dQ/dt for that interval; however, it differs in a number of important respects. When determining the direction of Q we are taking advantage of those times when (1) the value of dQ/dt remains the same during the entire interval of interest (i.e., Q is changing monotonically), and (2) the value of dQ/dt can be computed unambiguously. If the direction of Q cannot be easily determined it is left unknown. On the other hand, when determining the behavior of dQ/dt over time each ambiguity must be resolved. Furthermore, if dQ/dt changes value several times over the interval of interest, then this interval must be broken into a series of subintervals using transition analysis (which then attempts to determine dQ/dt's direction).

The qualitative relations used in modeling devices are built from equality, negation, addition and multiplication. Thus for each of these operations transition ordering contains a set of rules which place constraints on the direction (e.g., toward zero) and transition status (e.g., can't transition) of each quantity involved in the operation. The next section provides a few examples of these rules for each type of operation. In each example we assume that the relation holds over the interval of interest and the succeeding instant. A complete list of transition-ordering rules is presented in Appendix A.

4.2.1. *Transition-ordering rules*

If the signs of two continuous quantities are equivalent (i.e., $[A] = [B]$) over the open interval of interest and the following instant, then we know that if one of the quantities transitions to zero, then the other quantity must transition at the same time. If we know further that A is a monotone increasing function of B, then A and B are moving in the same direction. This may be viewed simply as a consistency check on equality. The above rule also holds for negation (e.g.,

$A = -B$), since negating a quantity does not change its direction with respect to zero.

The case where a quantity is the sum or difference of two other continuous quantities is more interesting. For example, assume that quantities A and C are moving towards zero and B is constant, where $[C] = [A] + [B]$. If A, B and C are positive, then A will transition to zero before C and C can be eliminated from the list of potential transitions.[22] On the other hand, if B is negative, then C will transition before A, and finally, if B is zero, then A and C will transition at the same time (since $[C] = [A]$). Also, consider the case where A and C are positive and B is negative but the direction of C is unknown (with the further restriction that $C = A + B$). If B is known to be constant and A is moving towards zero, then C must also be moving towards zero and will reach zero before A.

Finally, for multiplication (e.g., $[A] \times [B] = [C]$) we know that, if A and/or B transitions to zero, then C will transition to zero at the same time; otherwise, neither A nor B is transitioning and C won't transition.

Thus, transition ordering (1) factors the quantities into sets which transition at the same time, and (2) creates an ordering between these sets according to which transitions precede other transitions.

4.2.2. *Applying the transition-ordering rules*

Transition-ordering rules are applied using a constraint propagation mechanism similar to the one used in propagating qualitative values. If as the result of applying these inference rules it is determined that (1) all the remaining potential transitions will occur at the same time, and (2) the direction of these quantities is known to be toward zero, then the transitions occur at the end of the current interval. Otherwise, an ordering may be externally provided for the remaining potential transitions, or the system can try each of the remaining sets of possible transitions. More quantitative techniques which help resolve the remaining sets of possible transitions are currently being explored.

Section 4.3 provides an example of how transition recognition and transition ordering work together to describe how a simple circuit behaves over time.

4.3. Example

Using transition analysis, we can now describe the behavior of the RC example (Fig. 1.2) after Instant-0.[23] In Section 3.4, causal propagation was used to determine the values of the circuit's state variables at Instant-0. The results of

---

[22]If instead we had said that C transitioned to zero first then A would have to jump from plus to minus without crossing zero (i.e., $[A] = [C] - [B] = (0) - (-) = -$). This violates the Intermediate Value Theorem and, therefore, cannot occur.

[23]More complex examples of transition ordering are found in Sections 5.5 and 6.4.

this propagation were:

$$
\begin{array}{lll}
[\text{V(IN,GND)}] & = + & \\
\rightarrow [\text{I(T1(R1))}] & = + & \text{Resistor Model} \\
\rightarrow [\text{I(T1(C1))}] & = - & \text{Kirchoff's Current Law} \\
\rightarrow [\text{dV(IN,GND)}/\text{d}t] & = - & \text{Capacitor Model} \\
\rightarrow [\text{dI(T1(R1))}/\text{d}t] & = - & \text{Resistor Model} \\
\rightarrow [\text{dI(T1(C1))}/\text{d}t] & = + & \text{Kirchoff's Current Law}
\end{array}
$$

Since each quantity is non-zero at Instant-0, we know by the Continuity Rule that all the values will remain the same for an open interval (Interval-0) following Instant-0.

Next it must be determined whether or not any quantities will transition to zero at the end of Interval-0. By applying the Integration Rule to $[V_{IN,GND}] = +$ and $[\text{d}V_{IN,GND}/\text{d}t] = -$, we know that $V_{IN,GND}$ is moving towards zero. Using a similar argument, we determine that $[I_{T1(R1)}]$ and $[I_{T1(C1)}]$ are also moving towards zero.

The direction of $[\text{d} V_{IN,GND}/\text{d}t]$, $[\text{d}I_{T1(R1)}/\text{d}t]$ and $[\text{d}I_{T1(C1)}/\text{d}t]$, however, cannot be determined using the Integration Rule, since their derivatives (the second derivatives of V and I) are unknown. The direction of each of these quantities can be determined using the inference rules for equivalences described above. For example, we know that $[\text{d}V_{IN,GND}/\text{d}t]$ is moving towards zero, since $[I_{T1(C1)}]$ is moving towards zero and $[I_{T1(C1)}] = [\text{d}V_{IN,GND}/\text{d}t]$ from the capacitor model. In addition, it is deduced from KCL and the resistor model, which are both equivalences, that $[\text{d}I_{T1(R1)}/\text{d}t]$ and $[\text{d}I_{T1(C1)}/\text{d}t]$ are also moving towards zero.

Finally, since all of the quantities are qualitatively equivalent, they will all transition to zero at the same time. Since no other potential transitions exist, each of these quantities will transition to zero at the end of Interval-0.

Using the results of transition analysis, we know that the primary cause ($V_{IN,GND}$) at Instant-1 is zero, where Instant-1 immediately follows Interval-0. Causal propagation is then used to generate a causal account of why, for example, $[\text{d}V_{IN,GND}/\text{d}t]$ is zero at Instant-1.

The discussion, thus far, has assumed that all quantities behave continuously. The next section discusses how TQ analysis might be extended to deal with discontinuous behavior.

4.3.1. *Discontinuous behavior*

Although an engineer believes that circuits in the physical world exhibit continuous behavior, he often wants to model portions of their behavior discontinuously. For example, a voltage may rise sufficiently fast that the engineer wants to idealize the behavior as a step, simplifying his analysis.

Even when a circuit's behavior is modeled by a discontinuous function, the discontinuities are isolated to a few places and the rest of the function behaves continuously (e.g., a step is only discontinuous at one point). If the point at which a quantity is discontinuous can be identified, TQ analysis can deal with it simply by not applying transition analysis to the particular quantity at that point in time.

The remaining task, then, is to identify when a quantity may behave discontinuously. A discontinuity in one of the circuit's state variables may result from either a discontinuity in (1) an input, or (2) one of the device models. Discontinuities in state variables can be identified by propagating each discontinuity (or continuity) forward from the input (or device model) to the affected quantities. This propagation is performed using rules like: If $A + B = C$ where A is discontinuous at some point and B is not, then C is discontinuous at that point.[24]

Creating a set of rules which correspond to integration is more difficult since the integral of a discontinuous function may or may not be discontinuous, depending on the order of the singularity. For example, the integral of an impulse (a step) is discontinuous, while the integral of a step (a ramp) is continuous. To deal with integration the propagation mechanism for singularities must keep track of the order of the singularity as well. TQ analysis is currently being extended with a set of rules similar to the ones above which deal with discontinuities.

4.4. Summary

Key concepts:

(1) The behavior of real physical systems is continuous.

(2) Transition analysis may be viewed as a qualitative large-signal analysis.

(3) Transition analysis is built on a few simple theorems of calculus about intervals.

(4) Transition recognition determines the direction of a quantity with respect to zero using the Continuity Rule and the Integration Rule.

(5) Transition ordering uses the directions deduced during transition recognition, along with the qualitative relations between quantities to:
  – eliminate potential transitions which would violate the Zero-crossing Principle
  – determine, when possible, the direction of quantities not deduced by transition recognition.

(6) Transition analysis can be easily extended to deal with discontinuities.

5. Feedback Analysis

Feedback is an important property of most physical systems. Roughly speaking, feedback occurs whenever one of the inputs to a sum is a function of the sum's

---

[24]Usually we can say that the output of a qualitative expression is guaranteed to be continuous at some time as long as all of its inputs are continuous at that time.

output. A feedback path then exists between the sum's output and an input. Negative feedback is often used to add stability to amplifier gain and positive feedback is used in digital systems to provide sharp transitions and bi-stability. This section discusses how feedback and equations with simultaneities affect TQ analysis.

Instances of feedback can be found in remarkably simple circuits, such as the resistive current divider circuit (RR) shown in Fig. 5.1. Assuming that I_{IN} is initially zero, the following is one possible explanation for the response of the circuit to a rise in I_{IN}: An increase in I_{IN} produces an increase in I_{R1}, causing V_{IN} to rise. The rise in voltage is applied across R2, increasing I_{R2} and, hence, reducing the effect of the initial current increase on I_{R1}.

This is a simple example of negative feedback, where I_{R2} is the feedback quantity. Circuit analysts usually ignore feedback at this primitive level. Nevertheless, in qualitative analysis it is important to understand feedback at any level for two reasons. First, feedback is a special case which cannot be handled by the TQ mechanism discussed. Second, by understanding the properties which are particular to feedback, the power of TQ analysis is increased. In Sections 5.1 and 5.2 we discuss the effects of feedback on TQ analysis, and how TQ analysis can be augmented to deal with it.

5.1. The effects of feedback and simultaneities on TQ analysis

If TQ analysis is run on the RR circuit we immediately run into a problem. Initially all the circuit's state variables and their derivatives are zero. At the beginning of the first open interval, dI_{IN}/dt becomes positive. At this point the only applicable qualitative relation is Kirchoff's Current Law:

$$[dI_{IN}/dt] - [dI_{R2}/dt] = [dI_{R1}/dt] .$$

Unfortunately, either $[dI_{R1}/dt]$ or $[dI_{R2}/dt]$ must be known to solve this equation and there is no means of calculating them using purely local in-

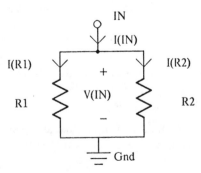

FIG. 5.1. RR current divider.

formation. We can see why this is not possible by looking at the overall structure of the causal relations between the circuit's state variables; this is shown in Fig. 5.2 and is called a *causal relation graph*. To deduce $[dI_{R1}/dt]$ from KCL we need to know $[dI_{R2}/dt]$; however, we can see from Fig. 5.2 that $[dI_{R2}/dt]$ is a function of $[dI_{R1}/dt]$. This results in a set of simultaneous relations; $[dI_{R2}/dt]$ cannot be calculated without knowing $[dI_{R1}/dt]$ and vice-versa.

The structure of the relations around a binary sum $(A + B = C)$ can be classified as one of two types: *direct sum* or *simultaneity*. A *direct* sum occurs when both inputs are independent of the output C. A *simultaneity* occurs whenever one of the inputs, A or B, is a function of its output C (and possibly some other inputs). The simultaneity is distinguished when one of the inputs is *only* a function of the output by calling it *feedback*.[25] An example of each type of sum is shown in Fig. 5.3. The point at which the feedback or simultaneity is summed is called a *comparison point*.[26] For the following discussion we will always use C as the *effect*, A as the independent *cause* and B as the *feedback* term.

The mechanism discussed thus far has assumed that all sums are direct. Earlier we found that if the result of a direct sum is ambiguous, the results of transition analysis can often be used to resolve this ambiguity. Similarly, if a sum is the comparison point of a simultaneity, the results of transition analysis can often be used to determine the value of a quantity which is the effect of a comparison point and continue the propagation based on that value. If the results of transition analysis cannot determine this value, we must look for the answer elsewhere. The next section examines the properties of feedback and shows how the resulting information is used to deduce the value for the effect of a comparison point.

5.2. Qualitative properties of feedback

Thus far TQ analysis has only used local information to determine the behavior of a circuit. In this section we examine the overall structure of the relations around a comparison point to determine the value of its effect.

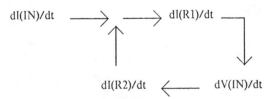

FIG. 5.2. Causal relation graph for RR current divider.

[25]This is a more restrictive definition than the one used in most texts; however, by doing so we are able to describe a number of interesting properties later on.

[26]A comparison point is a point in the relation graph, and does not necessarily correspond to any particular point in the circuit topology.

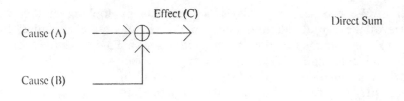

Direct Sum

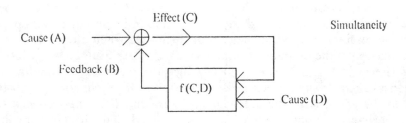

Simultaneity

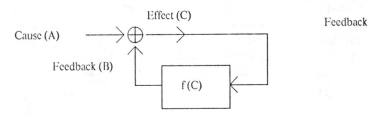

Feedback

FIG. 5.3. Support classification.

A feedback loop is described in general by the following two equations:

$$A + B = C, \quad B = \mathscr{F}(C).$$

If the sign of B is the same as A, then we have an instance of *positive feedback*. In this case the sign of C can be determined unambiguously and is the same as the sign of A. The result of positive feedback is to amplify the effect of any changes in A.

If the sign of B is the opposite of A, then we have an instance of *negative feedback*. The value of C is the difference between the magnitudes of A and B; this results in the sign of C being ambiguous. In a typical use of negative feedback, B dampens the effects of the input A on C, thus stabilizing the output. If $\mathscr{F}$ is a polynomial function, that is $\mathscr{F}$ only involves addition, negation and multiplication, then we say that it is *resistive*.[27] If the feedback is purely resistive then the magnitude of B will be less than A, except when A, B and C are zero: thus, the sign of A and C are the same. Intuitively, this means that, if there are no independent sources in the negative feedback loop, the feedback term will always be weaker than the input to the feedback loop. In order for the magnitude of the feedback term to be larger than the input, the gain of the function $\mathscr{F}(C)$ would have to be greater than one. An engineer's intuition says that such a gain can only be produced using an independent source of power.

Another way of viewing this concept is to consider there to be a finite delay along the feedback path and simulate the results of a change on the input. Assume that A, B and C are initially zero and $\mathscr{F}(C)$ is a negative constant gain such that $[B] = -[C]$. Now, if A becomes positive, then C becomes positive, since B is initially zero and $C = A + B$. This then causes B to become negative, reducing the effect of A on C. Now suppose that the magnitude of B becomes as large as A. This causes C to become zero, and since $[B] = -[C]$, B must also become zero. However, we are now back to the case where A is positive and B is zero, so C must instantaneously jump back to positive. By continuing this argument C appears to oscillate back and forth between positive and zero instantaneously. Such an oscillation violates continuity and cannot occur in real systems, thus C remains positive until A moves to zero.[28]

As we have seen above, for both types of feedback the sign of the effect is the same as the input. This is described by the following rule:

Resistive Feedback Rule. If $A + B = C$ and B is a resistive function of C, then the sign of C will always be the same as A ($[A] = [C]$).

The equivalence between A and B also supplies an additional constraint to transition ordering which is used to break simultaneities in the direction and transition constraints:

Resistive Feedback Transition Ordering Constraint. If $A + B = C$ and B is a resistive function of C, then A, B and C will transition to (from) zero at the same time.

Returning to the RR example (Fig. 5.1), we know that dI_{IN}/dt transitioned from 0 to + at the beginning of Interval-0. $[dI_{R1}/dt]$ cannot be deduced by KCL because $[dI_{R2}/dt]$ is unknown; furthermore, it is assumed that the value of $[dI_{R1}/dt]$ cannot be determined by transition analysis. We therefore assume that KCL produces a relation which is a feedback comparison point in the current divider's relation graph (Fig. 5.2). In addition we assume that dI_{R1}/dt is

---

[27]Intuitively, this means that the function is memoryless.

[28]Forbus uses this type of argument, which he refers to as "stutter", to model a person's naive intuition of simple feedback.

the effect of the comparison point and dI_{R2}/dt is the feedback term.[29] Under this assumption we assert that $[dI_{R1}/dt] = +$, since $[dI_{IN}/dt] = [dI_{R1}/dt]$ by the Resistive Feedback Rule, and eventually deduce by causal propagation that $[dI_{R2}/dt] = +$. This is a valid instance of feedback since the feedback term $([dI_{R2}/dt])$, is only a function of the effect $([dI_{R1}/dt])$. Furthermore, it is negative feedback since dI_{IN}/dt and dI_{R2}/dt are both positive, where $[dI_{IN}/dt] - [dI_{R2}/dt] = [dI_{R1}/dt]$.

After a period of time, I_{IN} stops rising and dI_{IN}/dt transitions to zero, marking the end of Interval-0. Using the Transition Ordering Constraint for resistive feedback we deduce that dI_{R1}/dt will transition to zero at the same time as dI_{IN}/dt, and dI_{R2}/dt will also transition at the end of Interval-0 since both dI_{IN}/dt and dI_{R1}/dt are transitioning and $[dI_{IN}/dt] - [dI_{R1}/dt] = [dI_{R2}/dt]$. Finally, dV_{IN}/dt will also transition to zero since $[dV_{IN}/dt] = [dI_{R1}/dt]$. Therefore, at the instant following Interval-0 all three currents are positive and constant and remain so until the input changes.

If a circuit includes an inductor or a capacitor along the feedback path then the function $\mathscr{F}$ will involve integration.[30] For a capacitor the relation $[dV/dt] = [I]$ makes it necessary to integrate dV/dt to get V, while the relation for the inductor, $[V] = [dI/dt]$ requires dI/dt to be integrated. A feedback path which requires voltage integration is called *capacitive feedback*, a path requiring current integration is called *inductive feedback*, and a path requiring no integration is called *resistive feedback*. The properties of resistive feedback have already been discussed above. The remainder of this section discusses the properties of feedback paths which involve integration.

An RC circuit exhibiting capacitive feedback is shown in Fig. 5.4, along with its relation graph. KCL, again produces a feedback comparison point in the relation graph with I_{R2} as the feedback term and I_{C1} as the effect. If V_{IN} is initially zero, then the Integration Rule tells us that V_{IN} will have the same sign

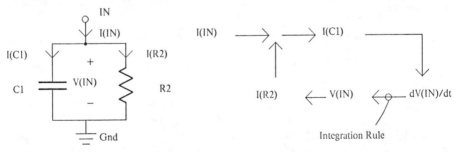

FIG. 5.4. RC current divider.

[29]In the RR example we also could have called dI_{R2}/dt the effect and dI_{R1}/dt the feedback term. A set of heuristics for selecting the effect and feedback term of a comparison point is discussed in Section 5.3.

[30]Intuitively a feedback path involving integration has memory.

as dV_{IN}/dt during the following time interval. This is depicted in the relation graph as $dV_{IN}/dt \rightarrow V_{IN}$.

When a negative-feedback path involves integration, it is not necessarily true that $[C] = [A]$ for all time. For example, if A is positive and begins to quickly drop, then A may become less than B and C becomes negative. The reason for this is that the integration along the feedback loop makes B sluggish and it can't respond quickly enough.

If, however, A, B and C are initially zero at some time instant (t_1) and A transitions from zero immediately after t_1, then the magnitude of B will be less than A for *an interval of time* (I_1) immediately following t_1.[31] Therefore, *the sign of C will be the same as A during I_1*. After this interval, the magnitude of B may become as large as A, in which case C will cross to zero and $[C] \neq [A]$. This is described by the following rule:

Integrating Feedback Rule. If
  (1) $A + B = C$,
  (2) B is a function of C involving integration,
  (3) $[A] = [B] = [C] = 0$ at some time instant, and
  (4) A transitions from 0 immediately after that instant,
then the sign of C will be the same as A i.e., $([A] = [C])$ for an interval of time immediately following that instant.

This rule can now be used to describe the behavior of the RC circuit (Fig. 5.4). Initially, it is assumed that the input current is zero and the capacitor is discharged, so that all the circuit's currents and voltages are constant at zero. At the beginning of some open interval the current I_{IN} becomes positive.[32] Using the Integrating Feedback Rule it is assumed that $[I_{C1}] = +$, allowing the following chain of deductions to be made:

$$([I(C1)] = +) \rightarrow ([dV(IN)/dt] = +) \rightarrow ([V(IN)] = +) \rightarrow ([I(R2)] = +)$$

Next we want to determine what transitions occur at the end of the interval. By the Integration Rule, V_{IN} is moving away from zero and cannot transition. I_{R2} also cannot transition since $[I_{R2}] = [V_{IN}]$. If I_{IN} is moving towards zero then, I_{C1} must reach zero before I_{IN} to satisfy the Intermediate Value Theorem in the relation $[I_{IN}] = [I_{C1}] + [I_{R2}]$; thus I_{IN} is eliminated. This leaves I_{C1} and dV_{IN}/dt, which must transition at the same time, since $[I_{C1}] = [dV_{IN}/dt]$. Since neither quantity's

---

[31]The integral of a continuous quantity Q is always less than Q for some interval starting at the beginning of the integration; therefore, the initial effect of the integration is to reduce the magnitude of the feedback term.

[32]It is interesting to note that the behavior of this circuit is deduced without knowing the derivative of the input. We will return to this example again in Section 5.7, using higher-order derivatives to produce a more detailed explanation.

direction is known, they may or may not transition. The former corresponds to the case where the input current levels off and the capacitor eventually stops charging. This matches our intuition since a capacitor acts like an open circuit at DC. The latter corresponds to the case where the input current continues to rise forever, and the capacitor never stops charging. The Integrating Feedback Rule also holds for inductive circuits; however, inductance is rarely considered in digital MOS circuits. The remainder of this section summarizes the steps involved in resolving ambiguities due to simultaneities.

During causal propagation, if one of the inputs to a sum cannot be determined and no further deductions can be made, it is assumed that the sum is a simultaneity and the results of transition analysis are used, if possible, to determine a value for C. If the value for C cannot be determined by transition analysis, it is assumed that the sum is part of a feedback loop and one of the above feedback rules is used to determine C.

Once the value for the feedback term (B) is deduced, this assumption is verified by looking at the causal chain supporting B. If C is encountered along B's causal chain then B is a function of C and the sum is a simultaneity. If all of the causal paths supporting B start at C then B is a function of C alone and the sum is further classified as feedback. Similarly, the feedback is further classified as positive or negative, and resistive, capacitive, inductive or both. Finally, if C is not encountered among B's supports, then B is not a function of C and we have a direct sum. If an assumption proves to be false it must be retracted. Verifying a simultaneity or feedback assumption is tricky for circuits with multiple feedback loops or cross coupled feedback loops and will not be discussed here.

5.3. Bi-directional comparison points

The problem addressed in this section is the determination of the effect and feedback terms of a comparison point. In the previous section we assumed that it was known which quantity was the effect and which quantity was the feedback term. However, if the comparison point of a feedback loop involves a bi-directional sum, the selection of these two quantities is not obvious. Although all of the feedback comparison points seen thus far have been a result of KCL, in general they can be produced by any relation involving a sum, either from a network law or a device model. Both of the network laws (KCL and KVL) contain bi-directional sums; however, none of the device models which we've encountered in the MOS domain contain bi-directional sums.[33]

Returning to the RR current divider example (Fig. 5.1) we notice that the circuit is symmetrical; R1 and R2 could be switched without changing the behavior of the circuit. This can also be seen in the relation graph (Fig. 5.2). An

---

[33]The mosfet model, presented later on, contains a relation involving a sum which can be used as a comparison point; however, the relation is uni-directional.

equally valid description of the circuit behavior would have been to use I_{R1} as the feedback term and I_{R2} as the effect. In this example the selection of a feedback term is arbitrary since the feedback path is bi-directional. This, however, is not the case in the RC current divider example (Fig. 5.4). We see from the relation graph that the causality along the feedback path can only run in one direction. I_{R2} must be the feedback term since the Integration Rule is uni-directional, allowing the causality to run only from dV_{C1}/dt to V_{C1}, but not the reverse.

One way of dealing with bi-directional comparison points is simply to try both possible directions. This, however, becomes costly, since most complex circuits have a large number of simultaneities. Furthermore, engineers appear to use a set of heuristics which allow them to significantly reduce the amount of backtracking which is performed while reasoning about feedback circuits.

Returning to the RC current divider, a circuit analyst might describe its behavior as follows:

> When the input current becomes positive, the capacitor initially acts like an incremental short and all the current goes into the capacitor. As the capacitor charges, this produces a positive voltage across the resistor, causing I_{R1} to be positive.

The important part of this dialogue is the viewpoint that C1 acts like an incremental short. We can understand this viewpoint by looking at the impedance of a capacitor. Initial changes in state variables are usually fairly sharp, involving a large high-frequency component. At high frequencies (ω), the impedance of the capacitor ($1/j\omega C$) becomes very small, causing the capacitor to act like an incremental short or 'battery'.

In this example the designer reasons that the current through the capacitor initially dominates over the resistor current, and selects the former as the effect of the comparison point. Looking at the circuit's relation graph, we see that the capacitor 'integrates' I_{C1}. The causality can only move from I_{C1} towards V_{IN} and not vice-versa; therefore, I_{C1} must be the effect of the comparison point. The opposite case occurs in the RC high-pass filter shown in Fig. 5.5. This circuit behaves as follows:

> When the input voltage begins to rise the capacitor initially acts like a 'battery', transmitting the change in the input voltage directly to the resistor's voltage. This produces a current through the resistor which charges the capacitor and causes V_{C1} to increase.

In this example the designer reasons that the capacitor is initially insensitive to any changes in voltage, and therefore selects it as the feedback term of the comparison point. Looking at this circuit's relation graph, we see that causality can only move from I_{C1} towards V_{C1} and not vice-versa; therefore, I_{C1} *must* be the feedback term in the comparison point.

If the capacitor is replaced with an inductor in the above two circuits, the

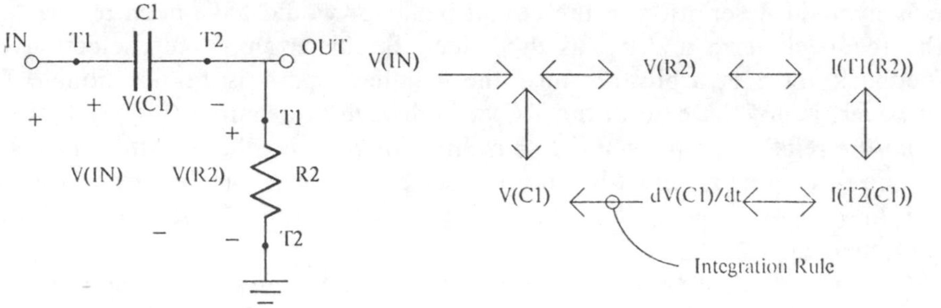

FIG. 5.5. RC high-pass filter.

behavior is exactly the opposite. At high frequencies (ω) the impedance of the inductor ($j\omega L$) becomes very large, causing the inductor to act incrementally like an open circuit or current source. Using the above analysis, we can construct the following heuristic:

Feedback Direction Heuristic. For each of the two unknown quantities in the comparison point:
(1) If the quantity is current (or one of its derivatives) then:
  – if the relation attached to the quantity is capacitive, the quantity is the effect of the comparison point;
  – if the relation attached to the quantity is inductive, the quantity is the feedback term of the comparison point.
(2) If the quantity is voltage (or one of its derivatives) then
  – if the relation attached to the quantity is inductive, the quantity is the effect of the comparison point;
  – if the relation attached to the quantity is capacitive, the quantity is the feedback term of the comparison point.
(3) If no relation, other than the comparison point, is attached to either quantity then feedback analysis is not appropriate.

Section 5.5.1 provides an example of how these heuristics are used to describe more complex circuits. The Section 5.4 discusses a means of restricting the number of sums which are treated as comparison points.

5.4. Localizing the effects of KVL

The KVL rule from Section 3 states that the sum of the voltages between *any* three nodes is zero, no matter how far or close the nodes are spaced. This differs from KCL and the device models in that its effects are non-local. This presents some serious problems when applying the feedback rules, since a change in voltage at one end of the network will produce a plethora of feedback assumptions across the network, few of which are of any use. Something is clearly wrong with this approach. An engineer doesn't suddenly jump back and forth from one end of a circuit to the other when describing its behavior. Instead he prefers to reason about circuit behavior in terms of local interactions. When a voltage is given with respect to a reference, it is often viewed as a node voltage (or potential) and the reference becomes implicit (e.g., $V_{IN,GND}$ becomes V_{IN}). A node voltage at node (N) may then be reasoned about as if it was a quantity local to N. To determine the effects of the node voltage, the analysts will look at the *branch* voltage (i.e. a voltage between two nodes) across devices which are directly connected to node N. In his Ph.D. Thesis, De Kleer identified the importance of reasoning about voltage locally when dealing with feedback, calling it the KVL Connection Heuristic. The following is a paraphrased version of the KVL Connection Heuristic: If the voltage at a node, which is connected to one terminal of a device, is increasing or decreasing, and nothing else is known to be acting on the device, then the device responds as if the unknown actions are negligible.

A statement of the KVL Locality Heuristic used in TQ analysis is shown below. The effect of the node voltage on the surrounding circuit is not stated in the KVL Locality Heuristic, but is determined by the feedback rules and heuristics outlined above. The resulting behavior of the KVL Locality Heuristic differs from the KVL Connection Heuristic in that the change in the node voltage *may* or *may not* be transferred across a locally connected device, depending on whether it is resistive, capacitive, or inductive. The latter case occurs in the RC example (Fig. 5.5) where the capacitor acts initially like a voltage supply, and the change in V_{IN} is produced across R2 rather than C1.

KVL Locality Heuristic. Only apply feedback analysis to a comparison point produced by KVL if the input to the comparison point is a node voltage (potential).

5.5. Examples

Using the rules and heuristics described in Section 5, it is now possible to describe the behavior of more complex circuits. In this subsection, TQ analysis is used to describe the behavior of two circuits: an RC ladder network and a Wheatstone bridge circuit. The first example combines the Integrating Feedback Rule with the Feedback Direction Heuristic to describe the behavior of a capacitive circuit over an interval of time. The second circuit provides a complex example of resistive feedback, and shows how feedback analysis interacts with transition ordering.

5.5.1. *RC ladder example*

An RC ladder network is shown in Fig. 5.6 along with its causal relation graph.

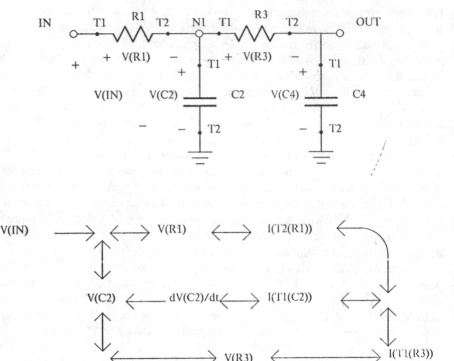

FIG. 5.6. RCRC ladder and causal relation graph.

This circuit has three comparison points, two from KVL and one from KCL, producing the three potential feedback loops shown in the network's causal relation graph. We assume that the voltage across the input and each capacitor is zero at Instant-0. At the beginning of the next interval (Interval-0), V_{IN} begins to rise and becomes positive. Using TQ analysis, we can predict the behavior of the circuit during Interval-0, as described below. Note that each phrase of the explanation is followed by a set of rules which were used to deduce that portion of the behavior:

> (1) As the voltage at node IN rises,
>   (*Input, KVL Locality Heuristic*)
> (2) C2 initially acts like a battery,
>   (*Feedback Direction Heuristic for voltages*)
> (3) and the voltage across the resistor (R1) connected to IN begins to increase.
>   (*Integrating Feedback Rule*)

(4) The positive voltage across R1 produces a current,
   (*Integration Rule, resistor model*)
(5) which flows into C2,
   (*KCL, Integrating Feedback Rule*)
(6) since C2 initially acts like an incremental short.
   (*Feedback Direction Heuristic for currents*)
(7) This causes C2 to charge, producing an increase in voltage at node N1.
   (*capacitor model*)
(8) This change in voltage in transferred across R3,
   (*same as* (1), (2) *and* (3))
(9) producing a current which flows into C4,
   (*resistor model, Integration Rule, KCL*)
(10) causing the capacitor to charge, and raising the voltage at node OUT.
   (*capacitor model*)

5.5.2. *Wheatstone bridge example*

Fig. 5.7 shows an example of a Wheatstone bridge, one of the more complex, purely resistive circuits used in engineering practice. Again, the voltage across the input, and therefore across each resistor, is assumed to be zero at Instant-0. At the beginning of the next interval (Interval-0), V_{IN} begins to rise and becomes positive. Causal propagation and feedback analysis are used to predict the behavior of the circuit during Interval-0. The arrows in the causal relation graph (Fig. 5.7) for the bridge circuit indicate the direction of causal flow resulting from the propagation.[34] The following is an explanation of I_{R5}'s behavior in response to the input:

(1) As the voltage at node IN rises,
   (*Input*)
(2) the voltage across R2 increases,
   (*KVL Locality Heuristic, Resistive Feedback Rule*)
(3) causing an increase in I_{R2},
   (*resistor model*)
(4) which flows into R4, producing an increase in I_{R4},
   (*KCL, Resistive Feedback Rule*)
(5) and causing V_{R4} to rise.
   (*resistor model*)
(6) Similarly, increasing V_{IN} causes an increase in V_{R1},
   (*KVL Locality Heuristic, Resistive Feedback Rule*)
(7) increasing I_{R1},
   (*resistor model*)
(8) which then flows into R3, producing an increase in I_{R3},
   (*KCL, Resistive Feedback Rule*)
(9) and causing V_{R3} to rise.
   (*resistor model*)

At this point an ambiguity arises; the voltage across R5 may become positive, negative, or remain zero. All three possibilities could occur, depend-

---

[34] All the relations for the Wheatstone bridge circuit are bi-directional.

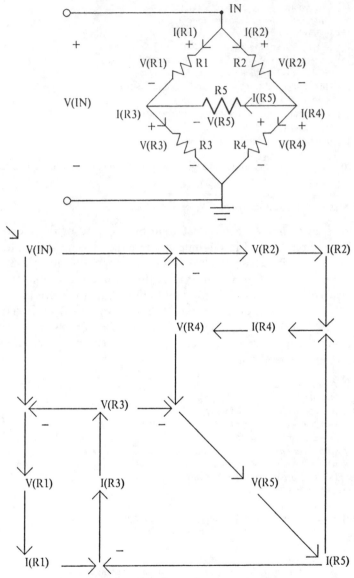

FIG. 5.7. Wheatstone bridge and causal relation graph.

ing on the relative magnitudes of V_{R4} and V_{R3}. These, in turn, depend on the specific values of the resistors in the network. For now we assume that $|V_{R3}| > |V_{R4}|$. Using this assumption the explanation can be completed:

(1) Assuming the increase in V_{R3} dominates over V_{R4}, then
    (*Assumption*)
(2) this causes an increase in V_{R5},
    (*KVL*)

(3) producing an increase in I_{R5}.
(*resistor model*)

Next, TQ analysis tries to determine whether or not any voltage or current can transition back to zero. At first glance, it seems likely that V_{R5} will go to zero, or oscillate back and forth between positive and negative, since its qualitative value was ambiguous in the above analysis. However, intuitively, an engineer knows that none of the circuit's voltages or currents should oscillate; because the circuit is purely resistive, there are no energy-storage units to support an oscillation. That is, none of the voltages or currents should transition to zero until the input voltage goes to zero. Combining transition ordering with the results of feedback analysis, shown below, TQ analysis is able to make a similar prediction.

Applying the Resistive Feedback Transition Ordering Constraint (Section 5.2) to the four feedback comparison points produces the following relations, where $t(X)$ denotes the time that X will transition to zero:

$$t(V_{IN}) = t(V_{R1}) = t(V_{R3}), \tag{5.1}$$

$$t(V_{IN}) = t(V_{R2}) = t(V_{R4}), \tag{5.2}$$

$$t(I_{R2}) = t(I_{R4}) = t(I_{R5}), \tag{5.3}$$

$$t(I_{R1}) = t(I_{R3}) = t(I_{R5}). \tag{5.4}$$

The resistor model provides the following additional constraint:

$$t(V_{Rn}) = t(I_{Rn}) \quad \text{for } n \text{ from 1 to 5}. \tag{5.5}$$

Using relations (5.1) and (5.2) above, we know that V_{R1} through V_{R4} will transition to zero exactly when V_{IN} transitions. In addition, from relations (5.3) and (5.4), I_{R1} through I_{R5} will also transition together. Finally, applying relation (5.5) to R5 and one of the other resistors (R1–R5), transition ordering determines that all of the currents and voltages in the circuit will transition to zero, exactly when V_{IN} does. This is precisely what we predicted above based on our intuition; thus V_{R5} can only oscillate if the input voltage oscillates.

Thus far we have discussed simultaneities which result in ambiguities at sums; in Section 5.6 we discuss how simultaneities can produce ambiguities which originate right at the primary cause.

5.6. Simultaneities involving primary causes

Returning to the parallel RC circuit described in the introduction, it has been determined thus far that $V_{IN,GND}$ is initially positive during Instant-0, and decreases during Interval-0, reaching zero at Instant-1. At Instant-1 the values of the voltage, currents and their derivatives are all zero. Intuitively we know that the voltage will remain zero during Interval-1, the interval following

Instant-1 (since any perturbation of $V_{\text{IN,GND}}$ off of zero will immediately decay back to zero). If $[dV_{\text{IN,GND}}/dt]$ is known during Interval-1, then $V_{\text{IN,GND}}$ can be determined using the Integration Rule. Unfortunately $[dV_{\text{IN,GND}}/dt]$ can only be deduced from $V_{\text{IN,GND}}$; i.e., the relations contain a simultaneity involving $V_{\text{IN,GND}}$ (Fig. 5.8). This situation is quite analogous to the feedback examples presented earlier. In fact the parallel RC circuit is identical to the RC high-pass filter (Fig. 5.5) when V_{IN} for the filter is zero. Because there is no independent source driving the feedback loop all quantities along the feedback loop will remain constant at zero. Feedback analysis deals with this type of simultaneity with the following rule:

Simultaneous Primary Cause Rule. If the value of a primary cause (Q), and its derivative (dQ/dt) are unknown during an interval and were both zero at the previous instant, then assert that Q is zero during that interval under the assumption that Q is part of a feedback loop with no source.

This rule is applied to any primary cause which is not independently driven as an input (i.e., the independent variable of a memory element, such as the voltage across a capacitor or the current through an inductor). It is then substantiated when dQ/dt is deduced by making sure that (1) $[dQ/dt] = 0$, and (2) $[dQ/dt]$ is a function of Q alone.

Applying the above rule to the parallel RC example, we assume that $[V_{\text{IN,GND}}] = 0$ during Interval-1. From this it is deduced that I_{R1}, I_{C1}, and finally $dV_{\text{IN,GND}}/dt$ are zero, thus substantiating the assumption. At this point all of the state variables and their derivatives are zero. Transition analysis determines that there are no more transitions and the system has reached steady state.

5.7. High-order derivatives

Thus far, we have described the complete mechanism, provided by TQ analysis, for analyzing networks of devices which are modeled by a single operating region. The examples presented have only involved voltage, current, and their first derivatives. TQ analysis, however, is not restricted to these quantities and

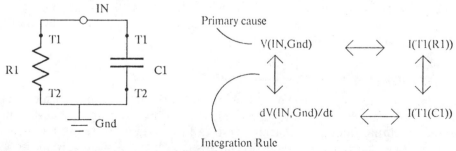

FIG. 5.8. Parallel RC circuit and causal relation graph.

can use higher-order derivatives when available. In this section we return to the RC current divider (Fig. 5.4) to show how higher-order derivatives may be used to provide more detailed predictions.

Recall from Section 5.2 that, assuming C1 of the divider is initially discharged, a positive input current, I_{IN}, starting at the beginning of an open interval (I_1), causes C1 to charge, making V_{IN} positive, which produces a current through R2. Knowing only the sign of the input current, TQ analysis is unable to determine whether or not the capacitor stops charging after a period of time, (i.e., does I_{C1} transition to zero?). The resolution of this ambiguity depends on more detailed characteristics of the input waveform which were not provided. Now we will provide some additional constraints on the input waveform and see how they affect the resulting prediction.

Instead of specifying just that the input is positive, it is assumed that the input current is monotonically increasing. This provides the additional constraint that the input current's derivative is positive during I_1. The relation graph corresponding to the additional input, dI_{IN}/dt, is the same as the one in Fig. 5.4, except that each quantity is replaced by its derivative. Again, applying the Integrating Feedback Rule to KCL, followed by constraint propagation, the following *additional* deductions are made:

$$([dI(IN)/dt] = +) \rightarrow ([dI(C1)/dt] = +) \rightarrow ([d^2V(IN)/dt^2] = +)$$
$$\rightarrow ([d^2I(R2)/dt^2] = +)$$

Using these deductions, it is now possible to determine what I_{C1} will do. Notice that, since both dI_{C1}/dt and I_{C1} are positive, I_{C1} is moving *away* from zero, thus, resolving the ambiguity about whether or not I_{C1} transitions. As long as dI_{C1}/dt stays positive, current will continue to flow and the capacitor voltage will rise monotonically. This resolves the ambiguity mentioned above; however, another ambiguity arises: dI_{C1}/dt may transition to zero. This transition might occur if the derivative of the input current oscillates sharply, while remaining in the positive region.

To resolve this new ambiguity, one final constraint is placed on the input current; the input waveform is a ramp. This corresponds to the second derivative of the input current being zero during I_1. Using causal propagation, the following deductions are made:

$$([d^2I(IN)/dt^2] = 0) - ([d^2I(R2)/dt^2] = +) \rightarrow ([d^2I(C1)/dt^2] = -)$$
$$\rightarrow ([d^3V(IN)/dt^3] = -)$$

This resolves the ambiguity about dI_{C1}/dt transitioning. Since its derivative (d^2I_{C1}/dt^2) is negative, dI_{C1}/dt is moving toward zero. Furthermore, transition ordering determines that, since dI_{C1} will reach zero first, it must transition. Once, dI_{C1}/dt reaches zero, I_{IN} and dI_{R2}/dt will both be rising ramps, where I_{R2} lags I_{IN} by the constant current I_{C1}. No further transitions will occur as long as the input current remains a ramp.

Above we saw that, by using higher-order derivatives, it was possible to resolve all ambiguity in response to the input. Furthermore, higher-order derivatives enabled us to describe the behavior of the circuit's state variables more precisely. For example, knowing only the sign of the input it was only possible to determine that I_{C1} was positive. By knowing the first and second derivatives of the input, we determined that I_{C1} was initially rising, but eventually leveled off to a constant value.

Using higher-order derivatives does not always reduce the number of ambiguities. If instead $[d^2 I_{IN}/dt^2]$ was positive, then it would have been ambiguous whether or not $[d^2 I_{C1}/dt^2]$ transitioned to zero. Furthermore, if the input was a rising exponential (e.g., $I_{IN} = e^t$), then all of the nth derivatives of I_{IN}, up to $n = \infty$ would be positive. For the exponential input, the addition of higher-order derivatives would result in replacing one ambiguity with another at a more detailed level. For this input one must use some other reasoning technique, such as induction, to resolve the ambiguity.

In this section we have seen that higher-order derivatives may be used to add detail to the prediction of the circuit's behavior. Furthermore, this additional information may sometimes be used to resolve ambiguities. However, the use of higher-order derivatives does not guarantee that all existing ambiguities will be resolved and may even add more ambiguities. In addition, these derivatives may add a level of detail into the explanation which the user would rather ignore or might find confusing.[35] A good theory of when it is profitable to pursue higher-order derivatives is important in qualitative analysis and is a topic of future research.

5.8. Summary

When TQ analysis encounters a situation where the input to a sum is a function of the sum's output, causal propagation cannot continue. The sum is assumed to be a simultaneity, and the results of transition analysis are used to deduce the output. If this is not possible, the sum is assumed to be a case of feedback and the qualitative properties of feedback can be used to determine the output. These properties are summarized by the Resistive Feedback Rule and the Integrating Feedback Rule. Finally, the assumption of simultaneity or feedback is verified.

At a bi-directional comparison point an additional complication arises: The cause and feedback terms must be identified. An engineer uses his intuition about capacitive and inductive relations to resolve this complication. This intuition is summarized in the Feedback Direction Heuristic. At present, bi-directional sums appear only in the KCL and KVL rules.

---

[35]The desired level of detail for an explanation depends on many factors, such as the domain and type of user. In the MOS domain, first and second derivatives have been found adequate for most circuits examined.

The number of potential feedback comparison points can be quite large due to the non-local behavior of KVL. A designer restricts this number by reasoning in terms of local interactions. This notion is captured in the KVL Locality Heuristic.

Finally, by viewing a circular set of relations as a feedback loop with a 'mythical cause', feedback analysis can be used to resolve the simultaneity.

6. Operating Regions and the MOS Transistor

The basic building block of MOS circuits is the Metal Oxide Silicon Field Effect Transistor or mosfet. This section develops a qualitative model for an enhancement n-channel mosfet and discusses how TQ analysis is extended to deal with this and other models which have more than one operating region.

The mosfet can be modeled at a number of levels from device physics to the switch-level abstraction. In this section we use a very simple analog model [22] which is adequate for modeling most digital circuits at the qualitative level. The mosfet model has three terminals which act as the gate, source and drain. In addition, this model is broken into two parts: *conduction* and *capacitance*, where conduction describes the relationship between $V_{G,S}$, $V_{D,S}$ and I_D, and capacitance describes the relationship between Q_G and the device's terminal voltages. Fig. 6.1 shows a high-level model of the mosfet where capacitance is modeled as an ideal capacitor from gate to source and conduction is modeled as a nonlinear dependent current source. The conduction model is broken into several operating regions (e.g., off, on, unsaturated, saturated, forward and reverse), and each region is described using a different set of constitutive relations. In this section we first discuss a mechanism for modeling devices with multiple operating regions, then develop the mosfet's conduction and capacitance models, and conclude with the analysis of a simple mosfet circuit.

6.1. Modeling devices with multiple operating regions

Thus far only the analysis of devices with a single operating region have been discussed. To analyze devices with multiple operating regions (e.g., diodes,

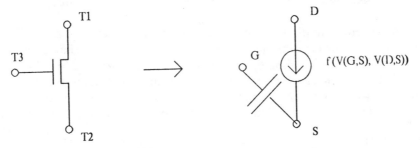

FIG. 6.1. n-mosfet large-signal model.

bi-polar transistors, JFETs, mosfets etc.), TQ analysis must be extended in two ways. First, it must be able to determine which region a device is currently operating in. This is necessary to determine which set of device relations is applicable. Second, TQ analysis must be able to determine when a device transitions from one operating region to another, identifying when one set of device relations must be exchanged for another.

An operating region is described by the set of boundaries which surround it. To determine the operating region which a device is currently in, it is necessary to determine the device's position with respect to each of these boundaries. To determine whether a device may transition between operating regions, one must determine the direction the device is moving with respect to each of these boundaries. When the device crosses one of these boundaries, it moves into a different operating region. In Section 4, we discussed a mechanism (transition analysis), for determining how a quantity transitions across the boundary *zero*, between the intervals, positive and negative. If a quantity is associated with each operating region boundary, which describes the device's distance from that boundary, then transition analysis can be used to determine the device's position and movement with respect to that boundary.

The remainder of this subsection describes the steps involved in defining the operating regions of a device and specifying their associated device relations. During this explanation each step will be demonstrated using the operating regions of the mosfet as an example.

The operating regions of the mosfet model can be broken into two sets: {Saturated, Unsaturated, Off} and {Forward, Symmetric, Reverse}. These regions are described by the following inequalities:

Forward:	$V(T1,T2) > 0$
Symmetric:	$V(T1,T2) = 0$
Reverse:	$V(T1,T2) < 0$
Off:	$(V(G,S) - V(Th)) \leqslant 0$
On:	$(V(G,S) - V(Th)) > 0$
Unsaturated:	$V(D,S) < (V(G,S) - V(Th))$
Saturated:	$V(D,S) \geqslant (V(G,S) - V(Th))$

A graphical representation of these operating regions is shown in Fig. 6.2.

The first step in creating an operating region involves defining the boundaries that separate it from other regions. A boundary and the half-planes above and below it can be described by the sign of a quantity; that is, the boundary's associated state variable.[36] This quantity is defined in terms of other state variables using the arithmetic operations: addition, negation, and multi-

---

[36]This state variable represents the distance from the device's current position in state space to the closest point on the boundary.

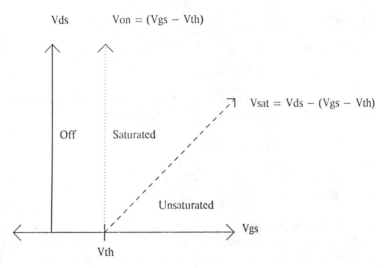

FIG. 6.2. n-mosfet operating regions.

plication. Graphically, these operations correspond to rotating and translating, reflecting, and scaling a linear boundary. In the mosfet model, the quantity describing the boundary between Forward and Reverse is just $V_{T1,T2}$ and already exists. For the boundary between On and Off we define the state variable V_{On}, where $V_{On} = V_{G,S} - V_{Th}$. Finally, the state variable V_{Sat} is used to describe the boundary separating Saturated and Unsaturated, where $V_{Sat} = V_{D,S} - V_{On}$.

Next we need to be able to determine whether or not a device is above, below, or at a particular boundary. This corresponds to asking whether or not the boundary's state variable is positive (>0), negative (<0) or zero ($=0$). In addition, the region name is a Boolean which is true if the device is in that region, false if the device is out of that region, and ? if undetermined. The Forward, Symmetric and Reverse regions are now defined as:

$$
\begin{aligned}
\text{Forward} \;\;&= \;\; (V(T1,T2) > 0) \\
\text{Symmetric} \;\;&= \;\; (V(T1,T2) = 0) \\
\text{Reverse} \;\;&= \;\; (V(T1,T2) < 0)
\end{aligned}
$$

If the behavior in a set of regions and boundaries can be described by the same set of relations, then those regions and boundaries can be combined. These regions are combined using union, intersection and complement, which correspond to ANDing, ORing and Negating the truth values associated with the particular regions being combined. For example, using $\lor$ or $\lnot$, two new predicates can be defined which combine a region and a boundary into a semi-closed region:

$$(A \geqslant 0) := (A = 0) \vee (A > 0)$$
$$(A \leqslant 0) := (A = 0) \vee (A < 0)$$

With these Boolean operations and predicates we can now define the remaining operating regions Off, On, Unsaturated and Saturated:

Off	$= (V(On) \leqslant 0)$
On	$= (V(On) > 0)$
Unsaturated	$= (V(Sat) < 0) \wedge On$
Saturated	$= (V(Sat) \geqslant 0) \wedge On$

Finally, each operating region can be associated with its corresponding relations using a set of conditional statements. For example, when a mosfet is off the current is zero and constant. This is expressed in the following statement:

If Off then $([I(D)] = 0) \wedge ([dI(D)/dt] = 0)$

Next a mechanism must be provided for determining how a device transitions from one operating region to another. Recall that each boundary is described by a corresponding state variable. The sign of this state variable determines where the device is operating with respect to that boundary. By computing the sign of the state variable's derivative, it is possible to determine the direction the device is moving with respect to its associated boundary. Transition analysis is then applied to determine when a device will transition between operating regions. For example if $[V_{On}] = +$ and $[dV_{On}/dt] = -$, then the mosfet is On and moving towards the On/Off boundary.[37] Transition analysis assumes that all quantities are modeled by continuous functions. Because of this, the relations in each operating region must be continuous across the region boundaries, or the discontinuity must be made explicit to transition analysis (Section 4.3.1). In the mosfet model this means that, since the current is zero in the Off region and at the boundary of On/Off, when a device moves from Off to On, the current at the edge of the On region can be 0^+, but could not jump discontinuously to 5 amps. The Shichman–Hodges model, which is used to derive the mosfet model in the next section, is continuous in current, voltage, and their first derivatives. In Section 6.2, the concept of multiple operating regions is used to model conduction in the n-channel mosfet.

[37]This also requires some modifications to the mechanism for verifying feedback loops which have not been discussed.

6.2. The mosfet-conduction model

The n-mosfet is a charge-controlled switch in which the three terminals, T1, T2 and T3, act as drain, source and gate respectively. When positive charge is placed on the gate of the n-mosfet a layer of negative charge forms between the gate and the substrate, which creates a channel between the source and drain and allows negative charge to flow from the source to the drain. The voltage at the time the channel is formed is called the threshold voltage (V_{Th}) and is measured between the gate and source. If $V_{G,S} \leqslant V_{Th}$, then the device is Off and no current flows between source and drain. If $V_{G,S} > V_{Th}$, then the mosfet is On and current may flow along the channel. The On operating region is subdivided into Saturated and Unsaturated regions which are described by the following quantitative relations:

Saturated: $I(D) = K(V(G,S) - V(Th))^2$
Unsaturated: $I(D) = K((V(G,S) - V(Th)V(D,S) - V(D,S)^2/2)$

If $V_{T1,T2}$ is zero then the source and drain are indistinguishable and no current flows through the channel.

The mental image most electrical engineers have for a mosfet is that voltage between the gate and source produces charge on the gate and in the channel, causing current to flow. Changes in drain and source current are viewed as the effect of the device's voltages and not the other way around. This means that the two current equations above should be modeled as uni-directional causal relations with the voltages, $V_{G,S}$ and $V_{D,S}$, as causes, and I_D as the effect. Furthermore, positive charge flows from drain to source so these equations have been written in terms of I_D rather than I_S. I_S is determined as an effect of I_D by three-terminal device KCL (Section 3.3.2.1).

The mosfet is a symmetric device in the sense that T1 and T2 switch between acting as drain and source, depending on whether the mosfet is in the Forward or the Reverse operating region. We, therefore, say that a particular terminal exhibits some behavior when *acting in the role* of source or drain, rather than a terminal *is* the source or drain. T3 always acts in the role of gate; however, the role of T1 and T2 may vary over time. The qualitative model for the n-mosfet is shown in Fig. 6.3. Note that the mechanism for associating between terminals, nodes and roles is left implicit. For the current I_D, D refers to the terminal acting in the role of drain and in $V_{D,S}$, D and S refer to the nodes connected to the terminals acting in the role of drain and source.

Three types of transistors commonly used in nMOS digital design are enhancement-mode, depletion-mode and zero-threshold mosfets. The threshold voltage for an enhancement-mode device is positive, for a depletion-mode device negative and for a zero-threshold device approximately zero. The model for the enhancement-mode n-mosfet is shown in Fig. 6.4. In Section 6.3

Model: n-channel-mosfet(M)
  Terminals: T1 T2 T3
  Corresponding Nodes: N1 N2 N3
  Roles: G S D
  Relations:
    $[I(G)] = 0$
    $[dI(G)/dt] = 0$
    $[V(On)] \leftarrow [V(G,S)] - [V(Th)]$
    $[dV(On)/dt] \leftarrow [dV(G,S)/dt] - [dV(Th)/dt]$
    $[V(Sat)] \leftarrow [V(D,S)] - [V(On)]$
    $[dV(Sat)/dt] \leftarrow [dV(D,S)/dt] - [dV(On)/dt]$
  Region: OFF: $[V(On)] \leq 0$
    Relations:
      $[I(D)] = 0$
      $[dI(D)/dt] = 0$
  Region: ON: $[V(On)] > 0$
    Region: SATURATED: $[V(Sat)] \geq 0$
      Relations:
        $[I(D)] \leftarrow [V(On)]^2$
        $[dI(D)/dt] \leftarrow [V(On)] \times [dV(On)/dt]$
    Region: UNSATURATED: $[V(Sat)] < 0$
      Relations:
        $[I(D)] \leftarrow ([V(On)] - [V(Sat)]) \times [V(D,S)]$
        $[dI(D)/dt] \leftarrow [V(D,S)] \times [dV(On)/dt] - [V(Sat)] \times [dV(D,S)/dt]$
  Assertions:
    three-terminal-device(M)
    Assume-initially (is-acting-in-the-role-of (T1(M) D(M)))
    Assume-initially (is-acting-in-the-role-of (T2(M) S(M)))
    Assert-always (is-acting-in-the-role-of (T3(M) G(M)))
  Region: FORWARD: $[V(T1,T2)] > 0$
    Assertions:
      is-acting-in-the-role-of (T1(M) D(M))
      is-acting-in-the-role-of (T2(M) S(M))
  Region: REVERSE: $[V(T1,T2)] < 0$
    Assertions:
      is-acting-in-the-role-of (T1(M) S(M))
      is-acting-in-the-role-of (T2(M) D(M))

FIG. 6.3. n-channel mosfet-conduction model.

Model: enhancement-n-channel-mosfet(M)
  Relations:
    $[V(Th)(M)] = +$
    $[dV(Th)(M)/dt] = 0$
  Assertions:
    n-channel-mosfet(M)

FIG. 6.4. Enhancement-mode n-channel mosfet-conduction model.

we discuss the capacitance which results from charge on the gate and along the channel.

6.3. Mosfet-capacitance model

Modeling mosfet capacitance is very difficult due to its nonlinearities. If MOS capacitance is modeled completely, then a capacitor should be connected between every terminal of the device, including the bias node. A digital designer, however, considers at most two of these capacitances, and usually only one. These capacitances are $C_{G,S}$ and $C_{G,D}$.[38] Usually $C_{G,D}$ is less than $C_{G,S}$ and is ignored. If the designer is interested in the detrimental effects of parasitic capacitance then he considers both of these capacitors, as they both have the ability of bootstrap. If the designer is explaining a bootstrap circuit, then he assumes that $C_{G,S}$ is dominant and ignores $C_{G,D}$. (An explicit capacitor may be added to the circuit to make sure that $C_{G,S}$ is dominant.) For more conventional designs, a designer usually explains the gate capacitance as a capacitor from gate to ground. This simplest model is adopted. Whenever a capacitor ($C_{G,S}$) is being used for bootstrapping, it will be made explicit.

As stated earlier, the gate capacitance on a mosfet is nonlinear. Below inversion (Off), there is no channel for charge to move into, and gate charge terminates on the substrate. This produces a very low capacitance. When the channel inverts ($V_{G,S} > V_{Th}$) charge moves into the channel and the capacitance jumps dramatically. To model this effect it would be necessary to add a qualitative MOS-gate-capacitor model. In this paper the ideal capacitor model given earlier is used. Next an explanation is shown which TQ analysis generates for a simple mosfet circuit using the model described above.

6.4. Mosfet example

By replacing the resistor in the parallel RC circuit (Fig. 1.2) with a mosfet we get the circuit shown in Fig. 6.5. Again we will assume that the voltage on the

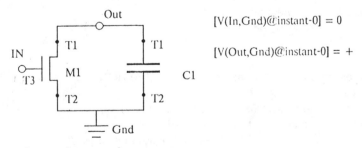

$[V(\text{In,Gnd})@\text{instant-0}] = 0$

$[V(\text{Out,Gnd})@\text{instant-0}] = +$

FIG. 6.5. n-mosfet-capacitor example.

[38] $C_{G,D}$ is often referred to as the Miller capacitance.

capacitor is some positive value; in addition, the input voltage is 0 and the mosfet is off. At some time instant (Instant-0) the input begins to rise. Eventually the mosfet turns on and the capacitor begins to discharge, decreasing $V_{OUT,GND}$. The following is an explanation using TQ analysis to determine why the $V_{OUT,GND}$ is decreasing:[39]

Explanation for FACT-210: dV(IN,GND)/dt @ Interval-1 is decreasing:

(1) It was given that V(OUT,GND) during Instant-0 is +.
(2) This causes M1 to be Forward,
      since from rule NMOS-OP-REGION: Forward if V12 > 0.
(3) This causes T1(M1) to act as Drain and T2(M1) to act as
      Source, from rule NMOS-FORWARD-BEHAVIOR.
(4) Also, it was given that V(IN,GND) during Instant-0 is 0.
(5) This causes V(On) to be −,
      since from rule NMOS-BEHAVIOR: [V(G,S)] − [V(Th)] → [V(On)].
(6) This and (1) cause V(Sat) to be +,
      since from rule NMOS-BEHAVIOR: [V(D,S)] − [V(On)] → [V(Sat)].
(7) also (5) causes M1 to be Off,
      since from rule NMOS-OP-REGION: Off if V(On) ⩽ 0.

Interval-0:

(8) It was given that dV(IN,GND)/dt during Interval-0 becomes +.
(9) This causes V(IN,GND) to be +,
      since from rule INTEGRATION: [dA/dt] → [A].
(10) Fact (8) also causes dV(On)/dt to be +.
      since from rule NMOS-BEHAVIOR: [dV(G,S)/dt] − [dV(Th)/dt] → [dV(On)/dt].
(11) This causes V(On) to move towards 0
      from rule INTEGRATION.

Instant-1:

(12) Eventually, V(On) becomes 0 at Instant-1
      by Transition Analysis on (11).

Interval-1:

(13) V(On) becomes + at Interval-1 by the INTEGRATION rule.
(14) This causes M1 to be On,
      since from rule NMOS-OP-REGION: On if V(On) ⩾ 0.
(15) This and (6) cause M1 to be Saturated,
      since from rule NMOS-OP-REGION: Saturated if On ∧ V(Sat) > 0.
(16) This and (13) cause I(T1(M1)) to be +,
      since from rule NMOS-SAT-BEHAVIOR: [V(On)] → [I(D)].

[39]This explanation is similar, in style to the output generated by the current implementation of TQ analysis.

(17)   This causes I(T1(C1)) to be −,
         since from rule 2-T-SKCL: ([I2]→ −[I1]).
(18)   This causes dV(OUT,GND)/dt to be −,
         since from rule S-CAPACITOR: [I1]→ [dV12/dt].
(19)   This causes V(OUT,GND) to move towards zero,
         from rule INTEGRATION.

The remainder of the explanation describes how the capacitor discharges to 0 volts and will not be given here.

The circuit shown in Fig. 6.6, is a simplified version of the bootstrap driver described in the introduction. The problem with many digital circuits is that their output rises slowly if the output load capacitance is large. One purpose of the bootstrap-driver circuit is to provide a strong current through the pullup (M2) to the output load capacitance, allowing the output to rise quickly. This is achieved by using a bootstrap capacitor to fix a voltage across the gate and source of M2, keeping it turned on hard. To keep the capacitor's voltage constant, the terminal of C_{boot} connected to node N1 is isolated, preventing any current from flowing into the capacitor. This isolation is performed by M3 which turns off when node N1 rises above the supply voltage. The digital behavior of the circuit's output is simply to invert the input.

The techniques described above make it possible to analyze the behavior of this circuit. Initially the input is high and the circuit has stabilized by Instant-0 with the following conditions:

M1: Unsaturated, [I(D)] = +
M2: Saturated, [I(D)] = +
M3: Saturated, [I(D)] = 0
[V(Cload)] = + (but close to zero)
[V(Cboot)] = +

Immediately   following   Instant-0   the   input   voltage   begins   to   fall

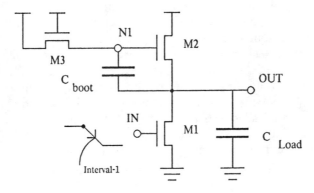

Fig. 6.6. Simple bootstrap circuit.

([dV_{IN}/dt @ Interval-1] = $-$). TQ analysis is then used to determine the response of the circuit to this input. Using the results of this analysis we can answer some interesting questions about the circuit's behavior, for example:[40]

What happens to V_{OUT} during Interval-1?
V_{OUT} increases.

Why?
A decrease in V_{IN} produces a decrease in $I_{D(M1)}$, causing I_{Cload} to increase and become positive. This causes C_{load} to charge, thus increasing V_{OUT}.

In addition we might be interested in how the bootstrap capacitor affects M2's drain current:

What happens to $I_{D(M2)}$ during Interval-1?
An increase in V_{OUT} (described above) causes an increase in V_{N1}, turning off M3. This causes $I_{T1(Cboot)}$ to be zero, holding $V_{G,S}$ across M2 constant, and, in turn, causing $I_{D(M2)}$ to remain constant.

In this explanation we see how M3 turning off isolates N1 which prevents current from flowing into C_{boot}. This holds V_{Cboot} constant which allows a change in V_{OUT} to be directly transferred to V_{N1}. Thus, C_{boot} is 'bootstrapping' V_{N1} from V_{OUT}.

6.5. Summary

This section first described a technique for modeling devices with multiple operating regions, using the qualitative arithmetic defined previously, along with a small set of predicates and Boolean operations. This technique takes advantage of the mechanism described in transition analysis to determine how a device moves between operating regions. Transition analysis places the constraint that the relations for a device must be continuous across region boundaries.

We then discussed the qualitative model for an n-mosfet which is broken into two parts: conduction and capacitance. Conduction is modeled as a nonlinear dependent current source described by the enhancement n-channel mosfet-conduction model (Section 6.2) and the capacitance is modeled as an ideal capacitor (Section 3.3.2.2) from gate to source or gate to ground. In the mosfet model, the notion was introduced that a relation can be written in terms of the *role* which a terminal is playing, as well as the terminal itself. Next these models were used to generate a detailed explanation for a simple MOS circuit. Finally, TQ analysis was used to describe some interesting characteristics of a simplified version of the bootstrap circuit presented in the introduction.

[40]The text of the explanation shown here is what we would eventually like to produce and was generated by hand from the rules discussed in this paper.

7. Discussion

This paper has presented a technique, temporal qualitative analysis, for analyzing the behavior of MOS circuits whose behavior straddles the analog and digital domains. Throughout this work, we have emphasized the close relationship between an expert's intuition and formal theory. To summarize:

(1) By assuming that quantities may be represented qualitatively as open regions separated by boundaries, we have been able to unify the representations for space, time, state variables, and device operating regions.

(2) Using the lumped-circuit approximation, circuit behavior has been modeled with a set of network laws and device relations. By looking at the electrodynamics which underlie circuit theory and understanding the limitations of the lumped-circuit approximation, we are able to impose a causal viewpoint on these relations (*causal propagation*).

(3) By assuming that physical quantities are modeled by continuous functions, we have been able to use a few simple theorems to determine how state variables move between qualitative regions (*transition analysis*). These theorems capture one's intuitive notion of continuity and integration.

(4) Overall structural patterns of the relations which describe a circuit's behavior, such as simultaneities and feedback, have been used to derive additional constraints. Furthermore, the intuitions designers use for feedback have been employed to determine the direction of a feedback path (*feedback analysis*).

(5) Because the boundaries of device operating regions are constructed from relations between state variables, the mechanism provided by transition analysis for determining state variable transitions is also applicable to determining how devices move between operating regions. In addition open regions and boundaries can be combined to describe more complex regions such as semi-open time intervals and closed operating regions.

7.1. Related work

7.1.1. QUAL *and envisioning*

Some of the most notable work on the qualitative analysis of electrical systems has been done by Johan De Kleer and John Seely Brown. In his Ph.D. Dissertation, De Kleer discusses incremental qualitative (IQ) analysis, a causal qualitative analysis technique that was the basis of a program, QUAL, for describing and recognizing the functionality of bipolar circuits [7]. De Kleer and Brown's recent work on envisioning [10, 11, 13] extends this earlier work to other domains, using the methodology provided by system dynamics for describing a variety of physical systems (e.g. electrical, mechanical, fluid and thermal systems) in terms of networks of lumped elements. As discussed below, this work also extends QUAL's theory in the areas of state, time, continuity and transitions.

7.1.1.1. *Operating regions and state*

QUAL provides the qualitative arithmetic and some of the basic framework for the propagation mechanism used in TQ analysis. However, the analog bipolar domain used by De Kleer and the digital MOS domain differ in a number of important respects.

First, when modeling an analog bipolar amplifier, the analyst is primarily concerned with the incremental response of the circuit to a small variation on the input. During the analysis it is assumed that each device in the circuit will remain within a single operating region and the initial perturbation will propagate across the circuit instantaneously; this corresponds to the circuit's small-signal behavior. When modeling digital MOS circuits the analyst is still interested in the instantaneous incremental response of the circuit; however, he is equally concerned with the circuit's large-signal behavior. This includes the long-term effects of a changing input such as a device moving between operating regions or a positive quantity becoming zero.

Second, the modeling of capacitive memory was not important in De Kleer's work since, during the small-signal analysis of bipolar circuits, large capacitors become incremental shorts and small, parasitic capacitances become open circuits. In the MOS domain circuit behavior is strongly dependent on charge flow and capacitive memory which results from charge storage.

Because De Kleer was primarily interested in incremental behavior, qualitative relationships were written only in terms of voltage and current derivatives. In TQ analysis this vocabulary is expanded to include any type of quantity such as charge, current, voltage, their first derivatives, second derivatives and any higher-order derivatives.

In QUAL the relationships among a device's different operating regions and the movement between them is represented by explicit statements like: "If the Diode is on and the voltage across the diode is decreasing then the diode will turn off." In addition, the persistence (inertia) exhibited by a device with memory is modeled by breaking the device into several explicit states that include statements describing the device's movement from one state to the next (e.g. two of the states for a capacitor are positively charging and constant). In QUAL, operating regions are not distinguished from state; the term 'state' is used to refer to both.

In TQ analysis a distinction is made between operating regions and state. State is viewed as a property of quantities (i.e., state variables) rather than the device itself; the state of a device is then described by the values of its independent state variables. The persistence exhibited by a device with memory results from the continuity of its state variables. State is then a property of continuous quantities, rather than devices, and is the qualitative region in which the state variable currently lies (e.g., $+$, 0 or $-$). For example, the notion that a capacitor is discharging is equivalent to saying that the capacitor's charge is positive and decreasing. Furthermore, if the change in a device's state variables is zero the device exhibits memory (e.g., a capacitor stores charge or a mosfet remains in a single operating region). Operating regions, on the other hand, are properties of the devices themselves and are described as a set of qualitative regions on the device's state variables.[41]

Transition analysis provides a single mechanism for determining how quantities move from one qualitative region to another. These regions may be as simple as positive and negative, or as complex as the operating regions: Saturated, Unsaturated and Cutoff. The mechanism depends on the properties of continuous quantities and the relationship between them, rather than properties specific to the device. Transition analysis is, therefore, independent of the model, the domain and even network theory.

In recent work by De Kleer and Brown state and operating regions are still indistinguishable; however, boundaries between device 'states' are modeled in terms of inequalities between 'qualitative variables'. The notions of qualitative calculus and continuity are then used to provide a mechanism for recognizing transitions between states (i.e., the inter-state behavior). The strong similarities between this mechanism and transition analysis suggests the possibility of unifying the two viewpoints.

7.1.1.2. *Feedback*

QUAL provided two heuristics for dealing with ambiguities introduced by simultaneities in network laws: the KVL Connection Heuristic (discussed in Section 5.4) and the KCL Heuristic. Recent work on ENVISION refers to these heuristics as the Component and Conduit Heuristics, respectively, and provides an additional heuristic for resolving ambiguities introduced by simultaneities in device models (i.e., the Confluence Heuristic). These two heuristics suggest a style of reasoning where ambiguities introduced by simultaneities are resolved heuristically using information local to the ambiguity. This style of reasoning is the motivation behind the feedback analysis portion of TQ analysis. Feedback analysis separates the general properties of simultaneous relations (e.g., Resistive Feedback Rule) from those properties which are specific to network theory (e.g., KVL Locality Heuristic). In addition, the feedback properties of systems with memory are exploited (Integrating Feedback Rule) and an engineers intuition about devices which introduce memory (e.g., capacitors and inductors) is used to determine the direction the feedback flows (Feedback Direction Heuristic).

7.1.2. *Qualitative process theory*

Forbus' qualitative process theory [14] provides a viewpoint where physical interactions are described through properties of processes, rather than properties of devices. A process is the basic vehicle for change in a physical system.

---

[41]Recall that a device is broken into several operating regions if the behavior of the device in each region is described by a different set of equations.

Examples of processes are heating, evaporating, stretching, and flowing. A process-centered viewpoint is quite natural for many physical domains where a device-centered model would be awkward; on the other hand, many domains, especially circuit analysis, naturally fit into a device-centered model and would be difficult to understand in terms of a process-centered model. QP theory and TQ analysis also differ in intent; qualitative process theory models commonsense reasoning about everyday physics. Temporal qualitative analysis models expert reasoning about electronics. TQ analysis tries to create a close link between the intuitions an expert has and the formal theory that his expertise is built upon (e.g. calculus, algebra, circuit theory, and feedback analysis). For example, QP theory describes the behavior of negative feedback in terms of an instantaneous oscillation called 'stutter' that results from the feedback term oscillating instantaneously between being equal to and less than the input to the feedback loop. An engineer doesn't consider these oscillations in complex circuits since they violate continuity (i.e., a quantity cannot jump instantaneously); however, he may use an argument similar to stutter to describe feedback to someone unfamiliar with the phenomena.[42]

In spite of these differences QP theory and TQ analysis have a number of similarities. In QP theory there is a clear separation between the properties of quantities, as defined by the 'quantity space', and the properties of processes. The clear division of quantities and processes motivated the separation of TQ analysis into its basic components. In TQ analysis the only knowledge that depends on a device-centered view is the device model and network laws which have been made explicit through causal rules. Furthermore, the mechanisms for determining transitions between operating regions or processes in each theory are domain-independent and have a number of features in common. The similarities between philosophy and underlying mechanism suggest that these two viewpoints can be unified into a single theory.

7.1.3. *Allen's temporal intervals*

In this paper we have discussed the temporal representation that an engineer uses in reasoning about circuits. Allen [2] describes an interval-based temporal representation and reasoning mechanism that, among other applications, could be used as the temporal component of naive physics. Time is represented as a set of intervals and the relationships between them. Allen argues that zero-width time points are counter-intuitive; therefore, the temporal intervals in his representation are neither open nor closed but are described as 'meeting'.

Allen supports this argument with the following example [2]:

> "...consider the situation where a light is turned on. To describe the world changing we need to have an interval of time during which the light was off, followed

---

[42]In fact, the description of the intuition behind the Resistive Feedback Rule in Section 5.2 is very similar to the stutter argument in QP theory.

by an interval during which it was on. The question arises as to whether these intervals are open or closed. If they are open, then there exists a time (point) between the two where the light is neigher on nor off. Such a situation would provide serious semantic difficulties in a temporal logic. On the other hand, if intervals are closed, then there is a time point at which the light is both on and off. This presents even more semantic difficulties than the former case".

The problem in this example is not with intervals being open or closed, but that a continuous process is being modeled discontinuously. Consider what really happens when the light switch is flipped. When the light switch is closed, current begins to flow through the switch into the light bulb and the filament begins to glow at a very small intensity. Initially the light bulb resists this current, due to inductance in the filament; however, eventually the light reaches a steady intensity and is considered 'on'. This process consists of a closed time interval where the light is off, followed by an open interval during which the light's intensity is increasing and ending with a closed interval when the light is 'on'. Of course this occurs too fast for the human eye to see. The process, therefore is collapsed into an instant and the light intensity is perceived as stepping from 'off' to 'on'. The reason for collapsing these series of events into an instant is that we are not interested in their details. The price that must be payed for this abstraction is that the process is no longer continuous, and if we look at the process too closely our intuitions about continuity will be violated (after all, how can a light be both on and off during the same instant?).

Allen also argues that "... given an event, we can always 'turn up the magnification' and look at its structure." This is certainly true in some cases. In the light switch example "by turning up the magnification" we see that the light intensity doesn't really step from off to on but changes continuously over a finite interval of time. The instant the light switches from off to on is a useful idealization, something which can't be looked inside of without changing magnification (i.e., abstraction level).

The notion that zero-width time points exist is not counter-intuitive to someone with a math background. Intuitions are developed from observations about the surrounding world. For example, it seems intuitively obvious that a person who wants to enter a building cannot walk through its brick walls, but must go through a door or some other opening. Early on in our math background many of us are told of such concepts as infinitely thin, one-dimensional lines and points with no dimensions. These are things which don't change appearance, no matter how much the magnification is turned up. Using these concepts as givens, our instructors teach us how they can be manipulated to understand and idealize many things that happen in the real world. Eventually notions such as zero-widths points become part of the intuitions of someone like an engineer or mathematician. For example, when a ball is thrown in the air, it is obvious to a physicist that the ball is at the top of its arc for only an instant independent of the magnification; to hang there longer would defy the laws of gravity.[43]

In spite of these differences the temporal representation used here has a number of similarities to that of Allen's. First, although instants play an important role in TQ analysis, they are viewed as a subset of closed intervals. Second, except for the parts of transition analysis which depend on the continuity of quantities, closed and open intervals are not differentiated (e.g., in causal propagation no distinction was made between the types of intervals). Finally, open and closed intervals may be viewed as meeting; however, continuity places the restriction that the closed end of an interval can only be met by the open end of another interval (i.e., time is dense). If continuity were ignored, the distinction between open and closed intervals would not be necessary.

Allen has provided a rich vocabulary for describing the relationships between intervals and a mechanism for reasoning about these relations. As discussed in Section 7.2, a 'temporal reasoner' based on open and closed intervals is currently being developed and will be incorporated into TQ analysis.

7.2. Limitations and future directions

As of this writing, all of the parts of TQ analysis have been implemented and tested except for feedback analysis. The system has been tested on simple R, L, C and mosfet circuits. The explanations for the parallel RC and mosfet-capacitor circuits given earlier in this paper were generated by the system. I am currently working towards generating a qualitative description of circuits similar to the bootstrap clock driver given in the introduction.

The representation for time in TQ analysis is in the process of being modified. The current representation of time as a linear sequence places a total ordering on all events. Such a global viewpoint is often not necessary or desirable, since it requires that an ordering be placed on unrelated events. A more realistic representation breaks time into a set of open and closed intervals in a temporal network. This creates a partial ordering on time intervals, rather than a total ordering. Two quantities, then interact only if they are locally connected in space and their time intervals (or instants) coincide.[44]

There are two major components of circuit analysis which have not been addressed in this work so far: the use of quantitative information and the use of cliches [3, 5].

In TQ analysis many of the ambiguities which arise during causal propagation can be resolved using non-numerical information such as continuity theorems or properties of feedback. There are, however, a number of am-

---

[43]Of course, this is an ideal ball which can't be held up by such things as rising gusts of wind!
[44]This is similar to Hayes' notion of histories [16].

biguities which cannot be resolved using these techniques. Many of these remaining ambiguities can only be resolved using some form of quantitative information. A circuit analyst, for example, often considers certain circuit parameters dominant, and might use phrases like the following when analyzing a circuit:

- The current drawn by $C_{G,S}$ is insignificant compared to $I_{D,S}$.
- The rise time of the output capacitance is much slower than the input.
- The pullup is much longer than the pulldown, allowing the inverter to meet a valid logic low level.

Quantitative comparisons such as these and other types of quantitative knowledge must at some point be integrated with TQ analysis.

A number of cliches are used by a designer in analyzing a circuit, such as the phrases 'isolation', 'precharging', and 'bootstrapping' used in the bootstrap clock driver example in the introduction. A cliche can either refer to a set of devices, such as 'precharge circuit' and 'bootstrap capacitor', or it can refer to a complex behavior, such as 'precharging the input node' or 'isolating the gate'. A cliche which refers to a device can be used to help determine which of a number of possible behaviors the designer intend the circuit to have. Furthermore, the ability to combine a series of events into a cliche is important in generating a qualitative summarization of a circuit's behavior.

If the behavior of a device within a particular operating region during a time interval is viewed as an episode, then a cliche may be described in terms of a sequence of episodes. This is similar to what Forbus refers to as an encapsulated history [14]. Cliches may then be used in analyzing the circuit's behavior to answer questions not yet addressed by TQ analysis such as:

- Why didn't the circuit behave as I expected?
- Which device parameters should I change to make it work?
- Which parameters should I change to increase the circuits performance (speed, power, voltage thresholds etc.)?

By answering these and similar questions we hope to create a versatile tool which provides the circuit analyst with expert advice on a wide class of circuits.

Appendix A. Transition-ordering Inferences

A.1. Predicates

- to-zero(Q): Q is moving monotonically towards zero during the current interval.
- not-to-zero(Q): Q is constant or moving away from zero during the current interval.
- transition(Q): Q will transition at the end of the current interval.
- not-transition(Q): Q cannot transition at the end of the current interval.

A.2. General

> not-to-zero(A) → not-transition(A)

A.3. Equality

Transition inferences: $[A] = (+/-)[B]$

> transition(A) iff transition(B)
>
> not-transition(A) iff not-transition(B)

Direction inferences: A is a monotone increasing (decreasing) function of B

> to-zero(A) iff to-zero(B)
>
> not-to-zero(A) iff not-to-zero(B)

A.4. Sums and differences

Transition inferences: $[A] + [B] + [C] = 0$ where $[A] = [B] = -[C]$

> transition(A) ∧ transition(B) → transition(C)
>
> not-transition(A) ∨ not-transition(B) → not-transition(C)
>
> transition(C) → transition(A) ∧ transition(B)
>
> not-transition(C) → not-transition(A) ∨ not-transition(B)

Direction inferences: $A + B = C$ where $[A] = [B] = -[C]$

> to-zero(A) ∧ to-zero(B) → to-zero(C)
>
> not-to-zero(A) ∧ not-to-zero(B) → not-to-zero(C)
>
> to-zero(C) → to-zero(A) ∨ to-zero(B)
>
> not-to-zero(C) → not-to-zero(A) ∨ not-to-zero(B)

A.5. Products

Transition inferences: $[A] \times [B] = [C]$

> transition(A) ∨ transition(B) → transition(C)
>
> not-transition(A) ∧ not-transition(B) → not-transition(C)
>
> transition(C) → transition(A) ∨ transition(B)
>
> not-transition(C) → not-transition(A) ∧ not-transition(B)

Direction inferences: $A \times B = C$

> to-zero(A) ∧ to-zero(B) → to-zero(C)
>
> not-to-zero(A) ∧ not-to-zero(B) → not-to-zero(C)
>
> to-zero(C) → to-zero(A) ∨ to-zero(B)
>
> not-to-zero(C) → not-to-zero(A) ∨ not-to-zero(B)

A.6. Resistive feedback

Relation: $[A] + [B] = [C]$ which is the comparison point of a feedback loop.
Idea: If A is the cause and C is the effect of a feedback loop then $[A] = [B]$
and all the inferences for equivalences apply.

ACKNOWLEDGMENT

The following people have provided advice during the development of this work: Howie Shrobe, Rich Zippel, Johan De Kleer, Daniel Bobrow, Ramesh Patil, Leah Ruby, Walter Hamscher, Ken Forbus, and Randy Davis.

REFERENCES

1. Allen, J., A general model of action and time, Tech. Rept. 97, University of Rochester Computer Science Department, Rochester, NY, 1981.
2. Allen, J., Maintaining knowledge about temporal intervals, *Comm. ACM* **26** (1983) 832–843.
3. Brotsky, D., Program understanding through cliche recognition, AI Working Paper 224, MIT, Cambridge, MA, 1981.
4. Cherry, J. and Roylance, G., A one transistor RAM for MPC projects, VLSI Memo 81–43, MIT, Cambridge, MA, 1981.
5. Cyphers, S., Programming cliches and cliche extraction. AI Working Paper 223, MIT, Cambridge, MA, 1982.
6. De Kleer, J., Doyle, J., et al., AMORD: A deductive procedure system, AI Working Paper 151, MIT, Cambridge, MA, 1977.
7. De Kleer, J., Causal and teleological reasoning in circuit recognition, Ph.D. Thesis, MIT, Cambridge, MA, 1979.
8. De Kleer, J. and Sussman, G., Propagation of constraints applied to circuit synthesis, *Circuit Theory Appl.* **8** (1980) 127–140.
9. De Kleer, J. and Brown, J.S., Mental models of physical mechanisms and their acquisition, in: J.R. Anderson (Ed.), *Cognitive Skills and their Acquisition* (Erlbaum, Hillsdale, NJ, 1981).
10. De Kleer, J. and Brown, J.S., Assumptions and ambiguities in mechanistic mental models, in: D. Gentner and A. Stevens (Eds.), *Mental Models* (*Erlbaum, Hillsdale, NJ*, 1983).
11. De Kleer, J. and Brown, J.S., The origin, form and logic of qualitative physical laws, in: *Proceedings Eighth International Joint Conference on Artificial Intelligence*, Karlsruhe, West Germany, August, 1983.
12. De Kleer, J. and Bobrow, D.G., Qualitative reasoning with higher order derivatives, in: *Proceedings National Conference on Artificial Intelligence*, Austin, TX, August, 1984.
13. De Kleer, J. and Brown, J.S., A qualitative physics based on confluences, *Artificial Intelligence* **24** (1984) this volume.
14. Forbus, K., Qualitative process theory, *Artificial Intelligence* **24** (1984) this volume.
15. Forbus, K., Measurement interpretation in qualitative process theory, in: *Proceedings Eighth*

International Joint Conference on Artificial Intelligence, Karlsruhe, West Germany, August, 1983.

16. Hayes, P., The naive physics manifesto, in: D. Michie (Ed), *Expert Systems in the Micro-Electronic Age* (Edinburgh University Press, Edinburgh, 1979).

17. Kuipers, B., Commonsense reasoning about causality: Deriving behavior from structure, *Artificial Intelligence* **24** (1984) this volume.

18. Kuipers, B., Getting the envisionment right, in: *Proceedings National Conference on Artificial Intelligence*, Pittsburgh, PA, August, 1982.

19. Loomis, L., *Calculus* (Addison-Wesley, Reading, MA, 1977).

20. Newton, A., Pederson, D., et al., Spice version 2G user's guide, Dept. of EECS, University of California, Berkeley, CA, 1981.

21. Shearer, J.L., Murphy, A.T. and Richardson, H.H., *Introduction to System Dynamics* (Addison-Wesley, Reading, MA, 1971).

22. Shichman, H. and Hodges, D.A., Modeling and simulation of insulated-gate field-effect transistor switching circuits, *IEEE J. Solid State Circuits* **3** (1968) 285–289.

23. Simmons, R., The use of qualitative and quantitative simulations, in: *Proceedings National Conference on Artificial Intelligence*, Washington, DC, August, 1983.

24. Stallman, R. and Sussman, G., Forward reasoning and dependency-directed backtracking in a system for computer-aided circuit analysis, *Artificial Intelligence* **9** (1977) 135–196.

25. Steele, G., The definition and implementation of a computer programming language based on constraints, Ph.D. Thesis, MIT, Cambridge, MA, 1980.

26. Thomas, G., *Calculus and Analytic Geometry* (Addison-Wesley, Reading, MA, 1968).

27. Williams, B.C., The use of continuity in a qualitative physics, in: *Proceedings National Conference on Artificial Intelligence*, Austin, TX, August, 1984.

Received October 1983

Diagnostic Reasoning Based on Structure and Behavior*

Randall Davis

The Artificial Intelligence Laboratory, Massachusetts Institute of Technology, Cambridge, MA 02139, U.S.A.

ABSTRACT

We describe a system that reasons from first principles, i.e., using knowledge of structure and behavior. The system has been implemented and tested on several examples in the domain of troubleshooting digital electronic circuits. We give an example of the system in operation, illustrating that this approach provides several advantages, including a significant degree of device independence, the ability to constrain the hypotheses it considers at the outset, yet deal with a progressively wider range of problems, and the ability to deal with situations that are novel in the sense that their outward manifestations may not have been encountered previously.

As background we review our basic approach to describing structure and behavior, then explore some of the technologies used previously in troubleshooting. Difficulties encountered there lead us to a number of new contributions, four of which make up the central focus of this paper.
– We describe a technique we call constraint suspension *that provides a powerful tool for troubleshooting.*
– We point out the importance of making explicit the assumptions underlying reasoning and describe a technique that helps enumerate assumptions methodically.
– The result is an overall strategy for troubleshooting based on the progressive relaxation of underlying assumptions. The system can focus its efforts initially, yet will methodically expand its focus to include a broad range of faults.
– Finally, abstracting from our examples, we find that the concept of adjacency *proves to be useful in understanding why some faults are especially difficult to diagnose and why multiple representations are useful.*

1. Introduction

The overall goal of this research is to develop a theory of reasoning that exploits knowledge of structure and behavior. We proceed by building programs that use such knowledge to reason from first principles in solving

*This report describes research done at the Artificial Intelligence Laboratory of the Massachusetts Institute of Technology. Support for the laboratory's Artificial Intelligence research on electronic troubleshooting is provided in part by the Digital Equipment Corporation and in part by the Defense Advanced Research Projects Agency.

problems. The initial focus is troubleshooting digital electronic hardware, where we have implemented a system based on a number of new ideas and tools.

Troubleshooting digital electronics is a good domain for several reasons. First, troubleshooting seems to be one good test of part of what it means to 'understand' a device. We view the task as a process of reasoning from behavior to structure, or more precisely, from misbehavior to structural defect: given symptoms of misbehavior, we are to determine the structural aberration responsible for the symptoms. Second, the task is interesting and difficult because the devices are complex and because there is no established theory of diagnosis for them. Third, the domain is appropriate because the required knowledge is readily available from schematics and manuals. Finally, the application itself is relevant and tractable.

Work with a similar intent has been done in other domains, including medicine [23], computer-aided instruction [6], and electronic troubleshooting [7, 18], with the 'devices' ranging from the gastro-intestinal tract, to transistors and digital logic components.

This work is novel in a number of respects, some of which have been reported in an earlier publication [8]. As noted there:
– We have developed languages that distinguish carefully between structure and behavior, and that provide multiple descriptions of structure, organizing it both functionally and physically.
– We have argued that the concept of *paths of causal interaction* is a primary component of the knowledge needed to do reasoning from structure and behavior.
– We have developed an approach to troubleshooting based on the use of a layered set of categories of failure and demonstrated its use in diagnosing a bridge fault.

This paper substantially expands and develops this line of work[1], reporting several new contributions:
– We describe a new technique called *constraint suspension*, capable of determining which components can be responsible for an observed set of symptoms.
– We show that the categories of failure, previously derived informally, can be given a systematic foundation. We show that the categories can be generated by examining the assumptions underlying our representation.
– This in turn gives us a new way to view our approach to troubleshooting: the methodical enumeration and relaxation of assumptions about the device.
– Finally, we describe the concept of *adjacency* and argue that it helps in

---

[1]For the sake of continuity and ease of presentation, parts of [8] are reprinted here, including the bridge-fault example and some of the background material (machinery for describing structure and function, and the introduction to troubleshooting). This material is reprinted with permission from [8], Copyright Academic Press Inc. (London) Ltd.

understanding both what it means to have a good representation, and why multiple representations can be useful.

Section 2 is introductory, supplying a brief review of the overall concerns, expanding on the ideas listed above as a preview of what is central to this work.

If we are to reason from first principles, we require: (i) a language for describing structure, (ii) a language for describing behavior, and (iii) a set of principles for troubleshooting that use the two descriptions to guide their investigation. The central part of the paper describes each of these components, paying particular attention to the nature of the reasoning that underlies troubleshooting.

Sections 3 and 4 explore our approach to describing structure and behavior, while Sections 5 through 9 deal with troubleshooting. In Section 5 we consider the machinery traditionally used to reason about circuits and show that it fails to solve the problem we face. We then show how a technique called discrepancy detection offers a number of useful advances, but claim that it must be used with care. We suggest that the potential difficulties center around implicit assumptions typically made when using the technique. We find a solution to the problems encountered by making those assumptions explicit, organizing them appropriately, and providing for a way to surrender them one by one, methodically expanding the scope of failure the program considers. Section 9 provides an example of these ideas in operation, showing how they guide the diagnosis of a bridge fault (an unintended electrical connection, often caused by extra solder running between two adjacent pins on a chip).

In Sections 10 and 11 we draw back from the specific example presented and attempt to generalize our methods. We argue that the concept of paths of interaction offers a useful framework for asking questions about a domain. We claim that the notion of 'adjacency' both explains some of the difficulty in reasoning about bridges and provides guidance in selecting and using multiple representations.

Section 12 reviews the machinery we have presented, pointing out is limitations and suggesting directions for future work. Finally, Section 13 compares our work to a number of previous approaches to similar problems.

2. Central Concerns

Some of the examples in later sections of this paper require a substantial amount of detail, yet the principles they illustrate are often relatively uncomplicated. In order to be sure that the important points are not lost in the detail, we describe the fundamental principles here briefly, enlarging on them in the remainder of the paper.

Candidate generation can be achieved by using a new technique we call constraint suspension.

Given the symptoms of a malfunction, we wish to generate candidate components, i.e., determine which components could plausibly be responsible for the malfunction. We model the intended behavior of a device as a network of interconnected constraints, where each constraint models the behavior of one of the components. If the device is malfunctioning, then the outputs predicted by the entire constraint network will not match the actual outputs. Normally, contradictions in constraint networks are handled by retracting one or more of the input values. Constraint suspension takes the dual view and asks instead: "is there some *constraint* (component behavior) whose retraction will leave the network in a consistent state?" Each such constraint that we find corresponds to a component whose misbehavior can account for all the observed symptoms. In many cases the technique will also supply the details of the component misbehavior (i.e., show how it is misbehaving). We describe the technique in detail in Section 6.1.

Paths of causal interaction play a central role in troubleshooting.

An important part of the basic knowledge needed for troubleshooting is understanding the mechanisms and pathways by which one component can affect another. Electronic components typically interact because they are wired together, but they can also interact due to heat, capacitive coupling, etc. We argue that viewing the problem in terms of paths of interaction is more useful and revealing than the fault models (e.g., stuck-ats) traditionally used.

In doing troubleshooting we are faced with an unavoidable problem of complexity vs. completeness.

To be good at troubleshooting, we need to handle many different kinds of paths of interaction. But this presents a serious problem. If we include all possible paths, candidate generation becomes indiscriminate: every component could somehow be responsible for the observed symptoms. Yet omitting any one kind of path would make it impossible to diagnose an entire class of faults.

One technique for dealing with this dilemma is enumerating and layering the categories of failure.

As experienced troubleshooters know, some things are more likely to go wrong than others. But what are the 'some things'? And what does 'more likely' mean? We make both of these notions more precise.

We show how to generate the 'things that can go wrong' by making explicit the assumptions underlying our representation; the result is a list of 'categories of failure'. The categories are organized by using the most likely first and adding additional, less likely categories only in the face of contradictions.

Associated with each category of failure is a collection of paths of interaction. Hence the ordered listing of categories produces an ordering on the paths of interaction to be considered. This allows us to constrain the paths we consider initially, making it possible to constrain candidate generation. But no path is permanently excluded, hence no class of faults is overlooked.

The result is a strategy for troubleshooting based on the methodical enumeration and relaxation of underlying assumptions.

This technique allows us to deal with a progressively wider range of different faults without being overwhelmed by too many candidates at any one step.

The categories of failure can be generated systematically by examining the assumptions underlying our representation.

As we demonstrate in Section 10, the categories can be derived by listing the assumptions implicit in the representation and considering the consequences of violating each in turn. Because the representation employs little more than the traditional notion of black boxes, the categories of failure deal with information transmission, and the results of this exercise have relevance broader than digital electronics. We suggest that the results may be applicable to software and speculate about wider applications.

The concept of 'adjacency' proves to be useful in both troubleshooting and the selection of representations.

We noted above that the possible pathways for device interaction are an important part of the knowledge required for troubleshooting. We take the view that devices interact because they are in some sense *adjacent*: electrically adjacent (wired together), physically adjacent (hence 'thermally connected'), electromagnetically adjacent (not shielded), etc. Each of these definitions can be used as the basis for a different representation of the device, different in its definition of adjacency. The multiplicity of possible definitions helps to explain why some faults are especially difficult to diagnose: *they result from interactions between components that are adjacent in a sense (representation) that is unusual or subtle.*

This concept appears to generalize in several ways. We view faults as modifications to the original design, and claim that changes that appear small and local in one representation may not appear small and local in another. We also suggest that adjacency can help determine what makes a 'good' representation: one in which the change can be seen as compact. It may also explain some of the utility of using multiple representations: they offer multiple different definitions of adjacency.

Adjacency is a useful principle to the extent that the 'single-initial-cause heuristic' holds true.

A commonsense heuristic suggests that malfunction of a previously working device generally results from a single cause rather than a number of simultaneous, independent events. When there is indeed a single cause, there will be some representation in which a compact change accounts for the difference between the good and faulty device.

The concept of a 'single point of failure' is not well defined without specification of the underlying representation.

A failure in a single physical component, for example, may manifest as multiple points of failure in the behavior of the overall device. Consider a single chip with four AND gates in it. If the chip is damaged (via over-voltage, heat, mechanical stress, etc.), we will have a single point of failure in the physical representation, but may find four different points of failure (the four AND gates) in the functional view of the device. We claim as a result that 'single point of failure' is by itself an under-determined concept, and that to make precise sense of the term we need to indicate both the nature of and the level of abstraction of the underlying representation to which 'point' refers. We claim further that the use of multiple representations can add diagnostic power by offering different ways of resolving apparently independent failures into a single cause.

3. Describing Structure

If we wish to reason about structure and behavior, we clearly need a way of representing both. We consider each of these in turn.

By structure we mean information about the interconnection of modules. Roughly speaking, it is the information that would remain after removing all the textual annotation from a schematic.

Two different ways of organizing this information are particularly relevant to troubleshooting: functional and physical. The functional view gives us the machine organized according to how the modules interact; the physical view tells us how it is packaged. We thus prefer to replace the somewhat vague term 'structure' by the slightly more precise terms *functional organization* and *physical organization*. As we will see, every device is described from both perspectives, producing two distinct, interconnected descriptions.

Our aim is to provide a means of encoding in one place all of the information about a circuit that is typically distributed across several different documents. To this end our approach provides a way of representing much of the information traditionally found in a schematic, as well as the hierarchical description often encoded in block diagrams.

The most basic level of our structure description is built on three concepts: *modules, ports,* and *terminals* (Fig. 1). A module can be thought of as a standard black box; ports are the places where information flows into or out of a module. Every port has at least two terminals, one terminal on the outside of the port and one or more inside. Terminals are primitive elements; they are the places we can 'probe' to examine the information flowing into or out of a

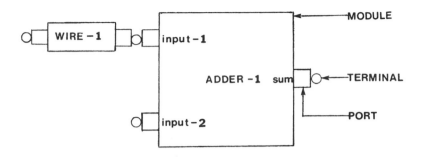

FIG. 1. The basic terms used in structure description.

device through a port, but they are otherwise devoid of interesting substructure.

Two modules are attached to one another by superimposing their terminals.
In Fig. 1, for example, wire-1 is a (wire) module that has been attached to the
input-1 port of adder-1 (an adder module) in this fashion.

The language is hierarchical in the usual sense: modules at any level may
have substructure. In practice, our descriptions terminate at the gate level in
the functional hierarchy and the chip level in the physical hierarchy, since for
our purposes these are black boxes—only their behavior (or misbehavior)
matters. Fig. 2 shows the next level of structure of the adder and illustrates why
ports may have multiple terminals on their inside: ports provide the important
function of shifting level of abstraction. It may be useful to think of the
information flowing along wire-1 as an integer between 0 and 15, yet we need to
be able to map those four bits into the four single-bit lines inside the adder.
Ports are the places where such information is kept. They have machinery
(described below) that allows them to map information arriving at their outer
terminal onto their inner terminals.

Since our ultimate intent is to deal with hardware on the scale of a
mainframe computer, we need terms in the vocabulary capable of describing
levels of organization more substantial than the terms used at the circuit level.
We can, for example, refer to *horizontal, vertical,* and *bit-slice* organizations,
describing a memory, for instance, as "two rows of five 1K RAMs". We use
these specifications in two ways: as a description of the organization of the
device and a specification for the pattern of interconnections among the
components.

Our eventual aim is to provide an integrated set of descriptions that span the
levels of hardware organization ranging from interconnection of individual
modules, through higher level of organization of modules, and eventually on up
through the register transfer and PMS [4] levels. Some of this requires
inventing vocabulary like that above, in other places we may be able to make
use of existing terminology and concepts.

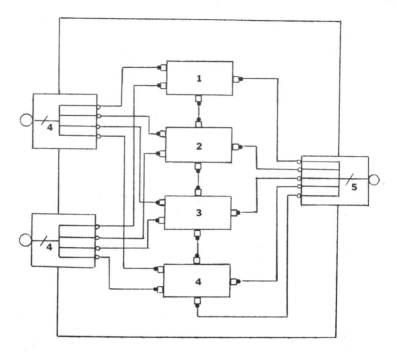

FIG. 2. Next level of structure of the adder, showing that it is implemented as a ripple-carry.

The structural description of a module is expressed as a set of commands for building it. The adder of Fig. 2, for example, is described by the instructions shown in Fig. 3. With NBitsWide bound to 4, the first expression indicates that we should repeat the following sequence of operations four times:
– create an adder slice;
– run a wire from the first input of the adder to the first input of the slice;
– run a wire from the second input of the adder to the second input of the slice;
– run a wire from the output of the slice to the output of the adder.
The next expression builds the carry chain and the last wires up the high-order bit.

```
(definemodule adder NBitsWide
  (repeat NBitsWide i
    (part slice-i adder-slice)
    (run-wire (input-1 adder) (input-1 slice-i))
    (run-wire (input-2 adder) (input-2 slice-i))
    (run-wire (output slice-i) (sum adder))
   (repeat (− NBitsWide 1) i (run-wire (carry-out slice-i)
                                       (carry-in slice-[i + 1])))
   (run-wire (carry-out slice-[NBitsWide − 1]) (sum adder)))
```

FIG. 3. Parts are described by a pathname through the part hierarchy, e.g., (input-1 adder).

These commands are executed by the system, resulting in the creation of data structures that model all the components and connections shown. These data structures are isomorphic to the diagram shown in Fig. 2. That is, the data structures are connected in the LISP sense in the same ways that the objects are connected in Fig. 2. As in real devices, information flow occurs as a result of these interconnections: slice-1 can place information on its end of the data structure modeling the carry-out wire, for example, because the two are superimposed. This information will then be propagated to the other end of the wire and pass into the data structure modeling slice-2 because those two are superimposed.[2] The utility of this approach is explored in Section 12.

The definition in Fig. 3 is thus a specification of a prototypical ripple-carry adder; invoking it with a specific value for the width parameter produces one particular instance. We have found it useful to maintain this prototype/instance distinction for several reasons. It allows the standard economy of representation, since information common to all instances can be stored once with the prototype. It also makes possible the parameterization illustrated above, allowing us to describe the overall structure of the device, capturing the generalization inherent in the standard pattern of interconnections. Finally, it allows us to build up a library of module definitions available for later use. There is considerable utility in assembling such a library, utility beyond the ease of describing more complicated devices. By requiring that we define modules outside of the context of their use in any particular circuit, we encourage an important form of 'mental hygiene' described further in Section 12.2.

Since our eventual aim is troubleshooting of devices as complex as a computer, the complete description of the device could become quite large. To deal with this we have made use of 'lazy instantiation': when an instance of a module is created, only the 'shell' is actually built at that time. For the adder in Fig. 2, for example, the outer 'box' and ports are built, but the substructure—the slices—are not built until they are actually needed. Only when we need to 'look inside' the box, i.e., drop down a level of structural detail, is additional structure actually built.

As a result, the system maintains a compact description of the device, expanding only where necessary. This can save a considerable amount of space. Even for the simple adder example (Fig. 2), there is a lot to describe: each slice is built from two half-adders and an OR-gate, each half-adder is built from an XOR- and an AND-gate. The initial instantiation is simply an adder with two inputs and an output, rather than four levels of detail and twenty gates. For more complex devices the savings can of course be greater.

The examples illustrate how we describe functional organization: an adder

---

[2]We do not, by the way, have any special mechanism for dealing with wires. They are simply another module, albeit one with a particularly simple behavior: information presented to either port will be propagated to the other.

composed of slices, which are in turn composed of half-adders, etc. Exactly the same module, port and terminal machinery is used to describe physical organization, but now the hierarchy of modules is cabinets, boards, and chips.

Since, as noted earlier, every component has both a functional and physical description, we have two interconnected description hierarchies. We represent this in our system by having the two hierarchies linked at their terminal nodes (Fig. 4).

We determine the physical location of any non-terminal entry in the functional organization by aggregating the physical locations of all of its leaves. These descriptions are available at various levels of abstraction. The physical location of slice-1, for example, is the list of all the locations of its gates (e.g., E1, E4, E7, etc.); alternatively we can also say simply that it is on board-1, if all of these chips are in fact on the same board.

By having available cross-links between the two descriptions, it becomes possible to answer a range of useful questions. For example, we can ask, "where physically do I find the (part that functions as the) address translation register", or, "what function(s) does this quad-and-gate chip perform?"

Our description language has been built on a foundation provided by a subset of DPL [3]. While DPL as originally implemented was specific to VLSI design, it proved relatively easy to 'peel off' the top-level of language (which dealt with chip layout) and rebuild on that base the new layers of language described in Fig. 4.

Since pictures are a fast, easy and natural way to describe structure, we have developed a simple circuit-drawing system that permits interactive entry of

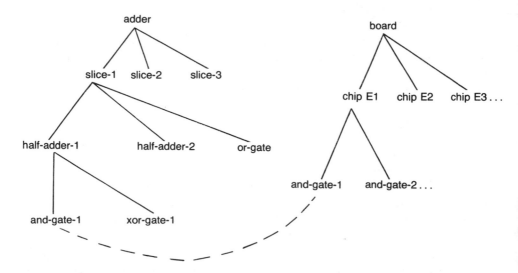

FIG. 4. Sample interconnection of functional and physical descriptions.

pictures like those in Figs. 1 and 2. Circuits are entered with a combination of mouse movements and key strokes; the resulting structures are then 'parsed' into the language shown in Fig. 3.

4. Describing Behavior

By behavior we mean the black box description of a component: how is the information leaving the component related to the information that entered it? A variety of techniques have been used in the past to describe behavior, including simple rules for mapping inputs to outputs, Petri-nets, and un-restricted chunks of code. Simple rules are useful where device behavior is uncomplicated, Petri-nets are useful where the focus is on modeling parallel events, and unrestricted code is often the last resort when more structured forms of expression prove too limited or awkward. Various combinations of these three have also been explored.

4.1. Simulation rules and inference rules

Our initial implementation is based on a constraint-like approach [30, 32]. Conceptually a constraint is simply a relationship. The behavior of the adder of Fig. 1, for example, can be expressed by saying that the logic levels of the terminals on ports input-1, input-2 and sum are related in the obvious fashion.

In practice, this is accomplished by writing a set of expressions covering all the different individual relations (the three for the adder are shown below) and setting them up as demons that watch the appropriate terminals. A complete description of a module, then, is composed of its structural description as outlined earlier and a behavior description in the form of rules that interrelate the logic levels at its terminals.

> to get sum from (input-1 input-2) do (+ input-1 input-2)
> to get input-1 from (sum input-2) do (− sum input-2)
> to get input-2 from (sum input-1) do (− sum input-1)

A set of rules like these is in keeping with the original conception of constraints, which emphasized the non-directional, relationship character of the information. When we attempt to use it to model behavior of physical devices, however, we have to be careful. This approach is well suited to modeling behavior in analog circuits, where devices are largely non-directional. But we can hardly say that the last two rules above are a good description of the *behavior* of an adder chip—the device doesn't do subtraction; putting logic levels at its output and one input does not cause a logic level to appear on its other input.

The last two rules really model the *inferences we make about the device.* Hence our implementation distinguishes between *simulation rules* that represent flow of electricity (digital behavior, the first rule above) and *inference rules* representing flow of inference (conclusions we can make about the device, the next two rules).

We find this distinction useful in part for reasons of 'mental hygiene' (the two kinds of rules deal with different kinds of knowledge) and in part because it contributes to the robustness of the simulation in the face of unanticipated events. Consider for example a circuit that included an adder, and imagine that a fault in that circuit resulted in some other component trying to drive the output of the adder. If we treated all rules the same, our simulation would suggest that the device did the subtraction described above, yet this simply doesn't happen.

4.2. Implementation

Our implementation accomplishes this distinction by using two parallel but separate networks, one containing the simulation rules modeling causality, the other containing the inference rules. We keep them distinct by giving each terminal two slots, one holding the value computed by the simulation rules, the other holding the value computed by the inference rules (Fig. 5). Each network then works independently, using the standard demon-like style of propagating values through its collection of slots.

In addition to firing rules to propagate information around the network, this rule-running machinery also keeps track of dependencies, allowing us to determine how the value in a slot got there. This is done by having each slot keep track of (i) every rule that uses this slot as an input, (ii) every rule that can place a value in this slot (i.e. uses it as an output) and (iii) which rule did, in fact, provide the current value (since, in general, more than one rule can set the value of a slot).[3]

This dependency network offers several advantages. As we explore below, it is one of the foundations of the discrepancy detection approach to trou-

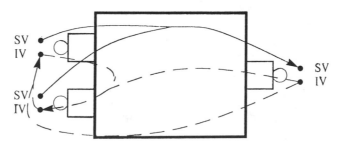

FIG. 5. Adder with one simulation rule (solid) and two inference rules (dashed). SV: simulation value; IV: inference value.

[3]The user can also set a value; this is most commonly done at the primary inputs.

bleshooting. As the work in [6] demonstrated, such a network also makes it easy to explore hypothetical situations. We can place a value in some terminal and observe the consequences, i.e., see what values propagate from it. When done with the exploration, removing the value at the terminal causes the dependency network to remove everything that depends on it as well. This mechanism makes it easy to discover the answer to some questions by simulation: we can get the device to a particular state, then explore multiple alternative futures from that point.

While all of the examples given thusfar deal with combinatorial devices, we can also represent and model simple devices with memory. This requires three simple augmentations of the approach described above. First, we use a global clock and timestamp all values. Second, we extend the behavior-rule vocabulary so that it can refer to *previous* values. For example, one simulation rule for a D flipflop would be

> To get output from (input previous-output clock)
>   do (if clock is high then input else previous-input)

Finally, our propagation machinery is extended to keep a history of values at each terminal (details are in [10]). This model of time is still very simple, but has allowed us to represent and reason about basic flipflops, memories, etc.

5. Troubleshooting

Having provided a way of describing functional organization, physical organization and behavior, we come now to the important third step of providing a troubleshooting mechanism that works from those descriptions. We develop the topic in three stages. In the first stage we consider test generation—the traditional approach to troubleshooting—and explain how it falls short of our requirements.

We consider next the style of debugging known as *discrepancy detection* and demonstrate why it is a fundamental advance. Further exploration, however, demonstrates that this approach has to be used with care in dealing with some commonly known classes of faults. We suggest that the difficulties arise from a number of implicit assumptions typically made when troubleshooting.

In discussing how to deal with the difficulties uncovered, we argue for the primacy of *models of causal interaction*, rather than traditional fault models. We point out the importance of making these models explicit and separate from the troubleshooting mechanism. The result is a strategy for troubleshooting based on the systematic enumeration and relaxation of underlying assumptions. This approach allows us to deal with a progressively wider range of different faults, without being overwhelmed by too many candidates at any one step.

We demonstrate the power of this approach on a bridge fault, a traditionally difficult problem, showing how our system locates the fault in a focused process that generates only a few plausible candidates.

5.1. The traditional approach

The traditional approach to troubleshooting digital circuitry (e.g., [5]) relies primarily on the process of path sensitization in a range of forms, of which the D-Algorithm [26] is one of the most powerful. A simple example of path sensitization will illustrate the essential character of the process. Consider the circuit shown in Fig. 6 and imagine that we want to determine whether the wire labeled A is stuck at 1. We try to put a zero on it by setting both x1 and x2 to 0. Then, to observe the actual value on the wire we set x3 to 1 thereby propagating the value unchanged through G2, and set x4 to 0, making the output of G3 = 0 allowing the value of A to propagate unchanged through G1.

Troubleshooting with this approach is then accomplished by running a complete set of such tests, checking for all stuck-ats on all wires.

For our purposes this approach has a number of significant drawbacks. Perhaps most important, it is a theory of *test generation*, not a theory of *diagnosis*. Given a specified fault, it is capable of determining a set of input values that will detect the fault (i.e., a set of values for which the output of the faulted circuit differs from the output of a good circuit). The theory tells us how to move from faults to sets of inputs; it provides little help in determining what fault to consider, or which component to suspect. Such questions are a central issue in our work because of complexity: the size of the devices we want to work with in the long run precludes the use of diagnosis trees—complete decision trees for all possible faults.

A second drawback of the existing approach is its lack of sharp distinction between *diagnosis* in the field and *verification* at the end of the manufacturing line. As a result of economic and historical forces, diagnostics written to verify the correct operation of a newly manufactured device have been pressed into service in the field. Yet the tasks are sharply different. We are not requesting verification that a machine is free of faults. The problem facing us is "Given

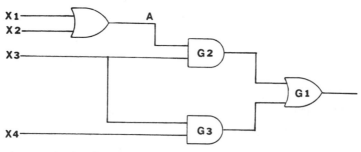

FIG. 6. Simple example of path sensitization.

the observed misbehavior, determine the cause". We know that the device has worked in the past, we know that some part of it has failed, and we know the symptoms of that failure. Given the complexity of the device, it is important to be able to use all of this information as a focus for further exploration. Only if this fails might it make sense to fall back on a set of diagnostics that, by design, start with no information and test exhaustively.

A final drawback of the existing theory is its unavoidable use of a set of explicitly enumerated fault models.[4] Since the theory is based on boolean logic, it is strongly oriented toward faults whose behavior can be modeled as some form of permanent binary value, typically the result of stuck-ats and opens. One consequence of this is the paucity of results concerning bridging faults.[5]

In solving the diagnosis problem, though, we have a significant luxury: we can treat as an error any behavior that differs from the expected correct behavior. The misbehavior need not be modelable in terms of any fixed set of faults, it need only be different from what should have resulted.

In summary, the technology often used for troubleshooting is oriented toward test generation and the task of verification. We, on the other hand, are concerned with troubleshooting, a process that makes use of test generation (for an example, see [27]), but which requires as necessary precursors the processes of candidate generation (determining which components may be failing) and 'symptom generation' (how they may be failing). The next section explores an approach that supports both of these.

6. Discrepancy Detection and Candidate Generation

One response to these problems has been the use of 'discrepancy detection' (e.g., [6, 11]). The two basic insights of the technique are (i) the substitution of violated expectations for specific fault models and (ii) the use of dependency records to trace back to the possible sources of a fault. Instead of postulating a possible fault and exploring its consequences, the technique looks for mismatches between the values it expected from correct operation and those actually obtained. This allows detection of a wide range of faults because

---

[4]Fault models are necessary in verification if we want to avoid the exponential effort of exhaustive testing. If we treat a device as a black box (e.g., saying only that it is an adder), we are forced to verify all of its behavior, a task that is potentially exponential in the number of inputs and amount of state. The most common way of avoiding this is by combining knowledge of the substructure of the device (e.g., that it is a carry-chain adder) with a specific set of faults to consider (e.g., stuck-ats on all wires), to produce tests for all such faults on all specified parts of the substructure. This task is at worst a product of the number of faults and wires.

[5]While the theory underlying verification may be limited in the range of faults it can describe, in practice it turns out to handle a large part of the problem: experience indicates that a large percentage of all faults turn out to be *detected* (but not diagnosed) by checking just for stuck-ats. Hence we can determine that something is wrong (satisfying the *verification* task); determining the identity and location of the error (*diagnosis*), however, is a different problem.

misbehavior is now simply defined as anything that isn't correct, rather than only those things produced by a stuck-at on a line.

The inspiration behind using dependency networks is that any component on the path from an input to an incorrect output could conceivably have been responsible for the faulty behavior. As we have seen, the simulator builds a dependency network by recording the propagation of values as it simulates the circuit. Using those records (or, equivalently, the original schematic) as a guide to which components to examine appears to be an effective way to focus attention appropriately. As we will see, it is in fact an interesting trap.

We work through a simple example to show the basic approach of discrepancy detection, then add to it the idea of constraint suspension. We comment on the strengths of the resulting procedure for candidate generation, then use the same example to illustrate difficulties that can arise.

Consider the circuit in Fig. 7.[6] If we set the inputs as shown, the system will use the behavior descriptions to simulate the circuit, constructing dependency records as it does so, and indicating that we should expect 12 at F.

If, upon measuring, we find the value at F to be 10, we have a conflict between observed results and our model of correct behavior. We trace back through the dependency network to enumerate the possible sources of the problem [11]. The dependency record at F indicates that the value expected there was determined using the behavior rule for the adder and the values emerging from the first and second multiplier. One of those three must be the source of the conflict, so we have three possibilities to pursue: either the adder-behavior rule is inappropriate (i.e., the first adder is broken), or one of the two inputs did not have the expected values (and the problem lies further back). Consideration of the first possibility immediately generates Hypothesis 1: adder-1 is broken.

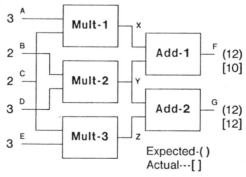

FIG. 7. Troubleshooting example using discrepancy detection.

[6]As is common in the field, we make the usual assumptions that there is only a single source of error and the error is not transient. Both of these assumptions are important in the reasoning that follows; we comment further on them below.

To pursue the second possibility, we assume that the second input to adder-1 is good. In that case the first input must have been a 4 (reasoning from the result at F, valid behavior of the adder, and one of the inputs), but we expected a 6. Hence we now have a discrepancy at the input to adder-1; we have succeeded in pushing the discrepancy one step further back along the dependency chain. The expected value there was based on the behavior rule for the multiplier and the expected value of its inputs. Since the inputs to the multiplier are primitive (supplied by the user), the only alternative along this line of reasoning is that the multiplier is broken. Hence Hypothesis 2 is that adder-1 is good and mult-1 is faulty.

Pursuing the third possibility: if the first input to adder-1 is good, then the second input must have been a 4 (suggesting that the second multiplier might be bad). But if that were a 4, then the expected value at G would be 10 (reasoning forward through the second adder). We can check this and discover in this case that the output at G is 12. Hence the value on the output of the second multiplier can't be 4, it must be 6, so the second multiplier can't be causing the current problem.

This style of reasoning can be described as the *interaction of simulation and inference*: simulation generates expectations about correct outputs based on inputs and knowing how devices work (simulation rules); inference generates conclusions about actual behavior based on observed outputs and device inference rules. The comparison of these two, in particular differences between them, provides a foundation for troubleshooting.[7]

6.1. Constraint suspension

In the discussion above, we glossed over the machinery used to determine when a candidate is consistent (as adder-1 was) and when it is inconsistent with all the available evidence (as mult-2 was). One of the novel contributions of this work is the development of the constraint-suspension technique as a way of providing an answer to this question.

To see how it works, consider once again the first step of the problem. When we examine the dependency record at F, we find that the value there resulted from the behavior rule for adder-1 and the values coming from mult-1 and mult-2. As above, the first possibility is that adder-1 is broken.

But this is a *local inference* (i.e., it is based only on the dependency record at F) and we have to be sure it's *globally consistent* with all the symptom data. More precisely, we want to ask whether there is *some* assignment of values to the ports of the adder that is consistent with all of the inputs and observed outputs. Is there any way in which adder-1 alone could be broken and produce the symptoms noted?

---

[7]The guided probe technique, in common use in industry, is based on a set of ideas that is closely related, though not identical. We discuss the differences in Section 13.

We can do this conveniently by using the 'constraint-like' character of our representation and the notion of *constraint suspension*. While the simulation and inference rules are usually kept distinct, for the moment we use the whole collection of them together, in effect a network of constraints that can indicate whether we have a consistent set of assignments to the inputs and outputs. If, for example, we were to try to assign to the network the inputs and *observed* outputs of Fig. 7, it would report a contradiction: there is no way for all the rules to be active (i.e., all the components working as expected) and for those inputs to have produced the observed outputs.

Normally contradictions in constraint networks are handled by retracting one of the values inserted into the network. But here we are sure of the values (the inputs we sent in to the circuit and the outputs we measured); what we are unsure of is the constraints (component behaviors). We therefore take a dual view, and rather than looking for a value we can retract, we look for a *constraint* whose retraction will leave the network in a consistent state. This is the basic idea behind constraint suspension.

To check the global consistency of adder-1, for example, we *suspend* (disable) all the rules in adder-1, assign the input values to input ports A through E, and assign the *observed* values to output ports F and G. We then allow the whole collection of rules to run to quiescence, determining for us whether there is *some* set of values on the ports of adder-1 consistent with the inputs and observed outputs.

If the network does reach a consistent state, we know that the candidate can account for the symptoms. In addition, we can examine the resulting state to see what values the candidate must have at its ports. In the case of adder-1, for example, the network indicates that the inputs must be 6 and 6, and the output 10. Thus in the process of determining the global consistency of a candidate, constraint suspension also produces symptom information about the misbehavior.

If the network reports an intractable contradiction, there is no assignment of values to the component that is consistent with all the symptoms, and hence no way for that component to account for the observed malfunction. For example, when we disable the rules of mult-2 and insert the inputs and observed outputs, an inescapable contradiction results. This demonstrates that mult-2 cannot account for all the observed values.

Fig. 8 provides a complete description of the candidate-generation process in a code-like notation (the procedure has been made easier to follow by ignoring the simulation/inference distinction for the moment and assuming we have a traditional constraint network). Candidate generation occurs in three basic steps: simulate the circuit and collect discrepancies, determine potential candidates using the dependency records; and finally, for each potential candidate determine global consistency and symptom values by using constraint suspension.

CANDIDATE GENERATION PROCEDURE

STEP 1: COLLECT DISCREPANCIES
   1.1 Insert device inputs into the constraint network inputs
     ; *e.g. insert 3, 2, 2, 3, and 3 at primary inputs A through E*
     ; *simulation predicts values at F and G*
   1.2 Compare predicted outputs with observed and collect discrepancies
     ; *e.g., prediction and observation differ at F.*
STEP 2: DETERMINE POTENTIAL CANDIDATES VIA DEPENDENCY RECORDS
   2.1 For each discrepancy found in Step 1:
      follow the dependency chain back from the predicted value
      to find all components that contributed to that prediction
     ; *these are all the components "upstream" of the discrepancy*
     ; *e.g., if we follow the dependency chain back from the 12*
     ; *at F, we find adder-1, mult-1, and mult-2*
   2.2 Take the intersection of all the sets found by Step 2.1
     ; *this yields the components common to all discrepancies (and*
     ; *hence potentially able to account for all discrepancies)*
     ; *(in the example above there is only one discrepancy)*
STEP 3: DETERMINE CANDIDATE CONSISTENCY VIA CONSTRAINT SUSPENSION
   3.1 For each component found in Step 2.2:
     3.1.1 Turn off (suspend) the constraint modeling its behavior
     3.1.2 Insert observed values at outputs of constraint network
      ; *(inputs were inserted earlier at Step 1.1)*
     3.1.3 If the network reaches a consistent state
      – the component is a globally consistent candidate
      – its symptoms can be found at its ports
      – add the candidate and its symptoms to the candidate list
      ; *e.g., adder-1 and its values of 6, 6, and 10*
      otherwise
       the candidate is not globally consistent, ignore it
       ; *e.g., mult-2*
     3.1.4 Retract the values at constraint network outputs
     3.1.5 Turn on the constraint turned off in Step 3.1.1
      ; *(these last two just get ready for the next iteration of 3.1)*

FIG. 8. Candidate generation via constraint suspension (assuming single point of failure).

As we explore further below, there are a number of important assumptions underlying this reasoning. But constraint suspension provides a mechanism that is both very useful and characteristic of a basic theme underlying this work: the careful management of assumptions. The traditional approach to diagnosis proceeds by assuming that it knows how the component might be failing: it is displaying one of the known misbehaviors found in the set of fault models. We, on the other hand, *proceed by simply suspending all assumptions about how a component might be behaving.* We then allow the symptoms to tell us what the component might be doing. By suspending the constraint in the adder, for example, we are in effect withdrawing all preconceptions about how that component is behaving. We then let the symptoms and the rest of the network tell us whether there is any behavior at all that is consistent with all our observations.

6.2. Advantages of discrepancy detection and constraint suspension

The combination of discrepancy detection and constraint suspension provides a very useful mechanism with a number of advantages:

(1) It is fundamentally a *diagnostic* technique, since it allows systematic isolation of the possibly faulty devices, and does so without having to pre-compute fault dictionaries, diagnosis trees, or the like.

(2) It reasons from the structure and behavior of the device: the candidate-generation process works from the schematic itself to determine which components might be to blame.

(3) Since it defines failure behaviorally, i.e., as anything that doesn't match the expected behavior, it can deal with a wide range of faults, including any systematic misbehavior. This is more widely applicable than a fixed set of models like stuck-ats.

(4) As we saw above, the technique yields symptom information about the malfunction: if adder-1 is indeed the culprit, then we know a little about how it is misbehaving. As will become clear, this information turns out to be useful in several ways.

(5) The approach allows natural use of hierarchical descriptions, a marked advantage for dealing with complex structures.

In the example above, for instance, we determined the relevant candidates at the current, fairly high level of description, never having to deal with lower-level descriptions (e.g., gate-level devices). We could now continue the process 'inside' either candidate, using the next level of description in exactly the same fashion, to determine what subcomponents might be responsible.

(6) Continuing the process at the next level might indicate that no sub-component could be responsible, ruling out that candidate.

We might, for example, find that, given how the adder is implemented, there may be no subcomponent of it that can logically account for the '6 plus 6 equals 10' symptom that the adder would have to be displaying. Thus the same candidate-generation machinery will either provide a set of candidate sub-components at the next level, or indicate that none can account for the inferred misbehavior, exonerating this candidate.

(7) This approach keeps knowledge about logical plausibility distinct from knowledge about physical plausibility. This helps simplify construction of the system.

Constraint suspension answers the question of logical plausibility of a candidate; it determines whether there is *any* set of values the component might display that could account for all the symptoms. The technique (by design) knows nothing about whether that set of values is in fact physically plausible.

Our candidate-generation machinery would, for example, consider a forked wire to be a plausible candidate if it inferred that the values at its three ports were 1 at the 'input' (the point where some device is driving the wire), and 0 and 1 at the two 'outputs' (where the wire in turn drives two other devices). Viewed at the black-box level, the wire is a three-port device that could well display the symptoms noted. To know that this is implausible requires understanding the physics of a specific technology: a wire will display different values at its ends as a result of breaks, but a broken wire in TTL will manifest as a high. Hence the pattern of values given can be ruled out by using knowledge of the particular technology.

The candidate generator thus provides a list of logically plausible components; further pruning of this list can then be done by invoking a distinct body of technology-specific knowledge. Keeping the two distinct simplifies the construction of both.

(8) The technique extends in straightforward fashion across multiple tests.

Each test of the overall device provides one set of symptoms which in turn yields one or more components with their suspected misbehaviors. The test in Fig. 7, for instance, gives us one misbehavior for adder-1 and one for mult-1; subsequent tests can provide additional misbehaviors. Two kinds of knowledge then relate results across tests.

The non-intermittency assumption indicates that if a component is misbehaving, that misbehavior is at least consistent and reproducible. Hence if a candidate has identical inputs in a later test, it must have an identical output. If, however, a later test were to indicate that adder-1 was a candidate with inputs 6 and 6, and an output of 13, those two test results (and the non-intermittency assumption) exonerate adder-1.

The second source of knowledge comes from additional information concerning faults physically plausible within a specific technology. Consider a situation in which Test 1 indicates that a particular wire is a candidate because it is getting a 0 but propagating a 1, while Test 2 indicates the wire is a candidate because it is getting a 1 but propagating a 0. Considered simply as a two-port device, this is logically consistent and the candidate generator will report it as such. But knowledge about TTL circuits tells us that there is no physically plausible fault which will cause a wire to start behaving as an inverter, hence the wire can be exonerated.

(9) This approach makes the $\langle N \rangle$-point-of-failure assumption both explicit and easily modified.

In Fig. 8 above the single-point-of-failure assumption appears in two places: at Step 2.2 where we intersected the sets, and at Step 3.1 where we disable the rules for exactly one component when checking candidate consistency. To deal with any specific $N > 1$, the simplest change is to take the *union* at Step 2.2 and take pairs, triples, etc., at Step 3.1.

While this does not in any sense solve the problem of multiple points of failure, it does demonstrate two important points. First, it shows that, unlike many approaches, our constraint-suspension technique is not limited to dealing with a single point of failure. Second, it does provide some aid in grappling with multiple failures, since we can methodically try possible single failures, then pairs, triples, etc.[8]

Unfortunately, as we demonstrate, the power of all of this mechanism is only part of the story.

6.3. Subtleties in candidate generation

Consider the slightly revised example shown in Fig. 9. Reasoning as before, we would discover in this case that there is only one hypothesis consistent with the values measured at F and G: the second multiplier is malfunctioning, outputting a 0.

Yet there is another quite reasonable hypothesis: the third multiplier might be bad (or the first).

But how could this produce errors at both F and G? The key lies in being wary of our models. The thought that digital devices have input and output ports is a convenient abstraction, not an electrical reality. If, as sometimes happens (due to a bent pin, bad socket, etc.), a chip fails to get power, its inputs are no longer guaranteed to act unidirectionally as inputs. If the third multiplier were a chip that failed to get power, it might not only send out a 0 along wire Z, but it might also pull down wire C to 0. Hence the symptoms result from a single point of failure (mult-3), but the error propagates along an 'input' line common to two devices.

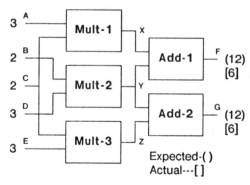

FIG. 9. Troublesome troubleshooting example.

[8]While *checking* pairs, etc. using constraint suspension (Step 3.1.3) is computationally simple, *generation* of appropriate pairs, triples, etc., (Step 3.1) is still an exponential process. This has not yet proved to be untenable, since both the number of faults considered and the number of components at any given level of description are relatively small. We are nevertheless exploring ways of improving the process. For example, some simple bookkeeping tricks can be used to rule out some of the pairs, triples, etc., very quickly.

The most immediate problem lies in our implicit acceptance of unidirectional ports—when checking the inputs to multi-1, we assumed that the inputs were machinery. We implicitly assumed that wires get information only from output ports—when checking the inputs to mult-1, we assumed that the inputs were 'primitive'. We looked only at terminals A and C, never at the other end of the wire at mult-3.

Bridges are a second common fault that illustrates another place where we need to be careful: the reasoning style used above can *never* hypothesize a bridging fault, again because of implicit assumptions and their subtle reflection in the reasoning. Bridges can be viewed as wires that don't show up in the design. But we traditionally make an implicit closed-world assumption: the structure description is assumed to be complete and anything not shown there 'doesn't exist'. Clearly this is not always true. Bridges are only one manifestation; wiring errors during assembly are another possibility.

Let's review for a moment. The traditional test-generation technology suffered from a number of problems: among others, it is a technology for test generation, not diagnosis, and it uses a limited fault model. The use of discrepancy detection and constraint suspension improves on this substantially by providing a diagnostic ability, by defining a fault as anything that produces behavior different from that expected, and by working directly from descriptions of structure and behavior. This seems to be perfectly general, but, as we illustrated, it has to be used with care:

Put simply, the virtue of the technique is that it reasons from the schematic; the serious flaw in the technique is that it reasons from the schematic *and the schematic might be wrong*.

We believe it is instructive to examine the basic source and nature of this problem.

7. Mechanism and Knowledge

In the example above we encountered some interesting situations because we failed to make explicit a number of important assumptions underlying the reasoning. In the power-failure example, we were assuming implicitly that there was only one possible direction of causality at an input port, and thus never examined the other end of wire C. Similarly, tracing back through the circuit from input X of adder-1, we looked only at mult-1, because that was the only apparent connection at that point. We never looked at, say mult-3, because there was no wire leading there, hence no reason to believe one might affect the other.

Note carefully the character of these assumptions: they concern the *existence of causal pathways, the applicability of a particular model of interaction*. In the power failure example we assumed implicitly that there was no way for mult-3 to affect mult-1 through wire C, yet such a path is possible. As we noted above in discussing the possibility of a bridge fault, there seemed to be no path in the schematic that would allow mult-3 to affect adder-1, yet a pathway is in fact possible.

The problem is not in the existence of such assumptions—they are in fact crucial to the reasoning process. The problem lies instead in the careful and explicit management of them. To see the necessity of having assumptions about causal pathways, consider the nature of the candidate-generation task. Given a problem noticed at some point in the device, candidate generation attempts to determine which modules could have caused the problem. To answer the question we must know by what mechanisms and pathways modules can interact. Without *some* notion of how modules can affect one another, we can make no choice, we have no basis for selecting any one module over another.

In this domain the obvious answer is 'wires': modules interact because they're explicitly wired together. But that's not the only possibility. As we saw, bridges are one exception; they are 'wires' that aren't supposed to be there. But we also might consider thermal interactions, capacitive coupling, transmission-line effects, etc.

Generating candidates, then, should not be thought of in terms of tracing wires (or dependency records). Rather, we claim, it should be thought of in terms of *tracing paths of causality*. Wires are only the most obvious pathway. In fact, given the wide variety of faults we want to deal with, we need to consider many different pathways of interaction.

And that leaves us on the horns of a classic dilemma. If we include every interaction path, candidate generation becomes *indiscriminate*—there will be some (possibly convoluted) pathway by which every module could conceivably be to blame. Yet if we omit any pathway, there will be whole classes of faults we will *never* be able to diagnose.

What can we do? We believe that two steps are important. First, we have to recognize that our inference mechanisms—in this case dependency detection and constraint suspension—are not the source of problem-solving power. The power is instead in the knowledge that we supply those techniques, i.e., the pathways of interaction.

And therein lies the second step: there is an important task in enumerating and organizing the pathways of interaction to be considered. How can we do this? We believe that human performance supplies a useful clue.

8. Organizing the Pathways of Interaction

We appear to be faced with an unavoidable dilemma, caught between the desire to be complete and the need to constrain the possibilities we consider. But people face exactly the same dilemma and seem to handle it. What do they do?

The answer seems be an instantiation of Occam's razor: an experienced engineer knows that some things are more likely to go wrong than others. He will, as a result, attempt to generate solutions that employ simpler and more likely hypotheses first, falling back on more elaborate possibilities only in the face of an intractable contradiction (i.e., given the current set of assumptions, there is no way to account for the observed misbehavior). There are three important points here.

(1) The engineer has a notion of 'the kinds of things that can go wrong'.

(2) There is an ordering criterion that indicates which category of hypotheses to entertain first.

(3) The categories are ordered but none is permanently excluded.

To capture this same sort of behavior in our program we need to (i) make precise the notion of 'what can go wrong', and (ii) determine what constitutes a 'simple' explanation. We consider both of these briefly here, as background for the example that follows, then address the issue in detail in Section 10.

To address the first of these, we need some methodical way to define and generate the possible kinds of failures. This is accomplished by enumerating the assumptions built into our 'module and information path' representation and then characterizing the variety of failure that results from violating each assumption. We refer to the resulting list as the *categories of failure*.

One such category is illustrated by the problem presented in Fig. 9. The implicit assumption there was that information flows in only one direction at an input (or output) port. If this assumption is violated, we get a category of failure we term an 'unexpected-direction' failure. The other categories generated in this way are described in Section 10.

Given such a notion of 'what can go wrong', we now need an appropriate metric for ordering the list. This is currently accomplished by relying on the experience of expert troubleshooters, who tell us which categories of failure are encountered more frequently than others. Stuck-ats are more likely than assembly errors, for example. While the ordering criterion may eventually need be more elaborate, its precise content is less an issue here than its character: it is a summary of empirical experience that helps us to order the kinds of hypotheses we consider. For our current domain, this approach produces the following list:

– localized failure of function (e.g., stuck-at on a wire, failure of a RAM cell),

– bridges,

– unexpected direction (e.g., the power-failure problem),

– multiple point of failure,

– intermittent error,

– assembly error,

– design error.

We start by attempting to generate candidates in the localized-failure category, assuming that the structure is as shown in the schematic, that there was only a single point of error, that information flowed only in the predicted directions, etc. Only if this leads to a contradiction are we willing to surrender an assumption (e.g., that the schematic was correct) and entertain the notion that a bridge might be at fault. If this too leads us down a blind alley then we would surrender additional assumptions and consider ever more elaborate hypotheses, eventually entertaining the possibility of multiple errors, an assembly error (every individual component works but they have been wired up incorrectly) and even design errors (the implementation is correct but cannot produce the desired behavior).

This mimics what we believe a good engineer will do: make all the assumptions necessary to simplify a problem and make it tractable, but be prepared to discover that some of those simplifications were incorrect. In that case, surrender some of those assumptions and be willing to consider additional kinds of failure.

In terms of the dilemma noted above, the categories of failure serve as a set of *filters*. They restrict the paths of interaction we are willing to consider, thereby preventing candidate generation from becoming indiscriminate. In using the localized-failure-of-function category, for example, we are assuming for the moment that the structure is as shown in the schematic, hence there are no additional paths of interaction (and thus no bridges). But these are filters that we have carefully ordered and consciously put in place. If we cannot account for the observed symptoms with the current set of filters in place, we remove one, leaving us with a set that is less restrictive, allowing us to consider additional interaction paths and hence more elaborate hypotheses.

There are of course no guarantees that this will lead us to the correct category of failure without any false steps. It is possible that all the evidence at a given point is consistent with, say, a localized failure of function in a single component, yet replacing that component may make it clear that the fault is elsewhere. As always with Occam's razor, our only assurance is that we are generating a hypothesis that is by some measure the simplest and most likely, and that's the best we can do. We may subsequently discover that the problem is in fact more complex. By making the ordering criteria explicit and accessible, we have at least provided a place for embedding knowledge that can make the choice of hypothesis category as informed as possible at each step.

9. Example: a Bridge Fault

As we have noted, traditional automated reasoning about circuits works from a predefined list of fault models and uses the mathematical style of analysis exemplified by boolean algebra or the D-Algorithm. As a result, it is strongly oriented toward faults that can be modeled as a permanent binary value. One problem with this is its inability to provide useful results concerning bridge faults.

In this section we show how our system works when faced with a bridge fault, illustrating a number of the ideas described above. While the example has been simplified for presentation, there is still unfortunately a fair amount of detail necessary. A summary of the basic steps will help make clear how the problem is solved.

(1) The device is a 6-bit carry-chain adder. The problem begins when we notice that the attempt to add 21 and 19 produces an incorrect result.

(2) The candidate-generation process outlined above generates a set S_1 of three candidates, any of whose malfunction can explain this result.

(3) A new set of inputs (1 and 19) is chosen in an attempt to discriminate among the three possibilities. The adder's output is incorrect for this set of inputs also. The candidate generator indicates that there are two candidates capable of explaining this new result.

(4) Neither of these two candidates are found in S_1. Thus we reach a contradiction: no component is capable of explaining the data from both sets of inputs.

(5) Put slightly differently, we have a contradiction *under the current set of assumptions and interaction models*. We therefore have to surrender one of our assumptions and use a different interaction model.

(6) The next model—bridge faults—surrenders the assumption that the structure is as shown in the schematic and considers one class of modifications to the structure: the addition of one wire between physically adjacent pins.

(7) The combination of functional information (the expected pattern of values produced by the fault) and physical adjacency provides a strong constraint on the set of connections which might be plausible bridges.

(8) The first application of this idea produces two hypotheses that are functionally plausible, but both are ruled out on physical grounds.

(9) Dropping down a level of detail in our functional description reveals additional bridge candidates, two of which prove to be both functionally and physically plausible. One of these proves to be the actual error.

A key point is the utility of ordering the paths of interaction to be considered. Starting with a very restricted category of failure, we discover that it leads us to a contradiction. We surrender an assumption, consider an additional category and hence an additional pathway of interaction: bridge faults. We show how knowledge of both structural and functional organization allows us to generate a select few bridge-fault hypotheses, eventually discovering the underlying fault.

9.1. The example

Consider the six-bit adder shown in Fig. 10 and imagine that the attempt to add 21 and 19 produces 36 rather than the expected value of 40. Invoking the candidate-generation process described above, we would find that there are three devices (SLICE-1, A2 and SLICE-2), any one of whose malfunction can explain the misbehavior.[9]

---

[9]The example has been simplified slightly for presentation.

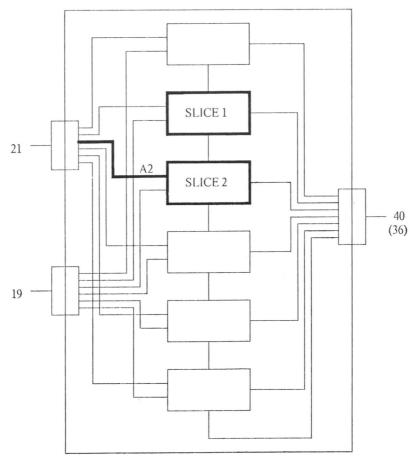

FIG. 10. Six-bit adder constructed from single-bit slices. Heavy lines indicate components implicated as possibly faulty.

A good strategy when faced with several candidates is to devise a test that can cut the space of possibilities in half. In this case changing the first input (21) to 1 will be informative: if the output of SLICE-2 does not change (to a 0) when we add 1 and 19, then the error must be in either A2 or SLICE-2.[10]

---

[10]This and subsequent test generation is currently done by hand. Work on automating test generation is in progress [27]. The reasoning behind this test relies on the single-fault assumption: if the malfunctioning component really were SLICE-1, both A2 and SLICE-2 would be fault-free. Hence the output of SLICE-2 would have to change when we changed one of its inputs. (Notice, however, if the output actually does change, we don't have any clear indication about the error location: SLICE-2, for example, might still be faulty.)

As it turns out, the result of adding 1 and 19 is 4 rather than 20. Since the output of SLICE-2 has not changed, it appears that the error must be in either A2 or SLICE-2.

But if we invoke the candidate generator, we discover an oddity: the only way to account for the behavior in which adding 1 and 19 produces a 4 is if one of the two candidates highlighted in Fig. 11 (B4 and SLICE-4) is at fault.

Therein lies our contradiction. The only candidates that account for the behavior of the first test are those in Fig. 10, the only candidates that account for the second test are those in Fig. 11. There is no overlap, so there is no single candidate that accounts for all the observed behavior.

Our current category—the localized failure of function—has thus led us to a

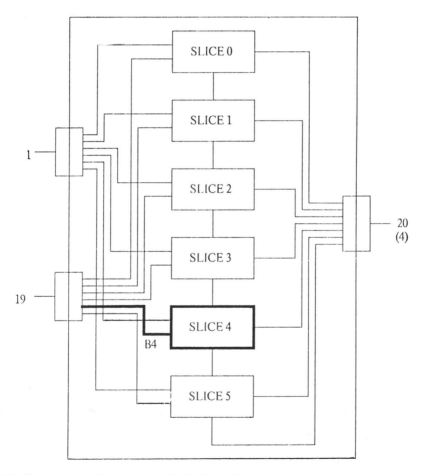

FIG. 11. Components indicated as possibly faulty by the second test.

contradiction.[11] We therefore surrender it and consider the next, less restrictive category, one that allows us to consider an *additional kind of interaction path*—bridging faults. The problem now is to see if there is some way to unify the test results, some way to generate a single bridge-fault candidate that accounts for all the observations.

Much of the difficulty in dealing with bridging faults arises because they violate the rather basic assumption that the structure of the device is in fact as shown in the schematic. But admitting that the structure may not be as pictured says only that we know what the structure *isn't*. Saying that we may have a bridge fault narrows it to a particular class of modifications to consider, but the real problem here remains one of *making a few plausible conjectures about modifications to the structure*. Between which two points can we insert a wire and produce the behavior observed?

To understand how we answer that question, consider what we have and what we need. We have test results, i.e., observations of *behavior*, and we want conjectures about modification to *structure*. The link from behavior to structure is provided by knowledge of electronics: in TTL, a bridge fault acts like an AND-gate, with ground dominating.[12]

From this fact we can derive a simple pattern of behavior indicative of bridges. Consider the simple example of Fig. 12 and assume that we ran two tests. Test 1 produced one candidate, module A, which should have produced a 1 but yielded a 0 (the zero is underlined to show that it is an incorrect output).

FIG. 12. Pattern of values indicative of a bridge. Heavy lines indicate candidates.

[11]Note that dropping down another level of detail in the functional description cannot help resolve the contradiction, because our functional description is a tree rather than a graph: in our work to date, at least, no component is used in more than one way. (If the functional description were in fact a graph, we could easily continue down it to see if the two candidate sets did indeed have a subcomponent in common).

[12]This is an oversimplification, but accurate enough to be useful. In any case, the point here is how the information is used; a more complex model could be substituted and carried through the rest of the problem. Note also that for notational convenience, we assume in the rest of the description that ground is equivalent to a 0.

Module B was working correctly and produced a 0 as expected. In Test 2 this situation is exactly reversed, A was performing as expected and B failed.

The pattern displayed in these two tests makes it plausible that there is a bridge linking the outputs of A and B: in the first test the output of A was dragged low by B, in the second test the output of B was dragged low by A.

We have thus turned the insight from electronics into a pattern of values on the candidates. It is plausible to hypothesize a bridge fault between two modules A and B from two different tests if: in Test 1, A produced an erroneous 0 and B produced a valid 0, while in Test 2, A produced a valid 0 while B produced an erroneous 0. Note that this can resolve the contradiction of non-overlapping candidate sets: it hypothesizes one fault that involves a member of each set and accounts for all the test data.

Thus, if we want to account for all of the test data in the original problem with a single bridge fault, we need a bridge that links one of the candidates from the first test (SLICE-1, A2, SLICE-2) with one of the candidates from the second test (B4, SLICE-4), and that mimics the pattern shown in Fig. 12.

Fig. 13 shows the candidate-generation results from both tests in somewhat more detail. As noted earlier, the candidate-generation procedure can indicate for each candidate the values that would have to exist at its ports for that candidate to be the broken one. For example, for SLICE-1 to be at fault in Test

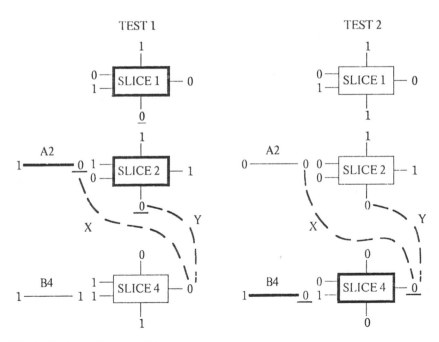

FIG. 13. Candidates and values at their ports.

1, it would have to have the three inputs shown, with its sum output a zero (as expected) and its carry output also a zero (the manifestation of the error, underlined).

In Fig. 13 there are two pairs of devices that match the desired pattern, yielding two functionally plausible bridge hypotheses:
– dotted line X, bridging wire A2 to the sum output of SLICE-4;
– dotted line Y, bridging the carry output of SLICE-2 to the sum output of SLICE-4.

But the faults have to be physically plausible as well. For the sake of

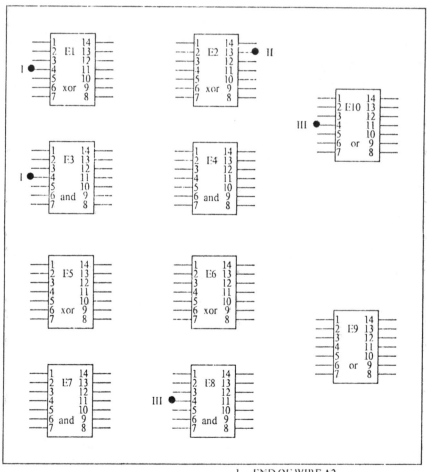

I   - END OF WIRE A2
II - SUM OUTPUT OF SLICE-4
III - CARRY-OUT OF SLICE-2

FIG. 14. Physical layout of the board with first bridge hypotheses indicated. (Slices 0, 2, and 4 are in the upper 5 chips, slices 1, 3, and 5 are in the lower 5.)

simplicity, we assume that bridge faults result only from solder splashes at the pins of chips.[13] To check physical plausibility, we switch to our physical representation, Fig. 14. Wire A2 is connected to chip E1 at pin 4 and chip E3 at pin 4; the sum output of SLICE-4 emerges at chip E2, pin 13. Since they are not adjacent, the first hypothesis is not physically reasonable. Similar reasoning rules out Y, the hypothesized bridge between the carry-out of SLICE-2 and the sum output of SLICE-4.

So far we have considered only the top-level of functional organization. We can run the candidate generator at the next lower level of detail in each of the non-primitive components in Fig. 13. (Dropping down a level of detail proves useful here because additional substructure becomes visible, effectively revealing new places that might be bridged.)

We obtain the components and values shown in Fig. 15. Checking here for the desired pattern, we find that either of the two wires labeled A2 and S2 could be bridged to either of the two wires labeled S4 and C4, generating four functionally plausible bridge faults.

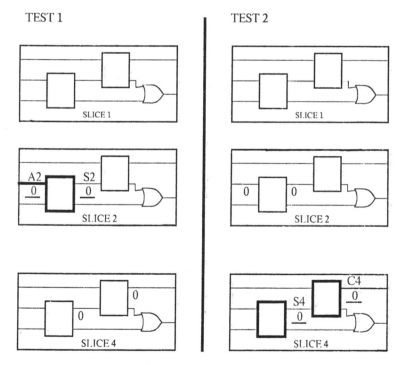

FIG. 15. Candidates at the next level of functional description. Each single-bit adder is built from two 'half-adders' and an OR-gate. (To simplify the figure, only the relevant values are shown.)

[13]Again this is correct but oversimplified (e.g., backplane pins can be bent or bridged), but as above we can introduce a more complex model if necessary.

Once again we check physical plausibility by examining the actual locations of A2, S2, S4, and C4 (Fig. 16).[14] As illustrated there, two of the possibilities are physically plausible as well: A2–S4 on chip E1 and S2–S4 on chip E2.

Switching back to our functional organization once more, Fig. 17, we see that the two possibilities correspond to (X) an output-to-input bridge between the XOR-gates in the rear half-adders of SLICE-2 and SLICE-4, and (Y) a bridge between two inputs of the XOR-gates in the forward half-adders of slices 2 and 4.

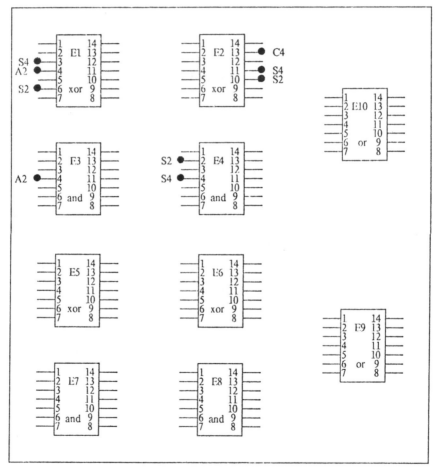

FIG. 16. Second set of bridge-fault hypotheses located on physical layout.

[14]Note that the erroneous 0 on wire S2 can be in any of three physical locations because S2 fans out (inside the module it enters on its right).

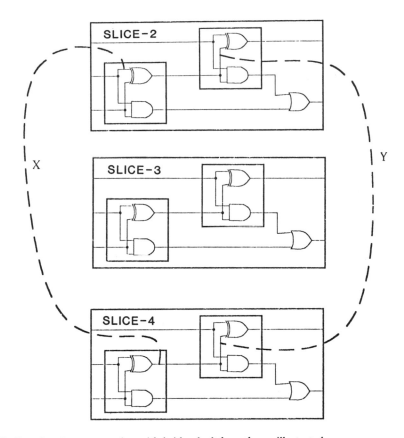

FIG. 17. Functional representation with bridge-fault hypotheses illustrated.

It is easy to find a test that distinguishes between these two possibilities:[15] adding 0 and 4 means that the inputs of SLICE-2 will be 1 and 0, with a carry-in of 0, while the inputs of SLICE-4 will both be 0, with a carry-in of 0. This set of values will show the effects of bridge Y, if it in fact exists: the sum output of SLICE-2 will be 0 if it does exist and a 1 otherwise. When we perform this test the result is 1, hence bridge Y is not in fact the problem.

Bridge X becomes the likely answer, but we should still test for it directly. Adding 4 and 0 (i.e., just switching the order of the inputs), is informative: if bridge X exists the result will be 0 and 1 otherwise. In this case the result is 0, hence the bridge labeled X is in fact the problem.[16]

---

[15]As above, tests are currently generated by hand.

[16]Had both been ruled out by direct test, then we would once again have had a contradiction on our hands and would have had to drop back to consider a still more elaborate model with additional paths of interaction.

9.2. The example: summary and comments

A fundamental point illustrated by the example is the utility of a layered set of models as a device for making explicit our simplifying assumptions and for dealing with complexity in candidate generation. Our original model, localized failure of function, incorporated the largest set of simplifying assumptions and was the most restrictive. It worked initially, but we eventually found ourselves unable to account for all the observations. At that point we surrendered one of our assumptions, adopted a less restrictive model, and considered an additional path of interaction. This allowed us to generate several bridge-fault hypotheses, one of which eventually proved to be correct. The notion of layers of inter-action models thus provided an important overall framework guiding the problem solving.

A second source of problem-solving power came from using multiple representations. This was particularly important in constraining the generation of bridge candidates. Faced with the original, apparently insoluble problem, we admitted the possibility of a bridge. But this left us with the difficult task of deciding where the bridge might be. The problem is quite similar to adding a new line to complete a proof in geometry and the difficulty is analogous: new constructions are difficult in general because they are relatively unconstrained [22].

The system's search for likely candidates turned out to be focused because we were able to derive useful constraints from each of our multiple represen-tations. Consider the physical representation, where the constraint is physical adjacency. We started by choosing a particular variety of adjacency, contiguity of pins on chips. This produced a significant reduction in the potential search space, but still left us with too many choices to produce an effective hypothesis generator: trying each pair of pins would be too unwieldy.

We then found a way to reduce the search using the functional represen-tation. We used knowledge about electronics to derive a link from behavior to structure, producing a pattern characteristic of bridges. This reduced the search space considerably, since the pattern had to include one candidate from each of the two sets (each of which is itself typically small), and since the pattern of 'alternating zeros' is relatively rare.

The result was sufficiently constrained to be an effective generator of bridge-fault hypotheses. We were then able to use the physical representation as a filter on the hypotheses generated.

In general then, our system produces a focused development of its solution by relying on several keys:

(1) The layered set of interaction models produced by methodical enumera-tion and relaxation of underlying assumptions constrained the categories of errors we were willing to consider, yet allowed us to consider more elaborate hypotheses when simpler ones failed.

(2) The availability of multiple representations allowed us to take advantage of constraints associated with each representation.

(3) We were able to use one representation as the basis for a constrained generator of hypotheses and use the other to filter the hypotheses generated.

In Section 11 we speculate on ways of generalizing the set of ideas used here. We consider the character of the representations used and ask what made them effective generators and filters. Our goal there is to produce a set of principles that will function as guidelines in selecting representations, making it possible to carry over this approach to other problems in other domains.

10. Categories of Failure

Since the categories of failure and paths of interaction play a significant role in our approach, two obvious questions concern their origin and ordering. Where do we get them, and how can we determine an appropriate ordering?

We want a methodical way to generate the categories so that we have some reason to believe that the result is systematic and hence reasonably complete. We need to define the criterion for simplicity so that we know how to order the categories to produce a sequence of successively more elaborate hypotheses.

10.1. Origins

The list in Section 8 of possibilities to consider is of course specific to our current domain. We believe that our overall framework does, however, offer a useful set of questions that we can ask about any domain to generate an analogous listing. Appropriately enough, many of the questions derive from examining carefully our simple 'module and information path' representation, asking what assumptions the representation makes about the world, and then asking what the consequences are of violating those assumptions.

The simplest assumption (indicated schematically in Fig. 18(a)) lies in believing that a module can be said to have a particular behavior. To say this is violated means, as we saw earlier, that the module isn't behaving in accordance with the assigned behavior, i.e., it is broken. This is the simple 'localized-failure-of-function' category that heads the list in Section 8. Simple examples in our current domain include the traditional stuck-at (a particular kind of failure of a wire module), as well as failures of primitive gates (e.g., a NOR-gate acting as an inverter), or even the use of an incorrect part during assembly (e.g., a NOR-gate chip instead of a NAND-chip).

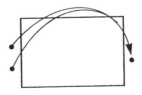

FIG. 18(a). Assigning behavior to a module.

Our representation also assumes that modules have ports, each with a specified direction (Fig. 18(b)). Yet as we saw above, this too can be violated. We term it an 'unexpected-direction' error, with the power-failure example as one instance.

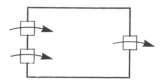

FIG. 18(b). Assuming that ports have a specified direction.

Treating a module as a black box means committing only to its behavior; when we drop down a level in the description, we are assuming that it has a specific substructure (Fig. 18(c)). But that may not be true; we refer to this as a 'structure error'. How could the substructure be different from what we expect? In our current domain there are a wide range of answers, i.e., a wide range of paths of interaction: bridges, thermal or transmission-line effects, as well as out-of-date schematics or a wiring error during assembly. Each of these has the effect of producing a substructure different from what we expected.

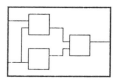

FIG. 18(c). Assuming that a substructure is as specified.

Finally, our representation assumes that the overall behavior of a module should be matched by the aggregate behavior of its substructure (Fig. 18(d)). Violating this assumption means there is a design error: all components work as specified, but they cannot produce the desired behavior.

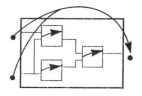

FIG. 18(d). Assuming that the overall behavior matches the aggregate of its substructure.

Thus, examining carefully the character of the assumptions built into our representation yields a set categories of failure. These in turn provide a number of questions we can ask about the domain, questions whose answers are the pathways of interaction to be considered. While we have answered these questions here for our digital circuits, we believe the questions are more broadly applicable, and may prove to be a useful way to think about other domains where the 'module and information path' view is appropriate.

One additional category derives from examining our candidate generator. As noted in Section 6.2, the single-point-of-failure assumption is embodied in the fact that we disabled the rules for exactly one component when checking candidate consistency. This too may be an incorrect assumption, yielding yet another category, multiple faults.

10.2 Ordering

The example in Section 9 used a very simple approach to ordering the categories: a fixed order based on frequency of occurrence as reported by experienced troubleshooters. While the program currently uses this approach, it is easy to imagine more sophisticated ordering schemes that still fit naturally into this framework. The remainder of this section speculates about a number of such possibilities.

More elaborate static-ordering criteria might take account of the age of the machine or the age of the design. We might want to indicate that assembly errors are more common in machines received from the production line recently, and design errors more likely if the device is a new model or has undergone substantial redesign.

Note that, were we willing to model enormously more of the world, we might be able to *infer* that design errors are less common in well-established designs, but this is beyond the scope of our efforts and the investment would be very large for a relatively modest return. As it stands, we are in this case willing to rely on some simple experiential observations for guidance, without bothering to model the causality in any detail.

The character of the reported misbehavior can be revealing as well. Small changes in external behavior are often suggestive of the local-failure-of-function category, while substantial variations in behavior can be suggestive of assembly and wiring errors. We might thus borrow from medicine the notion of a 'presenting complaint' and use information about the character of the misbehavior to reorder the categories to be considered.

An obvious further extension would make the ordering dynamic. We might start out as above, but reorder the categories in response to information gained as inference and testing proceeds.

Whatever the ordering criteria chosen, the overall point is that having an ordered set of fault categories provides a number of advantages. First, it offers a means of expressing and managing simplifying assumptions. Second, it provides a simple mechanism for dealing with complexity, by limiting the set of interaction paths to consider. Finally, it supplies a relatively natural site for embedding and using the empirical knowledge of an experienced engineer that might be difficult to represent at the level of first principles.

11. The Adjacency Principle

The bridge-fault example raises two interesting questions:
   (1) Why are bridge faults so difficult?
   (2) Why does the physical representation prove to be so useful?
   To see the answer, we start with the trivial observation that all faults are the result of some difference between the device as it is and as it should be. With bridge faults the difference is the addition of a wire between two physically adjacent points.
   Now recall the nature of our task: we are typically presented with a device that misbehaves, not one with obvious structural damage. Hence we reason from behavior, i.e., from the functional representation. And the important point is that for a bridge fault, the difference in question—the addition of a single wire—is not small and local in that representation. As the comparison of Figs. 16 and 17 makes clear, the new wire connects two points that are adjacent in the physical representation but widely separated in the functional representation.
   The difference is also not as simple in that representation: if we include in our functional diagram the AND-gate implicitly produced by the bridge (Fig. 19), we see that a single added wire in the physical representation maps into an AND-gate and a fanout in the functional representation.
   This view helps to explain why bridge faults produce behavior that is difficult to understand. Bridge faults are modifications that are simple and local in the physical description, but our reasoning is done using the functional description. Hence the dilemma:

   The desire to reason from behavior requires us to use a representation that does not necessarily provide a compact description of the fault.

   This non-locality and complexity should not be surprising, since devices physically adjacent are not necessarily functionally related. Hence there is no guarantee that a change that is compact in one will produce a change that is compact in the other. More generally, *changes compact in one representation are not necessarily compact in another.*
   We can turn this around to put it to work for us:

   Part of the art of choosing the right representation(s) for diagnostic reasoning is finding one in which the suspected change is *compact.*

   This explains the utility of the physical representation: it's the 'right' one

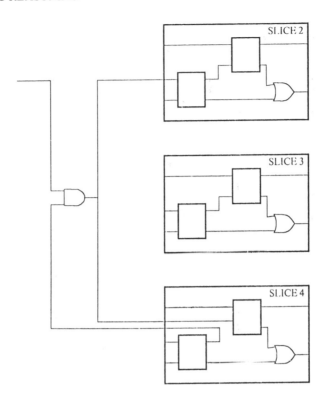

FIG. 19. Full functional representation of bridge fault X.

because it's the one in which the change is compact—the affected components are adjacent.

Going one step further, we might ask why adjacency is the relevant organizing principle. We believe the answer follows from two facts: (a) devices interact through physical processes (voltage on a wire, thermal radiation, etc.) and (b) physical processes occur locally, or more generally, causality proceeds between devices that are in some sense adjacent: there is no action at a distance. To make this useful, we turn it around:

The paths of interaction are one way to define adjacency. That is, each kind of interaction path can define a representation.

Bridge faults arise from *physical adjacency* and hence are local in the physical representation. The notion of *thermal adjacency* and a corresponding representation would be useful in dealing with faults resulting from heat conduction or radiation, *electromagnetic adjacency* would help with faults dealing with transmission line effects, etc.

Each of these produces a different representation, different in its definition of adjacency. And each will be useful for understanding and reasoning about a category of failure.

The paths of interaction are in effect a set of 'representation generators'. They can tell us what kinds of views to take of the device; how to represent it in order to make use of the fundamental belief that physical action proceeds between components that are adjacent in some way.

Finally, we can push this one step further, asking why we expect that there will in fact be some representation, some definition of adjacency, that 'makes sense' of the problem at hand. Why should there be some representation in which the fault appears to be a compact perturbation? The belief appears to be based on what we might call the 'single-initial-cause heuristic':

It is often the case that the malfunction of a previously working device results from a single cause, rather than a number of simultaneous, independent events.

When there is indeed a single cause, there will be some representation in which a small and local change accounts for the difference between the good and faulty device. To the extent that a malfunction results from multiple, *unrelated* events (e.g., multiple failures in an old machine; multiple problems inserted deliberately), it becomes far less likely that we can find a single representation that offers a unifying perspective for every fault at once.[17]

One additional illustration of the utility of multiple representations with multiple definitions of adjacency comes from considering devices with shared components. In some designs, one physical component (e.g., an AND-gate) may be used for two different purposes. We can model this by having two different modules in the functional representation that point to the same module in the physical representation (using the cross-links shown in Fig. 4). If the physical gate is bad, then the candidate generator may find that it needs two points of failure to account for the symptoms. But what looks like two failures in the functional representation can be resolved to a single point of failure by shifting to the physical representation.

Similarly, if a chip containing four AND-gates is completely bad, our candidate generator will find four apparently distinct candidates. Once again, shifting to the physical representation gives us a view in which the problem can be understood as a single failure.

In both cases shifting to a different definition of adjacency helps resolve the issue and provides alternate definitions of the notion a single point of failure. In the first case two modules distant in the functional representation are adjacent (in fact coincident) in the physical representation; in the second case four

---

[17]This work has not yet explored the problem of multiple, related failures, where one fault causes a cascade of other failures.

different functional modules become adjacent (same package) in the physical representation.

As this illustrates, the basic concept of a 'single point of failure' is not in fact well defined until we specify the representation. We should really speak of a single point with respect to a particular representation, since, as we have seen, what appears as multiple distinct points in one representation may be a single point in a different representation.

We still have substantial additional work to do on these topics, but we seem at least to be asking the right questions. The concept of pathways of interaction and the corresponding definitions of adjacency appear to make sense for a wide range of hardware faults.

The ideas also appear to work in other domains. When debugging software, for example, the pathways of interaction differ (e.g., procedure call, mutation of data structures), but the resulting perspectives appear to make sense and there are some interesting analogies. Unintended side effects in software, for example, are in some ways like bridge faults. An unexpected direction of information flow can result during a procedure call, by assigning a value to a parameter that turns out to be called by name rather than by value.

More generally still, there appears to be substantial breadth to this whole perspective of viewing different representations as embodying different definitions of adjacency. Consider software once again. Our typical view of software is functional, in flowcharts or dataflow diagrams. Yet there are faults where the notion of 'physical adjacency' is crucial in understanding the bug. Consider for example an out-of-bounds array addressing error. Full understanding of the bug may require knowing how the software is mapped physically into memory, so that we can determine which cell was actually referenced.

A similar phenomenon is apparent in speech: the classic 'recognize speech' vs. 'wreck a nice beach' confusion is entertaining in part because the two are so 'far apart' in meaning (distant in any semantic representation) yet adjacent in their phonetic representation. The idea even supports 'troubleshooting' in this domain. In reading an abstract recently, I encountered a number of phrases that made no sense in an otherwise coherent text. Then, considering the origin of the document, it became plausible that the text might have been dictated over a noisy (transatlantic) phone line. This suggested that a phonetic representation might be the 'correct' one for debugging, i.e., the one in which the errors could be seen as small and local changes. It was then easy to debug phrases like 'decorative representations' ('declarative representations') and 'rule space systems' ('rule-based systems').

Two widely accepted bits of wisdom about AI suggest that having the 'right' representation is an important key in problem solving and that multiple representations often contribute substantial power. We believe that the notion of adjacency as a way of defining representations is useful in understanding more about both of these ideas. In the effort to define what is meant by the 'right' representation, for example, a number of general guidelines have emerged, at the level of suggestions that appropriate representations 'make the important things explicit', and 'expose the natural constraints' (e.g., [34]). The notion of adjacency offers one additional level of detail to these catchphrases. It suggests that natural constraints arise because things are adjacent 'in some sense', and that 'in some sense' can have multiple different instantiations. We can generate a variety of representations by seeking out different definitions of adjacency. Finally, this in turn may help explain the utility of multiple representations: part of the power in using them arises because they provide us with multiple different definitions of adjacency.

12. Evaluation and Future Work

Since this work is still in its formative stages, there are still a number of interesting questions about its advantages and limits and appropriate directions for future work.

12.1. Advantages of reasoning from structure and behavior

There are several advantages in basing reasoning on knowledge of structure and behavior, rather than previous approaches like the empirical associations used in a number of earlier programs (e.g., MYCIN [9, 28], INTERNIST [24], or PROSPECTOR [17]). Reasoning from first principles provides a strong degree of machine independence, makes the system easier to construct and maintain, facilitates defining the program's scope of competence, and makes it capable of dealing with bugs that display novel symptoms.

Reasoning from first principles offers a significant degree of machine independence. The tools and techniques described above work directly from the descriptions of structure and behavior and make explicit their assumptions about those descriptions. This allows us to cover a wide range of devices built from digital logic components. Even more fundamentally, concepts like modules linked by causal pathways, expected behavior, etc., are widely useful, extending perhaps to include handheld calculators, digital watches, automobiles and software.

Rules, on the other hand, are typically strongly machine-specific. There is distressingly little carry-over from one machine to the next when we capture troubleshooting knowledge at the level of symptom/disease associations. Even simple changes to a single machine (e.g., design upgrades) can mean substantial changes in the rules. Diagnosing a new machine means even more difficulty. Each new system would require a new knowledge base with all of the difficulties that entails.

A system based on reasoning from first principles is easier to construct because there is a way of systematically enumerating the required knowledge: the structure and behavior of the device. A system based on empirical associations is more difficult to construct because the character of the knowledge makes it necessary to extract the rules on a case-by-case basis. To the extent that the knowledge is a distillation of the expert's experience, the best we can do is to assemble a representative collection of cases and ask an expert for the rules dealing with each case. No more systematic method of collecting rules is available and the process often continues for an extended period of time. This time lag is a particular problem in dealing with electronic hardware: the time necessary to accumulate the relevant experience is beginning to be longer than the design cycle for the next model of the machine.

A system based on reasoning from first principles is also easier to maintain, since modifications to the machine design are relatively easy to accommodate. We can update the structure and behavior specifications for each modified component, rather than having to determine how each change should modify the overall behavior and the troubleshooting strategy.

The ability to enumerate the knowledge systematically also aids in defining the program's scope and competence. We know what parts of the machine have been modeled and to what level of detail.

When building a system from empirical associations, it is more difficult to define precisely what such a program 'knows'. A precise answer to the question is often possible only for a problem that can be formalized, so almost every AI system suffers from this to some extent. But the more systematic our mechanism for enumerating the required knowledge, the more precise we can be about defining the program's competence. Deriving the knowledge strictly from a collection of case studies is one of the less systematic mechanisms, yet it is in such cases that rule-based systems are appropriate. As a result, often the best we can say about the system is that it has a set of rules dealing with one or another class of problems, with only a very informal measure of how thoroughly that class has been covered.

Finally, reasoning from first principles offers the possibility of dealing with novel faults. As we have seen, our system does not depend for its performance on a catalog of observed error manifestations. Instead it takes the view that any discrepancy between observed and expected behavior is a bug, and it uses knowledge about the device structure and behavior to determine the possible sources of the bug. As a result, it is able to reason about bugs that are novel in the sense that they are not part of the 'training set' and are manifested by symptoms not seen previously.

Since rules are a distillation of an expert's experience, a program built from them will be reasonably sure of handling only cases quite similar to those the human expert has already seen, solved, and communicated to the program. We have little reason to believe that the program will handle a bug whose outward manifestation is unfamiliar, even if the root cause is within the claimed scope of the system.

At times there may not be a choice: in domains where knowledge truly is anecdotal and experiential, a rule-based encoding may be appropriate. Where knowledge in the domain does admit some more basic model, however, we find the reasons above present a strong argument for capturing that level of understanding in the program.

12.2. Describing structure and behavior

12.2.1. *Previous representations*

There is a long history of attempts to represent structure and behavior in general and computer hardware in particular. Our approach has a number of features in common with that work. The primary points of overlap are the black-box view of modules and the use of hierarchical descriptions (both of which are found in [16, 33], for example). Major points of difference include (i) our distinction between, and explicit representation of, functional, physical and behavioral information, (ii) emphasis on the creation of a domain-specific language, and (iii) the ability to make multiple uses of our representations.

Many previous languages fail to include information about physical organization at all. This seems to have resulted from their origin in work on machine design, where physical packaging is sometimes considered only after functional design has been accomplished.

In some other description languages there is a significant intermixing of structure and behavior information, arising apparently from the use of traditional programming languages as foundations. There are many advantages to implementing a new language as a variant on some existing language (like ALGOL), including the availability of a compiler and other language development tools. But this makes it all too easy to carry over a set of habits that may be inappropriate. The temptation exists, for example, to use datatype declarations as a mechanism for expressing the existence of functional modules. Hence we see such things as

```
    STRUCTURE:

      DECLARE
      MEMORY[0: 1023]⟨0 : 15⟩
      ACCUMULATOR⟨0 : 16⟩
      PC⟨0: 11⟩
      IR⟨0: 15⟩;

    BEHAVIOR:

      IR := MEMORY[PC]
      IF IR⟨8: 11⟩ = 13    ; add instruction
       . . .
      etc.
```

There is a significant intermixing of structure and behavior here. The declarations are supposed to contain the structure information, but where is the indication that the instruction register (IR) is connected to the memory? It is indicated indirectly in the behavior section of the code, where we discover that the IR is capable of being loaded from memory. We prefer that such information be made explicit. Among other things, this permits more systematic fault insertion. In the current example, we would be able to simulate the effects of faulty behavior in the bus that links the memory and instruction register.

A second major difference in our approach lies in our creation of a domain-specific language, one that incorporates the concepts and vocabulary of computer architecture. As noted, several hardware description languages have used the black-box view and the module/port approach as a starting point. Simple interconnections of devices are easily accommodated in this scheme, but the attempt to describe even small real circuits soon presents problems. One common insight is that many circuits contain a substantial amount of regularity. The pattern of interconnections in memory or between slices of an ALU, for example, is often easily expressed as some form of iteration. One common response (see, e.g., [21]) is to adopt more of the traditional programming language constructs, like iterative loops.

But this presents problems. A bit-slice CPU, for example (Fig. 2), has a form of regularity different from that displayed by an array of memory chips. Using a **for** loop to express both of them ignores, or at best makes obscure, the important difference. The result is often difficult to interpret as well. It can take a considerable amount of study to determine that a tightly coded iterative loop in fact expresses a well-known organization.

We are pursuing an alternate approach, described in Section 3, of assembling a vocabulary of terms common to architects. Each such term labels a particular kind of organization and has associated with it information on how to wire up that configuration. The result is in effect a new, high-level language, with all of the standard benefits of such. It allows us to make explicit the nature of the organization in the circuit, as well as providing a compact, efficient, and easily understood language.

A third major difference in our approach is our ability to make use of descriptions in several different ways. The same description is used (i) as a basis for the troubleshooting module, (ii) as a database of facts about connectivity, part identity, etc., (iii) as a body of code that can be run to simulate the device, and (iv) as the basis for a display program for observing the device. This is possible because we have avoided the temptation to write code oriented toward a single purpose like simulation, and have instead produced a set of data structures (described in Sections 3 and 4) that can be used in all the different ways noted. This approach is not unknown in the hardware description language world—ISPS has been used quite profitably in this fashion [2]—but it is rare. We find that it offers sufficient leverage to be worth the additional effort.

12.2.2. *Advantages*

Our approach offers a number of features which, while not necessarily novel, do provide useful performance. For example, there is a unity of device description and simulation, since the descriptions themselves are 'runnable'. That is, the behavior descriptions associated with a given module allow us to simulate the behavior of that module; the interconnection of modules specified in the structure description then causes results computed by one module to propagate to another. Thus we don't need a separate description or body of code as the basis for the simulation, we can simply 'run' the description itself. This ensures that our description of a device and the machinery that simulates it can never disagree about what to do, as can be the case if the simulation is produced by a separately maintained body of code.

Our use of a hierarchic approach and the terminal, port, module vocabulary makes multi-level simulation very easy. In simulating any module we can either run the behavior associated with that module (simulating the module in a single step), or 'run the substructure' of the module, simulating the device according to its next level of structure. Enabling the behavior that spans the entire module gives us a one-step simulation; enabling the abstraction-shifting machinery that implements a port gives us a detailed simulation (by allowing information to propagate into the next lower level). Since the abstraction-shifting behavior of ports is also implemented with the constraint-like mechanism described in Section 4, we have a convenient uniformity and economy of machinery.

Varying the level of simulation is useful for speed (no need to simulate verified substructure), and provides as well a simple check on structure and behavior specification: we can compare the results generated by the module's behavior specification with those generated by the next lower level of simulation. Mismatches typically mean a mistake in structure specification at the lower level.

Work in [6] described the importance of the 'no function in structure' concept, essentially a point of methodology and 'mental hygiene', suggesting that device behaviors be defined independent of their use in any specific circuit. We have adopted this perspective and built a small library of component descriptions (adders, wires, AND-gates, etc.); a set of prototypical modules with structure and behavior descriptions independent of any particular circuit. Devices are then constructed by assembling and interconnecting instances of those prototypes, using the language described in Section 3.

A wire, for example, is a device whose behavior is a simple bi-directional propagation: information appearing at either one of its terminals will be propagated to the other. Any particular use of a wire typically has a single direction of propagation in mind, but our simulator runs the behavior description that reflects the 'actual' (bi-directional) behavior.

While this approach offers no formal guarantees that the behavior definitions are free of implicit assumptions, it does provide an environment that strongly encourages attention to the issue by (i) distinguishing clearly between behavior definition of an individual module and its intended use in a circuit, and (ii) by forcing every module of a particular type of share the same behavior specification. This approach is especially important in troubleshooting, since some of the more difficult faults to locate are those that cause devices to behave not as we know they 'should', but as they are in fact electrically capable of doing.

Finally, our approach offers a convenient mechanism for fault insertion. A wire stuck at zero, for example, is modeled by giving the wire a behavior specification that maintains its terminals at logic level 0 despite any attempt to change them. Bridges, opens, etc., are similarly easily modeled.

12.2.3. *Limitations*

The behavior-specification mechanism we have described is quite straightforward and some of its limits are well known. A set of constraints is, for example, a relatively simple mechanism for specifying behavior, in that it offers no obvious support for expressing behavior that falls outside the 'relation between terminals' view. A bus protocol, for example, would require additional machinery to represent the state-transition network describing the protocol. We might also want to describe and reason about behavior in higher-level terms like *enables*, or *inhibits*, suggesting the need for a vocabulary similar to the one developed in [25].

In addition, our current propagation mechanism works well when dealing with simple quantities like numbers or logic levels, but cannot deal with more elaborate symbolic expressions. What, for example, do we do if we know that the output of an OR-gate is 1 but we don't know the value at either input? We can refrain from making any conclusion about the inputs, which makes the rules easy to write but misses some information. Or we can write a rule which express the value on one input in terms of the value on the other input. This captures the information but produces problems when trying to use the resulting expression elsewhere. A simple but effective propagation of symbolic expressions is accomplished in [19], suggesting that the approach taken there may be a good starting point.

12.3. Limitations in candidate generation

This limitation in our propagation machinery is also responsible for the primary limitation in the candidate-generation facility. As we have seen, the basic technique works by looking for a contradiction: we 'turn off' the behavior rules for a single device and see if there is any set of assignments to its terminals that

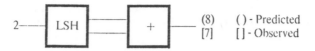

FIG. 20. Reconvergent error. There is no way for the input wire alone to account for the symptoms. (The first device shifts its input left one place and sends the result to both outputs.)

is consistent with the inputs and observed output symptoms. If no contradiction is reported, we consider the component to be a candidate.

But sometimes no contradiction is reported because the propagation machinery is too weak to discover it. One simple case can arise from reconvergent errors. In the simple circuit shown in Fig. 20, for example, our current system is unable to determine that the input wire could not be a consistent candidate. When, in using constraint suspension, we 'turn off' the behavior of the input wire, and insert the input (2) and observed output (7), several terminals end up with no values assigned. This is not considered a contradiction, so the input wire is put on the list of plausible candidates.

In principle, we should have been able to rule it out, but including it as a candidate does not present any serious problems. The candidate set will be larger than it should be, so our system may end up doing some additional work in narrowing the set later (e.g., running more tests than should strictly have been necessary). The net result is some inefficiency, but no intractable difficulties. Enhancing the propagation machinery to handle this situation would involve difficult problems, including propagating and manipulating symbolic expressions [32], and reasoning about such properties as integer solutions to equations.

12.4. Comments on the example

We chose a bridge example because they have traditionally been difficult; we considered the problem in TTL because of its common use. But this turns out to be a convenient choice. Bridges in TTL are easily modeled and the pattern easily checked for in the symptoms; we noted earlier the power this supplies in constraining the search space. In other technologies, unfortunately, the behavior of bridge faults is not so easily described. The reasoning is correspondingly more difficult and our system would be less focused in its generation of hypotheses.

A second problem highlighted by the example is the nature of the overall control of problem solving. Some parts are reasonably clear. The use of the categories of failure, for example, is to date at least fairly straightforward, starting with the most likely and moving toward the more exotic categories. We were also able to describe the overall strategy behind using and switching between multiple representations (using the functional as a hypothesis generator and the physical as a filter), but this is currently hardwired into the system. It would of course be better to have the system able to make this choice. Finally, we have yet to develop a globally defined strategy concerning the use of the description hierarchy. In general we work at the higher description levels before moving down, but this may not always be appropriate. It is not yet clear, for example, how 'deep' to pursue candidate generation before stopping to generate distinguishing tests.

Consider the example of Fig. 7. There we determined that either the first multiplier or first adder could be at fault. Should we now drop down a level and try generating candidates inside the adder and multiplier, or should we try another test vector to provide more symptom data? Either of these strategies might indicate which of the two candidates contains the broken component. As noted earlier, dropping down a level may demonstrate that no subcomponent of (say) the adder can account for the original set of symptoms, hence it cannot be at fault: running a second test provides additional symptom data that may distinguish between the candidates. The appropriate strategy presumably depends on the costs in the specific case at hand: when we are very near the 'bottom' of the description hierarchy, it may cost relatively little to go down the one final level; when tests are relatively cheap to generate and run, that may be the preferred approach.

12.5. The example: implementation

As we have noted, test generation in the example is currently done by hand, but all the rest has been implemented, in FRANZ LISP running on a VAX 780. The example shown requires approximately 3 minutes of CPU time, but since this is an early prototype, no attention has been given yet to producing efficient code.

The system is still a simple feasibility demonstration and as such lacks a number of design features necessary before it can be used as a serious tool. The current control structures, for example, are too deeply hardwired into the system. The sequencing through various categories of failure is currently embodied in a collection of procedure calls. Yet, given our emphasis on enumerating and keeping careful track of assumptions (as in Section 10), the selection of a failure category would more appropriately be accomplished with a general TMS system of the sort described in [15]. We do have a simple form of TMS in the dependency networks maintained by the simulation and inference rules, but it would be useful to construct a more general version and use it to keep track of the assumptions underlying the failure categories.

We are also working on a graphics interface that will allow dynamic display of the reasoning. As the sequence of figures shown earlier suggests, much of the process of candidate generation (for both the individual components and bridges) is easily understood in terms of diagrams. We are developing a system that will allow us to do this, displaying the results as they are generated.

12.6. Scaling: device complexity and time

With any initial demonstration of this size, the scaling issue is always of concern. We have demonstrated the feasibility of a particular technique on a small combinatorial circuit assembled from simple devices. What happens when the circuit gets considerably larger and the devices get more complex?

We believe that size alone is unlikely to be a disabling problem, arguing that the design task imposes a limit on complexity. In order to make the design task tractable, a circuit with several hundred or several thousand components must have some sort description more compact than a simple listing of the components. Without such a hierarchy, it is unlikely it could have been designed successfully.

Complex behavior is likely to present a more difficult problem. Describing the behavior of devices at the scale of gates and adders is relatively straightforward. Describing the behavior of a disk controller is likely to be considerably more challenging, but, by the design argument once again, we speculate that it will not be overwhelmingly so.

The significant problem with complex devices is likely to lie in the inference rules. It is one thing to describe what a disk controller should do, it may be quite another task to infer what some of its inputs were, given its outputs. One important subproblem we will encounter here is propagating symbolic expressions, since, as noted, many devices are not uniquely invertible.

A second problem lies in extending our work to deal with more elaborate models of time and more complex devices with state. Our current system uses only the simplest model of time, enabling us to deal with simple synchronous devices. There are several steps we need to take to elaborate this. We have to model propagation delays so we can deal with races. Since protocols play an important role in communication, we need to be able to represent and reason about them.

Reasoning about devices with memory will also require elaboration of our candidate generation machinery. Our planned approach will be in the spirit of the current effort: where discrepancy detection currently moves us backward in space through the circuit, we intend to extend it to move backward in time as well, inferring values at previous time slices.

In facing the problem of scaling this feasibility demonstration up to problems of practical size, then, we find two issues of central concern: how can we generate inference rules for complex devices, and how can we model time in a way that allows us to reason over a significant number of slices? Work on both of these is currently under way.

12.7. Limits of modeling: analog devices and incomplete models

Though we have set our sights here on reasoning from first principles, as with any representation we eventually encounter a level of detail not incorporated in our model. We have been working strictly in the digital world and as such cannot model or reason about analog phenomena. This is most obvious in the power-failure example: our representation makes it easy to *incorporate* the insight that input ports can behave as output ports, but reasoning at the level of the digital abstraction precludes *deriving* that insight. Marginal signals are a second example: the effects might be captured at the digital level but some of the reasoning would be outside our current abilities.

Since every representation incorporates some level of abstraction, the issue is not that we encounter limits, but rather how important those limits are to the current domain and how difficult it would be to press beyond them. In answer to the first of these, we simply need more experience to determine how much of the problem can be captured at the level of detail we use.

Concerning the second, previous work (e.g., [13]) suggests that dealing with analog circuits and their continuous variables requires confronting significant additional problems. One difficulty arises because most analog devices are bi-directional and this often makes candidate generation considerably less constrained. There are more paths of interaction to be considered and hence more components in the circuit that could have caused the fault. In the example of Fig. 9, for instance, allowing ports to be bi-directional widens the set of candidates (as it should) to include all the multipliers. Working in the digital domain means that most of our devices are uni-directional, keeping the set of candidate components smaller.

A second problem arising in analog circuits is the use of designs that rely on aggregate properties. The feedback or hysteresis in a device, for example, cannot be said to reside in or result from any one component. This produces difficulties when troubleshooting because some of the more interesting faults are those that are local to a single component but that disable the desired aggregate property. Tracing the fault from the disappearance of the aggregate property back to a single component can be difficult.

Finally, dealing with the continuous values present in analog devices presents its own set of problems, motivating much of the work on qualitative physics (e.g., [13]). We have to determine whether it will be possible to quantize the domain, developing and reasoning from a small vocabulary of labels like *high*, *low*, *float*, *rising*, and *falling*, or whether more complex machinery is necessary.

An equally pressing issue concerns the completeness of our models. Our system is focused in its efforts in part because its models of structure and behavior are complete: we knew, for example, exactly how the adder was constructed and how it behaved. Yet much real-world troubleshooting is done with incomplete models. Experienced engineers employ much the same sort of reasoning shown here even when the device is a mainframe computer and the behavior is on the scale of an operating system, yet they clearly are not using complete models of either. The ability to specify and use incomplete models would thus help address the scaling issue and would increase the likely scope of utility of our work to fields like medicine, where complete models are simply unavailable.

12.8. But that's not how it's *really* done

The performance of the program we have developed is in some ways noticeably different from the standard practice of a human expert. As expert systems work rather than cognitive science, the intent here is to be inspired by human performance without modeling it in detail. It is nevertheless useful to consider how our system differs from real practice.

While we argued earlier for the difficulty of troubleshooting based solely on empirical associations, it is clear that rules can serve useful roles. They might, for example, offer a form of memory to shortcut the process for problems previously encountered. This would clearly be an improvement on our current system, which will solve a problem from first principles every time, no matter how many times it is encountered. Such rules can also help focus the process by recognizing symptoms characteristic of particular kinds of malfunctions (e.g., power-supply failures), characteristic of particular locations of failures (e.g., memory, I/O bus, etc.), or characteristic of particular machines (e.g., the disk controllers on this model tend to fail sooner).

Real troubleshooting also typically involves extensive use of logic probes, an issue this work has not addressed at all yet. While it will clearly be important in the long run, we would argue that it is appropriately delayed for several reasons. First, we claim that inference is 'free', while measurement is often quite expensive. It's comparatively expensive in time: many inferences can be drawn in the time it takes to place a probe. More important, it's expensive in potential loss of information: it is often necessary to put cards on extenders or otherwise disturb the current state of the machine to make the measurement and the information lost can be crucial. The current trend in hardware speed makes this imbalance likely to continue.[18] As a result, we claim that it's well worth it to 'think as much as you can' before taking another measurement.

The real issue here is the longstanding problem of information gathering. Where, contrary to our current assumption, we do not have complete data available, the real problem is reasoning from the current stock of information and deciding what measurement to take next. Our current examples are small enough that complete information is reasonable, but we will clearly encounter the issue as we scale the problem up to larger devices.

Finally, we might ask what fraction of the troubleshooting problem is not currently handled by simpler, existing technology of the sort characterized by stuck-at models and state-of-the-art diagnostics. A significant percentage of the problem is solved in this fashion, but the fraction left unsolved turns out to be

---

[18]There is some countervailing trend in the design of hardware that offers visibility of internal machine state and the possibility of automated probing.

quite expensive. It is not unusual to find a strongly bi-modal distribution in which problems are commonly solved in either two hours or two days. There is thus a significant problem here, which, because of issues like decreasing design lifetimes, is likely to become worse.

13. Related Work

13.1. Hardware diagnosis

Two lines of work developed in the hardware-diagnosis community have some interesting overlap with the work described here: the guided probe [5] and the effect-cause analysis of Abramovici and Breuer [1].

The guided-probe technique has been in use in industry for some time and shares some basic ideas with our approach to troubleshooting. Both are based on the notion of discrepancy detection; both trace an error at an output back to its source by following the wiring of the circuit, and both use simulation to produce the correct values.[19]

One important difference arises because the guided-probe approach does not have anything analogous to our inference rules (it uses a logic probe to measure voltages at nodes interior to the circuit). Having inference rules is important because it allows us to separate candidate generation from probing. That is, we can determine the entire set of plausibly broken components before making any additional measurements on the circuit. This can be an advantage because, given the entire candidate set, we may be able to select a few (or even one) places to probe that best reduce the size of the candidate set (e.g., the usual half-split strategy). The standard guided-probe approach, by interleaving discrepancy detection with probing, in effect requires us to consider every candidate when it is first encountered.[20]

One further practical concern suggests additional utility of inference rules. Given the tendency toward increasingly exotic packaging technology, it is becoming more difficult to probe at random on a board. In such cases the inference rules become especially useful.

Finally, since the guided probe works directly from the schematic, it also inherits the fundamental problem noted earlier: the schematic may be wrong, and there is nothing in this approach capable of dealing with that problem.

Abramovici and Breuer have independently developed an approach to diagnosis that has a number of the features of a constraint-based system. Their deduction algorithm is similar to the use of inference and simulation rules in discrepancy detection, and they use multiple tests as we do to further prune the

---

[19]Some automatic testers use a board known to be good as the source of the correct values.

[20]The lack of inference rules and corresponding need to probe suggests that, where we earlier characterized our approach as the interaction of simulation and inference, the guided probe is analogously characterized as the interaction of simulation and measurement.

candidate set. One interesting result of their work is in its application to synchronous sequential circuits, where they show that this approach can diagnose a fault that prevents initialization (i.e., the initial states of the flipflops are unknown). This has long been a difficult roadblock for traditional fault-dictionary style diagnostics.

Drawbacks in the approach include its extensive use of inferences drawn from the fact that a wire can be labeled as 'normal' (i.e., it has been observed to take on all possible values). The label is easy to establish in the world of binary gates but clearly gets considerably more difficult for circuits modeled at higher levels. More seriously, the approach has been extensively explored for faults modelable as wires struck at 1 or 0, but does not appear to go beyond this. One of the examples in [1], for instance, produces a unique diagnosis for a circuit under the stuck-at model, but does not indicate that, among other possibilities, a malfunctioning OR-gate (*not* modelable as a stuck-at) is another, equally valid diagnosis. Finally, like other approaches that work solely from the schematic, it has no mechanism for considering that the schematic may be incorrect.

13.2. Fault models and categories of failure

In reviewing some of the traditional approaches to troubleshooting (Section 5), we noted several problems. We pointed out the historical trend toward using code originally designed for verification (proof that a device is totally free of faults) to do troubleshooting. We noted that code designed for verification requires fault models—if we are to avoid exhaustive testing, we need to limit our tests to errors produced by a pre-specified list of faults. We then claimed that we do not need traditional fault models when the task is diagnosis and when a fault is defined as anything different from the correct behavior.

Yet in doing discrepancy detection we found it necessary to come up with an apparently similar sort of list: we had to enumerate the categories of failure in order to limit the paths of interaction we considered. Have we in fact made any progress or have we simply substituted one list for another?

We claim that progress has been made along two fronts. First, by focusing on troubleshooting and defining a fault as any discrepancy, we can deal with a wider range of faults, including any systematic misbehavior. Second, we have taken a step toward providing a somewhat more formal way of generating the entries on the list. The traditional fault-model list is typically an informally generated listing of erroneous behaviors that have been observed in practice. Carefully examining the assumptions underlying our representation, as we did in Section 10, is in effect a 'generator' of categories. It produces a number of well-known categories (e.g., local failures like stuck-ats, assembly errors, design errors) and suggests some less obvious ones as well (e.g., direction of information flow errors). While it is still not a formally complete generator, we at least have some relatively systematic basis for enumerating categories of failure to consider.

13.3. Other AI work

As we have noted at several points above, a number of ideas developed in previous AI research have proved very useful in this undertaking.

13.3.1. Troubleshooting

From the work of Sussman and Steele on constraints, for example, we take the local propagation style of computation [32] and the maintenance of dependency networks [29]. Work by De Kleer first demonstrated [11] that a first-order theory of troubleshooting could be based on examining the dependency records left behind by a local propagator: any device on the path to a discrepancy should be considered a potential candidate; any device that participates in a 'corroboration' (a place where predicted and measured values agree) can be ruled out. We used the first half of this approach in our candidate generator, when Step 2 of Fig. 8 used the dependency network leading to a discrepancy to determine the potential candidates.

Our work moves beyond this in two ways: by viewing troubleshooting in the framework of methodical relaxation of assumptions, and by the use of constraint suspension. Relaxation of assumptions handles bridge faults, while the approach in [11] specifically excludes all such errors in topology. The approach there works by examining dependency records produced by the local propagator, but the propagator worked from the original schematic. Nothing in this approach provides a way of entertaining the idea that the original schematic was incorrect; there is no mechanism for hypothesizing additional paths of interaction not shown in the original description.

Constraint suspension provides two additional advantages. First, like the approach in [11], it determines which components might be at fault, but then it also determines symptom values for the candidates. This provided important information in solving the bridge fault problem in particular, and in general allows candidate generation to continue at successively lower levels of description.

Second, as noted in [11], the use of corroborations in the first-order theory above runs into trouble with any device whose behavior can inhibit propagation of an error (e.g., an AND-gate or multiplier whose other input is 0). Consider for example a slight modification to Fig. 7. If adder-2 were a fourth multiplier and input E were 0, we would get a corroboration at G (0 expected and observed), apparently exonerating mult-2. But in that circuit mult-2 would in fact be a valid candidate. Our constraint-suspension approach handles this situation without difficulty: by running the behavior descriptions of all but one component (the one being tested for candidacy), it effectively determines the appropriate consequences of all discrepancies and corroborations.

The approach in [11] was developed further in SOPHIE [6] to include knowledge of component-fault modes (e.g., resistors can be shorted, open, high or low), and to include knowledge about higher-level modules that was specific to the particular circuit and module. Our approach differs in using a uniform approach to device modeling and troubleshooting, where SOPHIE's troubleshooting of the high-level modules was handled using the circuit-specific knowledge (the first principles approach was used at the level of primitive components).

That system also noted the potential difficulties arising from implicit assumptions, and speculated about the use of a general truth-maintenance system to deal with the problem. This does not appear to have been implemented.

We have drawn from the work in [6] in some other respects, both for specific techniques and overall approach. That work demonstrated the use of simulation as a fundamental tool in troubleshooting (using it for example to predict observations from inputs and to predict consequences of failures). It showed how dependency chains could support hypothetical reasoning. The work also made clear the importance of 'mental hygiene' in building simulation models. Ideas like the 'no function in structure' concept were both directly useful (as noted in Section 12) and helped sensitize us to the importance of implicit assumptions.

That work also kept distinct the kinds of knowledge used in doing troubleshooting. The system relied on dependency records to generate the candidate set first, and only then used knowledge about component fault modes to prune the set.

13.3.2. Adjacency

The notion of adjacency has been pursued from several different directions, some of which proved useful in our own approach to the concept. The original conception of constraints [32] helped define the issue and characterize local propagation as a way of thinking about computation. Work by De Kleer [12] and De Kleer and Brown [13, 14] developed a number of principles involving local propagation when reasoning about cause and effect in physical devices.

A slightly different conception of adjacency underlies some of the work of Lenat [20]. There, syntactic changes to LISP descriptions produced useful new mathematical concepts because LISP and mathematics are languages that are 'close' together. That is, the primitives and method of composition are similar enough that the languages are structurally similar: concepts that are 'adjacent' mathematically often have LISP definitions that are quite similar. As a result, making small syntactic changes to a LISP expression that captured one mathematical concept often produced an expression embodying another meaningful mathematical concept.

This underscores the importance of the choice of representation language when making changes to a description: the changes will produce meaningful results to the extent that the languages share a definition of adjacency. A similar inspiration lies behind our analysis of the need for the 'right' representation in understanding different kinds of faults: the physical definition was appropriate for bridge faults because it provided the appropriate definition of adjacency.

In Section 11 we suggested that it can be useful to have several different definitions of adjacency, provided by the multiple representations (functional, physical, etc.) employed there. A related notion, multiple views of a circuit, shows up in the concept of slices [31] used in design. A central observation in that work was that simplifying the design task requires being able to have several different views of a circuit, each one packaging up things differently. The basis for the packaging is typically teleological: a particular section of a circuit is packaged up in a slice because it has an identifiable behavior that accomplishes a particular purpose. The design task can then be simplified by reasoning about the device using that abstraction, without being concerned about how that behavior is actually accomplished. Multiple slices can provide multiple views of the same section of the circuit; slices thus offer a mechanism for expressing multiple abstractions.

Our emphasis has been on using different definitions of what adjacent can mean in order to produce fundamentally different representations for troubleshooting. Slices may offer multiple different views of the circuit, but they are all functional views and share the same basic representational vocabulary (that of functional modules). We have both a functional representation with its definition of adjacency and its vocabulary, and a physical representation with its own distinct definition of adjacency and vocabulary (cabinets, boards, chips). Our focus is thus not on having multiple views of the device, but on having fundamentally different representations, and on carefully enumerating the different criteria (definitions of adjacency) that can be used as the basis for each representation. The definitions are in turn derived from the different pathways of interaction, since those pathways reflect the mechanisms by which faults manifest.

Finally, our categories of failure are similar in spirit to the class-wide assumptions in [13]. As pointed out there, it is impossible to write assumption-free descriptions of behavior. The problem manifests itself in the most basic terms in simply choosing a vocabulary. Any behavior description will be built from a finite vocabulary of terms, yet there is no obvious limit to the set of terms that *might* prove relevant (weight, color, flexibility, etc.). Since the vocabulary must be finite, it is important to provide at least an explicit, defensible set of selection criteria. The problem arises also in using a given vocabulary to describe a device. In describing a door bell, for example, the model in [13] needs to refer to the effect of the coil's magnetic field on the clapper, but it invokes the common assumption that the field is not strong enough to induce currents in nearby wires. Again there should be explicit, defensible grounds for making such assumptions.

The authors suggest that introductory physics provides a convenient and

routinely, if tacitly, used set of criteria; they term them 'class-wide assumptions'. These are assumptions about behavior whose utility (and credibility)
arises in part because they apply to whole sets of devices. Ignoring the effect of
the magnetic field on nearby wires, for example, is a reasonable assumption
because it applies to a wide class of devices.

Our categories of failure are similar in spirit. We are motivated by the same
original consideration, namely that it is impossible to create assumption-free
descriptions of structure and behavior. We have made the identification and
handling of such assumptions a primary concern and have been able to provide
a somewhat more systematic generation of the categories. Since De Kleer and
Brown are concerned with qualitative physics, they appropriately look to that
field for inspiration and have the task of identifying and accumulating the
assumptions. Our more tightly focused concern—troubleshooting—allows us to
examine what kinds of things can go wrong, and makes possible the relatively
systematic generation of assumptions accomplished by perturbing the
representation, as we did in Section 10.

This also reflects our concern with enumerating the pathways of interaction
as completely as possible. While class-wide assumptions reflect important
knowledge about the domain, that knowledge is often in the form of a reason
not to include a particular pathway of interaction (e.g., omitting the path from
the coil to nearby wires in the door-bell example). We want to press one step
further on by building a list of possible pathways that is as systematic as
possible, and then consider the variety of fault characterized by the existence
(or omission) of such a pathway.

14. Summary

We seek to build a system that reasons from first principles in understanding
how devices operate. We find troubleshooting of digital hardware to be a
tractable and fertile ground for exploration. We have developed languages
describing structure and behavior that distinguish carefully between them, and
provide information about structure that is organized both functionally and
physically.

We find that the traditional machinery for troubleshooting focuses primarily
on test generation and its use in verification of device behavior. Our problem is
better characterized as diagnosis in the presence of known symptoms, in
devices complex enough that it is important to use the symptoms to help guide
the troubleshooting.

We view the process as the interaction of simulation and inference, with
discrepancies between them driving the generation of candidates. Discrepancy
detection and tracing through dependency records gives us a foundation for
troubleshooting that identifies potential candidates. The technique of constraint
suspension extends this by supplying symptom values for the candidates and
handling both discrepancies and corroborations with a single mechanism.

In exploring this approach further, we find that the concept of paths of causal interaction plays a key role, supplying the knowledge that makes the machinery work. We need an explicit model of causal interactions in order to determine which components to consider. The amount of such knowledge then leads us to a fundamental dilemma: the desire to deal with a wide range of faults seems to force us to choose between an inability to discriminate among candidates and the inability to deal with some classes of faults.

In response we have developed a troubleshooting strategy based on the methodical enumeration and relaxation of underlying assumptions about the device. We were able to generate the assumptions in a relatively systematic fashion by examining the module and information path representation of hardware. By considering the consequences of violating each assumption, we were able to generate a collection of categories of failure.

We then invoked a version of Occam's razor, noting that some categories of failure are more likely than others. This provides a criterion for ordering the categories and pathways of interaction to be considered. We start with the simplest category of failure first and consider only one class of paths of interaction initially. If this fails to generate a consistent hypothesis, we surrender one of our underlying assumptions, adding the next category of failure, and consider an additional pathway of interaction.

We illustrated this approach by diagnosing a bridge fault. When our initial categorization—local failure of function—encountered a contradiction, we surrendered the assumption that the schematic was correct and considered one additional path, bridges. This staged relaxation of assumptions permitted a constrained generation of hypotheses. Within the bridge-fault category, additional restriction was then provided by using constraints associated with both the physical and functional representations.

Drawing back from this specific example, we explored several possible generalizations of the work. We found applicability in software, for example, for the notion of enumerating the assumptions in the representation and using this to generate categories of failure. While the particular pathways of interaction were different, the technique appears to phrase a relevant set of questions. We found that some errors in software are usefully thought of in terms of a set of pathways of interaction from that domain.

Our overall approach also suggests that part of the expertise of a domain lies in knowing how to simplify a problem, i.e., knowing what simplifying assumptions can be made, recognizing when an assumption has failed to help, and knowing how to recover and get the solution back on course. Enumerating and ordering the categories of failure provides one simple mechanism for expressing such knowledge.

A further generalization of this work came from examining the difficulty involved in dealing with bridge faults. We found that an important property of a representation is its definition of adjacency. In this view bridge faults are difficult because they are simple and local changes to the physical representation, but neither simple nor local in our original, functional representation. We started with the functional representation because we were presented with behavioral manifestations of a fault, and hence needed to reason from a representation organized according to behavior. But this proved to have an inappropriate definition of adjacency for the problem at hand, so we shifted representations. This in turn lead us to a useful guideline in choosing representations for diagnostic reasoning: we should attempt to find a representation in which the suspected change can be viewed as a compact modification affecting adjacent devices.

The underlying rationale for focusing on defining adjacency is a belief that faults manifest through processes that act locally, i.e., there is no action at a distance. We then found that we could define a number of useful kinds of adjacency by considering the paths of interaction. Each of these defines a different metric (Euclidean, thermal, electromagnetic, etc.), each generating a different representation.

We pursued this one additional step, asking why we believe there will in fact be some representation in which the fault can be seen as compact. The belief appears to rest on the heuristic that a malfunction in a previously operational device often results from a single cause rather than a number of independent events. Like any heuristic, this may not always be correct, since multiple, independent failures do occur. But it is true often enough and there are substantial advantages to choosing a representation with a good definition of adjacency.

Because our basic representation machinery employs little more than the traditional black-box notion of information transmission, we suggest that some of the central concepts in this work may have relevance of considerable breadth. The examination of assumptions underlying the representation and constraint suspension, for instance, appear to be applicable in a number of different areas. We noted above the potential use in software of examining underlying assumptions. We conjecture that both techniques may apply to any system that might be modeled in terms of information transmission, ranging from hardware, to software, to organizations. Organizations may have pathways of interaction other than those on the personnel chart, for example, and we might consider 'organization troubleshooting' via constraint suspension.

Finally, we observe that there has been growing focus on the power contributed by choosing a 'good' representation and the utility of multiple representations. We suggest that one of the characteristics of a good representation is that it provides a definition of adjacency that makes the fault appear compact, and that the utility of multiple representations arises in part from the multiple different definitions of adjacency they provide.

ACKNOWLEDGMENT

Contributions to this work were made by members of the Hardware Troubleshooting project at MIT, including: Howie Shrobe, Walter Hamscher, Mark Shirley, Harold Haig, Art Mellor, John Pitrelli, and Steve Polit.

Some of the initial inspiration for this work came from conversations with Ed Feigenbaum; periodic arguments with Mike Genesereth have helped sharpen vague intuitions and were an early source of specific examples. The presentation in this paper was improved by comments from John Seeley Brown, Johan De Kleer, Ken Forbus, Doug Hofstader, Mark Shirley, and Patrick Winston.

REFERENCES

1. Abramovici, M. and Breuer, M.A., Fault diagnosis in synchronous sequential circuits based on an effect-cause analysis, *IEEE Trans. Comput.* **31** (1982) 1165–1172.
2. Barbacci, M.R., Instruction set processor specifications (ISPS): The notation and its applications, Carnegie-Mellon University Tech. Rept. CMU-CS-79-123, Pittsburgh, PA, 1979.
3. Batali, J. and Hartheimer, A., The design procedure language manual, MIT AI Memo 598, Cambridge, MA, 1980.
4. Bell, G. and Newell, A., *Computer Structures: Readings and Examples* (McGraw-Hill, New York, 1971).
5. Breuer, M.A. and Friedman, A., *Diagnosis and Reliable Design of Digital Systems* (Computer Science Press, Rockville, MD, 1976).
6. Brown, J.S., Burton, R. and De Kleer, J., Pedagogical and knowledge engineering techniques in SOPHIE I, II and III, in: D.H. Sleeman and J.S. Brown (Eds.), *Intelligent Tutoring Systems* (Academic Press, New York, 1982).
7. Davis, R., Shrobe, H., Hamscher, W., Wieckert, K., Shirley, M. and Polit, S., Diagnosis based on structure and function, in: *Proceedings National Conference on Artificial Intelligence*, Pittsburgh, PA (August, 1982) 137–142.
8. Davis, R., Reasoning from first principles in electronic troubleshooting. *Internat. J. Man–Mach. Stud.* **19** (1983) 403–423.
9. Davis, R., Buchanan, B.G. and Shortliffe, E.H., Production rules as a representation in a knowledge-based consultation system, *Artificial Intelligence* **8** (1977) 15–45.
10. Davis, R. and Shrobe, H.E., Representing structure and behavior of digital hardware, *IEEE Trans. Comput.* **32** (1983) 75–82.
11. De Kleer, J., Local methods for localizing faults in electronic circuits, MIT AI Memo 394, Cambridge, MA, 1976.
12. De Kleer, J., The origin and resolution of ambiguities in causal arguments, in: *Proceedings Sixth International Joint Conference on Artificial Intelligence*, Tokyo, Japan (August, 1979) 197–203.
13. De Kleer, J. and Brown, J.S., Assumptions and ambiguities in mechanistic mental models, Xerox PARC Rept. CIS-9, Palo Alto, CA, 1982.
14. De Kleer, J. and Brown J.S., Naive physics based on confluences, Xerox Parc Rept., 1983.
15. Doyle, J., A truth maintenance system, *Artificial Intelligence* **12** (1979) 231–272.
16. Estrin, G., A methodology for design of digital systems—supported by SARA at the age of one, in: *Proceedings NCC* (1978) 313–324.

17. Gasching, J., Preliminary evaluation of the performance of the PROSPECTOR system for mineral exploration, in: *Proceedings Seventh International Joint Conference on Artificial Intelligence*, Vancouver, BC (August, 1981) 308–310.
18. Genesereth, M., The use of hierarchical models in the automated diagnosis of computer systems, Stanford HPP Memo 81-20, Stanford, CA, 1981.
19. Kelly, V. and Steinberg, L., The CRITTER system—Analyzing digital circuits by propagating behaviors and specifications, in: *Proceedings National Conference on Artificial Intelligence*, Pittsburgh, PA (August, 1982) 284–289.
20. Lenat, D., Heuretics: theoretical and experimental study of heuristic rules, in: *Proceedings National Conference on Artificial Intelligence*, Pittsburgh, PA (August, 1982) 159–163.
21. Lim, W.Y-P., HISDL—A structure description language, *Comm. ACM* **25** (1982) 823–830.
22. Newell, A. and Simon, H., *Human Problem Solving* (Prentice-Hall, Englewood Cliffs, NJ, 1972).
23. Patil, R., Szolovits, P. and Schwartz, W., Causal understanding of patient illness in medical diagnosis in: *Proceedings Seventh International Joint Conference on Artificial Intelligence*, Vancouver, BC (August, 1981) 893–899.
24. Pople, H., Heuristic methods for imposing structure on ill-structured problems, in: P. Szolovits (Ed.), *Artificial Intelligence in Medicine*, AAAS Selected Symposium 51, 1982.
25. Reiger, C.R. and Grinberg, M., A system for cause-effect representation and simulation for computer-aided design, in: J.-C. Latombe (Ed.), *Artificial Intelligence and Pattern Recognition in Computer-Aided Design* (North-Holland, Amsterdam, 1978) 299–334.
26. Roth, J.P., Diagnosis of automata failures: A calculus and a method, *IBM J. Res. Develop.* **10** (1966) 278–291.
27. Shirley, M. and Davis, R., Digital test generation from hierarchical models and symptom information, in: *Proceedings IEEE International Conference on Computer Design*, November, 1983.
28. Shortliffe, E., *Computer-Based Medical Consultations: Mycin* (American Elsevier, New York, 1976).
29. Stallman, R.M. and Sussman, G.J., Forward reasoning and dependency-directed backtracking in a system for computer-aided circuit analysis, *Artificial Intelligence* **9** (1977) 135–196.
30. Steele, G., The definition and implementation of a computer programming language based on constraints, MIT TR-595, Cambridge, CA, 1980.
31. Sussman, G.J., Slices: At the boundary between analysis and synthesis, in: J.-C. Latombe (Ed.), *Artificial Intelligence and Pattern Recognition in Computer-Aided Design* (North-Holland, Amsterdam, 1978) 261–299.
32. Sussman, G.J. and Steele, G., Constraints—a language for expressing almost-hierarchical descriptions, *Artificial Intelligence* **14** (1980) 1–40.
33. Van Cleemput, W.M., An hierarchical language for the structural description of digital systems, in: *Proceedings Fourteenth Design Automation Conference*, New Orleans, LA (1977) 377–385.
34. Winston, P., *Artificial Intelligence* (Addison-Wesley, Reading, MA, 2nd ed., 1984).

Received August 1983; revised version received November 1983

The Use of Design Descriptions in Automated Diagnosis

Michael R. Genesereth

Department of Computer Science, School of Humanities and Sciences, Stanford University, Stanford, CA 94305, U.S.A.

ABSTRACT

This paper describes a device-independent diagnostic program called DART. DART differs from previous approaches to diagnosis taken in the Artificial Intelligence community in that it works directly from design descriptions rather than MYCIN-like symptom-fault rules. DART differs from previous approaches to diagnosis taken in the design-automation community in that it is more general and in many cases more efficient. DART uses a device-independent language for describing devices and a device-independent inference procedure for diagnosis. The resulting generality allows it to be applied to a wide class of devices ranging from digital logic to nuclear reactors. Although this generality engenders some computational overhead on small problems, it facilitates the use of multiple design descriptions and thereby makes possible combinatoric savings that more than offsets this overhead on problems of realistic size.

1. Introduction

Continuing advances in the technology of design and manufacturing have led to artifacts of unprecedented complexity. Devices like VLSI chips, nuclear power plants, and jet aircraft are among the most complex physical objects ever created by man. Unfortunately, the physical components from which these devices are built are subject to failure; and, given current design practices, the failure of a single component can lead to the malfunction of an entire device. The key disadvantage of complexity is that it makes the diagnosis of such component failures more difficult.

The DART program is an automated diagnostician aimed at dealing with this complexity. The program is intended for use in conjunction with a tester that can manipulate and observe a malfunctioning device, as suggested by Fig. 1. The diagnostician accepts from the tester a description of an observed malfunction, prescribes tests and accepts the results, and ultimately identifies the faulty components responsible for the malfunction.

DART was developed in the context of moderately successful work on medical

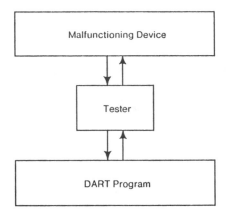

FIG. 1. Automated diagnosis of equipment failures.

diagnosis, as exemplified by such programs as INTERNIST [10, 11] and MYCIN [14]. However, there's a difference. These medical diagnosis programs both use 'shallow' theories of human pathophysiology in the form of 'rules' that associate symptoms with possible diseases. The DART program contains no rules of this form. Instead, it works directly from a 'deep' theory consisting of information about intended structure (a device's parts and their interconnections) and expected behavior (equations, rules, or procedures that relate the device's 'inputs', 'outputs', and 'state').

An important advantage of this approach is that it greatly simplifies the task of building diagnosticians for new devices. If a designer uses a modern computer-aided design system like PALLADIO [2], then when he is done there is an on-line description of his design. This description can be passed as data to the DART program to diagnose its faults. Similarly, this design information can be passed to a program to simulate the device, a program to verify and evaluate the design, a program to generate testing codes, and a program to generate fabrication instructions. See Fig. 2.

The idea of using design information in automated diagnosis is hardly a new one. Over the years a number of test-generation algorithms have been proposed in the domain of computer hardware [1], the most well-known of which is the d-algorithm [13]. The primary disadvantage of these algorithms is their specificity. For example, the d-algorithm is based on Boolean algebra (or, more precisely, Roth's 'd-calculus'), and so it is applicable only to devices whose behavior can be characterized in terms of ones and zeros.

By contrast DART uses a device-independent language for design description and a device-independent diagnostic procedure. All device-dependent information is contained in the design descriptions it uses. Because of this generality, DART can diagnose a wider class of devices than the d-algorithm, including non-digital and non-electronic devices.

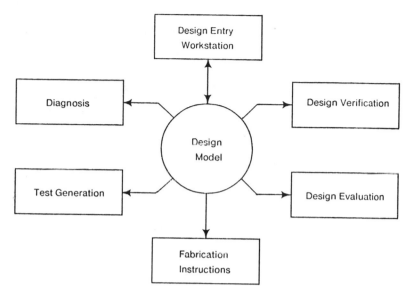

FIG. 2. An integrated-design environment.

Interestingly, this generality can also promote enhanced efficiency. The device-independence of the design language and diagnostic procedure makes it easy to apply the program at multiple levels of abstraction and thereby exploit the hierarchy inherent in most computer-system designs. The power of the design language and diagnostic procedure makes it easy to use symbolic constraint propagation techniques [17, 18] and thereby avoid unnecessary combinatorics.

This paper describes the DART program in detail and discusses the role of design descriptions in diagnosis. Section 2 shows how design can be formally described, and Section 3 formalizes the description of actual devices. The concepts of fault, symptom, and diagnosis are defined in Section 4, and the DART program is described in Section 5. Section 6 discusses the interrelationship between the choice of design description and the completeness and efficiency of diagnosis. The conclusion discusses the state of implementation and testing of DART, offers some directions for future work, and summarizes the key points of the paper. This paper is an expanded version of a previous publication [6].

2. Design Description

In this paper a *design* is broadly defined as any arrangement of the world that achieves a desired result for known reasons. The arrangement can be artificial (e.g. a computer system), or it can be natural (e.g. the human circulatory system). The desired result can be a specific situation, or it can be a behavior that varies from one situation to another. What differentiates a design from a coincidence is that its result is explanable in terms of an assumed theory of the world.

A digital circuit like the 'full-adder' is a good example. A full-adder is essentially a one-bit adder with carry-in and carry-out, and it is usually used as one of n elements in an n-bit adder. A graphical representation of its design is given in Fig. 3. It has three inputs and two outputs and consists of two XOR-gates (X1 and X2), two AND-gates (A1 and A2) and an OR-gate (O1). A tabular representation of its behavior is given in Fig. 4. In normal operation, the first output (the 'sum line') is 'on' if and only if an odd number of inputs is 'on'; and second output (the 'carry line') is 'on' if and only if at least two inputs are 'on'. Behavioral tables for the components in Fig. 3 are given in Fig. 5. Using this information, it is possible to prove that the design in Fig. 3 achieves the behavior in Fig. 4.

In DART all descriptions are written as propositions in a variant of prefix predicate calculus. Upper case letters are used exclusively for constants, function symbols, and relation symbols, while lower case letters are used for variables. Prefix universal quantifiers are dropped, and all free variables are universally quantified.

For example, the propositions in Fig. 6 constitute a design description for the device in Fig. 3. Each part is designated by an atomic name (e.g. A1). The structural type of each part is declared using type relations, as in the first five propositions: X1 and X2 are XOR-gates, A1 and A2 are AND-gates, and O1 is an OR-gate. The 'inputs' and 'outputs' (or 'ports') of each device are named using the functions IN and OUT. For example, (IN 2 F1) designates the second input of F1, and (OUT 2 F1) designates the second output of F1. Connections are made between the ports of devices. The remaining propositions specify the wiring diagram for F1. The sixth proposition states that the first input to F1 is connected to the first input of X1; the last proposition states that the output of O1 is connected to the second output of F1.

The propositions in Fig. 7 describe the behavior of a full-adder. The function

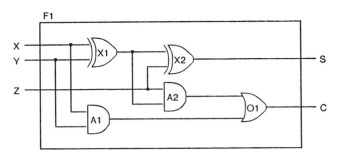

FIG. 3. Design of the full-adder F1.

X	Y	Z	S	C
0	0	0	0	0
0	0	1	1	0
0	1	0	1	0
0	1	1	0	1
1	0	0	1	0
1	0	1	0	1
1	1	0	0	1
1	1	1	1	1

FIG. 4. Behavior of the full-adder F1.

AND-gates		
0	0	0
0	1	0
1	0	0
1	1	1

OR-gates		
0	0	0
0	1	1
1	0	1
1	1	1

XOR-gates		
0	0	0
0	1	1
1	0	1
1	1	0

Connections	
0	0
1	1

FIG. 5. Behavior of various gates.

```
SD1:   (XORG X1)
SD2:   (XORG X2)
SD3:   (ANDG A1)
SD4:   (ANDG A2)
SD5:   (ORG O1)

SD6:   (CONN (IN 1 F1) (IN 1 X1))
SD7:   (CONN (IN 1 F1) (IN 1 A1))
SD8:   (CONN (IN 2 F1) (IN 2 X1))
SD9:   (CONN (IN 2 F1) (IN 2 A1))
SD10:  (CONN (IN 3 F1) (IN 2 X2))
SD11:  (CONN (IN 3 F1) (IN 1 A2))
SD12:  (CONN (OUT 1 X1) (IN 1 X2))
SD13:  (CONN (OUT 1 X1) (IN 2 A2))
SD14:  (CONN (OUT 1 A1) (IN 2 O1))
SD15:  (CONN (OUT 1 A2) (IN 1 O1))
SD16:  (CONN (OUT 1 X2) (OUT 1 F1))
SD17:  (CONN (OUT 1 O1) (OUT 2 F1))
```

FIG. 6. Structural description for the full-adder F1.

BD1: (IF (AND (VAL (IN 1 F1) t OFF) (VAL (IN 2 F1) t OFF) (VAL (IN 3 F1) t OFF))
     (AND (VAL (OUT 1 F1) t OFF) (VAL (OUT 2 F1) t OFF)))

BD2: (IF (AND (VAL (IN 1 F1) t OFF) (VAL (IN 2 F1) t OFF) (VAL (IN 3 F1) t ON))
     (AND (VAL (OUT 1 F1) t ON) (VAL (OUT 2 F1) t OFF)))

BD3: (IF (AND (VAL (IN 1 F1) t OFF) (VAL (IN 2 F1) t ON) (VAL (IN 3 F1) t OFF))
     (AND (VAL (OUT 1 F1) t ON) (VAL (OUT 2 F1) t OFF)))

BD4: (IF (AND (VAL (IN 1 F1) t OFF) (VAL (IN 2 F1) t ON) (VAL (IN 3 F1) t ON))
     (AND (VAL (OUT 1 F1) t OFF) (VAL (OUT 2 F1) t ON)))

BD5: (IF (AND (VAL (IN 1 F1) t ON) (VAL (IN 2 F1) t OFF) (VAL (IN 3 F1) t OFF))
     (AND (VAL (OUT 1 F1) t ON) (VAL (OUT 2 F1) t OFF)))

BD6: (IF (AND (VAL (IN 1 F1) t ON) (VAL (IN 2 F1) t OFF) (VAL (IN 3 F1) t ON))
     (AND (VAL (OUT 1 F1) t OFF) (VAL (OUT 2 F1) t ON)))

BD7: (IF (AND (VAL (IN 1 F1) t ON) (VAL (IN 2 F1) t ON) (VAL (IN 3 F1) t OFF))
     (AND (VAL (OUT 1 F1) t OFF) (VAL (OUT 2 F1) t ON)))

BD8: (IF (AND (VAL (IN 1 F1) t ON) (VAL (IN 2 F1) t ON) (VAL (IN 3 F1) t ON))
     (AND (VAL (OUT 1 F1) t ON) (VAL (OUT 2 F1) t ON)))

FIG. 7. Behavioral description for the full-adder F1.

TH1: (IF (AND (ANDG d) (VAL (IN 1 d) t ON) (VAL (IN 2 d) t ON))
      (VAL (OUT 1 d) t ON))
TH2: (IF (AND (ANDG d) (VAL (IN 1 d) t OFF))
      (VAL (OUT 1 d) t OFF))
TH3: (IF AND (ANDG d) (VAL (IN 2 d) t OFF))
      (VAL (OUT 1 d) t OFF))

TH4: (IF (AND (ORG d) (VAL (IN 1 d) t OFF) (VAL (IN 2 d) t OFF))
      (VAL (OUT 1 d) t OFF))
TH5: (IF (AND (ORG d) (VAL (IN 1 d) t ON))
      (VAL (OUT 1 d) t ON))
TH6: (IF (AND (ORG d) (VAL (IN 2 d) t ON))
      (VAL (OUT 1 d) t ON))

TH7: (IF (AND (XORG d) (VAL (IN 1 d) t ON) (VAL (IN 2 d) t ON))
      (VAL (OUT 1 d) t OFF))
TH8: (IF (AND (XORG d) (VAL (IN 1 d) t ON) (VAL (IN 2 d) t OFF))
      (VAL (OUT 1 d) t OFF))
TH9: (IF (AND (XORG d) (VAL (IN 1 d) t OFF) (VAL (IN 2 d) t ON))
      (VAL (OUT 1 d) t ON))
TH10: (IF (AND XORG d) (VAL (IN 1 d) t OFF) (VAL (IN 2 d) t OFF))
      (VAL (OUT 1 d) t OFF))

TH11: (IF (AND (CONN x y) (VAL x t z))
      (VAL y t z))

FIG. 8. Behavioral description of logic gates and connections.

symbol VAL is used to designate the signal value on a port at a given time. For example, the proposition (VAL (IN 2 F1) 3 ON) states that at time 3, the second input of F1 is 'on'. The proposition (VAL (OUT 2 F1) t OFF) states that the second output of F1 is always 'off'. The eight propositions in Fig. 7 capture the eight cases illustrated in Fig. 4.

The behavior of components can be expressed similarly. The propositions in Fig. 8 illustrate. The first three propositions describe the behavior of an AND-gate. The next three describe the behavior of an OR-gate. The four thereafter describe an XOR-gate. The final proposition describes the behavior of an ideal connection. A variation of this rule is discussed in Section 6.2.

3. Device Description

A *device* is any physical realization of a design. Unfortunately, due to fabrication errors and physical failures, the actual structure of a device may differ from its intended structure, and this can give rise to differences in behavior. The information in a device description comes from a variety of sources.

Theoretical information includes the definitions and theorems used in proving the correctness of a device. For example, in the case of the full-adder it would be relevant to include the propositions from Fig. 8 in F1's device description as well as its design description.

Achievable data are propositions that can be made true by a tester. This can include structural modifications of which the tester is capable, such as part swaps and the addition of testing equipment. More typically, it involves modifications to the environment of a device, such as setting the values of its inputs. For example, the propositions in Fig. 9 describe a sequence of inputs that a tester has applied to the full-adder F1.

Observable data are propositions that can be directly observed by a tester. In some cases the actual structure of a device can be observed. Boards can be visually inspected, and chips can be examined microscopically. However, observations of behavior are more common. For example, the propositions in Fig. 10 describe the output values resulting from the inputs in Fig. 9.

Unfortunately, it is not possible to diagnose all malfunctions using just theoretical, achievable, and observable data. And even when it is possible, it is

AC1: (VAL (IN 1 F1) 1 ON)
AC2: (VAL (IN 2 F1) 1 OFF)
AC3: (VAL (IN 3 F1) 1 OFF)

AC4: (VAL (IN 1 F1) 2 ON)
AC5: (VAL (IN 2 F1) 2 OFF)
AC6: (VAL (IN 3 F1) 2 ON)

FIG. 9. Achievable data concerning the full-adder F1.

OB1: (VAL (OUT 1 F1) 1 OFF)
OB2: (VAL (OUT 2 F1) 1 OFF)

OB3: (VAL (OUT 2 F1) 2 OFF)

FIG. 10. Observable data concerning the full-adder F1.

often impractical. For these reasons it is customary to augment this hard data with some assumptions about the malfunctioning device, as in Fig. 11.

A common example is the assumption that certain parts of the device's design description are correct. For example, the connections in a circuit may be guaranteed correct and the functionality of the components may be in doubt, or vice versa. In the examples below, all connections are assumed to be correct.

The single-fault assumption (SFA) states that there is at most one faulty component in a circuit. This idea can be formalized by stating that the failure of any component implies the functionality of the others. The next five propositions in Fig. 11 specify the single-fault assumption for the components of F1. The single-fault assumption can be stated more succinctly as a single proposition that applies to all components, but that rendition is slightly more complicated than the one given here.

The non-intermittency assumption (NIA) states that all devices behave consistently over time. This is patently false in general, for it implies that no part can ever fail. However, it is often a reasonable assumption to make for the

DA1:   (CONN (IN 1 F1) (IN 1 X1))
DA2:   (CONN (IN 1 F1) (IN 1 A1))
DA3:   (CONN (IN 2 F1) (IN 2 X1))
DA4:   (CONN (IN 2 F1) (IN 2 A1))
DA5:   (CONN (IN 3 F1) (IN 2 X2))
DA6:   (CONN (IN 3 F1) (IN 1 A2))
DA7:   (CONN (OUT 1 X1) (IN 1 X2))
DA8:   (CONN (OUT 1 X1) (IN 2 A2))
DA9:   (CONN (OUT 1 A1) (IN 2 O1))
DA10: (CONN (OUT 1 A2) (IN 1 O1))
DA11: (CONN (OUT 1 X2) (OUT 1 F1))
DA12: (CONN (OUT 1 O1) (OUT 2 F1))

DA13: (IF (NOT (XORG X1)) (AND (XORG X2) (ANDG A1) (ANDG A2) (ORG O1)))
DA14: (IF (NOT (XORG X2)) (AND (XORG X1) (ANDG A1) (ANDG A2) (ORG O1)))
DA15: (IF (NOT (ANDG A1)) (AND (XORG X1) (XORG X2) (ANDG A2) (ORG O1)))
DA16: (IF (NOT (ANDG A2)) (AND (XORG X1) (XORG X2) (ANDG A1) (ORG O1)))
DA17: (IF (NOT (ORG 01)) (AND (XORG X1) (XORG X2) (ANDG A1) (ANDG A2)))

DA18: (IF (AND (VAL (IN 1 d) s x) (VAL (IN 2 d) s y) (VAL (OUT 1 d) s z)
                (VAL (IN 1 d) t x) (VAL (IN 2 d) t y))
           (VAL (OUT 1 d) t z))

FIG. 11. Device assumptions for the full-adder F1.

duration of a diagnosis. A formal statement of the non-intermittency assumption follows the single-fault propositions in Fig. 11. It says that, if a device with specific inputs has a given output at one time, then given the same inputs it will have the same output at any other time.

Assumptions like these are extremely *important to* the efficiency of a diagnostic procedure like DART as well as to its competence in diagnosing difficult malfunctions. However, it is important to emphasize that they are not *part of* the procedure. They can be included or not at the discretion of the user. This flexibility is essential for situations in which the assumptions are wrong. For example, there may be more than one fault in a device, or the device may be malfunctioning intermittently. The inappropriateness of an assumption usually manifests itself as a contradiction. Davis [3] discusses some approaches to relaxing assumptions to deal with such contradictions.

4. Diagnosis

A *fault* is any discrepancy between the actual structure of a device and its design. In DART terms this corresponds to any proposition from the device's design description that is not true of the device itself and, therefore, is inconsistent with its device description. For example, if the component X1 of the full-adder F1 were broken, the proposition describing its type would be incorrect.

When a device is faulty, its behavior can differ from what is predicted from its design. In DART terms, a *symptom* is any observable proposition that, when added to a device description, makes it inconsistent with the device's intended behavior. For example, given the achievable data in Fig. 9, the first observation in Fig. 10 is a symptom of some fault in F1, because it disagrees with the behavioral description in Fig. 7.

The goal of *diagnosis* is to determine the fault or faults responsible for a set of symptoms. The diagnosis of a fault can be considered complete if the device description contains sufficient information to prove it. For example, from the information in Figs. 8, 9, 10, and 11, it is possible to prove (NOT (XORG X1)), i.e. that X1 is broken. Of course, a circuit may have more than one fault.

The purpose of diagnostic testing is to obtain sufficient information to complete a diagnosis. Of course, some faults are *undiagnosable* in that there is no set of achievable and observable data that allows them to be distinguished from each other.

The importance of design information in diagnosis can best be seen by thinking of the process as one of theory formation. Starting with a set of data about a device, the goal of diagnosis is to produce a description of its actual structure. Without the design description, diagnosing a device is indistinguishable from designing a device that exhibits the observed behavior. *A design description constrains the kinds of theories that the diagnostician can form by forcing it to consider only propositions from the design description or their negations.*

5. The DART Program

DART is a device-independent diagnostician that works directly from information about the design of a malfunctioning device. Given a set of symptoms, it generates tests, accepts the results, and ultimately pinpoints at least one fault in the device or an undiagnosable cluster containing a fault.

5.1. Overview

DART begins with a design description for a malfunctioning device and a partial

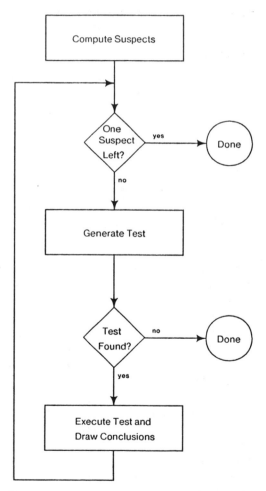

FIG. 12. Flowchart for the DART program.

device description. For device F1, the design description would include the propositions in Fig. 6. A typical device description might include the theoretical propositions and assumptions in Figs. 8 and 11 together with the achievable and observable propositions from Figs. 9 and 10 relevant to time 1.

A flowchart for DART appears in Fig. 12. The program first computes a set of suspect propositions. If this set contains only one element, the diagnosis is done. Otherwise, DART tries to generate a test to discriminate the suspects. If it is successful, the resulting test is executed, its consequences are computed, and the process repeats. Otherwise, the set of suspects is returned as value.

Note that DART does *not* generate a complete diagnostic tree before executing tests. The reason for this is efficiency. Although complete diagnostic planning has the advantage of minimizing the cost of test execution, the computational cost of constructing a complete diagnostic tree is usually prohibitive.

5.2. Computing suspects

The goal of suspect computation is to identify a subset of the design description within which some fault is guaranteed to lie. In computing a suspect set, DART starts with the observed symptoms and tries to deduce a proposition of the following form, where each p_i is a statement from the circuit's design description not already known to be true. Obviously, the smaller the set, the better.

(OR (NOT p1) . . . (NOT pn))

As an example, consider the symptom in Fig. 10 relevant to time 1. Since the first output of F1 is not 'on' and the output of X2 is connected to it, then the connection rule requires that the output of X2 must not be 'on' either. Since the output of X2 is not 'on', then either it is not a functioning XOR-gate or it is not the case that its two inputs are 'on' and 'off'. However, the second input must be 'off', since it is connected to the third input of F1, and that is known to be 'off'. If the first input is not 'on', then the output of X1 must not be 'on', and this could only be the case if X1 is not a functioning XOR-gate, since its inputs are known to be 'on' and 'off'. Thus, either X1 or X2 is broken.

(OR (NOT (XORG X1)) (NOT (XORG X2)))

One thing to note is that suspect computation is not simply a matter of tracing a design diagram backwards from a faulty output. On the one hand, this can lead to too many suspects. For example, tracing backwards from the second output of F1 leads to four components, yet an error in the second output with the input data above implies there is a fault in one of the three components A1, O1 and A2. X1 may have a fault, but it is not involved in this error and shouldn't be included in the suspect set.

On the other hand, simply tracing backwards can also lead to too few suspects. For example, it would rule out the possibility that components elsewhere in the circuit could have any bearing on the symptom and so would make it impossible to diagnose short circuits.

A second thing to note is that in some situations it is possible to derive several different suspect sets. There may be several symptoms, each giving rise to its own suspect set. For example, given inputs 'on', 'off', and 'on', an error in the first output of F1 would implicate X1 and X2, and a simultaneous error in the second output would implicate X1, A2, and O1. It is also possible to generate several suspect lists from a single symptom. For example, if all three inputs to F1 were 'off', an error in the second output of F1 would implicate X1, A2, O1, and A1 through one line of argument, and it would implicate just A2, O1, and A1 through a different line of argument.

When a device description includes the single-fault assumption, it is possible to intersect multiple suspect sets. In the first case, this would immediately identify X1 as the culprit. In the second case, it would narrow the suspect set to A1, A2, and O1. Note that in order to get as small a bound as possible on the suspects, it may be necessary to deduce and intersect all suspect sets. Due to the decidability of the suspect computation for most design descriptions, this is usually possible and frequently practical.

5.3. Generating tests

The goal of diagnostic testing is to gather data to help confirm or disconfirm the propositions in the suspect set. Of course, some data are more valuable than other data in this regard. Test generation is the process of deciding which data to gather.

In DART a *test* consists of zero or more propositions to be achieved and at least one proposition to be observed. One way to generate a test is to assume some set of possible faults, select a set of achievable propositions (e.g. input values), and simulate the circuit to predict an observable (i.e. an output value). The problem with this approach is that the resulting test may not depend on any of the suspects. The diagnostician may be forced to try numerous sets of achievables before coming upon one that supplies any information about the malfunction. This may be okay for small devices like the full-adder, but it is unacceptable for large devices like VLSI chips and entire computer systems, where the number of input combinations is astronomically large.

The alternative used by DART is to start with one of the suspect propositions and try to deduce a proposition of the following form, where each of the a_i is an achievable proposition, where each of the p_i is a suspect proposition, and where ob is an observable proposition.

```
(IF (AND a1 ... am ob)
    (OR (NOT p1) ... (NOT pn)))
```

As an example, consider the problem of computing a test to discriminate the suspects computed in the last section. DART begins the test-generation process with the tautologies

(IF (XORG X1) (XORG X1))   and   (IF (XORG X2) (XORG X2))

one for each suspect. Applying resolution residue (see Section 5.5) to the former of these leads to the test shown below. The right-hand side of the tautology unifies with the behavioral rules for X1, in particular the rule stating that, if the gate's two inputs are 'on' and 'off' respectively, its output is 'on'. This value propagates to the input of A2; and, if the third input to F1 is 'on', the value also propagates to the output of A2. It then propagates to the input of O1, to the output of O1, and finally to the second output of F1. In summary, if the inputs to F1 are 'on', 'off', and 'on', the second output must be 'on' so long as X1 is working properly. This is equivalent to saying that, if the inputs are 'on', 'off', and 'on' and the second output is *not* 'on', X1 is broken.

(IF (AND(VAL (IN 1 F1) t ON) (VAL (IN 2 F1) t OFF) (VAL (IN 3 F1) t ON)
        (NOT (VAL (OUT 2 F1) t ON)))
    (NOT (XORG X1)))

Of course, to have diagnostic value at all the outcome of a test must not be known, i.e. it must provide new information. Once DART generates a test, it is checked for novelty by trying to prove the propositions shown below. If it fails to prove either proposition, then the test provides new information.

(IF (AND a1 . . . am) ob)
(IF (AND a1 . . . am) (NOT ob))

The proposition below is an example of a test that DART might generate in this situation that provides no new information. The reason is that the output of the test is completely predictable. By the single-fault assumption, A1 and O1 are operational. Since the two inputs to A1 are 'on', its output and the second input to O1 must be 'on'. But then the output of O1 and, therefore, the second output of F1 must be 'on', whether or not the first input is 'on'. In short, the test is not 'sensitive' to any possible failure in X1 and so provides no new information.

(IF (AND (VAL (IN 1 F1) t ON) (VAL (IN 2 F1) t ON) (VAL (IN 3 F1) t ON))
        (NOT (VAL (OUT 2 F1) t ON)))
    (NOT (XORG X1)))

5.4. Drawing conclusions

Once DART generates an acceptable test, it instructs the tester what to achieve and what to observe. When the test's results are obtained, it then stores them in its device description. For example, if the test derived in the last section were applied to F1 and the corresponding result were observed, DART would store the propositions from Figs. 9 and 10 relevant to time 2.

DART also does a limited amount of deduction from its test results in an attempt to prune the set of suspects. The data in Figs. 9 and 10 make a simple example. The achievable and observable propositions added to the device description together with the test proposition from the last section allow DART to conclude that the XOR-gate X1 is faulty. Since this prunes the suspect set to a single element, the diagnosis is complete. In general, this would not be the case, and DART would continue to generate and execute tests until it failed to generate a test or until it eliminated all but one suspect.

5.5. Resolution residue

The key to DART's generality is its use of a device-independent inference procedure in all phases of the diagnostic process. The computation of suspects, generation of tests, and updating of suspects are all done by proving appropriate propositions. The inference procedure is a variation of resolution [12] called *resolution residue* [4].

Resolution residue is similar to resolution in that it operates on propositions in conjunctive normal form and uses the resolution rule of inference. However, unlike resolution, it is a direct proof procedure rather than a refutation method. The procedure begins with propositions known to be true and terminates only when it deduces a proposition that satisfies two criteria.

The first criterion concerns the form of the proposition. Resolution residue succeeds only when it deduces a disjunction in which each literal is in one of a small number of prespecified classes. In computing suspects, each literal must be the negation of a proposition from the malfunctioning device's design description, as described in Section 5.2. In generating tests, each literal must be the negation of an achievable proposition, an observable proposition or its negation, or the negation of a proposition from the design description, as described in Section 5.3. In drawing conclusions from the results of a test, each literal must be the negation of a proposition from the design description, as with suspect computation.

The second termination criterion is consistency. Each literal in a deduced proposition must be consistent with the global data base and the other literals in the proposition. This is important in computing suspects and drawing conclusions to be sure the result is not simply tautologous. It is important in generating tests to be sure that the conditions of the test can be achieved. Evaluating the consistency of a literal is a non-monotonic deduction accomplished by trying to prove its negation. If the proof attempt terminates unsuccessfully, the literal is consistent. Of course, this consistency test may not

```
CS1:   (NOT (VAL (OUT 1 F1) 1 ON))              OB1

CS2:   (OR (CONN x (OUT 1 F1))                  TH11
           (NOT (VAL x 1 ON)))

CS3:   (NOT (VAL (OUT 1 X2) 1 ON))              DA11

CS4:   (OR (NOT (XORG X2))                      TH8
           (NOT (VAL (IN 1 X2) 1 ON))
           (NOT (VAL (IN 2 X2) 1 OFF)))

CS5:   (OR (NOT (XORG X2))                      TH11  DA7
           (NOT (VAL (OUT 1 X1) 1 ON))
           (NOT (VAL (IN 2 X2) 1 OFF)))

CS6:   (OR (NOT (XORG X2))                      TH8
           (NOT (XORG X1))
           (NOT (VAL (IN 1 X1) 1 ON))
           (NOT (VAL (IN 2 X1) 1 (OFF))
           (NOT (VAL (IN 2 X2) 1 OFF)))

CS7:   (OR (NOT (XORG X2))                      TH11  DA1
           (NOT (XORG X1))
           (NOT (VAL (IN 1 F1) 1 ON))
           (NOT (VAL (IN 2 X1) 1 OFF))
           (NOT (VAL (IN 2 X2) 1 OFF)))

CS8:   (OR (NOT (XORG X2))                      AC1
           (NOT (XORG X1))
           (NOT (VAL (IN 2 X1) 1 OFF))
           (NOT (VAL (IN 2 X2) 1 OFF)))

CS9:   (OR (NOT (XORG X2))                      TH11  DA3
           (NOT (XORG X1))
           (NOT (VAL (IN 2 F1) 1 OFF))
           (NOT (VAL (IN 2 X2) 1 OFF)))

CS10:  (OR (NOT (XORG X2))                      AC2
           (NOT (XORG X1))
           (NOT (VAL (IN 2 X2) 1 OFF)))

CS11:  (OR (NOT (XORG X2))                      TH11  DA5
           (NOT (XORG X1))
           (NOT (VAL (IN 3 F1) 1 OFF)))

CS12:  (OR (NOT (XORG X2))                      AC3
           (NOT (XORG X1)))

CS13:  (ANDG A1)                                DA13  DA14

CS14:  (ANDG A2)                                DA13  DA14

CS15:  (ORG O1)                                 DA13  DA14
```

FIG. 13. Example of computing suspects.

```
GT1:   (OR (NOT (XORG X1)) (XORG X1))

GT2:   (OR (NOT (XORG X1))                          TH8
           (NOT (VAL (IN 1 X1) t ON))
           (NOT (VAL (IN 2 X1) t OFF))
           (VAL (OUT 1 X1) t ON))

GT3:   (OR (NOT (XORG X1))                          TH11  DA1
           (NOT (VAL (IN 1 F1) t ON))
           (NOT (VAL (IN 2 X1) t OFF))
           (VAL (OUT 1 X1) t ON))

GT4:   (OR (NOT (XORG X1))                          TH11  DA3
           (NOT (VAL (IN 1 F1) t ON))
           (NOT (VAL (IN 2 F1) t OFF))
           (VAL (OUT 1 X1) t ON))

GT5:   (OR (NOT (XORG X1))                          TH11  DA8
           (NOT (VAL (IN 1 F1) t ON))
           (NOT (VAL (IN 2 F1) t OFF))
           (VAL (IN 2 A2) t ON))

GT6:   (OR (NOT (XORG X1))                          TH1
           (NOT (VAL (IN 1 F1) t ON))
           (NOT (VAL (IN 2 F1) t OFF))
           (NOT (ANDG A2))
           (NOT (VAL (IN 1 A2) t ON))
           (VAL (OUT 1 A2) t ON))

GT7:   (OR (NOT (XORG X1))                          CS14
           (NOT (VAL (IN 1 F1) t ON))
           (NOT (VAL (IN 2 F1) t OFF))
           (NOT (VAL (IN 1 A2) t ON))
           (VAL (OUT 1 A2) t ON))

GT8:   (OR (NOT (XORG X1))                          TH11  DA6
           (NOT (VAL (IN 1 F1) t ON))
           (NOT (VAL (IN 2 F1) t OFF))
           (NOT (VAL (IN 3 F1) t ON))
           (VAL (OUT 1 A2) t ON))

GT9:   (OR (NOT (XORG X1))                          TH11  DA10
           (NOT (VAL (IN 1 F1) t ON))
           (NOT (VAL (IN 2 F1) t OFF))
           (NOT (VAL (IN 3 F1) t ON))
           (VAL (IN 1 O1) t ON))

GT10:  (OR (NOT (XORG X1))                          TH5
           (NOT (VAL (IN 1 F1) t ON))
           (NOT (VAL (IN 2 F1) t OFF))
           (NOT (VAL (IN 3 F1) t ON))
           (NOT (ORG O1))
           (VAL (OUT 1 O1) t ON))
```

FIG. 14. Example of generating tests.

```
GT11: (OR (NOT (XORG X1))                    CS15
          (NOT (VAL (IN 1 F1) t ON))
          (NOT (VAL (IN 2 F1) t OFF))
          (NOT (VAL (IN 3 F1) t ON))
          (VAL (OUT 1 O1) t ON))

GT12: (OR (NOT (XORG X1))                    TH11  DA12
          (NOT (VAL (IN 1 F1) t ON))
          (NOT (VAL (IN 2 F1) t OFF))
          (NOT (VAL (IN 3 F1) t ON))
          (VAL (OUT 2 F1) t ON))
```

FIG. 14. *Continued.*

terminate, in which case resolution residue fails. Fortunately, the problems that arise in diagnosing most computer-hardware faults are decidable.

Figs. 13–15 present examples of resolution residue in diagnosis. Each line is the result of resolving the previous line with the proposition named on the right. In some cases steps are skipped, but all propositions used in the omitted resolutions are named on the right. Fig. 13 shows the derivation of the suspect set described in Section 5.2 and illustrates the use of the single-fault assumption in exonerating all non-suspects. Fig. 14 shows the derivation of the test described in Section 5.3. Fig. 15 shows the derivation of the conclusion described in Section 5.4. In all cases the derived propositions are consistent with each other and the propositions in Figs. 8–11.

An important concern in using resolution in diagnostic reasoning is its potential for proliferating useless deductions. In order to minimize this problem, DART employs a variety of control schemes to focus its effort. It recognizes and separately solves independent subproblems. It uses the 'unit preference' strategy to draw simple conclusions before introducing disjunctions. It uses branchiness as a criterion in ordering subproblems [15]. It prunes deduction

```
DC1: (NOT (VAL (OUT 2 F1) 2 ON))             OB3

DC2: (OR  (NOT (XORG X1))                    GT12
          (NOT (VAL (IN 1 F1) 2 ON))
          (NOT (VAL (IN 2 F1) 2 OFF))
          (NOT (VAL (IN 3 F1) 2 ON)))

DC3: (OR  (NOT (XORG X1))                    AC4
          (NOT (VAL (IN 2 F1) 2 OFF))
          (NOT (VAL (IN 3 F1) 2 ON)))

DC4: (OR  (NOT (XORG X1))                    AC5
          (NOT (VAL (IN 3 F1) 2 ON)))

DC5: (NOT (XORG X1))                         AC6
```

FIG. 15. Example of drawing conclusions from tests.

paths on the basis of solution-set sizes [16]. It interleaves consistency checking with residue computation. Finally, it caches partial residues for use in subsequent computations [9].

6. Design Description and Diagnosis

The primary problem in diagnosing devices directly from design information is computational cost. In the world of digital circuits, the cost of executing a test is usually small and the number of tests needed to pinpoint a fault is at worst linear in the number of components [7]. However, the cost of generating appropriate tests usually grows nonlinearly, and in general the problem is NP-complete [8].

On the other hand, diagnosis is relative to the design description for the malfunctioning device, and by using a different design description it is frequently possible to achieve dramatic improvements in the efficiency of test generation. Fortunately, design descriptions of this sort are frequently available. Most designers begin with high-level design descriptions and successively refine them until the details are complete. The design descriptions produced in this process frequently contain sufficient information to generate diagnostic tests but suppress enough detail that the cost of test generation is far less than it would be if the full-blown descriptions were used instead.

This section describes some properties of design descriptions that lead to substantial efficiency improvements. *The advantage of the* DART *program over procedures like the d-algorithm is that it works with a wide enough class of design descriptions that it can exploit these properties to achieve enhanced efficiency.*

6.1. Structural abstraction

A structural abstraction of a design description is one in which much of the structural detail has been suppressed. The most common example is structural hierarchy. The structure of a complex device is often described in terms of high-level components, whose internal structure either is not specified at all or is specified separately. For example, the structure of an arithmetic circuit like the one in Fig. 16 is easily described in terms of adders and multipliers. The adders and multipliers can be separately described in terms of their subcomponents, and so on until one reaches the level of gates, transistors, etc.

The advantage of structural abstraction for diagnosis is that it is often possible to diagnose faults without considering the suppressed structural detail. For example, in digital electronics it is usually adequate to diagnose a device to the level of chips or boards rather than the level of individual gates, and this can often be done without knowing their substructure.

Even when the diagnosis must be done to the level of gates, the structural hierarchy can be valuable. For example, it is possible to diagnose the device in Fig. 16 at a high level of abstraction to determine the major subcomponent in

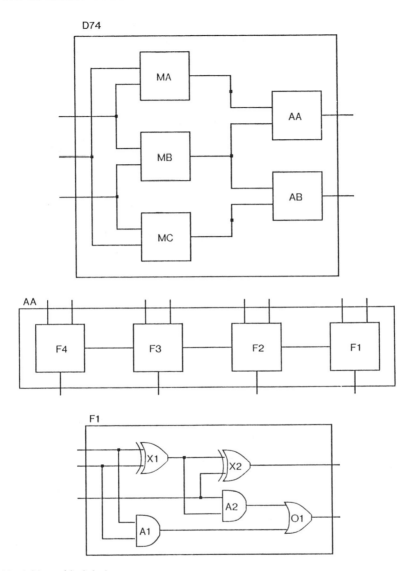

FIG. 16. A hierarchical design.

which the fault lies (e.g. the adder AA). This subcomponent can then be diagnosed to identify the fault at the next lower level (e.g. the full-adder F1), and so on until the lowest-level failure is determined (e.g. X1's output line stuck 'off'). By doing the diagnosis hierarchically, the number of components under consideration at any one time can be kept small; and, even though the higher-level components are often quite complex, the cost of test generation remains manageable.

Assuming that at each level the cost of diagnosis is some function F_i and the number of possible faults is N_i, the overall cost of hierarchical diagnosis can be expressed as follows, where H is the number of levels.

$$\sum_{i=1}^{H} F_i(N_i)$$

The computational advantage of hierarchical diagnosis is most apparent when the number of gates and the cost function are constant from level to level. Then, for a device of H levels, with N possible faults at each level, the cost of non-hierarchical diagnosis if $F(N^H)$, whereas for hierarchical diagnosis, the cost is only $H*F(N)$. This saving is of special importance when the cost function F is nonlinear, but even in the case of linear cost the hierarchical approach still offers a logarithmic advantage.

At first glance this efficiency gain may look illusory. Components at higher levels in the structural hierarchy have more complex behavior than components at lower levels; and, consequently, the diagnostic cost function F_i is not always constant. For example, going from the gate level to the arithmetic level in Fig. 16 decreases the number of parts but increases their complexity. Each component at the gate level has only four possible inputs, whereas each component at the arithmetic level has sixteen.

Fortunately, the increase in behavioral complexity as one ascends the structural hierarchy seldom grows as fast or faster than the decrease in structural complexity. So long as this is true, there is computational advantage in using the structural hierarchy. In some cases, the saving comes simply from the use of behavior tables for the higher-level components (e.g. the bit tables for a full-adder), rather than computing their behavior from lower-level components.

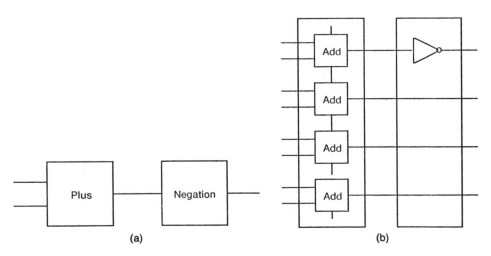

(a)   (b)

FIG. 17. (a) A undiagnosable design. (b) A diagnosable version of the design in (a).

In other cases, the saving comes from the exploitation of important behavioral properties of higher-level components as described in the next sections.

One problem with diagnosis using structural abstractions is that the loss of information can lead to undiagnosability. As an example, consider the circuit in Fig. 17(a). Without any information about the structure of the 'negation' device, this circuit cannot be diagnosed. However, given the additional information in Fig. 17(b), it's easy to generate discriminatory tests for many additional faults.

6.2. Behavioral abstraction

A behavioral abstraction of a design description is one in which much of the behavioral detail has been suppressed. Behavioral abstractions for many designs are determined by the structural hierarchy. The behavior of components at one level in the structural hierarchy is often described in different terms from the behavior of components at other levels. For example, the behavior of gates is best described in terms of 'ons' and 'offs' rather than voltages. The behavior of adders and multipliers is best described in terms of numbers rather than 'ons' and 'offs'. The behavior of computer networks is best described in terms of packets rather than characters.

A common example of behavioral abstraction is the consolidation of sets of values into single values. For example, in going from the level of transistors to gates, it is reasonable to divide the voltage continuum into discrete values. Similarly, the inputs and outputs of arithmetic devices can be characterized as prime and non-prime, even or odd, positive or negative. Considerable savings can be realized by computing with abstract values of this sort rather than by enumerating the lower-level values they summarize.

Another case of behavioral abstraction is the disregard of detail for the sake of simplification. A good example is the rule for the behavior of connections given in Fig. 8. The rule states that if a port x is connected to a port y and the signal value on port x is z, then the signal value on port y is z. As stated, the rule ignores the problem of contradictory values that might arise in the presence of shorts. This makes the tasks of suspect computation and test generation much easier, because it is unnecessary to consider connections other than those explicitly described in the design.

Unfortunately, abstracting away the dependence of signal values on other connections makes the diagnosis of shorts impossible. In computing suspects with the connection rule in Fig. 8, a program like DART has no way of hypothesizing the presence of undesirable connections, since their effect isn't documented. Of course, it is possible to describe the behavior of connections correctly and thereby cure this problem. One need only add a non-monotonic condition to the rule to make it dependent on the absence of connections other than those in the design. The disadvantage is that this drastically increases the number of suspects for any fault, since the rule would be applicable everywhere. Davis [3] describes some ways to keep this growth manageable.

6.3. Constraints

Another way of gaining efficiency in test generation is by formulating a device's design description in terms of interesting functions and relations rather than strictly in terms of values. For example, the behavior of the arithmetic devices in Fig. 16 can be described in terms of mathematical functions like addition and multiplication, as shown below, rather than in terms of value tables, like those in Fig. 8.

> (IF (AND (ADDER d) (VAL (IN 1 d) t x) (VAL (IN 2 d) t y) (= (+ x y) z))
> (VAL (OUT 1 d) t z))

The advantage of formulations like this is that these functions and relations can be used to encode constraints on a device's behavior, symbolic constraint propagation techniques can then be used in place of exhaustive enumeration of possibilities.

Consider, for example, the circuit in Fig. 16 and assume that for test-generation purposes it is necessary to get a 4 on the first output and a 6 on the second. One way of doing this is to work backwards from the desired values. For example, if the inputs to the adder A1 were 4 and 0, this would produce the 4 desired on the output. The consequences of this choice can then be propagated around the circuit. In this case, in order for there to be a 0 on the second input to A1, there must be a 0 on the output of M2 and a 0 on the first input to A2. In order for the output of A2 to be 6, the second input to A2 and the output of M3 must be 6. This can be accomplished by seeting the inputs to M3 to 6 and 1. In order for there to be a 6 on the first input to M3, there must

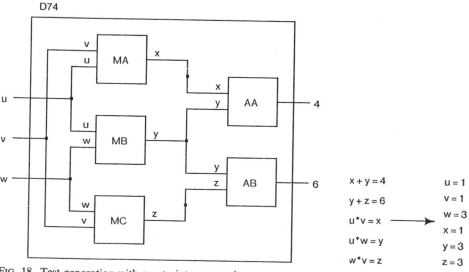

Fig. 18. Test generation with constraint propagation.

be a 6 on the second input to M2. In order to get a 0 on the output of M2, there must be a 0 on its first input and a 0 on the second input to M1. However, this means that the output of M1 must be 0, in contradiction with its previous setting to 4. In other words at least one of the arbitrary choices made at A1 and M3 must be undone and other values tried, until a consistent value assignment is found.

An alternative to this sort of exhaustive enumeration is the posting, propagation, and satisfaction of symbolic constraints. For example, in this case, rather than selecting specific values at each choice point, one could designate those values by variables and record appropriate constraints among them, as suggested in Fig. 18. These symbolic values can then be propagated and new constraints can be posted, until all relevant lines have been visited. The constraints accumulated during this process can then be solved to produce values for the variables.

In this approach, no backup is necessary in generating the constraints, and the constraints can often be solved quite efficiently. The cost of test generation without constraint propagation is exponential in the number of choices that must be made. For a device with N choice points and B alternatives at each point, the cost is B^N. Using symbolic-constraint propagation, the search of this space is replaced by the problem of solving a set of simultaneous equations in N variables. If the equations are linear, this can be done in time proportional to N^3.

Of course, the constraints produced during test generation are not always this inexpensive to solve; and when this is the case the value of constraint propagation is open to debate. On the one hand, constraint propagation is good because it breaks the test-generation problem into two parts, viz. the basic search cost and the cost of propagation. Although the basic search cost may not be improved, the cost of propagation is paid only once. On the other hand, the overhead of propagating symbolic constraints may outweigh this saving. The merit of constraint propagation appears to be situation dependent.

6.4. Conditional values

Another design-description reformulation of particular utility in generating tests for circuits is the use of 'conditional values' in the behavioral description of a design. A true–false conditional value consists of two signal values and an implicit condition. The presence of a true–false conditional value on a port means that the port has the first value if the condition is true, and it has the second value if the condition is false. An n-way conditional value consists of n signal values and an implicit condition with n possible outcomes, and its presence on a port means that the port has the first value if the first outcome is true, etc.

Conditional values are of particular use in generating bi-directional tests. A bi-directional test is one that is guaranteed to provide information about a set of faults whether it succeeds or fails. If it succeeds, the conclusion of the test can be assumed to be true. If it fails, the conclusion can be assumed false. In other words, the implication is bi-directional.

The d-algorithm provides an interesting implementation of this technique. Instead of propagating just 'ons' and 'offs', the d-algorithm employs an additional pair of symbols for each suspect. In order to generate a test for a component, one of these symbols is placed on the output line of the component. If the value of the line is supposed to be 'on' when the component is functioning properly, the 'positive' symbol (e.g. d) is placed on the line. If the output is supposed to be "off", the "negative" symbol (e.g. $\underline{d}$) is used instead. These values are then propagated through the circuit. The occurrence of a positive symbol on a line means that that line should be 'on' if the component corresponding to the symbol is working properly, and it should be 'off' otherwise. The occurrence of a negative symbol means that the line should be 'off' if the component is functioning properly and vice-versa. The arrival of a positive symbol at a primary output signals a bi-directional test for the associated component. The arrival of a positive symbol for one component and a negative symbol for another is discriminatory.

The advantage of conditional values like these is that they allow several uni-directional tests to be generated simultaneously. The cost of generating these tests is not substantially greater than the cost of generating a single test, but together they yield more information. Furthermore, conditional values make it easy for a diagnostician to recognize evolving bi-directional tests during test generation and give them control priority.

The disadvantage of conditional values is that the behavioral description of each component must be augmented to include propagation rules for these new symbols. Fortunately, this can be done automatically. Unfortunately, it expands the number of rules that a diagnostician must store and use. In preliminary experiments the computational benefit of this approach has not warranted the cost of these modified descriptions. However, the technique looks promising and warrants further study.

7. Conclusion

The DART program has been implemented and tested on a variety of examples. The implementation was done in MRS [5]. The test examples include simple circuits like the one in Fig. 3, more complex devices like the teleprocessing system of the IBM 4331, and non-electronic devices like the cooling system of a nuclear reactor. In all cases the program was able to generate tests and diagnose underlying faults. The time to diagnose each case was on the order of seconds or minutes. While this is not particularly good for small circuits, it is excellent for complex devices.

One limitation of DART in its present form is that it doesn't take into account the cost of tests. Some tests are more expensive than others. For example, it's easier to check a status light than to measure a voltage. It's easier to get information at a system terminal than to pore through a core dump. Unfortunately, the evaluation of test cost can be quite difficult because of dependencies on sequencing and grouping. For example, once a file has been deleted, it may be expensive or impossible to recreate. Once a piece of test equipment has been attached to a port, it's just as easy to get a set of values as it is to get an individual value.

DART also doesn't into account the diagnostic value of tests, beyond the novelty check described in Section 5.3, even though this can be extremely important in reducing the overall cost of diagnosis.

While DART is faster than the d-algorithm in generating tests for complex devices, computational cost remains a problem. Not all design descriptions are tuned for the task of diagnosis, and a bad description can lead to substantial inefficiency. One way of dealing with this problem is to automate the reformulation of design descriptions into more useful forms, like those suggested in Section 6.

A more drastic way of dealing with inefficiency is to 'compile' design descriptions into MYCIN-like symptom-fault rules. If it is possible to diagnose a device automatically, it should be possible to create a set of diagnostic tests automatically. The cost of this approach can be formidable since it must take into account all possible faults. However, the savings can also be dramatic, and the approach warrants further investigation.

One final issue worth mentioning is DART's absolute dependence on the existence of design information. Missing or inappropriately represented information can lead to extreme inefficiency and undiagnosability. While adequate information about the design of a device is usually available in the heads of its designers, it is a significant chore to express it in a machine-readable form. The problem can be mitigated by the creation of design tools that facilitate the entry of useful design descriptions. Unfortunately, design information is sometimes unavailable outside of the organization responsible for the design; and, whenever this is the case, the DART program is of little use.

In summary, the key contribution of this research is the DART program. DART differs from previous approaches to diagnosis taken in the Artificial Intelligence community in that it works directly from design descriptions. DART differs from previous approaches taken in the design-automation community in that is more general and in many cases more efficient. DART uses a device-independent language for describing devices and a device-independent inference procedure for diagnosis. The resulting generality allows it to be applied to a wide class of devices ranging from digital logic to nuclear reactors. Although this generality engenders some computational overhead on small problems, it makes possible combinatoric savings that more than offsets this overhead on problems of realistic size. For these reasons, the DART algorithm appears to be a promising way of coping with the increasing complexity of modern designs.

ACKNOWLEDGMENT

The idea of applying this research to computer hardware was first suggested by Ed Feigenbaum. Bob Joyce and Narinder Singh experimented with an early implementation of DART and explored many of the techniques for improving efficiency. Randy Davis critiqued the work at an early stage and pointed out the need for physical information in computing suspects. The work was done with the collaboration and support of the IBM Palo Alto Scientific Center and the Fairchild Laboratory for Artificial Intelligence Research. Additional funding was provided by the Office of Naval Research under contract number N00014-81-K-0004.

REFERENCES

1. Breuer, M.A. and Friedman, A.D., *Diagnosis and Reliable Design of Digital Systems* (Computer Science Press, Rockville, MD, 1976).
2. Brown, H., Tong, C. and Foyster, G., PALLADIO: An exploratory environment for circuit design, *IEEE Trans. Comput.* (1983).
3. Davis, R., Diagnosis based on description of structure and function, in: *Proceedings National Conference on Artificial Intelligence*, Pittsburgh, PA (August, 1982) 137–142.
4. Finger, J. and Genesereth, M.R., RESIDUE—a deductive approach to design, HPP-83-46, Stanford University Heuristic Programming Project, Stanford, CA, 1983.
5. Genesereth, M.R., Greiner, R. and Smith, D.E., MRS—a meta-level representation system, HPP-83-28, Stanford University Heuristic Programming Project, Stanford, CA, 1983.
6. Genesereth, M.R., Diagnosis using hierarchical design models, in: *Proceedings National Conference on Artificial Intelligence*, Pittsburgh, PA (August, 1982) 278–283.
7. Goel, P., Test generation cost analysis and projections, in: *Seventeenth Design Automation Conference Proceedings*, June, 1980.
8. Ibarra, O.H. and Sahni, S., Polynomially complete fault detection problems, *IEEE Trans. Comput.* 24 (1976) 242–250.
9. Lenat, D.B., Hayes-Roth, F. and Klahr, P., Cognitive Economy, HPP-79-15, Stanford University Heuristic Programming Project, Stanford, CA, 1979.
10. Pople, H., The dialog model of diagnostic logic and its use in internal medicine, in: *Proceedings Fourth International Joint Conference on Artificial Intelligence*, Tbilisi, USSR, August, 1975.
11. Pople, H., The formation of composite hypotheses in diagnostic problem solving—an exercise in synthetic reasoning, in: *Proceedings Fifth International Joint Conference on Artificial Intelligence*, Cambridge, MA (August, 1977) 1030–1037.
12. Robinson, J.A., A machine-oriented logic based on the resolution principle, *J. ACM* 12 (1965) 23–41.
13. Roth, J.P., Bouricius, W.G. and Schneider, P.R., Programmed algorithm to compute tests to detect and distinguish faults in logic circuits, *IEEE Trans. Electronic Computers* 16 (1967).
14. Shortliffe, E., *MYCIN: Computer-Based Medical Consultation* (American Elsevier, New York, 1976).
15. Smith, D.E. and Genesereth, M.R., Ordering conjuncts in problem solving, HPP-82-9, Stanford University Heuristic Programming Project, Stanford, CA, 1983.
16. Smith, D.E. and Genesereth, M.R., Finding all of the solutions to a problem, HPP-83-21, Stanford University Heuristic Programming Project, Stanford, CA, 1983.
17. Sussman, G.J. and Steele, G.L., Constraints—a language for expressing almost-hierarchical descriptions, *Artificial Intelligence* 14 (1980) 1–39.
18. Stefik, M., Planning with constraints, *Artificial Intelligence* 16 (1981) 111–140.

Received November 1983

VERIFY: A Program for Proving Correctness of Digital Hardware Designs

Harry G. Barrow

Fairchild Laboratory for Artificial Intelligence Research, Palo Alto, CA 94304, U.S.A.

ABSTRACT

VERIFY is a PROLOG program that attempts to prove the correctness of a digital design. It does so by showing that the behavior inferred from the interconnection of its parts and their behaviors is equivalent to the specified behavior. It has successfully verified large designs involving many thousands of transistors.

1. Introduction

1.1. The nature of the problem

When a hardware or software system is designed, there is always the problem of deciding whether the design meets its functional specification. There are currently three main approaches to doing so: develop the design from the specification by a methodology that ensures it cannot be incorrect; design the system and prove formally that it will satisfy the specification for all cases; design and build the system, or a simulation of it, and try it out on test cases.

The first approach is perhaps the most attractive, but it is also the most difficult. It requires codification of a great deal of knowledge about the design domain, from the most abstract levels of system description down to the most detailed levels of implementation. It faces a potentially astronomically large search space of design alternatives. In software design it is exemplified in principles of structured programming methodology [1], and in research into automatic or semi-automatic programming [2]. In hardware design, research has focussed on pieces of the problem that are most tedious and prone to human error, such as wire routing, or programmable logic array generation (see [3] for details). There have been some attempts at automatic design of entire integrated circuits, including microprocessors, and these have met with varying degrees of success [4]. However, these attempts begin with an essentially structural specification, rather than a functional one, and are limited to particular stylized architectures. Truly general-purpose design generation systems are still many years in the future.

The third approach, of building a system, or an accurate simulation of it, and trying it on test cases, is the current standard practice. As systems become more complex, however, it runs into practical and theoretical limitations. The greatest difficulty is that of selecting test cases. In all but the simplest systems, the space of possible inputs can be vast. For example, a simple multiplier that multiples two 16-bit integers can face over 4 000 000 000 different inputs, while a system that contains a single 32-bit register can potentially have over 4 000 000 000 different responses to *each* input. Clearly, we cannot hope to test a system on every possible input with every possible system state. We must select a subset of these from which we can extrapolate to conclude the correctness, or otherwise, of the design. Fortunately, the number of tests needed grows linearly with the number of components in the system, but unfortunately, the task of finding them is known to be NP-complete [5]. Methods of test generation that are nevertheless reasonably practical in most situations are under development. They require, however, that all the pieces of the design are known to meet their specifications!

Thus, we find that the second approach, formally proving that a design meets its specifications, is perhaps the most promising on any but the longest time-scale. Research into formally proving correctness of software has continued for many years, with some notable recent successes [6]. It is by no means sufficiently advanced, however, that program correctness proofs are common. The correctness of hardware design has received much less attention until recently, but it now seems that progress might be made fairly rapidly. Hardware is in some ways more constrained in its organization than software, which makes many problems more tractable. Of course, as systems become more complex, and much software is embedded within the hardware, the distinction between hardware and software becomes increasingly blurred, and the tractability diminishes. For the time being, however, we can apply correctness proof techniques to a broad enough range of hardware systems to be useful.

While the domain of design verification is of immense practical value, it is also of considerable interest in terms of its AI research content. In its most general form, it involves representing the structure and function of complex systems, along with some knowledge about the problems the system is intended to deal with. Inference mechanisms are needed which can perform competently, even expertly, in an astonomically large search space: Techniques must be developed for guiding reasoning in the search for a proof, perhaps along the lines of meta-level reasoning in MECHO [7]. Verification depends heavily upon general mathematical abilities, such as algebraic manipulation

[8, 9] and induction [10]. It also depends, to a lesser extent, upon understanding the functionality of designs, and perhaps also of the designer's intentions.

In a broader context, the ability to reason about system designs and make inferences about their behavior has application to issues other than verification. The same representations, knowledge, and inference mechanisms are required for abstract hierarchical simulation [11], generation of tests [12], diagnosis of failures [13, 14, 15], criticism and improvement of designs, and even design synthesis. The ultimate goal of much of the work in such areas is an integrated, intelligent design aid that can collaborate in the development of a design. Some current work at the Fairchild Laboratory for Artificial Intelligence Research (FLAIR) and Stanford University (and other places as well) is aimed in this direction. In this paper, however, we shall concentrate on only one piece, namely verification.

1.2. Approaches to hardware verification

As we noted above, hardware verification is currently done by simulation—indeed, the terms *verification* and *simulation* are often taken to be synonymous in the field of digital design. It is not feasible to perform an exhaustive simulation for any but very small systems, and it is hard to choose a subset of cases for selective simulation. One possible way to alleviate the difficulties is to perform symbolic simulation, that is, to use symbols representing one of many alternative values, instead of one particular value. This does not appear to have received much attention, perhaps because it involves algebraic manipulation of expressions. This manipulation would appear slower than conventional simulation, but may in fact be faster, since it effectively handles many alternative values simultaneously.

A potentially more valuable verification methodology is to formally prove correctness of the design, for all inputs and situations. The key notion is to provide both a structural description and a behavioral description of the design and to prove that they are equivalent. An early piece of research in this direction was performed by Wagner [16], who used a non-procedural functional language for description of the hardware, and a first-order logic proof checker to demonstrate correctness. The proof was directed entirely manually, and was limited by the description language to low levels of design.

Hanes developed a program which accepted functional and structural design descriptions in a higher-level language, translated them into predicate calculus clauses, and used a general-purpose theorem-prover to establish correctness [17]. The most complex example tackled was a 4-bit ripple-through adder, with seven components and two levels of descriptive hierarchy. The proof was accomplished with a set of rewriting rules for simplifying expressions. Hanes recognized the importance of hierarchical structure in designs as a means to reasoning about them, but did not exploit it very heavily.

The approach described in this paper was developed from Gordon's methods for modeling and verifying hardware [18], which concentrate upon the denotational semantics of designs and their behaviors. (See [19] for an exposition of denotational semantics.) Gordon has proved correctness of several example designs with multiple levels of hierarchy, at the gate and transistor levels, as well as architectural levels. Initially, proofs were made manually, but more recently, they were made using the LCF interactive proof-checking system [20, 21]. Shostak [22] has also followed Gordon's approach, and has attempted proofs of small systems involving loops (such as a Muller C-element) using STP, a semi-automatic prover [23].

Our work has aimed at developing a useful system that can deal with real designs. Consequently, our emphasis has been upon representation in a suitable notation, that captures such notions as bit-wise interconnection, and a reasoning system that has enough domain-specific and general mathematical knowledge to perform the proofs largely automatically. It would appear that the examples described in this paper represent the most complex verified automatically by any system so far.

The verification system we have implemented, called VERIFY, is a PROLOG [24] program embodying an initial, simplified version of Gordon's methodology (specifically, omitting the notion of behaviors as manipulatable objects). VERIFY has successfully proved correctness of a straightforward but very detailed design, involving many thousands of transistors.

2. An Example

By way of introduction to VERIFY and its problem domain, we shall consider a somewhat elementary example. Later we shall discuss the principles involved, and how they are currently implemented. We shall also present some more complicated examples.

In VERIFY, a design is comprised of a collection of modules, organized hierarchically, and modeled as finite state machines. A module has a set of input ports and a set of output ports. Each port has an associated signal type, which specifies the domain for signals passing through it. A module also has a set of state variables, each with its own signal type. The behavior of a module is specified by two sets of equations: one set gives output signals as functions of inputs and current internal state, and the other gives new internal states as functions of inputs and current state.

As an example, a simple type of module, called inc, which has no state variables, and whose output is simply its input plus one, may be declared as follows:

```
% Definition of module type Incrementer

module (inc).
```

```
port(inc, in(AnInc), input, integer).
port(inc, out(AnInc), output, integer).

outputEqn(inc, out(AnInc)) := 1 + in(AnInc)).
```

In this definition, AnInc is a PROLOG variable that stands for any instance of an incrementer, and in and out are functions from an instance to signals at its ports. := is an infix operator used to define the behavior of an output or state variable (on its left) as an expression (on its right).[1]

Similarly, a type of simple multiplexer, whose output is one of two inputs, according to the value of a control input, may be declared as:

```
% Definition of module type Multiplexer

module(mux).

port(mux, in0(AMux), input, integer).
port(mux, in1(AMux), input, integer).
port(mux, switch(AMux), input, boole).
port(mux, out(AMux), output, integer).

outputEqn(mux, out(AMux) :=
    if(switch(AMux), in1(AMux), in0(AMux))).
```

Here, AMux stands for any instance of a module of type mux, and

$$if(\langle condition \rangle, \langle true.expr \rangle, \langle false.expr \rangle)$$

is a conditional expression with the obvious semantics.

Finally, a module type that involves an internal state variable:

```
% Definition of module type Register

module(reg).

port(reg, in(AReg), input, integer).
port(red, out(AReg), output, integer).

state(reg, contents(AReg), integer).

outputEqn(reg, out(AReg) := contents(AReg)).
stateEqn(reg, contents(AReg) := in(AReg)).
```

---

[1]For readability, the notation for input is a slightly simplified version of the internal representation: here in and out appear as functions from module instances to signal values. Internally they become functions from module instances to signals, and the function value maps from signals to their values.

This describes a simple register, whose current contents are given by the state variable contents. The equations declare that the output of the register is the current value of its contents, and that the new value of its contents is whatever is the current input. This register thus can be viewed as depending on an implicit clock (which is not necessarily the same as the system clock): at each tick of the clock, the contents are updated, and the output follows the input, but is delayed by one tick.

The incrementer, multiplexer, and register are all primitive modules. That is, their specification is assumed to accurately characterize their behavior. Compound modules now can be defined, declaring their parts as instances of the primitives, and specifying the internal interconnections.

We can, for example, specify a loadable counter, shown in Fig. 1, as follows:

% Definition of module type Counter

module(counter).

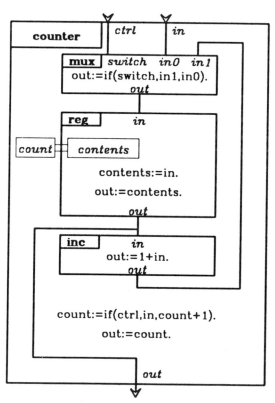

FIG. 1. A loadable counter.

```
port(counter, in(Acounter), input, integer).
port(counter, ctrl(Acounter), input, boole).
port(counter, out(Acounter), output, integer).

part(counter, muxA(Acounter), mux).
part(counter, regA(Acounter), reg).
part(counter, incA(Acounter), inc).

connected(counter, ctrl(Acounter), switch(muxA(Acounter))).
connected(counter, in(Acounter), in1(muxA(Acounter))).
connected(counter, out(muxA(Acounter)), in(regA(Acounter))).
connected(counter, out(regA(Acounter)), in(incA(Acounter))).
connected(counter, out(incA(Acounter)), in0(muxA(Acounter))).
connected(counter, out(regA(Acounter)), out(Acounter)).

% Behavior specification:

state(counter, count(Acounter), integer).
stateMap(counter, count(Acounter), contents(regA(Acounter))).

outputEqn(counter, out(Acounter) : = count(Acounter)).

stateEqn(counter, count(Acounter) : =
    if(ctrl(Acounter), in(Acounter), count(Acounter) + 1)).
```

In this definition, muxA, regA, and incA are functions that select a particular component of an instance of a counter. Thus muxA(Acounter) yields the multiplexer of the counter Acounter, and hence in0(muxA(Acounter)) yields the signal at its input in0.

Connections are declared between a source and a destination. A source can be an input to the current module, an output of one of its parts, or a state variable. Similarly, a destination can be an input of a part, an output of the module, or a state variable.

The state variable, count(Acounter), declared in the behavior specification above is for the purpose of describing the counter as a black box. It actually corresponds to the state variable of the register, contents(regA(Acounter)), and the renaming is accomplished by the stateMap declaration.

When the above module descriptions are loaded into VERIFY and the user types in the request to verify the module type counter, VERIFY first recursively attempts to verify the module's components, then derives its own description of the module's behavior from its structural description, and finally tries to prove the equivalence of the derived behavior and the specified behavior. The following trace results:

```
| ?- verify(counter).

)))))) Attempting to verify counter ))))))
Verifying components of counter

    )))))) Attempting to verify inc ))))))
    inc is primitive (needs no verification).
    (((((( Success! Behavior of inc meets its specification.

    )))))) Attempting to verify reg ))))))
    reg is primitive (needs no verification).
    (((((( Success! Behavior of reg meets its specification.

    )))))) Attempting to verify mux ))))))
    mux is primitive (needs no verification).
    (((((( Success! Behavior of mux meets its specification.

Verifying counter as whole
Determining specified behavior of counter
Specified behavior is:

Module: counter
Inputs: ctrl(counter), in(counter)
States: count(counter)
Output equations:
    out(counter) = count(counter)
State equations:
    count(counter) = if(ctrl(counter), in(counter), count(counter) + 1)

Determining behavior of counter from structure.
    Determining behavior of inc as primitive.
    Determining behavior of reg as primitive.
    Determining behavior of mux as primitive.
Constructed behavior is:

Module: counter
Inputs: ctrl(counter), in(counter)
States: count(counter)
Output equations:
    out(counter) = count(counter)
State equations:
    count(counter) = if(ctrl(counter), in(counter), 1 + count(counter))

Trying to show behaviors are equivalent.
Considering equations for out(counter)
We must show that
```

value(count(counter)) = value(count(counter))

Trivial identity: true

Considering equations for count(counter)
We must show that

```
if(value(ctrl(counter)),
   value(in(counter)),
   value(count(counter)) + 1)
=
if(value(ctrl(counter)),
   value(in(counter)),
   1 + value(count(counter)))
```

Complexity: 25 subterms.
Trying symbolic manipulation.
Canonicalizing the identity. . .
Canonical form is:
   1
Identity has been established.
⟨⟨⟨⟨⟨ Success! Behavior of counter meets its specification.

yes

3. The Principles of VERIFY

One key principle underlying VERIFY is that, given the behaviors of components of a system and their interconnections, it is possible to derive a description of the behavior of the whole system [18, 25]. This derived behavior can then be compared with a specification of the intended behavior of the system. If the structural design (the components and interconnections) or the functional specification (the behavioral equations) contains an error, a discrepancy can be detected and corrected. Of course, there is still the possibility that the design and the specification agree, but the specification is incorrect: that is, however, the error of designing the wrong system, an error of a different order.

In our current work, behaviors of systems or their component modules are specified in detail, rather than via general assertions (as in [26]). A module is considered as a finite state machine (FSM) which has some inputs, some outputs, and some internal variables that contain its state. For conciseness, the FSM is described by a set of equations, rather than an exhaustive table. For each output, there is an equation that determines the value of the output as a function of the inputs and state variables. Similarly, for each state variable, there is an equation that determines its next value as a function of the inputs and the current values of the state variables. These equations embody the notion of an implicit clock: at each tick, the state variables are updated and the outputs are updated immediately afterwards. If the system has a single synchronous clock, we may choose to identify it with the implicit clock of our finite state model. Alternatively, we may represent it explicitly, as just another signal propagated within the system, perhaps generated by a module whose behavior is also described as a finite state machine in terms of the implicit clock.

The internal structure of a module is specified by declaring the names of its components, their types, and how they are interconnected and connected to the inputs and outputs of the system.

The structural description is readily translatable into a behavioral description. Each component module has its own set of equations specifying its behavior, and each connection determines an equation relating an output of one component module to an input of another, or relating a component input or output to a system input or output. We thus have a set of equations from which component module inputs and outputs can be eliminated, yielding output and state variable equations for the system.

Having derived a behavioral description from the structural description, we now wish to compare it with the behavioral specification. The problem is to determine the correspondence between two finite state machines. In the basic case, the behaviors of the two machines are actually identical, but the equations differ somewhat in form. Mathematical knowledge of the functions involved in the equations is used during algebraic manipulation to prove equivalence. In more complex cases, the machines may be structurally or behaviorally homomorphic (or both). They are structurally homomorphic when a mapping can be found from variables of one machine to variables of the other, and they are behaviorally homomorphic when a mapping can be found from sequences of states of one to sequences of states of the other.

Another key principle, which gives VERIFY much of its power, is to exploit the hierarchical structure of a design. The exploitation results in a number of benefits. First, the design is effectively broken into manageable pieces with simply representable behavior. The general verification strategy can then be applied recursively. Second, with the structural hierarchy comes a signal abstraction hierarchy, in which signals may be regarded as voltage levels, or as numbers, or even higher-level objects. The semantics of higher structural and signal levels allow more succinct description, greater leaps of inference, and much suppression of unnecessary detail. Third, the correctness of each type of module can be recorded when it is established so that the proof need not be repeated. The work done in proving the correctness of a complete system is therefore linear in the number of types of module in its design, rather than linear in the number of primitive components. For complex designs involving many thousands of primitive components, the computational saving obtained can be very great indeed.

4. Representation in VERIFY

4.1. Signal abstraction

Signals in a digital system are viewed differently according to the context and conceptual level in which they are considered. At the lowest level, signals are considered as representing voltages and currents; at the next, logic levels with various strengths; at the higher levels, bits, numbers, addresses, or even computational objects. We naturally wish to think of and describe a system as performing certain operations upon objects (represented by transformations applied to signals). We therefore need to capture some of the semantics of those objects and transformations, and how they map to the signal domain.

In the current implementation, signals may have one of several types: boole, Boolean truth values (0 and 1); bit, binary digits (0 and 1); integer(N), integers in the range 0 to $2^{N+1} - 1$; and integer, arbitrarily large positive integers (the natural numbers). Since in hardware design outputs are often connected together in a common bus, it is necessary to allow some signals to take an additional state, hiZ, or high impedance. Thus there are signal types booleZ, bitZ, integerZ(N), and integerZ, which are unions of the former types with type Z that represents just high impedance signals.

4.2. Module structure

We have seen in Section 2 that module structure is described in terms of ports (each with its own direction and signal type), parts (each of a particular module type), and connections. The description language also supports several additional useful constructs: constants, parameters, part and port arrays, and bit-wise connections.

Constants can be declared by specifying their name, type, and value. Connections can then be specified from the constants to input ports of parts. Explicit declaration of constants means that they are prominently visible in a description, and their values are not embedded in expressions, which makes design editing much less error-prone.

Parameters may be provided to module declarations, so that a single description may cover several distinct types of module. For example, one parameter might indicate the width of inputs and outputs in bits, while another might be the value of a built-in constant. Parameters are expressed by adding arguments to the module type name, such as adder(N) for an (N + 1)-bit adder.

Arrays of parts, ports, state variables, and constants are easily represented by adding subscripts to the arguments of selector functions. For example in(AModule, I) refers to the Ith in port of module AModule.

Bit-wise connections are specified by use of a function bit, as in bit(I, x), which represents the selection of the Ith bit of a signal, x, or as in bit(I: J, x), which represents selection of bits I through J of x. The selection can be applied to a source or to a destination. In the latter case, VERIFY recognizes that it must construct an expression for the destination signal after collecting together all the relevant bit-wise connections.

Parameters, constants, arrays, and bit-wise connections can be best understood by considering an example. In the following, an adder is constructed from a collection of fullAdders, each of which has inputs inx, iny, and cin (the carry in), and outputs sum and carry.

```
% Definition of an (N + 1)-bit adder in terms of fullAdders

module(adder(N)).

port(adder(N), inx(Adder), input, integer(N)).
port(adder(N), iny(Adder), input, integer(N)).
port(adder(N), out(Adder), output, integer(N1))
    :- N1 is N + 1.

constant(adder(N), carryin(Adder), 0, bit).

part(adder(N), fa(Adder, I), fullAdder) % an array of parts
    :- range(0, I, N).

connected(adder(N), bit(I, inx(Adder)), inx(fa(Adder, I)))
    :- range(0, I, N).
connected(adder(N), bit(I, iny(Adder)), iny(fa(Adder, I)))
    :- range(0, I, N).
connected(adder(N), carryin(Adder), cin(fa(Adder, 0))).
connected(adder(N), carry(fa(Adder, I)), cin(fa(Adder, I1)))
    :- range(1, I1, N), I is I1-1.
connected(adder(N), sum(fa(Adder, I)), bit(I, out(Adder)))
    :- range (0, I, N).
connected(adder(N), carry(fa(Adder, N)), bit(N1, out(Adder)))
    :- N1 is N + 1.

% Behavior specification:

outputEqn(adder(N), out(Adder): = inx(Adder) + iny(Adder)).
```

In this example, N is a parameter specifying the number of bits in the inputs to the adder (i.e. the most significant bit represents 2^N). The adder is composed of N + 1 fullAdders, specified in the part declaration. Note that the declarations exploit the expressive power of PROLOG, using a single rule to represent a collection of assertions. For example, the construct range(0, I, N) means simply that I may take any value from 0 to N. Other terms on the right-hand side of the rule express constraints among variables.

Individual bits of the inputs are connected to the fullAdders, and their outputs are bit-wise connected to the adder output. The equation describing the behavior of the adder is the specification, and is concerned only with input/output behavior, not reflecting any of the internal structure.

4.3. Basic design checks

Experience has shown that, before verification proceeds, it is well worth investing a small amount of time in checking for basic design errors.

Checks can be made to ensure that no line is driven by two outputs simultaneously (unless they are tri-state outputs), that every line has an output and an input, and that every output and state variable is accounted for by some equation.

The signal types of connected outputs and inputs are checked for compatibility in the signal abstraction hierarchy, and a type conversion is made where appropriate, or the user is warned where not. For example, boole, bit, and integer(0) signals can be freely interconnected; sources of integer(2) signals can be connected to integer(5) destinations, but not vice versa, since information would be lost. A special form of 'type-conversion' occurs when bit-wise connections are made: integer outputs are embedded in bit-selection functions, and bit inputs are collected into integers as terms in a power series. Permissible type-conversions are governed by a set of rules, which also specify what appropriate type-conversion functions should be inserted.

In a similar way, the argument and result types of functions used in behavior specifications can be declared and the argument and result types of subexpressions in behavior equations can be type-checked.

Design checking has proved to be extremely useful in finding mistakes in module structure and function specifications. Many typing errors have been found in this way during the development of VERIFY.

4.4. Module behavior

Module behavior, as we have seen in previous sections, is represented by a FSM description, with equations giving output and new state values in terms of inputs and current state. The vocabulary of functions that can be used in equations is still being developed, with new functions added as they are needed to deal with new types of example. The current vocabulary includes logical and arithmetic functions and relations, the conditional, if, and special functions for such operations as combining signals in buses and for storing and fetching data in memories. When a new primitive function is added, its argument and result types must be declared, and rules provided for evaluating and simplifying expressions in which it occurs. A define declaration can be used to define non-primitive functions in a manner very similar to LISP. For example,

```
define(joinfn(X, Y),
        if(X = hiZ, Y, if(Y = hiZ, X, if(X = Y, X, undefined)))).
```

defines joinfn as a function that yields the result of wiring two output signals together.

To facilitate subsequent computations, module behavior descriptions are converted from the 'human-convenient', parametrized notation above into a more explicit form, with instantiated parameters and explicit sets of equations. For example, the generic adder behavior description might be converted into specific descriptions of 3- and 5-bit adders, if these were required in the course of verification. The notation for expressions is modified slightly, replacing the names of signals by PROLOG variables so that it is easy to substitute values or build compound expressions. The conversion is only done once, when needed, and the results are cached.

The behavior descriptions (whether given in the specification, or constructed from the structure) are useful for many purposes. Values can be supplied for input signals and state variables, and output values can be determined by the evaluation and simplification mechanism described later. It is not necessary to supply literal values for all variables: values can be left as variables. Thus we can simplify output expressions for such purposes as optimization, or specialization. We can also perform symbolic simulation, propagating symbols for variables which have definite, but unknown, values. For example, by symbolic simulation we can show that in the multiplexer primitive defined above, when switch is true, the output is in1, regardless of the actual value of in1. This approach has the potential for much faster checking of a design by simulation than instantiating values for all variables, as is currently done. In this work, however, the major purpose of constructing behavior descriptions is so that they may be compared with the specified behavior and the design verified.

5. Inferring Behavior from Structure

The first major step in verifying a module is to infer a behavioral description from its structural description. Each component module has a set of behavioral equations, and each connection implies an equation relating an output signal to an input signal. (Each stateMap declaration also implies an equation relating a state variable of the module to a state variables of its parts.) The set of all these equations is, indeed, a behavioral description, but it is unnecessarily complex. It involves internal variables (signals at ports inside the module) which should be eliminated.

For modules in which any internal feedback loops are broken by state variables (typically registers), elimination of intermediate variables can be accomplished by simple substitution. Fortunately, this is a very common case: it is even a principle in the Mead–Conway nMOS design methodology [27]. There are, however, modules that we may wish to consider in which unbroken feedback loops exist. To deal with these in a fully general way requires solution of simultaneous equations, and possibly the introduction of new state variables to account for the different modes of behavior of the loops. For example, when two NOR gates (which have no state variables of their own) are cross-coupled to form a bistable latch, a new state variable must be introduced. (See [22] for another approach to designs with loops.)

VERIFY currently derives behavioral descriptions by simple substitution, and is not able to do general simultaneous equation-solving or state variable introduction. It does sometimes construct very large equations that have perhaps three thousand terms, but, so far, these can be handled by the rest of the proof mechanism. It may be advantageous, however, not to eliminate all the intermediate variables, even when no unbroken feedback loops exist, to avoid constructing even larger equations.

The end-result to this stage of verification is a set of constructed equations that describe the module outputs and new values for state variables as functions of the module inputs and current values of state variables.

6. Proving Equivalence of Behavioral Descriptions

6.1. The nature of the equivalence

Having derived a behavioral description of the module from its structural description, we can now attempt to prove that it is equivalent to the behavioral specification. The most basic case is to show that the two finite state machines are, in fact, identical by showing that corresponding equations are identical. This is, in general, a hard problem, because arbitrary mathematical knowledge may be required. For example, one equation may involve a multiplication of two variables, $x \times y$, while the other may involve bit-wise decomposition of x and y, logical operations, and bit-wise reconstitution to form the product. However, it appears possible to capture enough knowledge to deal with many cases that arise in real designs. Equations may be given in terms of recursively or iteratively defined functions, in which case inductive proofs of equivalence may be needed.

In more complex cases, the correspondence between the machines may be a homomorphism, rather than exact equivalence, and the homomorphism may have a structural or a behavioral form. Structural homomorphism occurs when the two machines are effectively functionally identical, but their descriptions reflect a variation of organization. For example, one machine may have several outputs (or inputs, or state variables), while the other has the same information packed into one; alternatively, one machine may have redundant, or constant, state variables or outputs which are ignored in the other. It is a fairly straightforward matter, if the nature of the structural difference is known, to define a transformation from one machine to the other, and thus reduce the problem to showing exact equivalence. Finding the transformation when it is unknown, however, can increase the complexity considerably.

Behavioral, or temporal, homomorphism occurs when the two machines represent two views of the same machine, but viewed with different time-scales. For example, one machine may represent the behavior of a computer at the instruction sequence level, while the other represents the same computer at the microcode sequence level. In this case it is necessary to show that one step of the instruction-level machine is equivalent to a sequence of steps of the microcode-level machine. Sequences of operations allow the possibility of the machine cycling an indefinite number of times, depending on the input data. In such cases, it may be necessary to use inductive proofs. In the most complex cases, the form of a homomorphism may be structural and behavioral combined.

VERIFY currently handles identity of machines and, as we shall see, certain types of behavioral homomorphism.

7. Verifying the Design of a Module: Behavioral Identity

When presented with a module to be verified, the VERIFY system first checks to see whether correctness of this module type has been proved already, in which case it can return successfully. Otherwise, if the module is primitive, that is, has no internal structure, its correctness can be assumed. Finally, if correctness of the module is unknown, the system recursively verifies each of its parts, and then attempts to verify the module itself, deriving a behavioral description from its structure and comparing it with the specified behavior.

The behaviors are compared by considering the outputs, and state variables, in turn. For each output, the two behaviors give two expressions purporting to describe its function. the expressions are equated and an attempt is made to prove that the equation is an identity (i.e. holds for all possible values of inputs and states). The module is correct if this can be done for all outputs and state variables.

In work on verification, Shostak has developed a decision procedure for quantifier-free Presburger arithmetic (no multiplication, except by constants) extended to include uninterpreted functions and predicates [28]. Such a decision procedure seems to be applicable in many cases of program verification, and could be a useful component of our design verification system, but has not been implemented. Instead, a more general proof mechanism is used which performs algebraic manipulation to transform an equation through a sequence of steps into 'true' or 'false', in much the same way as the simplification procedures in MACSYMA [8, 9] and REDUCE [29, 30]. VERIFY goes somewhat beyond those systems in having a variety of different methods for both strategies and tactics, and using (currently simple) meta-level reasoning at several levels to determine which are appropriate.

The equation is first checked to see whether it is recognized as a trivial identity, of the form '$X = X$' or 'true', or whether it is a trivial non-identity, such as '$a = b$', where a and b are constants. If the equation is not trivial, an enumerative approach is considered. The size of the domain space of the equation is determined by finding the cardinality of the domains of the input and state variables occurring in it. If the space size is sufficiently small (less than about 40 combinations of variable values), the equation is tested by enumeration: each combination of variable values is generated and substituted into the equation, which is then simplified to 'true' or 'false'. This 'brute-force' approach is surprisingly useful. Complex designs are frequently composed of many simple pieces that are amenable to proof by enumeration, but which would require much additional mathematical knowledge and algebraic manipulation to prove by other means.

When the domain space it too large for enumeration, VERIFY considers proving identity by algebraic manipulation, provided the complexity of the equation is not too great (typically several hundred to a thousand subterms). The algebraic manipulation strategy incorporates several operations: evaluation, simplification, expansion, canonicalization, and case analysis.

Evaluation involves recursively considering subexpressions, such as '$1 + 2$', to see whether they can be replaced by constants, such as '3'. It is implemented with a general recursive PROLOG procedure that evaluates the arguments in an expression, and a set of rewriting rules that are applied to the result. To deal with arithmetic, PROLOG's evaluable predicates are used, after checking that the arguments are indeed numbers. Some examples of evaluation rules are:

```
evaluate1(not(true), false).
evaluate1(not(false), true).

evaluate1(if(true, X, Y), X).
evaluate1(if(false, X, Y), Y).

evaluate1(X + Y, Z)
   :- integer(X), integer(Y), Z is X + Y.
```

Simplification is an extension of evaluation that can replace a subexpression by a simpler one. For example, 'and(true, x)' is simplified to 'x'. This operation is also implemented with a set of rewriting rules, which are invoked by the evaluation mechanism. Simplification can be used for more than partial evaluation. Lemmas, such as De Morgan's laws or trigonometrical identities, often can be expressed as rewriting rules and are thereby easily invoked.

Expansion occurs when a function is observed on one side only of the equation. The definition of the function is then substituted for its call, and the resulting expression evaluated and simplified. Although expansion leads to larger expressions, it is much simpler to implement and control than attempting to contract the other side of the expression. Bit-wise connection of signals is a special case which is looked for by the meta-level routines. The observation of bit(i, x) on one side of the equation can lead to the expansion of x as a power series of its bits on the other side. Bit-expansion is used fairly frequently in the examples tried so far.

Canonicalization attempts to deal with certain combinatorial problems of proof. In particular, it attempts to handle associativity and commutativity of functions (such as '+', '×', 'and', and 'or') and their identities and zeros. Nested expressions involving an associative function are first flattened. A generalization of cancellation is performed in which two terms may be combined to yield a single result: 'x' and 'not(x)' are combined in an 'and' expression to yield 'false', while in an 'or' expression they yield 'true'. Identity elements of the function (such as 'true' for 'and') are then discarded, and any occurrence of a zero element of the function (such as 'false' for 'and') causes the entire expression to be replaced by the zero. The terms in the flattened expression are then lexically ordered, resulting in similar terms being grouped together. In particular, numbers are collected and the expression function can be evaluated over them (which was not possible when they were distributed over different subexpressions). Finally, the nested expression structure is rebuilt.

Other normalizations are also performed during canonicalization: logical expressions are put into a normal form, and conditional expressions are pulled to the outside. This is accomplished using more rewriting rules that deal with relations between expressions. For example, one rule rewrites 'not(if(C, X, Y))' to 'if(C, not(X), not(Y))'.

Case analysis is performed when the equation involves conditionals, which by this time are outermost in the expression, to determine whether the expression is a tautology. The analysis descends recursively through the conditionals, substituting truth for the condition in the true-expression, and falsity for it in the false-expression. For example, if the condition is '$x = 1$' then '1' can be substituted for 'x' in the true-expression, and 'false' for '$x = 1$' in the false-expression: If 'x' is known to be a Boolean variable, then '0' can be substituted in the false-expression. In its present form, VERIFY handles these cases, but does not deal with all the ramifications of the condition in both branches.

Evaluation, simplification, expansion, canonicalization, and case analysis can be applied repeatedly until they no longer have any effect. (In practice some care has been taken in the implementation to apply them in ways that avoid large amounts of wasted effort.) If the resulting expression is trivial, identity will have been proved or disproved.

If the automatic algebraic manipulation strategy does not manage to produce an answer, an interactive mode is entered. It was originally intended that the interactive mode would be the primary means of proof, with the user specifying the strategy (collect terms, substitute, simplify, etc.) and the system executing the tactics and doing the necessary bookkeeping. The interactive facility has not yet been fully implemented, partly because surprisingly much progress has been made using the automatic strategy described above! If VERIFY resorts to asking for help, the user currently can over-ride too much caution by insisting that it attempt algebraic manipulation or enumeration, can suggest enumeration upon just a few of the variables, can suggest that it try decomposing the problem into several cases, or can simply tell VERIFY to assume the identity is true, false or unknown.

8. A More Complex Example: D74

The most ambitious example that has been attempted is the module known as D74, decomposed in Fig. 2. The example was taken from Genesereth [13], a paper which addresses the problem of fault diagnosis. However, our version is enormously more detailed. At the top level, D74 contains three multipliers and two adders. The multipliers are composed of slices, each of which contains a one-bit multiplier, a shifter, and an adder. The adders are built from full-adders, which are built from selectors, which are built from logic gates. The logic gates are themselves described at two levels: an abstract Boolean function level, and a level closer to an underlying nMOS transistor model, involving tri-state signals and stored charge.

Enhancement and depletion-mode transistors, along with signal-joining nodes and ground, are the primitives upon which the entire design rests. The model used for transistors is a variation of one used by Gordon [21], and is a simplified switch model. Transistors are treated as uni-directional devices with one bit of internal state, representing the charge on the gate:

```
% Basic nMOS FET

module(eFet).

port(eFet, source(AneFet), input, booleZ).
port(eFet, drain(AneFet), output, booleZ).
port(eFet, gate(AneFet), input, booleZ).

state (eFet, charge(AneFet), boole).

outputEqn(eFet, drain(AneFet) : =
          if(or(and(gate(AneFet) = hiZ, charge(AneFet) = 1),
              gate(AneFet) = 1),
            source(AneFet), hiZ)).

stateEqn(eFet, charge(AneFet) : =
        if(gate(AneFet) = hiZ,
          charge(AneFet), gate(AneFet))).
```

D74 is parametrized in the number of bits in its input data. An instance that has three 9-bit inputs involves 49 different types of module, from 9-bit multipliers, 18-bit adders, 17-bit adders, and so on, down to transistors, with 9 levels of structural hierarchy. There are 29 538 primitive parts in the fully instantiated design, including 18 180 transistors. The design specification of D74 occupies about 400 PROLOG assertions.

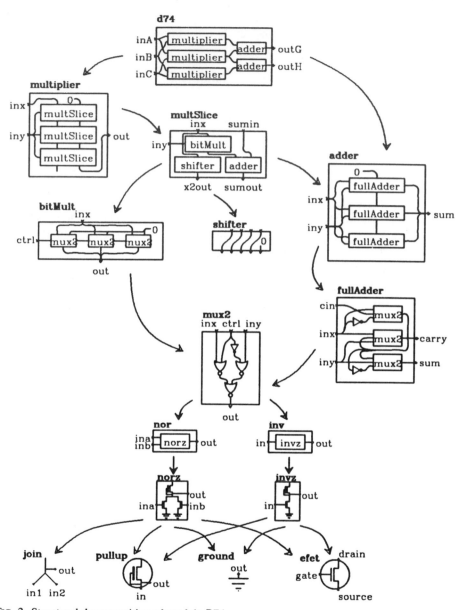

FIG. 2. Structural decomposition of module D74.

VERIFY can automatically prove the correctness of the design of D74, taking about 10 minutes of CPU time on a DEC 2060 running compiled PROLOG. Of this time, more than 25% is spent in pretty-printing expressions for monitoring. The entire proof trace occupies about 4800 lines of output, so we shall refrain from including it here! We shall, however, give a few interesting excerpts.

When VERIFY is asked to prove the correctness of the design, it recurses through the structure of the design until it reaches the primitives and then comes back up verifying correctness of each module as it does so:

```
| ?- verify(d74(8)).

))))) Attempting to verify d74(8) )))))
Verifying components of d74(8)
   ))))) Attempting to verify multiplier(8) )))))
   Verifying components of multiplier(8)
     ))))) Attempting to verify multSlice(16) )))))
     Verifying components of multSlice(16)
       ))))) Attempting to verify adder(16) )))))
       Verifying components of adder(16)
         ))))) Attempting to verify fullAdder )))))
         Verifying components of fullAdder
           ))))) Attempting to verify mux2 )))))
           Verifying components of mux2
             )))))) Attempting to verify nor2 ))))))
             Verifying components of nor2
               ))))) Attempting to verify nor )))))
               Verifying components of nor
                 ))))) Attempting to verify ground )))))
                 ground is primitive (needs no verification).
                 ((((( Success! Behavior of ground meets its specification.
                 ))))) Attempting to verify eFet )))))
                 eFet is primitive (needs no verification)
                 ((((( Success! Behavior of eFet meets its specification.
                 ))))) Attempting to verify join )))))
                 join is primitive (needs no verification).
                 ((((( Success! Behavior of join meets its specification.
                 ))))) Attempting to verify pullup )))))
                 pullup is primitive (needs no verification).
                 ((((( Success! Behavior of pullup meets its specification.
```

Having determined that the components of module type nor are correct, VERIFY finds its specified behavior, and then derives a new behavioral description from its structural description.

```
Verifying nor as whole

Determining specified behavior of nor
Specified behavior is:

Module: nor
Inputs: in2(nor), In1(nor)
```

States: charge2(nor), charge1(nor)
Output equations:
  out(nor)

   =

  not(or(if(in1(nor) = hiZ, charge1(nor), in1(nor)),
       if(in2(nor) = hiZ, charge2(nor), in2(nor)))))
State equations:
  charge2(nor) = if(in2(nor) = hiZ, charge2(nor), in2(nor))
  charge1(nor) = if(in1(nor) = hiZ, charge1(nor), in1(nor))

Determining behavior of nor from structure.
Determining behavior of ground as primitive.
Determining behavior of eFet as primitive.
Determining behavior of join as primitive.
Determining behavior of pullup as primitive.
Constructed behavior is:

Module: nor
Inputs: in2(nor), in1(nor)
States: charge2(nor), charge1(nor)
Output equations:
  out(nor)

   =

  if(joinfn(if(or(and(in1(nor) = hiZ, charge1(nor) = 1), in1(nor) = 1),
        0,
        hiZ),
      if(or(and(in2(nor) = hiZ, charge2(nor) = 1), in2(nor) = 1),
        0,
        hiZ))

   =

  hiZ,
  1,
  joinfn(if(or(and(in1(nor) = hiZ, charge1(nor) = 1), in1(nor) = 1),
       0,
       hiZ),
      if(or(and(in2(nor) = hiZ, charge2(nor) = 1), in2(nor) = 1),
       0,
       hiZ)))
State equations:
  charge2(nor) = if(in2(nor) = hiZ, charge2(nor), in2(nor))
  charge1(nor) = if(in1(nor) = hiZ, charge1(nor), in1(nor))

Notice that the derived behavioral description is rather more complex than the specification: it contains different functions, such as joinfn, and it has not been simplified in any way.

The next step is to consider the outputs and states, one by one, equating the behavior expressions and trying to prove identity. In the first case, for the output, VERIFY elects to use an enumeration strategy (printing a ∗ for each case as it is considered and evaluated.

> Trying to show behaviors are equivalent.
>
> Considering equations for out(nor)
> We must show that
>
>   not(or(if(value(in1(nor)) = hiZ,
>   value(charge1(nor)),
>   value(in1(nor))),
>   if(value(in2(nor)) = hiZ,
>   value(charge2(nor)),
>   value(in2(nor)))))
>   =
>   if(joinfn(if(or(and(value(in1(nor)) = hiZ, value(charge1(nor)) = 1),
>   value(in1(nor)) = 1),
>   0,
>   hiZ),
>   if(or(and(value(in2(nor)) = hiZ, value(charge2(nor)) = 1),
>   value(in2(nor)) = 1),
>   0,
>   hiZ))
>   =
>   hiZ,
>   1,
>   joinfn(if(or(and(value(in1(nor)) = hiZ, value(charge1(nor)) = 1),
>   value(in1(nor)) = 1),
>   0,
>   hiZ),
>   if(or(and(value(in2(nor)) = hiZ, value(charge2(nor)) = 1),
>   value(in2(nor)) = 1),
>   0,
>   hiZ)))
>
> Trying enumeration.
> ∗
> Identity has been demonstrated.

The two state variables lead to trivial identies:

> Considering equations for charge2(nor)

We must show that

if(value(in2(nor)) = hiZ, value(charge2(nor)), value(in2(nor)))

=

if(value(in2(nor)) = hiZ, value(charge2(nor)), value(in2(nor)))

Trivial identity: true

Considering equations for charge1(nor)
We must show that

if(value(in1(nor)) = hiZ, value(charge1(nor)), value(in1(nor)))

=

if(value(in1(nor)) = hiZ, value(charge1(nor)), value(in1(nor)))

Trivial identity: true
⟨⟨⟨⟨⟨ Success! Behavior of nor meets its specification.

And proof of module type nor is complete.

The next module considered, nor2, is a specialization of nor with inputs constrained to be boole, rather than tri-state booleZ. Once more, an enumerative proof is used:

Verifying nor2 as whole

Determining specified behavior of nor2
Specified behavior is:

Module: nor2
Inputs: in2(nor2), in1(nor2)
Output equations:
  out(nor2) = not(or(in1(nor2), in2(nor2)))

Determining behavior of nor2 from structure.
Constructed behavior is:

Module: nor2
Inputs: in2(nor2), in1(nor2)
Output equations:
  out(nor2)

  =

  not(or(if(in1(nor2) = hiZ, charge1(norA(nor2)), in1(nor2)),
         if(in2(nor2) = hiZ, charge2(norA(nor2)), in2(nor2))))

Trying to show behaviors are equivalent.

Considering equations for out(nor2)

We must show that

not(or(value(in1(nor2)), value(in2(nor2))))

=

not(or(if(value(in1(nor2)) = hiZ,
           charge1(norA(nor2)),
           value(in1(nor2))),
        if(value(in2(nor2)) = hiZ,
           charge2(norA(nor2)),
           value(in2(nor2))))))

Trying enumeration.
* * * *
Identity has been demonstrated.
⟨⟨⟨⟨⟨ Success! Behavior of nor2 meets its specification.

While verification via enumeration would be out of the question for the top-level module of the design, with $(2^9)^3 = 134\,217\,728$ cases to consider, it is a useful strategy when dealing with small fragments of a design. From a practical standpoint, it can be fairly fast, and it can also finesse the need for detailed rules, definitions, or lemmas relating different levels of function: only evaluation rules are required. As a simple example, the natural way to specify the behavior of module type mux2 is using the conditional, if, but the way to build it is using nor and inv gates. Thus,

We must show that

if(value(ctrl(mux2)), value(in1(mux2)), value(in0(mux2)))

=

not(or(not(or(value(in0(mux2)), value(ctrl(mux2)))).
        not(or(value(in1(mux2)), not(value(ctrl(mux2)))))))))

Trying enumeration.
* * * * * * * *
Identity has been demonstrated.
⟨⟨⟨⟨⟨ Success! Behavior of mux2 meets its specification.

When the verifier reaches module adder(16) things become more interesting. adder(16) is a instantiation of the parametrized adder shown in Section 4.2. It is built from fullAdders, whose behavior is specified as:

Module: fullAdder
Inputs: cin(fullAdder), iny(fullAdder), inx(fullAdder)

Output equations:
carry(fullAdder)

=

bit(1, inx(fullAdder) + iny(fullAdder) + cin(fullAdder))

sum(fullAdder)

=

bit(0, inx(fullAdder) + iny(fullAdder) + cin(fullAdder))

These equations are used in deriving the behavior of adder(16) from its structure, leading to a fairly complex output equation, which expresses the output in terms of individual bits of the inputs. (The pretty-printer does not show all the subterms when it prints large expressions.)

In order to show that this module meets its specification ...

We must show that

value(inx(adder(16))) + value(iny(adder(16)))

=

bits($\cdots + \cdots + \cdots * \cdots + 2 \uparrow 4 *$ bit(0, ...) $+ 2 \uparrow 3 *$ bit(0, $\cdots + \cdots$))

    +

    $2 \uparrow 2 *$ bit(0, $\cdots + \cdots +$ bit(1, ...)))

    +

    $2 \uparrow 1 *$ bit(0, bit(1, ...) + bit(1, ...) + bit(1, $\cdots + 0$))

    +

    $2 \uparrow 0 *$ bit(0, bit(0, value(...)) + bit(0, value(...)) + 0))

This equation is too complex for enumeration, so algebraic manipulation is attempted. The verifier recognizes the need to expand the left-hand side in terms of individual bits, and then puts the resulting expression into a canonical form, which reduces to a trivially true identity.

Complexity: 2840 subterms.
Trying symbolic manipulation.
Bit-expanding the left side...
Bit-expanded form is:
bits($\cdots + \cdots + \cdots * \cdots + 2 \uparrow 13 *$ bit(0, ...) $+ 2 \uparrow 14 *$ bit(0, $\cdots + \cdots$))

    +

    $2 \uparrow 15 *$ bit(0, $\cdots + \cdots +$ bit(1, ...)))

    +

    $2 \uparrow 16 *$ bit(0, bit(16, ...) + bit(16, ...) + bit(1, $\cdots + \cdots$)))

    +

    $2 \uparrow 17$

    *

    bit(1,

$$\text{bit(16, value(. . .)) + bit(16, value(. . .))}$$
$$+$$
$$\text{bit(1, } \cdots + \cdots + \text{bit(1, . . .))))}$$
$$=$$

bits($\cdots + \cdots + \cdots * \cdots + 2 \uparrow 4 * \text{bit(0, . . .)} + 2 \uparrow 3 * \text{bit(0, } \cdots + \cdots)$

$$+$$
$$2 \uparrow 2 * \text{bit(0, } \cdots + \cdots + \text{bit(1, . . .))}$$
$$+$$
$$2 \uparrow 1 * \text{bit(0, bit(1, . . .)) + bit(1, . . .) + bit(1, } \cdots + 0))$$
$$+$$
$$2 \uparrow 0 * \text{bit(0, bit(0, value(. . .)) + bit(0, value(. . .)) + 0))}$$

Canonicalizing the identity. . .
Canonical form is:

1

Identity has been established.
⟨⟨⟨⟨⟨ Success! Behavior of adder(16) meets its specification.

Canonicalization is not always sufficient by itself. For example, when the verifier deals with module type bitMult(16), after canonicalization it finishes up with an expression of the form:

```
if(value(ctrl(bitMult(16))),
  . . .
  +
  bit(2, value(in(. . .))) * value(ctrl(bitMult(16))) * 4
  +
  bit(1, value(in(bitMult(16)))) * value(ctrl(bitMult(16))) * 2
  =
  . . .
  +
  bit(2, value(in(bitMult(16)))) * 4
  +
  bit(1, value(in(bitMult(16)))) * 2,
  0
  =
  . . .
  +
  bit(2, value(in(. . . .))) * value(ctrl(bitMult(16))) * 4
  +
  bit(1, value(in(bitMult(16)))) * value(ctrl(bitMult(16))) * 2
```

The problem is that ctrl occurs only on one side of the two equalities inside the if. However, the value of ctrl is also the condition to be tested. To determine if the expression is a tautology, we should substitute Boolean values 1 and 0 for ctrl in the true and false branches of the condition. VERIFY does this, resulting in trivially true equalities after further simplification. Hence, the whole expression is true.

> Doing case analysis. . .
> Final form is:
>   1
> Identity has been established.
> ⟨⟨⟨⟨⟨ Success! Behavior of bitMult(16) meets its specification.

After a great deal more work, dealing with all the different parameterizations of the modules involved, VERIFY is able to show the correctness of the 9-bit multiplier and then the 18-bit adder. It is finally ready to deal with the top-level module of D74.

> Verifying d74(8) as whole
>
> Determining specified behavior of d74(8)
> Specified behavior is:
>
> Module: d74(8)
> Inputs: inC(d74(8)), inB(d74(8)), inA(d74(8))
> Output equations:
>   outH(d74(8)) = inA(d74(8)) * inC(d74(8)) + inB(d74(8)) * inC(d74(8))
>   outG(d74(8)) = inA(d74(8)) * inC(d74(8)) + inA(d74(8)) * inB(d74(8))
> Determining behavior of d74(8) from structure.
> Constructed behavior is:
>
> Module: d74(8)
> Inputs: inC(d74(8)), inB(d74(8)), inA(d74(8))
> Output equations:
>   outH(d74(8)) = inA(d74(8)) * inC(d74(8)) + inC(d74(8)) * inB(d74(8))
>   outG(d74(8)) = inB(d74(8)) * inA(d74(8)) + inA(d74(8)) * inC(d74(8))
> Trying to show behaviors are equivalent.
>
> Considering equations for outH(d74(8))
> We must show that
>   value(inA(d74(8))) * value(inC(d74(8)))
>   +
>   value(inB(d74(8))) * value(inC(d74(8)))
>   =
>   value(inA(d74(8))) * value(inC(d74(8)))
>   +
>   value(inC(d74(8))) * value(inB(d74(8)))

Domain space >512 cases. Too big to enumerate.
Complexity: 39 subterms.
Trying symbolic manipulation.
Canonicalizing the identity. . .
Canonical form is:
    1
Identity has been established.

Considering equations for outG(d74(8))
We must show that

   value(inA(d74(8))) * value(inC(d74(8)))
   +
   value(inA(d74(8))) * value(inB(d74(8)))
   =
   value(inB(d74(8))) * value(inA(d74(8)))
   +
   value(inA(d74(8))) * value(inC(d74(8)))

Domain space >512 cases. Too big to enumerate.
Complexity: 39 subterms.
Trying symbolic manipulation.
Canonicalizing the identity. . .
Canonical form is:
    1
Identity has been established.
⟨⟨⟨⟨⟨ Success! Behavior of d74(8) meets its specification.

In these last steps of the proof, the specified and derived behaviors differ only in the ordering of terms, which is easily handled by the canonicalization process. Module D74 has at last been proved to meet its specification!

We can now ask to see what has been accomplished:

```
yes
| ?- printverified.
    ground        true
    eFet          true
    join          true
    pullup        true
    nor           true
    nor2          true
    inv           true
```

inv2	true
mux2	true
fullAdder	true
adder(16)	true
shifter(16, 1)	true
bitMult(16)	true
multSlice(16)	true
adder(15)	true
shifter(15, 1)	true
bitMult(15)	true
multSlice(15)	true
adder(14)	true
shifter(14, 1)	true
bitMult(14)	true
multSlice(14)	true
adder(13)	true
shifter(13, 1)	true
bitMult(13)	true
multSlice(13)	true
adder(12)	true
shifter(12, 1)	true
bitMult(12)	true
multSlice(12)	true
adder(11)	true
shifter(11, 1)	true
bitMult(11)	true
multSlice(11)	true
adder(10)	true
shifter(10, 1)	true
bitMult(10)	true
multSlice(10)	true
adder(9)	true
shifter(9, 1)	true
bitMult(9)	true
multSlice(9)	true
adder(8)	true
shifter(8, 1)	true
bitMult(8)	true
multSlice(8)	true
multiplier(8)	true
adder(17)	true
d74(8)	true

```
yes
| ?– printparts(d74(8)).
   eFet      11358
   ground    6822
   join      4536
   pullup    6822
   Total     29538

yes
| ?– Transistors is 11358 + 6822.
Transistors = 18180
yes
```

9. Representation Revisited

9.1. Special types of module

The example of D74 has shown that our representation framework can deal with many levels of description, from complex modules down to individual transistors. There are, however, a few kinds of module which we have not yet discussed and which deserve some consideration: buses and memories. Such modules are key elements of architectural-level designs, but need a little care to avoid pitfalls.

9.2. Buses

A bus is a set of signal lines shared among a group of modules. Several modules can output data to the bus, and several can read data from it. From an electrical viewpoint, it is necessary to ensure that outputs do not fight each other. If one is attempting to drive the line high while another is attempting to drive it low, high currents can occur with possible subsequent damage to transistors. This situation can be avoided by arranging that outputs are less dogmatic, in one of two ways. We can insist that outputs only drive strongly towards one level, say low. If any output drives low, the signal line is driven low, and any other outputs attempting to drive it high are simply forcibly counteracted with no ill effects. This arrangement is called a *wired-or*: the nor gate defined earlier operates in precisely this way. An alternative arrangement is to allow outputs to drive strongly towards either high or low, but to insist that only one output at a time can do so. When an output is not driving strongly, it drives very weakly to an intermediate level; it is then said to be in a *high-impedance* state. An output that can be in a high-impedance state is a *tri-state* output. The constraint that only one output can drive at a time is not enforced by the bus in any way, but by the logical relations between the modules in the system.

In order to represent buses for VERIFY, we introduced (in section 4.1) the high-impedance state, hiZ, and a set of tri-state types, booleZ etc. We also need to introduce a function, busfn, that determines how two tri-state output signals combine. It is defined as:

```
evaluate1(busfn(X, hiZ), X),
evaluate1(busfn(hiZ, X), X).
evaluate1(busfn(X, X), X).
```

Note that a busfn expression cannot be simplified if its arguments are different and neither is hiZ. We can now define a bus module:

```
% Definition of a bus.

module(bus(Type, Inputs)).

port(bus(Type, Inputs), in(Abus, I), input, Type)
   :- range(0, I, Inputs)
port(bus(Type, Inputs), out(Abus), output, Type).

outputEqn(bus(Type, Inputs), out(Abus) := OutExpr)
   :- busOutExpr(Abus, Inputs, OutExpr).
```

In this description, note that the bus is parametrized in the type of signal it carries (which must be tri-state, such as integerZ(7)). Since the number of inputs to the bus is also a parameter, it is necessary for the output equation to be computed using a simple PROLOG function, busOutExpr, which constructs nested busfn expressions involving all the inputs. For example, the output equation for busV, a bus with 5 inputs is:

```
out(busV)
=
busfn(in(busV, 4),
      busfn(in(busV, 3),
            busfn(in(busV, 2),
                  busfn(in(busV, 1),
                        in(busV, 0)))))
```

The output of a bus can be connected to an input of a module, even when that module supplies one of the inputs to the bus (subject, in the current implementation of VERIFY, to the feedback loop constraint discussed in Section 5).

9.3. Memories

Another key component in systems is memory, either read-only or read-write memory. We need to be able to represent the storage and retrieval of large amounts of data in a convenient way.

A read-only memory (ROM) has a particularly simple description. It has one input, the address, and one output, the data. A particular ROM is specified by the number of words of storage it contains, the number of bits in each word, and the data stored in it. For VERIFY, a general-purpose ROM has the form:

```
% Microcode rom

module(rom(Words, Bits, Data)).

port(rom(Words, Bits, Data), address(Rom), input, integer(N))
    :- numBits(Words, N).
port(rom(Words, Bits, Data), data(Rom), output, integer(Bits)).

outputEqn(rom(Words, Bits, Data),
          data(Rom) := rfetch(address(Rom), Data)).
```

In this specification, numBits is a PROLOG function that determines how many bits of address are required to access the given number of words of store.

The lookup function, rfetch maps the address and something that represents the contents of the memory into the appropriate data. We have many alternative ways to represent the contents: as a vector, as a simple list, as a binary tree, and so on. The format affects only performance and not the logic of the lookup function. We have chosen, initially, to represent contents as a simple list of address and data pairs, for reasons which will be clearer shortly. It is also convenient not to embed the list (or other data structure) as a parameter in the module type name, since that is often printed. Instead we use a symbol that represents the data and have an assertion, such as

```
romContents(rom(511, 7, someData), [(0, 147), (1, 23), . . . , (511, 0)]).
```

that relates the ROM type rom(511, 7, someData) to its contents. As we shall see later, the contents of a ROM can easily be specified in a higher-level language, and a simple microcompiler used to compile them into a list of address and data integer pairs.

To represent read-write random-access memory is only a little more difficult. The contents of the memory can change over time, so we now need state variables to hold the contents. If the memory is sufficiently small, we can afford to define it in the obvious way:

```
% Simple random-access memory.

module(memory(Words, Bits)).

port(memory(Words, Bits), address(Mem), input, integer(N))
    :- numBits(Words, N).
```

```
port(memory(Words, Bits), datain(Mem), input, integer(Bits)).
port(memory(Words, Bits), write(Mem), input, boole).
port(memory(Words, Bits), dataout(Mem), output, integer(Bits)).

state(memory(Words, Bits), contents(Mem, I), integer(Bits))
   :- range(0, I, Words).

outputEqn(memory(Words, bits), dataout(Mem) : =
   contents(Mem, address(Mem))).

stateEqn(memory(Words, Bits), contents(Mem, I) : =
   if(and(write(Mem), I = address(Mem)),
      datain(Mem),
      contents(Mem, I))).
```

When the memory is large, however, it becomes cumbersome to represent all of its locations explicitly. Instead, we use a single state variable, in which we keep a data structure that represents current memory state. As in the case of the ROM, we use a list of address and data pairs to represent memory state.

```
% Concise random-access memory.

module(memory(Words, Bits)).

port(memory(Words, Bits), address(Mem), input, integer(N))
   :-numBits(Words, N).
port(memory(Words, Bits), datain(Mem), input, integer(Bits)).
port(memory(Words, Bits), write(Mem), input, boole).
port(memory(Words, Bits), dataout(Mem), output, integer(Bits)).

state(memory(Words, Bits), contents(Mem),
        list(pair(integer(N), integer(Bits))))
   :- numbits(Words, N).

outputEqn(memory(Words,Bits), dataout(Mem) : =
   fetch(address(Mem), contents(Mem)).

stateEqn(memory(Words, N), contents(Mem) : =
   if(write(Mem),
      store(address(Mem), contents(Mem), datain(Mem)),
      contents(Mem))).
```

Here, fetch is a function that maps from an address and a memory state to the appropriate data, by looking it up in the list of pairs, just like rfetch above. When storing data, the function store takes an address, a memory state, and the data to be stored, and returns a new memory state to be stored in contents. The new memory state is easily computed by prepending a new pair to the old state.

Just as in a LISP association list, the semantics are correct if the retrieval function returns only data from the first pair with the correct address that it finds. If the address is not found in the association list, a special default value, such as 'undefined' or '0', can be returned.

10. Another Example: A Simple Computer—Part 1

By way of illustrating the use of memories, buses, and other architectural-level modules, and to raise some further basic issues in verification we shall consider another example. This example is taken from [21] and is a register-transfer level description of a simple computer. The computer has lights and switches, a knob, and a button, as shown in fig. 3.

Like many other simple computers, the knob, switches, and button can be used to set internal registers and start a program. When the button is pressed, if the knob is in position 0, the program counter is loaded from the switches; when it is in position 1, the accumulator is loaded; when it is in position 2, the memory location pointed to by the program counter is loaded with the contents of the accumulator; and when it is in position 3, the program is started, beginning at the address currently in the program counter. If a program is running and the button is pushed, the computer is halted.

The instruction set of the computer is fairly simple, having only 8 operations:

```
0: halt          % Halt the computer
1: jmp   addr    % Jump to address
2: jzro  addr    % Jump if accumulator is zero
3: add   addr    % Add memory into accumulator
4: sub   addr    % Subtract memory from accumulator
5: ld    addr    % Load accumulator from memory
6: st    addr    % Store accumulator into memory
7: nop           % No operation
```

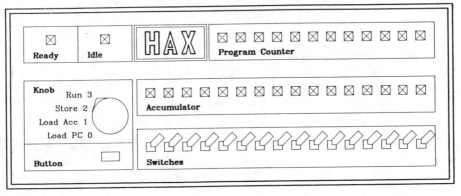

Fig. 3. A simple computer.

The architecture of the computer is shown in Fig. 4. It is divided into a control section and a data section. The data section is built upon a single data bus for 16-bit integers, with 6 registers connected to it: pc, the (13-bit) program counter, acc, the accumulator, ir, the instruction register, arg, an argument register, buf, a buffer register, and mar, the (13-bit) memory address register. In addition an arithmetic-logic unit, alu and a read-write random-access memory, mem, are connected to the bus, and the input from switches can also be routed onto it.

The control section contains a microprogram ROM, mprom, a microprogram counter, mpc, and a microinstruction decoder, mpdecode. When a microstruction is read from the ROM, the decoder sets various control signals in the data section and supplies a new microprogram address to mpc. The value of the new address may be conditional on the result of various tests: whether the button is currently pressed, whether the contents of the accumulator are zero, or what is the opcode of the instruction currently in the instruction register.

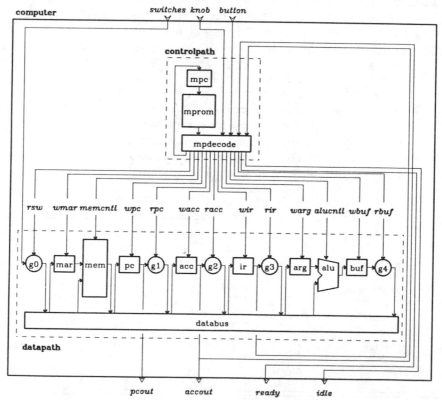

FIG. 4. Architecture of the simple computer.

The microcode to implement the required behavior of the computer is very small, consisting only of 26 microinstructions. The microinstructions are expressed in a semi-symbolic notation from which an elementary micro-assembler can generate the data actually stored in the microcode ROM.

```
% Contents of microcode rom

romSource(microrom, [
0: (ready, idle        ;if(button, 1, 0)),     % loop until button pressed
1: (0                  ;knob + 2),             % decode knob position
2: (rsw, wpc           ; 0),                   % switches → pc
3: (rsw, wacc          ; 0),                   % switches → acc
4: (rpc, wmar          ; 7),                   % pc → mar
5: (ready              ;if(button, 0, 6)),     % begin fetch-decode-execute
6: (rpc, wmar          ; 8),                   % pc → mar
7: (racc, write        ; 0),                   % acc → mem(mar)
8: (read, wir          ; 9),                   % mem(mar) → ir
9: (0                  ;opcode + 10),          % decode
10: (0                 ; 0),                   % halt
11: (rir, wpc          ; 5),                   % jmp: ir → pc
12: (0                 ;if(acc = 0, 11, 17)),  % jzro:
13: (racc, warg        ;19),                   % add: acc → arg
14: (racc, warg        ;22),                   % sub: acc → arg
15: (rir, wmar         ;24),                   % ld: ir → mar
16: (rir, wmar         ;25),                   % st: ir → mar
17: (rpc, inc, wbuf    ;18),                   % pc + 1 → buf
18: (rbuf, wpc         ; 5),                   % buf → pc
19: (rir, wmar         ;20),                   % ir → mar
20: (read, add, wbuf   ;21),                   % arg + mem(mar) → buf
21: (rbuf, wacc        ;17),                   % buf → acc
22: (rir, wmar         ;23),                   % ir → mar
23: (read, sub, wbuf   ;21),                   % arg-mem(arg) → buf
24: (read, wacc        ;17),                   % mem(mar) → acc
25: (racc, write       ;17),                   % acc → mem(mar)
26: (0                 ; 0),
27: (0                 ; 0),
28: (0                 ; 0),
29: (0                 ; 0),
30: (0                 ; 0),
31: (0                 ; 0)
],
[idle = 0, ready = 1, rbuf = 2, inc = 3, add = 4, sub = (3, 4),
warg = 5, rir = 6, wir = 7, racc = 8, wacc = 9, rpc = 10, wpc = 11,
read = 12, write = 13, wmar = 14, rsw = 15, wbuf = 16]).
```

The microinstruction is divided into high and low parts. The high (left) part consists of bits that specify control signals on various gates, given as symbols whose definition as a bit number is given in the third argument to romSource. The low (right) part consists of two address fields and a test to decide between them. In the above listing, the high and low parts are separated by a semi-colon.

The proof of correctness of the simple computer proceeds by recursing down through the structural hierarchy, through the control section until it reaches the primitives buffer(4), rom(25, 29, microm), and decode. We have already described the representation of the first two of these (buffer(4) is just a 5-bit register, like reg of Section 2). The behavior of decode is quite simple; it takes a micro-instruction as input, and outputs control signals and a next microprogram address. The next address depends upon the tests according to the semantics of the microinstruction format:

```
outputEqn(decode, nextaddr(M) : =
  if(and(bit(0 : 2, lo(data(M))) = 1, button(M)),
    bit(3 : 7, lo(data(M))),
  if(and(bit(0 : 2, lo(data(M))) = 2, acc(M) = 0),
    bit(3 : 7, lo(data(M))),
  if(bit(0 : 2, lo(data(M))) = 3,
    knob(M) + bit(8 : 12, lo(data(M))),
  if(bit(0 : 2, lo(data(M))) = 4,
    bit(13 : 15, ir(M)) + bit(8 : 12, lo(data(M))),
    bit(8 : 12, lo(data(M)))
    ))))).
```

where data is the microinstruction input, and lo a function that selects the right-hand part of it.

Having found the primitives, VERIFY pops up to the next level of module control(microrom). This module is described as a FSM interpreting microin-structions, but with no particular set of microinstructions in its ROM. It has a state variable, wrd, for the microprogram counter, which is updated by nextaddr from the decoder.

```
stateEqn(control(Rom), wrd(M) : =
  if(and(bit(0 : 2, lo(rfetch(wrd(M), Rom))) = 1, button(M)),
    bit(3 : 7, lo(rfetch(wrd(M), Rom))),
  if(and(bit(0 : 2, lo(rfetch(wrd(M), Rom))) = 2, acc(M) = 0),
    bit(3 : 7, lo(rfetch(wrd(M), Rom))),
  if(bit(0 : 2, lo(rfetch(wrd(M), Rom))) = 3,
    knob(M) + bit(8 : 12, lo(rfetch(wrd(M), Rom))),
```

```
    if(bit(0:2, lo(rfetch(wrd(M), Rom))) = 4,
      bit(13:15, ir(M))
      +
    bit(8:12, lo(rfetch(wrd(M), Rom)))),
    bit(8:12, lo(rfetch(wrd(M), Rom)))
    ))))).
```

The constructed behavior for control is easily shown to be identical to the specified behavior, as should be clear from the similarity of the above two equations, and the focus of the proof moves up a level to module controlpath. This module is really just a different view of control, which it has as its only part. The difference is that controlpath is described taking the contents of the microcode ROM into account. For example, its state variable (also called wrd) is described by the equation:

```
    stateEqn(controlpath, wrd(M)) :=
      if(wrd(M) = 0, if(button(M), 1, 0),
      if(wrd(M) = 1, knob(M) + 2,
      if(or(wrd(M) = 2, or(wrd(M) = 3, or(wrd(M) = 7, wrd(M) = 10))), 0,
      if(wrd(M) = 4, 7,
      if(wrd(M) = 5, if(button(M), 0, 6),
      if(wrd(M) = 6, 8,
      if(wrd(M) = 8, 9,
      if(wrd(M) = 9, bit(13:15, ir(M)) + 10,
      if(or(wrd(M) = 11, wrd(M) = 18), 5,
      if(wrd(M) = 12, if(acc(M) = 0, 11, 17),
      if(wrd(M) = 13, 19,
      if(wrd(M) = 14, 22,
      if(wrd(M) = 15, 24,
      if(wrd(M) = 16, 25,
      if(wrd(M) = 17, 18,
      if(wrd(M) = 19, 20,
      if(or(wrd(M) = 20, wrd(M) = 23), 21,
      if(or(wrd(M) = 21, or(wrd(M) = 24, wrd(M) = 25)), 17,
      if(wrd(M) = 22, 23,
        0)))))))))))))))))))).
```

Proving the correctness of controlpath amounts to proving that this is indeed an alternative view of control. For each of the 15 output control lines, this is achieved simply by enumerating over all of the possible microprogram addresses. For the state variable, wrd, which depends also on inputs from the knob, button, instruction register, and accumulator, as well as its own previous value, the search space is too large to consider all possible cases. Examination of the equation, however, shows that it contains the term

rfetch(value(wrd(controlpath)), microrom).

Unfortunately, when the value of an expression depends on the contents of a memory, we must generally treat memory lookup as an unstructured function mapping from addresses to unrelated values. We thus have little alternative but to consider all the cases, and this is just the strategy that VERIFY chooses to adopt. It enumerates over all the possible values of wrd, but keeps knob, button, ir, and acc as variables. This strategy is successful, and so controlpath is shown to be equivalent to control.

The next module to be considered is datapath, built from gates, registers, an alu, a memory, and a bus. The structure and behavior are straightforward but laborious to specify. The behavior description of the whole module is, in this case, no simpler than the compounding of the behaviors of its parts. Writing a behavior specification would amount to manually deriving it from the structure, and VERIFY can do this derivation more reliably. We therefore declare that this module has no behavior specification, by the assertion nospec(datapath), and pass the buck up one level in the structural hierarchy. This does not incur any penalty: all we are doing is using the description of datapath like a macro in the description of the next higher module. When VERIFY encounters a nospec module, it merely assumes it is correct, and proceeds, using the derived behavior instead of the specified behavior when it is needed to derive behavior of other modules. We shall see another example of this in Section 13.

The final step in this phase of proving the correctness of the computer is to prove the correctness of module host, which is a description of the entire computer at the microinstruction level. The structure of host is just controlpath and datapath connected together. The behavior is described in terms of a FSM which runs at the microinstruction rate. Output equations describe the values displayed by the panel lights, idle, ready, accout, irout, and pcout, and state equations describe the changes to all the internal registers, including the microprogram counter.

The proof of correctness of host proceeds smoothly through the output equations, but when the state equations are encountered, VERIFY runs into a little difficulty and asks for help.

Considering equations for bufcont(host)

We must show that

if(value(mpccont(host)) = 17,
   1 + value(pccont(host)),
   ...)
=

```
                if(hiZ = if(hiZ = busfn(if(if(. . . , 2 , . . .) = 1,
                                    fetch(value(. . .), value(. . .)), hiZ),
                                  busfn(if(or(. . . , . . .), value(. . .), hiZ),
                                    busfn(if(. . . , . . . , hiZ),
                                      busfn(. . . , . . .)))),
              undef,
              . . .),
            value(bufcont(host)),
            if(or(value(mpccont(host)) = 17,
                or(value(mpccont(host)) = 20,
                  value(mpccont(host)) = 23),
              . . . ,
              value(bufcont(host))))
```

Complexity: 2016 subterms. Too big to manipulate.
Let's try it together!

VERIFY now enters an interactive proof mode with a theorem to prove, namely the identity, and prints a theorem name, the names and types of variables involved, and the theorem itself.

```
To prove: th1

th1
    unknown [switches(host) : integer(15),
                bufcont(host) : integer(15),
                argcont(host) : integer(15),
                ircont(host) : integer(15),
                acccont(host) : integer(15),
                pccont(host) : integer(12),
                marcont(host) : integer(12),
                memcont(host) : list(integer(15)),
                mpccont(host) : integer(4)]
    if(value(mpccont(host)) = 17,
      1 + value(pccont(host)),
      . . .)
    =
    if(hiZ = if(hiZ = busfn(if(if(. . . , 2 , . . .) = 1,
                            fetch(value(. . .), value(. . .)), hiZ),
                          busfn(if(or(. . . , . . .), value(. . .), hiZ),
                            busfn(if(. . . , . . . , hiZ),
                              busfn(. . . , . . .)))),
                undef,
                . . .),
```

```
  value(bufcont(host)),
  if(or(value(mpccont(host)) = 17,
      or(value(mpccont(host)) = 20,
          value(mpccont(host)) = 23)),
    . . . ,
      value(bufcont(host))))
Prove |
```

The interactive prover is only partially implemented at present. The intention is that the user should supply the strategy, in the form of high-level commands like "simplify this", "collect terms in x", "substitute the definition of this function for its call", or "split the proof into cases on the basis of..." and the prover should execute the tactics. It also keeps track of the sequence of steps in the proof, and the intermediate results, so that it can be used to explore different strategies. A truth maintenance system is incorporated, so that the consequences of different branches of the proof are propagated, and assumptions can be made and disproved or proved.

The user has currently a rather limited repertoire of commands. He can insist that the prover proceed with algebraic manipulation, or full enumeration, if he judges that VERIFY has been too timid in the face of complexity; He can tell it to assume truth or falsity of the theorem; Or he can ask it to try enumerating over the values for a subset of the variables. In this particular case, VERIFY is told to enumerate over the possible addresses in the microprogram counter, and verify that the equation reduces to true each time.

```
Prove | enumerate(th1, mpccont(host)).
* * * * * * * * * * * * * * * * * * * * * * * * * * * * * * * * *
th1 is true    enumerated

Thank you. We have proved identity.
```

The same piece of advice (enumerate over program counter addresses) is needed for verifying each of the state equations. To enable VERIFY to decide for itself that this approach is necessary should not be difficult. Inspection of the identity reveals that tests are made for specific values of mpccont in many subterms. This alone suggests that enumeration would greatly simplify the expression. A little domain knowledge also indicates that program counters may often need such enumeration since they index into memory.

When the last state equation has been verified, we have proved the correctness of the computer at the microinstruction level. It now remains to bridge the gap between microinstructions and macroinstructions.

11. Verifying the Design of a Module: Behavioral Homomorphism

Proving the correctness of computer microcode is one example of proving that two behavior descriptions are homomorphic. In this case, we wish to show that a sequence of microinstructions is equivalent to a single macroinstruction. There are many analogous situations. For example: multiplier/dividers in computers often iterate to compute their results; longtitudinal parity checking is inherently iterative; digital signal processing is often implemented in serial hardware. To reason about such modules and systems it is necessary to introduce the notion of sequences of inputs, actions, and outputs. In the general case, the sequences of actions and outputs depend in both form and content upon the inputs: for example, a module might need to cycle N times to compute the factorial of N.

To handle sequential computation properly, we need more powerful mathematical techniques, such as induction. Fortunately, however, there are many cases where we can obtain useful results without such power. The number of cycles required may be constant, as for serial arithmetic, or at least tightly bounded. We can readily make the transition from micro- to macro-behavior by unrolling the iterations, composing behavior descriptions, the output from one being the input to the next. (Intuitively, we do the equivalent of constructing a chain of identical modules, each of which computes the result of a single iteration.) We then compare the unrolled behavior with the specified behavior, just as before.

The unrolling process has the odor of simulation about it, but it is not as undesirable as conventional hardware simulation, insofar as signals are still represented symbolically: the number of cycles to be unrolled is usually much more limited than the number of possible input combinations at a given instant. To decide when to stop unrolling is not a problem when the number of cycles is fixed, but in other cases it is necessary to observe the results of each unrolling step. For example, if a module outputs zero until it has finished computing and then outputs the result, we need to examine the output expression to determine when it is no longer zero. In general, after each iteration the termination condition may or may not hold, so that the constructed behavior description will be tree-structured with two branches at each node corresponding to the two cases of the termination condition.

The question arises as to whether inputs may change during the microcycles, and the answer depends on how we choose to view the computation carried out by the hardware. We may view the macrosteps as defining the time-scale for inputs, implying that inputs are constant during a macrostep. In this case, during the unrolling, inputs are assumed to have always the same values. Alternatively, we may view the microsteps as defining the time-scale, in which case inputs may change from microstep to microstep. We must then introduce the notion of input at a particular time. We can readily modify our notation for signals from value(in(AModule)) to value(in(AModule), t) to distinguish the different values of an input at different times in a behavior expression. Naturally, this has ramifications to notation for state variables and outputs too, but the extension is straightforward. The current version of VERIFY assumes that inputs are constant during unrolling, but it is intended that future versions will represent time explicitly (as is done in DART [13]).

One further complication is that several different states at the step level should possibly be considered the same state at the sequence level. For example, the contents of registers used to hold intermediate results may be immaterial—indeed, the very existence of such a register may be ignored at the sequence level (as for arg and buf in the simple computer). In the computer example above, it is convenient to describe the behavior of the system as obeying console commands or executing the program, while at the microlevel these correspond to the microprogram counter containing an address less than or equal to 4, or greater than 4.

To deal with this mapping of states between two levels, we can simply define states at the higher level to be functions of those at the lower level. The proof mechanism needs then to be extended so that it can handle the resulting ambiguity. In VERIFY mappings are currently implemented explicitly, listing pairs of corresponding values for state variables at the two levels, and all the possible alternative situations are considered notionally in parallel. Possible initial states of the microlevel system at the start of a macrostep are declared (although they could be computed under some circumstances), and the unrolling process starts with these, continuing until a termination condition specifying the end of a macrostep is met. VERIFY does not currently handle the full complexity of sequential computation, in particular, cases where induction is essential, but it does handle a fairly useful subset.

12. Another Example: A Simple Computer—Part 2

Having established the correctness of the description of the computer at the microinstruction level, it is now necessary to verify it at the macroinstruction level. The behavior specification at the macroinstruction level includes port declarations, a part declaration to indicate the microinstruction level specification, host, and declarations that relate the two levels:

```
part(computer, hostH(c), host).
stateCorresp(computer, execute(C), host, mpccont(hostH(C)),
                [(0, 0), (1, 5)]).
init(computer, [([mpccont(hostH(C)) = 0], [execute(C) = 0]),
                ([mpccont(hostH(C)) = 5], [excute(C) = 1])]).
until(computer, ready(hostH(C)) = 1).
```

Here, the stateCorresp declaration says that the execute state variable of computer corresponds to the mpccont state variable of host and gives the explicit mapping between them. (It is only necessary to map the values of mpccont that can actually exist at the end of a macrostep.) The init statement gives the possible states at the start of a macrostep, and the until statement gives the step termination condition. In principle, it is possible to infer the initial condition from the termination condition, or vice versa, but this has not yet been done.

The verification of the computer continues, as follows:

Verifying computer as whole
Determining specified behavior of computer
Specified behavior is:

. . .

Determining behavior of computer from sequencing module

To determine the behavior from the microlevel description, VERIFY begins to unroll its behavior, starting from the two possible initial states, and looking for the termination condition.

*** Unfolding cannot go on because the following formula
cannot be evaluated to check for halting conditions:

if(button(hostH(computer)), 0, 1)

From the definition of the microcode, this conditional expression is what determines the next microprogram address: if the button is pressed, the address is 0 and the unrolling can halt; if not, the address is 1 and unrolling must continue. VERIFY must therefore consider both possibilities, but since it is currently cautious, it asks the user for advice about proceeding.

Please enter a variable for enumeration : button(M).

The process continues until:

*** Unfolding cannot go on because the following formula
cannot be evaluated to check for halting conditions:

or(bit(13:15, fetch(pccont(hostH(computer)),
memcont(hostH(computer)))) + 10 = 0,
bit(13:15, fetch(pccont(hostH(computer)),
memcont(hostH(computer)))) + 10 = 5)

Please enter a variable for enumeration : opcode(M).

This expression can never be true, since bit returns a positive integer, but VERIFY does not yet have the appropriate mathematical ability to realize that fact.

For the next microinstruction, the microcode dispatches to the rom address opcode + 10 (which is where the above expression originated). It is possible to determine by inspecting this expression that the cases to be considered are the 8 possible values of bit(13:15,...), rather than the 2^{13} values of pccont or the enormously many values of memcont. However, VERIFY asks for advice, and the user instructs it to enumerate over possible values of opcode, opcode is a function whose body expands to

$$\text{bit}(13:15, \text{fetch}(\text{pccont}(\text{hostH}(\text{computer})),}$$
$$\text{memcont}(\text{hostH}(\text{computer}))))).$$

When the unrolling process is complete, a description of the computer's behavior can be constructed:

Constructed behavior is:

Module: computer
Inputs: switches(computer), button(computer), knob(computer)
States: execute(computer), acccont(computer),
        pccont(computer), memcont(computer)
Output equations:
  idle(computer)   -
    =
  if(and(execute(computer) = 0, button(computer) = 0),
     1,
    if(and(execute(computer) = 0,
           and(button(computer) = 1, knob(computer) = 0)),
       1,
      if(and(execute(computer) = 0,
             and(button(computer) = 1, knob(computer) = 1)),
         1,
        if(and(execute(computer) = 0,
               and(button(computer) = 1, knob(computer) = 2)),
           1,
          if(and(execute(computer = 0, and(. . . . = 1, . . . = 3)),
             0,
            if(and(. . . = 1, and (. . . , . . .)),
               1,
              if(and(. . . , ...), 0, if(. . . , 0, . . .))))))))).
  ready(computer)
    =
    . . .

The constructed behavior equations are rather complex, since they were derived by an enumerative case analysis, and have not been simplified to any great extent.

Trying to show behaviors are equivalent.

Since the constructed behavior is built from enumeration,
the proof will be based on the same enumeration:
Variable(s) to be enumerated are:
[execute(computer), button(computer),
 knob(computer), opcode(computer)]
Considering equations for idle(computer)
We must show that

    if(and(value(execute(computer)),
         or(value(button(computer)),
            value(opcode(computer)) = 0)),
     1,
     if(and(not(value(execute(computer))),
         and(value(button(computer)),
            value(knob(computer)) = 3)),
       0,
      not(value(execute(computer)))))
   =
   if(and(value(execute(computer)) = 0,
       value(button(computer)) = 0),
     1,
     if(and(value(excute(computer)) = 0,
        and(value(button(computer)) = 1,
          value(knob(computer)) = 0)),
      1,
      . . .))

Enumerate on: [execute(computer), button(computer),
              knob(computer), opcode(computer)]. . .

* *
* *
* *
We have demonstrated that this is an identity.

Similarly, the equations for the other output and state variables are dealt with by enumeration over the same set, until

   . . .
We have demonstrated that this is an identity.
⟨⟨⟨⟨⟨ Success! Behavior of computer meets its specification.

The computer has now been verified at the instruction level, and our proof is complete. The proof required about 6 minutes of CPU time on a DEC 2060.

13. Towards Assertions about Behavior

Our approach to hardware verification is extremely promising and it appears applicable to a wide range of real designs. One factor seems to be an inherent limitation, however, and that is the need to provide a total specification of each module. It is a limitation because behavior can be extremely complex, and providing a total specification may be extremely difficult: We have seen in the previous example how it was preferable not to provide a specification at all for datapath, but to pass the buck to the next level above. We would perhaps prefer to relax the totality and make more general assertions about outputs and states.

One way in which we might make things easier is to introduce a constant, unspecified, into our description language, with the semantics that it is meant to represent 'the right behavior'. For example, in

```
output(Module) : =
    if(input(Module) = 73, factorial(19), unspecified).
```

we are prepared to say what happens if input has a particular value, but not otherwise. We could then arrange that our verification mechanism would take account of this new construct, verifying only the specified parts of the description. This approach seems problematic and unlikely to provide what we really need.

Replacing the total specification with a set of assertions might help in some situations, but it brings its own difficulties. In order to verify the correctness of a module, we would presumably use assertions about its component modules (and their interconnections), but we would need to be very careful in our selection of those assertions. An assertion about a component module might lead to a proof when the module was used in system A, but not when used in system B.

There is another approach, which has some of the good features of total functional specification and assertional specification. It is best illustrated with an example.

Consider an error detecting and correcting module, edac, whose block diagram is given in Fig. 5(a). The inputs are a 32-bit data word and a 7-bit parity code. The parity code for the input data is computed internally, and the resulting 7-bit code is compared with the input code by an exclusive-or operation. If the data has not been corrupted, the two codes will be identical, and the exclusive-or will be zero. If the data is corrupt, however, the exclusive-or will be non-zero: each single-bit corruption will give rise to a unique 7-bit signature. The signature is then decoded to give a 32-bit word in which a single

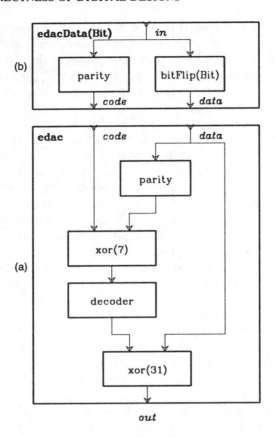

FIG. 5. Verifying an error detecting and correcting module.

bit is set, namely the one that was corrupted in the data. Finally, the exclusive-or of the decoded word with the input data flips the corrupted bit and produces corrected data for the output.

To specify the behavior of this module is difficult. It is not at all clear even how to describe succinctly what it means for the data to be corrupt and not agree with the parity code. We can, of course describe the output purely as an extremely complicated function of the inputs, ignoring all notions of any relationship between the input data and code. Since each of the 32 bits of output depends on all 7 bits of the signature, and each of these depends on roughly 16 of the input bits, there will be thousands of terms involved. How might we cope with this complexity?

One solution we give here is a hardware analog of a principle used by Boyer and Moore in their program verification system [10]. We consider another module, edacData(BadBit), which computes data for the error-correcting module. It is shown in Fig. 5(b). It takes a 32-bit input, computes a 7-bit parity code in exactly the same way as the error-correcting module, and passes that to one output. It also takes the input data and passes it through a component which corrupts the data in a controlled way, namely by flipping one bit. The bit in question is specified by the parameter BadBit. Specification and verification of this module is comparatively easy.

We now build a composite system, testEdac(BadBit), from the error-introducing and error-correcting modules, feeding the outputs of the former directly to the inputs of the latter. We can now readily specify the behavior for the composite: the output is just the same as the input—it has no net effect on the data! We can now tell our verifier that we are not prepared to specify behavior for the error-correcting module and that it should use the behavior description it builds from the structure. We then ask it to prove the correctness of the composite. If it can do so no matter which bit is corrupted internally, we know the design of the error-correcting module is correct.

This problem has been presented to VERIFY and correctness has been proved in two different ways. The first way is to specify the parity encoding and decoding operations in full detail. The constructed equations for the output bits of the composite are very large, but they are readily simplified down to just the input value. (The equations are so large that VERIFY can only hold three bits' worth at a time.) This is repeated for each of the 32 possible single-bit corruptions of the data. Of course, the input data is a symbolic variable, rather than any particular numerical value, so the proof holds for all of the 2^{32} inputs.

The second way in which correctness has been proved is to represent the encoding and decoding operations by functions parityCode and decode, so that two of the output equations of the component modules become:

outputEqn(parity, out(AP)) : = parityCode(in(AP))).

outputEqn(decoder, out(AD)) : = decode(in(AD))).

In the first way, we would have defined these functions as complex expressions involving the xor of individual bits of their arguments. Now, however, we only need to partially define them by giving two lemmas:

define(parityCode(xor(IN1, IN2)),
        xor(parityCode(IN2), parityCode(IN1))).
define(decode(parityCode(2 ↑ J)), 2 ↑ J).

When asked to prove correctness of the composite, testEdac(badBit), VERIFY builds a specification which is much simpler, and the resulting identity to be proved is:

$$value(in(testEdac(badBit)))$$
$$=$$
$$xor(xor(value(in(testEdac(badBit))), 2 \uparrow badBit),$$
$$decode(xor(parityCode(xor(value(in(testEdac(badBit))),$$
$$2 \uparrow badBit)),$$
$$parityCode(value(in(testEdac(badBit)))))))$$

This identity is simplified and put into canonical form, and in doing so the definitions of parityCode and decode given in the lemmas are substituted for their calls, and the equation collapses down to true. Note that in this case badBit is a symbol, rather than a particular integer, so the proof holds no matter which bit is corrupted.

Verification of hardware by embedding it in a larger system with more manageable characteristics has not yet been formalized, nor have its limitations been explored. It promises to be a very useful technique.

14. Discussion

14.1. Performance and competence

VERIFY is a large PROLOG program, occupying about 4200 lines of source text, with about 1000 clauses in 300 predicates. On the DEC 2060, it results in 48 600 words of compiled code. It also runs (interpreted) on a VAX 11/780.

VERIFY has been applied to only a few large systems (such as D74 and the simple computer), but about 60 different classes of module have now been verified. Verification proceeds quite rapidly, with less than 10 minutes of CPU time being required for a 9-bit version of D74, of which 25% is spent in planning pretty-printing. The main restriction on the complexity of examples which currently can be tackled is the amount of workspace required by PROLOG. To deal with large systems, it is necessary to verify them a piece at a time, or to restart verification when it aborts due to lack of space. Since VERIFY records which modules have been verified in the database, restarting does not result in duplication of work.

The high speed of verification and the large scale of designs that can be tackled stem primarily from the hierarchical decomposition of design descriptions. The complexity of proofs varies with the number of types of module, rather than the number of primitive component instances. The decomposition also allows an enumerative strategy to be used more frequently, which reduces the likelihood that the verifier becomes stuck for lack of mathematical knowledge.

The competence of VERIFY is a function of the amount of domain knowledge and general mathematical knowledge it contains. Development of the program is being accomplished by trying it on examples and extending it if inadequacies are found. It is certainly easy to prevent verification by writing behavior descriptions that exploit some piece of mathematics about which VERIFY is ignorant. On the other hand, it is usually possible to find a way of writing the description that enables a proof to be found. Clearly, we wish to provide the program with sufficient knowledge that it can handle the behavior descriptions that are natural in hardware design.

14.2. Limitations and extensions

VERIFY is limited in a number of ways: It is limited fundamentally in the type of behavior descriptions that it can handle; and it is limited by its mathematical abilities.

Currently only functional verification can be performed, with no consideration of timing. Timing problems are often highly significant in real designs, and it is desirable to locate potential race and hazard conditions. We would certainly like to include eventually some representation of delays and relative timing in our descriptions. It is fairly straightforward to introduce such things into our notation. It is only slightly harder to add the appropriate inferential machinery: For example, to determine the value of a signal may involve determining its value at an earlier time, and then showing that it has not changed since then.

Once some basic capabilities for dealing with time are incorporated, we can turn some attention to reasoning about sequences of inputs and outputs. The facilities for dealing with temporal homomorphism are too specialized for this purpose and need to be extended. Sequences might be dealt with by a mechanism similar to unrolling, but for full generality we need to introduce inductive proofs for sequences of indeterminate length. Dealing with truly asynchronous systems, however, requires a rather different approach, and some revision of the basic representation as well as proof mechanisms. One approach is to use temporal logic to make assertions about a module, since it is hard to provide a total specification of behavior over time where asynchronous systems are concerned. Moszkowski has used temporal logic to describe asynchronous modules [31, 32], while Fujita et al. have used a variant of PROLOG for verifying small asynchronous systems by verifying assertions about states and transitions between them [33].

More generally, assertions provide a useful alternative to total specification even for synchronous systems. The proofs of correctness then become proofs of general tautologies, rather than identities. Assertions are attractive because they seem simpler to write, but since they say much less than total functions, there is considerable potential for proofs stalling through lack of information: It is not always easy to know what assertions about component modules will be needed when considering a higher-level module.

The mathematical abilities of VERIFY, while fairly general, would certainly benefit from extension and a little revision. In case analysis, much more can be inferred from the assumption of truth or falsity of the condition in an if expression. In the unrolling process for computer, relatively little effort is required to handle the tautologies (or negations of tautologies) that were encountered.

We should reconsider the derivation of behavior descriptions from structural ones, to deal with over-complex expressions and loops. In the former case, we can retain some of the equations for internal variables, instead of substituting for them immediately, but that means dealing with sets of equations. In the latter case, new variables may need to be introduced and new mathematical abilities are required for simultaneous solution of equations.

Another mathematical ability we should attempt to introduce is induction. Induction is required for reasoning about sequences when the number of steps depends on the data. It would also be very useful for proving correctness of parametrized modules, such as an N-bit adder, instead of resorting to proving correctness of all the module specializations with particular values of parameters. The latter application is less significant, however, than the former.

As we contemplate the many extensions and improvements to the mathematical abilities of VERIFY, it seems we are heading towards a general-purpose mathematical expert subsystem. Such a subsystem would be given an equation, or set of equations, and be asked to verify certain fundamental assertions about them, such as an expression being a tautology (with identity as a special case), or to solve algebraically a set of simultaneous equations, or to find a homomorphism between two sets of equations. Such an enterprise is of interest in its own right, and is more in the spirit of MECHO than of MACSYMA, since we need to capture strategic expertise, rather than just algorithms for manipulation.

Finally, we are aiming at developing a truly useful system. Part of the apparent competence of VERIFY stems from the fact that we are developing a specialist system for verification of designs, which tends to bound what needs to be done much more than developing a more general system for mathematical manipulation. This implies, however, that we need to provide the means for describing designs succinctly and mathematical knowledge of the notation and functions used in the description. We need to improve upon the current specification syntax (which is also the internal representation format) to make it easier to use. We need also to extend the vocabulary of functions used in specifications to cover all that a designer might want to say.

15. Conclusion

VERIFY is only a first attempt at implementing a design verification system that is founded on a clear mathematical model, and that can deal with designs of an interesting degree of complexity. The knowledge provided to the present version is tuned in a few places to handle some special cases, and much must be done before it can be made into a real design tool. However, hints of the potential of this approach, and particularly the virtues of structured designs, are already evident.

In the course of this work, we have found that quite rapid progress can be made and large designs can be approached. Hardware appears to be more constrained than software in a number of ways, at least, at the levels we have been considering so far. For example, a module has very well defined interfaces with the outside world, and modules can only affect each other *via* inputs and outputs. Of course, when modules become highly complex and include computers and memories containing programs, the distinctions between hardware and software evaporate. In the meantime, however, it seems that there is much we can accomplish.

In the immediate future, VERIFY will be applied to more designs, especially real ones, and it will be extended to deal with them. The mathematician expert subsystem will be developed further, and the range of problems with which it can deal will be increased. In a broader context, VERIFY is but one component of a larger system that can act as an interactive consultant to a designer. There is synergy to be gained by putting together programs currently under development for design entry, simulation, verification, test generation and diagnosis ... but that is the subject of a future paper.

ACKNOWLEDGMENT

This work owes an intellectual debt to Michael Gordon, who showed how structured designs can be verified at many levels using denotational semantics, with laborious manual proofs.

Richard Sheng contributed to this research by exploring the problem of behavioral homomorphism and writing an initial implementation of microcode verification for the simple computer.

REFERENCES

1. Dahl, O.-J., Dijkstra, E.W. and Hoare, A.R., *Structured Programming* (Academic Press, London and New York, 1972).
2. Rich, C., Shrobe, H.E. and Waters, R.C., An overview of the programmer's apprentice, in: *Proceedings Sixth International Joint Conference on Artificial Intelligence*, Tokyo, Japan, August, 1979.
3. *Proceedings, 20th Design Automation Conference*, Miami Beach, FL, June, 1983.
4. Johannson, D., Silicon compilation, Ph.D. Thesis, Department of Computer Science, California Institute of Technology, Pasadena, CA, 1981.
5. Ibarra, O.H. and Sahni, S., Polynomially complete fault detection problems, *IEEE Trans. Comput.* **24**(3) (1976) 242–250.
6. Schwartz, R.L. and Melliar-Smith, P.M., Formal specification and mechanical verification of SIFT: A fault-tolerant flight control system, SRI International, Menlo Park, CA, TR CSL-133, 1982.
7. Bundy, A., Byrd, L., Luger, G., Mellish, C., Milne, R. and Palmer, M., Solving mechanics problems using meta-level inference, in: *Proceedings Sixth International Joint Conference on Artificial Intelligence*, Tokyo, Japan, August, 1979.
8. Martin, W.A. and Fateman, R.J., The MACSYMA system, in: *Proceedings Second Symposium on Symbolic Manipulation*, Los Angeles, CA (1971) 59–75.
9. Fateman, R.J., Essays in algebraic simplification, Ph.D. Thesis, Department of Electrical Engineering, MIT, Cambridge, MA, 1972.

10. Boyer, R. and Moore, J., *A Computational Logic* (Academic Press, London and New York, 1979).
11. Singh, H., MARS: A multiple abstraction rule-based simulator, Fairchild Laboratory for Artificial Intelligence Research, Palo Alto, CA, FLAIR Tech. Rep. No. 17, 1983.
12. Singh, N., Private communication, Fairchild Laboratory for Artificial Intelligence Research, Palo Alto, CA, 1982.
13. Genesereth, M.R., Diagnosis using hierarchical design models, in: *Proceedings National Conference on Artificial Intelligence*, Pittsburgh, PA, August, 1982.
14. Davis, R., Diagnosis via causal reasoning: Paths of interaction and the locality principle, in: *Proceedings National Conference on Artificial Intelligence*, Washington, DC, August, 1983.
15. Gabriel, J.R., A diagnostic automation, Argonne National Laboratory, Argonne, IL, ANL/MCS-TM-10, 1983.
16. Wagner, T.J., Hardware verification, Ph.D. Thesis, Department of Computer Science, Stanford University, Stanford, CA, 1977.
17. Hanes, L.H., Logic design verification using static analysis, Ph.D. Thesis, Department of Electrical Engineering, University of Illinois at Urbana-Champaign, IL, 1983.
18. Gordon, M., Two papers on modelling and verifying hardware, Computer Laboratory, Cambridge University, Cambridge, England, 1981.
19. Stoy, J.E., *Denotational Semantics: The Scott–Strachey Approach to Programming Language Theory* (MIT Press, Cambridge, MA, 1983).
20. Gordon, M., Milner, R. and Wadsworth, C., *Edinburgh LCF* (Springer, Berlin, 1979).
21. Gordon, M., Proving a computer correct, Computer Laboratory, Cambridge University, Cambridge, England, Tech. Rept. No. 42, 1983.
22. Shostak, R.E., Verification of VLSI designs, in: *Proceedings Third Caltech Conference on VLSI* (Computer Science Press, Rockville, MD, 1983).
23. Shostak, R.E., Schwartz, R.L. and Melliar-Smith, P.M., STP: A mechanized logic for specification and verification, in: *Proceedings Sixth Conference on Automated Deduction*, Courant Institute, New York, 1982.
24. Clocksin, W. and Mellish, C., *Programming in PROLOG* (Springer, Berlin, 1981).
25. Foster, M.J., Syntax-directed verification of circuit function, in: H. Kung, B. Sproull and G. Steele (Eds.), *VLSI Systems and Computations* (Computer Science Press, Carnegie-Mellon University, Pittsburgh, PA, 1981) 203–212.
26. Floyd, R.W., Assigning meanings to programs, *Proc. Amer. Math. Soc. Symp. Appl. Math.* **19** (1967) 19–31.
27. Mead, C. and Conway, L., *Introduction to VLSI Systems* (Addison-Wesley, Reading, MA, 1980).
28. Shostak, R.E., A practical decision procedure for arithmetic with function symbols, *J. ACM* **26**(2) (1979) 351–360.
29. Hearn, A.C., REDUCE: A user-oriented interactive system for algebraic simplification, in: *Interactive Systems for Experimental Applied Mathematics* (Academic Press, London and New York, 1967).
30. Hearn, A.C., REDUCE users' manual, University of Utah, Salt Lake City, UT, UCP-19, 1973.
31. Moszkowski, B.C., A temporal logic for reasoning about hardware, in: *Proceedings Sixth International Symposium on Computer Hardware Description Languages*, Carnegie-Mellon University, Pittsburgh, PA (1983) 79–90.
32. Moszkowski, B.C., Reasoning about digital circuits, Ph.D. Thesis, Department of Computer Science, Stanford University, Stanford, CA, 1983.
33. Fujita, M., Tanaka, H. and Moto-oka, T., Verification with PROLOG and temporal logic, in: *Proceedings Sixth International Symposium on Computer Hardware Description Languages*, Carnegie-Mellon University, Pittsburgh, PA (1983) 103–114.

Received December 1983

Index

Numbers in boldface are inclusive page numbers for chapters.

Abramovici, M., 401, 402
Aiello, N., 110
Allan, J., 94, 102, 165, 340
Amarel, S., 172
Asbell, I., 115, 155n

Barbacci, M. R., 393
Barrow, Harry G., 3, 4, 174, **437–490**
Batali, J., 356
Bee, N., 154
Bell, G., 353
Bobrow, Daniel G., **1–5,** 270, 273, 274,
    304, 306
Bovricius, W. G., 412
Boyer, R., 439, 485
Breuer, M. A., 360, 401, 402, 412
Brotsky, D., 342
Brown, John Seely, 2, 3, 4, 5, **7–82,** 12,
    13, 18, 90n, 164, 173, 189, 205, 213n,
    224, 239, 250, 254, 273, 278, 292n,
    337, 338–339, 348, 359, 361, 394,
    399, 403, 404, 405, 412
Buchanan, B. G., 390
Bundy, A., 438
Bunge, M., 154n
Burton, R. R., 18, 164, 278, 348, 359,
    361, 394, 403, 404
Byrd, L., 438

Caramazza, A., 187, 195, 201
Cherry, J., 282
Chi, M. T. H., 171
Clocksin, W., 440
Cochin, I., 14, 26
Collins, A., 110
Conway, L., 450
Cyphers, S., 342

Dahl, O. J., 437
Davis, Randall, 3, 4, 18, 174, **347–408,**
    348, 348n, 359, 361, 374n, 390, 419,
    431, 439
de Kleer, Johann, 2, 3, 4, 5, **7–82,** 12,
    13, 18, 35, 90n, 91, 92, 110, 115,
    135, 153, 154n, 169, 172, 173, 189,
    205–279, 205, 213n, 218, 224, 230,
    239, 244, 249, 250, 252, 254, 263,
    270, 273, 274, 275, 278, 285, 290n,
    292n, 294, 304, 306, 337, 338–339,
    348, 359, 361, 362, 394, 399, 403, 404
Dijkstra, E. W., 437
DiSessa, A. A., 38, 119n, 154
Dosoer, C. A., 212, 227
Doyle, J., 252, 294, 397

Eliot, C., 171
Estrin, G., 392

Fateman, R. J., 439, 452
Feeher, C., 163
Feltovich, P. J., 171
Feynman, R. P., 63
Fikes, R., 87
Finger, J., 424
Floyd, R. W., 445
Forbus, Kenneth, 2, 3, 4, 5, 13, 21, 42,
    85–166, 88n, 89n, 90, 91, 92, 115,
    119n, 135, 137n, 144, 151, 154n, 157,
    166, 172, 173, 189, 211, 290n, 339
Forrester, J. W., 164, 174
Foster, M. J., 445
Foyster, G., 86
Friedman, A., 360, 401, 412
Fujita, M., 488

Gabriel, J. R., 439
Gasching, J., 390
Genesereth, Michael R., 3, 4, 174, 348,
    411–436, 413, 424, 427, 428, 434,
    439, 455, 480

Gentner, D., 90, 119n, 166, 189
Glaser, R., 171
Goel, P., 428
Gordon, M., 440, 445, 455, 471
Gray, P. E., 209, 212, 230
Green, B., 187, 195, 201
Greiner, R., 434
Grinberg, M., 153, 172, 395

Hamscher, W., 18, 174, 348
Hanes, L. H., 439
Harris, J. N., 209
Hartheimer, A., 356
Hayes, P. J., 3, 4, 13, 14, 58, 87, 92, 97, 102, 119, 122, 124, 173, 189, 342
Hayes-Roth, F., 428
Hearn, A. C., 452
Heise, D. R., 154n
Hendrix, G., 164
Hoare, A. R., 437
Hodges, D. A., 299, 327
Hollan, J., 155n
Hopfield, J. J., 77

Ibarra, O. H., 428, 438

Johannson, D., 438

Karnopp, D., 14
Kassirer, J., 165, 170
Kelly, V., 395
Klahr, P., 428
Kuh, E. S., 212, 227
Kuipers, Benjamin J., 2, 3–4, 5, 13, 165, **169–202,** 170, 171, 173, 176, 189
Kulikowski, C. A., 172

Langley, P., 157
Larkin, J., 172
Leighton, R. B., 63
Lenat, D. B., 64, 428
Lim, W. Y.-P., 393
Loomis, L., 299n, 300
Luger, G., 438

McAllester, D., 252
McCarthy, J., 87
McCloskey, M., 134n, 187, 195, 201
McDermott, D., 88n, 165, 172
McDermott, J., 172
McDonald, D., 163
Martin, W. A., 439, 452

Mead, C., 450
Melliar-Smith, P. M., 438, 440
Mellish, C., 438, 440
Miller, D., 163
Miller, M., 110
Milne, R., 438
Milner, R., 440
Minsky, M., 87, 142
Mokwa, J., 154
Moore, J., 439, 485
Moore, R., 110
Moszkowski, B. C., 488
Moto-oka, T., 488
Murphy, A. T., 213n

Nagel, L. W., 275
Newell, A., 353, 382
Newton, A., 282
Newton, Isaac, 12
Nillson, N., 87

Palmer, M., 438
Patil, R., 348
Pederson, D. O., 275, 282
Pew, R., 163
Polit, S., 18, 174, 348
Pople, H., 390, 412
Poston, T., 15

Reiger, C. R., 395
Reiter, R., 110
Rich, C., 437
Richardson, H. H., 213n
Rieger, C., 153, 172
Riley, M., 154
Robinson, J. A., 424
Rosenberg, R., 14
Roth, J. P., 360, 412
Roylance, G., 282

Safir, A., 172
Sahni, S., 428, 438
Sands, M., 63
Schneider, P. R., 412
Schwartz, R. L., 438, 440
Schwartz, W., 348
Searle, C. L., 209, 212, 230
Shearer, J. L., 14, 213n
Shirley, M., 18, 174, 348, 361, 374n
Shortliffe, E. H., 390, 412
Shostak, R. E., 440, 451, 452
Shrobe, H., 18, 174, 348, 359, 437

Simmon, R., 90n
Simmons, R., 166
Simon, D. P., 172
Simon, H. A., 172, 382
Singh, H., 439
Smith, D. E., 427, 428, 434
Stallman, R., 110, 218, 403
Stanfill, C., 90n
Stansfield, J., 164
Steele, G. L., 191, 218, 357, 396, 403,
    404, 413
Stefik, M., 413
Steinberg, L., 395
Stevens, A., 155n, 189
Stewart, I., 15
Stoy, J. E., 440
Suppes, P. S., 50
Sussman, G. J., 35, 110, 218, 275, 357,
    396, 403, 404, 405, 413
Szolovits, P., 348

Tanaka, H., 488
Thomas, G., 303
Tong, C., 412

Van Cleemput, W. M., 392
Van Lehn, K., 189

Wadsworth, C., 440
Wagner, T. J., 439
Waldhaver, F. D., 230
Warnock, E., 110
Waters, R. C., 437
Weiss, S. M., 172
Weld, D., 166
Wieckert, K., 18, 174, 348
Wiener, N., 73
Williams, Brian C., 2, 3, 4, 5, 224, **281–
345,** 286
Williams, M., 155n
Winston, P., 390

Zdybel, F., 164